The Australian Women's WEEKLY

FAMILY HEALTH
AND
MEDICAL
GUIDE

The Australian Women's Weekly

FAMILY HEALTH
AND
MEDICAL GUIDE

The A-Z complete guide to
family health for your home

MEDICAL EDITOR: DR FRANCES MACKENZIE
GENERAL EDITOR: SANDRA SYMONS

VIKING O'NEIL

Viking O'Neil
Penguin Books Australia Ltd
487 Maroondah Highway, PO Box 257
Ringwood, Victoria 3134, Australia
Penguin Books Ltd
Harmondsworth, Middlesex, England
Viking Penguin Inc.
40 West 23rd Street, New York, N.Y. 10010, U.S.A.
Penguin Books Canada Ltd
2801 John Street, Markham, Ontario, Canada L3R 1B4
Penguin Books (N.Z.) Ltd
182–190 Wairau Road, Auckland 10, New Zealand

First published by Penguin Books Australia Ltd, 1987
Copyright © Concept and form, Penguin Books Australia Ltd, 1987
Copyright © Name and form, *Australian Women's Weekly*,
    Australian Consolidated Press Limited, 1987
Copyright © Text of 'A-Z Of Family Health' and 'Medical Tests And
    Examinations', Sandra Symons, 1987
Copyright © All other text sections, Penguin Books Australia Ltd, 1987
Copyright © Illustrations for 'How The Body Works',
    Quarto Publishing Limited, 1985
Copyright © All other illustrations, Penguin Books Australia Ltd, 1987

Produced by Viking O'Neil
56 Claremont Street, South Yarra, Victoria 3141, Australia
A division of Penguin Books Australia Ltd

Typeset in Century Old Style and Helvetica by
    Abb-typesetting Pty Ltd, Collingwood, Victoria
Printed and bound in Hong Kong through Bookbuilders Ltd

National Library of Australia
Cataloguing-in-Publication data

Family health and medical guide.

    Includes index.
    ISBN 0 670 90048 6.

    1. Family — Health and hygiene — Dictionaries. 2. Medicine,
    Popular — Dictionaries. 3. Health — Dictionaries.
    I. Mackenzie, Frances. II. Title: Australian women's weekly.

613'.03'21

This is the great error of our day: that physicians separate the soul from the body. The cure of the part should not be attempted without the treatment of the whole.

Plato (427–347 B.C.)

CONTENTS

INTRODUCTION

For over fifteen years I have been writing medical columns and answering readers' questions in Australian magazines. It has been a rewarding and informative experience.

In private practice, I have always thought it important to encourage people to talk comfortably about themselves. I enjoy the privilege of close personal contact with people's lives that working as a doctor allows me. I feel that giving clear information and being open to questions are among the most important things I can offer.

Anyone who needs to see a doctor will want to know as much as possible about what is wrong, the cause of the problem, what can be done about it, the possible outcomes and how to prevent similar problems in the future.

Until recently, the way in which our bodies work in health and illness has been shrouded in mystery and secrecy. Many people accepted medical diagnoses and treatments as their fate, and the word of doctors and other health professionals was taken without question. People felt that they had no right to ask questions about their illnesses and the treatments prescribed for them.

Fortunately this attitude is changing. More people today want to know what is happening to their bodies when they are sick. More doctors are realising that well-informed patients respond better to their care than do those who are anxious through ignorance.

I have found that people who understand the cause and possible effects of their illness and its treatment can take an active part in making decisions about how their health problems may be solved in the present, and prevented in the future.

Answering 'Dear Doctor' letters has been a real eye-opener for me. I quickly learned that, in spite of my belief that the old mystique about medicine is disappearing, many people are still nervous and embarrassed about talking with their doctors. I have been constantly astonished that people feel the need to write to an anonymous stranger to ask questions about illnesses that could have profound effects on their lives and those close to them. I wondered why the family doctor could not be asked these questions.

When you are consulting your doctor because you are ill, you may feel too unwell, anxious or embarrassed to ask about certain things. You may not know what questions to ask or the questions may not occur to you until later.

Many people, I think, feel that they should not take up a busy doctor's time with questions. If you do ask, your doctor may answer in terms that are difficult to understand and you may be hesitant about asking for further information.

It is understandable that confusion exists. During the last thirty years there has been an explosion of knowledge and understanding about how the body works in health and illness. There have also been huge leaps forward in technology to aid in the diagnosis and treatment of disease.

New developments in the health sciences are reported by the media immediately after having been published in scientific journals. Journalists often attend meetings of specialists and may report research findings to the public even before these appear in medical journals or books. The news reports are of great value for the information they give to the public. However, health news items may overemphasise and sensationalise the controversial and exotic aspects of medical practice.

One of the aims of *The Australian Women's Weekly Family Health And Medical Guide* is to fill in the gaps between health news items and what your doctor tells you, and to provide all the other information you need to know about health problems that affect you and your family.

In this guide we have set out to answer the basic questions about the common and serious diseases, as well as about all the main symptoms of illness and their possible causes. With this knowledge we hope that you will be better prepared to ask the right questions when dealing with your doctor, such as the following: what is the cause of my symptoms? Can the illness be passed on to others? What is the best treatment? Are there any side-effects of treatment? How long will it be before I feel better? Should I be off work and for how long, and what is the outlook for the future?

To understand illness, it is essential to have some knowledge of normal anatomy and physiology. We have included a special section to help you to understand how the systems of our bodies function and interact with one another to perform the miracle that is human life.

In my experience people are often confused or baffled by the many tests and examinations which aid in accurate diagnosis and the monitoring of treatment. We have provided a comprehensive section on the subject, suggesting questions you might wish to ask your doctor about any tests ordered for you.

We have also included a first aid section to give clear, concise and easily-found information to help you in an emergency while you are waiting for the doctor or ambulance to arrive.

It must be emphasised that this guide is not intended to take the place of a medical consultation. No book can ever replace medical knowledge and experience. Although home care and simple remedies are suggested for common minor ailments, we tell you when it is necessary for you to see your doctor.

I hope this book will make it easier for you to talk with your doctor, to seek more information, and to ask more specific questions about your health. Your doctor will be encouraged by your interest and may volunteer additional information. Understanding more about your body fosters a cooperative effort between you and your doctor in restoring and maintaining your health.

Dr Frances Mackenzie

HOW TO USE THIS BOOK

The human body is a marvellous piece of machinery which is, nevertheless, subject to a variety of illnesses and disorders. The aim of *The Australian Women's Weekly Family Health And Medical Guide* is to help you understand the functions of a healthy body, how disease may affect it, and the nature of disease and diagnosis.

There are five main sections in the guide, each with its own careful system of cross-reference. You may find that your needs focus mainly on the alphabetical listing of illnesses and disorders and the emergency first aid section. But the other sections are there for you to expand further your knowledge.

1   HOW THE BODY WORKS

This detailed, illustrated section is divided into ten categories based on the different but interrelated body systems essential to maintaining life. The way each individual system works is explained in a comprehensible, forthright way. In many cases you will be referred to How The Body Works from other sections in the book when we think you will benefit from further, more detailed information.

2   A-Z OF FAMILY HEALTH

Set apart from the rest of the book by its distinctive pink-edged pages, this is one of the most important sections in the guide, for here you will find illnesses and disorders defined and explained. All the disorders and diseases are listed alphabetically. Words in SMALL CAPITAL LETTERS within an entry indicate other relevant entries in the A-Z guide. You will also see cross-references to How The Body Works, Medical Tests And Examinations, and First Aid For Emergencies, where you will find additional information on the entry you have just looked up. In some cases, you will be directed to our special section, Medical And Health Support Organisations, which provides the names, addresses and telephone numbers of organisations and agencies which offer on-going information, help and support.

3 MEDICAL TESTS AND EXAMINATIONS

There is an enormous range of tests and examinations available today to assist in both the diagnosis and treatment of disease and disorders. People may often be confused about why their doctor has ordered a particular test and what will be involved in the procedure. Some tests are simple and may be carried out in your doctor's surgery; others require more specialised procedures in a laboratory or hospital. This section is divided into categories according to the parts of the body and body systems, such as Bones, Joints And Muscles; The Circulatory System; The Respiratory System. Within each of these categories you will find the relevant tests discussed: for example, tests for thyroid function appear under the heading, The Endocrine System. Within individual test entries, there may be other tests mentioned which appear in SMALL CAPITAL LETTERS. To follow these up you will need to turn to the alphabetical contents list at the beginning of this section to find the number of the page on which these are discussed.

4 FIRST AID FOR EMERGENCIES

This important section of the guide (with its distinctive red-edged pages) gives alphabetical coverage of how to deal with both minor emergencies and situations in which you may need to act promptly and correctly in order to save a life or prevent serious injury. Words in SMALL CAPITAL LETTERS indicate other entries within the first aid section which will give you more information on what to do until the doctor or ambulance arrives.

5 MEDICAL AND HEALTH SUPPORT ORGANISATIONS

This invaluable resource section has been divided into State-by-State listings for Australia and main regional listings for New Zealand. All the organisations and agencies are listed alphabetically and most of the disorders and diseases dealt with have special entries in the A-Z Of Family Health. This resource guide has been collated to serve the needs of all members of the community. However, there are gaps of information for some States where we found it difficult to find the necessary information or where certain organisations have yet to be established. Every effort has been made to make the lists as comprehensive as possible.

Finally, an all-encompassing GENERAL INDEX helps the reader to refer quickly to information on desired topics.

ACKNOWLEDGEMENTS

The research and compilation of *The Australian Women's Weekly Family Health And Medical Guide* has been a long, hard haul. It has also been enormously pleasurable. One of the most enjoyable aspects of the project has been working with a team of colleagues and friends who so generously offered information and advice — and endless patience.

Affectionate, special thanks to Sue Wendt and Patricia Rolfe (both formerly of the *Australian Women's Weekly* Special Projects department) for their encouragement when the book was but a 'brilliant, sure-fire success' idea.

Thanks also to Margaret Barca, who initially got the project under way, to book editors Maggie Taylor and Lesley Dunt, to researchers Sue Cater, Susan Brierley and Jill Rivers, and to illustrators Vera Thomas and Geoff Kelly. Sydney medical writer Shaun McIlraith gave a practical demonstration of how a true professional works in the expert, adept way he researched and collated the chapter, How The Body Works. The handsome symmetry of the guide was elegantly and thoughtfully created by graphic designer Leonie Stott.

Our huge workload was greatly reduced by that wondrous invention — the computer. We were inducted into the mysteries of this magical technology through the constant and often bemused help of George Bray (Logical Solutions) and Marco Orlando (Dick Smith Electronics). Never once did they flinch at the call for a midnight consultation.

We leave our final, heartfelt thanks to the project coordinator Helen Duffy. Hers was not always such a pleasurable task, especially as deadlines thundered towards us, but always Helen was kindly, warm of heart and, as they say, gracious under pressure.

Dr Frances Mackenzie
Sandra Symons

EDITORIAL AND PRODUCTION

Editorial and production coordination by Helen Duffy and
Margaret Barca.

Additional research by Shaun McIlraith, Lesley Dunt,
Susan Brierley, Sue Cater, Jill Rivers.

Editorial assistance by Maggie Taylor, Felicity Anderson,
Nati Sangiau, Janet Mau.

Design by Leonie Stott.
Additional design by Sandra Nobes.
Jacket design by Guy Mirabella.
Design assistance by Gary Devine and Ruth Ashwin.

Colour illustrations in How The Body Works are copyright Quarto
Publishing Limited, London. Some have appeared in a different
form in *The Australian Family Health Encyclopedia* published in
1985 by Doubleday Australia Pty Limited.

Illustrations (A-Z Of Family Health and First Aid For
Emergencies) by Vera Thomas.
Additional illustrations by Geoff Kelly.
Photography and photographic reference by Bruce Postle.
General Index by Fay Donlevy of Pryor Medical Typing.

The publishers would also like to thank the following organisations
and individuals for their assistance and advice: The St John
Ambulance Association, NSW and Victoria (special thanks to
Norman Hutton, Howard Modin, Bill Cafferty and
Julie Blackshaw); Sydney AIDS Clinic; The Family Planning
Association, NSW and Victoria; Drug and Alcohol Education and
Resource Unit (NSW Department of Health). The publishers offer
their thanks to the Australian Resuscitation Council for their help
and advice on the First Aid chapter of the book.

MEDICAL ABBREVIATIONS

The following common medical abbreviations have been used in this book. They have been spelt out in full on their first use, but on subsequent use, the initials only have been used.

ACTH   adrenocorticotrophic hormone
ADH   antidiuretic hormone
AHF   anti-haemophilic factor
AID   artificial insemination donor
AIDS   acquired immune deficiency syndrome
AIH   artificial insemination husband
ATP   adenosine triphosphate
BMR   basal metabolic rate
CAT   computer axial tomography
CCF   congestive cardiac failure
CNS   central nervous system
CSF   cerebrospinal fluid
D and C   dilation and curettage
DNA   deoxyribonucleic acid
DVT   deep venous thrombosis
ECG   electrocardiogram
EEG   electroencephalogram
ESR   erythrocyte sedimentation rate
FSH   follicle stimulating hormone
GPI   general paralysis of the insane
hCG   human chorionic gonadotrophin
HGH   human growth hormone
HIV   human immunodeficiency virus
HRT   hormone replacement therapy

HSVI   herpes simplex virus I
HSVII   herpes simplex virus II
IRT   infra-red thermography
IUD   intrauterine device
LASER   light amplification by stimulated emission of radiation
LH   luteinising hormone
LSD   lysergic acid diethylamide
MS   multiple sclerosis
NMR   nuclear magnetic resonance
NSAIDS   non-steroid anti-inflammatory drugs
NSU   non-specific urethritis
OT   oxytocin
PID   pelvic inflammatory disease
PIH   pregnancy-induced hypertension
PMS   premenstrual syndrome
PMT   premenstrual tension
RSI   repetitive strain injury
SIDS   sudden infant death syndrome
STD   sexually transmitted diseases
SUDS   sudden unexplained death syndrome
TB   tuberculosis
TIA   transient ischaemic attack
TSH   thyroid stimulating hormone
TV   *Trichomonas vaginalis*
VD   venereal disease

PUBLISHERS' NOTE

The publishers acknowledge with gratitude the cooperation of Australian Consolidated Press Ltd and the *Australian Women's Weekly* in the production of this FAMILY HEALTH AND MEDICAL GUIDE. In particular, they are grateful to the *Weekly*'s medical writer, Dr Frances Mackenzie, for her editorial supervision of the medical content. While every care has been taken in researching and compiling the medical information in this guide, it must never take the place of professional medical advice. Neither the publishers, the *Australian Women's Weekly* nor Australian Consolidated Press Ltd may be held responsible for any action or claim resulting from the use of this book or any information contained in it.

HOW THE BODY WORKS

BONES, JOINTS AND MUSCLES

The living sculpture of the human body is fashioned on a framework that provides far more than mere strength. The solid part, the skeleton, is cunningly articulated to allow a freedom of movement that Michelangelo's *David* suggests but no automaton can capture. The skeleton ultimately determines a person's height. Wreathing it are muscles which influence our shape and provide the power to move the bones at the joints. Binding and supporting the whole human structure is connective tissue.

BONE FORMATION

The basic framework is laid down in the sixth or seventh week of the life of the embryo, when the fibrous membrane and cartilage models which foreshadow the skeleton begin to transform to bone. In this ossification process special bone-forming cells called osteoblasts cluster in the fibrous membrane. They secrete a protein mesh or matrix and deposit in it a mineral, calcium. The open latticework of 'spongy bone', the repository of red marrow, then develops. Oxygen and building materials are supplied to the site by a network of blood capillaries. At the same time osteoblasts are at work on the embryonic cartilage, turning its outer membrane, the perichondrium, into spongy bone. The cartilage within degenerates, leaving hollows which merge to form the marrow cavity of long bones.

Around the light, yet resilient inner core of spongy bone, hard or compact bone forms in concentric rings, like the bark of a tree. Compact bone is an engineer's dream: it can adapt its shape and strength to suit the function required of it. Riddling the hard bone is a system of tunnels carrying blood vessels, lymph vessels and nerves.

BONE GROWTH

By the time a baby is born the only cartilage left from the ossification process is at the ends of each bone. Bone growth continues under the influence of hormones, the growing points being near the ends of the bones. This is where the diaphysis, or shaft of the bone, meets the thicker ends, or epiphyses. Separating the two parts of the bone is a cartilage plate. The diaphysis lengthens by converting some of this cartilage to bone, while on the other side of the junction new cartilage cells are formed. This goes on until bone growth is complete at about age 18 for boys and 16 for girls.

HOW WE MOVE

The skeleton can move with the grace of the ballet dancer or the explosive energy of the 100 metres sprinter thanks to the efficiency of its joints and the precise control exerted on them by the muscles.

Wherever two bones meet is a joint. Between some bones it is fixed as in the bones of the skull. Other joints allow anything from a little movement to rotation through a number of different planes. The self-lubricating joints of the limbs turn freely in gliding, pivoting, hinge and other actions subtle and supple. Their articulating surfaces are lined with hyaline cartilage, a hard, clear, bluish tinted material more friction-free than ice. Its common name is gristle. Especially strong cartilage known as fibro-cartilage is found in the knee joint and the discs between the vertebrae of the spine.

The self-lubricating or synovial joints, including the elbow, the knee and the hip, are bathed continually in an oiling fluid. Like egg white in consistency, this is secreted by the joint lining into the small space between the cartilage surfaces of the opposing bones.

One joint which is mainly rigid but must move on occasion is the pubic symphysis between the pubic bones in the female. In childbirth – as the baby is delivered – it widens a little to allow passage, then closes again. The baby's skull, prepared for the squeeze, is able to compress as it goes through because some of the joints, or sutures, between its bones have still to close. These gaps, called fontanelles, begin to close one or two months after birth but do not seal permanently until the baby is about a year old.

MUSCLES

The muscles which swathe the skeleton and are present in many other tissues supply the power for all the body's movements, from walking and running to breathing and digestion. The skeletal muscles contract to move bones about their joints like levers on a fulcrum. This is putting it in the simplest terms. In reality, nearly all bodily movements require the interplay of muscle groups, with the contraction of the prime mover being balanced by the relaxation of complementary muscles.

The skeletal muscles, being under conscious control, are called 'voluntary'. Another term for them is striated muscles. This refers to the appearance of the bundles of fibres of which they are made. As in all muscle, each fibre is a single cell. In the voluntary muscles, however, the fibres contain many overlapping strands of two different filaments: one containing the protein, actin; the other a different protein called myosin. Under the light microscope the overlap of the two filaments within a skeletal muscle fibre shows up as a dark band against the lighter colour of the rest. Hence the name, striated. The arrangement of muscle fibres varies according to the function of the muscle. A muscle with a twisting action, such as the trapezius in the back, for example, has its fibres arranged in spirals.

Our control over the voluntary muscles is non-specific. When we wish to move an arm or a leg, it is the brain which automatically notifies the particular muscles involved. The message it sends induces the release of a chemical, acetylcholine, at nerve endings. Acetylcholine initiates a chemical reaction within the muscle fibre, causing actin microthreads

THE SKELETON

Adults have 206 bones arranged in a framework called the skeleton. (At birth humans have 350 bones, but many of these fuse in infancy.) The skeleton is divided into a vertical axis of skull, spinal column and rib cage (80 bones), with the pelvis and shoulder girdles and attached limbs hanging from it (126 bones). Males tend to have larger, stronger bones, broader shoulders and a longer rib cage than females. The pelvis in women has a wider opening to allow for childbirth.

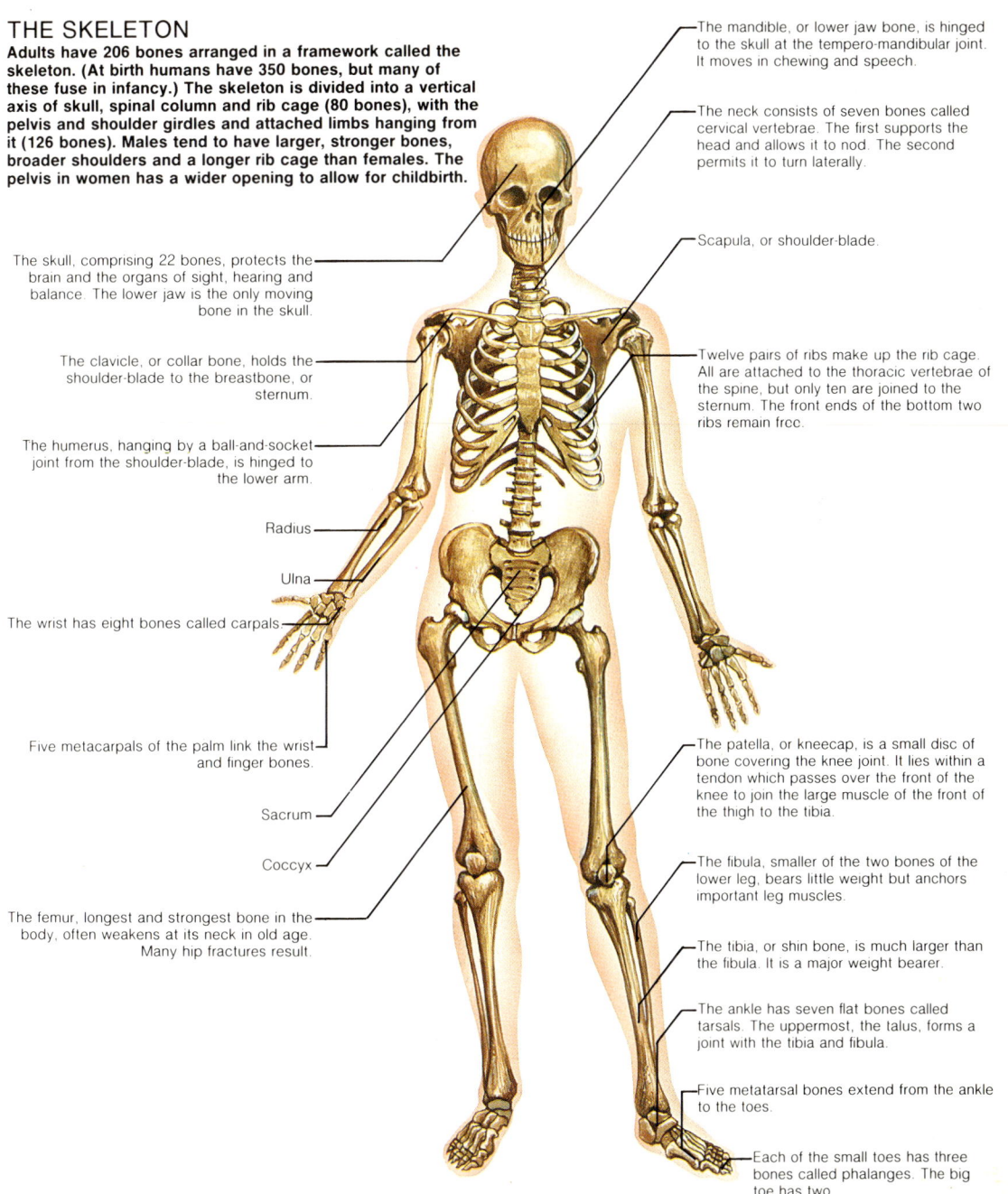

The mandible, or lower jaw bone, is hinged to the skull at the tempero-mandibular joint. It moves in chewing and speech.

The neck consists of seven bones called cervical vertebrae. The first supports the head and allows it to nod. The second permits it to turn laterally.

The skull, comprising 22 bones, protects the brain and the organs of sight, hearing and balance. The lower jaw is the only moving bone in the skull.

Scapula, or shoulder-blade.

The clavicle, or collar bone, holds the shoulder-blade to the breastbone, or sternum.

Twelve pairs of ribs make up the rib cage. All are attached to the thoracic vertebrae of the spine, but only ten are joined to the sternum. The front ends of the bottom two ribs remain free.

The humerus, hanging by a ball-and-socket joint from the shoulder-blade, is hinged to the lower arm.

Radius

Ulna

The wrist has eight bones called carpals

Five metacarpals of the palm link the wrist and finger bones.

The patella, or kneecap, is a small disc of bone covering the knee joint. It lies within a tendon which passes over the front of the knee to join the large muscle of the front of the thigh to the tibia.

Sacrum

The fibula, smaller of the two bones of the lower leg, bears little weight but anchors important leg muscles.

Coccyx

The tibia, or shin bone, is much larger than the fibula. It is a major weight bearer.

The femur, longest and strongest bone in the body, often weakens at its neck in old age. Many hip fractures result.

The ankle has seven flat bones called tarsals. The uppermost, the talus, forms a joint with the tibia and fibula.

Five metatarsal bones extend from the ankle to the toes.

Each of the small toes has three bones called phalanges. The big toe has two.

to slide towards myosin microthreads, contracting the muscle. During contraction lactic acid is created as a by-product. Cramp and muscle fatigue result from accumulation of lactic acid during strenuous exercise: the blood cannot deliver enough of the oxygen required to break it down.

The many muscles under control, not of the conscious mind, but of the autonomic nervous system are divided into two categories: the cardiac muscle of the heart wall, and smooth muscle, which performs a variety of unsung tasks in the body. Both types are involuntary, but cardiac is striated whereas smooth muscle is not.

Cardiac muscle puts man-made engines in the shade, commonly working non-stop for seventy years to keep blood flowing around the body. Smooth muscle, to mention just some of its jobs, moves food through the digestive canal, expels wastes from the urinary bladder and babies from the uterus, and controls blood flow in the arteries and veins.

BODY MUSCLES

Attached to the bones are nearly 700 skeletal muscles which control movement, maintain the posture of the body and generate heat to help keep it warm.

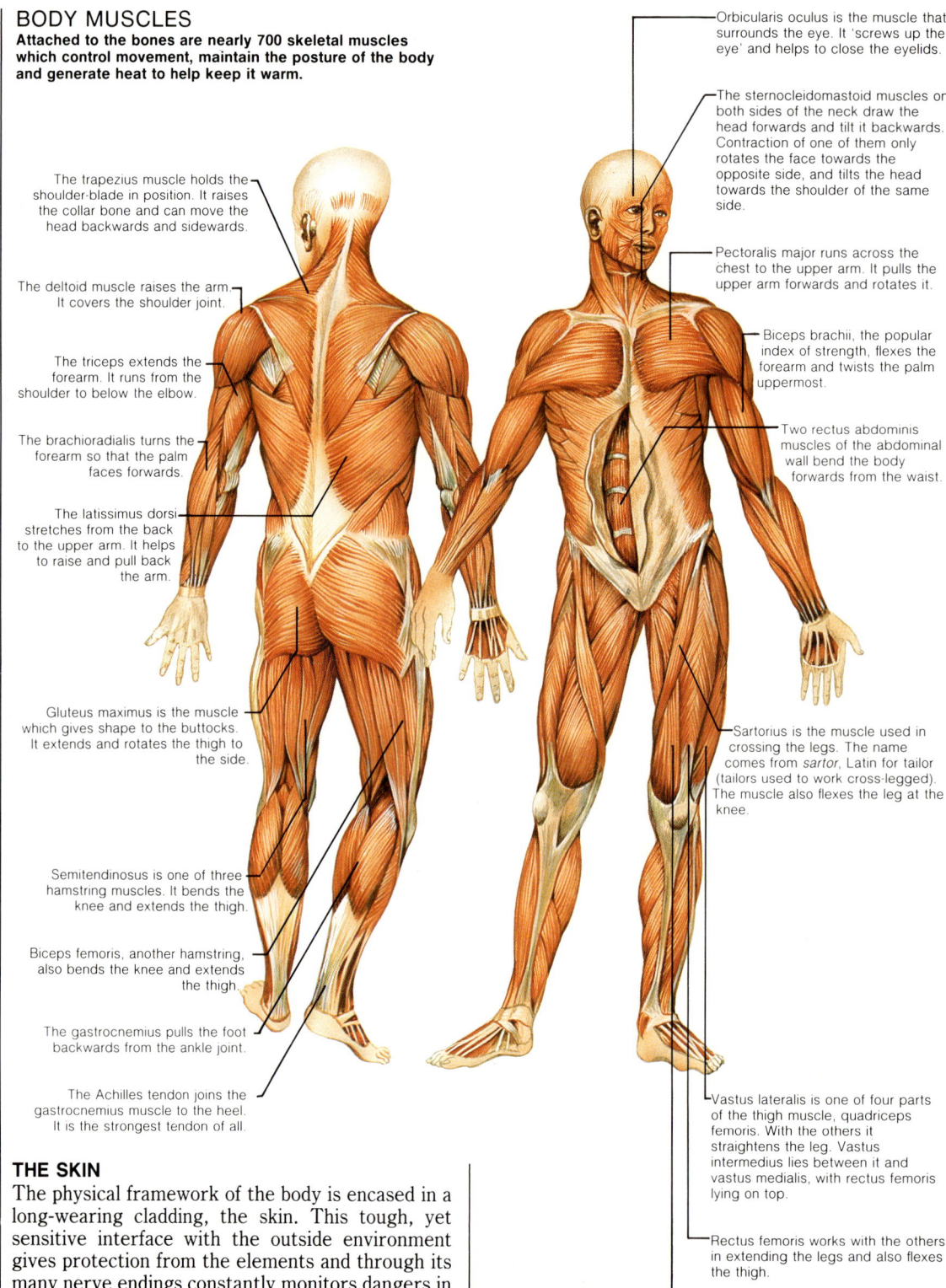

The trapezius muscle holds the shoulder-blade in position. It raises the collar bone and can move the head backwards and sidewards.

The deltoid muscle raises the arm. It covers the shoulder joint.

The triceps extends the forearm. It runs from the shoulder to below the elbow.

The brachioradialis turns the forearm so that the palm faces forwards.

The latissimus dorsi stretches from the back to the upper arm. It helps to raise and pull back the arm.

Gluteus maximus is the muscle which gives shape to the buttocks. It extends and rotates the thigh to the side.

Semitendinosus is one of three hamstring muscles. It bends the knee and extends the thigh.

Biceps femoris, another hamstring, also bends the knee and extends the thigh.

The gastrocnemius pulls the foot backwards from the ankle joint.

The Achilles tendon joins the gastrocnemius muscle to the heel. It is the strongest tendon of all.

Orbicularis oculus is the muscle that surrounds the eye. It 'screws up the eye' and helps to close the eyelids.

The sternocleidomastoid muscles on both sides of the neck draw the head forwards and tilt it backwards. Contraction of one of them only rotates the face towards the opposite side, and tilts the head towards the shoulder of the same side.

Pectoralis major runs across the chest to the upper arm. It pulls the upper arm forwards and rotates it.

Biceps brachii, the popular index of strength, flexes the forearm and twists the palm uppermost.

Two rectus abdominis muscles of the abdominal wall bend the body forwards from the waist.

Sartorius is the muscle used in crossing the legs. The name comes from *sartor*, Latin for tailor (tailors used to work cross-legged). The muscle also flexes the leg at the knee.

Vastus lateralis is one of four parts of the thigh muscle, quadriceps femoris. With the others it straightens the leg. Vastus intermedius lies between it and vastus medialis, with rectus femoris lying on top.

Rectus femoris works with the others in extending the legs and also flexes the thigh.

Vastus medialis lies on the inside of the thigh opposite to vastus lateralis.

THE SKIN

The physical framework of the body is encased in a long-wearing cladding, the skin. This tough, yet sensitive interface with the outside environment gives protection from the elements and through its many nerve endings constantly monitors dangers in our surroundings. If you could take it off and stretch it out, it would measure about 1.5 square metres.

If the skeleton and muscles are the framework of the body, the blood and lymph systems are the service conduits which carry the necessities of life and vital instructions to the millions of cells of which the body is made. At the delivery end of the conduit, oxygen, nutrients and messenger substances called hormones pass through the walls of tiny blood capillaries into the interstitial fluid bathing the cells. Carbon dioxide and other wastes from the cells are picked up in exchange. Security agents in the form of white blood cells and antibodies travel through the conduit to fight invading organisms.

BLOOD

The tissue called blood is about 45 per cent cells and 55 per cent a straw-coloured fluid called plasma. Most of the cells are erythrocytes, or red blood cells, which carry oxygen and give blood its colour. Each cubic millilitre of blood in a healthy male contains about 5.4 million red blood cells. In a healthy female the figure is about 4.5 million. Scattered through the red cell population are white blood cells, outnumbered about 700 to 1, and platelets, outnumbered some fifteen to twenty times. The white cells, or leucocytes, are the body's defence against infectious disease and foreign matter generally. The function of the platelets is to maintain the closed circuit of the circulation by hastening to seal leaks in blood vessels and to initiate clotting.

RED BLOOD CELLS

In adults, red blood cells are made in the red bone marrow of the breastbone, ribs, vertebrae and pelvis. In children, many are also made in the marrow of the limb bones and in the spleen. Each cell lives for about 120 days after which it is broken down in the liver and spleen. Normally red cell production and red cell destruction proceed at the same pace. The need for more red cells is noticed by certain kidney cells as the oxygen content of the blood falls. The kidney cells release a forerunner of a hormone called erythropoietin, which stimulates the bone marrow to make more red cells.

The formation of healthy red cells depends on an adequate supply of vitamin B_{12} and folic acid absorbed from food. Iron, also obtained from food, furnishes haem, a pigment which combines with the protein, globin, to form haemoglobin, the cargo of the cell. As blood passes through the lungs, oxygen from the air combines with the iron of the haemoglobin, turning it red. When the red cells release their oxygen to the tissues, the carbon dioxide waste from the body cells is taken up in its place by the globin. On reaching the lungs on the return trip, the carbon dioxide is discharged.

WHITE BLOOD CELLS

There are five different types of white cells, each with its own function and each differing from red blood cells in possessing a nucleus. Most also differ from red cells in being able to squeeze through capillary walls into the tissues.

Best known of the white cells are the lymphocytes which defend against invading organisms either by releasing special proteins known as antibodies or by attaching to the invader and killing more directly. The first function is performed by B lymphocytes, the second by T lymphocytes. They are produced by the spleen, tonsils and other lymphatic organs.

Two other types of white cell, monocytes and neutrophils, actually gobble up bacteria. Cells which do this are known as phagocytes. A fourth type of white cell, the eosinophils, are believed to produce allergy antibodies, while a fifth type, basophils, are thought to be involved in the allergic reaction, entering the tissue and liberating histamine and the anticoagulant, heparin.

PLASMA

More viscous than water, though largely made of it, plasma carries the products of digestion to the cells of the body. These products include amino acids (from protein), glucose (from carbohydrates) and fatty acids and glycerol (from fats). Plasma contains a great many other substances in solution, including gammaglobulin antibodies, fibrinogen and other clotting factors, enzymes to catalyse chemical reactions and hormones to regulate the growth and metabolism of the body.

CARDIOVASCULAR SYSTEM

To reach every part of the body the blood travels along a network of blood vessels which branch to narrower and narrower passages as they near delivery sites, then enlarge again going away. The blood is driven from one end of this maze to the other by the pumping of the heart. The vessels which carry blood away from the heart are the arteries. Those bringing it back are the veins. The heart and blood vessels make up the cardiovascular system.

THE HEART
The heart lies slightly askew between the lungs. About two-thirds of its mass projects to the left of centre behind the breastbone. Its position vertically is from just below the second pair of ribs at the top to the sixth pair at the bottom.

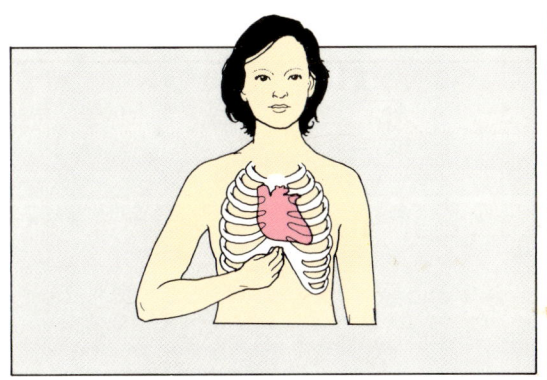

BLOOD CIRCULATION

A network of arteries and veins carries blood around the body to service the cells. Arteries carry blood from the heart; veins take it back. One complete journey for the five or so litres in the system takes about 60 seconds and 28 heartbeats. Blood velocity is about 40 cm a second at the aorta, but much slower in the smaller vessels.

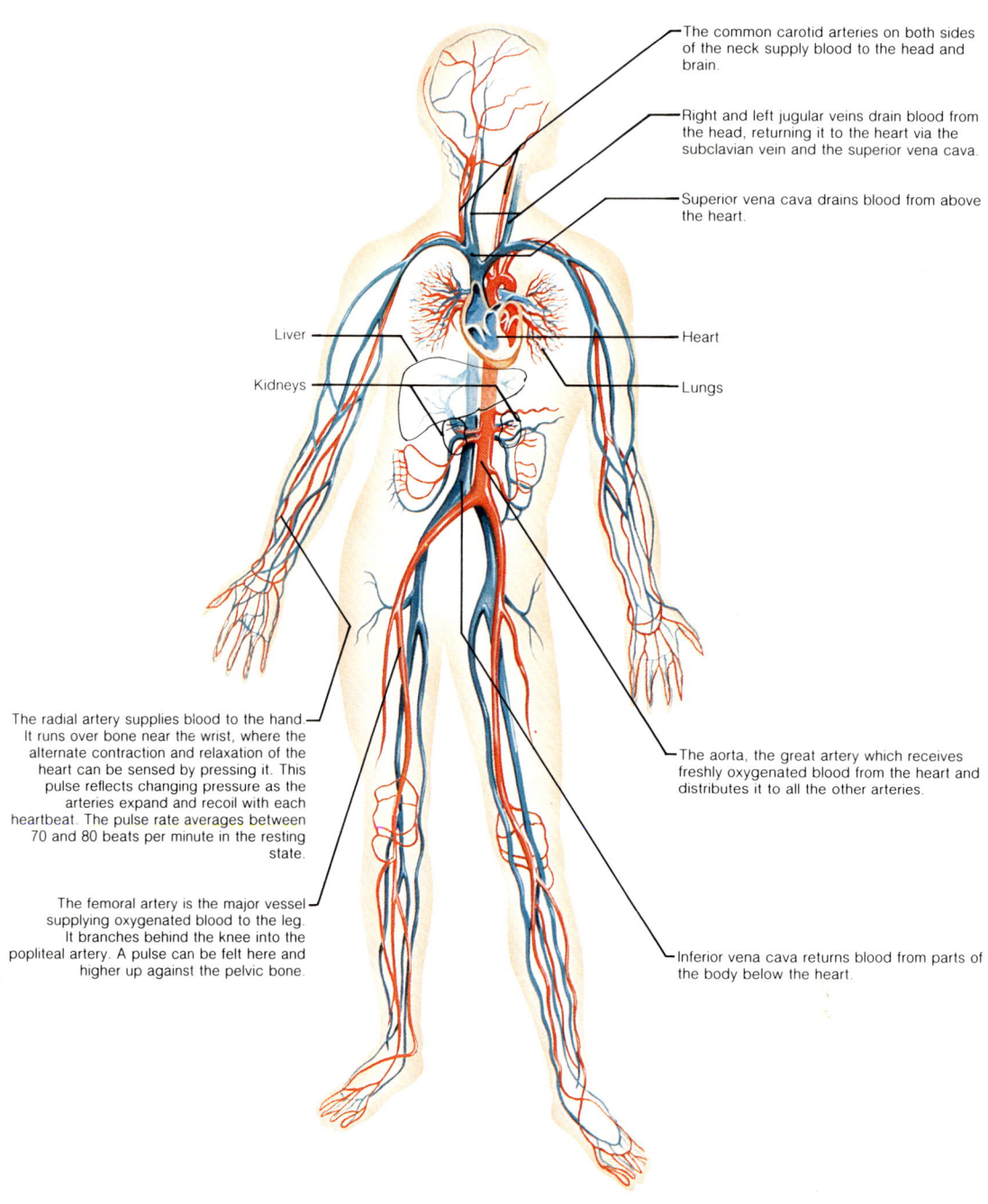

The common carotid arteries on both sides of the neck supply blood to the head and brain.

Right and left jugular veins drain blood from the head, returning it to the heart via the subclavian vein and the superior vena cava.

Superior vena cava drains blood from above the heart.

Heart

Lungs

Liver

Kidneys

The radial artery supplies blood to the hand. It runs over bone near the wrist, where the alternate contraction and relaxation of the heart can be sensed by pressing it. This pulse reflects changing pressure as the arteries expand and recoil with each heartbeat. The pulse rate averages between 70 and 80 beats per minute in the resting state.

The aorta, the great artery which receives freshly oxygenated blood from the heart and distributes it to all the other arteries.

The femoral artery is the major vessel supplying oxygenated blood to the leg. It branches behind the knee into the popliteal artery. A pulse can be felt here and higher up against the pelvic bone.

Inferior vena cava returns blood from parts of the body below the heart.

BLOOD FLOW THROUGH THE VEINS
In the veins, where blood pressure is greatly reduced, there are valves to stop backflow of blood. Skeletal muscles contracting around veins in the extremities force open the valves, which close again when the muscles relax. The action is called 'milking'.

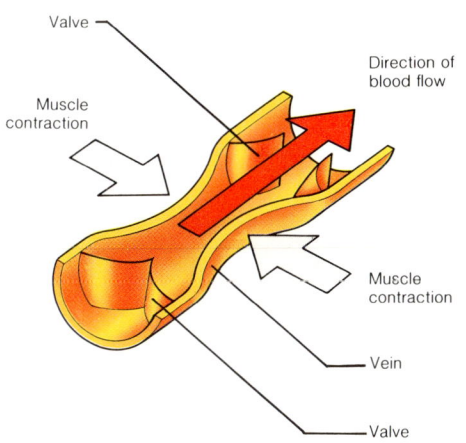

Valve

Direction of blood flow

Muscle contraction

Muscle contraction

Vein

Valve

With each contraction of the heart, blood freshly oxygenated in the lungs is forced into the great artery, the aorta, and thence to all the other arteries and their branches. As blood spurts from the heart the strong walls of the arteries, laminated with smooth muscle and elastic fibres, stretch to accommodate the flow. As the heart relaxes the arteries recoil, forcing the blood on. This is the pulse. The pressure in the arteries, the so-called blood pressure, is governed by the volume of blood expelled from the heart at each stroke and by peripheral resistance of the blood vessels. During the heart muscle contraction, or systole, the pressure in a young, healthy adult varies from about 90–120 mm of mercury. During relaxation, or diastole, when the heart is refilling, the pressure ranges between 60–80 mm. The reading is taken with a sphygmomanometer and expressed as, say, 90/60 or 120/80. Blood pressure tends to increase with age, but this effect can be considerably reduced by maintaining cardiovascular fitness. The body has its own mechanism for regulating blood pressure. Specialised nerve cells in the aortic and carotid arteries can bring about changes in pressure by influencing heart contractions and/or the dilation and contraction of the arteries.

After leaving the heart, blood flows through the arteries to the smaller branches, the arterioles, and finally to microscopic capillaries, 10 000th of a millimetre in diameter – that is, just wide enough to admit one cell at a time. The walls of these vessels are one cell thick. Fluid bearing oxygen, nutrients, hormones and other substances seeps through them

into the fluid around the cells. At the same time carbon dioxide and other waste products of the cells flow the other way through the capillary walls. Blood pressure and osmosis – the movement of water across a permeable membrane from more dilute to more concentrated solutions – govern this exchange.

Laden with the cellular wastes, the blood begins the return journey to the heart through narrow vessels called venules, then through small veins to bigger veins and finally to the two vena cavae which empty into the right side of the heart. Blood pressure in the veins is much lower than in the arteries. Blood might fall back but for valves in some of the veins. Skeletal muscles help to keep it moving by contracting around the veins running through them. The pressure opens the valves in an action called 'milking'. If valves become defective, blood accumulates in a distortion known as varicose veins.

LYMPHATIC SYSTEM
Protein-containing fluid that seeps from the blood capillaries cannot be directly reabsorbed by the cardiovascular system. It is removed from around the cells by the complementary lymphatic system. This has two other main functions: to transport fats from the digestive tract to the bloodstream and to produce infection-fighting lymphocytes. The lymph vessels ultimately carry their fluid to two large ducts, the thoracic and right lymphatic, which empty into large veins in the chest and neck.

At intervals throughout the lymph system are small decontamination centres, or nodes, where resident phagocytic cells cleanse the lymph of bacteria, foreign material and cell debris. The nodes are also important sites for the manufacture of lymphocytes. As well as the hundreds of tiny lymph nodes are three big ones: the tonsils, the spleen and the thymus gland.

A LYMPH NODE

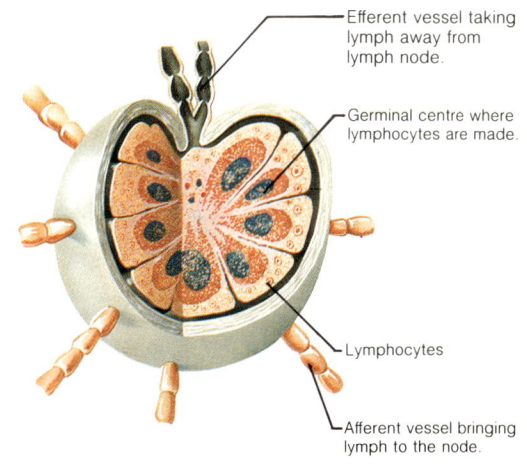

Efferent vessel taking lymph away from lymph node.

Germinal centre where lymphocytes are made.

Lymphocytes

Afferent vessel bringing lymph to the node.

THE LYMPHATIC NETWORK

The network of lymphatic vessels is part of the lymphatic system's defence against infectious disease. Certain white cells (lymphocytes) produced in the system kill invading organisms by direct contact or with antibodies. The lymphatic network is linked with many tiny lymph nodes and three big glands, the tonsils, the spleen and the thymus. Tissue fluid is collected into the lymphatics and is filtered in the nodes before being returned to the blood via the thoracic duct.

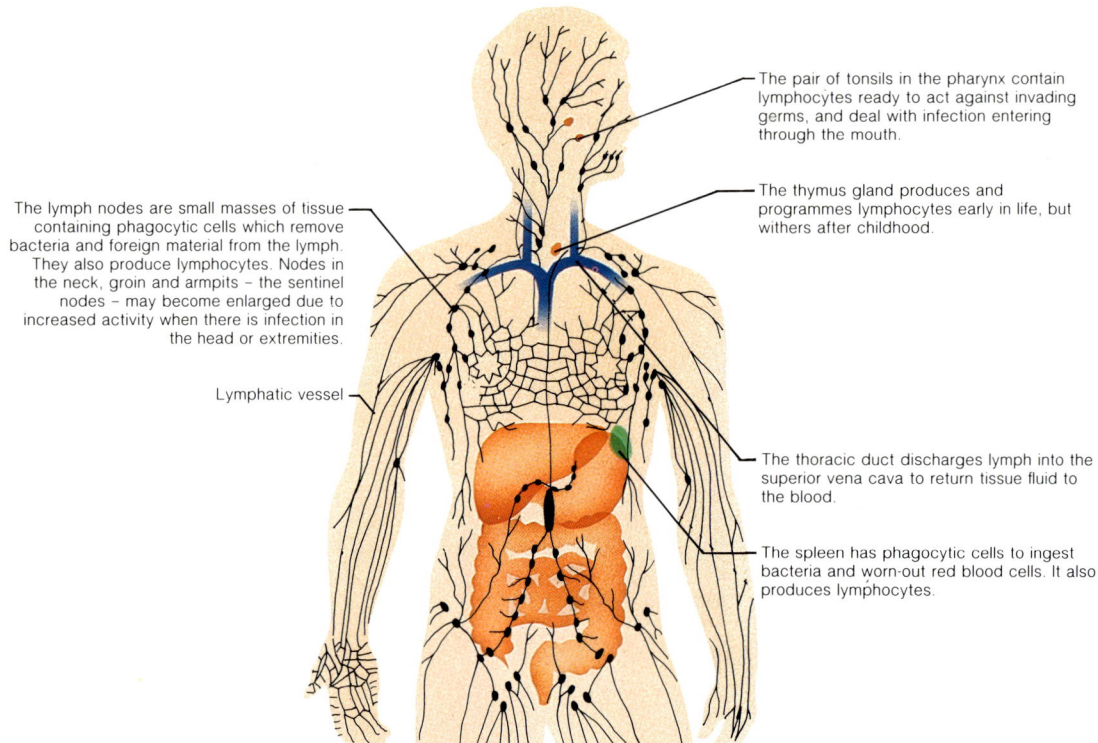

The pair of tonsils in the pharynx contain lymphocytes ready to act against invading germs, and deal with infection entering through the mouth.

The thymus gland produces and programmes lymphocytes early in life, but withers after childhood.

The lymph nodes are small masses of tissue containing phagocytic cells which remove bacteria and foreign material from the lymph. They also produce lymphocytes. Nodes in the neck, groin and armpits – the sentinel nodes – may become enlarged due to increased activity when there is infection in the head or extremities.

Lymphatic vessel

The thoracic duct discharges lymph into the superior vena cava to return tissue fluid to the blood.

The spleen has phagocytic cells to ingest bacteria and worn-out red blood cells. It also produces lymphocytes.

HOW THE HEART FUNCTIONS

The powerhouse for the complicated process of feeding, cleansing and protecting the body cells is a natural pump about the size of a man's fist, which keeps working for decades without maintenance. As already described, blood from the veins enters its right upper chamber, the right atrium. From here it is pumped through the tricuspid valve into the lower chamber, the right ventricle. As the heart contracts again, the blood is forced through the pulmonary valve towards the lungs to discharge carbon dioxide and pick up oxygen. Freshly oxygenated blood from the lungs returns to the left side of the heart, entering the left atrium and passing through the mitral valve into the lower chamber, the left ventricle. This last is the most powerful of the four chambers. When it contracts it sends blood through the aortic valve into the aorta with enough force to carry it around the body.

The heart is a two-stroke pump. On one stroke the two atria – right and left – contract, sending venous blood into the right ventricle and oxygenated blood from the lungs into the left ventricle. On the following stroke the two ventricles contract, sending venous blood to the lungs and oxygenated blood to the body. These contractions are electrically controlled by the heart itself through a conduction pathway beginning at an area of specialised cells called the sinoatrial node, or 'pacemaker'. The impulse arising here spreads over both atria and down to the atrioventricular node, which relays it to the ventricles. These self-generated impulses can be picked up from the skin surface with an electro-cardiograph, or ECG machine, providing evidence of how well a patient's heart is performing.

Working as hard as it does, the heart needs a copious blood supply, which it gets from two arteries springing from the aorta just outside the left ventricle. These branch and wreath the heart like a crown. Hence their name – the coronaries.

HOW THE HEART FUNCTIONS

The heart is actually just an exceptionally good pump. About the size of a man's fist, it consists principally of the body's most hard-working muscle. It beats over 100 000 times a day.

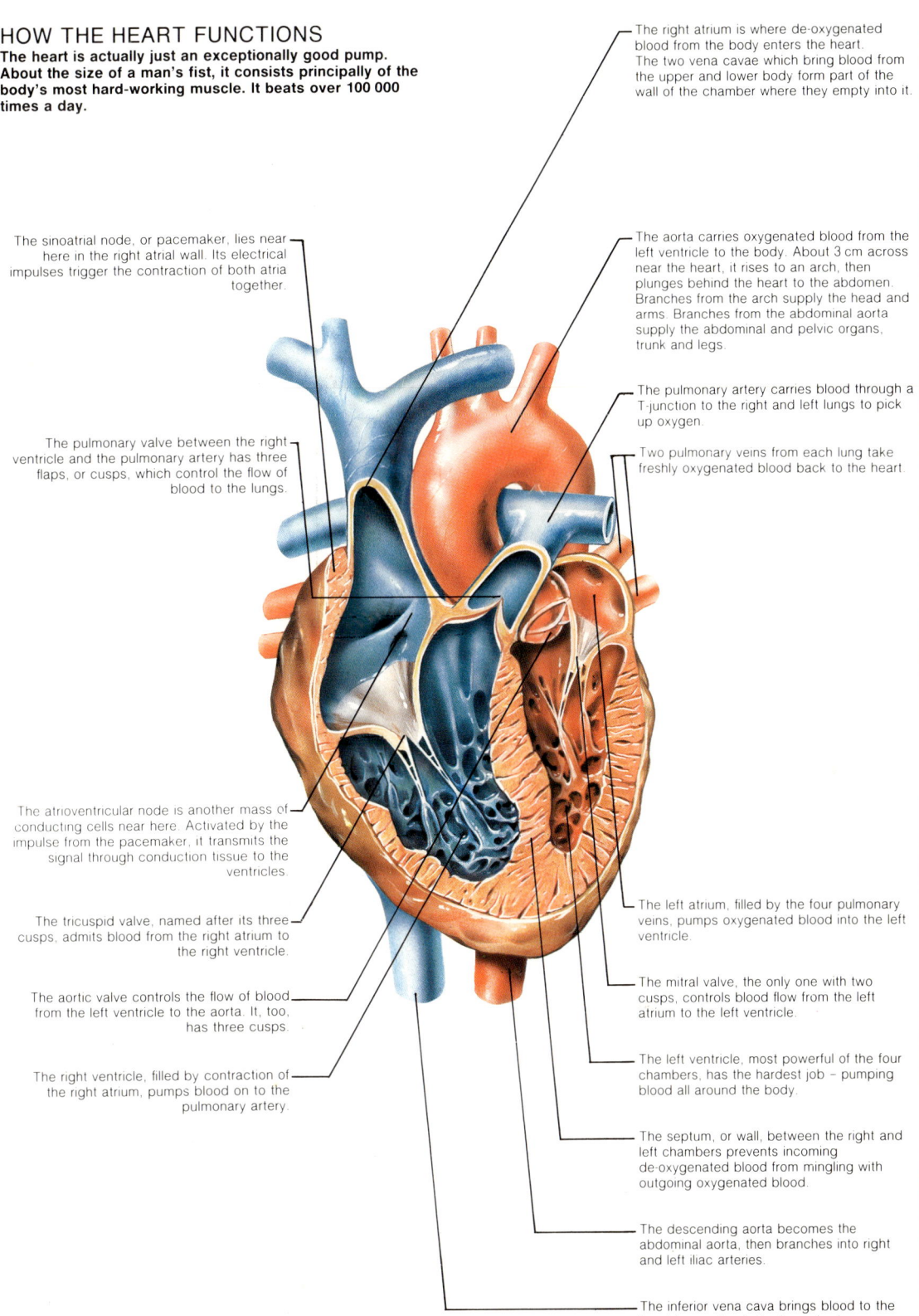

The right atrium is where de-oxygenated blood from the body enters the heart. The two vena cavae which bring blood from the upper and lower body form part of the wall of the chamber where they empty into it.

The sinoatrial node, or pacemaker, lies near here in the right atrial wall. Its electrical impulses trigger the contraction of both atria together.

The aorta carries oxygenated blood from the left ventricle to the body. About 3 cm across near the heart, it rises to an arch, then plunges behind the heart to the abdomen. Branches from the arch supply the head and arms. Branches from the abdominal aorta supply the abdominal and pelvic organs, trunk and legs.

The pulmonary valve between the right ventricle and the pulmonary artery has three flaps, or cusps, which control the flow of blood to the lungs.

The pulmonary artery carries blood through a T-junction to the right and left lungs to pick up oxygen.

Two pulmonary veins from each lung take freshly oxygenated blood back to the heart.

The atrioventricular node is another mass of conducting cells near here. Activated by the impulse from the pacemaker, it transmits the signal through conduction tissue to the ventricles.

The tricuspid valve, named after its three cusps, admits blood from the right atrium to the right ventricle.

The aortic valve controls the flow of blood from the left ventricle to the aorta. It, too, has three cusps.

The right ventricle, filled by contraction of the right atrium, pumps blood on to the pulmonary artery.

The left atrium, filled by the four pulmonary veins, pumps oxygenated blood into the left ventricle.

The mitral valve, the only one with two cusps, controls blood flow from the left atrium to the left ventricle.

The left ventricle, most powerful of the four chambers, has the hardest job – pumping blood all around the body.

The septum, or wall, between the right and left chambers prevents incoming de-oxygenated blood from mingling with outgoing oxygenated blood.

The descending aorta becomes the abdominal aorta, then branches into right and left iliac arteries.

The inferior vena cava brings blood to the heart from veins in the lower body.

THE RESPIRATORY SYSTEM

The demand for oxygen by the billions of cells that comprise the body drives a largely unconscious behaviour that lasts from birth to death. We breathe. If we stop for more than three or four minutes cells begin to die, with those in the brain succumbing first.

RESPIRATORY CENTRE

The cells' claim to an adequate oxygen supply is jealously pursued by a small focus of nervous tissue in the medulla at the base of the brain. This is the respiratory centre, where reports from various bodily monitoring stations are continuously assessed. The respiratory centre controls breathing without the conscious brain's knowing. From specialised nerve cells called chemoreceptors in the aortic and carotid arteries, reports may come in that the level of carbon dioxide in the blood is high. A major waste product of cells is not being cleared efficiently. Out from the respiratory centre will go messages to the respiratory muscles to increase the breathing rate. More air entering the lungs carries away more carbon dioxide and the balance of blood gases reverts towards normal.

The respiratory centre also processes reports on blood oxygen levels and blood pressure. At a sudden rise or fall in blood pressure the centre orders breathing either to slow or speed up. Connections between the centre and the cerebral cortex in the conscious brain allow us to take charge of our own breathing when we choose.

The lungs, within which we extract oxygen from the air and release carbon dioxide in exchange, are bags of spongy tissue lying immediately inside the rib cage. The pleural cavity each occupies is airtight. Surrounding them is a double pleural membrane, the outer layer fixed to the wall of the cavity, the inner layer covering the lungs themselves. A film of fluid in the space between the two membranes helps them slide easily over each other in breathing.

INSPIRATION AND EXPIRATION

The muscles of breathing controlled by the respiratory centre in the medulla are those of the chest wall and the diaphragm, a dome-shaped structure separating the chest from the abdomen. There are two phases of breathing: inspiration when air is drawn in, and expiration when it is let out. In inspiration the diaphragm flattens and the chest muscles push the ribs upwards and outwards. The joint effect is to increase the volume of the pleural cavity. The further effect is that air pressure in the lungs falls below atmospheric pressure outside the body. Air from outside immediately rushes in to equalise. In other words, we breathe in. Expiration is a purely passive process most of the time. As the breathing muscles relax, the higher pressure in the lungs and their recoil force air from the chest.

UPPER AND LOWER RESPIRATORY TRACTS

The lungs draw air from without through an airway divided into the upper and lower respiratory tracts. The upper tract consists of the nose, mouth, pharynx and larynx, also known as the voice-box. As air passes down, impurities and organisms are filtered from it by the hairs of the nostrils and the mucous membrane of the nose and mouth. Lymphocytes from the tonsils and adenoids also attack incoming bacteria. The mouth and pharynx serve as an entry for food as well as air. Food is prevented from proceeding further down the airway by a flap of cartilage, the epiglottis, which swings across the entrance to the larynx during swallowing.

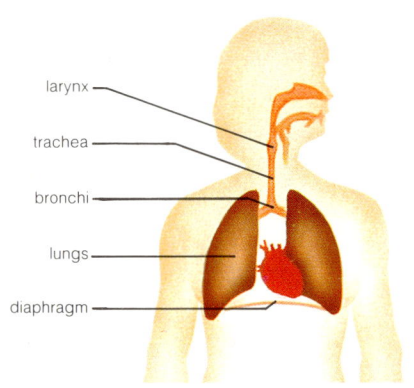

larynx

trachea

bronchi

lungs

diaphragm

Below the larynx runs the lower respiratory tract, beginning with the trachea, or windpipe, a tube about 25 cm long held open by strong rings of cartilage. At its lower end the trachea divides into two other tubes, the left and right bronchi, which enter the left and right lungs. Within the lungs the bronchi branch and branch again, forming a bronchial tree with the smallest twigs, the bronchioles, only 0.2 mm across. The bronchioles lead to clusters of alveoli, or air sacs, over which the capillary network of blood vessels runs. The lungs contain an estimated 300 million alveoli, providing a surface area of about 70 square metres for the exchange of oxygen and carbon dioxide.

Blood arriving at the capillary network of the alveoli is oxygen starved. Oxygen from the air reaching the alveoli is attracted through the capillary walls by diffusion. Entering the red blood cells, the oxygen turns the dark blue haemoglobin red again. At the same time carbon dioxide passes the other way from the blood to the alveoli, to be released to the air.

Each breath we take does not renew all the air in the lungs. It merely adds to a stock of about 3 litres, known as the 'resting respiratory level'. The air drawn in is known as the 'tidal volume' and at normal resting breathing amounts to about 500 ml. Only

HOW THE LUNGS WORK

The left lung has been dissected in this diagram to expose the bronchial tree. At its extremities oxygen passes from air passages (the alveoli) into blood capillaries and carbon dioxide is exchanged.

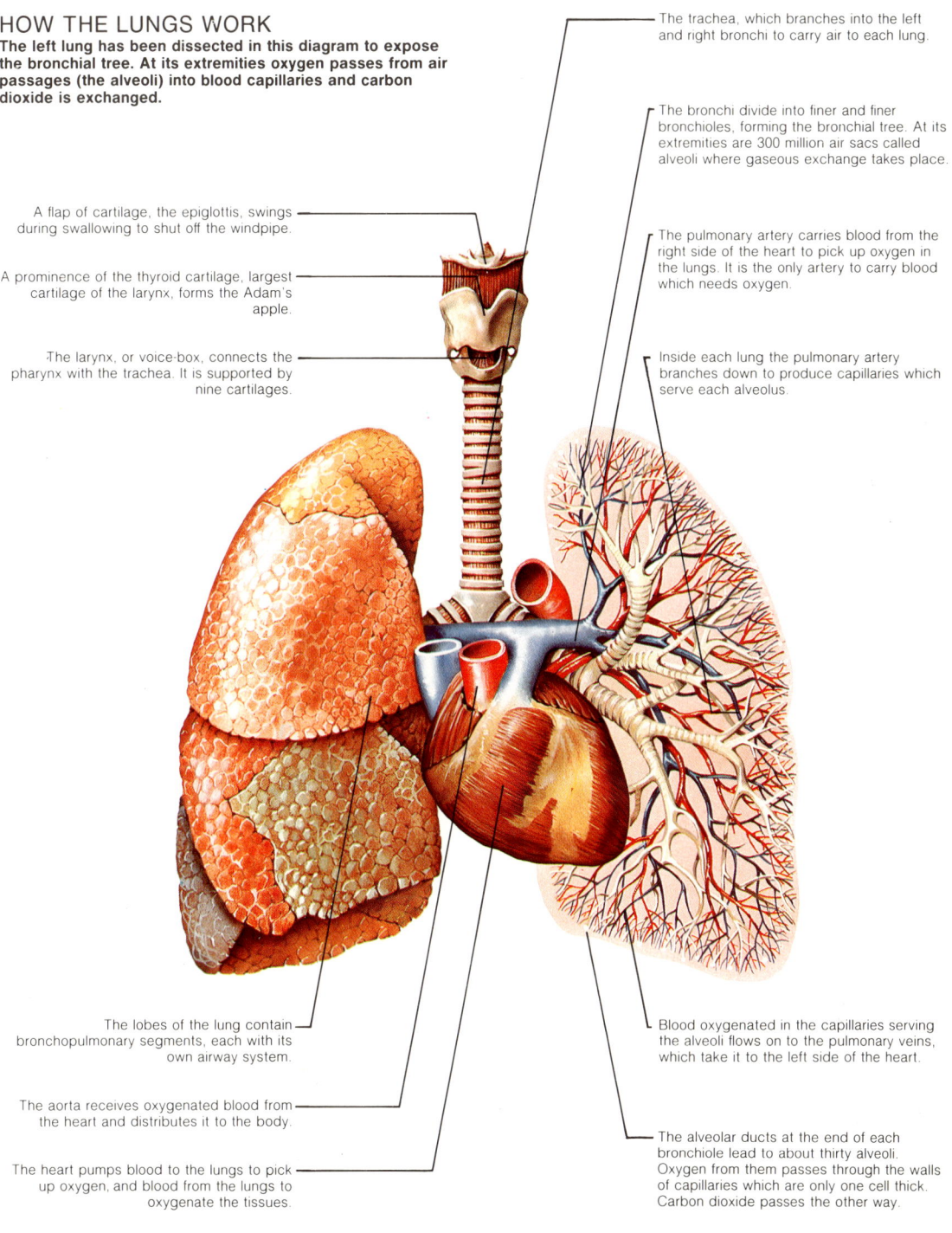

The trachea, which branches into the left and right bronchi to carry air to each lung.

The bronchi divide into finer and finer bronchioles, forming the bronchial tree. At its extremities are 300 million air sacs called alveoli where gaseous exchange takes place.

The pulmonary artery carries blood from the right side of the heart to pick up oxygen in the lungs. It is the only artery to carry blood which needs oxygen.

Inside each lung the pulmonary artery branches down to produce capillaries which serve each alveolus.

A flap of cartilage, the epiglottis, swings during swallowing to shut off the windpipe.

A prominence of the thyroid cartilage, largest cartilage of the larynx, forms the Adam's apple.

The larynx, or voice-box, connects the pharynx with the trachea. It is supported by nine cartilages.

The lobes of the lung contain bronchopulmonary segments, each with its own airway system.

The aorta receives oxygenated blood from the heart and distributes it to the body.

The heart pumps blood to the lungs to pick up oxygen, and blood from the lungs to oxygenate the tissues.

Blood oxygenated in the capillaries serving the alveoli flows on to the pulmonary veins, which take it to the left side of the heart.

The alveolar ducts at the end of each bronchiole lead to about thirty alveoli. Oxygen from them passes through the walls of capillaries which are only one cell thick. Carbon dioxide passes the other way.

about 350 ml reaches the alveoli, the rest occupying 'dead space' in the airway. Breathe through a snorkel and the added dead space will force you to breathe harder. Down at the alveoli each new breath brings about 21 per cent oxygen to boost the oxygen content of the residual air stock.

When oxygen is being used up quickly during exercise the respiratory centre will detect the falling level in the blood and signal for quicker, stronger breathing. In vigorous physical activity the resting reserve volume as well as the tidal air volume will be used – that is, up to about 6 litres of air at a time.

THE NERVOUS SYSTEM

The nervous system, with its command post the brain, oversees the functions of the body, monitors and responds to the outside environment and is the essence of our being – harbouring our thoughts, attitudes and emotions. By comparison the most elaborate computers lack initiative, creativity, feeling and the ability to reprogramme themselves. The human nervous system, distinguished from that of all other species by its powers of analytical thought and decision-making, is moreover more spontaneous and unobtrusive than any computing apparatus.

TWO NETWORKS OF NERVES

We are largely unaware of being programmed from birth to fit our environment and much of the work of the nervous system, the humdrum tasks of maintaining the body and adjusting to what is going on around it, proceeds without our being aware of it. That fact suggests, correctly, that there are two networks of nerves: one under conscious control; one carrying out its duties of regulating digestion, heart rate, breathing and so on without needing to inform us. Both networks consist of two pathways, distinguished by the directions in which they convey nervous impulses. One is the sensory pathway which picks up signals from the environment, and from every cranny of the body, and carries the information to the central nervous system, made up of the brain and spinal cord. The other is the motor pathway which carries instructions from the command centres outwards to every part of the body.

However, human beings are not automatons and there is some flexibility in the way the various components of the nervous system operate. In breathing, for example, the brain can consciously override the unconscious control of the lungs by deliberately deciding, say, to take deeper breaths. There is a limit to how far that overlap will stretch. One cannot kill oneself by holding one's breath. The unconscious system will not allow it.

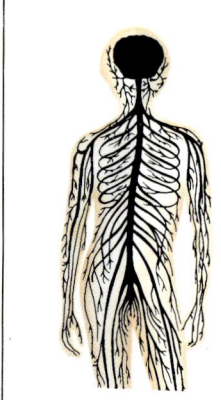

The nervous system has two principal divisions: the central nervous system and the peripheral nerves. The first consists of the brain and spinal cord. The peripheral network consists of 31 pairs of spinal nerves.

SENSORY SYSTEM

What is happening to the body and in the body from its surface to the bowels is detected continuously by an army of receptors of the sensory nervous system. There are receptors in the skin, the muscles and the joints. There are receptors monitoring respiration, blood pressure, levels of oxygen and carbon dioxide in the blood and the performance of the heart. There are receptors that register external heat, that give us the sense of touch, make us feel hunger and thirst, that analyse body chemistry and transmit other signals from a cut or bruise that make us feel pain. The four main sense organs, the eyes, ears, nose and tongue, are part of the overall sensory system.

MOTOR SYSTEM

The responses to messages transmitted inwards by the sensory system are transmitted outwards to the muscles and glands by the motor network. If the sensory message was 'skin too hot', the motor system tells the sweat glands to start secreting. If a burning ember falls on a bare foot, a millisecond later the leg muscles are ordered to leap from the fire.

Many of these responses are initiated without reference to the conscious brain. The motor system has two pathways – conscious and unconscious. The first is called the somatic pathway, the second the autonomic (a name given in the mistaken belief that it was autonomous, with no input from the central nervous system). The somatic nerves carry messages dictated by our conscious brains that tell striated skeletal muscles to get us out of our chair or lift a fork to our lips. The autonomic nerves get on with the business of running the body, dilating and constricting blood vessels, changing the size of the pupils and doing hundreds of other chores. Their signals go to the smooth muscles of the viscera, the heart muscle and the glands, and the activities they promote largely escape our attention.

The autonomic pathway is itself divided into two: the sympathetic and parasympathetic systems. Many organs are served by both. In general, impulses from the sympathetic division stimulate the organ to start or increase activity, while impulses from the parasympathetic tone down the activity.

CENTRAL NERVOUS SYSTEM

The central office for nearly all incoming and outgoing nervous impulses is the brain. But the spinal cord is an important relay station, passing incoming messages to the brain and conveying outgoing messages to the peripheral nervous system. The brain and spinal cord make up the central nervous system (CNS).

The structures we call nerves belong only to the peripheral system. They are bundles of fibres which are actually extensions of single nerve cells. There are two types of fibres: dendrites which carry impulses towards the nerve cell, and axons which carry them away. Some axons measure only a few

HOW THE BODY REACTS

The special senses of sight, smell, hearing and taste keep the brain informed of what is going on in the external environment. Other sensory nerves give the brain a constant update on what is happening inside the body. In situations of danger, such as the threat of being run down (right), the brain processes incoming signals in a flash. Through the motor nerves it transmits impulses telling the skeletal muscles to remove the body fast.

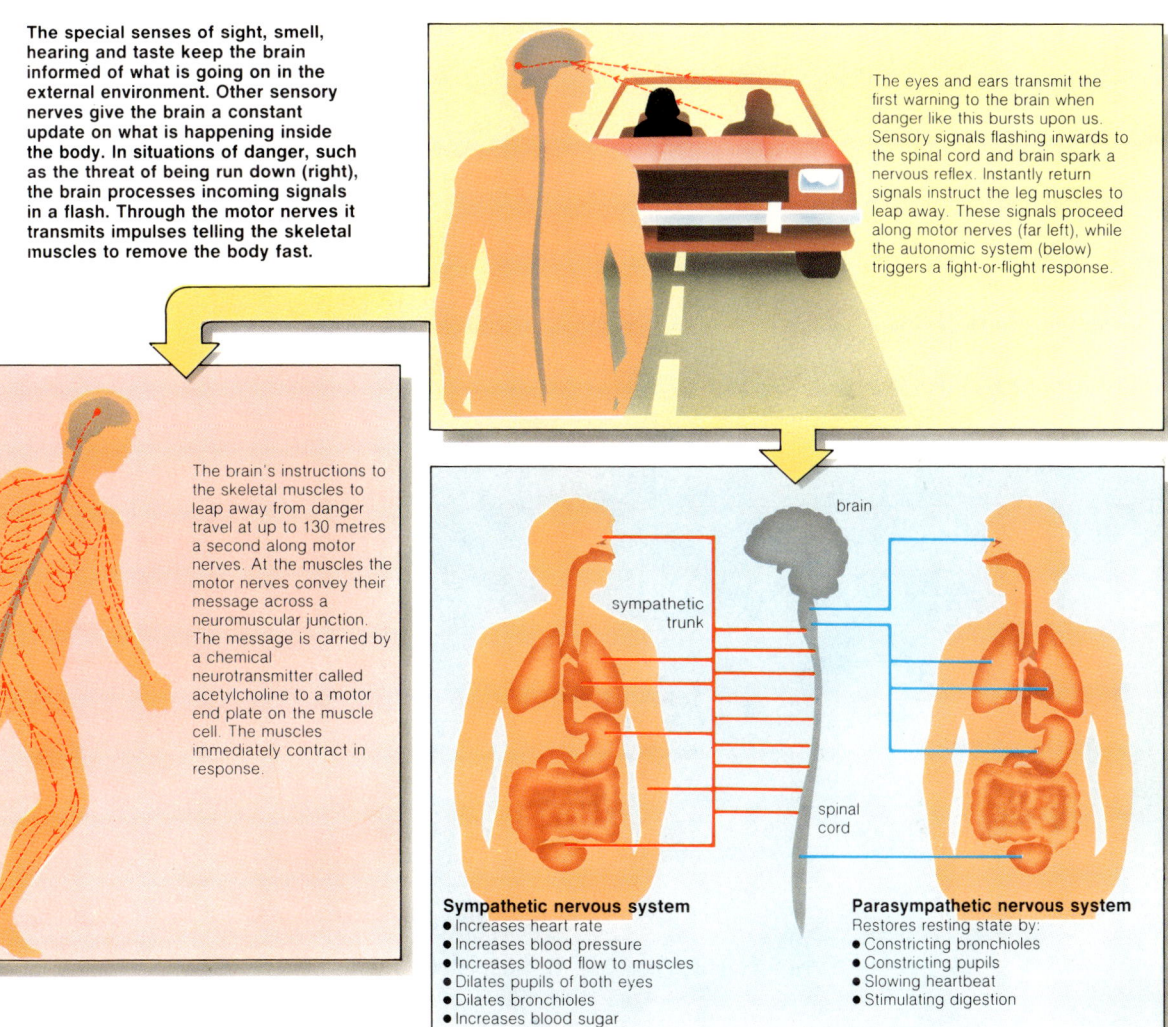

The eyes and ears transmit the first warning to the brain when danger like this bursts upon us. Sensory signals flashing inwards to the spinal cord and brain spark a nervous reflex. Instantly return signals instruct the leg muscles to leap away. These signals proceed along motor nerves (far left), while the autonomic system (below) triggers a fight-or-flight response.

The brain's instructions to the skeletal muscles to leap away from danger travel at up to 130 metres a second along motor nerves. At the muscles the motor nerves convey their message across a neuromuscular junction. The message is carried by a chemical neurotransmitter called acetylcholine to a motor end plate on the muscle cell. The muscles immediately contract in response.

brain

sympathetic trunk

spinal cord

Sympathetic nervous system
- Increases heart rate
- Increases blood pressure
- Increases blood flow to muscles
- Dilates pupils of both eyes
- Dilates bronchioles
- Increases blood sugar
- Slows digestion

Parasympathetic nervous system
Restores resting state by:
- Constricting bronchioles
- Constricting pupils
- Slowing heartbeat
- Stimulating digestion

millimetres; others like those from the spinal cord to the toes can be more than a metre long. Sensory fibres carrying impulses inwards and motor fibres transmitting outwards are often contained within the same nerve. As nerves travel inwards from the periphery they unite with other nerves, becoming thicker and thicker until they enter the spinal cord. Or, looking from the other direction: from the spinal cord issue thirty-one pairs of large nerve trunks which branch to thinner and thinner nerves on the way to the parts they supply. The transmission of signals to and from the brain within the spinal cord is carried out by spinal tracts, which are bundles of nerve fibres akin to nerves. Ascending tracts carry sensory impulses to the brain; descending tracts carry motor impulses to the body.

The importance of the central nervous system is reflected in the strength of its shielding – the skull and the spinal vertebrae. There are thirty-three vertebrae ringing the spinal cord, although those in the lower back and the coccyx are usually fused into pairs or greater numbers of bones. The twenty-six unfused bones between the neck and pelvis are separated by intervertebral discs – fibrous rings which absorb vertical shock.

In addition to its bony armour, the CNS has three protective membranes called meninges. The outer membrane is the dura mater, or tough layer, the middle the arachnoid, or spider layer, and the inner, the pia mater, or delicate layer. Between the arachnoid and pia mater, in what is called the subarachnoid space, flows the cerebrospinal fluid.

HOW THE BRAIN WORKS

The cerebrum, largest mass of brain tissue and centre of decision-making, consists of two matching hemispheres. Our illustration looks at the right hemisphere from the middle of the brain.

The limbic system, seat of the emotions, borders on the cerebrum and the hypothalamus.

The hypothalamus controls the autonomic nervous system, regulates body temperature, responds to hunger and registers thirst.

The cerebral cortex is the outer 2–4 mm of grey matter covering the cerebrum. Containing roughly 15 000 million cells, it is the most highly evolved part of the brain. Its many folds increase its surface area by about thirty times.

The thalamus, two oval-shaped masses above the midbrain, relays all sensory impulses except smell to the cerebral cortex. It interprets other sensory impulses, such as those of pain, temperature, crude touch and pressure.

The corpus callosum is a large bundle of fibres connecting the two hemispheres of the cerebrum. It is the communications channel between the two.

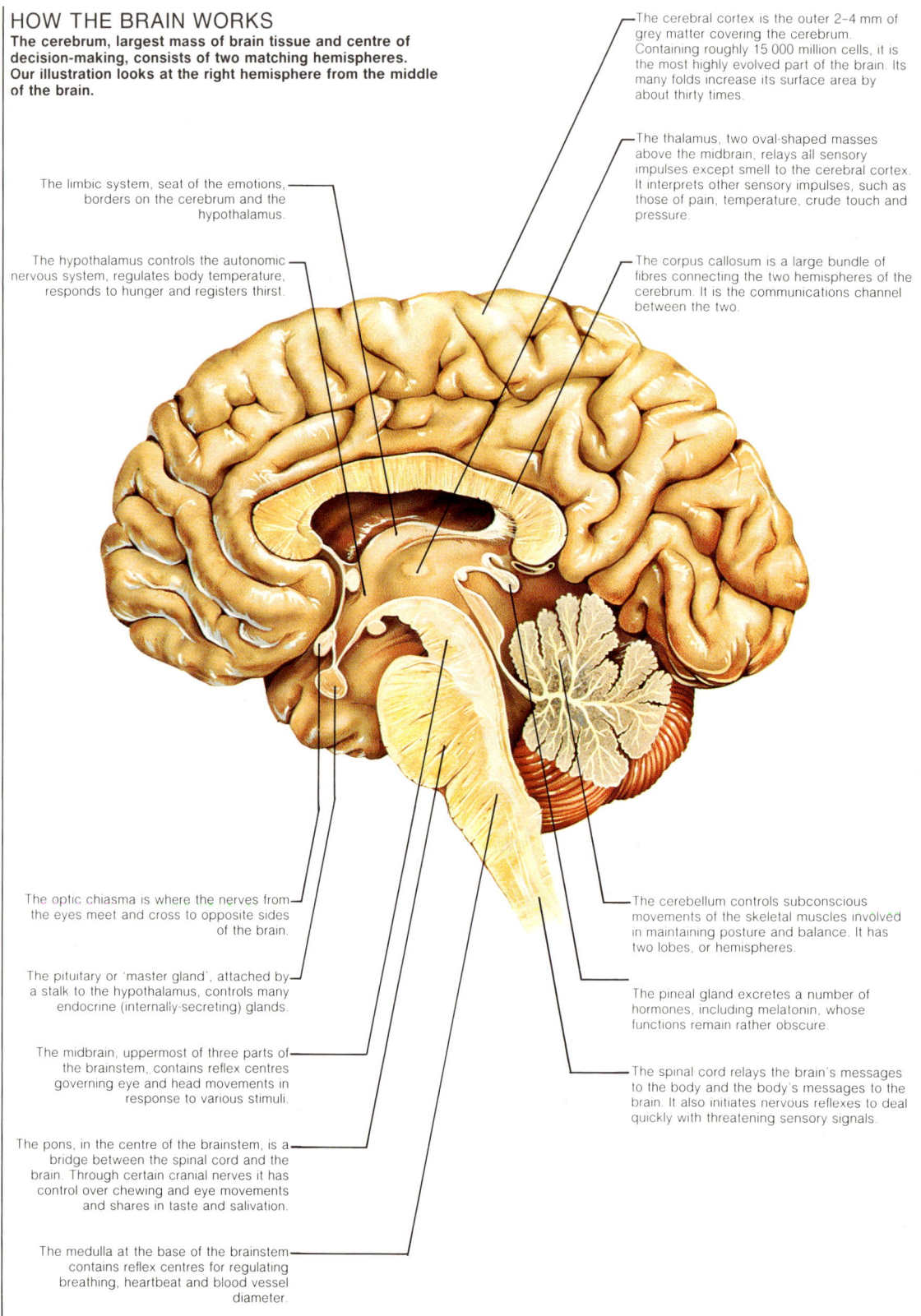

The optic chiasma is where the nerves from the eyes meet and cross to opposite sides of the brain.

The pituitary or 'master gland', attached by a stalk to the hypothalamus, controls many endocrine (internally-secreting) glands.

The midbrain, uppermost of three parts of the brainstem, contains reflex centres governing eye and head movements in response to various stimuli.

The pons, in the centre of the brainstem, is a bridge between the spinal cord and the brain. Through certain cranial nerves it has control over chewing and eye movements and shares in taste and salivation.

The medulla at the base of the brainstem contains reflex centres for regulating breathing, heartbeat and blood vessel diameter.

The cerebellum controls subconscious movements of the skeletal muscles involved in maintaining posture and balance. It has two lobes, or hemispheres.

The pineal gland excretes a number of hormones, including melatonin, whose functions remain rather obscure.

The spinal cord relays the brain's messages to the body and the body's messages to the brain. It also initiates nervous reflexes to deal quickly with threatening sensory signals.

SPINAL CORD

The cord itself is composed of white and grey matter. A cross-section shows the grey matter forming a rough letter H in the centre of an oval of white matter. The white matter, made up of nerve fibres, contains the ascending and descending sensory and motor tracts. The grey matter comprises mainly nerve cells, some with a sensory function, others involved in motor tasks. It routes incoming sensory impulses to the appropriate ascending tracts and steers motor impulses from the brain to the appropriate peripheral nerves.

The grey matter is also involved in the spinal reflex, an immediate reaction to anything upsetting the body's internal or external equilibrium. To revert to the example of the burning ember falling on the bare foot: the sensory distress signal from the foot does not go all the way to the brain; it activates a motor nerve cell in the cord which tells the leg muscles to get away fast. When your doctor asks you to cross your legs then taps the upper one just below the kneecap, he is testing the stretch reflex. If it is working, stretch receptors in a thigh muscle attached to a kneecap ligament flash a message to the grey matter in the cord. A reflex arc is created, the muscle contracts and the leg kicks forwards.

THE BRAIN

The grey matter and the white matter of the cord extend into the brain, the highest, most intricate organisation of nervous tissue. Weighing around 1300 grams, the brain constitutes about 2 per cent of body weight. Protected by the meninges and cerebrospinal fluid, it has a rich blood supply, consuming 20 per cent of the oxygen used by the body.

The spinal cord and the brain are contiguous, running into each other at the brainstem. This consists of three parts: the medulla, the pons and the midbrain. Sensory and motor tracts of white matter from the cord cross as they pass through the medulla with the result that control of functions in either side of the body rests in the opposite side of the brain.

The medulla encompasses important control centres of the autonomic nervous system which regulate breathing, heartbeat and the diameter of blood vessels. Swallowing, vomiting, coughing, sneezing and hiccuping are also coordinated here. The pons, as the name implies, is a bridge connecting the spinal cord with the brain and parts of the brain with each other. It is also the command post of nerves involved in chewing, taste, salivation and facial expression. The midbrain contains reflex centres governing movements of the eyeballs and head in response to visual and other stimuli. It also shares functions of touch with the medulla and pons.

CEREBELLUM

Behind the brainstem lies the cerebellum, whose twin hemispheres give it a rough butterfly shape. The cerebellum plays an important part in the coordination of unconscious movements involved in maintaining posture and balance. Information about how the parts of the body are disposed, such as whether there is a lean to the left or right, is sent to the cerebellum from the inner ear. The cerebellum corrects the lean by stimulating the requisite muscle contractions. It also coordinates delicate conscious movements such as playing the piano.

CEREBRAL CORTEX

Above the brainstem, like a mushroom on its stalk, is the cerebrum, with its outer rind, the cerebral cortex. Consisting of grey matter 2–4 mm thick, the cortex is the most highly evolved part of the highest centre of the brain. It is concerned with consciously locating parts of the body from which sensory stimuli are received, sorting out sensory data received from lower parts of the brain, despatching instructions to the muscles and glands, and with intellectual processes and emotional responses. Among its 15 000 million nerve cells are some dedicated to storing memories of previous sensory experiences so that comparisons with the past can be made. The cortex covers both hemispheres of the cerebrum, buckling into many folds called gyri or convolutions which increase its surface area for decision-making by about thirty times.

Deep within the cerebrum and extending into two other underlying structures, the thalamus and hypothalamus, is the limbic area where emotions such as rage, pleasure, pain, fear, sexual desire and affection are thought to be generated.

AREAS OF THE CEREBRAL CORTEX
Particular areas of the cerebral cortex are concerned with various body functions – as designated in the diagram.

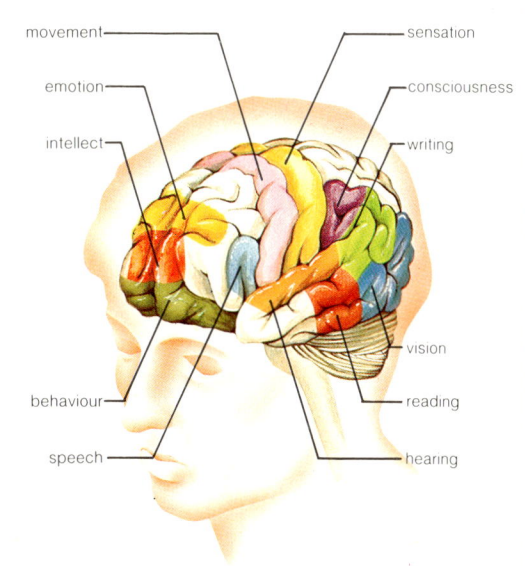

For sustenance for its cells and the energy to permit them to perform their vital functions the body must first process the food it is offered to meet their requirements. Digestion is needed to convert food into the small molecules which will pass through the walls of the intestines into the blood and lymph streams to nourish the cells.

BREAKING DOWN FOOD

Food is digested during a journey through a canal some 10 metres long, starting at the mouth and ending at the anus. This gastrointestinal tract, or alimentary canal, bulges in places such as the stomach and colon, but is uninterrupted.

Even before food reaches the mouth the body prepares to break it down into its basic components, mainly carbohydrates (sugars and starches), fats and protein. The sight or smell of food or the sounds of a meal being prepared will stimulate the parotid and other glands to secrete saliva into the mouth in anticipation of what is to come. Saliva contains an enzyme, or organic catalyst, which assists chemical changes. Called salivary amylase, it starts the breakdown of starches. Saliva also lubricates food during chewing so that it can be swallowed more easily. The salivary glands produce from a litre to a litre and a half of fluid every day for digestion and to moisten the mucous membrane of the mouth and lubricate the tongue and lips during speech. Excess production is swallowed and reabsorbed.

Chewing merely prepares food for swallowing. It serves no digestive purpose. When the teeth have broken food into small lumps, the tongue rolls them into a bolus, or soft mass that can be swallowed. Any conscious influence on digestion ceases once food is swallowed. We are blissfully unaware of most of the following events as the bolus slips into the throat and the unconscious centres of the brain take over.

OESOPHAGUS

The conscious act of swallowing involves other unconscious muscular movements: the soft palate closes off the airway from the nose, the larynx rises and a flap of cartilage, the epiglottis, swings across the opening to the trachea and the lungs. Like changing points on a railway track, that leaves one way for the food to go – down the oesophagus. This is the part of the gastrointestinal tract leading to the stomach. Wave-like contractions and dilations of the muscular wall of the oesophagus, called peristalsis, squeeze the bolus down to the J-shaped ballooning of the food tract below.

STOMACH

The stomach lies quite high in the abdomen, just beneath the diaphragm. About the size of a large sausage when empty, it serves two main functions: it stores food, releasing it slowly according to the digestive capacity of the intestines; and it plays a part in digestion by producing enzymes.

The taste, sight, smell or even thought of food triggers the gastric glands to secrete several substances into the stomach. This preparatory action is a nervous reflex involving the medulla in the brainstem and parasympathetic fibres in the vagus nerve. The substances secreted include hydrochloric acid, pepsinogen and mucus. The mucus protects the stomach lining from attack by the hydrochloric acid, while the acid converts pepsinogen into the active enzyme, pepsin. The acid also kills most micro-organisms in food. Pepsin breaks down proteins by splitting their long amino acid chains into smaller units called peptides.

While alcohol, a small amount of water and certain drugs are absorbed directly from the stomach into the bloodstream, the rest of its contents is churned with gastric secretions in a peristaltic movement of the stomach muscle called mixing waves. The thin liquid resulting is known as chyme. This moves slowly to the bottom of the J shape, then a little at a time through the pyloric sphincter, a ring of smooth muscle which controls admission to the duodenum, the next section of the alimentary canal.

Carbohydrates tend to pass through first, clearing the stomach in about two hours, followed by protein (three hours) and fat (four hours). Various gastric hormones regulate passage of foods by inhibiting gastric secretions and stomach movement.

DUODENUM

Digestion and absorption begin in earnest in the duodenum, the beginning of the small intestine. It leads to two other parts: the jejunum; then the ileum where digestion continues. As the chyme moves through the duodenum its composition is analysed by specialised cells in the intestinal wall, which stimulate the secretion of chemicals to process it. Some of these are released by the small intestine itself, others by the pancreas, liver and gall-bladder. On contact with chyme the intestinal lining secretes an enzyme called enterokinase whose function is to convert another enzyme from the pancreas, trypsinogen, to trypsin. Trypsin digests protein. The reason its activation is delayed until food has actually arrived is that it might otherwise start working on the protein of intestinal cells. The pancreas provides the alkali, sodium bicarbonate, to neutralise any excess of acid in the duodenum and the enzymes, amylase and maltase, to break down carbohydrates to simple sugars and lipase to break down fats to triglycerides.

High in fats, chyme provokes a reaction which causes the gall-bladder to release some of its store of bile – a thick, yellow, brownish or olive green liquid produced in the liver. Bile entering the duodenum through the bile duct breaks down fat globules to tiny droplets called micelles.

ABSORPTION INTO BLOOD AND LYMPH

As digestion proceeds in the duodenum and later the

THE PROCESS OF DIGESTION

Digestion involves several organs and many metres of intestines. It starts in the mouth and proceeds throughout most of the gastrointestinal tract. It breaks down food progressively to furnish the small molecules needed by the cells for energy, growth and repair.

The stomach churns food into a thin liquid called chyme and, with the digestive enzyme, pepsin, starts breaking down protein into smaller amino acid sequences. The churning action slowly forces chyme into the beginning of the small intestine, the duodenum.

Saliva starts the digestive process in the mouth, where food mixed with it and torn by the teeth is formed into a bolus by the tongue so it can be swallowed.

Saliva comes from three pairs of glands which deliver their secretions into the mouth.

A rippling muscle movement called peristalsis forces food down the oesophagus to the stomach.

The small intestine is where food is digested, then absorbed into the blood and lymph streams. Digestion proceeds as chyme passes through its three segments, the duodenum, jejunum and ileum. Absorption occurs at millions of tiny projections in the intestinal wall called villi. Each is served by blood capillaries and a small lymphatic vessel called a lacteal. Proteins pass into the blood as amino acids, carbohydrates as small molecules of sugar, mainly glucose. Fats pass into the lacteals as minute droplets.

The duodenum secretes an enzyme called enterokinase as food, turned to chyme, moves in from the stomach. Enterokinase converts another enzyme from the pancreas from trypsinogen to trypsin. Trypsin digests protein. Two other enzymes from the pancreas, amylase and maltase, break down carbohydrates to simple sugars. Bile from the gall-bladder breaks down fat to tiny droplets.

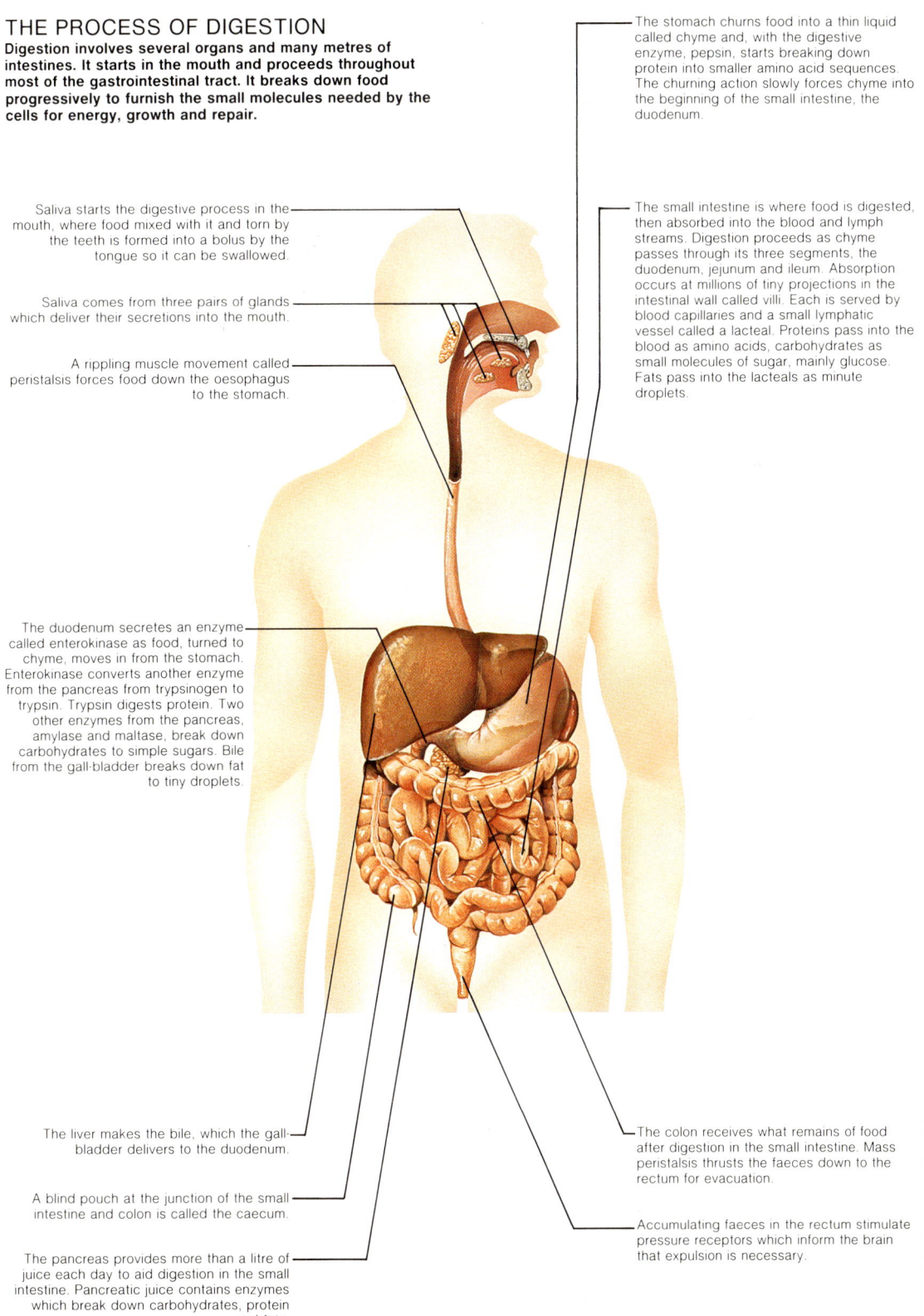

The liver makes the bile, which the gall-bladder delivers to the duodenum.

A blind pouch at the junction of the small intestine and colon is called the caecum.

The pancreas provides more than a litre of juice each day to aid digestion in the small intestine. Pancreatic juice contains enzymes which break down carbohydrates, protein and fats.

The colon receives what remains of food after digestion in the small intestine. Mass peristalsis thrusts the faeces down to the rectum for evacuation.

Accumulating faeces in the rectum stimulate pressure receptors which inform the brain that expulsion is necessary.

jejunum and ileum, its breakdown products are absorbed through the intestinal wall into the blood and lymph. Absorption depends on the surface area available for it, which explains the extraordinarily corrugated structure of the lining of the small intestine. This is broken into 4–5 million tiny projections called villi, and each villus has even tinier, finger-like projections called microvilli. Together they give the 3 metres of small intestine an absorption area of about 40 square metres.

Each villus contains a small artery and vein, a capillary network and a small lymphatic vessel called a lacteal. The millions of villi are junctions where digested nutrients diffusing from the intestine are shipped away in the blood or lymph. Small molecules of sugar and amino acid pass through the walls of capillaries and are carried by the blood, first to the liver, then through the heart into the general circulation. Tiny droplets of fat are carried off in the lymph to the thoracic duct, where they enter the bloodstream to proceed to the liver. Each day, also, about 7 litres of water from secretions produced by glands and organs of the digestive tract are reabsorbed into the blood. About a litre or so of fluid drunk is absorbed, too, and any surplus fluid not needed by the body is filtered from the blood by the kidneys and discharged in urine.

THE FUNCTION OF THE KIDNEYS
The kidneys, situated above the waist at the back of the abdomen, filter the blood and produce urine. Each kidney is about 10–12 cm long and 5–7.5 cm wide. Oxygenated blood from the aorta is delivered to each kidney by the renal artery. Blood passing from the kidneys is carried to the inferior vena cava by the renal veins. Each kidney has about one million cleansing units called nephrons. In each nephron there is a glomerulus where blood is filtered and a convoluted tubule which processes the filtrate and carries urine away. Urine from each kidney is taken by a ureter to the bladder.

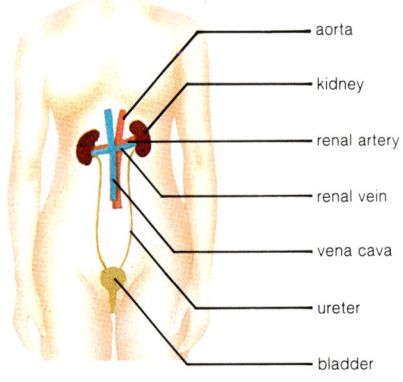

- aorta
- kidney
- renal artery
- renal vein
- vena cava
- ureter
- bladder

LARGE INTESTINE
Absorption is almost complete by the time what is left of the digested food reaches the large intestine. Peristalsis forces it from the ileum through the

STRUCTURE OF THE KIDNEYS

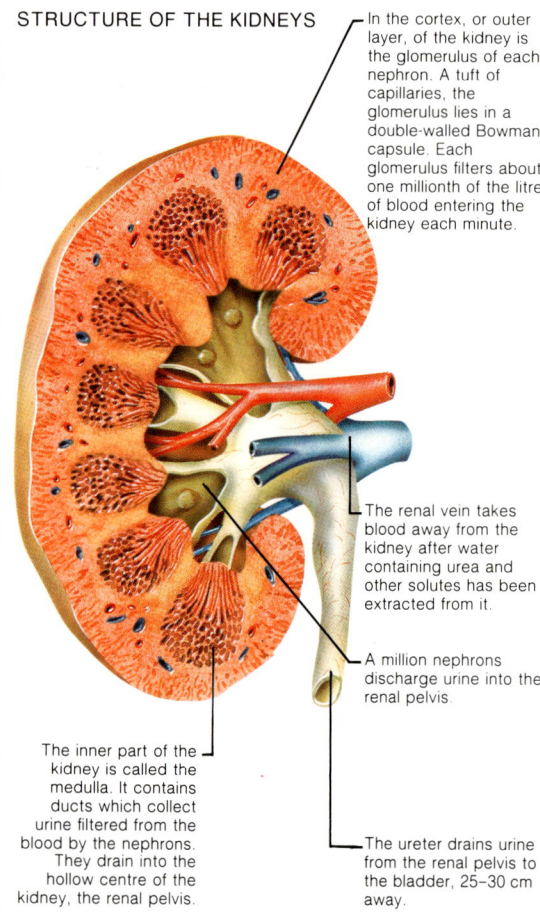

In the cortex, or outer layer, of the kidney is the glomerulus of each nephron. A tuft of capillaries, the glomerulus lies in a double-walled Bowman's capsule. Each glomerulus filters about one millionth of the litre of blood entering the kidney each minute.

The renal vein takes blood away from the kidney after water containing urea and other solutes has been extracted from it.

A million nephrons discharge urine into the renal pelvis.

The inner part of the kidney is called the medulla. It contains ducts which collect urine filtered from the blood by the nephrons. They drain into the hollow centre of the kidney, the renal pelvis.

The ureter drains urine from the renal pelvis to the bladder, 25–30 cm away.

ileocaecal valve into the ascending colon just above a blind pouch called the caecum which ends in the appendix. In the large bowel, more water and salts are absorbed from the chyme, and the bacteria normally present ferment any remaining carbohydrate and break down further any remaining protein. The resulting residue, the faeces, is thrust towards the end of the large intestine by the churning propulsive action of the muscles in its wall. The amount of faeces varies according to the amount eaten and drunk, and the type of diet.

DEFAECATION
Peristalsis eventually pushes enough faecal material into the rectum to distend the rectal wall, stimulating pressure receptors to inform the brain that defaecation is necessary. Evacuation is performed as a conscious action by contracting the abdominal muscles, tightening the diaphragm and holding the breath. The anal sphincter, a tight ring of muscle around the anus, opens under the pressure and the faeces pass out. In the first year or two of life the anal sphincter opens unconsciously in an involuntary nervous reflex. In later infancy the brain brings the action under conscious control.

Digestion is only the first step in providing new sources of energy and sustenance to keep the body alive and in good working order. The nutrients absorbed from the gastrointestinal tract must undergo further change before they can serve the needs of the cells. They must be drawn into the scheme of living chemistry that rules the body. They must take part in metabolism. This process is the sum total of all the chemical reactions of the body, both those that break down substances to release energy and those that require energy to build simpler substances into more complex ones. Food and the air we breathe provide the basic chemicals for these processes.

ELEMENTS OF NUTRITION

By the time it reaches the blood and lymph systems, the food we eat has been transformed into small molecules of mainly carbohydrates, proteins and fats. Like all living things, these nutrients are made up principally of the chemical elements, carbon, hydrogen and oxygen. These three, plus nitrogen, constitute 96 per cent of body weight.

Carbohydrates entering the bloodstream after digestion do so in the form of simple sugars, predominantly glucose. Glucose is made up of molecules of six atoms of carbon, twelve of hydrogen and six of oxygen. Proteins are broken down in

digestion to twenty different amino acids, each containing atoms of carbon, hydrogen, oxygen and nitrogen. Fats enter the lymph then the bloodstream as minute globules, but still essentially fats. Later, however, they are reduced to simpler compounds made up of carbon, hydrogen and oxygen.

PROVIDING ENERGY

The three elements – carbon, hydrogen, oxygen – are involved in the chemical reactions which provide energy for cells to perform their functions. Heat to maintain the constant warm temperature of the body is created as part of the process. The waste products, carbon dioxide and water, are produced at the same time. The fuel for these energy-generating reactions lies handy in the compounds of mainly carbon, oxygen, hydrogen and nitrogen atoms which reach the fluid bathing the cells via the blood.

ROLE OF THE LIVER

Before delivery to the cells the nutrient products of digestion pass through the liver, which has an important role in regulating how they are used. Glucose and other simple sugars arriving from the small intestine via the portal vein are released only as the body requires them. If the level of glucose in the blood is such that only part of the new consignment is needed, the liver converts the rest to glycogen in a synthetic, or building up process. Glycogen is stored in the liver and muscles. When

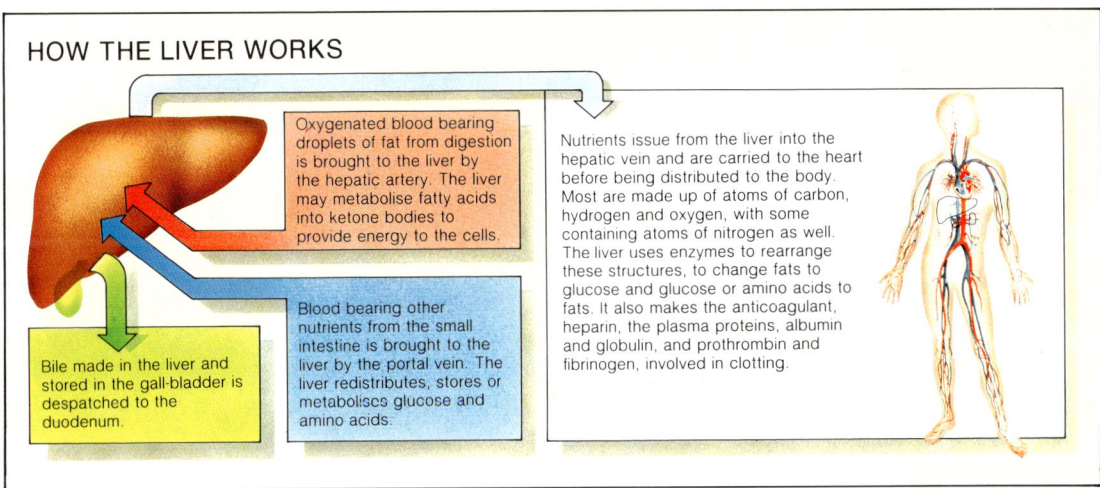

HOW THE LIVER WORKS

Oxygenated blood bearing droplets of fat from digestion is brought to the liver by the hepatic artery. The liver may metabolise fatty acids into ketone bodies to provide energy to the cells.

Blood bearing other nutrients from the small intestine is brought to the liver by the portal vein. The liver redistributes, stores or metabolises glucose and amino acids.

Bile made in the liver and stored in the gall-bladder is despatched to the duodenum.

Nutrients issue from the liver into the hepatic vein and are carried to the heart before being distributed to the body. Most are made up of atoms of carbon, hydrogen and oxygen, with some containing atoms of nitrogen as well. The liver uses enzymes to rearrange these structures, to change fats to glucose and glucose or amino acids to fats. It also makes the anticoagulant, heparin, the plasma proteins, albumin and globulin, and prothrombin and fibrinogen, involved in clotting.

The liver is a versatile chemical factory, able to transform substances by juggling atoms of carbon, hydrogen, oxygen and nitrogen. It is a storage depot as well. Its main tasks are as follows:
● It manufactures bile salts used in the small intestine to break down fats.
● It transforms poisons into less harmful substances. Ammonia produced by the burning of amino acids for energy is converted by the liver into urea, which is excreted in the urine.
● It turns glucose into glycogen for storage. When blood glucose level falls or when more energy is needed the liver breaks glycogen down to glucose again.

● When it runs out of glycogen it may make glucose from protein and fats.
● When the body begins to run out of carbohydrates the liver can turn fats into ketone bodies to provide a quick source of energy to the cells.
● If excessive carbohydrate consumption produces a surplus of glucose the liver changes it into fats.
● It stores copper, iron, vitamins A, D, E and K. It also stores some poisons that cannot be broken down. That is why the pesticide DDT is found in human and animal liver.
● It generates phagocytic cells which destroy worn-out red and white blood cells and some bacteria.

HOW METABOLISM WORKS

The liver, a detoxifying and nutrient-processing organ, has a double blood supply. The hepatic artery, a branch of the aorta, brings oxygenated blood and fats from the lymph stream. From the portal vein the liver receives blood from the small intestine containing digested protein and carbohydrate.

The oesophagus transports food to the stomach by its muscular action.

The liver weighs about 1.4 kg and is divided into right and left lobes. Each lobe is made up of microscopic lobules, which are clumps of cells radiating from a central vein. These veins carry products of liver cells and nutrients to the hepatic vein for transport to the heart.

The stomach, where digestion starts.

The gall-bladder, a pear-shaped sac at the bottom of the liver, collects and concentrates bile made in the liver. A hormone from the duodenum stimulates the gall-bladder to contract and release bile for digestion. The gall-bladder is about 7–10 cm long.

The duodenum, the start of the small intestine.

The common bile duct carries bile from the gall-bladder to the duodenum to split fats into tiny droplets.

The inferior vena cava takes blood from the liver to the heart.

The aorta delivers oxygenated blood from the heart to the hepatic artery.

The hepatic artery provides blood containing oxygen and digested fats to the liver cells.

The portal vein carries blood laden with digested carbohydrates and protein to the liver from the small intestine.

the level of blood sugar falls, the pancreatic hormone, glucagon, orders glycogen in the liver store to be changed back to glucose and released. When the level of blood sugar gets too high, another pancreatic hormone, insulin, speeds the transport of glucose into the cells and the conversion of glucose to glycogen for storage.

Proteins arriving at the liver by the portal vein in the form of amino acids may depart as something else. If there is a shortage of glucose the liver will combine the amino acids with fat to make extra sugar. The destiny of most amino acids, however, is to be reassembled as protein by the cells which need protein for many essential purposes, such as maintaining their own structures and making enzymes, antibodies and hormones.

Fats, which enter the lymph stream as globules of triglyceride coated with protein, reach the liver through the hepatic artery. If not immediately needed for energy, they may be stored there or in adipose (fatty) tissue. Or the liver may combine them with protein to make glucose.

THE CELLS

The glucose, fats and amino acids that enter the tissue fluid soon after digestion, pass through the walls of cells into a thick chemical suspension called the cytoplasm. Each cell is its own chemical factory. It has its own battery in a molecule called ATP (adenosine triphosphate), which stores energy released by the breakdown of glucose. It has powerhouses called mitochondria, where glucose is decomposed to make ATP. And it has a transport system called acetyl coenzyme A. This consists of an enzyme which initiates the conversion of nutrient molecules and a molecule called a coenzyme which carries end products to their target site.

BASAL METABOLIC RATE

The body is never at rest: the heart keeps beating, the lungs keep extracting oxygen from the air and those billions of tiny chemical factories, the cells, keep breaking down substances and building up new ones. The rate at which energy is consumed to keep the body ticking over in its quietest period is called the basal metabolic rate (BMR). The rate varies between individuals, which helps to explain why some people eat a lot without getting fat. On average, however, the adult BMR is about 330 kilojoules per hour, with the male's rate usually slightly higher because of his bigger body. During exercise the amount of energy expended may rise to fifty times the BMR. Another very effective way of altering the energy balance is to eat less. If the body needs more energy than is being supplied in food, stored fat in the liver and adipose tissue is released to make up the deficiency.

HOW THE CELLS WORK

Each cell's job is to contribute to the processes which keep the body alive. For this purpose it requires energy sources, which are provided in nutrients from digestion and oxygen from the lungs. Cells expend energy in contracting muscles and making products such as hormones and blood proteins. In the process they produce wastes, including carbon dioxide, which are carried by the blood to the lungs and kidneys for disposal.

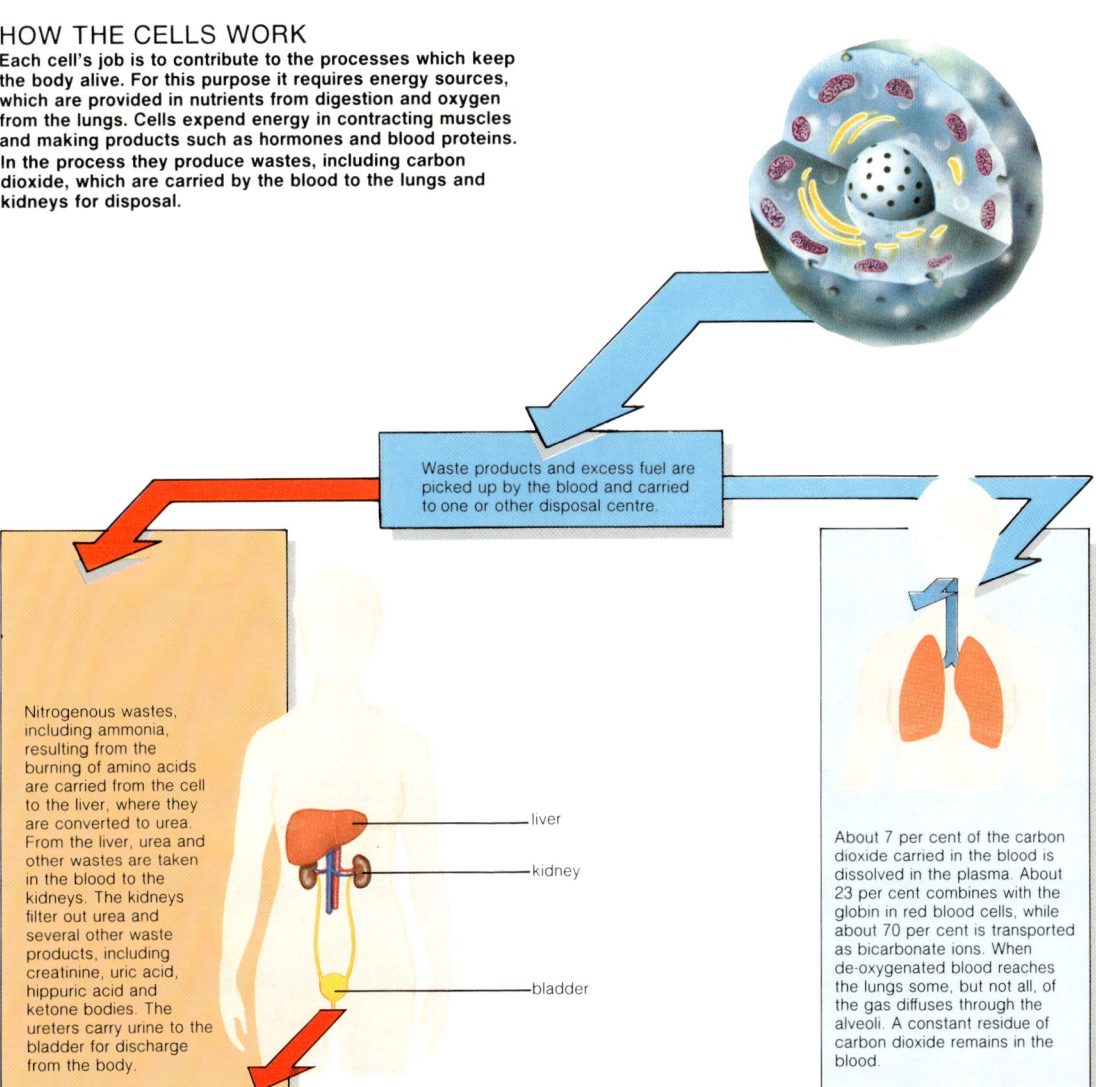

Waste products and excess fuel are picked up by the blood and carried to one or other disposal centre.

Nitrogenous wastes, including ammonia, resulting from the burning of amino acids are carried from the cell to the liver, where they are converted to urea. From the liver, urea and other wastes are taken in the blood to the kidneys. The kidneys filter out urea and several other waste products, including creatinine, uric acid, hippuric acid and ketone bodies. The ureters carry urine to the bladder for discharge from the body.

liver

kidney

bladder

About 7 per cent of the carbon dioxide carried in the blood is dissolved in the plasma. About 23 per cent combines with the globin in red blood cells, while about 70 per cent is transported as bicarbonate ions. When de-oxygenated blood reaches the lungs some, but not all, of the gas diffuses through the alveoli. A constant residue of carbon dioxide remains in the blood.

THE ENDOCRINE SYSTEM

While the nervous system controls activities of the body through electrical impulses, the endocrine system exerts a complementary control with chemical messengers called hormones. Both systems are concerned with maintaining homeostasis: that is, with trying to preserve a balance between the vital functions going on in the body and stresses coming from within and without. Cold is a cause of stress from without, high blood pressure a cause of stress from within.

ENDOCRINE GLANDS IN THE BODY

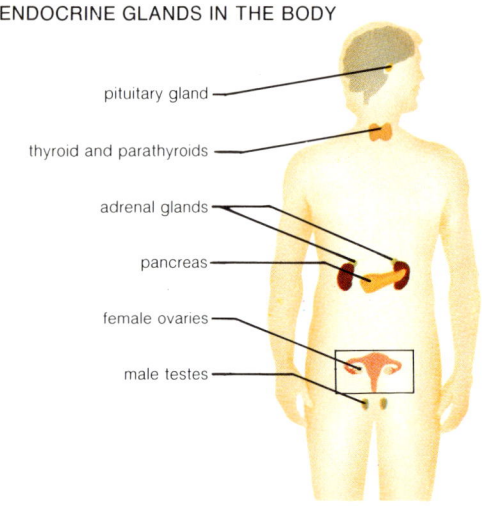

pituitary gland

thyroid and parathyroids

adrenal glands

pancreas

female ovaries

male testes

ROLE OF THE ENDOCRINE GLANDS

Nervous impulses to the muscles and glands demand swift, usually brief action. The endocrine or internally secreting glands initiate slower changes often lasting much longer. For example, they control growth from the child to the adult. Specialised clusters of cells found in the endocrine glands release hormones into the bloodstream to be carried to other glands, muscles and organs. Hormone comes from the Greek, *hormon*, meaning to stir up. Hormones stimulate the required response by acting on receptors either on the surface of or inside target cells at their destinations. The level of hormone secretion is delicately adjusted to avoid too much or too little, the mechanism principally involved being negative feedback control. For example, when the level of calcium in the blood is too low this is brought to the notice of the parathyroid glands. They release a hormone which acts on various parts of the body to restore calcium level to normal. As soon as blood calcium begins to rise above normal, this fact, too, is referred to the parathyroids, which stop releasing the hormone.

The principal endocrine glands are the pituitary, the thyroid, the parathyroids, the ovaries, the testes, the adrenal glands, the pancreas and, in pregnant women, the placenta.

PITUITARY GLAND

The pituitary, which lies at the base of the brain below the hypothalamus, has been called the 'master gland' because it regulates so many activities, including those of several other endocrine glands. It secretes nine different hormones. Seven of these are produced in the front of the gland, which is called the adenohypophysis, and two in the hind part, or neurohypophysis. Many of the secretions from the front of the gland are trophic, meaning that they activate other endocrine glands, specifically the thyroid, ovaries, testes, breast and the adrenal glands. All seven secretions are stimulated or inhibited by regulatory secretions from the hypothalamus. All are essential, but none more important than human growth hormone (HGH), which increases the rate of growth by increasing protein synthesis. It acts primarily on the skeleton and skeletal muscle. Too little HGH in childhood can lead to pituitary dwarfism, too much to gigantism.

The hind part of the pituitary secretes oxytocin (OT) and antidiuretic hormone (ADH). The former stimulates contraction of smooth muscles in the uterus during childbirth, the latter regulates the volume of urine. When the body becomes dehydrated, ADH tells the kidneys to reduce urine output so that water can be reabsorbed into the body. Too much water in the blood results in suppression of ADH and increased output of urine.

STRIKING A HORMONE BALANCE
In controlling other endocrine glands the pituitary is itself controlled by a negative feedback system (below). A fall in the blood level of a hormone stimulates the hypothalamus to release a regulating factor. This factor stimulates the pituitary to send a stimulating hormone through the blood to the gland concerned. In response, the gland secretes more hormone. When secretion of the hormone starts becoming excessive, this is fed back to the hypothalamus, which orders the pituitary to produce an opposite (negative) effect by stopping hormone secretion.

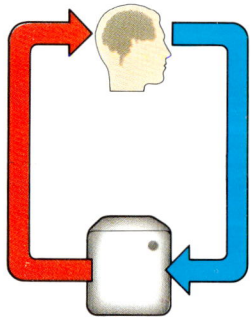

THYROID GLAND

The thyroid gland, sitting around the trachea, or windpipe, just below the voice-box, has a wide-ranging job of regulating metabolism, growth and development and the activity of the nervous system.

FUNCTION OF THE PITUITARY GLAND

Four of six hormones secreted by the anterior pituitary are trophic, meaning they stimulate other endocrine glands. All six secretions are under control of the hypothalamus, mainly through a negative feedback mechanism. In such a system the response mounted by the gland is opposite to the stimulus that invokes it. For example, if the blood sugar level rises too high the hypothalamus orders the pituitary to produce the opposite effect – reduction in blood glucose through stopping release of growth hormone.

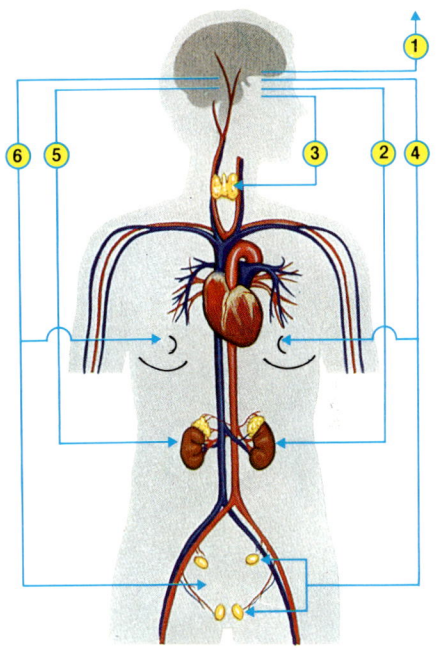

One of the six anterior pituitary hormones, growth hormone, 1, stimulates cell growth, increasing the release of glucose in the process. Adrenocorticotrophic hormone (ACTH), 2, controls the adrenal glands, and thyroid stimulating hormone (TSH), 3, the thyroid gland. Three of the six hormones, prolactin, follicle stimulating hormone (FSH) and luteinising hormone (LH), 4, are concerned with reproduction. Prolactin stimulates the female breast to secrete milk, FSH initiates the development of ova each month, and LH stimulates the release of one of them. The two hormones of the posterior pituitary are antidiuretic hormone (ADH), 5, which prompts the kidneys to reabsorb water, and oxytocin, 6, which stimulates uterine contractions and the nipples to eject milk.

Its hormones, thyroxine and triiodothyronine, are formed from iodine compounds derived from food, and are secreted on orders from the hypothalamus, relayed through the pituitary gland. The message arrives from the pituitary in the shape of thyroid-stimulating hormone (TSH). On release, the thyroid hormones trigger the breakdown of nutrients, increasing the basal metabolic rate. Early in life they combine with growth hormone to accelerate body development. They also prompt the nervous system to increase blood flow and strengthen the heart beat. A third thyroid hormone, calcitonin, prevents calcium level in the blood from rising too high.

PARATHYROID GLANDS

Four small, round masses of tissue called the parathyroid glands – two on each side behind the thyroid – also serve as watch-dogs over blood calcium levels. The hormone they secrete is known as parathyroid hormone, or parathormone. The parathyroids may fail to perform properly either by not maintaining adequate blood levels of calcium (hypoparathyroidism) or by permitting it to rise too much (hyperparathyroidism). In the first case, nerve cells, which need calcium to preserve their normal resting state, may over-react causing severe muscle spasms called tetany. In the second, the

excessive secretion of parathormone may result in calcium being leeched from bones.

ADRENAL GLANDS

The two adrenal glands, one sitting on top of each kidney, are divided into an outer part, the adrenal cortex, and an inner part, the adrenal medulla. The adrenal cortex secretes aldosterone, which acts on the kidneys to reabsorb salt and water from the urine. The purpose is to restore blood volume after dehydration or haemorrhage. Aldosterone is part of a complex control system. On sensing a fall in blood pressure due to loss of blood volume, the kidneys secrete an enzyme called renin. Renin reacts with a plasma protein from the liver to form angiotensin I. Converted to angiotensin II in the lungs, this stimulates the adrenal cortex to produce aldosterone. Thus initial action of the kidneys culminates in restoration of blood volume and blood pressure.

A second group of hormones from the adrenal cortex called glucocorticoids are concerned with normal metabolism and resistance to stress. They include cortisol and cortisone. By assisting the conversion of amino acids and fats to glucose they provide a quick source of energy to combat fright, temperature extremes, infection and trauma. They are also anti-inflammatory agents. Their secretion is

FUNCTION OF THE THYROID

Unique in its ability to store hormones, the thyroid sits in front of the trachea. Its two lobes secrete thyroxine and calcitonin. At the back of the thyroid lie four parathyroid glands. The hormone they secrete is called parathormone.

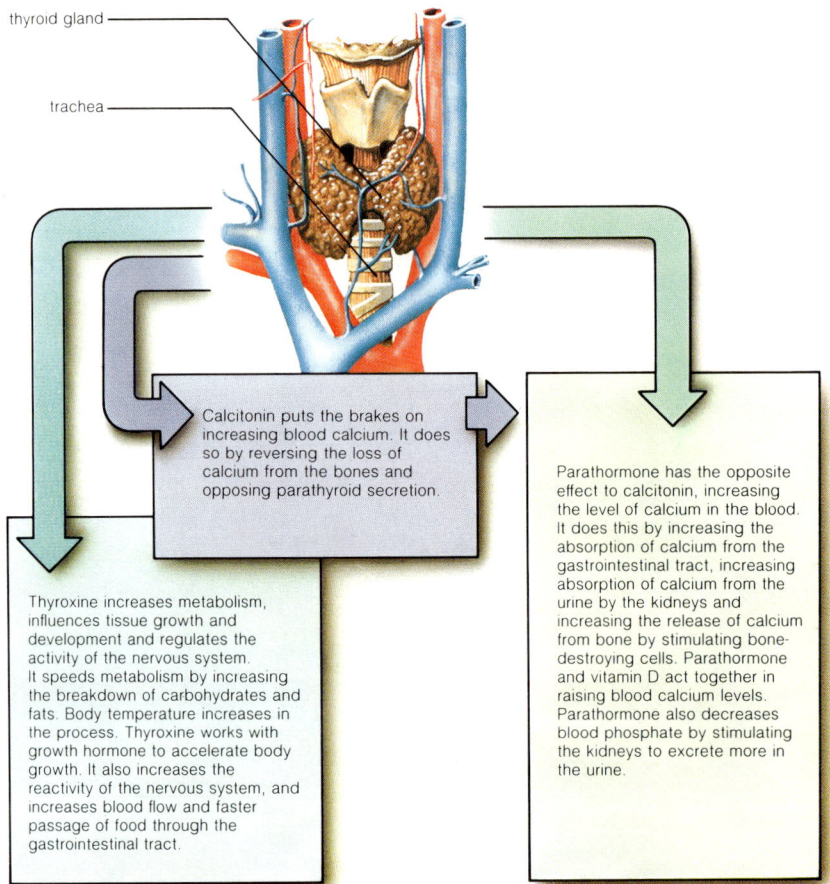

thyroid gland

trachea

Calcitonin puts the brakes on increasing blood calcium. It does so by reversing the loss of calcium from the bones and opposing parathyroid secretion.

Parathormone has the opposite effect to calcitonin, increasing the level of calcium in the blood. It does this by increasing the absorption of calcium from the gastrointestinal tract, increasing absorption of calcium from the urine by the kidneys and increasing the release of calcium from bone by stimulating bone-destroying cells. Parathormone and vitamin D act together in raising blood calcium levels. Parathormone also decreases blood phosphate by stimulating the kidneys to excrete more in the urine.

Thyroxine increases metabolism, influences tissue growth and development and regulates the activity of the nervous system. It speeds metabolism by increasing the breakdown of carbohydrates and fats. Body temperature increases in the process. Thyroxine works with growth hormone to accelerate body growth. It also increases the reactivity of the nervous system, and increases blood flow and faster passage of food through the gastrointestinal tract.

controlled by the hypothalamus, which directs the pituitary to send adrenocorticotrophic hormone (ACTH) to the adrenal cortex to summon their release.

The adrenal medulla secretes two hormones, adrenalin and noradrenalin, which literally spurt from the gland when fear, anger, a severe injury or some other cause of stress assaults the brain. The glandular reaction is part of the fight-or-flight response. Impulses from the hypothalamus travelling along fibres of the sympathetic division of the unconscious nervous system, jolt the adrenal medulla into discharging its hormones. They accelerate breathing and heart rate, divert blood from the periphery to the skeletal muscles by constricting blood vessels of the skin, increase blood sugar level and bring about other changes which prepare the body for immediate action.

THE PANCREAS

The pancreas sits in a bend of the duodenum, conveniently placed for its work in digestion. In its other role as an endocrine gland, it makes two hormones which regulate the everyday fluctuations in blood glucose levels. They come from two different clusters of cells in the islets of Langerhans. When glucose enters the blood after a meal, insulin is secreted to limit its level. It does this mainly by speeding the entry of glucose into the cells. It also accelerates the conversion of glucose to glycogen for storage.

The other pancreatic hormone, glucagon, has the opposite effect. Secreted when the level of blood glucose falls below normal, it accelerates the conversion of glycogen in the liver to glucose and helps the liver to convert other nutrients such as amino acids and fats into glucose.

The ultimate biological purpose of sex is reproduction. If sexual union were not a compelling instinct for all species, animal life on Earth might have died out. The subtle mechanisms of the human mating instinct are tuned by the senses of sight, smell and touch and by psychological conditioning to ensure that sexual activity regularly takes place. Because female ovulation occurs only once a month, much sexual intercourse between men and women, though important in bonding prospective parents, is without prospect of achieving a reproductive outcome. The sexual organs and functions of men and women are necessarily complementary and arise in embryonic life from the same tissues, which are directed by genes and hormones to differentiate into male or female systems.

FEMALE SYSTEM

The female's reproductive organs lie mainly in the shelter of the pelvis. The opening of her genital tract, the vulva, has two gateways: the outer lips or labia majora, and the inner labia minora. The latter vary considerably in size, and may normally protrude outside the labia majora or be hidden by them.

Both pairs of lips surround a space called the vestibule. This contains the entrance to the vagina – the introitus – and the opening of the urethra, the tube that carries urine from the bladder. Hooded by the junction of the labia minora in front is the clitoris, a small (5 mm) knob of nerve-packed tissue which is the centre of female sexual sensation. In infancy and childhood the entrance to the vagina is partly closed

FEMALE SYSTEM

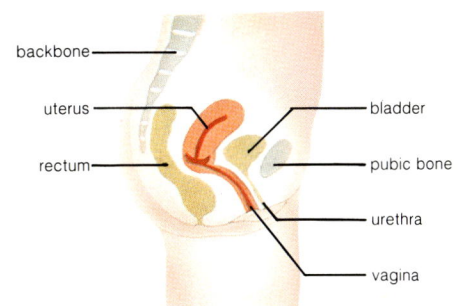

backbone
uterus
rectum
bladder
pubic bone
urethra
vagina

by a thin membrane, the hymen, which is stretched or broken by the first sexual penetration.

The vagina is a flask-shaped tube, 8–10 cm in length, running upwards and backwards towards the uterus. Its folded lining and the muscle in its wall allow for considerable expansion during intercourse and childbirth. The lining is kept moist by a watery fluid which seeps from capillaries beneath the surface, increasing in amount during sexual arousal.

The vagina meets the uterus at the cervix, the neck or narrowed entrance to the gestation chamber. The uterus, about 7.5 cm long and 5 cm wide, is shaped like an inverted pear. Its strong, muscular walls are about 1 cm thick, and its lining, the endometrium, is specialised for gestation. The uterus is a very mobile organ, being loosely tethered to the pelvic walls by four sets of ligaments. It leans forwards when the rectum is full, backwards when

FEMALE REPRODUCTIVE ORGANS

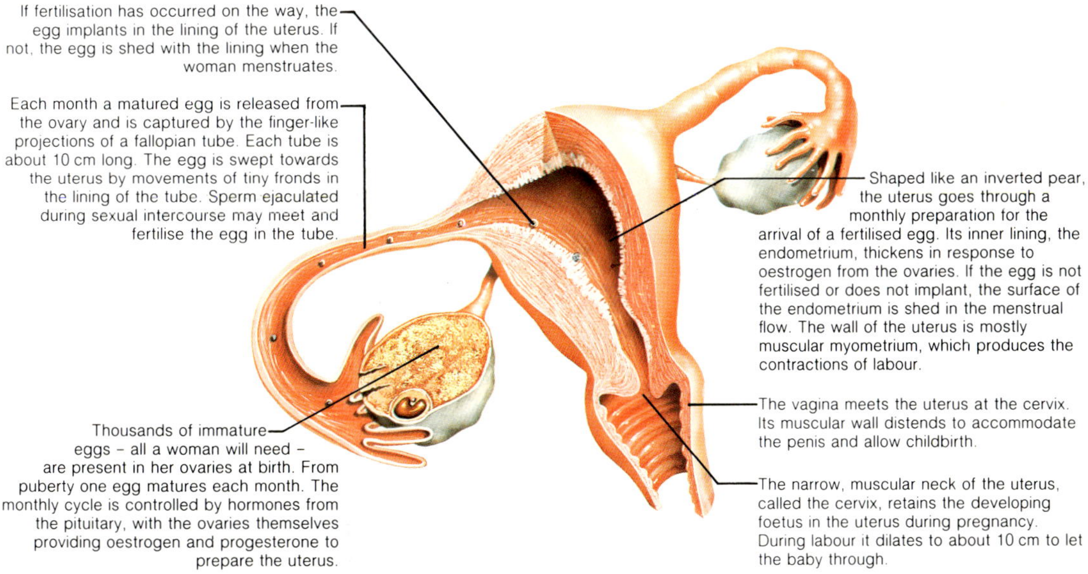

If fertilisation has occurred on the way, the egg implants in the lining of the uterus. If not, the egg is shed with the lining when the woman menstruates.

Each month a matured egg is released from the ovary and is captured by the finger-like projections of a fallopian tube. Each tube is about 10 cm long. The egg is swept towards the uterus by movements of tiny fronds in the lining of the tube. Sperm ejaculated during sexual intercourse may meet and fertilise the egg in the tube.

Thousands of immature eggs – all a woman will need – are present in her ovaries at birth. From puberty one egg matures each month. The monthly cycle is controlled by hormones from the pituitary, with the ovaries themselves providing oestrogen and progesterone to prepare the uterus.

Shaped like an inverted pear, the uterus goes through a monthly preparation for the arrival of a fertilised egg. Its inner lining, the endometrium, thickens in response to oestrogen from the ovaries. If the egg is not fertilised or does not implant, the surface of the endometrium is shed in the menstrual flow. The wall of the uterus is mostly muscular myometrium, which produces the contractions of labour.

The vagina meets the uterus at the cervix. Its muscular wall distends to accommodate the penis and allow childbirth.

The narrow, muscular neck of the uterus, called the cervix, retains the developing foetus in the uterus during pregnancy. During labour it dilates to about 10 cm to let the baby through.

THE VULVA

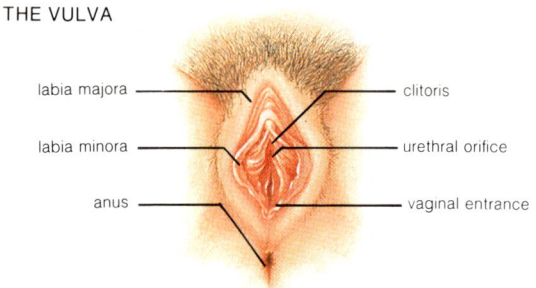

labia majora — clitoris

labia minora — urethral orifice

anus — vaginal entrance

the bladder is full, and can expand up to the diaphragm during pregnancy.

The uterus is joined on either side near the top by the fallopian tubes. These narrow passageways, about 10 cm long, open out in finger-like projections near the surface of the ovary. Their sweeping movements will pick up the ovum as it is released to be transported down the tube to the uterus.

The almond-shaped ovaries have two functions: maturing and release of eggs and production of hormones. At birth the ovaries contain many thousands of ova in a resting, immature state. Each ovum is surrounded by a layer of specialised cells, forming an ovarian follicle. Starting from puberty, the brain begins to order a few of these follicles to develop each month, the instruction being carried by follicle stimulating hormone (FSH) from the pituitary gland. The egg cells begin to mature, and the surrounding cells multiply and start to manufacture the hormone oestrogen. This hormone prepares the female body for pregnancy by stimulating growth of the lining of the uterus and development and maintenance of all other female secondary sex characteristics. Each month only one of the ripening follicles reaches full maturity. This takes about two weeks, during which time fluid accumulates within the follicle around the ovum. Eventually, increasing amounts of oestrogen produced by the cells of the follicle wall trigger release of luteinising hormone (LH) from the pituitary. Under the influence of LH the follicle bursts to release the ovum (ovulation), which is captured by the tube to be swept towards the uterus and any sperm that may be coming the other way.

After ovulation LH directs the remains of the follicle to transform into the corpus luteum, a gland which secretes an additional hormone, progesterone, which halts growth of the endometrium and transforms the uterine lining into a lush secretory layer, rich in blood supply and perfectly designed for implantation of a fertilised ovum. If there is no conception, the corpus luteum degenerates after twelve to fourteen days, oestrogen and progesterone levels fall and the endometrium dies and is shed. This is menstruation. The menstrual discharge consists of the liquefied dead endometrium mixed with some blood which is lost as the tissue breaks down. The usual amount of the

menstrual flow is 40–80 ml. This monthly cycle continues from the first period or menarche until the menopause at about 50 years of age.

MALE SYSTEM

The functions of the male reproductive system are to make sperm, semen, and male reproductive hormones, and to deliver the semen to the female.

The male gonads or sex glands, the testes, are housed outside the body in the scrotum because sperm production requires a temperature about 2° Celsius below internal body heat. Each testis, about 5 cm long and 2.5 cm in diameter, is wrapped in a firm fibrous coat called the tunica albuginea. Prongs from this tunic divide the testis into 200–300 compartments, each containing several seminiferous tubules – fine tubes in which sperm develop.

Sperm production, called spermatogenesis, starts at puberty when on command from the brain, the pituitary releases FSH to initiate the process. At the same time, LH stimulates special cells around the tubules to secrete the male hormone testosterone, responsible for development and maintenance of male sexual characteristics and function. Sperm are produced at a rate of about 300 million per day. From the seminiferous tubules sperm move into the epididymis, a small comma-shaped organ (in fact, a fine coiled tube about 6 metres in length) attached to the back of the testis. Here they mature and are stored to await a summons to complete their journey. Mature sperm, now able to swim, pass from the epididymis into the 45 cm tube, the vas deferens, which ascends from each testis through the scrotum into the pelvis and loops around the bladder to join

MALE REPRODUCTIVE ORGANS

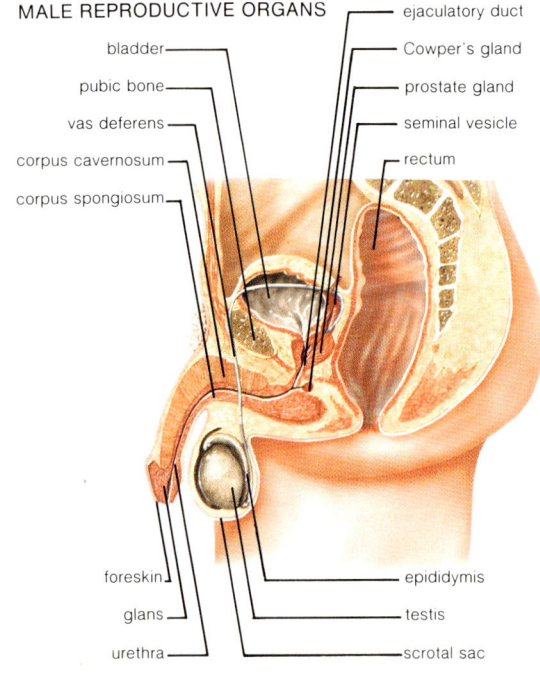

bladder — ejaculatory duct

pubic bone — Cowper's gland

vas deferens — prostate gland

corpus cavernosum — seminal vesicle

corpus spongiosum — rectum

foreskin — epididymis

glans — testis

urethra — scrotal sac

CROSS-SECTION OF THE TESTIS

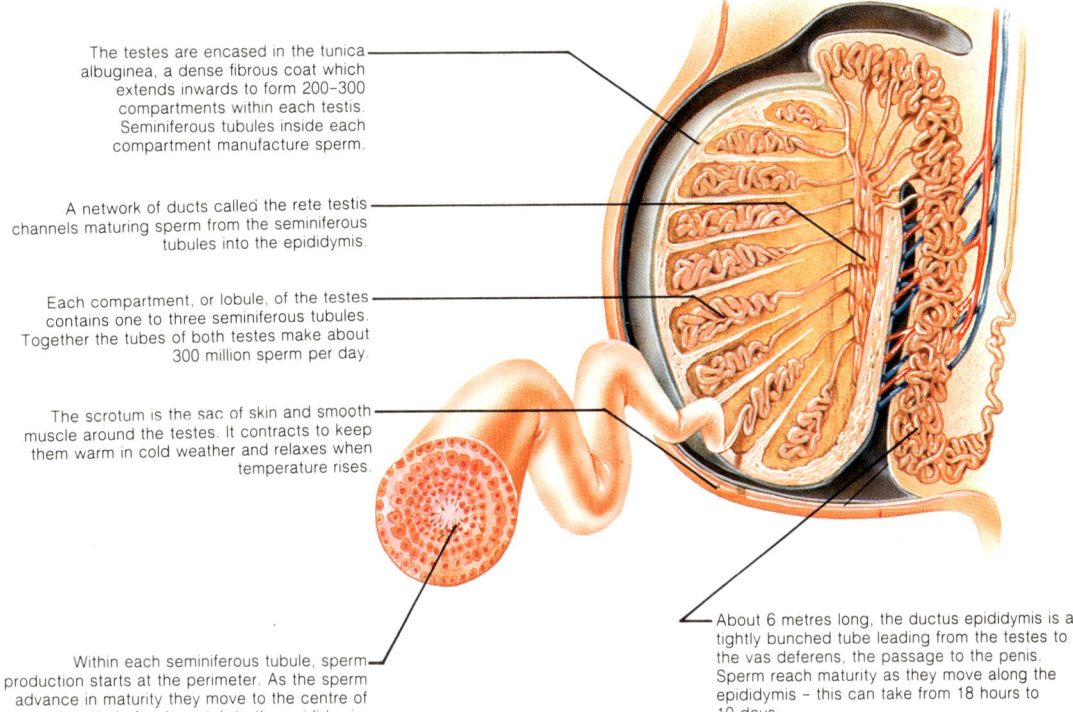

The testes are encased in the tunica albuginea, a dense fibrous coat which extends inwards to form 200–300 compartments within each testis. Seminiferous tubules inside each compartment manufacture sperm.

A network of ducts called the rete testis channels maturing sperm from the seminiferous tubules into the epididymis.

Each compartment, or lobule, of the testes contains one to three seminiferous tubules. Together the tubes of both testes make about 300 million sperm per day.

The scrotum is the sac of skin and smooth muscle around the testes. It contracts to keep them warm in cold weather and relaxes when temperature rises.

Within each seminiferous tubule, sperm production starts at the perimeter. As the sperm advance in maturity they move to the centre of the tubule for despatch to the epididymis.

About 6 metres long, the ductus epididymis is a tightly bunched tube leading from the testes to the vas deferens, the passage to the penis. Sperm reach maturity as they move along the epididymis – this can take from 18 hours to 10 days.

the urethra as it passes through the prostate gland. During their journey from the testis, sperm acquire the liquid vehicle necessary for completion of their mission. The fluid comes from the vas, the seminal vesicles beneath the bladder and the prostate.

The penetrating organ, the penis, is at most times a soft tube hanging limply below the abdomen. Unerect penises may vary in size. The erect penis measures about 10 cm. The head, or glans, at the end of the penis is a highly sensitive zone in which are initiated most of the sensations of sexual arousal. It is protected by the foreskin, which in some societies is removed soon after birth by circumcision.

The shaft of the penis is composed of three cylinders of erectile tissue: two cavernous bodies uppermost and the spongy body, through which the urethra runs, behind. Erectile tissue has a rich blood supply which runs through blood sinuses or channels where blood can stockpile. Sexually arousing stimuli evoke unconscious nervous impulses which dilate the arteries in the penis. Blood rushes into the sinuses, which expand to block drainage through the veins and an erection results.

SEXUAL INTERCOURSE

The process of sexual arousal, or preparation of the male and female bodies for intercourse, is the complex result of biological instincts and reflexes largely outside conscious control. Seeing, touching, smelling and other erotic stimuli act on unconscious parts of the brain or through reflex arcs in the spinal cord to attract and to alert the sex organs. The conscious brain perceives pleasureable sensations which augment the response. The effects are basically similar in the two sexes. The penis of the male starts to swell as its arteries dilate. It becomes tumescent, or half erect, then fully erect. Blood rushing into the female pelvis causes swelling of the clitoris and the tissues around the entrance to the vagina, and expansion of the upper vagina.

Lubrication for penetration comes mainly from an increase of fluid seeping through the walls of the vagina. Initial moistening of the head of the penis comes from glands in the urethra near the base of the penis. Orgasm (climax) in the male comes at the height of sexual arousal, when a nervous reflex from the spinal cord triggers forceful waves of contraction in the muscular walls of the vas, seminal vesicles and prostate, and rhythmic contractions of the muscles at the base of the penis. This flings the semen into the urethra and out through the penis. The female orgasm shares similar convulsive features, with rhythmic contraction of muscles of the pelvic floor and vaginal wall. Orgasm in both sexes is accompanied by intensely pleasurable sensations throughout the body, and followed by overwhelming feelings of euphoria and relaxation. The latter are believed to be most important in couple bonding.

The woman who has new life developing inside her can find that time one of joy and revelation. Her feelings about pregnancy and childbirth will be influenced by many factors, however, including her upbringing, her general state of health and her knowledge of what having a baby entails. Uncertainty about what lies ahead, particularly in regard to the labour of childbirth, can generate unnecessary fears. Understanding what is happening within her body and how her baby will be ushered into the world will help her to find an unrivalled contentment in her condition.

STAGES IN FOETAL GROWTH
At the twelfth week of pregnancy the top of the uterus is still low in the abdomen. It rises by about two finger widths every two weeks from then until week 20 when it is just below the navel. The rise then slows to about two fingers every four weeks.

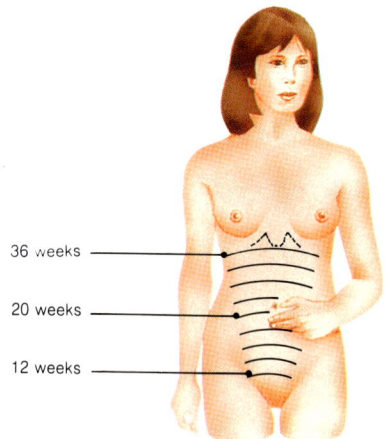

36 weeks
20 weeks
12 weeks

DIAGNOSIS OF PREGNANCY

Menstruation ceases after conception, providing one of the first signs of pregnancy – a missed period. (Some women experience other early signs of pregnancy such as swelling of the breasts, darkening of the nipples and early morning nausea.) When a period is overdue by two weeks a woman should have a test for pregnancy. This involves checking a sample of her urine collected in the early morning to see if it contains a hormone called human chorionic gonadotrophin (hCG). This hormone is secreted by the placenta early in pregnancy and can be detected in the urine from about the eighth day after the missed period. Although test kits are available from chemists, it is advisable to see a doctor in case there is any doubt about the test result.

HOME OR HOSPITAL DELIVERY?

The 1970s witnessed a vigorous debate in Australia about where and in what manner women should have their babies. While a divergence of opinion remains, the debate did induce a number of maternity

hospitals to change their practices. In some cases more homely birthing centres were introduced where women can have their babies in less intimidating surroundings with the husband and other family members present. The advocates of home birth still regard the typical hospital birth as unnecessary medicalisation of a normal condition, although they do recognise that women with any sign of impending complications should have their babies in hospital. Nevertheless, this country does not provide the range of back-up services necessary to take care of any emergency that might arise during childbirth at home. For most women, therefore, the safest place to give birth is in hospital. The Childbirth Education Association and Parents Centres (Australia) can provide information about the various alternatives available to the woman who wants to make a considered choice. A woman's doctor will be only too willing to advise her.

PREPARING FOR BIRTH

To ensure she and her baby coexist healthily and to improve her childbirth education, a woman should have regular ante-natal care from early in pregnancy. She may obtain this from her own doctor or by attending an ante-natal clinic at a hospital. These appointments should be every four weeks for the first 30 weeks of pregnancy, then fortnightly until the 36th week and weekly thereafter until the baby arrives. A complete medical history will be taken on the first visit, which will also include a full medical examination. Details of previous illnesses, particularly conditions which might affect her pregnancy, such as high blood pressure, are recorded. A blood sample is taken from the woman to check her blood group and to exclude anaemia.

The doctor will offer advice about diet, exercise and general health care during pregnancy to ensure the best outcome for mother and baby. These days doctors invariably warn pregnant women about the possible consequences of smoking and drinking. In fact, all drugs including prescribed medicines should be avoided in pregnancy unless there are strict medical indications for taking them.

During the initial physical examination the doctor will also assess the size and position of the uterus, and check the abdominal and pelvic organs and the breasts. Routine blood pressure and weight measurements, urine analysis and assessment of uterine size will be repeated at all ante-natal visits. In the later months of pregnancy the position of the baby can also be felt by abdominal examination. Special investigations such as blood tests, ultrasound or amniocentesis may be arranged, if indicated, to check the health of mother and baby and the progress of the pregnancy. Termination of pregnancy may be offered if any serious genetic or congenital defect is found in the baby.

Ante-natal classes, often attended by husbands as well as mothers-to-be, give the couple a better understanding of what to expect as the woman nears the end of pregnancy. Such classes also advise the prospective parents on how to prepare for care of the new baby. The woman is taught breathing exercises which help her to respond better to her contractions during labour.

LABOUR AND DELIVERY

The first sign of labour varies between women and between pregnancies. It may be regular contractions of the uterus becoming stronger and more frequent. It may be the 'breaking of the water' when the sac which surrounds the baby in the uterus breaks, releasing amniotic fluid. Some women notice a discharge of slightly blood-stained mucus which was the plug sealing the cervix during the nine months of gestation. Any of these signs is usually taken as notice to prepare for the birth of the baby, which usually means a journey to hospital.

Labour has three stages which culminate respectively in full dilation of the cervix to allow the

FORTY MOMENTOUS WEEKS

By the 8th week of pregnancy the embryo is beginning to exhibit human characteristics. The forerunners of eyes, limbs and digits are clearly visible. The principal organs are formed. The heart has been beating for about 4 weeks. From now on it will be known as a foetus. By the 12th week ears can be seen and the nose has developed a bridge. The heartbeat can be detected. At 20 weeks the head is less disproportionate to the rest of the foetus and the body is covered with fine hair. Usually the foetus is beginning to move. By 28 weeks it weighs about 1130–1360 grams and is likely to be moving much more. At 36 weeks it has developed a layer of fat beneath the skin, and finger nails extend to the tips of the fingers and sometimes beyond. Birth is usually between 38 and 41 weeks.

baby through, expulsion of the baby, and expulsion of the placenta. The onset of labour and its progression are under hormonal control.

The relief available to women in labour varies from light to general suppression of the pains of contraction. An important principle in the modern management of labour is to avoid clouding the woman's consciousness too much. One method, affording light relief, is to provide the mother with a mask through which she breathes a mixture of nitrous oxide and oxygen. Nitrous oxide used to be known as laughing gas and was first used by dentists. An injection of the narcotic, pethidine, will certainly mask pain but may blur the mother's perception of what is going on. Epidural anaesthesia was introduced as a means of effectively blocking the pain from the pelvic region without seriously reducing the woman's awareness and ability to participate in the birth of her baby.

When the joyful moment comes and baby arrives, usually head first, into the world, the first thing the mother wants to do is hold her child. Today, she is promptly granted her wish and the doctor quickly estimates the baby's APGAR score. This is a brief physical check of colour, respiration, heart rate, muscle tone and reflexes.

Maternity hospitals now recognise the importance of allowing mothers to maintain close contact with their new-born babies. The days when babies were routinely placed in the hospital nursery and released to their mothers only at feeding time are fortunately over. It can be confidently said that generally mothers and babies in hospital are happier and more comfortable than they used to be.

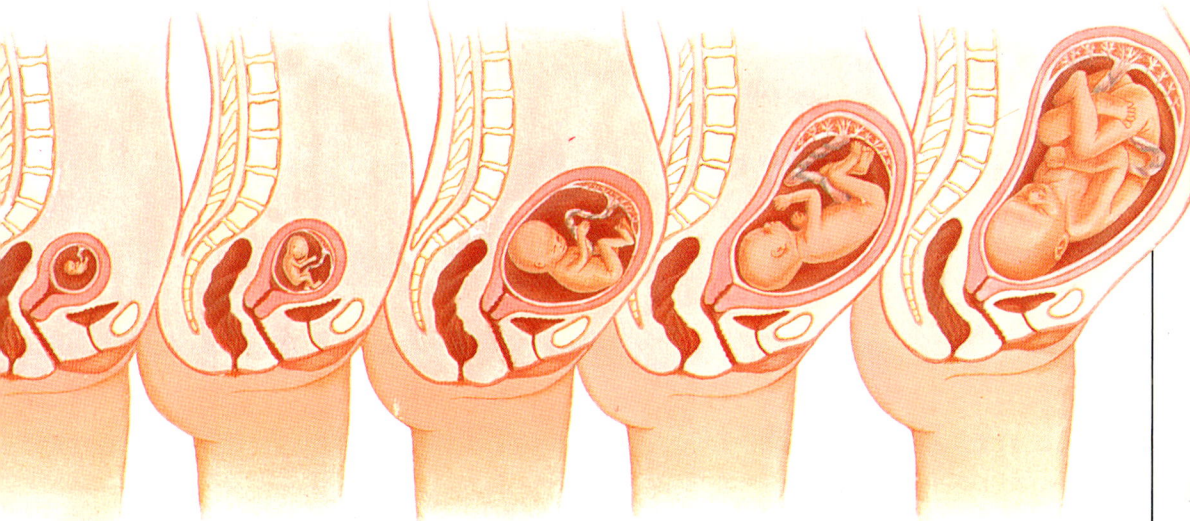

8 weeks   12 weeks   20 weeks   28 weeks   36 weeks

THREE STAGES OF LABOUR

Towards the end of pregnancy a woman's hormonal balance changes to prepare for the birth of her baby. Relaxin, a hormone from the placenta and ovaries, relaxes the neck of the uterus. The baby has settled head down in the pelvis (below). Labour is about to begin. The three stages of labour take the baby from its home of nine months to the outside world.

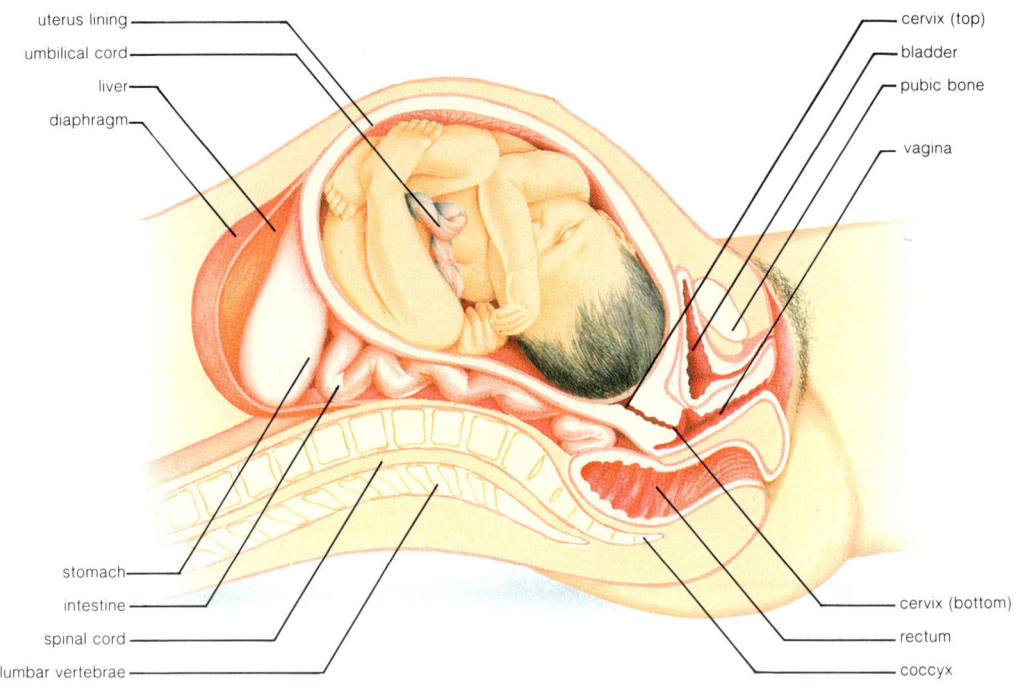

uterus lining
umbilical cord
liver
diaphragm

cervix (top)
bladder
pubic bone
vagina

stomach
intestine
spinal cord
lumbar vertebrae

cervix (bottom)
rectum
coccyx

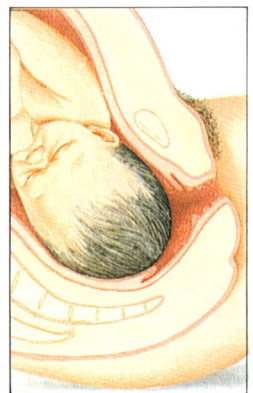
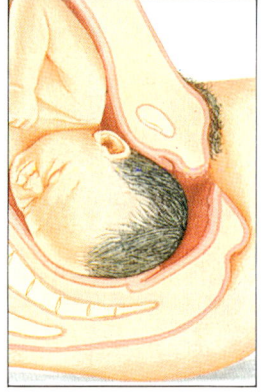
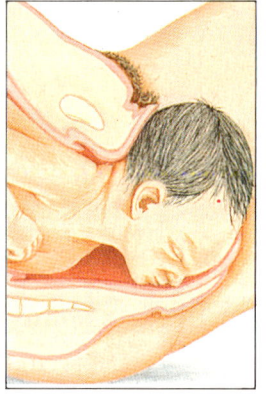
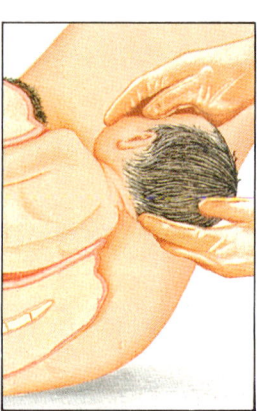

STAGE 1 (first two frames above) begins with regular wave-like contractions of the uterus and extends to when the cervix has fully dilated to about 10 cm. The wave-like contractions become more intense and more rapid as this stage progresses. The amniotic sac surrounding the baby usually breaks towards its end, releasing a gush of fluid through the vagina. The first stage usually lasts eight or nine hours but can take a longer or shorter time.

STAGE 2 begins with the baby's head being forced through the cervix into the vagina and ends with the baby's delivery (last two frames above). The uterine contractions continue during this

stage, pushing the baby through the vagina. The mother can help by actively contracting her abdominal muscles and diaphragm to increase the downwards pressure. The baby usually twists as it emerges from the vagina so that it is side-on for delivery. In this position the shoulders come through more easily. The umbilical cord ceases to beat and is cut, and the baby is given to the mother.

STAGE 3 is the time after delivery when the placenta, or 'after birth', is expelled from the body. The uterus contracts powerfully in doing this. The contractions also serve to constrict blood vessels to the placenta, reducing maternal blood loss.

Everywhere in our environment – in the air, in the water, in the soil, in our food – are microbes looking for a host. Our bodies offer food and substance in which to breed to bacteria, viruses, fungi and other disease-producing micro-organisms. Their ceaseless efforts to colonise would certainly have destroyed our species had we not developed a variety of ingenious defences against them.

MECHANICAL AND CHEMICAL DEFENCES

Some of the defences are mechanical: the sticky mucus covering the linings of body cavities, for example. It traps invading bacteria as swamps have trapped human armies. Other defences are chemical, while the most highly organised and accurate resistance is conducted by the cells of the immune system.

The unbroken skin is pretty well impermeable to micro-organisms, which is why they concentrate on body openings. Germs which do settle on the body surface are met by the mechanical defence of sebum, the oil secretion from the sebaceous glands of the skin. Tears spreading over the eyeballs each time we blink wash germs from the eyes. Saliva washes bacteria from the teeth and kills them with a bactericidal enzyme called lysosyme. Urine passing from the body hoses down the urethra as it goes, carrying invaders with it.

The airway, a favourite port of entry for many germs, has strong mechanical defences. Thick, mucus-coated hairs in the nose filter inhaled air, trapping microbes, dust and pollutants. Mucus in the upper respiratory tract does a similar job and hair-like projections in the tract called cilia sweep the

HOW THE IMMUNE SYSTEM WORKS

To resist invading micro-organisms the body relies on a variety of defences, both simple and complex. Germs which evade mechanical barriers, such as skin and tiny hairs in the breathing passages, may survive to face the guided missiles of the immune system.

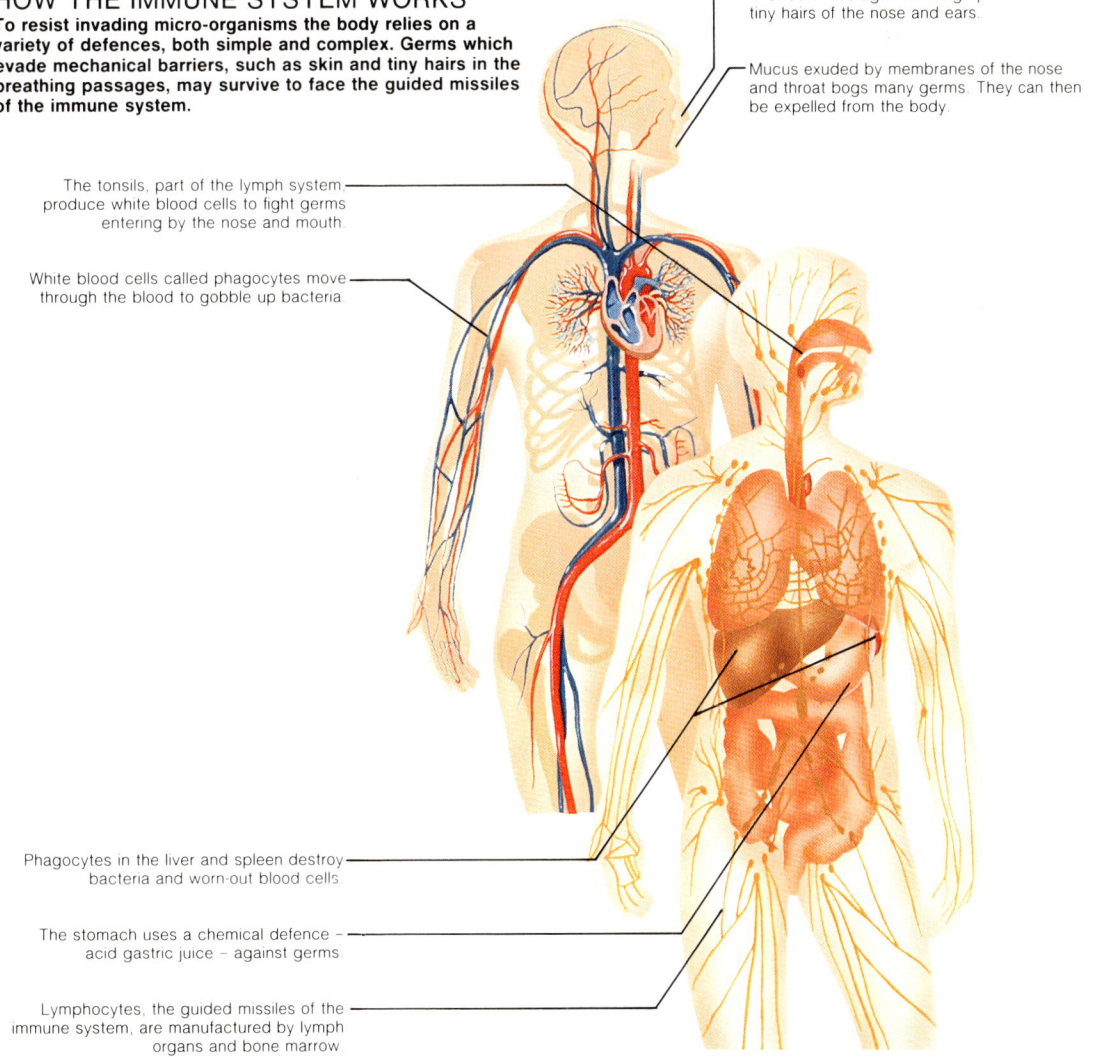

First defences against foreign particles are tiny hairs of the nose and ears.

Mucus exuded by membranes of the nose and throat bogs many germs. They can then be expelled from the body.

The tonsils, part of the lymph system, produce white blood cells to fight germs entering by the nose and mouth.

White blood cells called phagocytes move through the blood to gobble up bacteria.

Phagocytes in the liver and spleen destroy bacteria and worn-out blood cells.

The stomach uses a chemical defence – acid gastric juice – against germs.

Lymphocytes, the guided missiles of the immune system, are manufactured by lymph organs and bone marrow.

THE ROLE OF ANTIBODIES

Most antibodies fight particular antigens. Like a key fitting a lock, they combine exactly with the antigen's chemical structure (below). Phagocytes then ingest the antibody–antigen complex.

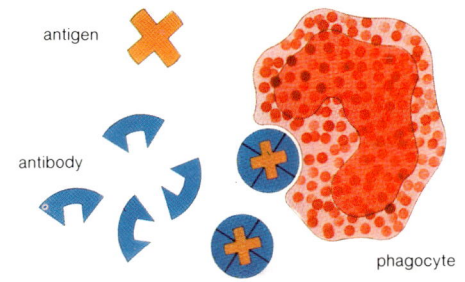

Another type of antibody tackles several antigens at the same time. The antibodies form a latticework with the antigens (below). Phagocytes then swallow the lot. Lymphocytes which secrete antibodies remember antigens once encountered and act much quicker against a second invasion.

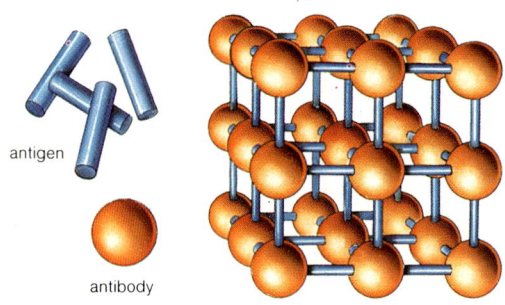

germ-laden mucus towards the throat in a movement called the 'ciliary escalator'. The escalator shifts mucus at 1–3 cm an hour. Coughing or sneezing speeds it up. Germs that divert down the oesophagus, or food tract, are likely to be killed by the acid in the stomach.

MACROPHAGES

Despite these frontline defences, many germs do succeed in penetrating the tissues and entering the bloodstream. Protein complexes in the blood such as antibodies and interferon do their best to destroy them. In many tissues, such as the liver, lungs, brain, spleen, lymph nodes and bone marrow, fixed macrophages lie in wait for them. These are cells capable of gobbling up bacteria and dead matter, an activity known as phagocytosis. The spleen, the largest mass of lymphatic tissue, has a major phagocytic function, cleansing the blood of foreign organisms, worn-out red blood cells and platelets.

Other white cells made in the bone marrow and lymphoid tissue move through the blood to engulf bacteria. First to arrive at the site of an impending infection are a type of granular white cell called neutrophils. Granular refers to their grainy struc-

ture inside. These are followed by agranular white cells called monocytes, which enlarge and become macrophages on the way. They are called wandering macrophages because they leave the blood and enter the tissues to do battle with adversaries. These phagocytic cells are undiscriminating about what they swallow. They are part of the general, non-specific system of resistance to disease.

THE IMMUNE RESPONSE

A second, specific defence system called immunity is much more selective in its targets. It operates against particular enemies which are identified and remembered by the immune system cells involved. If the enemies return the response is immediate.

The assault troops of specific immunity are white blood cells known as lymphocytes. There are two brigades of these troops, the so-called B cells and T cells, and their battle tactics are quite different. The spearhead of the T cell brigade, the killer T cells, are close-quarter fighters: they lock on to the enemy, sometimes a cell invaded by a virus, and secrete chemicals to destroy it. They are primed to recognise the antigen, or chemical characteristics of the invader. Having attached to the enemy, they emit other substances which summon other T cells and macrophages to the attack.

B cells stand off and fight the invader with antibodies, proteins which exactly complement the chemical structure of the invading antigen. The antibodies combine with the antigen and initiate its destruction. Each B cell can secrete about 2000 antibodies per second.

A certain type of both B cells and T cells remembers any antigen after an initial encounter. If the same organism invades a second time these cells initiate a much swifter reaction than on the first occasion. This process can confer lifetime natural immunity to some diseases, such as measles.

VACCINATION AND IMMUNISATION

Without understanding the mechanisms of immunity, Dr Edward Jenner in the late 18th century turned it to the service of medicine when he vaccinated his patients against smallpox with the similar virus of cowpox. He had acted on the popular belief in his part of Gloucester that people who contracted the much milder cowpox were thenceforth immune to smallpox. In our century artificial immunisation has become the most effective protection against many infectious diseases. It takes two forms: passive immunisation in which the patient is inoculated with serum containing antibodies to a particular disease organism; and active immunisation in which the inoculant used contains live or killed virus, or more often a weakened strain of the virus. The nature of immunity is under increasingly intensive study as medical scientists strive to improve the results of organ transplantation, now limited by the patient's immune reaction to foreign tissue.

2

A–Z
OF
FAMILY
HEALTH

ABDOMINAL PAIN

The abdomen contains all the important organs of digestion and excretion – the stomach, intestines, liver and gall-bladder, pancreas, kidneys and ureters – as well as the spleen (important in blood cell formation and breakdown) and the adrenal glands. The lower abdomen or pelvis contains the internal organs of reproduction – the ovaries, fallopian tubes and uterus in women and the seminal vesicles and prostate in men – and the bladder. (See How The Body Works, pp. 25–27.) Abdominal pain may be caused by disorders in any of these organs. The severity, speed and circumstances of onset, site and accompanying symptoms of the pain will usually give a good indication of whether its cause is a minor or serious disorder.

Consult a doctor immediately:
• If pain follows a blow or injury to the abdomen or back.
• If the pain remains severe or gets worse over 2 hours.
• If the pain is associated with vomiting (especially vomiting blood), fever or fainting.
• If pain occurs in a woman who is or may be pregnant, especially if it is accompanied by dizziness or fainting and/or any abnormal bleeding from the vagina.

See a doctor as soon as possible:
• If pain is bad enough to interfere with sleep or usual daily activities.
• If bouts of pain are recurrent.
• If there have been previous attacks of similar pain due to PEPTIC ULCERS, GALLSTONES, KIDNEY STONES or suspected APPENDICITIS.
• When there is persistent pain, even if not severe, in a child under 6 or an elderly person.

Possible causes of abdominal pain:
• Disorders of the alimentary canal, including GASTRIC or DUODENAL ULCERS, GASTROENTERITIS, APPENDICITIS, COLITIS, DIVERTICULITIS, INDIGESTION, BOWEL obstruction or PERFORATION.

• Disorders of the digestive glands, such as HEPATITIS, CHOLECYSTITIS, GALLSTONES, PANCREATITIS.
Digestive system pain may be felt in the upper, middle or lower abdomen: it is often colicky and may be accompanied by nausea, vomiting or diarrhoea.
• Urinary disorders, including NEPHRITIS, PYELO-NEPHRITIS, urinary stones, CYSTITIS. Kidney pain is usually felt in the small of the back. Bladder disorders cause pain in the lower abdomen or genitals.
• Disorders of the reproductive system. In women the commonest causes are DYSMENORRHOEA (cramps associated with normal menstruation), disorders of early pregnancy such as ABORTION (miscarriage), ECTOPIC PREGNANCY, SALPINGITIS and other pelvic infections, ENDOMETRIOSIS, OVARIAN CYSTS and OVULATION pain. These conditions usually cause lower abdominal or lower back pain, and may be accompanied by abnormal bleeding or discharge from the vagina. In men the commonest reproductive disorder causing abdominal pain is PROSTATITIS.

ABORTION

The premature ending of any process before it reaches its natural conclusion. Medically, abortion refers to a pregnancy finishing before the FOETUS is mature enough to survive.
There are two categories of abortion:

Spontaneous abortion – also called miscarriage – happens when pregnancy terminates without any outside interference, and usually to the great disappointment of the parents. The reason for miscarriage is often obscure, but thought to be due to a defect in the foetus, placenta, uterus or cervix, or the hormonal support of the pregnancy. It may also be caused by fever or viral illness in the mother. The symptoms of impending abortion are bleeding from the uterus, usually accompanied by lower abdominal cramps. When this happens during pregnancy, consult a doctor without delay. Several terms are used to describe spontaneous abortion:

• Threatened abortion. Bleeding from the uterus in the early or middle months of pregnancy without death of the foetus. The bleeding may settle and the pregnancy survive.

• Incomplete abortion. Part of the conception has been expelled from the uterus. The remaining part causes bleeding – often severe. The remaining conceptus must be removed by suction or CURETTAGE so that bleeding will stop.

• Inevitable abortion. When there has been much bleeding and the cervix has dilated, there is no possibility of the pregnancy surviving.

• Missed abortion. The foetus has died but remains in the uterus.

• Habitual abortion. Spontaneous abortion occurring in three or more successive pregnancies.

• Septic abortion. Miscarriage associated with infection in the uterus. In septic incomplete abortion it may be impossible to know whether infection is the cause or the result of the miscarriage.

Induced abortion. The deliberate termination of a pregnancy, either by surgical removal of the conception from the uterus or by inducing premature labour so that contractions of the uterus expel the pregnancy. In skilled medical hands abortion carries minimal risk of complication: indeed it is the safest of all surgical procedures. The legal position regarding induced abortion in Australia varies from State to State. Any woman seeking termination of pregnancy should see her doctor as early as possible for information and advice about the appropriate medical and legal requirements. (See Medical And Health Support Organisations – PREGNANCY, ABORTION, CONTRACEPTION.)

ABRASION
A scrape on the skin with surface bleeding or seepage of blood. Abrasions should be gently and thoroughly cleansed then covered with a sterile dressing. If redness, swelling and pus formation occur, see your doctor.

ABSCESS
A painful, swollen pocket of pus, which forms as a result of tissue destruction complicated by infection. An abscess can occur in any organ or tissue. Common examples are found in the skin (BOIL or FURUNCLE caused by infection entering through a hair follicle) or when a decayed tooth and its socket become infected. The pus must be drained from an abscess before healing can take place.

ACHE
A dull pain that lasts for a while in contrast to an ACUTE pain that is sharp and sudden.

ACHILLES TENDON
The strong, powerful tendon at the back of the ankle connecting the heel bone to the calf muscles.

ACIDOSIS
A metabolic disturbance resulting from accumulation of acid in or loss of alkali from the body. It is characterised by drowsiness, nausea and increased rate of breathing. The condition is serious and may occur as a complication of DIABETES, lung and KIDNEY DISORDERS and other severe illnesses. Acidosis is treated by attention to the cause and by correcting the body's acid-base balance with oral or intravenous fluids.

ACNE
An inflammation of the skin centred in the SEBACEOUS GLANDS. Acne is usually found where the sebaceous glands are most active – on the face, neck and upper trunk. At puberty, male hormones (ANDROGENS – produced in both males and females) stimulate increased growth of skin cells and increased production of SEBUM. Sebaceous ducts may become blocked by skin overgrowth to form a WHITEHEAD, or by plugs of sebum which darken on exposure to air, forming a BLACKHEAD. When the sebum trapped in a whitehead or blackhead is forced into the deeper skin layers an inflammatory reaction causes a red lump called a papule. If infection follows, pus collects and a classic pimple (PUSTULE) is seen. When the inflammatory reaction is severe, large, painful cysts may form.

It is not clear why some people suffer from constant or frequent acne while others have it rarely or never. There seems to be an inherited tendency for skin and sebaceous glands to over-react to androgens, which explains why acne tends to run in families. Acne remains a source of misery for many young people. There are many effective treatments which can reduce the frequency and severity of eruptions. All acne sufferers should see their doctor or a dermatologist for an assessment of the most suitable treatment.

Some important points about acne:
• It is definitely stress related, so you are more likely to have a flare-up when you are under any sort of physical or emotional strain.

• Avoid picking and squeezing, which may force more sebum into deep skin layers, causing increased inflammation. Fingers may also introduce infection.

• You won't see the benefit of any treatment for at least six weeks, so persevere and be patient.

• There is no connection at all between diet and acne, in spite of all you'll hear about it being caused by everything you like. Nevertheless, a well-balanced diet is good for everyone.

• Moderate exposure to sunlight usually helps acne.

• Don't scrub. Scrubbing stimulates overgrowth of skin cells, aggravating the condition. Wash twice a day with plain soap, and dry gently.

• Blackheads do not result from uncleanliness or the use of cosmetics.

• Disguising an unsightly spot with a water-based cover cream won't aggravate the condition and is good for your morale.

• Wearing your hair in a fringe does not cause acne on the brow.

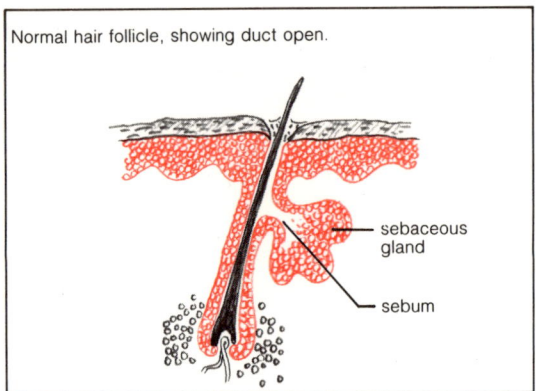

Normal hair follicle, showing duct open.

sebaceous gland

sebum

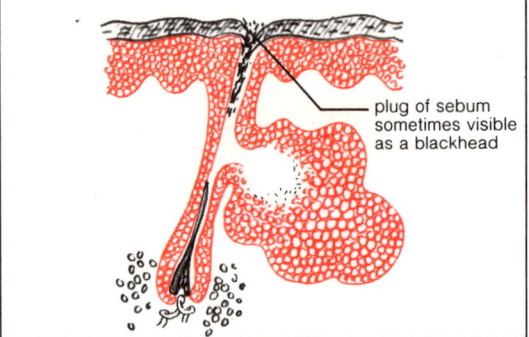

Hair follicle and sebaceous gland in acne patient. The duct wall is thickening and the increased sebum secretion rate causes damming back of sebum.

plug of sebum sometimes visible as a blackhead

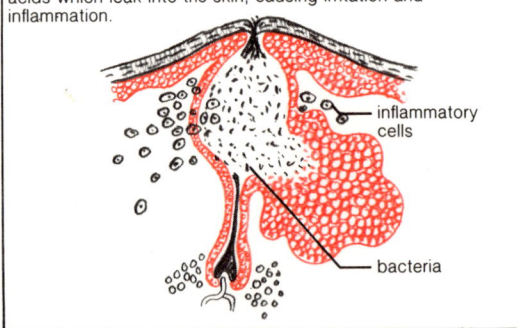

The trapped sebum is converted by bacteria into free fatty acids which leak into the skin, causing irritation and inflammation.

inflammatory cells

bacteria

Acne is an inflammation of the skin centred in the sebaceous gland.

ACQUIRED IMMUNE DEFICIENCY SYNDROME (AIDS)

See AIDS (ACQUIRED IMMUNE DEFICIENCY SYNDROME).

ACROMEGALY

Abnormal enlargement of the extremities of the skeleton – nose, jaw, fingers and toes – due to over-production of growth hormone in adulthood. The excess growth hormone is produced by a benign (non-cancerous) tumour of the pituitary gland. Early symptoms are changed appearance, tightening of shoes and gloves, and sometimes headache and visual disturbances. Treatment involves removing the gland surgically or destroying the tumour by radiotherapy. Excessive growth hormone in children results in a different condition, GIGANTISM.

ACROPHOBIA

An abnormal, excessive fear or dread of high places in which the sufferer may be illogically afraid in, say, a room in a high building even though there is no chance of falling. It is a disabling condition since the sufferer will often refuse to go to work or a function that involves going into a high building or a place high above the ground. As with other PHOBIAS, the sufferer may go into analysis to determine the possible cause of the phobia. Desensitisation, in which the sufferer is taught techniques of relaxation when confronted with high places, may also be helpful.

ACTINOMYCOSIS

An infection caused by a parasitic micro-organism, *Actinomyces israelii.* The microbe is commonly found in the mouth of many healthy people. When actinomyces gets into the tissues through a decayed tooth, or after the removal of a tooth or other injury to the jaw, it causes slowly progressive tissue destruction and pus formation. If infected pus is swallowed, inhaled, or enters the bloodstream, it may cause actinomycotic abscesses in the digestive tract, the liver, spleen, kidneys and lungs. Early treatment with antibiotics is usually effective although surgery may be necessary to drain accumulated pus.

ACUPUNCTURE

A traditional method of treatment used in China for several thousand years, acupuncture means 'piercing with a needle'. The Chinese theory is that a life force flows through the body along the meridian lines which are quite distinct from the lines followed by the nerves. Fine needles are inserted into the skin along the meridian lines at specific points which represent various organs. The rotation of the needles is believed to restore the balance between opposing energy forces. Recent scientific studies show that acupuncture causes the release of

ENDORPHINS and ENCEPHALINS whose effects include, among other things, reduction in pain perception.

ACUTE
A term used to describe a disease, disorder or illness that has a rapid onset, severe symptoms and a short course.

ADAM'S APPLE
A prominent piece of cartilage at the front of the neck surrounding the voice-box, also known as the LARYNX.

ADDICTION
An overwhelming and uncontrollable physical or psychological craving for a substance (such as drugs, alcohol) or activity (such as gambling, exercise). The need to have whatever it is that addicts crave prevents them from leading normal lives; all the addict's activities become directed towards satisfying the craving, to the detriment of health, family and other interpersonal relationships, and work. With some addictions, the body becomes so dependent on the substance that its withdrawal causes physical and mental illness. Addiction can be treated by psychotherapy using analysis, group therapy and various behaviour modification techniques. In some drug addictions, the prescription of less addictive drugs is used to relieve the symptoms of withdrawal. See also DRUG ABUSE, ALCOHOLISM, NARCOTICS (and Medical And Health Support Organisations – ALCOHOL & DRUG DEPENDENCE).

ADDISON'S DISEASE
First described by the 19th-century English physician Thomas Addison, this condition occurs when the adrenal glands do not produce sufficient quantities of the hormones called corticosteroids. In most cases this drop in production is caused when the body's defences react against the adrenal glands, slowly destroying them. Occasionally the glands may be damaged by tumours or by chronic infection such as TUBERCULOSIS.

Symptoms are weakness, tiredness, vomiting, weight loss, low blood pressure and a darkening of the mucous membranes and those areas of the body, like the elbows and palms, where there is friction on the skin. Treatment is by replacement of corticosteroids orally, by injection or by implantation under the skin.

ADENITIS
Inflammation of any glands, but the term usually refers to the lymph glands (lymphadenitis) in the neck, armpit and groin (sentinel lymph glands). These glands help the body's defences against infection. Mostly adenitis is caused by spread of bacterial infection from parts of the body drained by the lymph glands. Lymphadenitis also occurs in generalised viral infections such as infectious MONONUCLEOSIS (glandular fever) and RUBELLA (German measles). (See How The Body Works, p. 7.)

ADENOIDS
One or more small masses of lymphatic tissue, similar to the tonsils, that lie behind the nasal cavity close to where it joins the mouth cavity. They reach their maximum size around the ages 6–8, then begin to shrink until they have entirely disappeared by adolescence. Sometimes in childhood the adenoids become infected and grossly enlarged as a result of repeated throat and respiratory infections. In such cases adenoids may cause obstruction to breathing through the nose, thick nasal speech, snoring and repeated ear infections which may lead to deafness. Unless there is severe and troublesome blockage to the EUSTACHIAN TUBES which connect the throat with the middle ear, surgeons these days usually don't remove adenoids, preferring instead to treat infections as they occur and to allow the natural process of shrinkage to eventually solve the problem.

ADENOMA
A benign (non-cancerous) tumour caused by localised overgrowth of the cells of any gland. Adenomas vary in size from microscopic to larger than a football. Symptoms may be cosmetic, or because the tumour presses on nearby organs and tissues, or because the adenoma produces an excess of the usual secretion of the gland. Generally adenomas are removed surgically because a definite diagnosis that the tumour is non-cancerous cannot be made until it is examined under a microscope. If the tumour proves to be malignant (cancerous), it is known as an adenocarcinoma.

ADHESION
Fibrous tissue joining two surfaces that are not usually connected. Adhesions may be the result of inflammation (such as PERITONITIS, PERICARDITIS or PLEURISY) of the smooth internal membranes lining the body cavities, or of abnormal healing of a wound or surgical incision. They are usually harmless but may restrict movement in affected areas (for example, pleural adhesions may interfere with proper expansion of the lungs) or create difficulties in any future surgery in the same body cavity.

ADIPOSE TISSUE
Connective tissues specialised for fat storage. Adipose tissue is mainly found under the skin, especially of the upper arm, abdomen, buttocks and thighs, and in the omentum (the fold of peritoneum hanging from the lower border of the stomach). It acts as a buffering and insulating layer and as an

energy store. Too much fat storage leads to OBESITY, which is a danger to health.

ADOLESCENCE

The process of development from childhood to adulthood. See PUBERTY.

ADRENAL GLANDS

Sitting on top of the kidneys, this pair of endocrine glands secrete various hormones including corticosteroids and adrenalin. (See How The Body Works, pp. 22–24.)

ADRENALIN

More commonly known as the 'fright, flight or fight' hormone, it is produced by the adrenal glands and causes the entire body to be ready for immediate physical or mental effort.

AFTERBIRTH

See PLACENTA, UMBILICAL CORD.

AGORAPHOBIA

A pathological fear of open spaces. It can be a crippling condition when a sufferer is too afraid to do simple things, like go shopping. Agoraphobia is often successfully treated with behavioural therapy and relaxation techniques.

AIDS (ACQUIRED IMMUNE DEFICIENCY SYNDROME)

An infectious disease caused by a virus, the AIDS virus, or more properly the human immuno-deficiency virus (HIV). AIDS was first recognised in 1980 and in the second half of the decade is responsible for a world-wide epidemic which has claimed thousands of lives and is still growing. At first the epidemic spread most rapidly among homo-sexual and bisexual men, but now the greatest area of concern world-wide is the spread of the infection by heterosexual transmission and intravenous drug abuse.

AIDS is the most baffling disease of our times. In spite of intensive research, experts are still grappling with its mysteries, and to date no effective treatment, cure or preventive vaccine is in sight. One of the many extraordinary features of the HIV is the very long incubation period between infection and illness. This is so far known to be up to four years and suspected to be up to twenty years. Millions of people around the world (including an estimated 50 000 Australians) have already been infected with the virus. Infected people develop an antibody to HIV which circulates in the blood: they are described as being AIDS- or HIV-antibody positive. Whether all those who are antibody positive will eventually develop AIDS is at present quite unknown. Progression from infection to disease has so far been

10–30 per cent. Even if the spread of infection stopped now, we would be dealing with AIDS for at least the next two generations.

Why is AIDS such a serious disease?

The HIV virus attacks the body's natural defence against disease, the immune system, making it impossible to fight off other serious illness. It also affects the brain and other parts of the nervous system. AIDS patients usually die of infections such as pneumonia, or of cancer or nervous system failure. So far, all victims have died within three years of the development of full-blown AIDS.

How is AIDS diagnosed?

When an HIV-antibody positive person becomes ill due to infection by organisms which don't normally cause illness in humans, and/or develops certain rare cancers (lymphoma, Kaposi's sarcoma), and/or shows certain typical nervous system deterio-rations, AIDS is suspected. The finding of typical abnormalities in the blood count confirms the diagnosis.

How does AIDS spread?

The infection is spread when an infected person's blood, sexual secretions or other material containing the virus gets into another person's blood. This can happen via blood transfusion, by injection with a contaminated needle or syringe, by sexual trans-mission or by transmission from mother to baby across the placenta or during birth. AIDS does *not* spread by ordinary social or domestic contact. There are *no* reported cases transmitted through touching, hugging, kissing, sharing clothing, food or utensils, sneezing, coughing, or by using public drinking fountains, toilets or swimming pools.

How can the spread of AIDS be prevented?

The only hope for halting the spread of the epidemic is for people to adopt new standards of hygiene, especially safe sex (the use of condoms; avoiding any exchange of body fluids) and the avoidance of contact with other peoples' bodily fluids, particularly blood and sexual secretions. All blood used for transfusion in Australia is carefully tested and treated to remove any risk of AIDS transmission. (See Medical And Health Support Organisations.)

ALCOHOLISM

Excessive, persistent and compulsive drinking of alcohol resulting in personal and social problems and breakdown of health. People who become addicted to alcohol usually begin to drink heavily to find relief from personal, social or work stress. The more they drink, the less tension they can tolerate without alcohol. When a person cannot get through the day without a drink, and needs alcohol to make himself feel normal, chronic alcoholism with physical and psychological dependence has developed. Alco-holism leads to loss of appetite and malnutrition, and eventually the liver, digestive system, heart, reproductive system and nerves are affected. The cure is complete abstinence from alcohol with vitamin supplements and a good diet to correct the effects of poor nutrition. There are a number of social agencies which have been established to deal specifically with the problems faced by alcoholics and their families. (See Medical And Health Support Organisations.)

ALLERGY

A condition in which the body's immune system produces antibodies to certain substances (known as allergens) which don't normally cause antibody formation. Common allergens are pollens, animal hair, feathers, house dust, and certain foods and drugs. When an allergy is established, exposure to the allergen causes the antibodies to affect mast cells, (which are scattered widely throughout the body) causing them to release histamine, the culprit chemical in allergic reactions. Histamine causes various local or generalised disturbances of blood flow and involuntary muscle activity. Common manifestations of allergic reaction are ASTHMA, HAY FEVER, ECZEMA, contact DERMATITIS and URTICARIA. Treatment is by avoidance of the allergen, and if this is unknown or impossible, the use of ANTIHISTAMINE medication or attempts at desensitisation.

ALOPECIA

Baldness or loss of hair from areas where it normally grows. Hair is lost when hair follicles cease function. This may be temporary or permanent. Temporary baldness, which may be general or patchy, can occur in severe debilitating illness, or may be due to drugs, poisons, irradiation, hormonal disorders and emotional stress. Hair will regrow when the hair follicles are no longer influenced by whatever caused their temporary failure.

The pattern of permanent baldness in men is determined by heredity. In the presence of male hormones the hair follicles gradually disappear from certain parts of the scalp. The drug minoxidil has recently been used in an attempt to halt or reverse this change, with reported success in some cases.

ALZHEIMER'S DISEASE

Permanent, progressive DEMENTIA due to gradual degeneration of the cerebral cortex. The cause is unknown, but it may be one of the natural degenerations of ageing. About 20 per cent of people over 80 suffer from some degree of dementia. Alzheimer's disease is diagnosed when all other known (and possibly treatable) causes of dementia have been excluded. Forgetfulness is an early sign. All old people are somewhat forgetful, but in Alzheimer's disease the loss of memory for recent events becomes progressively worse and leads to

confusion, agitation, delusions, hallucinations and inappropriate emotions such as suspicion, hostility and aggression. There is no known treatment. (See Medical And Health Support Organisations.)

AMENORRHOEA

The absence of menstrual periods at any time between MENARCHE and MENOPAUSE. Amenorrhoea is normal or physiological during pregnancy and breast feeding. There are two types of abnormal or pathological amenorrhoea:

Primary amenorrhoea – failure to menstruate at PUBERTY. Australian girls usually start to menstruate between 13 and 14 years of age. If other developments of puberty seem normal there is generally no need to worry if the onset of periods is delayed. Late menstruation is especially likely in girls who are very underweight for their height. Other causes are failure of the uterus or ovaries to develop, imperforate hymen and certain genetic and hormonal disorders. If menstruation has not started by age 17 a girl should see her doctor.

Secondary amenorrhoea – no menstruation for more than eight weeks for reasons other than pregnancy or lactation. The most common causes are:
• Change of environment. The part of the brain controlling the reproductive cycle is very sensitive and may be disturbed by sudden changes in how you live, such as moving house, travelling, going on night-shift. Periods usually resume when your body adjusts to your new life-style.
• Excess weight loss. A certain amount of body fat is necessary to support a pregnancy. If you lose too much weight – especially if you lose it quickly – your body recognises that you are in no fit condition for pregnancy and you stop ovulating and menstruating. Crash diets play havoc with the menstrual cycle. Each woman has a 'minimal menstrual weight', determined by height and build. When women with ANOREXIA NERVOSA fall below a certain weight, their periods stop. This type of amenorrhoea is also seen in women undertaking intense athletic training, who replace most of their body fat with muscle.
• Hormonal disorders. Any disturbance to the menstrual cycle's hormonal control may result in amenorrhoea.

Any woman with eight weeks or more of amenorrhoea should see her doctor to exclude pregnancy, and so that other causes can be diagnosed and treated.

AMNESIA

A loss of memory that may be total or partial, temporary or permanent. It can follow brain damage from injury, infection, metabolic disease, poisoning, tumours, or can occur as a consequence of severe emotional shock. Specialised psychiatric treatment is most often suggested when amnesia follows psychological trauma.

AMNIOCENTESIS

Removal of a sample of the amniotic fluid during pregnancy for the purpose of testing the foetal cells it contains, to see whether a genetic or other foetal disorder exists. The fluid is obtained by inserting (under local anaesthetic and with ULTRASOUND monitoring) a hollow needle through the abdominal wall and the wall of the uterus into the amniotic sac. Amniocentesis cannot be performed until the fifteenth week of pregnancy or later. A more recently developed technique, amniotic villus sampling, allows removal of a fragment of the outer wall of the amniotic sac by passing a slender instrument through the mother's cervical canal. This can be performed before the twelfth week of pregnancy – a more satisfactory time for the diagnosis of foetal abnormalities. (See also Medical Tests And Examinations.)

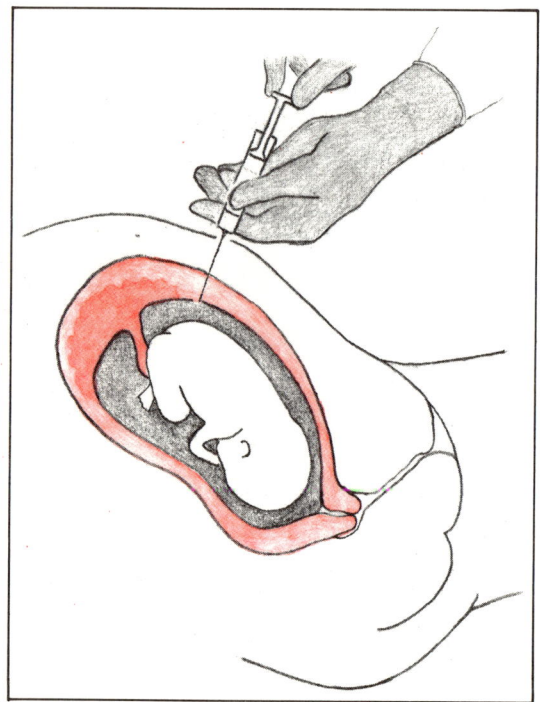

Amniocentesis is a test in which a sample of amniotic fluid is taken during pregnancy to check for genetic or foetal disorders.

AMNION

The membrane which lines the sac containing the amniotic fluid in which the FOETUS floats. During the first or second stage of labour the sac usually ruptures to release the fluid (breaking of the waters). Occasionally the foetus is delivered with the sac intact ('born in a caul'). In the past this was thought to be a sign that the new-born child would never die from drowning, and thus a favourable omen for a life at sea.

AMOEBIASIS

An infection of the large bowel (COLITIS) caused by the parasite *Entamoeba histolytica*. The infection is contracted by drinking water contaminated by the parasite and is prevalent where water supplies are unsanitary, particularly in hot climates. Symptoms are severe, watery, often blood-stained DIARRHOEA leading to dehydration, prostration and malnutrition. Diagnosis is by identification of the amoeba in stools. Amoebic dysentery, as it is commonly known, was previously the frequent cause of chronic ill health and death in tropical countries, but now effective antibiotic treatment is available.

AMOEBIC DYSENTERY

See AMOEBIASIS.

AMPHETAMINES

A family of drugs which stimulate the central nervous system, producing feelings of alertness, energy and exhilaration. After the effects of amphetamines wear off there is a reaction period in which low mood and extreme tiredness are felt. In the past the drug was used to combat fatigue in, for example, night workers, long-distance truck drivers, students cramming for exams. Because amphetamines also supress appetite they have been used in the treatment of obesity. Amphetamines became freely available on the pharmaceutical market during the 1950s. Like many other mood-altering drugs they were soon abused, with disastrous health consequences for the habitual user. Severe anxiety, distorted judgement, paranoia with delusions and hallucinations, deep depression (often suicidal), chronic exhaustion from lack of sleep, and malnutrition were common symptoms of 'speed' addiction. Because of abuse, amphetamines have now been banned in many countries, including Australia. See DRUG ABUSE.

AMYL NITRITE

A vasodilator drug used mainly in the treatment of ANGINA, but also subject to abuse for its brief exhilarating and muscle-relaxing effects.

AMYTAL

A medium-acting BARBITURATE.

ANAEMIA

A condition of reduced oxygen-carrying capacity of the blood. Oxygen is transported around the body by the iron-containing pigment HAEMOGLOBIN contained in the blood's red cells (erythrocytes), and released to the tissues as the blood passes through the capillaries. Oxygen-depleted red cells are returned in the veins to the right side of the heart, from where blood is pumped to the lungs for recharging with oxygen. Anaemia can be caused by an insufficiency or abnormality of the haemoglobin in the red cells, or by an inadequate number of red cells in the circulation. The many different causes of anaemia can be classified into two main groups:

Anaemias due to an insufficiency or abnormality of the haemoglobin in red cells. A common example of reduced haemoglobin anaemia is iron deficiency anaemia, due to an inadequate intake of iron in the diet or the excessive loss of iron from the body, such as occurs in bleeding lesions of the bowel (ulcers, cancers), chronic MENORRHAGIA, and closely repeated pregnancies and lactations. Abnormalities of haemoglobin occur in the hereditary anaemias (for example, thalassaemia, sickle cell anaemia), and in certain poisonings which change the haemoglobin so that it cannot carry oxygen properly.

Anaemias due to inadequate red cells in the circulation. The red cell count may fall in aplastic anaemia when insufficient red cells are produced by the bone marrow (as in bone marrow suppression by irradiation or drugs, or bone marrow destruction by primary or secondary cancer); or it may fall in pernicious anaemia and some hereditary anaemias when red cells are fragile and are destroyed too rapidly (the normal life of a red cell is 120 days).

The symptoms of anaemia are pallor, lethargy and fatigue, shortness of breath on exertion, headache, dizziness. The diagnosis of anaemia is made on a simple blood examination. Further tests may be necessary to identify the cause. When the cause of anaemia can be eliminated or corrected, treatment is entirely satisfactory. Otherwise the only treatment is by blood transfusion.

ANAESTHESIA

Meaning, literally, 'without feeling', anaesthesia is the loss of sensation when a nerve supplying any part of the body is damaged by injury or disease. Anaesthesia may also be induced deliberately by various means, including the use of drugs known as anaesthetics, so that surgery or dental treatment may be performed without any sensation of pain. General anaesthesia makes a patient unconscious so that sensations are not perceived. Drugs to induce general anaesthesia are administered by inhalation or by intravenous injection. Local anaesthesia is achieved by injecting the anaesthetic drug around the nerve supplying the part to be treated, to block the transmission of sensory impulses along the nerve to the brain.

ANALGESIC

A drug that relieves pain without causing loss of consciousness. Analgesics vary in strength from ASPIRIN to MORPHINE. They do not cure the cause but simply block the perception of pain. Use of analgesics other than occasionally, should be under medical supervision.

ANDROGENS

Male sex HORMONES that are responsible for the development of male sexual characteristics in an adolescent boy. Androgens are largely secreted by cells in the TESTES, with smaller quantities being manufactured by the ADRENAL GLANDS and the OVARIES. Too much androgen in women causes masculinisation while too little in men results in a lessening of male sexual characteristics. Both conditions can be successfully treated.

ANEURYSM

An abnormal swelling due to localised weakening of the wall of an artery resulting from congenital defect, injury, or disease such as SYPHILIS or ARTERIOSCLEROSIS. Congenital aneurysms may affect the arteries supplying the brain, where rupture may result in SUBARACHNOID HAEMORRHAGE in young, otherwise healthy people. Aneurysms secondary to disease most frequently occur in the aorta. A ruptured aortic aneurysm can be fatal because of internal bleeding. Recently there have been considerable advances in surgical techniques to correct aneurysms.

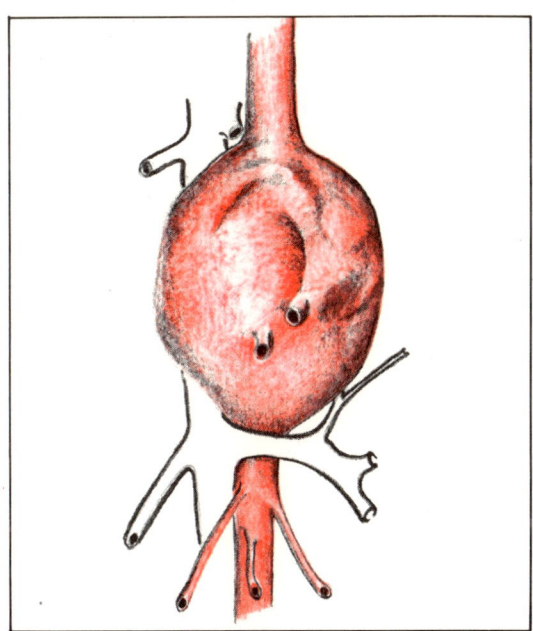

An aneurysm is an abnormal distension which forms in a weak part of an artery.

ANGINA

Any type of spasmodic pain that sometimes produces a feeling of suffocation.

ANGINA PECTORIS

A severe and constricting pain in the chest which may move to the shoulders, jaw and left arm. It occurs when there is insufficient blood supply to the heart, usually as a result of narrowing of the coronary arteries by ATHEROMA. Generally the pain is described as being constricting or like a heavy weight on the chest. There may be a sensation of suffocation with palpitations and dizziness. Angina pectoris most often occurs after physical exertion and is relieved by rest. It may also be brought on by other circumstances which increase the work of the heart, such as fever, heavy meals, exposure to cold and strong emotions. Treatment is by avoiding the known causes, and the use of drugs which increase the blood flow through the coronary arteries. Severe, progressive angina may be treated by CORONARY ARTERY BY-PASS surgery.

ANGIOGRAPHY

The introduction of a special dye into blood vessels to make them show up on an X-ray. The process reveals the site of defects such as ANEURYSM, narrowing or blockage so that corrective surgery may be carried out. (See Medical Tests And Examinations – CARDIAC ANGIOGRAPHY.)

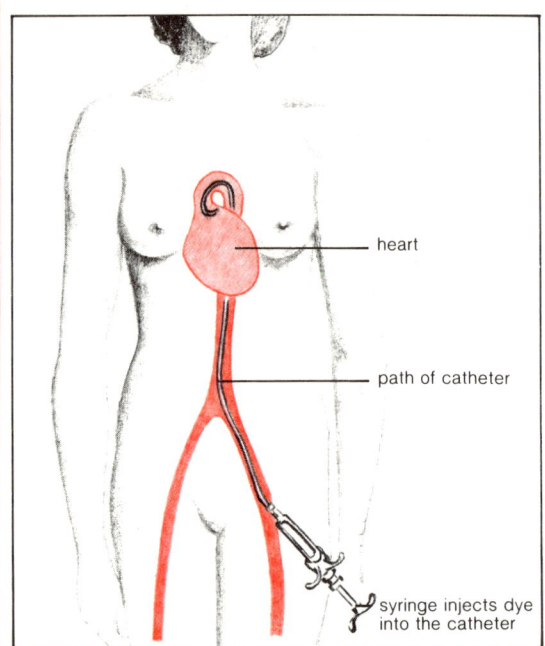

heart

path of catheter

syringe injects dye into the catheter

Angiography is a special test in which a radiopaque dye is injected into the arteries in order to make them show up on an X-ray.

ANKYLOSING SPONDYLITIS

A form of spinal arthritis which mainly affects men under 30, and which progresses to fusion of the spinal joints. The cause of ankylosing spondylitis is unknown, but an inherited predisposition is suspected. Treatment is by non-steroidal anti-inflammatory drugs (NSAIDS) and physiotherapy.

ANKYLOSIS

Loss of mobility in a joint due to fusion (growing together) of adjacent bones of the joint. Ankylosis may occur after severe inflammatory or infective ARTHRITIS or following destructive injury to joints.

ANOREXIA

Lack or loss of appetite. Temporary anorexia can occur in most infectious and other severe illnesses and in some emotional states such as anxiety and grief.

ANOREXIA NERVOSA

Abnormal lack or suppression of appetite. This is a psychological disorder of great complexity which mainly affects young women. Inability or refusal to eat, or habitual forced vomiting after eating, can lead to malnutrition, emaciation, AMENORRHOEA, IMPOTENCE in males and sometimes death. As soon as anorexia nervosa is suspected medical help should be sought so that the diagnosis may be confirmed and other causes of emaciation excluded. Skilled, sympathetic psychiatric treatment is usually successful. See also BULIMIA. (See Medical And Health Support Organisations.)

ANOVULATION

Failure to ovulate (release eggs from the ovary). This may be primary (if a woman has never ovulated) or secondary (if a woman stops ovulating). Primary and secondary anovulation can be caused by the same disorders as primary and secondary AMENORRHOEA. However, a woman may have periods without ovulating – called anovulatory cycles. This is likely to happen at the extremes of reproductive life – soon after the MENARCHE and as MENOPAUSE approaches. Failure to ovulate may be treated by drugs which stimulate the ovaries.

ANTACID

An alkaline substance which neutralises the acidic digestive juices of the stomach. Antacids are usually used to ease the discomfort of INDIGESTION and PEPTIC ULCERS. The habitual use of antacids can mask the symptoms of serious but treatable disease. Anyone needing to use them for more than a few days at a time should see a doctor for diagnosis of the cause of symptoms.

ANTIBIOTIC

An antibacterial drug, either natural or synthetic, that inhibits the growth of micro-organisms in the body. The name 'antibiotic' means, literally, 'against life'. Some antibiotics are used to treat specific infections while other broad-spectrum antibiotics destroy a wide range of micro-organisms. Antibiotics are of immense importance in treating bacterial and fungal infections, and are in fact the only drugs which eradicate the cause of any disease. However, unwise and unnecessary use of antibiotics may encourage the development of resistant strains of micro-organisms.

ANTIBODIES

Special proteins produced in the blood or tissues by the immune system to protect the body against invasion by harmful bacteria, viruses, foreign blood cells and other substances. In infectious illnesses – such as viral infections – for which there is no antibiotic treatment, recovery depends on the development of sufficient antibodies to overcome the invading organism. Some antibodies remain in the body throughout life to give permanent immunity (protection against a second attack of measles or mumps, for example). IMMUNISATION is deliberate, controlled exposure to dangerous agents (for example, polio, tetanus, diphtheria) so that antibodies will be produced to prevent future infection. Abnormal antibody formation occurs in ALLERGY and AUTOIMMUNE DISEASE.

ANTICOAGULANT

A drug that slows down or prevents the clotting of blood. Anticoagulants are used to prevent DEEP VENOUS THROMBOSIS in immobilised patients (for example, after certain types of surgery or after STROKE) and to prevent extension of established thrombosis, which may lead to EMBOLISM.

ANTICONVULSANT

A drug used to prevent or control convulsions, especially in EPILEPSY and TETANUS.

ANTI-D ANTIBODY

This prevents the formation of antibodies to the RHESUS (Rh) FACTOR in the blood of Rh-negative women who are carrying an Rh-positive foetus. It is given to all Rh-negative mothers after abortion, or after delivery of an Rh-positive baby so that there will be no blood incompatibility between mother and baby in future pregnancies.

ANTI-DEPRESSANT

A drug used to correct or modify the symptoms of DEPRESSION.

ANTIDOTE

A remedy that counteracts the effects of a poison.

ANTIGEN

A substance which, when it enters the body, causes the production of ANTIBODIES by the immune system.

ANTIHISTAMINE

A drug used in allergic disorders to counteract the effects of histamine. The side-effects of some antihistamines may include drowsiness, dizziness, dry mouth and a feeling of weakness. They should be taken according to direction.

ANTISEPTIC

A substance that prevents the growth of, or kills, bacteria and other micro-organisms. Antiseptics are used to disinfect the skin and surgical instruments.

ANURIA

A serious condition where the kidneys do not produce urine. It may imply either KIDNEY FAILURE or a blockage of the URETERS.

ANUS

The lower opening of the bowel.

ANXIETY

A feeling of intense fear, dread and distress in the absence of real danger. A state of anxiety may cause tension, tiredness, pounding heart, trembling, dry mouth, sweating and anorexia. Low-level rational anxiety in a real, stressful situation is normal and usually diminishes when the immediate problem is solved. Deep, irrational anxiety, when a state of apprehension is out of proportion to the real situation, is more serious and should be most properly treated by a psychiatrist.

AORTA

The largest artery of the body which conducts oxygen-rich blood from the left ventricle of the heart to distribute it via the circulation. Small and large arteries branch off the aorta to carry blood throughout the body.

APHASIA

Impairment or inability to express oneself through speech, or failure to understand the meaning of words. It is usually the result of damage to the dominant side of the brain, by STROKE, tumours or injury.

APOPLEXY

A STROKE caused by CEREBRAL HAEMORRHAGE. Paralysis and loss of consciousness may occur without warning, although premonitory symptoms often include numbness of one arm and leg, sudden blurred vision, giddiness and difficulty in speaking.

APPENDICITIS

Acute inflammation of the APPENDIX. Often one of the first signs of appendicitis is a severe pain around the umbilicus (navel) which later moves to the lower right-hand side of the abdomen. There may also be loss of appetite, nausea and, perhaps, vomiting. The most distinctive sign of appendicitis is extreme tenderness in the lower right abdomen. An inflamed appendix should be removed without delay by a relatively simple operation known as an appendicectomy.

APPENDIX

A small, tube-like organ branching off from the large intestine. It has no known function.

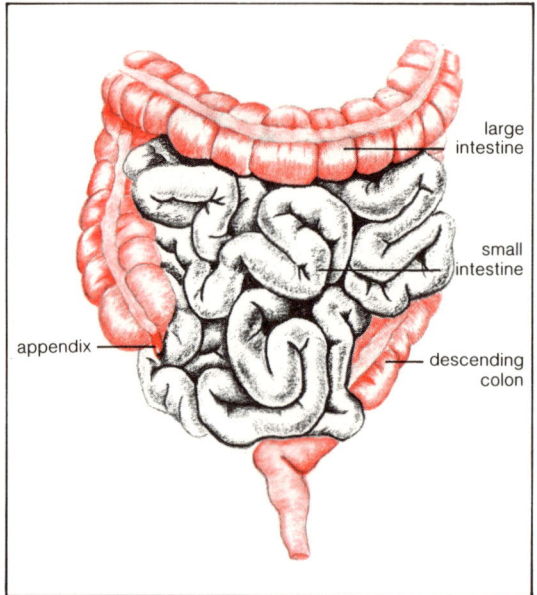

The appendix is a tube-shaped organ protruding from the large intestine. An inflamed appendix is often indicated by pain around the navel, moving later to the lower right-hand side of the abdomen.

APPETITE

The desire to eat food (in contrast to hunger which is a physical need for food). There is no such thing as a 'normal' appetite since each person's age, build, metabolism, daily activities, eating habits and attitude to food and stage of life influence appetite. A 'large' appetite is normal during certain stages of life, as in pregnancy or a child's peak growth periods.

Appetite usually reflects the state of physical and mental health. It is reduced in illness and increased during recovery. Appetite is abnormally reduced in ANOREXIA NERVOSA and abnormally increased in BULIMIA.

AREOLA

The coloured area around the nipple.

ARRHYTHMIA

A disturbance of the regularity of the heartbeat, resulting in an irregular pulse. Physically fit people and young people have a faster pulse when breathing in than when breathing out, a condition known as sinus arrhythmia. Arrythmias such as atrial or VENTRICULAR FIBRILLATION usually indicate serious disease.

ARTERIOSCLEROSIS

This means (and is commonly called) hardening of the arteries. Arteriosclerosis is caused by the gradual build-up of deposits of minerals and fibrous tissue in the arterial walls, making them thicker and less flexible. The loss of elasticity in the vessel walls increases the resistance to blood flow which causes blood pressure to rise. The increased blood pressure causes further damage, leading to further SCLEROSIS in the arterial walls – a vicious cycle. Some degree of arteriosclerosis is inevitable with ageing. When mild it usually doesn't cause health problems. Severe arteriosclerosis can lead to the formation of ANEURYSMS.

ARTERY

Any blood vessel that carries oxygenated blood from the heart to the rest of the body. The one exception is the PULMONARY artery which carries de-oxygenated blood from heart to lungs.

ARTHRITIS

A general term to describe a range of diseases in which the joints become inflamed causing swelling, pain and difficulty of movement. Two of the most common are OSTEOARTHRITIS, caused by the wearing away of the cartilage of the joints, and RHEUMATOID ARTHRITIS, where the joint linings become inflamed and the joints swollen and painful. Early treatment of arthritis with anti-inflammatory medication and physiotherapy will reduce the risk of limitation of movement and crippling deformity.

ARTIFICIAL INSEMINATION

The introduction of SEMEN into the uterus by artificial means in order for conception to take place. When the husband's semen is used, the procedure is known as AIH (artificial insemination husband) and when the semen comes from another, often anonymous man, it is known as AID (artificial insemination donor).

ASBESTOSIS

A debilitating disease affecting the lungs. Asbestosis is a form of PNEUMOCONIOSIS. It is usually an occupational disorder caused by breathing in minute particles of asbestos. The asbestos causes an inflammatory reaction which results in the destruction of lung tissue. Severe asbestosis can lead to EMPHYSEMA and obstructive airways disease.

ASCITES

Also known as dropsy, it is an abnormal build-up of fluid in the peritoneal cavity leading to swelling of the abdomen. It can occur as a result of diseases of the heart, liver or kidneys.

ASCORBIC ACID

Vitamin C. See VITAMINS.

ASPHYXIA

Interference with the respiratory function of the lungs, leading to an increase in the carbon dioxide level and a decrease in the oxygen level in the blood. It may be caused by obstruction of the airways (suffocation), entry of fluid into the lungs (drowning), collapse of the lungs, crushing or compression injuries to the chest, or breathing of air containing insufficient oxygen. If first aid isn't given immediately to a suffocating person, brain damage will occur if the cells of the brain are not given oxygen within 3 or 4 minutes. (See also First Aid.)

ASPIRIN

A drug usually prescribed as an ANALGESIC (painkiller). It is the basic ingredient of many pain-relieving tablets and is also effective in reducing fever and reducing inflammation. Because of its mild anticoagulant properties, aspirin is also useful in the prevention of thrombotic stroke. When used properly, aspirin is relatively safe.

ASTHMA

A condition in which the sufferer has difficulty breathing because of spasm of the muscles in the bronchial walls. It seems that asthma sufferers lack certain chemical and allergic defence agents which usually protect the bronchi from irritating trigger factors which cause an asthma attack. There are many factors which trigger bronchial spasm, including emotional stress and allergens like animal hair, pollen, dust, certain foods, drugs and chemicals. There are various effective drug treatments now used to prevent and reverse asthma attacks. (See Medical And Health Support Organisations.)

ASTIGMATISM

A vision disorder, caused by irregularities of the curvature of the lens or cornea of the eye, in which the image of an object is distorted or blurred. It is easily corrected with glasses or contact lenses.

ATHEROMA

Thickening of the lining of the arteries by fatty deposits, such as cholesterol.

ATHEROSCLEROSIS

The combination of ATHEROMA and ARTERIOSCLEROSIS. These conditions usually go together, because arterial walls damaged by atheroma are more likely to become sclerosed, and the increased blood pressure that goes with arteriosclerosis makes blood vessels more liable to atheroma. This process is one of the normal degenerations of ageing, and is progressive throughout adult life, though the degree varies greatly between individuals. When atherosclerosis is mild it causes no problems. Extensive fatty deposits can cause narrowing and irregularity of the lumen of the artery which may reduce or cut off the blood supply to the organ or tissue beyond the narrowing. Conditions secondary to arteriosclerosis are ANGINA PECTORIS, HEART ATTACK (coronary occlusion), STROKE, CLAUDICATION and GANGRENE. The rate of development of arteriosclerosis is believed to be influenced by heredity, diet and life-style. The National Heart Foundation advises that, to reduce the risk of arteriosclerosis, we should exercise regularly, stop smoking, reduce obesity, watch blood pressure and stick to a diet low in fats and salt and high in complex carbohydrates and fibre (unrefined grains and other plant foods).

ATHLETE'S FOOT

A fungal infection of the skin of the feet causing splitting, scaling and blisters, especially around and between the toes. It is most likely to occur when feet are sweaty and moist. The infection often spreads among people who use the same bathrooms or change-rooms. It can be effectively treated with anti-fungal creams and powders.

ATRIUM

The upper chambers of the heart, also called auricles. The right atrium receives de-oxygenated blood from the body, the left atrium receives oxygenated blood from the lungs. (See How The Body Works, pp. 5–9.)

ATROPHY

The wasting away, or reduction in size, of part of the body, usually caused by an inadequate nutritional supply or by loss of function (for example, atrophy of the muscles in POLIOMYELITIS or during prolonged immobilisation).

AURA

Feelings or signs which precede physical or mental disorders.

AUSCULTATION

Listening to the sounds made by various organs of the body, particularly the heart, lungs and intestines, to detect any irregularities.

AUTISM

A psychosis in children, cause unknown, characterised by an indifference to people, surroundings, noise, pain. Autistic children withdraw into themselves and live in a closed world of their own making. While often not responding to care and affection, an autistic child will sometimes show repetitive, ritualistic play. Although not necessarily mentally deficient, an autistic child may appear to be so because of intense withdrawal. Although complete recovery is rare, many advances have recently been made in understanding and treating autism. (See Medical And Health Support Organisations.)

AUTOIMMUNE DISEASE

A disease where the body cannot distinguish between foreign substances and those it produces itself, the result being that antibodies are produced that attack and destroy parts of the body.

AUTONOMIC NERVOUS SYSTEM

The part of the nervous system regulating the unconscious functions of the body such as breathing, the beating of the heart and bodily reactions to emotional states such as blushing. It consists of two parts: the sympathetic nervous system and the parasympathetic nervous system. The two balance each other so that the body can cope with many different situations and stresses. (See also How The Body Works, pp. 12–15.)

AUTOPSY

Also known as POST MORTEM, this is the examination of a body by dissection to discover the cause of death.

AVERSION THERAPY

A form of behaviour therapy in which an unpleasant sensation or association is linked, in the patient's mind, with behaviour considered socially or medically unacceptable.

AZOOSPERMIA

An absence of sperm in the seminal fluid. It may be the result of undescended testes, inadequate blood supply to the testes, obstruction of the seminal passages, infections of the testes, alcoholism, hormonal disorders, irradiation and certain poisonings. Temporary azoospermia may follow high fever, with recovery after two to three months.

B

BACKACHE

Most people suffer from backache at some time during their lives. Each year in Australia over 5 million days are lost from work because of back pain. The majority of backaches are not symptoms of serious disease. Most cases are the result of minor strains or injuries: about 70 per cent of sufferers will have recovered within a week and over 90 per cent within a month.

The spine is a very complex structure which is never still. The slightest movement, including breathing, involves the spine. Most back pains are the result of disturbances of spinal movements due to minor strains or injuries to the joints between the vertebrae or the surrounding muscles and ligaments. Man's upright posture puts additional stress on the neck and lumbar regions, which are the commonest sites of back pain. The pain may be sharp and sudden in onset, or an ache may develop gradually over several hours or overnight. There is often an obvious cause such as unaccustomed activity, or a strain during strenuous movement (lifting, digging, twisting the trunk), but many back pains come on without relation to any particular activity.

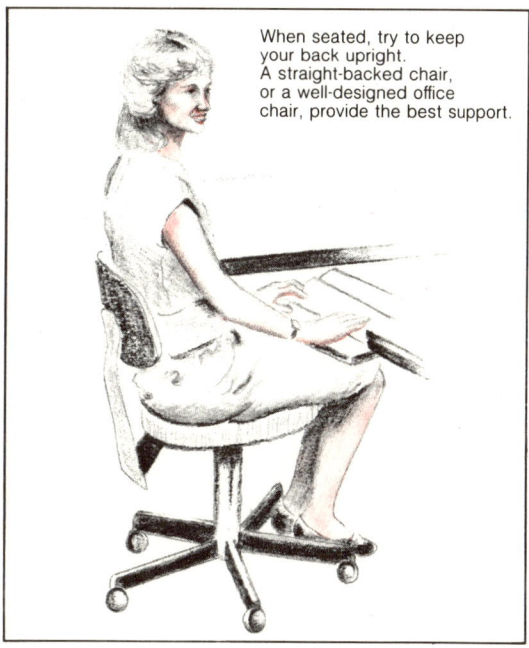

When seated, try to keep your back upright. A straight-backed chair, or a well-designed office chair, provide the best support.

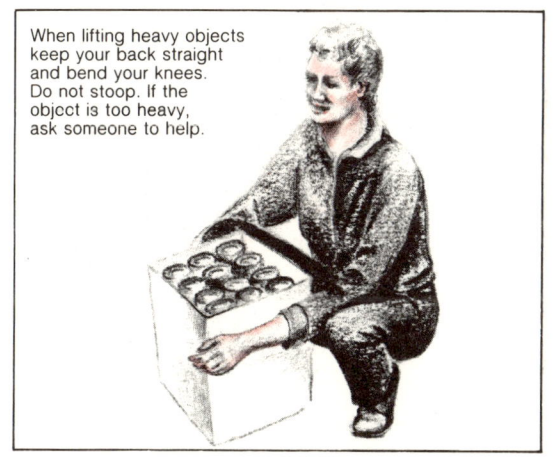

When lifting heavy objects keep your back straight and bend your knees. Do not stoop. If the object is too heavy, ask someone to help.

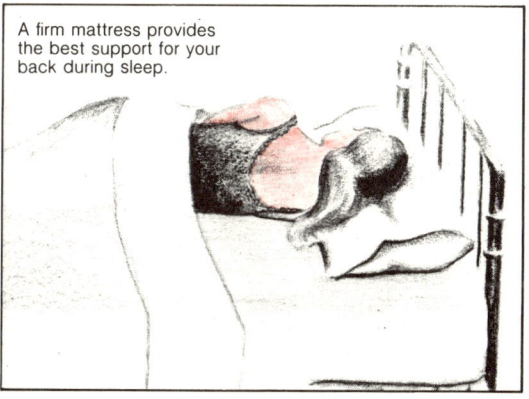

A firm mattress provides the best support for your back during sleep.

Backache is a common complaint which, in the majority of cases, is caused by minor strains or injuries.

Treatment of acute attacks consists traditionally of rest, local heat and simple painkillers such as aspirin. If pain is severe enough to keep you on your back, or if it hasn't improved considerably in two or three days, consult your doctor. Early physiotherapy or manipulation often speeds recovery, and your physiotherapist will recommend exercises, postural correction and care in movements to prevent or reduce further back problems.

Chronic backache should always be investigated as it may be a symptom of disease of the vertebrae or spinal joints. Occasionally back pain may be caused by disorders of the abdominal or pelvic organs, especially the kidneys and reproductive organs.

BACKBONE
See SPINE.

BACTERIA
Micro-organisms consisting of a single cell without a nucleus. Bacteria are found wherever life exists. Most bacteria live in harmony with other life forms. Some, for example those that are normally found in the human bowel and vagina, are essential for health. Bacteria which cause disease in animals or plants are described as pathogenic. Pathogenic bacteria cause disease by causing inflammation (for example, staphylococcus as a cause of wound infection), by invading and disturbing or destroying cells or tissues (for example, tubercle bacillus), or by producing toxins which enter the bloodstream and cause poisoning, (for example, BOTULISM).

BAD BREATH
See HALITOSIS.

BAG OF WATERS
The membranous sac (AMNION) containing amniotic fluid which surrounds the developing baby in the uterus.

BALANITIS
Inflammation of the glans (head of the) penis, usually as a result of bacterial, fungal or viral infection. Some forms of balanitis are sexually transmitted, such as HERPES, THRUSH and TRICHOMONIASIS. Other causes of balanitis are allergy, chemical or mechanical irritation, and the various dermatitises. Balanitis is more common in uncircumcised males, especially if the foreskin is tight. Symptoms are pain, redness and swelling of the glans, often with discharge of pus. Treatment is by rest, analgesics, bathing to remove discharges, antibiotics if appropriate. Further attacks can mostly be avoided by good hygiene. If the foreskin is difficult to retract because it is too long or too tight, circumcision may be necessary.

BALDNESS
Loss of hair. See ALOPECIA.

BARBER'S RASH
Infection of the hair follicles in the beard area, which may spread into the surrounding skin resulting in IMPETIGO. Treatment is by local or oral antibiotics.

BARBITURATES
A family of drugs that depress the central nervous system (CNS) to cause sedation (calmness and relaxation) or to act as hypnotics by inducing sleep. The various barbiturates differ in their degree of speed, duration and degree of depression of the CNS. The short-acting barbiturates rapidly induce sleep and are used for general anaesthesia. The medium-acting barbiturates are used to get a person off to sleep or to maintain a full night's sleep. Slow-acting barbiturates act as mild sedatives or anticonvulsants (phenobarbitone is commonly used to prevent or reduce the frequency of epileptic seizures). In recent years barbiturates have become somewhat disreputable because of careless prescribing and abuse. Like all CNS depressants, they involve some risk of overdose, side-effects, habituation, tolerance and addiction. To avoid these problems it is recommended that barbiturates (excepting those used to prevent epilepsy) should be used only for short periods (two to four weeks) and should be taken strictly at the prescribed dose. If there is any suspicion of barbiturate overdosage (slow shallow breathing, twitching muscles, blueness of the skin, coma), call an ambulance immediately.

BARIUM ENEMA/BARIUM MEAL
A procedure where a patient swallows or is given an enema of a barium sulphate solution so that the interior of the intestinal tract can be X-rayed. Since X-rays cannot go through barium, the cavities of the organs containing it show up clearly. Such disorders as ulcers, tumours, hiatus HERNIA, DIVERTICULOSIS and COLITIS may be revealed. (See Medical Tests And Examinations – BARIUM SULPHATE X-RAY STUDIES.)

BATTERED BABY SYNDROME
A situation where a child is repeatedly brought for medical attention because of injuries claimed to be accidental but in fact inflicted by the parent(s). It occurs in families where there is considerable emotional stress and instability, often aggravated by marital discord, poverty and drinking. In the last decade this condition has gained greater recognition and as a result more help is available than in the past, via medical treatment, and emergency 'help-line' services, psychological counselling and social services assistance for the parents and children. (See Medical And Health Support Organisations – CHILD ABUSE.)

BEDSORE
A condition in which ulceration develops on areas of

skin where there is continual pressure. Bedsores occur in bedridden people who are unable to move. Under prolonged pressure there is inadequate blood circulation to the skin and underlying soft tissue, which begin to break down to form ulcers which may become infected. Bedsores are much easier to prevent than cure. Any bedridden person who cannot move should be helped to change position and the pressure areas massaged at least every two hours.

BED-WETTING
At about the age of 5, 10 per cent of children still wet the bed. By the age of 8, most children are dry at night, though occasionally bed-wetting persists into adulthood. Bed-wetting occurs when the nervous control of the bladder is slow to mature. It can also happen with children who are heavy sleepers and who don't wake when their bladders are full. In some cases emotional upheavals such as the arrival of a new baby in the household or a family argument will cause bed-wetting in a child who has previously been dry. Occasionally, congenital abnormalities of the bladder or urinary infections (PYELITIS or CYSTITIS) are the cause.

After any obvious cause has been corrected, most bed-wetters will become dry with patience and encouragement. Scolding and punishment are likely to aggravate the problem. For heavy sleepers, interval training may cure bed-wetting. For several nights the child should be woken every hour and taken to the toilet to empty his bladder. The period between visits to the toilet should then be gradually lengthened by 15 minutes per night until the child remains dry until morning. If these simple measures have no success, consultation with a paediatrician is recommended.

BEE STING
(See First Aid – BITES AND STINGS.)

BELL'S PALSY
The sudden onset of paralysis of the muscles of one side of the face. The cause is unknown, but the paralysis is presumed to be due to swelling of the facial nerve as it emerges through the skull. Bell's palsy is usually painless, but it may cause severe embarrassment, loss of confidence and withdrawal because of uncontrollable dribbling and weeping from the affected side, difficulties in speaking and eating, and loss of control of facial expression. There is no specific treatment, but the use of anti-inflammatory medication will help to prevent further swelling of the nerve (and further paralysis), and physiotherapy will help to keep the paralysed muscles in good condition. Recovery is usually spontaneous, but can take from a few weeks when paralysis is partial, to many months when paralysis is extensive.

BENIGN
A term usually used to describe a growth or TUMOUR that is not dangerous or MALIGNANT. Benign tumours do not invade adjacent tissue or spread to other parts of the body, and are unlikely to grow again after removal.

BERI-BERI
A disorder caused by deficiency of vitamin B_1 (thiamine). Symptoms are loss of appetite, tiredness, irritability, aching muscles and disturbances of heart function. See VITAMINS.

BETA BLOCKERS
Drugs which have been developed during the last twenty years and are now among the most commonly prescribed medications. The action is to counteract some of the effects of the sympathetic division of the AUTONOMIC NERVOUS SYSTEM. Beta blockers may be used to treat HYPERTENSION and some other cardiovascular disorders, including ANGINA and TACHYCARDIA, and may be useful in some cases of tremor, migraine, thyroid disorder, anxiety and other psychiatric disorders.

BILE
A greenish, bitter alkaline fluid which is produced in the liver and stored in the GALL-BLADDER. When fatty foods are eaten, and the fat leaves the stomach and enters the small intestine, a flow of bile from the liver and the gall-bladder is stimulated to help in the digestion and absorption of those fats. (See also How The Body Works, pp. 16–18.)

BILIARY COLIC
See GALLSTONES.

BILIOUS
The term 'bilious' means to do with BILE and describes the taste and sensation of bile being brought up from the stomach into the mouth. 'Bilious attack' describes brief digestive upsets associated with NAUSEA and VOMITING because of the small amounts of bile which are often brought up.

BIOPSY
The removal of a small piece of tissue for examination under the microscope, to help in the diagnosis of disease. Common sites of biopsy are skin, breast, cervix, liver and kidneys. Biopsy is especially important in the early diagnosis of cancer. (See Medical Tests And Examinations.)

BIRTH
(See How The Body Works, pp. 28–30.)

BIRTH CONTROL
See CONTRACEPTION.

BIRTHMARK

A blemish or mark present on the skin at birth, also known as a NAEVUS. The cause of most birthmarks is not known. The commonest birthmarks are those due to clusters of abnormally dilated blood vessels (strawberry mark and PORT WINE STAIN), and those due to patches of excessive pigmentation of the skin (brown to black marks). Some birthmarks fade with time; others can be removed by surgery and skin-grafting. Some can only be camouflaged with cosmetics.

BISEXUALITY

The sexuality of a person who is sexually attracted to both males and females.

BITES

(See First Aid.)

BLACKHEAD

A tiny plug of hardened SEBUM, secreted by the sebaceous glands of the skin, which clogs up a pore

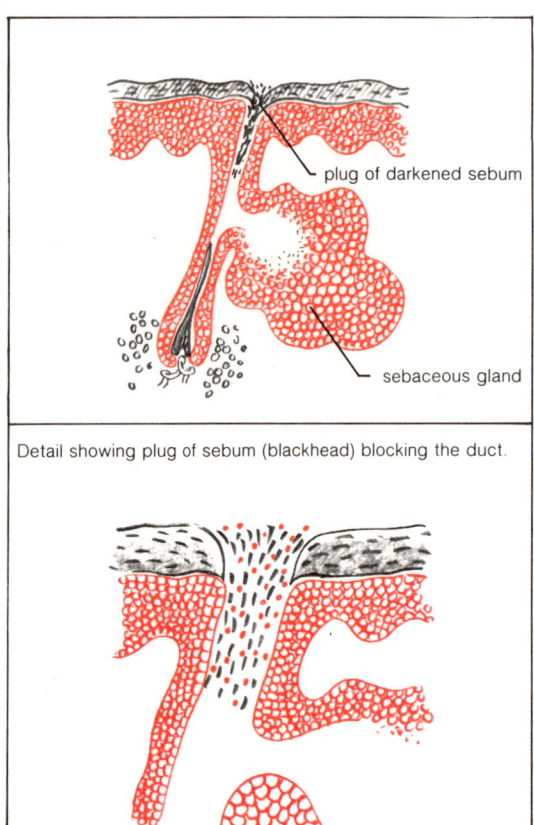

Detail showing plug of sebum (blackhead) blocking the duct.

— plug of darkened sebum

— sebaceous gland

A blackhead forms when a plug of sebum blocks a sebaceous duct.

and goes black with exposure to air. Blackheads should not be harshly and carelessly picked or squeezed as they may become infected. See also ACNE.

BLACKOUT

Another term for FAINTING.

BLADDER

A part of the URINARY TRACT consisting of a hollow muscular organ where URINE is collected. Urine excreted by the KIDNEYS passes through the URETERS to the bladder. As the bladder fills up, there comes the urge to urinate. Common disorders of the bladder are CYSTITIS, urinary INCONTINENCE, urinary RETENTION. (See also How The Body Works, pp. 16–21.)

BLEEDING

(See First Aid.)

BLEPHARITIS

Inflammation of the eyelids, most often caused by bacterial infection, chemical or mechanical irritation, or allergy. Treatment is by counteracting the cause (antibiotic drops or ointment, antihistamines, avoidance of allergens) and relief of acute symptoms by local warmth, bathing, use of dark glasses. Consult your doctor if blepharitis is not relieved after two days. Chronic blepharitis is often associated with DANDRUFF.

BLINDNESS

Partial or total loss of vision. There are many different causes of blindness. Some people are born blind, others lose their vision through injury to or some abnormality of the cornea, lens, retina, optic nerve or brain. See also GLAUCOMA, DETACHED RETINA, TRACHOMA and CATARACT. (See also Medical And Health Support Organisations.)

BLISTER

A collection of fluid under the surface layers of the skin. Blisters are caused by injury to the skin, and by infections and other skin disorders. Small blood vessels in the base of a blister may rupture, making the blister fluid blood-stained (blood blister). Blisters due to skin disorders usually have specific diagnostic features, such as those of CHICKEN-POX, HERPES, SHINGLES, ECZEMA.

BLOOD

The fluid that flows through the arteries and veins to all the organs and tissues of the body. Blood is made up of red and white cells, called corpuscles, and platelets suspended in PLASMA. The blood's many functions are complex and varied: it supplies OXYGEN and nourishment to the cells; transports CARBON

DIOXIDE from the tissues to the lungs; carries nourishment from the intestines to the liver and tissues; takes waste products from the liver to the kidneys; helps in the defence of the body against infection; carries hormones from the glands to the various organs; controls the body's chemistry and distributes body heat evenly. It has the ability to clot, so that bleeding from damaged blood vessels is limited. Disorders of the blood include ANAEMIA, LEUKAEMIA, bleeding disorders, RHESUS disease, HAEMOPHILIA and THROMBOSIS. (See also How The Body Works, pp. 5–9.)

BLOOD CLOT

Also called a THROMBUS. Blood clots form when the fluid blood becomes a solid mass by the process of COAGULATION. The normal purpose of coagulation is to seal a break in the wall of a blood vessel to limit blood loss. See also HAEMOPHILIA, THROMBOSIS, EMBOLISM.

BLOOD COUNT

An examination in which the red and white cells and platelets in a given volume of the blood are counted. (See Medical Tests And Examinations – FULL BLOOD COUNT.)

BLOOD GROUP

There are over thirty blood group systems, the most important being the ABO system. The ABO system contains groups A, B, AB and O. The classification of blood groups is based on whether or not particular ANTIGENS are present on the surface of the red blood cells. Group A has the A antigen, group B the B antigen, Group AB has both the A and B antigens and group O has neither A nor B antigens. ANTIBODIES in the blood plasma correspond to the missing antigens so that group A has B antibody and group B has A antibody. Group AB has no A or B antibodies. A person receiving a blood transfusion must be given blood of his or her own or a compatible group. When incompatible blood types are mixed, the donor's antigens and the recipient's antibodies clash, with resulting destruction of donor red cells. Incompatible transfusion is potentially lethal.

Before giving a transfusion, a doctor always checks the patient's blood group for compatibility. A person with group AB blood can receive a transfusion of any blood group, so group AB is known as the universal recipient. Group O, having neither A nor B antigens, can be given as a transfusion to any other blood group and so is known as the universal donor. People with blood group A can receive A and O; group B can receive B and O; group AB can receive A, B, AB and O; group O can receive only group O. People with group A can give blood to A and AB; group B can give to B and AB; group AB can give only to AB; group O can give to groups A, B, AB and O.

Blood groups are inherited according to a complicated pattern and while they are sometimes used to test paternity suits, it is not possible to tell that a particular man is a child's father but only to tell that the man is *not* a child's father. See also RHESUS (Rh) FACTOR (and How The Body Works, pp. 5–9.)

BLOOD POISONING

Also known as SEPTICAEMIA, this condition occurs when micro-organisms or their toxins enter and persist in the circulating blood, so that the whole body is affected.

BLOOD PRESSURE

A measure of the force exerted on the walls of the larger arteries by the blood flowing through them. Blood pressure is measured by an instrument called a SPHYGMOMANOMETER and expressed in millimetres of mercury. Two measurements are always given when blood pressure is recorded. The higher (systolic) is the pressure in the arteries at the moment the heart contracts; the lower (diastolic) measures the pressure during the relaxation of the heart between beats. The diastolic reading is the more significant indication of whether or not an abnormality of blood pressure exists. The difference between the systolic and diastolic pressures is called the pulse pressure. The main factors which control the blood pressure are the force of the heartbeat, the internal diameter and flexibility of the blood vessels, and the volume of blood in the circulation. The term 'blood pressure' is often used to mean high blood pressure (HYPERTENSION). Low blood pressure is HYPOTENSION. It is recommended that all adults should have regular blood pressure checks so that abnormalities may be recognised early and steps taken for correction. (See also How The Body Works, pp. 5–9.)

BLOOD TEST

(See Medical Tests And Examinations.)

BLOOD TRANSFUSION

See TRANSFUSION.

BLOOD VESSEL

A channel (ARTERY, VEIN or CAPILLARY) through which blood travels around the body. (See How The Body Works, pp. 5–7.)

BLUE BABY

A baby born with an abnormal channel connecting the right and left sides of the heart, which causes some of the dark venous blood to bypass the lungs and be recirculated without being recharged with the oxygen that makes the blood bright red. The baby has a bluish tinge (CYANOSIS) of lips and skin. The condition is corrected by surgery.

BODY ODOUR

All animals have distinctive body odours. These smells are important in giving other animals of our own and different species important information about our identity, emotional state (fear, anger, aggression, etc.), state of sexual arousal and health. Body odours are produced by sweat and other FEROMONES, and are not normally offensive. Sweat is odourless when secreted and normally evaporates quickly. When sweat cannot evaporate because of climatic conditions or because it is trapped where air cannot circulate freely (armpits, groin, feet), an offensive smell can develop because of the action of normal skin bacteria which break down certain chemicals in sweat. Unpleasant perspiration smells can be prevented by washing regularly in hot, humid weather, by avoiding synthetic clothing which prevents the absorption and evaporation of sweat, and by the appropriate use of deodorants.

BOIL

An ABSCESS in the skin caused by bacterial infection of a hair follicle which has spread and destroyed tissue beyond the anatomical boundary of the follicle (as opposed to a pimple, which is confined to the follicle). The central core of the boil, consisting of dead tissue and pus, is usually discharged onto the skin before healing begins. Because tissue destruction has extended beyond the skin boundary, a scar is left after healing. A blind boil is one in which the skin over the core of the abscess doesn't break down to release the pus. Surgical opening is usually necessary to prevent deeper spread of the infection. The pus discharged by a boil may spread to nearby or distant hair follicles resulting in clusters of, or recurrent, boils. For this reason it is best that the pus from a boil should be cultured to identify the bacteria causing the infection (usually staphylococci) and the appropriate antibiotic used to eradicate it.

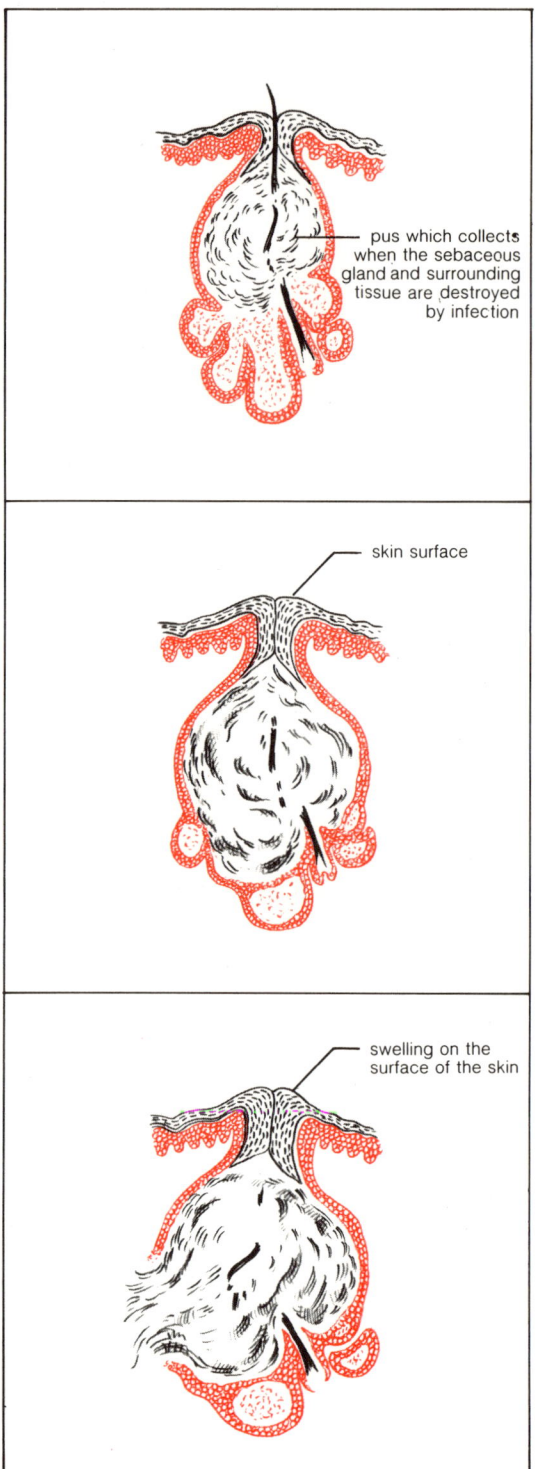

pus which collects when the sebaceous gland and surrounding tissue are destroyed by infection

skin surface

swelling on the surface of the skin

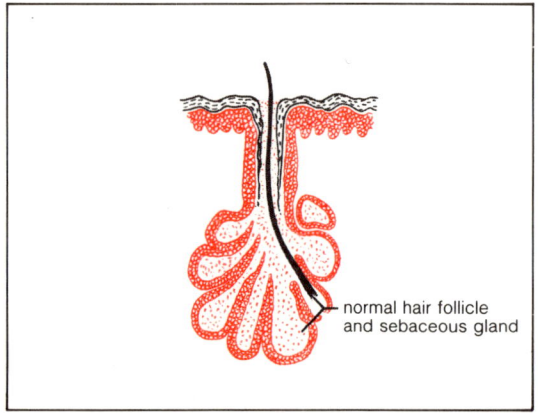

normal hair follicle and sebaceous gland

A boil is a red, painful swelling filled with pus, caused by bacterial infection of a hair follicle and sebaceous gland.

BONE

The hard, dense tissue that makes up the skeleton which is the framework of the body. The bones of the central skeleton form the head and trunk and the bones of the peripheral skeleton form the arms and legs. (See How The Body Works, pp. 2–4.)

BONE MARROW

The soft core of bones. It consists of tissue specialised for the production of blood cells (haemopoesis). Sometimes a sample of bone marrow is taken to help in the diagnosis of a blood disorder. (See Medical Tests And Examinations – BONE MARROW BIOPSY, and How The Body Works, pp. 2–4.)

BOOSTER INJECTION

An injection of vaccine given some time after a previous vaccination to strengthen or renew immunity.

BOTULISM

A rare but very serious form of food poisoning caused by the bacterium *Clostridium botulinum*, which may grow in canned or bottled foods which have been inadequately sterilised. This bacterium, normally present in small numbers in soil, flourishes without oxygen (hence in full, closed containers) to produce a powerful toxin which poisons the nervous system to cause difficulty in swallowing, speaking and breathing, and extreme muscular weakness. Botulism is often fatal. Instruction for adequate sterilisation should be followed strictly for all home preserving, and preserved food should never be eaten from any container which bulges or from which gas under pressure escapes on opening.

BOWEL

Another name for the large INTESTINE.

BRADYCARDIA

Slowing of the heartbeat to a rate of less than 60 per minute. In health, a slow heart rate at rest is often found in fit athletes, where it is an index of the heart's capacity to respond to the need for increased effort during strenuous physical activity. Bradycardia is a health problem only when the heart rate is too slow to maintain the blood pressure and adequate circulation. This happens briefly in FAINTING and permanently in disorders of the cardiac PACEMAKER or of the heart's conducting system.

BRAIN

The large, soft mass of nerve tissue within the skull. It weighs about 1.3 kg and is the centre of the nervous system. It is the seat of consciousness, the subconscious, memory, emotion and reason. (See How The Body Works, pp. 12–15.)

BREAST LUMPS/BREAST CANCER

Because the breast is the most common site of cancer in women (1 in every 15 women in Australia will be affected), it is recommended that women examine their breasts regularly. Early detection is essential for successful treatment of breast cancer. Ask your doctor to show you how to examine your breasts and to give you a pamphlet on breast self-examination. If you get to know the feeling of your normal breast tissue you will recognise any change early and can ask your doctor to check it. In most cases the doctor will suggest further tests (such as X-RAY, ULTRASOUND and BIOPSY), to be certain about whether any lump or change in the breast is benign or malignant. The majority of breast lumps are benign, being CYSTS, ADENOMAS or FIBROADENOMAS.

BREATHLESSNESS

Known medically as dyspnoea, breathlessness can be the normal result of intense physical activity. Otherwise it can be a symptom of ASTHMA, BRONCHITIS, EMPHYSEMA, PNEUMONIA, PLEURISY, ANAEMIA and HEART DISEASE. Anyone who is short of breath at rest or on mild exertion should see a doctor.

BREECH BIRTH

The birth of a baby feet and buttocks first.

BRIGHT'S DISEASE

See NEPHRITIS.

BRONCHIECTASIS

Abnormal dilatation of the bronchi and bronchioles – the passages which carry air into the alveoli of the lungs. This condition may be congenital but most commonly is a complication of chronic infection (such as BRONCHITIS or TUBERCULOSIS) or any condition which restricts air flow into the lungs (such as tumours, inhaled foreign bodies or infectious swellings). Bronchiectasis can rarely be reversed but can be prevented from worsening by vigorous steps to eliminate infection, and by physiotherapy aimed at improving breathing efficacy and draining accumulated secretions.

BRONCHITIS

Inflammation of the larger air passages (bronchi). Acute bronchitis is caused by bacterial or viral infection and is often a complication of upper respiratory infections (COMMON COLD) or generalised viral illness such as INFLUENZA or MEASLES. Symptoms are fever, noisy or wheezy breathing, shortness of breath, cough, phlegm production (often purulent). Acute bronchitis is usually self-limiting in otherwise healthy people, with complete recovery within three weeks. In babies, the elderly and those debilitated by other illness, acute bronchitis should be treated by antibiotics and physiotherapy to prevent the development of BRONCHOPNEUMONIA, chronic bronchitis or BRONCHIECTASIS.

In chronic bronchitis there is irreversible inflammatory damage to the bronchial walls, usually as a result of repeated attacks of acute bronchitis or caused by inhaled irritants such as cigarette smoke and other air pollutants. Symptoms are shortness of breath and the production of large amounts of purulent sputum. Chronic bronchitis sufferers should seek immediate treatment of any superimposed acute infection and should have regular physiotherapy which will help to drain secretions and to improve breathing efficiency. These measures will help to prevent the development of EMPHYSEMA.

BRONCHOPNEUMONIA

Inflammation of the lungs due to spread of bacteria via the smaller air passages (bronchioles). Bronchopneumonia is a common complication of viral UPPER RESPIRATORY INFECTION in infants, debilitated people and the elderly.

BRONCHOSCOPE

An instrument used for the internal examination of the air passages of the lungs. (See Medical Tests And Examinations – BRONCHOSCOPY.)

BRONCHUS

The main branches of the TRACHEA (windpipe) which carry air into the lungs. Inflammation of the bronchi is known as BRONCHITIS. (See How The Body Works, pp. 10–11.)

BRUISE

Purplish-blue discolouration in or beneath the skin due to the seepage of blood into the tissues, usually following a blow or severe pressure, but sometimes due to disorders of the capillary walls or disorders of the blood clotting process. Over about ten days, a bruise will turn green and then yellow before fading completely. Anyone who bruises too often or too easily should see a doctor for a blood check. See also HAEMATOMA.

BUERGER'S DISEASE

A deterioration of the circulation of blood in the extremities, mainly the legs and feet, because of progressive inflammatory narrowing and eventually obliteration of the small blood vessels. This disease affects men over 40 who are heavy smokers. Otherwise there is no known cause. Symptoms, which are intermittent and aggravated by exercise (see CLAUDICATION), are pain, numbness, coldness and discolouration. When the blood supply is totally inadequate, GANGRENE may occur, requiring amputation. Treatment consists of stopping smoking,

scrupulous care of the feet, anti-inflammatory drugs and a carefully graded physiotherapy programme to encourage the development of new blood channels.

BULIMIA

Excessive eating due to a disorder of the normal feelings of hunger and satiation. Bulimia is usually a complication of the emotional disturbances associated with depression, anxiety and other psychoneuroses. Bouts of bulimia often occur in people with ANOREXIA NERVOSA, who alternate between starving themselves and going on eating binges, the latter often followed by forced vomiting. Death from rupture of the stomach can occur in extreme bulimia. Treatment is that of the underlying disorder, usually by PSYCHOTHERAPY. (See also Medical And Health Support Organisations – ANOREXIA NERVOSA & BULIMIA.)

BUNION

A deformity of the head of the first metatarsal bone where it joins the big toe. The condition is usually caused by chronic pressure on the area from ill-fitting shoes. Initially, a painful BURSITIS develops which leads to an overgrowth of the underlying bone and distortion of the joint. Often there is CALLUS formation in the overlying skin, which adds to the pain and makes shoe fitting even more difficult. Treatment is surgical removal of the bony overgrowth followed by chiropody to prevent recurrence.

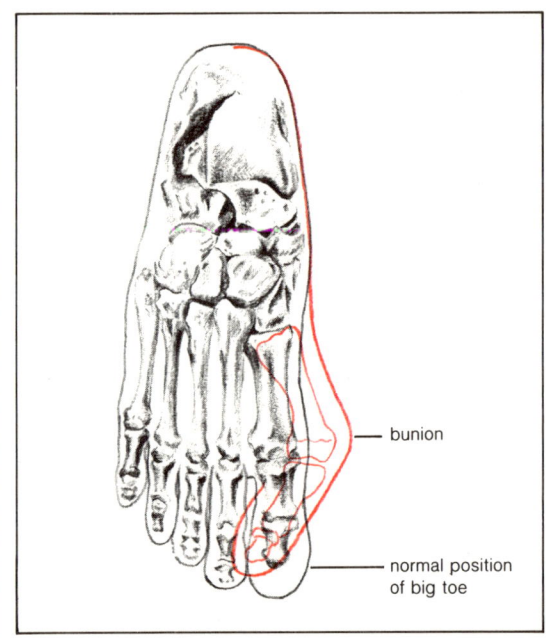

— bunion

— normal position of big toe

A bunion is a painful deformity of the base of the big toe caused by chronic pressure on the joint.

BURNS
(See First Aid.)

BURSITIS
Inflammation of a bursa – the fluid-filled cavities which surround tendons where they pass over bony prominences, usually close to joints. Bursitis may develop at the site of chronic or recurrent pressure (for example, housemaid's knee, student's elbow, coachman's bottom, bunion), but often occurs for no obvious reason (for example, around the shoulder joint). Bursitis is rarely caused by infection unless there has been a penetrating injury. Symptoms are pain, swelling and tenderness over the bursa and restriction of movement of the joint. Treatment is by rest, anti-inflammatory medication and, in some cases, injection of corticosteroids into the bursa. During recovery, a graded exercise programme helps to speed up the return of full movement.

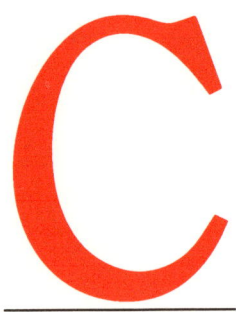

CAESAREAN SECTION

A surgical procedure for delivering a baby when a normal delivery through the birth canal would be dangerous or impossible. An incision is made through the lower abdominal wall and then through the lower part of the uterus. The baby is taken from the uterus through the incisions, which are then carefully repaired with SUTURES. The operation is carried out with general or epidural (spinal) anaesthesia. The main reasons for caesarian delivery are:

• The birth canal being too narrow for normal delivery.
• The progress of labour being unsatisfactory.
• Conditions of the mother or baby which would make normal delivery dangerous.

The name of the operation is believed to be derived from the method by which Julius Caesar was said to be born, though some authorities state that it comes from the Latin word meaning 'to cut'.

CALCIFICATION

The hardening of tissue due to the deposit of calcium and calcium salts. Calcification is a normal process in the development and growth of bones. Abnormal calcification, also called calcinosis, may occur in any organ or tissue following injury or inflammation, and in certain tumours. Common examples of calcification are ARTERIOSCLEROSIS and ANKYLOSIS of joints.

CALCIUM

An essential element. Calcium is necessary for the formation of healthy bones and teeth, and dissolved calcium salts in the blood are essential for normal function of the heart and all other muscles. We need 0.5–1.5 grams of calcium per day in the diet. Children, pregnant and lactating women and elderly people need the larger amounts. The richest dietary sources of calcium are milk and milk products, small fish (where you eat the bones), and some greens.

Too little calcium results in dental decay, bone diseases such as RICKETS and OSTEOPOROSIS, and disorders of heart and other muscles.

CALCULUS

A hard mass or stone, formed in the body from mineral salts. The most common and troublesome are KIDNEY STONES and GALLSTONES.

CALLUS

A hard and thick patch of skin, usually caused by pressure or friction. A common example is a CORN.

CALORIE

A unit of heat, often used as a measurement of the energy value of foods. It has now been replaced by the KILOJOULE.

CANCER

A MALIGNANT tumour which develops when the process of cell division gets out of control. The aberrant cells multiply in an uncoordinated way to form a tumour. A malignant tumour may invade and destroy adjacent organs and tissues, and malignant cells may spread to other parts of the body via the bloodstream or the lymph vessels to form secondary cancers, in a process called METASTASIS. Malignancy affecting the skin or mucous membranes is known as CARCINOMA. Other malignancies include SARCOMA – found in the connective tissue such as bones and muscle – and LEUKAEMIA, which affects the blood-forming (haemopoetic) tissues. See also BREAST CANCER, LUNG CANCER, STOMACH CANCER, CERVICAL CANCER. Although there is no certain cure for cancer, if it is found early enough it may be successfully treated with surgery, radiation therapy or drugs. (See Medical And Health Support Organisations.)

CANNABIS

A drug which when swallowed or smoked causes a

feeling of contentment and euphoria and which, in heavy doses, may produce hallucinations. Also known as pot, hemp, grass, hash and MARIJUANA. Its sale and use are illegal in Australia. See also ADDICTION, NARCOTIC (and Medical And Health Support Organisations – ALCOHOL & DRUG DEPENDENCE).

CAPILLARY

The most minute blood vessels in the body which form a network in tissues to allow the exchange of OXYGEN, CARBON DIOXIDE and other chemicals between the blood and cells. They are the connecting links between ARTERIES and VEINS. (See also How The Body Works, pp. 10–11.)

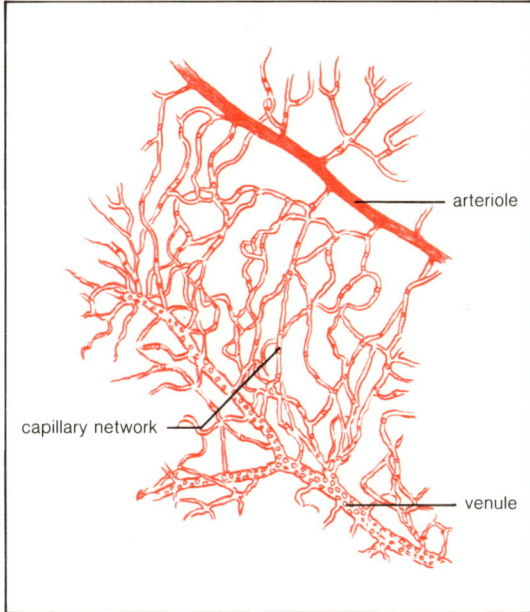

The capillaries are minute blood vessels connecting the smallest arteries with the smallest veins.

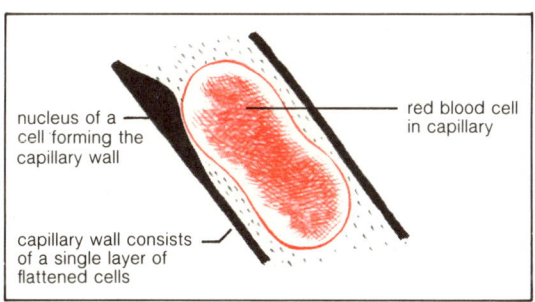

nucleus of a cell forming the capillary wall

red blood cell in capillary

capillary wall consists of a single layer of flattened cells

CARBOHYDRATE

A compound of carbon, hydrogen and oxygen. Carbohydrates are one of the three main constituents of food, the others being FAT and PROTEIN.

One of the main sources of KILOJOULES, they can either be used immediately to provide energy or converted to fat for storage. Foods rich in carbohydrates include grains, root vegetables, pulses, fruits and sugar.

CARBON DIOXIDE

A gas formed in the tissues and carried in the blood to the lungs where it is released and breathed out. (See How The Body Works, pp. 10–11.)

CARBUNCLE

A painful abscess under the skin formed from a cluster of adjacent boils. Carbuncles are usually the result of infection by *Staphylococcus aureus*, and are most often found on the chest, neck and face, buttocks and armpits. Treatment is by oral or injected antibiotics, surgical drainage of pus and analgesics.

CARCINOGEN

A substance that may cause the development of cancer.

CARCINOMA

A malignant TUMOUR in the skin, mucous membranes and glands. See also CANCER.

CARDIAC ARREST

Stopping of the heartbeat and the main cause of death from cardiac INFARCTION. When the heart muscle stops beating completely it is called asystole, and when it quivers rapidly but does not pump blood it is called VENTRICULAR FIBRILLATION. A heart that stops in asystole may be started again with external heart massage (see First Aid – RESUSCITATION). Stoppage through ventricular fibrillation can only be properly treated with an electric current being passed through the heart. See also DEFIBRILLATOR.

CARDIAC DISEASE

Disease of the heart. See ANGINA PECTORIS, CORONARY HEART DISEASE, MYOCARDIAL INFARCTION, HEART DISEASE.

CARDIOVASCULAR SYSTEM

The circulation of blood through heart, arteries, capillaries and veins.

CARIES

The medical term for the decay of teeth and bones.

CAROTID ARTERY

One of the two main arteries which rise up on either side of the neck to supply blood to the head. (See How The Body Works, pp. 5–9.)

CARTILAGE

Dense connective tissue which forms part of the skeleton. Cartilage is found in the nose, LARYNX, ears, between the vertebrae and over the moving surface of joints. (See How The Body Works, pp. 2–3.)

CASTRATION

The surgical removal of the GONADS (TESTES or OVARIES) because of disease or in some cases to combat certain cancers which are dependent on reproductive hormones, such as cancer of the prostate or breast.

CAT SCAN

Computerised axial tomography (CAT) is a diagnostic procedure whereby an image of the organs and tissues of the body can be made from any plane. (See Medical Tests And Examinations.)

CATARACT

Opacity of the lens of the eye which causes blurred vision. Cataracts most often develop in elderly people. If not treated, eventually all sight in the eye will be lost. Cataracts can be removed in a relatively simple operation.

CATARRH

Inflammation of the MUCOUS MEMBRANES, usually of the nose and throat, resulting in over-production of mucus. See COMMON COLD, HAY FEVER, RHINITUS, SINUSITIS.

CATATONIC

A term used to describe abnormal behaviour characterised by long motionless periods, repetitive complicated movements and sounds, phases of stupor and excitement, unresponsiveness and unawareness of people and surroundings. A person suffering catatonia needs psychiatric help.

CAUTERISE

To destroy diseased or damaged tissue with the application of heat or cold, acid, electric current or laser.

CELLULITIS

An infectious inflammation of the cellular and connective tissue of the skin causing a painful, red, shiny diffuse swelling. Treatment is by the appropriate antibiotic.

CEREBELLUM

Second largest part of the brain located under the CEREBRUM. (See How The Body Works, pp. 12–15.)

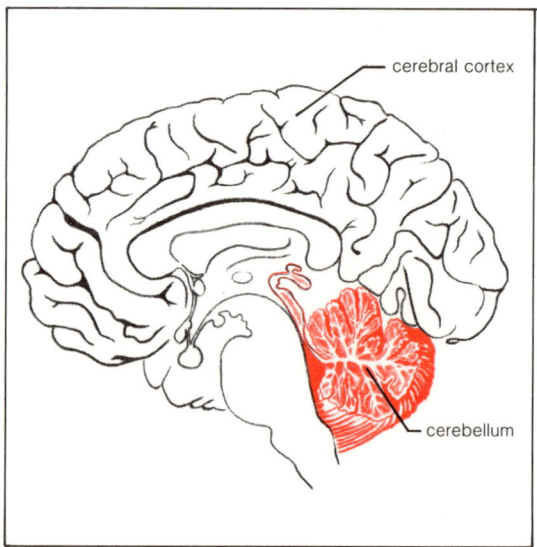

cerebral cortex

cerebellum

The cerebellum is made up of grey and white matter. Nervous impulses relating to muscle tone, balance and coordination of movement originate in this part of the brain.

CEREBRAL HAEMORRHAGE

Rupture of a blood vessel in the brain, usually an artery weakened by congenital ANEURYSM or ARTERIOSCLEROSIS. Temporary or permanent damage to the nearby brain may follow as a result of the pressure of the leaked blood, causing partial or complete paralysis of certain parts of the body. See APOPLEXY, STROKE.

CEREBRAL PALSY

Non-progressive SPASTIC paralysis due to damage to the brain, which occurs before, during or soon after birth. The cause may be obscure or may be traced to lack of oxygen during birth, injury during birth, RHESUS incompatibility or such diseases as MENINGITIS and ENCEPHALITIS in early infancy. A treatment programme aimed at improving the disability includes physiotherapy, speech training and specialised care. (See Medical And Health Support Organisations.)

CEREBRAL TUMOUR

A MALIGNANT or BENIGN mass in the brain. Surgical treatment or radiotherapy is usually necessary.

CEREBRUM

The main part of the brain, divided into two hemispheres which are in turn divided into four lobes. All thinking takes place in the cerebrum with different regions of the lobes dictating particular kinds of mental activity. (See How The Body Works, pp. 12–15.)

CERVICAL BARRIERS

Contraceptive devices worn in the vagina to cover the vaginal end of the cervical canal. Their action is twofold: sperm cannot enter the cervical canal, and cervical mucus is prevented from entering the vagina and mixing with semen to promote sperm movement and survival. The most commonly used cervical barriers are the DIAPHRAGM (Dutch cap) and the vault cap (Dumas). Most cervical barriers are used with a spermicide.

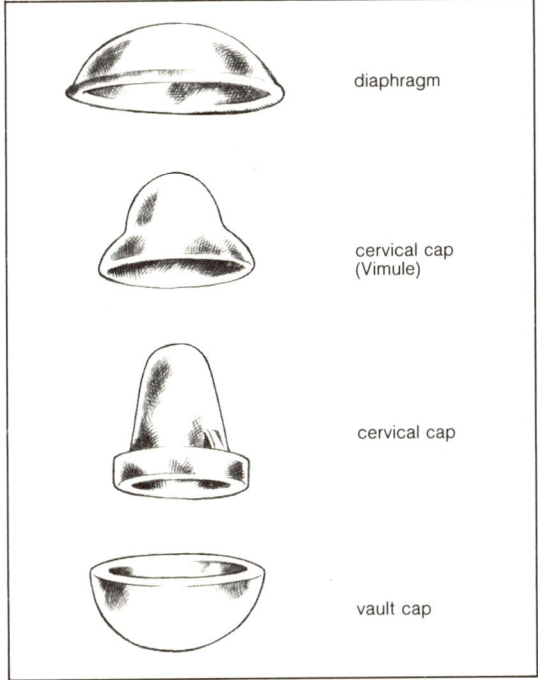

diaphragm

cervical cap (Vimule)

cervical cap

vault cap

Four kinds of intravaginal barriers.

CERVICAL CANCER

Cancer of the CERVIX, or neck of the uterus. See also SMEAR TEST.

CERVICAL CYTOLOGY

See SMEAR TEST.

CERVICAL EROSION

A term used to describe the appearance to the naked eye of the uterine cervix when the lining of the cervical canal extends on to the vaginal part of the cervix. The membrane lining the canal appears red and irregular compared with the smooth pink covering of the vaginal cervix, and before the advent of the COLPOSCOPE, was thought to indicate ulceration. It is now known that this condition is normal at certain stages of life (birth, puberty and pregnancy), so the term has been discarded in favour of the more accurate cervical eversion.

CERVICAL SMEAR

See SMEAR TEST.

CERVICITIS

Inflammation, usually due to infection, of the uterine cervix. See GONORRHOEA, CHLAMYDIA.

CERVIX

The neck of the uterus, which projects into the VAGINA. (See How The Body Works, pp. 25–27.)

CHANCRE

A painless ulcer that is the first sign of SYPHILIS. Chancres appear within four weeks after the disease has been contracted and are usually on the genitals, buttocks, lips, tongue and eyelids.

CHANGE OF LIFE

See MENOPAUSE.

CHEILOSIS

Thickening and cracking in the corners of the mouth due to a lack of vitamin B. See VITAMINS.

CHEMOTHERAPY

The use of drugs to treat or control disease. The term is usually understood to mean the treatment of infectious diseases and cancer with chemicals that destroy the disease-causing micro-organisms and cancer cells without harming surrounding, normal tissue.

CHEST PAIN

Pain in the chest may be caused by injury to or disease of the bones and soft tissues of the chest wall. It may also be a sign of respiratory disorders such as PLEURISY, or digestive disorders such as hiatus HERNIA. It is a major symptom of HEART DISEASE. All chest pain should be checked by a doctor to exclude serious disease.

CHICKEN-POX

Chicken-pox is a highly contagious disease caused by the *Herpes zoster* virus. It is most common in childhood. Incubation period is about two weeks. The illness is usually ushered in by mild fever, loss of appetite, headache and lethargy, followed shortly by the appearance of a skin eruption characterised by crops of raised red spots capped by blisters. When the blisters break extremely itchy scabs form, which take up to two weeks to fall off. Chicken-pox is self-limiting, and complications are rare. The aggravating itch can be relieved with a simple remedy like calamine lotion. The patient is infectious from the beginning of symptoms until all scabs have disappeared. After chicken-pox, most people are immune to the disease, though in some the virus may remain latent to cause SHINGLES later in life.

CHILBLAIN

A local inflamed swelling on the fingers, toes, ears and nose caused by skin damage following exposure to cold. When a chilblain becomes warm, it starts to itch and burn. Treatment is by relieving the itch and keeping the part warm so that healing may take place.

CHIROPRACTIC

Manipulation of the bones of the spine to correct displaced vertebrae. The question of whether disorders of internal organs can be corrected by manipulation of the vertebrae is controversial.

CHLAMYDIA

A group of micro-organisms which cause a variety of diseases in humans and animals. Chlamydia has recently been identified as the most common cause of non-specific URETHRITIS (NSU) in men and PID (PELVIC INFLAMMATORY DISEASE) in women.

CHLOASMA

Pigment marks which some women develop on the face and/or neck during pregnancy or while taking the contraceptive pill. The hormone oestrogen causes an over-reaction of the pigment-forming cells of the skin in response to sunlight. Chloasma may be prevented by wearing ultraviolet filter preparations on the face.

CHOKING

Obstruction of the LARYNX or TRACHEA (windpipe) so that air cannot enter the lungs, causing suffocation. (See First Aid.)

CHOLECYSTECTOMY

Removal of the GALL-BLADDER.

CHOLECYSTITIS

Inflammation of the GALL-BLADDER caused by either a bacterial infection or by GALLSTONES.

CHOLECYSTOGRAPHY

X-ray examination of the GALL-BLADDER. The patient swallows a mixture of iodine compounds which enter the gall-bladder making it radiopaque so that it shows up on an X-ray. If GALLSTONES exist, they too will show up.

CHOLELITHIASIS

The formation of GALLSTONES in the GALL-BLADDER.

CHOLERA

A disease caused by the micro-organism *Vibrio cholera* and transmitted by water or food that has been contaminated by the FAECES of infected people. The main symptoms are severe vomiting and violent DIARRHOEA followed by extreme DEHYDRATION. Cholera can be fatal if treatment to replace body fluids and administer antibiotics is not given quickly. The disease is rare in western countries because of high standards of hygiene and sanitation. Anyone travelling to a country where cholera exists should be vaccinated against the disease.

CHOLESTEROL

A substance similar to fat, found in the blood, brain and all other body tissues. It is produced chiefly by the liver and adrenal glands and is one of the key factors in the body's chemistry. In ATHEROSCLEROSIS, the ATHEROMA that thickens the walls of the arteries contains large amounts of cholesterol. Whether dietary intake of cholesterol-rich foods encourages the development of atherosclerosis is controversial, but it has been found that the disease is more common in people with a raised blood level of cholesterol.

CHOREA

An involuntary twitching and writhing of the muscles caused by diseases affecting the nervous system. Senile chorea sometimes affects the elderly while Sydenham's chorea, or ST VITUS'S DANCE, is a disorder associated with rheumatic fever in childhood. The most serious form of the condition is HUNTINGTON'S CHOREA which is hereditary, appears between the ages 30 to 50 and damages the brain causing dementia as well as chorea.

CHORIOCARCINOMA

Cancer of the placenta.

CHORION

One of the membranes which surround the developing foetus. At the site of attachment to the uterine wall, the chorion undergoes special development to form the placenta.

CHROMOSOMES

Structures present in the nucleus of every cell. Chromosomes consist of strings of special proteins, the GENES, which determine the HEREDITARY characteristics of each individual, such as colour of hair and eyes, height, build and all other features that we inherit from our parents. There are forty-six chromosomes in every cell, arranged into twenty-three pairs. One chromosome in each pair comes from the mother and the other from the father.

CHRONIC

A term that means to last for a long time without rapid change. Chronic is the opposite of ACUTE. To describe a disease or disorder as chronic doesn't necessarily mean that the disease is severe but rather that it is slowly persistent.

CIRCADIAN RHYTHM

Meaning 'about a day', circadian rhythm refers to the body's internal 24-hour clock, which controls the rhythm of appetite, alertness and sleep. This rhythm is set by daylight and darkness, and may be disturbed by such irregular events as a long plane trip over many time zones or night-shift work.

CIRCULATION

See CARDIOVASCULAR SYSTEM. (See also How The Body Works, pp. 5–9.)

CIRCUMCISION

Removal of the FORESKIN, the fold of skin covering the glans penis. Although once carried out on Australian baby boys as a matter of routine, circumcision in most cases is not regarded as warranted these days. A religious practice of great antiquity, circumcision remains a religious obligation and ritual among Australian Aboriginals, Jews and Moslems.

CIRRHOSIS

A chronic disease of the LIVER resulting in the destruction of liver cells and their replacement by a network of fibrous scar tissue. Cirrhosis may be the result of ALCOHOLISM, HEPATITIS, certain poisons, poor nutrition, heart failure. It is a serious condition which cannot be reversed, but if the process of liver destruction is halted in time, the remaining undamaged liver tissue may regenerate so that liver function remains adequate.

CLAUDICATION

Severe intermittent cramp-like pain in the legs caused by an insufficient supply of blood to the calf and leg muscles, usually as a result of narrowing of arteries by ATHEROSCLEROSIS. The pain is usually brought on by walking. Claudication may be treated by the use of vasodilator drugs and an exercise programme designed to encourage the development of alternate blood channels to the legs. If these measures fail, arterial grafting may be necessary.

CLAUSTROPHOBIA

An obsessive fear of enclosed places which may be so extreme that it prevents a person from having a normal life. It may be a sign of neurosis or PSYCHOSIS and a person with such irrational, overpowering fears should talk with a doctor.

CLAVICLE

The bone which connects the breastbone to the shoulder-blade. Fracture of the clavicle, or collar bone, is fairly common but it usually mends well within a month.

CLEFT PALATE

A split or cleft in the roof of the mouth, due to failure of the two halves of the palate to join during foetal development. It is often associated with HARELIP. Both can be successfully corrected by surgery.

CLITORIS

A small, pea-sized organ found where the inner lips of the female genitals meet in front. The clitoris contains many nerves which, when stimulated, produce sexual arousal. (See also How The Body Works, pp. 25–27.)

CLOT

The thickening of a liquid, for example blood, to form a soft, jelly-like mass. See COAGULATION.

CLUBFOOT

Also known as talipes, this is a congenital deformity of the joints of one or both feet which prevents standing with the sole flat on the ground. The foot may be twisted either inwards, outwards, up or down at the ankle. All new-born babies are examined to see whether any such deformity exists. If treatment by manipulation or splinting is started when a baby is just a day or two old, the deformity can usually be completely corrected. If, however, the condition persists, treatment involves further manipulation, a plaster cast to support and hold the foot in the correct position, exercises to strengthen muscles and tendons and, perhaps, specially fitted shoes. More severe cases may require orthopaedic surgery.

CLUSTER HEADACHE

A series of severe headaches which occur in clusters over several weeks, and then do not reappear for months or even years. The headache, which often begins during sleep, is typically intense, continuous rather than throbbing, and located behind one eye. It is associated with a weeping eye, running nose, and swelling of the face on the affected side. Cluster headache, unlike migraine, is not associated with nausea and vomiting. The pain, which may be quite debilitating, usually lasts an hour or two and several such headaches may occur in a day. The attack may be triggered by stress, dietary factors or hormonal changes. Treatment is by analgesics plus ergot and often BETA BLOCKERS. Sufferers are often prescribed preventative medication to be taken regularly at bedtime.

COAGULATION

The process of changing from a liquid into a soft, jelly-like mass as in blood clotting or milk curdling.

COARCTATION

Stricture or narrowing. For example, coarctation of the aorta: a localised malformation marked by deformity of the aortic wall, causing narrowing of the vessel.

COCAINE

A narcotic drug obtained from the leaves of the South American coca plant. Although it has been used in the past for its medicinal properties as a local anaesthetic, most doctors are now wary of its harmful side-effects. It is a powerful stimulant which produces short-lived excitement, euphoria and often pleasant hallucinations. Overdose causes delirium, convulsions, respiratory failure and even death. Cocaine is illegally used by drug-dependent persons in spite of the risk of adverse effects. Although it does not cause physical addiction (there are no withdrawal symptoms when the drug is stopped), users become psychologically dependent on its effects. Cocaine is taken in many ways, including chewing or smoking the coca leaves, inhaling the crystalline pure substance distilled from the leaves, or by injection. Crack is a somewhat purer and more concentrated form of regular cocaine. It is dried and broken into tiny chunks known as crack rocks. The little pellets are usually smoked in glass pipes. See also DRUG ABUSE, ADDICTION (and Medical And Health Support Organisations – ALCOHOL & DRUG DEPENDENCE).

COCCYX

The tailbone, attached to the sacrum at the lower end of the SPINE.

COCHLEA

The fluid-filled spiral cavity, in the shape of a coiled shell, lying in the inner ear and containing the organs of hearing.

COELIAC DISEASE

A disorder in which the lining of the small intestine is so adversely affected by glutens, the proteins found in wheat, rye and barley, that food cannot be properly digested. The disease tends to run in families and is usually diagnosed early in life, though in mild cases may not cause great health disturbance until adulthood, when ANAEMIA develops due to failure to absorb essential vitamins and minerals. Symptoms in infants include pot belly, loose, foul smelling stools, failure to thrive and irritability. In adults there may be bouts of diarrhoea, flatulence and abdominal distension, wasting and weakness. Effective treatment is a gluten-free diet. (See Medical And Health Support Organisations.)

COITUS

See SEXUAL INTERCOURSE.

COITUS INTERRUPTUS

Also called 'withdrawal'. A contraceptive method where the penis is withdrawn from the vagina before ejaculation so that no semen can enter the cervix. As a means of contraception this method is generally unreliable (about 20 per cent failure rate), although many couples have successfully used it to space their children.

COLD

See COMMON COLD.

COLD SORE

See HERPES.

COLIC

A severe, cramping pain in the abdomen, caused by spasm of muscles in the wall of hollow organs. Colic may be caused by constipation or distension of the bowel; any disorder that irritates the intestine, such as infection and certain poisonings; and partial or complete obstruction of the bowel. Biliary colic is due to obstruction of the bile ducts, usually by a gallstone. Urinary colic is due to obstruction of the ureter by a gallstone or tumour. See also ABDOMINAL PAIN.

COLITIS

Inflammation of the large intestine, the colon. Mucous colitis, also known as spastic colon, is a disorder often caused, or aggravated, by overuse of laxatives and is easily treated by stopping laxatives and taking a well-balanced, high fibre diet. See also ULCERATIVE COLITIS.

COLLAR BONE

See CLAVICLE.

COLLES' FRACTURE

A fracture of the forearm bones, just above the wrist. It is often caused by a fall on to the outstretched hand.

COLON

The lower part of the digestive tract. The colon and the rectum make up the large intestine, where water is absorbed from food residue, which is then discharged as faeces.

COLOSTOMY

A surgical procedure in which an artificial opening, or stoma, is made in the wall of the abdomen and connected to part of the colon. The contents of the large bowel are expelled into a colostomy bag attached to the stoma, instead of passing out through the rectum. A colostomy may be performed when part of the colon or rectum is removed because of CANCER, and in certain diseases of the large bowel. (See Medical And Health Support Organisations.)

COLOSTRUM

The protein-rich pale yellow fluid produced in the breasts during the latter part of pregnancy and in the first days after the birth of a baby, before the true milk starts flowing. Colostrum contains antibodies which help protect the baby against infection.

COLPOSCOPE

A magnifying instrument used to examine the cervix when pre-cancerous or cancerous conditions are suspected. (See Medical Tests And Examinations.)

COMA

A deep state of unconsciousness from which a person cannot be roused. It indicates serious brain disturbance and can be the result of head injury, disturbance of the blood supply to the brain, poisoning, alcoholism, drug overdose and such diseases as DIABETES, URAEMIA and MENINGITIS. Coma is serious and requires immediate medical attention. (See First Aid – UNCONSCIOUSNESS.)

COMMON COLD (CORYZA)

An acute viral infection of the upper respiratory passages in which the MUCOUS MEMBRANES of the nose, throat and larynx become inflamed. Early symptoms include sneezing, mild fever, blocked or running nose, headache and perhaps sore throat, hoarseness and cough. Symptoms usually appear within two days of infection and may last between a few days and several weeks. The best treatment is rest, aspirin, cough linctus if necessary, and plenty of fluids. Complications such as SINUSITIS, OTITIS media, BRONCHITIS and BRONCHOPNEUMONIA are rare, occurring mainly in infants and debilitated people. The common cold is the most widespread contagious disease, most people getting one or two colds per year. Prevention means keeping away from infected people.

COMMUNICABLE DISEASE

A disease that can be caught by one person from another.

COMPOUND FRACTURE

A FRACTURE where the broken end(s) of bone protrudes through the skin.

COMPUTERISED AXIAL TOMOGRAPHY

See CAT SCAN.

CONCEPTION

The beginning of pregnancy, when a fertilised egg implants in the uterus.

CONCUSSION

Injury to the brain from a severe blow, jolt or fall which may result in temporary disturbance or loss of consciousness. Symptoms include dizziness, headache, temporary loss of memory, difficulty in concentrating, depression, anxiety. Anyone who has been knocked out or suffers the symptoms of concussion should see a doctor. (See First Aid.)

CONDOM

Latex rubber sheath worn over the penis during sexual intercourse to catch the semen and prevent it from entering the vagina or cervical canal. Condoms (sheaths, French letters) also help to prevent the spread of sexually transmitted diseases.

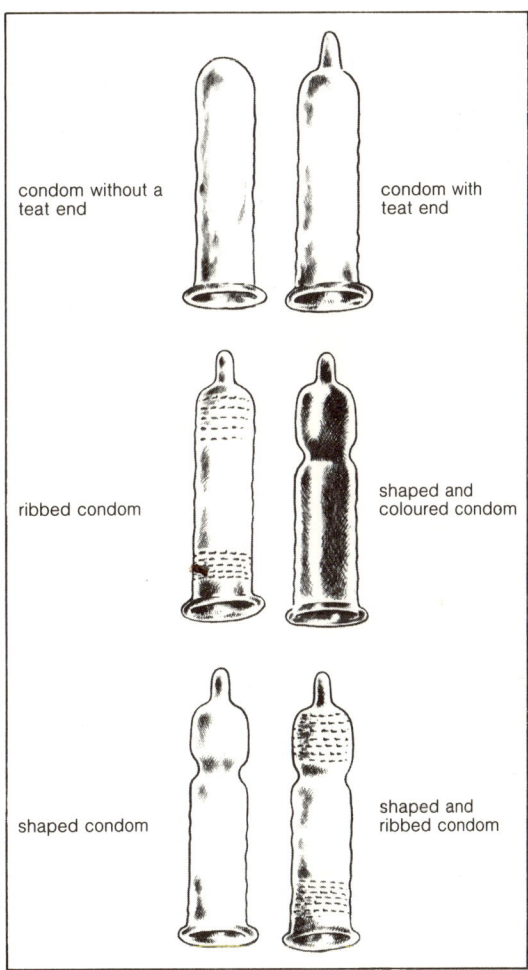

condom without a teat end

condom with teat end

ribbed condom

shaped and coloured condom

shaped condom

shaped and ribbed condom

Types of condoms are illustrated above. Condoms are used to prevent impregnation or infection and, theoretically, condom method failures should only occur if the condom breaks during sexual intercourse because of careless handling, the pressure of ejaculation or friction caused by inadequate lubrication.

CONGENITAL

Any condition existing at birth. A congenital defect may be due to a chromosomal abnormality, as in DOWN'S SYNDROME, or it may be the result of adverse influences on pre-natal development, as in RUBELLA.

CONGENITAL DISLOCATION OF THE HIP

A condition discovered at birth or shortly after, caused by instability of the hip joint. In previous days this condition may not have been detected until the infant began to stand, by which time there would be inevitable deformity. Now all new-born are examined to exclude congenital dislocation of the hip. If it is found, early treatment ensures prevention of deformity and disability.

CONGESTIVE HEART FAILURE

See HEART FAILURE.

CONJUNCTIVA

The membrane which lines the eyelids and the anterior part of the eyeball.

CONJUNCTIVITUS

Inflammation of the conjunctiva caused by infection, allergy or chemical irritation. Conjunctivitis due to bacterial infection is usually very contagious, especially among children. Early treatment with antibiotic drops will prevent spread. Allergic conjunctivitis responds to local or oral antihistamines.

CONSTIPATION

Difficulty in emptying the bowel, usually because the faeces have passed too slowly through the colon and have become hard and rather dry. Frequency of bowel movement is sometimes rather over-emphasised. One bowel movement every day is the average but one every several days or even once a week can be quite normal. As long as the stools are fairly soft and passed without discomfort, there is nothing to worry about. Plenty of fluids and a healthy, high fibre diet will ensure regular, easy bowel movements and help to overcome chronic constipation. It is not a good idea to rely on laxatives. A person of previously regular bowel habit who becomes constipated for no obvious reason should see a doctor.

CONTAGIOUS

A term used to describe a disease that is passed from person to person. All contagious diseases are infectious (in other words, due to infection by micro-organisms) but not all infectious diseases are contagious. Malaria, for example, is an infectious disease transmitted by mosquitoes, but it is not contagious.

CONTRACEPTION

An intervention to prevent pregnancy. This can be achieved in many ways. The following classification describes various interventions, in order, from sperm formation to implantation of the fertilised ovum.
• Prevent sperm formation. There is no satisfactory way to do this yet.
• Keep sperm out of the semen by cutting, tying or otherwise blocking the spermatic ducts. See VASECTOMY.
• Keep semen out of the vagina by abstinence, ejaculation outside the vagina (see COITUS INTERRUPTUS), or by catching the semen in a CONDOM.
• Keep semen out of the vagina when fertilisation could occur by predicting when ovulation will take place, and abstaining from coitus for seven days before and 36 hours after that event, or by abstaining from the beginning of menstruation until after ovulation. This method is called periodic abstinence. The various methods of predicting ovulation are known as mucus, Billings, basal temperature and symptothermal methods.
• Kill sperm in the vagina by using SPERMICIDES.
• Prevent sperm from passing through the cervical canal by using a CERVICAL BARRIER or by using hormones to change the cervical mucus so that it becomes impenetrable to sperm (the mini-pill).
• Prevent sperm from reaching the egg by cutting, tying or otherwise blocking the fallopian tubes, as in female STERILISATION.
• Prevent ovum formation by using hormones (pill or injection) to prevent egg maturation and release.
• Prevent implantation of a fertilised egg by using an IUD. This can also be done by post-coital administration or hormones (the morning-after pill).
(See Medical And Health Support Organisations – FAMILY PLANNING; PREGNANCY, ABORTION, CONTRACEPTION.)

CONVULSION

Sometimes called a fit or a seizure, a convulsion is a violent involuntary contraction of the muscles. Convulsions may occur for a variety of reasons such as brain injury, insufficient blood to the brain, brain tumours, excessive alcohol, drugs, EPILEPSY, overdose of insulin in DIABETES, brain inflammation from such diseases as MENINGITIS and ENCEPHALITIS. Severe fever in a child will sometimes cause convulsions. Whatever the reason for convulsions, call a doctor. (See First Aid.)

CORN

A type of CALLUS caused by badly-fitting shoes which, by pressing on and rubbing the skin, produce thickened, painful areas. The only prevention is by wearing shoes that fit correctly. If corns are really troublesome, see a doctor or podiatrist.

CORNEAL GRAFT

See KERATOPLASTY.

CORONARY ARTERIES

From the Latin word *corona* meaning 'a crown', these are the blood vessels that supply the heart and surround it like a crown. The right and left coronary arteries branch off the aorta. (See How The Body Works, pp. 5–9.)

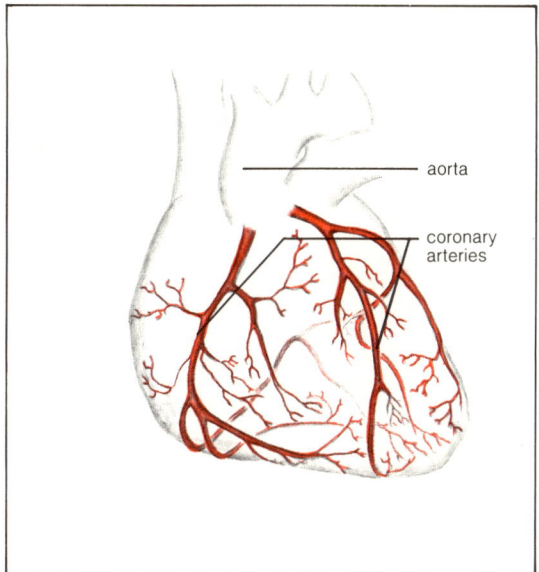

The coronary arteries carry oxygen and nutrients to the heart muscle.

CORONARY ARTERY BY-PASS

Two recent advances in medical technology have greatly improved the outlook for the future health and life expectancy for sufferers of CORONARY HEART DISEASE. The first is the technique of cardiac angiography (see Medical Tests And Examinations), in which the interior of the coronary arteries may be outlined and X-rayed. Thus the diagnosis of coronary disease may be confirmed and the exact site of the arterial narrowing located before the disease has proceeded to complete blockage of the vessel and MYOCARDIAL INFARCTION. Secondly, the development and refinement of the heart–lung machine has made open heart surgery possible. In this technique, the chest is opened and the heart exposed. Venous blood returning to the heart is diverted to the heart–lung machine, which does the work of the lungs by re-oxygenating the blood before it is returned to the aorta and the general circulation. When the hook-up to the heart–lung machine is complete, the patient's heart is stopped while surgical procedures, such as coronary by-pass or replacement of faulty heart valves, are carried out. On completion of the operation, the heart is stimulated to start beating again, the heart–lung machine is disconnected and the normal circulation resumes.

In a by-pass operation, healthy arteries are taken from another part of the body (usually the leg) and grafted onto the diseased coronary artery above and below the site of narrowing, which has been accurately located by angiography. The blood diverted through the graft restores the normal blood supply to the cardiac muscle.

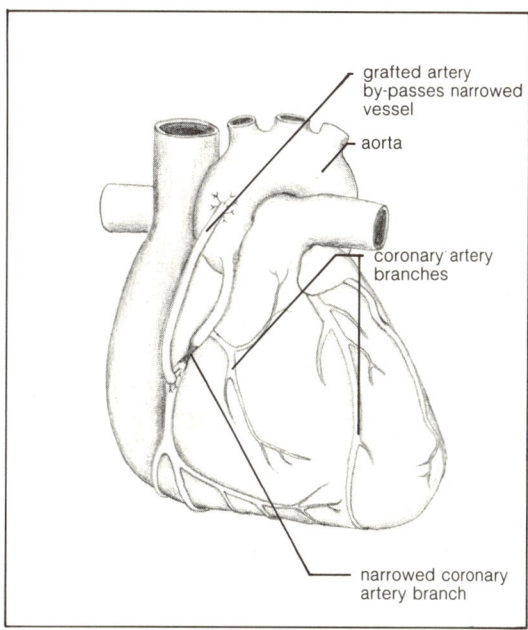

grafted artery by-passes narrowed vessel

aorta

coronary artery branches

narrowed coronary artery branch

CORONARY HEART DISEASE

Blockage or narrowing of the coronary arteries which supply blood to the heart with the result that the heart muscle receives inadequate blood supply to work efficiently. Most often the disease is caused by ATHEROSCLEROSIS (build-up of fatty deposits on the walls of the arteries) although it can be the result of RHEUMATIC FEVER, EMBOLISM, SYPHILIS and congenital heart disease. When the blood supply to the heart is reduced, the condition is known as coronary insufficiency, which causes ANGINA. When the artery is completely blocked, it is known as coronary occlusion, which results in MYOCARDIAL INFARCTION. High levels of cholesterol in the blood, HYPERTENSION, DIABETES, heavy cigarette smoking, stress and OBESITY increase susceptibility to coronary heart disease. Heredity is another factor. Coronary heart disease has been a common cause of premature death among Australian men. The future may be brighter because of improved knowledge about prevention and advanced techniques of CORONARY ARTERY BY-PASS surgery. (See Medical And Health Support Organisations – HEART DISEASE.)

CORONARY THROMBOSIS

A blood clot forming in the arteries supplying blood to the heart. See CORONARY HEART DISEASE and THROMBOSIS.

CORPUSCLE

One of the cells in the blood. Cells make up 45 per cent of the blood and include red cells, which carry oxygen to the tissues and waste carbon dioxide to the lungs, and white cells which destroy invading bacteria and help to resolve inflammation. (See How The Body Works, p. 21.)

CORTISONE AND CORTICOSTEROIDS

Natural steroid hormones produced by the ADRENAL GLANDS. Synthetic cortisone (corticosteroid drugs) is used as an anti-inflammatory and immuno-suppressant agent, and to treat ADDISON'S DISEASE, a condition in which the adrenal glands are under-active. Cortisone may have several adverse side-effects such as water retention, high blood pressure and diabetes, so it is used with caution.

COT DEATH

Also known as sudden infant death syndrome (SIDS), it occurs suddenly and unaccountably during sleep in about 1 in 600 babies under the age of six months. It seems that there are a variety of causes but often no cause can be identified. Cot death is more common in low income families, in babies born prematurely, in low birth weight infants and in babies whose mothers smoked during pregnancy. (See Medical And Health Support Organisations – SUDDEN INFANT DEATH SYNDROME.)

COUGH

A protective reflex response that helps rid the respiratory passages of irritants or mucus. Coughing is a symptom of respiratory disorder so anyone with a persistent cough should see a doctor.

CRAB LICE

Lice which infest the pubic hair. They are usually transmitted by sexual or close physical contact. The crabs are 1 mm in diameter. When they lay their eggs (nits) near the roots of the hairs, there is intense itching. Effective treatment is simple, using lotions on which your doctor or chemist will advise you.

CRACK

See COCAINE.

CRAMP

A painful spasm of muscle, often in the abdomen. See ABDOMINAL PAIN, COLIC. Cramp is also common in the legs and feet. Causes of cramp include poor cir-culation, abnormal salt balance, exhaustion and stress.

CRANIOTOMY

Surgical opening of the skull.

CRETINISM

A condition caused by congenital lack of thyroid hormone, and characterised by severely retarded physical and mental development.

CROHN'S DISEASE

A severe inflammation of parts of the intestine, cause unknown. It is also known as regional ILEITIS. Symptoms include abdominal pain, diarrhoea (often blood-stained), weight loss and often fever and general debility. Treatment is non-specific. Measures to control diarrhoea, improve nutrition and build up the general health are important. Sometimes corticosteroid drugs are used, and occasionally surgical removal of the affected segment of bowel is necessary.

CROSS EYES

A disorder in which one or both eyes turn in towards the nose. Most very young babies tend to have crossed eyes, but if the condition persists after six months consult a doctor so that corrective measures can be planned. See also STRABISMUS.

CROUP

An acute respiratory condition, common in young children, in which the breathing is noisy, difficult and painful, with a hoarse, raspy voice and a barking cough. It is the result of either a viral or bacterial infection of the larynx and trachea. Croup often strikes during the night in a child who has gone to bed with a slight cold. See a doctor if symptoms persist in the morning. In the meantime, croup can be relieved with steam and menthol inhalations.

CRYOSURGERY

Removal of tissue by freezing.

CRYPTORCHIDISM

The medical term for undescended TESTES.

CURETTAGE

Scraping a body cavity or surface with an instrument called a curette to remove abnormal tissue or growths. See BIOPSY, D AND C.

CURVATURE OF THE SPINE

See SPINAL CURVATURE.

CUSHING'S SYNDROME

A condition in which the ADRENAL GLANDS overproduce corticosteroid hormones as a result of overactivity or tumour in the adrenal or pituitary glands. Symptoms include fat deposits around the face, neck and trunk, tiredness, muscular weakness, high blood pressure, diabetes, salt and water retention, acne, excess hair growth. Treatment outlook is poor, unless the cause is a benign tumour which can be easily removed.

CYANOSIS

A blue or purple tinge to the skin, lips and mucous membranes indicating a lack of oxygen in the blood. Causes include respiratory failure, heart failure and congenital heart disease. See also BLUE BABY, BREATHLESSNESS.

CYST

A fluid-filled structure. Cysts can form anywhere in the body when the drainage of a hollow structure becomes blocked. Cysts are mostly benign, but may cause concern if they are seen or felt (for example, skin or breast cysts), and if they become large enough to cause pressure, obstruction or displacement of adjacent body parts. Particular cysts are those which may form in the ovaries, and parasitic cysts (when parasites such as amoebas and TAPEWORMS infest certain organs). Some cysts can become maligant and it is wise to have them properly checked by a doctor.

CYSTIC FIBROSIS

A serious although rare hereditary disease which affects 1 in 2000 children. Cystic fibrosis is a result of malfunction of the sweat and mucus-secreting glands. The abnormal mucus secretion adversely affects the lungs and the pancreas. Symptoms are respiratory infection, STEATORRHOEA, weight loss and malnutrition due to faulty digestion from lack of pancreatic enzymes. Treatment includes supplementation of digestive enzymes, antibiotics for respiratory infection, physiotherapy and use of a mist tent or respiration machine to loosen mucus in the air passages. (See Medical And Health Support Organisations.)

CYSTITIS

Inflammation of the bladder. Acute cystitis causes lower abdominal pain, burning, painful urination, occasionally blood-stained urine, and if associated with PYELITIS or PYELONEPHRITIS, fever, chills and backache. Cystitis is usually caused by bacteria which may enter the bladder from the kidneys via the URETERS, from the bloodstream or by way of the URETHRA. It most commonly affects women who are newly sexually active, pregnant or past the menopause. Bladder infections respond promptly to appropriate antibiotics, drinking lots of fluid and taking something to make the urine alkaline. If there are repeated attacks of cystitis, investigation of the bladder and urethra (usually by CYSTOSCOPY) is necessary so that the cause may be discovered and corrected.

CYSTOGRAM

(See Medical Tests And Examinations.)

CYSTOSCOPY

Examination of the bladder by means of a fine magnifying instrument, fitted with lights and mirrors, which is passed through the URETHRA. (See Medical Tests And Examinations.)

D

D AND C

Short for dilatation and CURETTAGE of the uterus. This is the second most commonly performed surgical procedure in Australia. It involves enlarging the canal through the cervix (dilatation) by inserting through it rods of gradually increasing diameter until a curette (a spoon-like instrument with a sharp edge) can be passed through into the uterine cavity. The curette is used to scrape the lining (endometrium) from the uterus to remove abnormal tissue or to take a sample for examination under the microscope. This can often help to diagnose the cause of abnormal uterine bleeding.

DANDRUFF

The common name for seborrhoea of the scalp, describing small flakes and scales of sebum and skin cells which catch in the hair. Dandruff is harmless and almost universal. It can be reduced or eliminated by anti-dandruff lotions which your chemist will recommend.

DEAFNESS

A partial or total loss of hearing. There are many possible causes of deafness which can be divided into two main groups.

Conductive deafness is the result of something interfering with the passage of sound waves to the inner ear. This may be anything which blocks the auditory canal, such as a plug of hard wax (cerumen); a boil or a foreign object blocking the ear canal; and disturbances of the middle ear such as infection (OTITIS media), perforated ear-drum; or conditions which block the Eustachian tube linking the middle ear with the throat, such as TONSILLITIS or ADENOIDS.

Perceptive deafness is the result of malfunction in the nerves supplying the ear or damage to the inner ear. Possible causes include congenital defects such as those which occur in a child whose mother has had RUBELLA during pregnancy, or the effects of MEASLES or MUMPS in childhood; viral infections of the ear; head injuries; MENIÈRE'S DISEASE; or prolonged exposure to loud noise. For unknown reasons, hearing also deteriorates with age. Perceptive deafness is difficult to treat and is nearly always permanent, although a hearing aid may help.

It is important that partial or complete deafness in infants and hearing loss in adults are recognised early and a specialist consulted so that all possible assistance may be given. See also EAR DISORDERS (and Medical And Health Support Organisations).

DECONGESTANT

Something used to reduce congestion and swelling of body tissues. Decongestants work by counteracting inflammation and normalising blood flow. Common examples are drops, sprays and inhalations for reducing congestion in the air passages in colds and HAY FEVER, and drops for reducing redness of the eyes in CONJUNCTIVITIS.

DEEP VENOUS THROMBOSIS (DVT)

The formation of blood clots (thrombi) in the veins, most commonly in the deep veins of the calf. There is a tendency to DVT during immobilisation after major surgery and stroke, and sometimes after childbirth. DVT is potentially dangerous because of the possibility of pieces of the thrombus breaking off and causing pulmonary EMBOLISM.

DEFAECATION

The process of passing solid waste material or FAECES from the body. (See also How The Body Works, p. 18.)

DEFIBRILLATOR

A machine that restores normal heart rhythm through the application of electric current to the chest. It is used in VENTRICULAR FIBRILLATION.

DEHYDRATION

A condition which can occur when there is excessive loss or inadequate intake of fluid, as in excessive perspiration, vomiting, diarrhoea or blood loss. Fluid replacement is the obvious treatment. In severe cases of dehydration, saline solution, blood plasma or whole blood may be given intravenously.

DELIRIUM

An acute mental disturbance characterised by great physical and mental restlessness, often accompanied by HALLUCINATIONS. Causes include high fever, toxins produced by bacteria in certain severe infections, INSULIN shock, withdrawal from drug addiction (as in CANNABIS, AMPHETAMINES and LSD) and withdrawal from alcohol (known as delirium tremens). In any case of delirium, medical treatment should be sought. See also ALCOHOLISM, DRUG ADDICTION.

DELUSION

An erroneous or exaggerated belief that does not change in response to reasoned argument. Delusions occur in PARANOIA, SCHIZOPHRENIA, MEGALOMANIA.

DEMENTIA

Serious impairment or loss of normal thought and reasoning capabilities. Dementia may be temporary, as in DELIRIUM, or gradually progressive and permanent, as occurs in such disorders or diseases as SENILITY, SYPHILIS, ALCOHOLISM, brain tumour and ARTERIOSCLEROSIS in the brain. A person with dementia needs medical help and patient, loving care.

DEPRESSION

A state of feeling sad and dispirited, most likely to occur at those stages of life of emotional upheaval and tumult, such as adolescence, during pregnancy and after birth, at menopause, during personal disappointment or bereavement. Relatively mild depression in response to adverse circumstances is normal and eventually passes. Pathological depression is characterised by overwhelming feelings of black despair with the future looking bleak, even hopeless. A depressed person may be constantly tired, have little appetite, suffer from inertia, INSOMNIA and loss of LIBIDO. Suicidal thoughts and attempts are common. In such cases, the person should see a doctor who may prescribe antidepressant drugs and psychiatric counselling. Loving, reassuring care from family and friends can be a great help.

DERMATITIS

Inflammation of the skin. Dermatitis is classified according to the cause, which may be infectious, allergic, physical or chemical trauma or nervous disorder. Treatment is symptomatic and specific to the cause, if this can be identified. See ECZEMA.

DETACHED RETINA

A condition in which the RETINA (the delicate film of light-sensitive cells which lines the inner surface of the eye) becomes partly or totally separated from its underlying tissue, causing a blank area in the field of vision. Detachment may be the result of an eye injury or it may happen spontaneously, especially in elderly people. If neglected it can result in permanent loss of vision, but if treated promptly most detached retinas can be successfully corrected with surgery.

DIABETES

There are two unrelated diseases carrying this name: diabetes mellitus and diabetes insipidus.

Diabetes mellitus, often known as sugar diabetes, occurs when the body is unable to control the use of sugars as a source of energy because of inadequate production by the pancreas of the hormone INSULIN. When foods containing sugar and starch are digested, they are absorbed into the blood as glucose, causing the PANCREAS to release insulin which enables the glucose to be used and stored in the tissues. Without sufficient insulin, the blood sugar level rises causing such symptoms as thirst, frequent urination, weight and energy loss. Severe diabetes may result in COMA and even death. It is not known why the body fails to make sufficient insulin but diabetes is a common disease in Australia. It is most likely to occur in young people with a family history of diabetes, and in middle to old age in overweight people. Depending on the diabetic person's requirements, the disease can be controlled by injections of insulin or by oral antidiabetic medication. (See also Medical And Health Support Organisations.)

Diabetes insipidus is a rare disease that has nothing in common with diabetes mellitus. It occurs when the PITUITARY GLAND does not produce enough antidiuretic hormone which limits the production of urine. The result is that the sufferer passes copious amounts of urine and has a constant thirst. Diabetes insipidus is controlled with HORMONE REPLACEMENT THERAPY.

DIAGNOSIS

The identification of a patient's disease given his or her particular series of symptoms, medical, occupational and social history, family medical background, the findings of physical examination and sometimes other tests.

DIALYSIS

A procedure in which a particular substance is separated from a solution by passing it over a membrane. It is often used to describe the procedure used in KIDNEY failure, when a patient's blood is pumped through a renal dialysis machine which

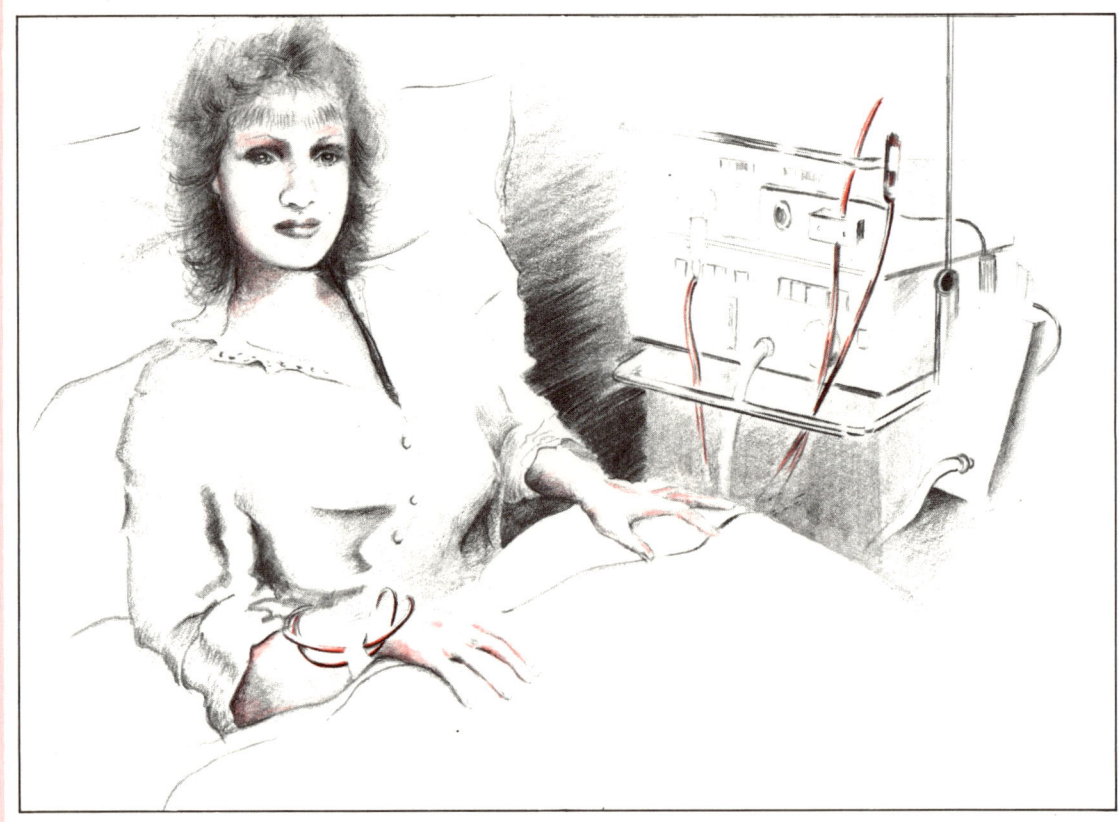

The dialysis machine does the kidneys' job of filtering waste products from the blood in cases of renal failure.

cleanses the blood in imitation of the filtering action performed by the kidneys.

DIAPHRAGM

The strong muscular partition between the thorax, or chest, and the abdomen. It contracts and relaxes rhythmically, playing an important role in breathing.

Diaphragm is also the name of a contraceptive device which fits over a woman's cervix to prevent sperm entering the womb. See CONTRACEPTION, CERVICAL BARRIERS.

DIARRHOEA

The frequent and excessive passage of watery STOOLS from the bowel. The main problem caused by diarrhoea is DEHYDRATION due to loss of water and salts. It has many different causes including inflammation of the intestines, (ENTERITIS), sensitivity to certain foods, FOOD POISONING, digestive disorders and disorders of the nervous control of the bowel, as occurs in unusual stress and excitement. In the case of severe or persistent diarrhoea, especially in children, see a doctor.

DIASTOLE

The period of rhythmic relaxation and dilation of the heart between contractions, when the chambers of the heart (atria and ventricles) are filling with blood. (See also How The Body Works, pp. 5–9.)

DIGESTIVE SYSTEM

The food tract from mouth to anus in which food is broken down into nutrients to be absorbed into the bloodstream, and food residue is processed and stored ready to be passed out of the body. (See also How The Body Works, pp. 16–18.)

DILATATION AND CURETTAGE

See D AND C.

DIPHTHERIA

An acute, contagious disease of the upper respiratory tract and throat caused by diphtheria bacteria. This infection causes acute pharyngitis and laryngitis resulting in high fever, sore throat and hoarseness. A membranous EXUDATE forms which may obstruct the larynx, causing choking. The bacteria produce a dangerous toxin which affects the heart muscles and nerves, so that swallowing is difficult, vision disturbed and pulse weak. If untreated, diphtheria can be fatal. Once a cause of serious epidemics, it occurs less commonly these days because most children are immunised at an early age. See IMMUNISATION.

DIPLOPIA
Double vision, usually as a result of weakness or paralysis of the external eye muscles.

DISC
A pad of cartilage and fibre, known as an intervertebral disc, which separates the vertebrae of the spinal column. Through deterioration with age or injury, a disc may rupture or move out of place as a SLIPPED DISC. (See also How The Body Works, pp. 2–3.)

DISCHARGE
An abnormal seepage of fluid from a body opening or surface, usually indicating disorder of underlying organs or tissues. A small amount of discharge from the vagina is normal. Any discharge which is unusual, excessive, irritating or bad smelling should be investigated by a doctor.

DISLOCATION
The displacement, usually caused by injury, of one or more bones from the normal anatomy of a joint. Shallow, very flexible joints, such as the shoulder, tend to be more easily dislocated than others. Careful, expert manipulation followed by a period of immobilisation is the usual treatment.

DISSEMINATED SCLEROSIS
See MULTIPLE SCLEROSIS.

DIURETIC
A substance that increases the production of urine by the kidneys. Diuretics are often prescribed in cases of heart failure and in kidney disease when fluid is retained in the body and accumulates in the tissues causing OEDEMA.

DIVERTICULOSIS AND DIVERTICULITIS
Diverticulosis is a common condition in the large intestines of older people. Small pouches in the mucous membrane lining protrude through gaps in the muscular outer wall of the bowel. Diverticulitis occurs when the pouches become inflamed and infected causing abdominal pain, either DIARRHOEA or CONSTIPATION, fever and blood in the FAECES. If a pouch ruptures, PERITONITIS is the result.

Successful treatment of diverticulosis includes a high fibre diet and high fluid intake. Diverticulitis needs rest, antibiotics and occasionally surgery.

DIZZINESS
A sensation of giddiness and whirling, which may be caused by a middle or inner ear disorder, or indicate

sudden reduction of blood supply to the brain. See also VERTIGO, MENIÈRE'S DISEASE.

DNA
An abbreviation for deoxyribonucleic acid, DNA is found in the nucleus of every cell and is the basis of heredity.

DOUBLE VISION
See DIPLOPIA.

DOWN'S SYNDROME
A congenital condition, sometimes called mongolism, named after the British doctor John Down. It is caused by a chromosomal abnormality. Down's syndrome is characterised by slanted eyes, short broad face, protruding tongue, short fingers, weak muscles and some degree of mental retardation. There is no cure for Down's syndrome but very often those affected have happy, gentle natures and with patient, loving care can be taught simple, rewarding tasks. (See Medical And Health Support Organisations.)

Down's syndrome is a congenital condition caused by a chromosomal abnormality, which ranges from mild (illustrated) to severe physical and intellectual retardation.

DRIP

See INTRAVENOUS DRIP.

DROPSY

A common name for OEDEMA or swelling due to excessive fluid in the tissues.

DROWNING

(See First Aid.)

DRUG ABUSE

Drug abuse is the habitual use of drugs other than for therapeutic purposes. See ADDICTION. (See also Medical And Health Support Organisations – ALCOHOL & DRUG DEPENDENCE.)

DRUG ADDICTION

See ADDICTION, DRUG ABUSE.

DT (DELIRIUM TREMENS)

See DELIRIUM.

DUODENAL ULCER

A peptic ulcer of the duodenum (the first and shortest part of the small intestine), caused by the action of the gastric acid on the duodenal lining. Anxiety and stress, which increase the production of gastric acid, are thought to be possible contributing causes. The main symptom is a gnawing, burning, upper abdominal pain. Milk and antacids help to relieve the pain and specific drugs may be used to reduce the secretion of gastric acid.

DUPUYTREN'S CONTRACTURE

Thickening of the tissues of the palm of the hand, leading to shortening of the tendons to the fingers. This causes the fingers to curl inwards, and if advanced may result in deformity and disability. Treatment is by surgical reconstruction.

DWARFISM

Abnormally stunted stature due to a variety of causes including poor nutrition, thyroid deficiency (CRETINISM), Vitamin D deficiency (RICKETS) which disturbs bone growth, and deficiency of production of growth hormone by the PITUITARY GLAND. The body may be either well proportioned (as in pituitary dwarfs) or deformed, and mental development may or may not be normal, depending on the cause and type of dwarfism. The most common type is achondroplastic dwarfism, an inherited disorder of the growth of long bones, in which the head and body are normal size and the arms and legs foreshortened.

DYSENTERY

An infection of the intestinal tract, marked by severe DIARRHOEA in which there may be blood and mucus, caused by either a bacterial infection (bacillary dysentery) or a parasitic infection (amoebic dysentery). Both can be successfully treated with special drugs.

DYSLEXIA

A learning disorder involving reading and writing and in some cases, numbers. Dyslexia does not often indicate low intelligence and special education programmes have had considerable success. (See Medical And Health Support Organisations.)

DYSMENORRHOEA

Painful MENSTRUATION. There are two types:

Primary dysmenorrhoea. Pain due to cramps or spasm of an otherwise normal uterus. The spasm is caused by substances (PROSTAGLANDINS) released when the mucous membrane that lines the uterus breaks down at the end of the menstrual cycle. (See How The Body Works, pp. 25–26.) Primary dysmenorrhoea most often affects young women who have not had children, and rarely persists after the first pregnancy. It is not known why dysmenorrhoea affects some women and not others. Pain begins with the onset of bleeding and rarely lasts more than a day or so. It may be accompanied by nausea and vomiting, diarrhoea and, in severe cases, fainting. Mild cramps may be relieved by rest and simple ANALGESICS such as aspirin or paracetamol. More severe dysmenorrhoea, such as that which causes absences from school or work, usually responds well to anti-spasmodic or anti-prostaglandin medication, and is usually eliminated by taking the contraceptive pill (one of the good side-effects of the pill). Any woman who suffers from severe dysmenorrhoea should have a thorough gynaecological check to make sure that there is no cause for the pain other than uterine spasm.

Secondary dysmenorrhoea. Painful menstruation in a woman who has previously had painless periods. Pain tends to be constant and severe, and often begins before and lasts throughout bleeding. Common causes include PID (PELVIC INFLAMMATORY DISEASE), FIBROIDS of the uterus and ENDOMETRIOSIS. Secondary dysmenorrhoea should always be investigated so that the cause can be treated.

DYSPAREUNIA

Painful intercourse in women. Deep pain is caused by inflammation or other disorder, such as ENDOMETRIOSIS, of the pelvic organs. Entry pain occurs in VULVITIS and VAGINITIS, and when there is inadequate lubrication due to loss of LIBIDO or diminished sexual response.

DYSPEPSIA

Also known as indigestion. Symptoms include upper

abdominal distension, a burning sensation in the chest, belching, nausea and vomiting. It can be caused by anxiety and stress, eating too quickly, rich foods and alcoholic excess, but it may also be a sign of GASTRIC or DUODENAL ULCERS.

DYSPHAGIA
Difficulty in swallowing, caused by obstruction of the throat or oesophagus, anxiety, and disorders of the nervous control of the swallowing reflex.

DYSPLASIA
Pre-cancerous change in cells.

DYSPNOEA
See BREATHLESSNESS.

DYSTROPHY
Usually meaning a wasting or disordered growth of tissue.

DYSURIA
Pain and difficulty in urinating, often a symptom of CYSTITIS, URETHRITIS, VENEREAL DISEASE, PROSTATITIS.

EARACHE

The commonest cause of earache is infection, either of the outer ear (OTITIS externa) or the middle ear (otitis media). The middle ear is closely connected with the nose and throat (see How The Body Works, p. 10) and an inflammation in any of these parts easily spreads to the middle ear. Thus, earache may be a complication of the COMMON COLD, TONSILLITIS, INFLUENZA or the infectious fevers of childhood. Children often can't convey that they have pain in the ear. If a young child is crying, unwell, feverish, pulling at the ear or has a red ear, suspect earache. Occasionally pain in or near the ears may be a symptom of neuralgia, tooth abscess or other facial conditions. All cases of earache should be seen by a doctor, who has the proper equipment to examine the ears to see what the problem is, and to provide the correct treatment.

EAR DISORDERS

EARACHE, DEAFNESS and DIZZINESS, discharge and ringing noises (TINNITUS) are all symptomatic of disorders of the ear. All ear symptoms should be checked by a doctor.

ECG

See ELECTROCARDIOGRAM.

ECLAMPSIA

A rare but serious complication of pregnancy. It is an advanced stage of pregnancy-induced hypertension (PIH – previously called TOXAEMIA). If PIH is not detected and treated early it may progress to eclampsia, with severe HYPERTENSION, protein in the urine (this is why blood pressure is measured and a urine specimen is tested at each ante-natal visit), OEDEMA, and if uncontrolled, kidney and liver damage, CONVULSIONS and COMA. Death of the baby and mother can result. The cause is unknown. The early recognition of PIH and the prevention of eclampsia are the most important reasons for having regular ante-natal checks.

ECTOPIC PREGNANCY

Meaning, literally, 'out of place', an ectopic pregnancy occurs when the embryo implants elsewhere than in the uterus, usually in the FALLOPIAN TUBE. Rarely, implantation may be on the ovary or in the abdominal cavity. Although there are a few bizarre reports of ectopic pregnancy being maintained long enough for a live baby to be delivered by abdominal surgery, the outcome is usually rupture of the pregnancy sac within the first three months. This results in severe bleeding into the abdomen, usually a life-threatening situation. Any pregnant woman with abdominal or shoulder-tip pain, vaginal bleeding, weakness or dizziness should urgently seek medical help. Surgical removal of the pregnancy and replacement of blood will save the mother's life. The cause of ectopic pregnancy is often obscure: there may be a history of pelvic infection (PERITONITIS or SALPINGITIS), but sometimes there is no explanation.

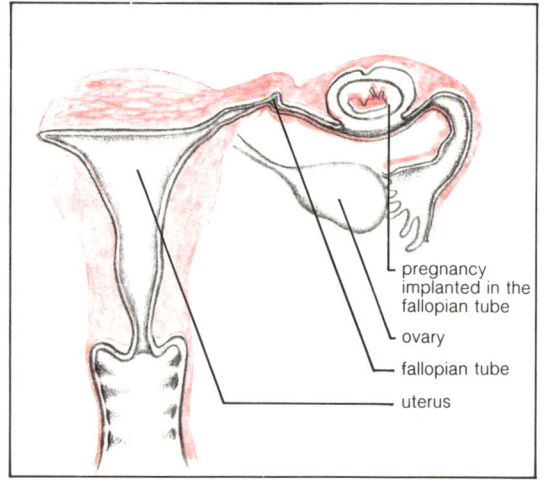

pregnancy implanted in the fallopian tube

ovary

fallopian tube

uterus

Ectopic pregnancy occurs when a fertilised egg implants in the fallopian tube instead of the uterus.

ECZEMA

An inflammation of the skin marked by red, itchy patches, often with blistering, crusting and scaling. It may be caused by ALLERGY, sensitivity to certain drugs or conditions of inadequate blood supply to the skin (varicose eczema). When eczema affects infants, an allergic tendency is suspected. Treatment includes identifying and removing the cause, if possible, applications to relieve itch and the use of corticosteroid creams to reduce inflammation.

EEG

See ELECTROENCEPHALOGRAM.

EGO

A term used to describe the conscious mind, that part of the personality that deals with the outside world.

EJACULATION

The forceful discharge of SEMEN, the sperm-bearing fluid, from the penis. See SEXUAL INTERCOURSE.

ELECTRA COMPLEX

A Freudian concept describing an excessive, repressed sexual love of a daughter for her father.

ELECTROCARDIOGRAM (ECG)

A tracing or graph of the electric impulses of the heart. Electrodes running from an instrument called an electrocardiograph are placed over the heart and on the arms and legs to detect the electrical activity produced by the beating heart. An ECG will reveal any abnormality of the heart. It is a short, painless procedure. (See Medical Tests And Examinations.)

ELECTROCUTION

(See First Aid – ELECTRIC SHOCK.)

ELECTROENCEPHALOGRAM (EEG)

A tracing or graph of the electrical activity of the brain. Electrodes from a machine called an electroencephalograph are taped to the scalp to record the electrical waves generated by the brain's nerve cells. In this way abnormal electrical activity is detected and may indicate epilepsy, brain tumour or other disorders of the central nervous system. An electroencephalogram is also used to establish brain death. (See Medical Tests And Examinations.)

ELECTROLYSIS

A method of permanently removing unwanted hair. A small electric needle is inserted into a hair follicle and an electric current is passed through the needle to destroy the root of the hair. Electrolysis should be performed by a trained practitioner.

ELEPHANTIASIS

Mostly found in the tropics, elephantiasis is caused by parasitic worms which inflame and obstruct the lymphatic ducts, eventually causing obstruction of lymph flow, with swelling of the tissues and overgrowth of the skin. The lower limbs and external genitals, in particular, may become hugely enlarged.

EMBOLISM

Blockage of a blood vessel caused by a blood clot, a ball of fungus, a clump of bacteria, a fat globule, a bubble of air or some such obstruction. The blockage prevents blood circulation to the parts beyond, resulting in an infarct (a region of dead tissue caused by blocking of blood circulation). See also STROKE, PULMONARY EMBOLISM, INFARCTION, GANGRENE.

EMBRYO

The product of conception from implantation until the eighth week of pregnancy. During these first weeks all major body systems start to form. After the eighth week the developing baby is known as a FOETUS. (See also How The Body Works, pp. 28–30.)

EMPHYSEMA

A chronic condition in which the air sacs of the lungs (alveoli) become over-distended and the oxygen–carbon dioxide exchange in the lungs inefficient. Symptoms may include wheezing, shortness of breath and a cough which brings up sputum. The condition may be found in elderly people (as the lung tissue loses elasticity with ageing), people who suffer from asthma or bronchitis, heavy smokers and people who live or work in areas with heavy pollution. There is no specific treatment for emphysema, though respiratory function may be improved by breathing exercises, measures to help get rid of sputum and removal of aggravating factors such as smoking.

EMPYEMA

A condition in which pus accumulates in a body cavity, such as the chest (pleural) or abdominal (peritoneal) cavities. It usually follows an infection of organs or tissues within the cavity. Treatment is by antibiotics and drainage of pus.

ENCEPHALINS

Like ENDORPHINS, these natural chemicals, manufactured in the brain, relieve pain in much the same manner as opiates such as MORPHINE.

ENCEPHALITIS

Inflammation of the brain, usually the result of viral infection. Depending on what part of the brain is most affected, symptoms may include fever, headache, coma, paralysis, convulsions, memory loss, uncoordinated movement and behaviour disturbances. Sometimes encephalitis is a complication of such illnesses as measles, mumps, influenza and glandular fever (infectious MONONUCLEOSIS).

ENDEMIC

A term used to describe disease or infection that frequently occurs in a particular geographical area or among a particular group of people. For example, MALARIA is endemic in some tropical regions of the world.

ENDOCARDITIS

Inflammation of the membrane lining of the inner cavities of the heart. See also HEART DISEASE.

ENDOCRINE GLAND

A ductless gland that secretes its hormones into the bloodstream, so that they may act on distant organs and tissues. Examples are THYROID, PITUITARY, ADRENAL GLANDS, and the OVARIES and TESTES. (See also How The Body Works, pp. 22–24.)

ENDOMETRIOSIS

A condition in which cells from the lining of the uterus (endometrium) grow outside the uterus, usually in and around the fallopian tubes, on the ovaries or on the lining of the pelvic cavity. This ectopic endometrium undergoes the same cyclic changes as if it were within the uterus: dying and bleeding at the end of each menstrual cycle. The bleeding causes inflammation and results in blood-filled cysts surrounded by scar tissue and adhesions. Symptoms are pelvic pain reaching a peak just before and during menstruation, pain on intercourse and pain with bowel movements. Scar tissue and adhesions may reduce fertility. The cause is usually obscure. Treatment is by the use of hormones which suppress the growth of the endometrium and by surgery to remove ectopic tissue.

ENDOMETRITIS

Inflammation of the endometrium.

ENDORPHINS

A group of neurotransmitters – natural chemicals manufactured in the brain that transmit impulses from one nerve to another. Together with ENCEPHALINS, endorphins are believed to influence feelings of well-being and response to pain.

ENEMA

Introduction of a liquid through the anus to clear the rectum and colon of FAECES. An enema is usually given before an operation on the bowel.

ENTERITIS

Inflammation of the small intestine, caused by either a viral or bacterial infection, food poisoning or such other disorders as CROHN'S DISEASE, COLITIS. The main symptoms are DIARRHOEA and ABDOMINAL PAIN.

ENURESIS

See BED-WETTING.

ENZYME

A substance that acts as a catalyst to help speed up biological processes. Thousands of different enzymes are present in the body. One of the most important groups plays an important role in digestion. (See How The Body Works, pp. 16–18.)

EPIDEMIC

The outbreak of an infectious disease in a community, with many people becoming infected over a short time. Sensible precautions are the best means of reducing the likelihood of an epidemic – through individual VACCINATION against infectious diseases where possible, and public health measures to promote high standards of hygiene.

EPIDERMIS

The outer layer of the SKIN.

EPIGLOTTIS

The leaf-shaped flap of cartilage at the back of the tongue. It acts as a valve, so that during swallowing the opening to the air passages is closed and food is prevented from getting into the windpipe, or TRACHEA. (See also How The Body Works, pp. 10–11.)

EPILEPSY

A condition in which there is a disturbance of the normal electrical activity of the brain. Epilepsy affects about 1 in 200 people, and in about half those cases the malfunction is the result of a head injury, a birth injury or an infection. Sometimes a stroke or a tumour is responsible. In the other cases, the cause is unknown. Epilepsy is characterised by seizures. In grand mal seizures there is a fit of abnormal jerky movements followed by unconsciousness. The seizure usually lasts a couple of minutes. Petit mal seizures are less severe and are most often seen in children. During petit mal, the person seems to go into another, private world with only a little twitching or blinking, the state lasting only a few seconds. Epilepsy is diagnosed by the symptoms as well as ELECTROENCEPHALOGRAMS, X-rays and other tests. It may be successfully controlled with anticonvulsant drugs. (See Medical And Health Support Organisations.)

EPISIOTOMY

An incision made in the perineum (the area between the vagina and the anus) during childbirth to ease delivery of the baby's head, and to prevent damage to the pelvic floor by overstretching and ragged tearing. After delivery is complete, the cut is repaired with sutures.

EPISTAXIS

Nose bleeding, usually caused by the rupture of a small blood vessel, either following a blow to the nose or as a result of inflammation or excessive picking. Sometimes nosebleeds in children are spontaneous and are of little significance. In mature adults, a nosebleed could be an indication of a serious health disorder. If the blood loss is severe, or occurs too often, see a doctor. (See First Aid – NOSEBLEEDS.)

ERECTION

The rigid state of the PENIS during sexual excitement. During mental or physical erotic stimulation, blood fills the erectile tissue causing the penis to grow longer and firm, and capable of entering the vagina in SEXUAL INTERCOURSE.

ERYSIPELAS

A dark red, patchy and painful inflammation of the skin, accompanied by feverish illness. It is caused by a streptococcal infection. The skin feels as hot as it looks and there may be red lines running from the affected area to the nearest lymph glands. Erysipelas is extremely contagious but is rare nowadays because of successful early treatment of skin infections with antibiotics.

ERYTHEMA

Abnormal redness of the skin caused by an excess of blood in the surface vessels. It may indicate infection or inflammation.

ERYTHROCYTES

The red blood cells. They are formed in the bone marrow and spend about 120 days in the bloodstream before being broken down in the liver and spleen. Erythrocytes are red because they contain the iron-based protein HAEMOGLOBIN which carries oxygen from the lungs to the cells of the body. They also help take carbon dioxide from the tissues to the lungs where it is breathed out. See ANAEMIA. (See also How The Body Works, p. 5.)

EUPHORIA

A sensation of comfort, security and sweet well-being. The word is often used to describe a state induced by means other than the body's natural health and happiness. Euphoria may be the result of alcohol or drugs such as AMPHETAMINES and NARCOTICS.

EUSTACHIAN TUBES

The tubes linking the middle ear to the PHARYNX at the back of the throat. The tubes act as a regulating device to equalise air pressure in the middle ear with atmospheric pressure. Inflammation of these tubes, as often happens with a head cold or other UPPER RESPIRATORY INFECTIONS, can result in swelling of the lining and blockage leading to earache and OTITIS media (an infective inflammation of the middle ear). (See also How The Body Works, pp. 10–11.)

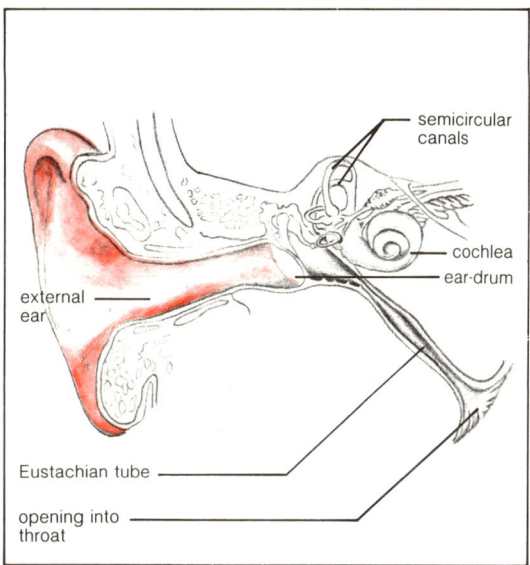

semicircular canals

cochlea
ear-drum

external ear

Eustachian tube

opening into throat

The Eustachian tube connects the middle ear to the back of the throat and equalises air pressure on the ear-drum.

EUTHANASIA

The act of causing or allowing someone to die painlessly. Advocates of euthanasia maintain that very old people or terminally ill people suffering great pain should have the right to determine when and how they should die. It is a controversial subject with organised religion and many members of the medical profession opposed to the idea.

EXCRETION

The elimination of waste material, such as URINE, FAECES, SWEAT and CARBON DIOXIDE from the body. It is also used to describe the waste material itself. (See also How The Body Works, p. 18.)

EXFOLIATION

The peeling off or shedding of dead tissue. Exfoliation of the skin may occur as a result of frostbite or sunburn, after certain infectious diseases such as MEASLES or after the application of certain chemicals.

EXHAUSTION
See FATIGUE.

EXHIBITIONISM
Most often used to describe a person who enjoys showing off, but as a medical definition it refers to a person, usually a man, who takes sexual pleasure in exposing his genitals.

EXOPHTHALMOS
Abnormally protruding eyes. The condition may be caused by swelling behind the eyeball due to a tumour, an infection or injury, or by the increase in connective tissue behind the eye which occurs in THYROTOXICOSIS.

EXPECTORANT
A substance, usually in a syrup form, which encourages and helps in the coughing up of phlegm.

EXTRAUTERINE PREGNANCY
See ECTOPIC PREGNANCY.

EXUDATE
A fluid rich in WHITE BLOOD CELLS that seeps into injured tissue from small blood vessels at the site of inflammation. It is part of the body's normal defence system. (See also How The Body Works, pp. 31–32.)

EYE DISORDERS
Symptoms of eye disorders are disturbances of vision, headache, discharge, red and painful eyes. See BLEPHARITIS, BLINDNESS. CATARACT, CONJUNCTIVITIS, DETACHED RETINA, DIPLOPIA, EXOPHTHALMOS, GLAUCOMA, STRABISMUS, STYE, TRACHOMA.

FAECES

The waste material discharged by the bowels after the digestion of food. As well as food residue the faeces, or STOOLS, also contain bile, mucus and large quantities of bacteria that have helped in the process of digestion. The two most common associated problems are CONSTIPATION and DIARRHOEA. Blood in the stools is an indication of some abnormal condition and should be reported to your doctor. (See also How The Body Works, pp. 16–18.)

FAINTING

Suddenly becoming unconscious, usually only for a short time, due to a brief, temporary reduction of blood supply to the brain, usually as a consequence of a sudden fall in blood pressure. A fainting spell may occur for any number of reasons: emotional shock, fear, pain, lack of food, lack of air or may be associated with such conditions as cardiovascular disease, anaemia, haemorrhage. The person about to faint feels weak and nauseated and breaks out in a sweat before vision blurs and recedes. (See also First Aid.)

FALLOPIAN TUBES

The tubes which connect the OVARIES to the womb or UTERUS. It is through the fallopian tubes, also known as oviducts, that the egg cell, or ovum released from the ovary, travels to the uterus. FERTILISATION takes place when a SPERM cell is united with the ovum in the tube. See also ECTOPIC PREGNANCY.

FAMILY PLANNING

See CONTRACEPTION. (See also Medical And Health Support Organisations.)

FAT

An essential element in the diet, supplying energy in concentrated form. Fats occur in all meats, whole milk, milk products like butter and cheese, nuts and fruits. Excessive intake of animal fats may lead to such disorders as ATHEROSCLEROSIS.

FATIGUE

A feeling of extreme tiredness. Fatigue is most commonly the result of strenuous exercise or activity and the cure is simple: rest and relaxation. However, unexplained fatigue may be a warning sign of oncoming illness such as viral infection; it may be associated with emotional stress, heavy menstruation, pregnancy or with such serious disorders as ANAEMIA, DIABETES, heart disease, kidney disease or cancer. A person who persistently feels tired for no apparent reason should see a doctor.

FEMINISATION

A condition in which men develop female sexual characteristics. Facial and body hair diminishes and the breasts develop. It may be the result of liver disease or ENDOCRINE and CHROMOSOMAL abnormalities. In the case of sex change, it is a desired result of hormone therapy.

FEMUR

The thigh-bone, which is the largest and strongest bone in the body.

FEROMONES

Substances produced by the body of one animal to affect another animal of the same or different species, usually by smell. See BODY ODOUR.

FERTILISATION

The union of SPERM and egg cell, or OVUM, to form a new individual. Fertilisation usually takes place in one of the fallopian tubes. The fertilised egg then moves through the tube into the uterus, where it implants and the embryo starts to develop.

FERTILITY

The ability to reproduce. A woman is fertile from the time she begins menstruation (MENARCHE) to the time menstruation ceases (MENOPAUSE). The most fertile time in the reproductive cycle is during

OVULATION which usually occurs fourteen days before menstruation. A healthy young woman has about a 25 per cent chance of conceiving during any menstrual cycle. Fertility may be reduced just after menarche and close to the menopause, but don't rely on it if you don't want to conceive. In most cases men retain their fertility as long as they are sexually potent. See also CONTRACEPTION, INFERTILITY.

FEVER

An abnormal rise in body temperature most often caused by a viral or bacterial infection. It is often associated with other symptoms such as dry skin, chills, a feeling of weakness and light-headedness, aching muscles and joints, loss of appetite and increased pulse rate. Fever with a sore throat may indicate INFLUENZA, TONSILLITIS, PHARYNGITIS, MUMPS or GLANDULAR FEVER. Aspirin taken several times a day, and plenty of fluids, will help reduce a mild fever. In the case of a high or persisting fever, a doctor should be consulted. In the meantime, sponging with cool water will help to lower body temperature.

FIBRILLATION

Rapidly repeated, weak contractions or tremors of a muscle, the term usually referring to the heart. Fibrillation is a sign of a heart disorder or disease. For example, VENTRICULAR FIBRILLATION may occur during a heart attack when the damaged ventricle cannot properly contract to pump blood into the circulation. The onset of ventricular fibrillation is often associated with loss of consciousness. This is a serious condition which needs immediate medical attention. Treatment is by use of a DEFIBRILLATION machine and drugs which regulate the heart's rhythm.

FIBROADENOMA

A benign tumour composed of a mixture of fibrous and gland tissues. Fibroadenomas are common in the breast, where they form firm, moveable, round or oval lumps. Like all breast lumps, their benign nature should be confirmed by biopsy.

FIBROIDS

BENIGN tumours of the connective and muscle tissue of the uterus. Often they remain quite small and cause no symptoms, being discovered on routine examination. Sometimes a fibroid grows to such an extent that it causes pain, heavy menstrual bleeding and disturbances due to pressure on or displacement of surrounding organs. In such cases it may need to be removed surgically. It is rare for these TUMOURS to become MALIGNANT.

FIBROSITIS

A term commonly used to describe pain caused by inflammation in muscular and connective tissues, especially those around the spine and large joints. The affected and surrounding muscles go into spasm, which is the main source of pain and limitation of movement. See also BACKACHE, LUMBAGO, RHEUMATISM.

FIBULA

One of the two long leg bones between knee and ankle.

FIRST AID

(See p. 193.)

FISSURE

A narrow break in the surface of the skin, a membrane or an organ. The most common fissures are usually found in the corner of the mouth, often as a result of a vitamin deficiency, and in the anus, the result of constipation. Fissures should be promptly treated by attention to the cause and with appropriate measures to prevent infection and relieve pain.

FISTULA

An abnormal tunnel-like passage connecting two internal organs, or an organ and the surface of the body. A fistula may be CONGENITAL (present at birth) or it may be the result of injury or infection, or may develop following abdominal surgery. Fistulas most often occur around the anus and rectum, between the loops of the bowel or between the bowel and the skin. See CROHN'S DISEASE, DIVERTICULITIS and COLITIS. Sometimes fistulas form between the vagina and bladder or rectum following difficult childbirth. Fistulas are treated by antibiotics which get rid of infection, and by surgical repair.

FIT

Another word for CONVULSION. See also EPILEPSY.

FLAT FEET

A condition where the arch of the instep flattens out and the entire sole of the foot is flat to the ground. Flat feet, or fallen arches, may be due to congenital looseness or weakness of the ligaments of the arch of the foot, or may be caused by stretching of these ligaments by being overweight or by standing for long periods without correctly fitted shoes to give good foot support. In some cases, they may occur after a crushing injury to the foot. Properly fitted arch supports and exercises are the usual treatments.

FLATULENCE

The uncomfortable presence of air or WIND in the stomach or intestines, causing excessive passing of wind through the mouth or ANUS. Flatulence may be the result of the nervous habit of swallowing air, DYSPEPSIA, or eating too many gas-producing foods such as beans, onions, cucumbers, cabbage and eggs. Attention to diet and eating habits will correct this problem.

FLOODING
A common term for MENORRHAGIA, or very heavy menstrual periods.

FLU
See INFLUENZA.

FLUORIDATION
The addition of a small amount of fluoride to the water supply in order to prevent tooth decay. Although some water supplies are rich in natural fluorides, there are many places in Australia and New Zealand where fluoride is considered inadequate and has been added to the water supply, usually in the proportion of one part fluoride to a million parts of water. In areas where the water supply is not fluoridated, protection against tooth decay may be gained through fluoride tablets or drops. See your dentist for advice.

FOETUS
The term used to describe an unborn baby two months or more after conception. For the first eight weeks after conception, the baby is described as an EMBRYO. From the third month of development, the foetus' heart is pumping blood and most of the internal organs are well formed. (See How The Body Works, pp. 28–30.)

FOLIC ACID
Folic acid is an essential dietary element. In the case of a deficiency, red cell formation and tissue growth are impaired. Symptoms are those of ANAEMIA and CHEILOSIS. Sources of folic acid are liver, green leafy vegetables, fruit and yeast.

FOLLICLE
A pouch-like depression or cavity found in many parts of the body, the most commonly known being hair follicles and ovarian follicles.

FOLLICULITIS
Inflammation of hair follicles, usually due to infection. See ACNE, BOIL.

FONTANELLE
The soft areas of cartilage between the bones of a baby's skull. Most of the fontanelles have become bony and hard by the baby's first birthday. The largest one on the top of the head has closed by the time the baby is eighteen months old.

FOOD POISONING
An acute illness resulting from eating contaminated foods and characterised by stomach cramps and pains, VOMITING and DIARRHOEA. Most cases of food poisoning are caused by BACTERIA or their TOXINS. See also BOTULISM, GASTROENTERITIS, SALMONELLA (and First Aid).

FORAMEN
A natural hole, especially in a bone, through which blood vessels or nerves pass.

FORCEPS
A tong-like instrument used for grasping and pulling. There are many different types of forceps used by doctors, dentists and surgeons. Obstetricans, for example, may use specially designed forceps to grasp the baby's head to help delivery.

FORESKIN
The fold or flap of skin, also known as the prepuce, that covers the head of the PENIS. See also CIRCUMCISION.

FRACTURE
A break in a bone which may be simple (where the break is clean and the surrounding tissues and skin intact), compound (where the skin and tissues are damaged and the bone protrudes through the skin), complicated (where the broken bone penetrates or presses on an internal organ or vessel), or comminuted (where the bone is broken into several small pieces). A greenstick fracture is commonly seen in children when the pliable bone bends rather than breaks. A fracture is usually the result of direct, sharp pressure, as in a blow or fall, and is indicated by pain, deformity and inability to move the part. If a fracture is suspected, call a doctor. (See First Aid.)

FRATERNAL TWINS
Non-identical twins occurring as a result of fertilisation of two separate egg cells. See also TWINS.

FRECKLE
A harmless brown pigmented spot on the skin. When fair skin is exposed to the sun there may be patchy, excessive development of the pigment melanin. People with fair, sensitive skin should apply a sunscreen lotion or cream before going out into the sun. So-called freckle-removing preparations are ineffective and possibly harmful to the skin. See also CHLOASMA.

FREUD
Austrian psychoanalyst Sigmund Freud (1856–1939) developed a branch of psychiatry based on the

existence of the subconscious mind, the importance of dreams and the effect of subconscious drives and motivations on behaviour. Freud believed that through PSYCHOANALYSIS, subconscious motivations could be liberated and thus neuroses cured.

FRIGIDITY

In women, a lack of sexual desire (LIBIDO) and an inability to experience pleasure from SEXUAL INTERCOURSE. It may be the result of physical pain on intercourse, called DYSPAREUNIA, insufficient lubrication of the genitals, fear of becoming pregnant, emotional and physical stress and general illness and lethargy. It may also be due to hostility and unconscious feelings of fear and guilt regarding sex. Sympathetic, expert sexual counselling is the best treatment.

FROSTBITE

Injury to the skin and tissues, particularly those of the ears, nose, toes and fingers, following prolonged exposure to extreme cold. Blood flow to the tissues stops and the skin cells are damaged. Symptoms include numbness, pallor and later blisters and pain. A doctor should treat frostbite. (See First Aid.)

FUGUE

An emotional state in which a person wanders aimlessly about, both mentally and physically separated from the normal environment. It may be associated with HYSTERIA and some organic mental disorders.

FUNCTIONAL DISORDER

A condition or illness that is PSYCHOSOMATIC, or emotional, rather than physical. Functional disorders cause symptoms as real as those of physical illness.

FUNGUS

A group of organisms that include mushrooms, toadstools, moulds, mildews, yeasts. Fungi are found everywhere in the soil and air. They reproduce by spore formation. There are about fifty different fungi recognised as causes of disease in human beings. Some cause local inflammation of skin and membranes, as in RINGWORM and ATHLETE'S FOOT, THRUSH. Effective anti-fungal remedies are available.

FURUNCLE

Another name for a BOIL.

G

GALL-BLADDER

The 7–10 cm long pear-shaped sac, lying below the liver in the right upper abdomen, which stores BILE from the liver. The gall-bladder releases bile into the duodenum to help with the digestion of fats. The most common problems affecting the gall-bladder are acute and chronic inflammation or CHOLECYSTITIS, and GALLSTONES. (See also How The Body Works, pp. 19–20.)

GALLSTONES

Hard, pebbly masses (calculi) usually comprised of cholesterol, bile and protein which may form in the

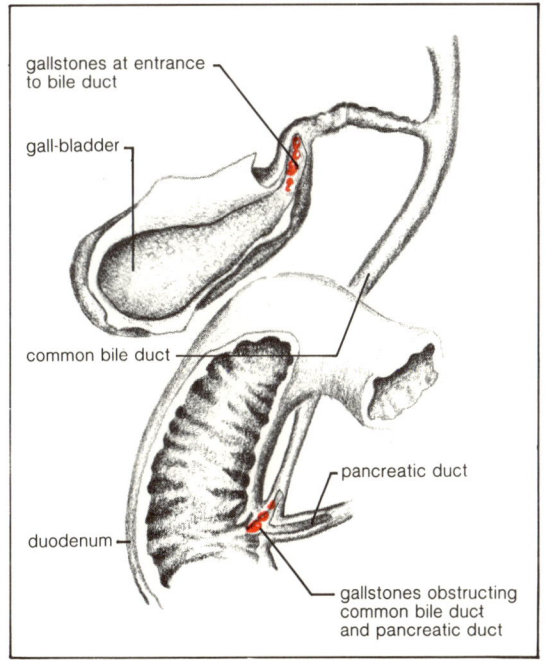

Gallstones may cause obstruction at various places in the bile duct system.

GALL-BLADDER. In many cases (about 70 per cent), gallstones cause no problems and are discovered by chance in an abdominal X-ray. When associated with inflammation of the gall-bladder, they may cause NAUSEA, dyspeptic symptoms and upper abdominal pain. When a gallstone blocks a bile duct, there may be severe abdominal pain and jaundice. Gallstones are detected by X-ray examination (CHOLECYSTO-GRAPHY) and, if causing symptoms, the gall-bladder and stones are usually removed surgically.

GAMMA GLOBULINS

Proteins found in blood plasma. ANTIBODIES essential to the body's defence system against infection are made up of gamma globulin.

GANGLION

A group of nerve cells.

GANGLION CYST

A small, firm, fluid-containing swelling found under the skin, usually connected to a tendon near a joint such as the wrist or ankle. Such swellings usually give no pain or trouble. Quite often they disappear of their own accord.

GANGRENE

The death of tissue, usually followed by bacterial invasion and putrefaction, which occurs when arterial blood supply to the area is cut off. Common causes are EMBOLISM, injury, diabetic blood vessel disease or FROSTBITE. The affected part, most often the feet or hands, becomes moist and swollen, and may turn black and separate. When there is no putrefaction the condition is dry gangrene, in which the part darkens and shrivels before separation. In gas gangrene, gas and toxin-forming bacteria called *Clostridium welchii* (which live without oxygen) infect a deep wound where there is a poor supply of blood. The infection can spread rapidly unless anti-biotics are given and the wound opened to allow aeration. Sometimes amputation of the gangrenous part is necessary.

GASTRECTOMY
Surgical removal of part or all of the stomach. Reasons for gastrectomy include GASTRIC ULCER or CANCER.

GASTRIC ULCER
Ulceration of the mucous membrane lining the stomach, similar in nature to DUODENAL ULCER. Gastric ulcers may be caused by injury to the stomach lining by alcohol, drugs such as aspirin or NSAIDS, or hyperacidity. These ulcers are more common in males and usually occur over the age of 40. Ten per cent of gastric ulcers are associated with stomach cancer. Symptoms may be vague or absent, or there may be gnawing upper abdominal pain relieved by ANTACIDS. Occasionally gastric ulcer causes vomiting of blood (HAEMOPTYSIS). Treatment is by medication which blocks production of gastric acid. Surgery is sometimes necessary.

GASTRITIS
Inflammation of the membrane lining the stomach, usually the result of chemical irritation by alcohol and certain drugs (aspirin, NSAIDS), ALLERGY or FOOD POISONING. Symptoms include upper abdominal bloating and cramp, nausea and vomiting. An infectious, epidemic gastritis ('gastric flu') causes similar symptoms plus chills, fever and later DIARRHOEA. Treatment is by rest and a light, bland diet. Gastritis is usually brief and self-limiting over a day or two.

GASTROENTERITIS
Inflammation of the stomach and intestines, usually caused by a bacterial or viral infection, allergy or food poisoning. Symptoms include stomach cramps, colic, fever, vomiting and DIARRHOEA. Treatment is a restricted diet (dry toast, grated apple, clear broth) and plenty of liquids for a day or two. Since DEHYDRATION is a common complication of gastroenteritis in infancy, children suffering from it should be watched carefully and given frequent drinks of water, soft drink and broth. If there is no improvement in 24 hours, see your doctor.

GASTROSCOPY
Examination of the stomach using an instrument called a gastroscope, which is fed through the mouth and into the stomach. Through a complex, delicate arrangement of lenses in the gastroscope, the doctor can examine the lining of the stomach to see whether a tumour, ulcer or other abnormal condition is present. (See Medical Tests And Examinations.)

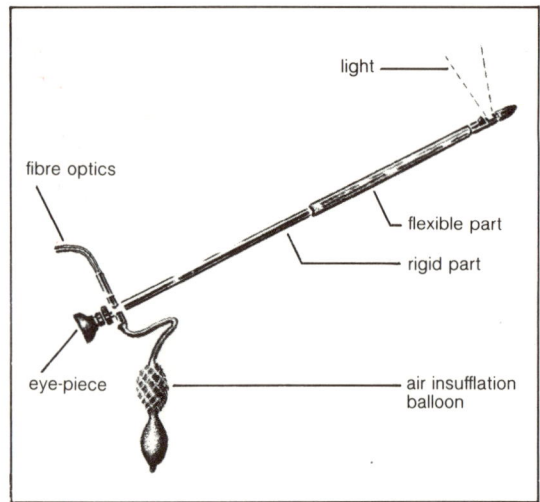

The special fibre optic cables in the gastroscope, used to view the interior of the stomach, allow the stomach lining to be illuminated, and transmit an image of the area back to the doctor.

GENES
Basic units of HEREDITY, which determine the form and function of all cells, and which carry information dictating all the characteristics of an individual, such as sex, colouring, shape of nose, chin, eyes, ears, etc., pattern of fingerprints, degree of intelligence and so on. Genes are arranged together to make the thread-like structures known as CHROMOSOMES, which are found in the nucleus of every living cell. The arrangement of the genes is called the genetic code. The reproductive gametes (SPERM and OVUM) each contains half (23) of the total number of chromosomes (46). When sperm and ovum combine, the two genetic codes are brought together with the developing baby getting half the full chromosomal number from the father and the other half from the mother. Dominant genes are always carried from parent to child (for example, the gene for brown eyes is dominant over that for blue eyes which is known as a recessive gene), although a recessive gene is still passed on and may show up several generations later. Mutations (changes in the genetic code) occur all the time in all living organisms, a mechanism by which evolution proceeds. Sometimes a genetic disorder may occur through a chance abnormal mutation taking place during cell division.

GENITALS
The external organs of reproduction: in a man, the TESTES and the PENIS, and in a woman, the labia majora and labia minora (lip-shaped folds of skin at the entrance of the VAGINA), the HYMEN and the CLITORIS. (See How The Body Works, pp. 25–27.)

GERIATRICS

The special medical area dealing with the diseases and problems associated with old age. As medical technology has improved, people are living longer so that study and research in geriatrics are increasingly important. The scientific study of the ageing process is called gerontology.

GERM

Commonly used to describe a micro-organism capable of causing disease. Such micro-organisms include BACTERIA, VIRUSES, rickettsia (a life form somewhere between bacteria and viruses) and protozoa (one-celled organisms like amoebas).

GERMAN MEASLES

See RUBELLA.

GIARDIASIS

A gastrointestinal disorder caused by the single cell (protozoal) parasite *Giardia lamblia* and contracted by eating contaminated food. Often symptoms are mild or absent, but may include abdominal bloating, anorexia, nausea, flatulence, colic and diarrhoea. It is effectively treated with antiprotozoal drugs such as tinidazole and metronidazole.

GIDDINESS

True giddiness, or VERTIGO – the sensation of the world spinning around – is caused by disturbance of the organs of balance in the inner ear. This is a normal consequence of rapid rotation of the body. Pathological giddiness may occur in MENIÈRE'S DISEASE, and in infections, disturbances of blood supply and tumours involving the inner ear. Also, giddiness may be a symptom when the brain is momentarily starved of blood and oxygen just before FAINTING.

GIGANTISM

Abnormal and excessive growth of the bones of the arms and legs, as a result of over-production of growth hormone in the PITUITARY GLAND during childhood. Gigantism is caused by a BENIGN or non-cancerous pituitary tumour, which can usually be removed by surgery or with irradiation.

GINGIVITIS

Inflammation of the gums beginning around the teeth and causing pain and bleeding. Causes include poor dental hygiene, excessive tartar build-up on teeth, decaying teeth, poorly fitted dentures and poor health and nutrition. Regular dental checks and good dental hygiene prevent gingivitis.

GLAND

An organ or cell group that secretes and releases vital substances to keep the body functioning properly. The many glands in the body can be divided into two main types: the exocrine glands which are those with ducts which deliver their secretions directly to particular parts of the body, such as sweat and salivary glands; and the endocrine or ductless glands such as pituitary, thyroid and adrenal, which secrete hormones directly into the bloodstream. (See How The Body Works, pp. 22–24.)

GLANDULAR FEVER

See MONONUCLEOSIS.

GLAUCOMA

A serious eye disorder caused by increased pressure of fluid within the eyeball, due to inadequate drainage of fluid from the anterior chamber of the eye. Glaucoma affects people of middle age and beyond. The eye becomes red and painful and in severe cases the RETINA and optic nerve may be so damaged that sight is destroyed. Although the precise causes of glaucoma are not fully understood, treatment with drugs or surgery to promote better drainage, if started early enough, is successful in preventing loss of vision. Thus it is important to have regular checks of eye pressure from age 50 onwards.

GLUCOSE

A sugar, found in the blood, which is derived from carbohydrate foods during the digestive process. Glucose is stored in the liver in the form of glycogen, and when needed is readily converted back into glucose to be absorbed into the bloodstream as a major source of energy. The level of glucose in the blood is controlled by the hormone INSULIN. Too much or too little insulin causes changes in blood glucose levels as in HYPOGLYCAEMIA or HYPER-GLYCAEMIA, the latter a symptom of DIABETES. (See also How The Body Works, pp. 16–18.)

GLUCOSE TOLERANCE TEST

Used in the diagnosis of DIABETES, this test, in which the patient eats a certain amount of glucose, determines through examination of the urine and blood how the patient's body deals with sugars. (See Medical Tests And Examinations – BLOOD SUGAR TESTS.)

GOITRE

Abnormal swelling of the thyroid gland. Goitre most often occurs in HYPOTHYROIDISM, when the gland is not making enough thyroid hormone (thyroxine), or when it is making too much (HYPERTHYROIDISM). Goitre may be caused by a deficiency of iodine, or by thyroid tumours.

A goitre is an abnormal swelling in the front of the neck caused by an enlargement of the thyroid gland.

GONADS
The glands which produce the cells and hormones necessary for reproduction: in men, the TESTES which produce SPERM; and in women, the OVARIES. (See How The Body Works, pp. 25–27.)

GONORRHOEA
A sexually transmitted disease caused by the bacteria *Neisseria gonorrhoeae*, which infects the membranes of the genital and lower urinary tracts. Symptoms of gonorrhoea appear about a week after infection and include frequent burning urination and a profuse yellow discharge from penis or vagina, though women with gonorrhoea may have no symptoms. If the disease is not diagnosed and treated promptly, it may lead to complications such as ARTHRITIS, ENDOCARDITIS, PROSTATITIS, inflammation of the testes, SALPINGITIS and INFERTILITY. Antibiotics cure gonorrhoea quickly and effectively.

GOUT
A disease in which there is an excess of uric acid (a breakdown product of proteins) in the blood, which can lead to deposits of acid and crystals (urates) in body tissue, particularly cartilage. In an acute attack of gout, one or more joints (classically the big toe), is affected. The gouty joint becomes hot, swollen and severely painful. The tendency to gout may be hereditary (1 in 5 sufferers has a close relative affected). An attack of gout may be brought on by surgery, a diet rich in proteins and fat, certain drugs or damage to a joint already affected by the disease. Treatment today is excellent and involves using dietary control, drugs to promote increased excretion of uric acid, and anti-inflammatory medication to prevent progressive damage to joints.

GRAFT
The transplanting of an organ, or part of an organ, to replace one that does not function efficiently. See SKIN GRAFT, TRANSPLANT.

GRAND MAL
See EPILEPSY.

GRASS
Another name for MARIJUANA.

GREENSTICK FRACTURE
An incomplete break in a bone, seen mostly in children. See FRACTURE.

GRIPE
Colicky intermittent abdominal pain, often caused by wind in babies. See COLIC.

GROUP THERAPY
A form of PSYCHOTHERAPY in which a number of people with a similar problem attend a series of meetings to discuss and analyse their problems. The idea of such meetings is that participants will learn to talk about themselves, interact with one another, learn from the others' experiences and so overcome their troubles. Group therapy is often helpful in the treatment of such disorders as ALCOHOLISM.

GUTHRIE TEST
A simple method of testing the blood of all new-born babies for the inherited disorder PHENYL-KETONURIA.

GYNAECOMASTIA
Enlargement and tenderness of breast tissue in males, which may affect one or both breasts. It is usually the result of hormone imbalance. Gynaecomastia is common in adolescent boys, in whom it often causes embarrassment and anxiety. At about age 12, boys should be told that they may notice some breast changes over the next few years, and

assured that this is part of the hormonal upheaval of puberty and will settle down within six months to three years. Causes of gynaecomastia in adult men include tumours of the testis and adrenal glands, ACROMEGALY, KLINEFELTER'S SYNDROME and advanced CIRRHOSIS of the liver. Breast enlargement may also occur as a side-effect of some drugs, especially OESTROGEN given to sufferers of prostatic cancer and when oestrogen-containing creams are used on the scalp to prevent baldness. Treatment depends on the cause. The breasts will subside after correction of hormone imbalance or stopping the drug responsible for the enlargement. In Klinefelter's syndrome, the breasts may be surgically removed.

HAEMANGIOMA
See BIRTHMARK.

HAEMATOMA
An accumulation of blood which has leaked into the tissues from damaged blood vessels, usually as a result of injury. Common haematomas are those occurring around fractures or in the tissues around the eye following a blow (the classic shiner). The most dangerous haematoma occurs beneath the outer membrane (dura) surrounding the brain following head injury.

HAEMATURIA
The presence of blood in the urine, usually obvious, but sometimes the blood may not be visible to the naked eye and is only detected by microscopic examination of urine. The causes of haematuria include kidney stone or tumour, NEPHRITIS, CYSTITIS, bladder tumours, inflammation or tumours of the PROSTATE GLAND. Blood in the urine should be immediately reported to the doctor for diagnosis of the cause and appropriate treatment.

HAEMOGLOBIN
A complex compound of protein and iron carried within the red blood cells, or ERYTHROCYTES. Haemoglobin, which carries oxygen from the lungs to the tissues, is the red pigment which gives blood its colour. (See How The Body Works, p. 5.)

HAEMOLYTIC DISEASE
A condition in new-born babies in which the baby's red blood cells are destroyed by antibodies in the mother's blood, which have formed because of a Rhesus blood group incompatibility between mother and baby. This may happen if the mother is Rh-negative and the baby is Rh-positive, and there is some mingling of maternal and foetal blood during pregnancy (see BLOOD GROUP). As a result the baby can suffer from ANAEMIA, JAUNDICE or brain damage.

Routine blood tests during pregnancy can detect the formation of antibodies in the mother's blood and anticipate the problem. In severe cases an exchange transfusion (in which the baby's blood is completely changed) is carried out on the FOETUS, or immediately after delivery (see RHESUS (Rh) FACTOR). These days haemolytic disease of the new-born rarely occurs, as now all mothers are screened for Rh group early in pregnancy and if necessary, anti-D antibody is given to prevent the problem.

HAEMOPHILIA
An inherited disorder in which the blood clots very slowly due to a deficiency in one of the factors in blood plasma, known as AHF or anti-haemophilic factor, that helps in the process of blood clotting. A person with haemophilia, unless cared for properly, may suffer from severe HAEMORRHAGE as a result of cuts, injuries, bruises or bumps. Haemophilia is caused by a genetic defect passed on by women, but occurring exclusively in males. It is treated by administration of concentrated preparations of AHF, which is purified from donated blood. (See Medical And Health Support Organisations.)

HAEMOPTYSIS
The spitting up of blood or blood-stained phlegm. It is usually a sign of a serious disease, such as CANCER, PNEUMONIA, TUBERCULOSIS, HEART DISEASE, LEUKAEMIA, and should be reported immediately to your doctor.

HAEMORRHAGE
Severe loss of blood due to injury to blood vessels or blood clotting disorders such as HAEMOPHILIA. Rapid loss of large amounts of blood results in shock, and even death, unless the blood is replaced by transfusion. (See First Aid – BLEEDING.)

HAEMORRHOIDS
Commonly known as piles, haemorrhoids are en-

larged veins in the RECTUM. They are more likely to occur in middle age and result from increased pressure in the pelvis, sometimes as a result of constipation, overuse of LAXATIVES, pregnancy, tumours or large cysts. Symptoms are discomfort or pain and sometimes bleeding on DEFAECATION. Mild cases of piles need no treatment or may be simply treated with special soothing creams or suppositories, but in more severe cases they may be injected with a special substance which makes them close up. Occasionally surgical treatment is required.

HAIR LOSS
See ALOPECIA.

HALITOSIS
The medical term for bad breath, which may be the result of smoking, tooth decay or abscess, chronic GINGIVITIS, disorders of the tonsils, nose or sinuses, stomach and intestines and, more seriously, diseases of the lungs and liver. Correct dental hygiene is an obvious treatment but if halitosis persists, check with your doctor.

HALLUCINATION
A vivid, waking perception that something, such as visions or voices, is real when it is not. Hallucinations (which can involve all the senses including taste, smell and touch) may be caused by alcohol, hallucinogenic drugs such as LSD, illnesses such as SCHIZOPHRENIA or extreme emotional stress or fatigue. A person experiencing hallucinations needs medical help.

HAMSTRING
One of the two groups of tendons at the back of the knee attaching the muscles of the back of the thigh to the bones of the lower leg.

HANGOVER
The unpleasant result of drinking too much alcohol. Alcohol is a toxic substance affecting the entire body and the after-effects may include headache, nausea, dizziness, thirst, anxiety and disorientation. Obvious remedies include painkillers for headache, mild antacids for stomach upset, plenty of fluids and a little sensible, soothing peace and quiet. 'Hair of the dog' or a morning-after drink is not recommended. A hangover is the body's warning to exercise future restraint. See also ALCOHOLISM.

HARDENING OF THE ARTERIES
See ARTERIOSCLEROSIS.

HARELIP
A birth defect of the upper lip, often associated with a CLEFT PALATE, in which the two sides of the lip fail to join properly. Although potentially disfiguring, a harelip can be successfully repaired (usually in conjunction with cleft palate) by cosmetic surgery during childhood, leaving only a minor scar.

HAY FEVER
Inflammation of the membranes lining the nasal passages and sinuses due to an allergic response to any number of inhaled substances, chiefly pollen from grasses, plants and trees as well as fungal spores, animal hair, house dust and even certain foods. Symptoms are running nose and eyes, and sneezing. Antihistamine drugs and decongestant sprays or drops usually relieve the problem although people with recurrent hay fever may be given a special course of injections in an attempt to desensitise them to the allergens (allergy-causing substances). See also ALLERGY.

HEADACHE
The most common is tension headache which is associated with extreme tenseness of the muscles of the head and neck, usually the result of emotional stress. Other headaches may be the result of changes of pressure within the sensitive blood vessels inside the skull (vascular headache), eye strain, SINUSITIS, INFLUENZA, feverish illness, high blood pressure, fatigue, too much smoking or drinking, hormonal changes, excessive noise. Headaches are most effectively dealt with by treating the cause rather than the symptoms. Persistent headaches warrant a visit to your doctor. See MIGRAINE.

HEART ATTACK
See CORONORY HEART DISEASE, MYOCARDIAL INFARCTION and HEART DISEASE. (See also First Aid.)

HEARTBURN
This is another common name for INDIGESTION.

HEART DISEASE
There are many different kinds of disease that affect the heart: certain parts of the heart may become inflamed in conditions such as MYOCARDITIS and ENDOCARDITIS; RHEUMATIC FEVER or SYPHILIS may cause the valves to become diseased; there may be loss of flexibility in the arteries in ARTERIOSCLEROSIS or build-up of fatty deposits in ATHEROSCLEROSIS; the blood supply may be affected in such conditions as ANGINA PECTORIS, coronary THROMBOSIS and EMBOLISM; it may become enlarged in HYPERTENSION or in PULMONARY HEART DISEASE resulting from asthma, bronchitis or emphysema; the heartbeat may become abnormally slow in BRADYCARDIA or fast in TACHYCARDIA. (See How The Body Works, pp. 5–9.)

HEART FAILURE
Heart failure does not mean that the heart has ceased to beat, but rather that it cannot meet the demands for blood made on it by the body. Heart failure is also called congestive cardiac failure (CCF) or cardiac insufficiency. The condition may be secondary to HEART DISEASE, lung disease, HYPERTENSION. Symptoms may include breathlessness, fluid accumulation in the legs, abdomen (dropsy) and lungs, giddiness and fainting. Many cases of heart failure can be successfully treated with drugs such as digitalis and diuretics and a sensible routine of rest and gentle exercise. See also PULMONARY HEART DISEASE.

HEART MASSAGE
More commonly known as external cardiac compression, this is an emergency treatment technique used to restore the beating of a heart that has stopped. (See First Aid – RESUSCITATION.)

HEART MURMUR
An unusual sound made by the heart as blood moves through the valves, which is usually detected by use of a STETHOSCOPE. While it might be an indication of some defect in the heart or its valves, many heart murmurs are nothing to worry about.

HEART STOPPAGE
See CARDIAC ARREST.

HEMIPLEGIA
A form of PARALYSIS, usually the result of a STROKE, in which only one side of the body is affected. PHYSIOTHERAPY, OCCUPATIONAL THERAPY and speech therapy are the usual means of treatment and rehabilitation.

HEPATITIS
Inflammation of the LIVER, usually caused by viral infection. There are many types of hepatitis, the commonest being types A and B. Hepatitis A is transmitted by food or drink contaminated by the faeces of infected persons, and is usually associated with poor sanitation. Its incubation period is two to six weeks. Symptoms are usually mild, with recovery after two to four weeks and subsequent lifelong immunity from hepatitis A infection.

Hepatitis B (previously called serum hepatitis) is transmitted by blood or blood products, or by other exchange of body fluids, including sexual intercourse. It is common among intravenous drug abusers. Incubation period is six to twenty-six weeks. Symptoms may be mild or severe. In many cases recovery is complete with future immunity. In other cases, where the affected person becomes a carrier and potential source of infection to others, the VIRUS may remain active in the body to cause chronic relapsing hepatitis leading to CIRRHOSIS of the liver. Thus hepatitis B is a potentially dangerous disease.

Symptoms of hepatitis from any cause include fever, malaise, nausea and vomiting, upper right abdominal pain, JAUNDICE, dark urine and pale faeces. There is no specific treatment for hepatitis. Rest and careful nourishment assist recovery, and it is important to avoid any liver toxins, including alcohol, until recovery is complete.

HEREDITY
The process by which children inherit physical and mental characteristics from their parents. Genetic characteristics are passed on through GENES.

HERNIA
A condition occurring when part of an organ bulges through a weak section in the surrounding tissue, usually muscle. Hernias are generally described according to where they occur: for example, inguinal hernia, occurring in the groin when the intestines are pushed through a break in the muscle layers. A strangulated hernia happens when the herniated intestine becomes constricted so that its blood flow is cut off. It requires surgical correction immediately to prevent possible GANGRENE or PERITONITIS. Other types of hernia include femoral (in the upper part of the thigh), hiatus (where the stomach protrudes through the muscles of the diaphragm), umbilical (where the abdominal contents bulge out around the navel – mostly found in children). In some cases, a supportive truss will hold back a hernia, but usually repair surgery is performed.

HEROIN
A highly addictive narcotic drug. It is the most dangerous drug of addiction used illegally today. See also ADDICTION, DRUG ABUSE (and Medical And Health Support Organisations – ALCOHOL & DRUG DEPENDENCE).

HERPES SIMPLEX
The name of a VIRUS which causes painful, blistering skin lesions commonly known as COLD SORES. There are two types, herpes simplex virus I and herpes simplex virus II (HSVI and HSVII). It used to be thought that HSVI caused cold sores around the mouth and HSVII caused genital herpes. It is now known that either virus can cause herpes lesions in either location. Infection occurs when a moist broken surface comes in contact with the virus, which enters the body, finds the nearest nerve, and migrates up the nerve to its root near the spinal cord. Here it lives for the life of the infected person.

Incubation period: from the time of infection it takes 48 hours to about twenty-one days to the first (primary) attack, which is usually quite severe.

Symptoms: painful red swellings appear on the skin, and a day or so later blisters develop on the surface. The blisters break to form ulcers, which often join to form larger ulcers. The glands draining the area become swollen and painful, and there are usually generalised symptoms of fever and malaise. There may be secondary bacterial infection of the ulcers, which makes everything worse. After five to twenty days the ulcers heal and the swelling subsides.

Treatment of the primary attack includes rest, local and oral analgesics, keeping the affected area clean, use of antiseptics to reduce bacterial infection of ulcers, and warm salty baths to reduce swelling. Herpes lesions near the urethra may cause difficulty passing urine; it may be necessary to empty the bladder while sitting in a warm bath. In extreme cases catheterisation is needed.

Recurrence: during the primary attack some antibodies are formed in the blood and tissues, which reduce the severity of recurrences and sometimes prevent them altogether. Recurrence, which is always at or around the same spot, is most likely when resistance is lowered by other illness, stress or local tissue damage. Oral herpes sufferers know that recurrence is likely if the mouth is sunburned or chapped, and during respiratory infections (hence the name 'cold sores'). Warning of recurrence is an itching, tingling sensation in the area. The blisters appear the following day. The infection can be passed on to another person from the time of first warning until the lesion heals.

There is no cure for herpes, but some of the new anti-viral medications may reduce the duration of an attack and the frequency of recurrence. See your doctor for information and counselling about herpes simplex.

HERPES ZOSTER
See SHINGLES.

HETEROSEXUAL
A person whose exclusive sexual preference is for members of the opposite sex.

HIATUS HERNIA
A condition in which a part of the stomach protrudes through a weak spot in the muscular wall of the diaphragm. See HERNIA.

HICCUP (HICCOUGH)
A spasmodic, involuntary contraction of the diaphragm (the muscle between the chest and abdomen) which occurs when the diaphragm and the epiglottis (the flap of cartilage which closes off the opening to the windpipe) get out of rhythm. Usually hiccups are harmless and are the result of eating or drinking too quickly, faulty swallowing or nervous tension. Sometimes, however, they may be a sign of more serious disorders including PLEURISY, ENCEPHALITIS, URAEMIA, ALCOHOLISM. Hiccups in babies, especially after a feed, are normal and harmless.

HIGH BLOOD PRESSURE
See HYPERTENSION.

HIP REPLACEMENT
An operation in which the head of the long bone of the thigh (femur) is replaced with an artificial one made of metal or a combination of metal and plastic. In recent years there have been great advances in this form of treatment for people who have had the joint seriously damaged through such diseases as ARTHRITIS or fracture. More than 90 per cent of hip replacements are successful nowadays.

HIRSUTISM
Excessive growth of body and facial hair. If hirsutism begins at puberty, it is usually inherited. When superfluous hair appears later in life, it may be caused by an excess of male hormones, which can be corrected. Hereditary hirsutism is best dealt with by shaving, plucking or bleaching the unwanted hair, or removal by depilatories or ELECTROLYSIS.

HIVES
An acute allergic reaction in the skin resulting in red, raised lumps which itch and burn. The round weals may be small or as large as a saucer. Usually hives are the result of a sensitivity to certain foods (such as tomatoes, shellfish, strawberries), certain drugs (such as penicillin), dust and pollens. Home remedies to help relieve the irritating itch include calamine lotion, and a compress dipped in cold milk. Hives usually disappear as soon as the allergen is withdrawn. See ALLERGY.

HOARSENESS
A husky, croaking pitch of voice, sometimes associated with a sore throat, that is the result of an overworked or inflamed larynx. Persistent hoarseness should be checked by your doctor. See LARYNGITIS.

HODGKIN'S DISEASE
A tumour of lymphoid tissue, occurring for no known reason and mostly in young adults, which affects the LYMPH nodes, spleen, liver and bone marrow. Also known as lymphadenoma, Hodgkin's disease is indicated by swelling of the lymph nodes in the neck, armpits and groin, a characteristic fever, sweating, weakness, weight loss, anaemia and itching. It may be successfully treated with RADIOTHERAPY in its early stages. Later treatment involves a combination

of drugs, radiotherapy and surgery, often with good results.

HOMEOPATHY
A system of treating diseases based on the principle 'like cures like', in which very small doses of those drugs that produce the same symptoms as a particular disease are used to treat that disease.

HOMOSEXUAL
Exclusive sexual preference for members of the same sex. A homosexual relationship between women is known as lesbianism.

HORMONE
A chemical messenger substance, released into the blood by the endocrine glands, which stimulates specific responses in various target hormones. (See How The Body Works, pp. 22–24.)

HORMONE REPLACEMENT THERAPY (HRT)
The replacement of ovarian hormones after production has come to an end at the MENOPAUSE, or when removal or destruction of both ovaries has brought about an artificial menopause. Many different natural or synthetic oestrogens may be used. Usually a progestogen is added for ten to fourteen days each month to prevent any unbalanced effects on the reproductive organs. HRT relieves menopausal symptoms and helps to prevent the development of OSTEOPOROSIS in older women. The small balanced doses recommended are very safe.

HUNTINGTON'S CHOREA
A rare, incurable hereditary disease, occurring between the ages of 30 and 50, in which there are degenerative changes in the brain. Symptoms include those known as chorea: jerky, involuntary movements of the face, neck and arms and unsteady mobility, often accompanied by emotional and intellectual disturbances. Tranquillisers and sedatives help relieve symptoms.

HYDRONEPHROSIS
A condition whereby the kidney becomes distended with accumulated urine because urinary outflow is obstructed. The blockage may be in the ureter, bladder or urethra, and may be the result of a kidney stone, an enlarged prostate gland, a tumour, an infection or a birth defect. It is usually necessary to treat the cause of the blockage.

HYMEN
The membrane, also known as the maidenhead, that partly covers the entrance of the VAGINA. (See How The Body Works, p. 25.)

HYPERGLYCAEMIA
An increase in the level of sugar in the blood because the pancreas is not producing enough of the hormone INSULIN. It is a feature of DIABETES mellitus. Symptoms are excessive thirst, increased urine production, weight loss, nausea, vomiting and, if untreated, KETOSIS, COMA and death.

HYPERTENSION
Also known as high blood pressure, this condition (in which the fluid pressure generated by the heart's pumping action is too high for the body's needs) puts a strain on the heart and may gradually damage the small blood vessels in heart, brain, kidneys and eyes. Hypertension may be a result of disorders and diseases of the kidneys, the circulation, brain, tumours of the adrenal glands and arteriosclerosis (hardening of the arteries). However, a specific cause is found in only about 1 out of 10 cases. Most other cases, where the cause is unknown, are described as essential hypertension. To some extent, the tendency to hypertension may be hereditary. It is more common in men over forty. In those cases where hypertension is the result of a known cause, treatment involves correcting or relieving the cause. In essential hypertension, overweight patients are put on an appropriate diet and special anti-hypertensive drugs are prescribed, together with life-style review.

HYPERTHYROIDISM
See THYROTOXICOSIS.

HYPERTROPHY
Overgrowth of any tissue or organ.

HYPNOSIS
A trance-like, or sleep-like state that is induced by a trained therapist, physician or hypnotist. A person in a hypnotic trance may respond to the suggestion that he or she will feel no pain and the technique is sometimes used when an anaesthetic cannot be used. A hypnotised person may also remember events and incidents that he or she cannot recall when awake and so the technique can be of value in PSYCHIATRY. About 80 per cent of people can be put into a light trance in which everything is remembered. Hypnotherapy is sometimes successfully used in the treatment of drug addiction.

HYPOCHONDRIA
An abnormal preoccupation with health. Sensible concern over health is normal but a hypochondriac is disturbed about feared or imagined symptoms and illnesses.

HYPOGLYCAEMIA
An abnormally low level of sugar in the blood, usually

due to an excess of the hormone INSULIN. It may occur in a person suffering from DIABETES who hasn't had enough to eat or who has had an excessive dose of insulin. Symptoms include sweating, weakness, dizziness, anxiety, manic behaviour and eventual loss of consciousness. A person showing the first signs of hypoglycaemia should be given a lump of sugar to eat. Hypoglycaemia may also be the result of fasting and can obviously be relieved by giving some quickly absorbed source of blood sugar, such as a sweetened drink.

HYPOTENSION

Low blood pressure. Hypotension may be normal in some people or it may be due to HAEMORRHAGE, or heart attack, pulmonary EMBOLISM or disease of the endocrine glands, the circulation or the central nervous system. Where hypotension becomes SHOCK as in haemorrhage or heart attack, it must be treated quickly. Generally, people who normally have low blood pressure do not develop arteriosclerosis and lead healthier, longer lives than people with high blood pressure. Brief, temporary drop in blood pressure results in FAINTING.

HYPOTHALAMUS

(See How The Body Works, pp. 14–15.)

HYPOTHERMIA

A condition in which body temperature is well below normal as may happen when a person, particularly a baby or someone elderly, is exposed to cold. Prolonged hypothermia can lead to COMA and perhaps death. The term is also used to describe the technique of deliberately lowering body temperature in order to lessen the body's oxygen requirements during surgery on the heart or the brain.

HYPOTHYROIDISM

Underactivity of the thyroid gland. In adults, it is marked by decreased metabolic rate, tiredness and lethargy. See also MYXOEDEMA.

HYSTERECTOMY

Surgical removal of the UTERUS and CERVIX, usually because of disease of the uterus or abnormal bleeding which cannot be controlled by other treatment. The operation requires eight to fourteen days in hospital and a further two to three weeks of convalescence. After a hysterectomy, it takes about four weeks for the inner end of the VAGINA to heal. There is usually some blood-stained discharge until healing is complete. When the discharge ceases, sexual intercourse may be resumed. After hysterectomy there is no more MENSTRUATION and pregnancy is no longer possible. The ovaries are not removed (unless they are also diseased) so that normal hormone production continues until the end of ovarian function at about age fifty. Although hysterectomy means the end of fertility, it is *not* castration, and should not have any effect on feminity or sexuality.

HYSTERIA

When properly used in its medical sense, the term refers to a neurotic condition in which symptoms and signs of organic disease are reproduced by the unconscious action of the mind. Often hysteria is an overaction of the nervous system and a defence mechanism against an unbearable situation. It is not a premeditated pretence; an hysterical patient really believes that the symptoms are due to disease. Symptoms may include loss of sensation, paralysis, blindness, deafness, dumbness, aches and pains, dizziness, fainting. Although hysteria is more common in women, it affects both sexes particularly in adolescence. Treatment is by PSYCHOTHERAPY.

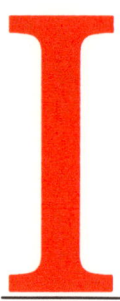

IATROGENIC DISEASE

A disease or disorder that is the result of treatment. Many drugs have side-effects that cause health problems in addition to, or worse than, the original condition for which they were prescribed. Some surgical procedures, manipulations and alternative health care treatments can also cause iatrogenic disease.

ID

A term used in psychoanalysis to describe the instinctive part of the mind. The originator of psychoanalysis, Sigmund FREUD, declared that the psyche is made up of three parts: the id or sub-conscious mind controlling primitive drives relating to birth, life and death; the EGO, the conscious, rational mind; and the super-ego, the moral conscience which helps the ego keep the id socially acceptable.

IDENTICAL TWINS

TWINS who develop from the splitting of a single fertilised egg cell.

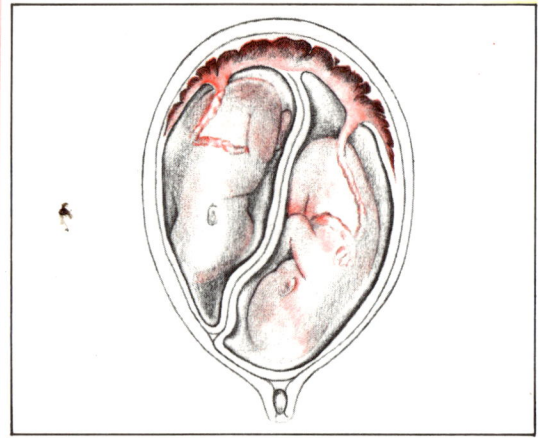

Identical twins share a single placenta.

IDIOPATHIC

Without known cause or reason.

ILEITIS

Inflammation of the ileum (the lower part of the small bowel) and sometimes other parts of the intestine. One form of ileitis is also known as CROHN'S DISEASE. The inflammation causes swelling and ulceration of the lining of the ileum. Ulcers may perforate, resulting in PERITONITIS. In the long term, scarring in and around the affected parts may cause narrowing or blockage of the bowel.

Ileitis usually affects young adults, men and women equally. The cause is unknown, but the disease tends to run in families. Symptoms include severe diarrhoea, abdominal pain, fever, and the manifestations of MALABSORPTION – weight loss, anaemia and other deficiency diseases. Diagnosis is confirmed by X-ray of the bowel. Treatment consists of anti-diarrhoeal medications, courses of corti-costeroids to reduce the inflammatory process and measures to combat nutritional deficiency. When ileitis is complicated by scarring or perforation, surgery may be necessary to remove the affected bowel or to rest it by ILEOSTOMY.

ILEOSTOMY

A surgical operation which joins part of the small intestine, or ileum, to an opening (called a STOMA) in the abdominal wall. The contents of the intestine empty into a special bag attached to the stoma. The operation is necessary in some cases of severe COLITIS, CROHN'S DISEASE and other disorders of the small and large intestines. A person who has had an ileostomy can have, after recovering from the operation, a normal daily routine. (See Medical And Health Support Organisations.)

IMMUNISATION

The process of deliberately creating resistance or

Recommended childhood immunisation schedule

AGE	DISEASE	VACCINE	METHOD OF ADMINISTRATION
2 months	diphtheria tetanus whooping cough	triple antigen	injection
	poliomyelitis	Sabin vaccine	oral
4 months	diphtheria tetanus whooping cough	triple antigen	injection
	poliomyelitis	Sabin vaccine	oral
6 months	diphtheria tetanus whooping cough	triple antigen	injection
	poliomyelitis	Sabin vaccine	oral
12–15 months	measles/mumps	measles/mumps	injection
18 months	diphtheria tetanus whooping cough	triple antigen	injection
5 years (prior to school entry)	diphtheria tetanus	combined diphtheria and tetanus	injection
	poliomyelitis	Sabin vaccine	oral
10–15 years (females only)	rubella (German measles)	rubella vaccine	injection
15 years or prior to leaving school	diphtheria tetanus	adult diphtheria tetanus	injection

immunity to various diseases by means of INOCULATION or VACCINATION with specialised VACCINES. Vaccines consist of specially treated infectious organisms which, when introduced into the body, stimulate the production of ANTIBODIES. Immunising vaccines are administered by various routes: for example, the Sabin vaccine for polio is usually taken orally; smallpox vaccine is given through a scratch in the skin; typhoid vaccine is given by injection. Immunisation in childhood is recommended for such diseases as DIPHTHERIA, WHOOPING COUGH, TETANUS, POLIOMYELITIS, MEASLES, MUMPS and, for prepubescent girls, RUBELLA.

IMMUNOSUPPRESSANT
Any drug or other treatment which suppresses the body's immune response. Immunosuppressants are used to prevent the rejection of grafts or transplants.

IMPETIGO
A staphylococcal skin infection, common in babies and children and usually found on the face. It causes the formation of crusty, yellow sores which spread rapidly to adjacent skin. It is extremely contagious and should be treated promptly with antibiotics.

IMPOTENCE
The inability of a man to effectively perform sexual intercourse, due to either a physical or emotional problem. Physical causes of impotence include hormonal disorders, disorders of genital nerves or blood supply, alcoholism, certain drugs, or abnormality of the sex organs. Such impotence can often

be corrected by treating the cause. Treatment of impotence due to emotional disorder is more complex, but PSYCHOTHERAPY may help.

INCONTINENCE
Loss of control of outflow from the bladder (urinary incontinence) or bowel (faecal incontinence). Incontinence may occur in any disorder of the nervous or muscular control of the bladder or rectum. Total incontinence may result from spinal cord injury, dementia, or severe degenerative nerve and muscle disease.

Stress incontinence is the involuntary passage of urine when pressure inside the abdomen increases, as in coughing, sneezing, laughing or jumping. It is common in women whose pelvic floor muscles have been damaged during childbirth or weakened by oestrogen deficiency after the menopause. Treatment is by physiotherapy and, in some cases, repair surgery.

Urge incontinence is the inability to hold the urine when the urge to urinate is felt. It is often the result of chronic inflammation of the bladder and urethra. Treatment of the inflammation and bladder retraining will usually correct urge incontinence.

INCUBATION PERIOD
The time between the contraction of an infection and the development of symptoms. Many infectious diseases have characteristic incubation periods which may range from one to four days for INFLUENZA, to up to many years for slow virus infections such as AIDS.

INDIGESTION
The common term used to describe minor upsets of the upper digestive system (OESOPHAGUS, STOMACH, duodenum). Indigestion, also known as DYSPEPSIA, may result from a number of causes including over-eating, gulping down food quickly, eating while emotionally upset, alcoholic excess and heavy smoking. Some people find that certain foods are likely to cause symptoms which include heartburn, a full feeling in the upper abdomen, and excessive burping (eructation). This uncomfortable condition can usually be relieved by taking ANTACIDS and can be avoided with a sensible diet and sensible eating habits.

INFARCTION
The death of tissue that occurs when its arterial blood supply is cut off. Usual causes include development of a blood clot in the artery (THROMBOSIS) and EMBOLISM. Infarction can happen in any tissue, but the term is most commonly used to describe the result of blockage of the coronary arteries (MYOCARDIAL INFARCTION).

INFECTIOUS DISEASE
See COMMUNICABLE DISEASE.

INFECTIOUS MONONUCLEOSIS
See MONONUCLEOSIS.

INFERTILITY
Couples who have not conceived after twelve months of trying are considered to be subfertile. The reason for subfertility is found to be due to the male in 40 per cent of cases, 40 per cent to the female, and in 20 per cent of cases subfertility is found in both. In men, subfertility may be due to absence or insufficiency of SPERM in the semen, blockage of the ejaculatory ducts or inability to ejaculate. In women, the problem may be failure to ovulate, blockage of the tubes or a defect of the uterus. Also, there may be factors in the seminal fluid or in the cervical mucus which cause the sperm to lose their motility, and thus prevent them from reaching the OVUM in the tube.

Investigations and treatments for subfertility are:

• Analysis of the semen. If the sperm count is less than 20 million per millilitre, the cause may be sought and treated if possible.
• Tests to see whether the woman is ovulating. These usually include keeping a basal body temperature chart, observing the cervical mucus, and measuring blood hormones.
• Post-coital test. Some mucus is taken from a woman's cervix within 2 hours of intercourse. If moving sperm are found in this mucus it is certain that there are healthy sperm in the semen, that the semen is being deposited in the right place, and that there is no incompatibility between the seminal fluid and the cervical mucus.
• Tests to see whether or not the tubes are blocked. This may be done by X-ray (hysterosalpingogram), or by LAPAROSCOPY or LAPAROTOMY. If a blockage is found it may be able to be corrected by surgery.
• Sperm migration tests. The man's semen is tested with the woman's cervical mucus and donor cervical mucus to measure the progress of sperm through the mucus. If sperm movement is impeded in the partner's mucus, the cause (such as antibodies, infection) can be sought and treated.

About 10–12 per cent of couples are subfertile. For half of these couples the cause can be remedied. For those who remain infertile, possible options may be adoption, artificial insemination or IN-VITRO FERTILISATION.

INFLAMMATION
The body's reaction to infection, allergy or other injury – such as chemical, heat or mechanical injury. The affected part becomes swollen, red, tender and

hot to the touch and its function is disturbed. The suffix 'itis' is used to signify inflammation, as in APPENDICITIS, DERMATITIS, ARTHRITIS.

INFLUENZA (FLU)
An acute infectious disease caused by the influenza virus, of which there are many strains. Symptoms include chills and fever, headache, muscular aches and pains, loss of appetite, weakness and INFLAMMATION of the mucous membranes of nose and throat. Flu carries a high risk of complication by secondary bacterial infection of inflamed tissues, such as BRONCHITIS, OTITIS media and SINUSITIS. Although there are no specific drugs for treating influenza, complications may be treated with antibiotics. Otherwise treatment is by rest, aspirin to reduce fever, light diet and plenty of fluids. A degree of immunity against the most prevalent strains of the influenza virus can be given by vaccination and many doctors recommend such inoculation for elderly and frail people.

INOCULATION
See IMMUNISATION.

INSOMNIA
Inability to fall asleep or to remain asleep for long enough to be refreshed. Nearly everyone suffers from insomnia at one time or another. There are any number of causes including too much noise, too much light, too many or too few bedclothes, an uncomfortable mattress, too many cups of stimulating drinks such as coffee and tea close to bedtime, excitement, anxiety, depression and pain. Sleeping tablets may help in a brief crisis, but are potentially habit-forming. It is better to deal with the cause of the problem. If insomnia becomes a chronic problem, see your doctor.

INSULIN
A hormone, produced by the PANCREAS, which controls the process by which sugar in the blood is converted into energy. In DIABETES, there is either too little or a complete absence of insulin so that people with diabetes must have regular injections of insulin. Too much insulin in the blood causes HYPOGLYCAEMIA; too little results in HYPERGLYCAEMIA. (See How The Body Works, pp. 19–20.)

INTERCOURSE
A common abbreviation for SEXUAL INTERCOURSE. (See How The Body Works, p. 27.)

INTESTINE
The long coiled tube of the digestive system, commonly called the gut, running from stomach to anus and divided into two main parts, the small intestine (consisting of the duodenum, jejunum and ileum) and the large intestine (made up of the caecum, appendix, colon and rectum). (See How The Body Works, pp. 16–18.)

INTRAUTERINE DEVICE (IUD)
A contraceptive device which is inserted into the uterus to prevent pregnancy. The IUD works by causing a foreign body reaction in the lining of the uterus which prevents implantation of a fertilised egg. IUDs provide contraception for up to five years, though many doctors recommend that the device should be changed after two years. IUDs seem to suit about 75 per cent of women. The remainder experience menstrual or other problems which lead to removal of the device. See your doctor for complete information, and for assessment of whether this method of contraception would be suitable for you.

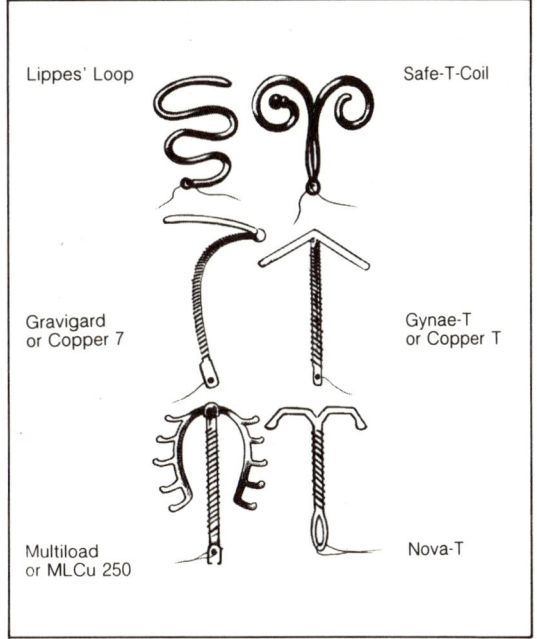

IUDs in common use.

INTRAVENOUS DRIP
A technique for replacing lost body fluids by introducing measured amounts of fluid into the bloodstream at a controlled rate. It may also be used to feed a very sick patient with liquid food such as glucose solution, or to administer drugs. The fluid is fed into the body through a tube fitted to a needle inserted into a vein, usually in the patient's arm.

INTROVERT
A person who is shy and quiet and mainly concerned with his or her own life and thoughts. Such a person

is usually happy when alone, values solitude and enjoys the inner satisfaction of reading and listening to music. The opposite type is the extrovert, an outgoing person who enjoys, and often needs, the company of other people.

IN-VITRO FERTILISATION

The fertilisation of an ovum outside the body, also known as extracorporeal fertilisation. This technique involves a mature egg being removed from the ovary (using a long hollow needle inserted through a laparoscope – see LAPAROSCOPY) and being fertilised under carefully controlled conditions in the laboratory. The fertilised ovum is returned to the woman's uterus at the four- or eight-cell stage, via a fine plastic tube inserted through the cervix. If the timing is right, the fertilised egg will implant in the lining of the womb and develop in the same way as a naturally fertilised egg. It is a delicate and complex procedure with no guarantees of success. There is a risk of spontaneous abortion within the first twelve weeks of gestation but generally around 25 per cent of women who receive extracorporeal fertilisation have successful pregnancies. There have been many such births since the first 'test tube baby' was conceived and born as a result of extracorporeal fertilisation in 1978.

IRIS

The coloured area surrounding the pupil of the eye. The colour of the iris, often dark blue in new-born babies, may later change to the colour determined by heredity. The iris expands and contracts to alter the size of the pupil so that the amount of light entering the eye through the pupil is controlled.

IRRADIATION

See RADIOTHERAPY.

ISCHAEMIA

A deficiency in the blood supply to a part of the body which may be the result of injury, narrowing or blockage of blood vessels, compression of tissue or severe anaemia. The results may be GANGRENE when a limb is affected, INFARCTION in the brain or lungs, or ANGINA or MYOCARDIAL INFARCTION when there is ischaemia in the muscles of the heart.

ITCHING

See PRURITUS.

JAUNDICE

This is not a disease itself but rather a symptom of disease or disorder. People with jaundice have a characteristic yellowish tinge to their skin and the whites of their eyes due to excessive amounts of bile pigment, known as bilirubin, in the blood and tissue fluids. There may be many different causes of jaundice, but the main ones include HEPATITIS where the liver is unable to deal with bile in the normal way, GALLSTONES which may block the bile duct, and the excessive breakdown of red blood cells (haemolysis) which may be due to certain poisons, infections such as malaria or some forms of anaemia. This last form of jaundice is frequently found in new-born babies when the liver is not developed enough to cope with the normal breakdown of red blood cells. It usually clears up in a couple of days. A serious cause of jaundice in new-born babies is RHESUS (Rh) FACTOR incompatibility, which results in haemolytic disease of the new-born. Jaundice from any cause subsides when the cause is corrected.

JOINT

The point where two bones come into contact, generally understood to mean the movable joints (the skull and the three bones of the pelvis are examples of fixed, or immovable, joints). Joints, which are lined with CARTILAGE, lubricated by a special synovial fluid and held in position by ligaments, can be divided into four basic groups: hinge joints such as in the fingers, knees and elbows; ball-and-socket joints such as in hips and shoulders; sliding joints such as those in the wrists and ankles; and pivot joints such as that between the head and the vertebrae of the neck. Joints may be affected by a number of disorders and diseases including sprains, fractures and dislocations, OSTEOARTHRITIS, RHEUMA-TOID ARTHRITIS, BURSITIS and GOUT. (See How The Body Works, pp. 2–3.)

JUGULAR VEIN

Among the largest in the body, the jugular is one of four veins, arranged in two paired internal and external branches, taking blood from the head and neck to the chest. The jugular is a sort of pressure gauge from which a doctor can obtain crucial information about the performance of the right side of the heart.

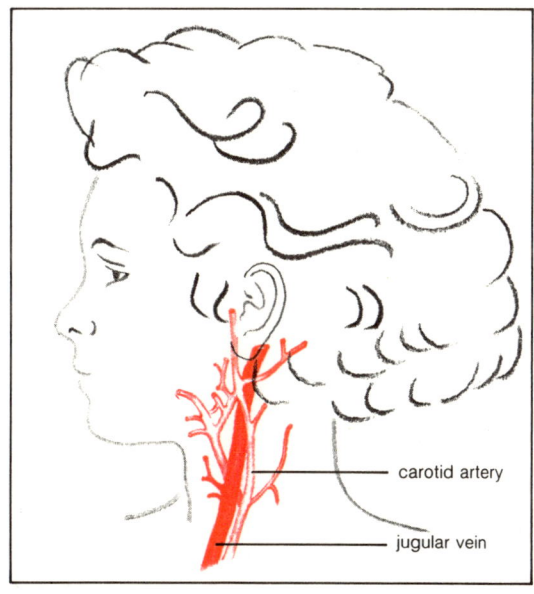

carotid artery

jugular vein

The jugular vein is not normally noticeable, but in right-sided heart failure it becomes distended with blood and is easily visible in the neck.

KELOID

An overgrowth of scar tissue in the skin during healing of a wound, burn or incision. The result is a raised, red, rubbery lump. It is more common in people with dark skin. Although not harmful, a keloid can be unsightly. With time it may become softer and less noticeable. Plastic surgery can usually correct disfiguring keloid.

KERATIN

The substance formed by skin cells which provides a waterproof layer on the surface of the skin. Modified keratin forms hair and nails and in other species, fur, feathers and scales.

KERATITIS

Inflammation of the cornea, due to infection, injury or deficiency of vitamin A. Symptoms include severe pain, sensitivity to light and watering and redness of the eye. Depending on the cause, it is treated with antibiotics, CORTISONE or vitamin A supplements. See VITAMINS.

KERATOPLASTY

A corneal graft. A delicate operation in which the cornea from a donor who has recently died is grafted on the patient's eye, replacing that person's own, non-functioning cornea. See also TRANSPLANT.

KERNICTERUS

A condition in babies with severe JAUNDICE in which the brain, particularly the nerve centres at the base of the brain, turn yellow. Symptoms include difficulty in breathing, writhing of the limbs and twitching of the face. It is most often associated with RHESUS disease, and with prompt diagnosis at or before birth can be effectively treated by phototherapy (exposure to special light) or exchange transfusion.

KETONES

Chemical compounds usually produced in the liver through the partial oxidation of protein and fat. Under normal circumstances, sugar rather than fat is metabolised to produce energy, but when fat is metabolised, a ketone called acetone is produced giving the breath a distinctive sharp, sweet smell. Excessive ketones in the body cause KETOSIS.

KETOSIS

A condition in which KETONE production reaches such a level that the body tissues cannot cope and the sufferer develops fast, panting breathing, nausea and vomiting, sometimes has the distinctive sweet smell of acetone on the breath and may go into a coma. The most common cause is DIABETES mellitus, when the body, unable to metabolise sugar for energy in the usual way, metabolises fat and produces ketones. Ketosis also occurs in starvation when the body needs to metabolise fat from its own stores. Ketosis in diabetics is corrected with injections of INSULIN.

KIDNEYS

A pair of organs lying high against the back wall of the abdomen, one each side of the spine. They filter and purify the blood with the waste products being passed out through the bladder as urine. (See How The Body Works, p. 18.)

KIDNEY DISORDERS

There are numerous diseases and disorders of the kidneys: some caused by infections such as PYELO-NEPHRITIS and PYELITIS; through inflammation as in NEPHRITIS; distension if the passage of urine is blocked as in HYDRONEPHROSIS; or by obstruction of urine drainage as in KIDNEY STONES; accidental injury; and other diseases such as ARTERIOSCLEROSIS, MALARIA, DIABETES and GOUT. CONGENITAL abnormalities include CYSTS which may be so severe in the kidneys of a foetus that the baby doesn't live long after birth, two kidneys on the same side of the body or lower down than normal – the last two conditions causing no problems if the out-of-place kidneys are otherwise normal. When kidneys become severely damaged the result is RENAL FAILURE, and DIALYSIS or kidney TRANSPLANT may be necessary. (See also Medical And Health Support Organisations.)

KIDNEY FAILURE
See RENAL FAILURE.

KIDNEY MACHINE
People with kidney failure (RENAL FAILURE) must regularly use this machine to purify their blood. The machine, which is connected to the patient by tubes inserted in blood vessels in the arm or leg, contains a dialysing fluid and a special membrane which holds back blood cells and proteins and allows through water and waste products. See also DIALYSIS. (See also Medical And Health Support Organisations.)

KIDNEY STONE
A solid mass variously made up of calcium salts, oxalates, phosphates, uric acid or the amino acid, cystine, which may develop as a result of kidney infections, excessive increase of calcium in the blood, certain metabolic diseases and even too much milk or alkaline substances in the diet. Some people seem to have a tendency to develop kidney stones and while very small particles may be passed out in the urine without the sufferer knowing, large stones may cause severe COLIC that runs through the groin and thighs and, in men, into the tip of the penis. Large stones are usually removed surgically or by litholapaxy or lithotripsy, and the patient given appropriate drugs and a special diet ·to prevent formation of more stones.

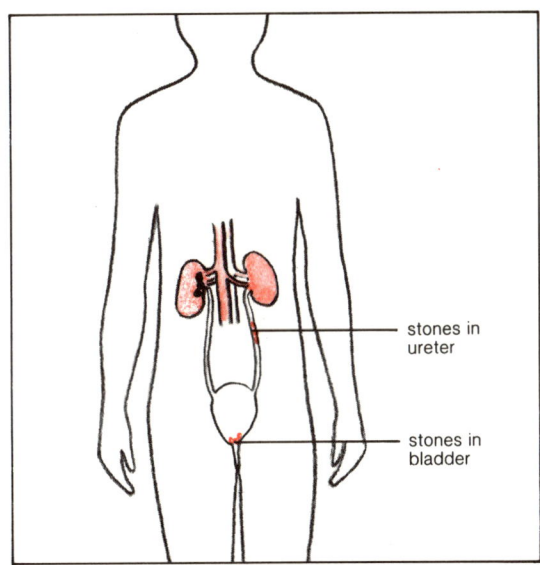

stones in
ureter

stones in
bladder

Stones may lodge anywhere in the urinary system. When a stone obstructs the flow of urine, severe colicky pain is felt in the abdomen, back or genitals.

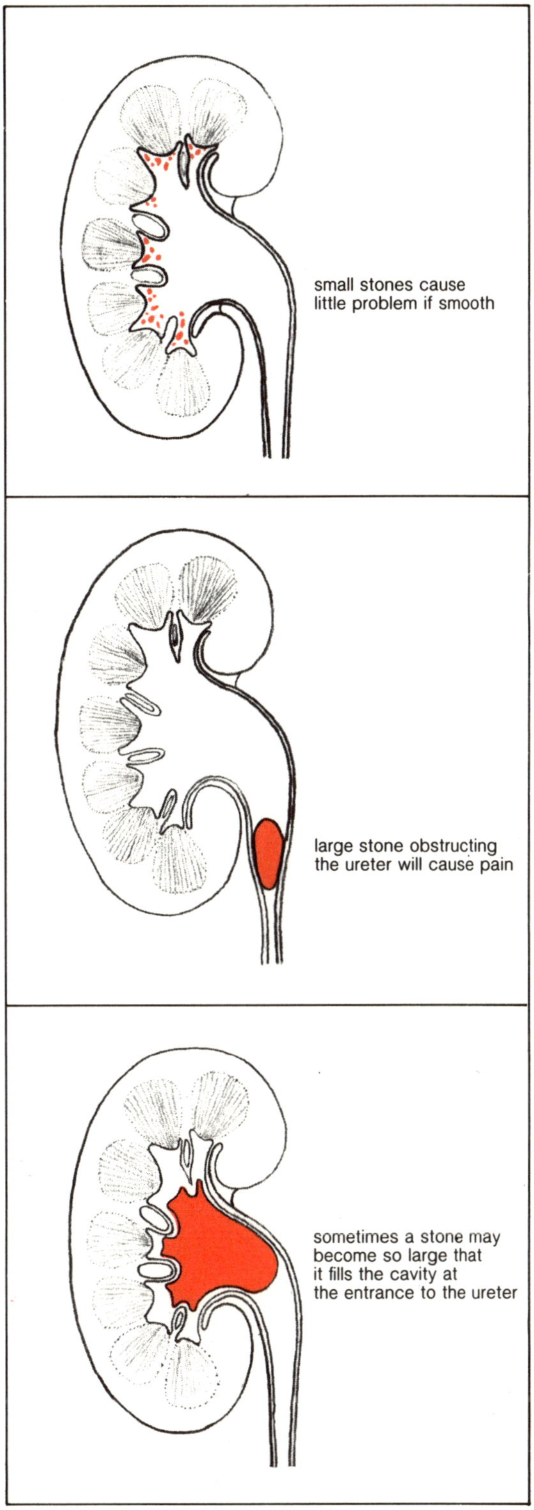

small stones cause little problem if smooth

large stone obstructing the ureter will cause pain

sometimes a stone may become so large that it fills the cavity at the entrance to the ureter

Types of kidney stone.

KILOJOULE

A unit, replacing the calorie, expressing the energy value of food.

KISS OF LIFE

Another term for mouth-to-mouth/expired air resuscitation. (See First Aid – RESUSCITATION.)

KLINEFELTER'S SYNDROME

A congential disorder of the CHROMOSOMES, in which a man has an extra X chromosome giving the combination XXY instead of XY (the normal male combination). Men with Klinefelter's syndrome are usually tall and thin with small TESTES which do not produce SPERM, and little body or facial hair.

KNOCK KNEE

A disorder, which starts in early childhood, in which the legs curve inwards so that the knees touch. The ankles are pushed further apart than usual and the feet may be flat. It may be caused by RICKETS, weak LIGAMENTS or injury to the soft bone ends of the knees. Children often outgrow the condition; otherwise it can be helped with special supports for the legs, exercise, manipulation and, in severe cases, surgery.

KOPLIK'S SPOTS

Small red spots with bluish-white centres which form in the MUCOUS MEMBRANES of the mouth in MEASLES, usually before the characteristic body rash appears.

KYPHOSIS

Excessive outward curvature of the spine, resulting in a hump on the upper back. Although it may be caused by severe back injury, congenital malformation or such diseases as TUBERCULOSIS and SPONDYLITIS, it is most often found today in old people, especially women (the 'dowagers' hump'), whose vertebrae become thin and collapse because of OSTEOPOROSIS.

LABOUR

The final stage of pregnancy, during which the products of conception (foetus, membranes, placenta) separate from the mother and are delivered into the outside world. There are three stages of labour. The **first stage** starts with rhythmic contractions of the uterus and is completed when the cervix is fully dilated. During the **second stage**, further contractions of the uterus push the infant through the dilated cervix and vagina to the outside world. The **third stage** lasts until the placenta and membranes are expelled and the rhythmic contractions cease. (See also How The Body Works, pp. 28–30.)

LABYRINTHITIS

Inflammation of the inner ear, usually caused by viral infection. Symptoms include giddiness, loss of balance, nausea and vomiting, and TINNITUS. There is no specific treatment. Rest and relief of symptoms are usually followed by spontaneous recovery.

LACERATION

A break in the surface of the skin or any organ or tissue, made by any tearing, cutting or deforming force.

LACTATION

The production of milk by glands in the breast, which begins about three days after the birth of a baby. Immediately after birth, the breast produces a fluid called COLOSTRUM which nourishes the baby until lactation is established. The act of the baby suckling stimulates the PITUITARY GLAND to produce the hormone prolactin which in turn stimulates the production of milk. As long as breast-feeding is continued, milk will be produced.

LAPAROSCOPY

Endoscopic examination of the abdominal or pelvic cavities. (See Medical Tests And Examinations.)

LAPAROTOMY

The exploratory, surgical opening of the abdomen in order to examine the organs for signs of suspected disorder or disease.

LARYNGITIS

Inflammation of the voice-box or LARYNX, causing hoarseness or loss of voice and, in severe cases, harsh and wheezy breathing. There are many causes of laryngitis including bacterial or viral infection, allergy, irritation from inhaled pollutants, and even too much talking or shouting. The best treatment is to address the cause, plus resting the voice.

LARYNX

The organ that produces speech, also known as the

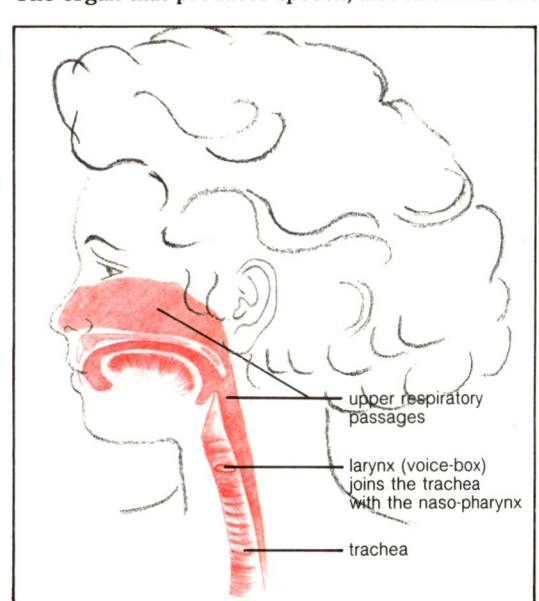

The upper respiratory passages are indicated by the shaded area. Upper respiratory infections are often complicated by laryngitis.

voice-box, in the upper part of the respiratory passages. The larynx is made up of cartilage, muscles and ligaments, the largest cartilage making the Adam's apple. The two most important ligaments, the vocal cords, can be vibrated by air passing through them to make sound and thus speech.

LASER

An acronym for Light Amplification by Stimulated Emission of Radiation, the laser is a device for generating a very narrow, concentrated beam of light energy. Because it can be focused with great precision, it is used in medicine for operations that must be performed on a very small area without the surrounding tissue being touched.

LAXATIVE

A medicine that is given to help empty the contents of the bowels. There are several types. Bulk laxatives, such as unprocessed bran and certain vegetables and fruit fibres containing much cellulose, cause the FAECES to become softer and bulkier and therefore easier to pass; some, such as senna and castor oil, cause the intestinal muscle to contract, so forcing the waste matter along the gut; while others, like liquid paraffin, soften the faeces and lubricate the bowel. Prolonged use of laxatives for CONSTIPATION is not a good idea. Rather the cause of constipation should be investigated and then treated. Quite often a high-fibre, well-balanced diet and plenty of fluids solve the problem.

LEAD POISONING

The absorption of lead, or lead salts, by the body resulting in symptoms such as anaemia, stomach cramp, weight loss, constipation and convulsions. Lead poisoning may occur through inhalation of car exhaust fumes, inhalation of lead dust or absorption of lead through the skin (as might occur in some manufacturing industries using lead), or, in children, chewing on objects that have a coating of lead-based paint.

LEGIONNAIRE'S DISEASE

A newly recognised, severe, infectious lung disease caused by BACTERIA (*Legionella pneumophila*) which may breed in warm stagnant water and may be spread by air-conditioning systems. It was first identified as a result of an outbreak at an American Legion convention in Philadelphia in 1976. Symptoms include headache, muscular aches and pains, fever, chest pain, chills, cough and sometimes nausea, vomiting, diarrhoea and abdominal pain. As yet there is no effective immunisation, but the disease can usually be successfully treated with antibiotics.

LEPROSY

Also called Hansen's disease, it is a chronic infectious bacterial disease of the skin, nerves, muscles and bones, which develops over a long period and can result in loss of sensation, tissue destruction, paralysis and deformity. The disease can now be cured by specific sulphone drugs, though treatment must be continued for several years.

LESBIANISM

Sexual love of one woman for another. See also HOMOSEXUALITY.

LEUCOCYTES

(See How The Body Works, p. 5.)

LEUCOCYTOSIS

When the body's normal defence mechanism to fight disease and infection is in progress, the number of white blood cells, or leucocytes, rapidly increases. A raised white cell count is known as leucocytosis.

LEUCORRHOEA

An abnormal white or yellowish mucous discharge from the VAGINA. Some clear mucous discharge is normal but excessive vaginal discharge associated with itching and an unpleasant smell could indicate VAGINITIS.

LEUKAEMIA

A form of cancer affecting the bone marrow and other blood-forming tissues causing over-production of leucocytes (white blood cells). Leukaemia can be either acute or chronic. In acute lymphoblastic leukaemia, which affects children, leukaemic cells replace the normal cells of the bone marrow. Acute myeloblastic leukaemia usually occurs in middle age; chronic myeloblastic leukaemia, in which the liver and spleen become enlarged, and chronic lymphatic leukaemia, in which liver, spleen and lymph nodes may become enlarged, mostly affect elderly people. In general, leukaemia causes suppression of the production of red blood cells and other blood constituents resulting in ANAEMIA, recurrent infections, pains in joints and bones, bleeding disorders such as nosebleeds and bruising, weight loss, fever, night sweats and lack of energy. The cause of leukaemia is unknown, but treatment with anti-leukaemic drugs, RADIOTHERAPY, blood transfusions and sometimes bone marrow transplants, will often result in remission. (See also Medical And Health Support Organisations – CANCER.)

LIBIDO

The natural sex urge which is directed towards the achievement of pleasure in the form of sexual climax. Libido is part of the instinctive reproductive drive. It may be reduced by certain prescribed drugs, alcoholism, drug addiction, age, illness, anxiety, stress and emotional and psychosexual problems.

LICE

Wingless insect parasites which may infest people by clinging to the hair and sucking blood from the skin. There are three different kinds of lice which affect people: body lice, or *Pediculus corporis*, which usually live and lay eggs in clothing; head lice, or *Pediculus capitus*, which live in the scalp; and pubic lice, or *Phthirus pubis*, commonly called crabs, which live in the pubic hair and sometimes other body hair such as in the armpits. The tiny eggs (nits) of pubic and head lice stick to the hairs. Lice are passed on by direct contact and cause uncomfortable itching. There are a number of proprietary preparations which simply and effectively get rid of them.

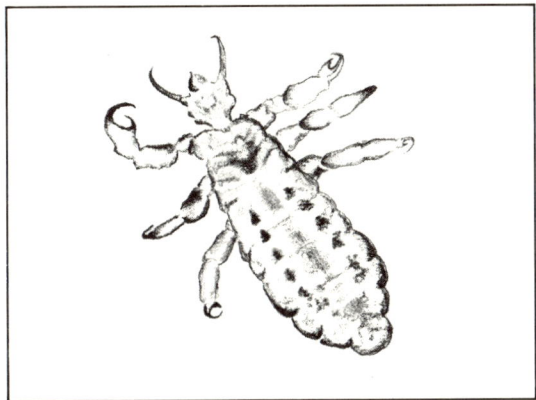

The body louse, 3–6 mm long, lives and lays its eggs in clothing and bites the body to suck blood.

LIGAMENT

A band of tough connective tissue which binds together the ends of bones where they form joints. Ligaments may strengthen and support the bones of a joint and help limit its movements to those for which it was designed. Ligaments also help keep an organ of the body in place. Sometimes through sprain, fracture or excessive physical activity, the ligaments may become stretched or torn. A torn ligament can be as serious as a broken bone and must be well rested with the joint carefully and firmly supported until the ligament is completely healed.

LIPOMA

A benign TUMOUR of adipose (fatty) tissue appearing as soft lumps under the skin.

LITHOTOMY

In correct medical terms, a surgical operation to remove CALCULUS, or stone, from any organ or duct, though usually referring to the bladder, ureter or urethra. Small stones may be removed in a non-surgical procedure known as litholapaxy or lithotrity, whereby a special instrument, inserted into the bladder through the urethra, crushes the stones so that they can be easily flushed out.

LIVER

(See How The Body Works, pp. 19–21.)

LOCHIA

The discharge from the VAGINA which lasts for a week or so following childbirth. Made up of mucus, shed tissue and blood, it is a reddish brown colour at first and gradually becomes paler as it decreases in quantity.

LOW BLOOD PRESSURE

See HYPOTENSION.

LSD

An extremely powerful drug causing HALLUCINATIONS. Its name is derived from the three words of its chemical name: lysergic acid diethylamide. It is commonly known as 'acid'. It alters normal emotions, perception and judgement and its unauthorised possession is prohibited by law in most countries.

LUMBAGO

A general term used to describe pain in the lower back, caused by a variety of strains, sprains and other disorders. See also BACKACHE, SLIPPED DISC, ARTHRITIS.

LUMBAR PUNCTURE

A procedure in which a sample of cerebrospinal fluid is taken from the spinal canal using a hollow needle which is inserted in the lumbar region (small of the back), usually between the fourth and fifth lumbar vertebrae. It is used as an aid to diagnosis and may help detect such diseases and disorders as MENINGITIS and brain HAEMORRHAGE. (See Medical Tests And Examinations – SPINAL TAP.)

LUNGS

A pair of organs located in the chest and responsible for respiration. Every organ in the body needs oxygen and the lungs play a crucial role in providing the body's life-giving supply of oxygen. (See How The Body Works, pp. 10–11.)

LUNG CANCER

One of the most common forms of CANCER, and most often found in heavy smokers, particularly men over 45. A person who smokes a packet of cigarettes a day is fifteen times more likely to get lung cancer than a non-smoker. There are relatively few symptoms in the early stages, but later there may be a persistent cough, weight loss, shortness of breath, wheezing and blood-stained phlegm. Untreated lung cancer spreads to other parts of the body through the lymphatic system. Treatment includes surgical removal of the tumour, RADIOTHERAPY or drug therapy.

LUNG DISORDERS
See ASTHMA, BRONCHITIS, EMPHYSEMA, PNEUMONIA, PLEURISY, LUNG CANCER.

LYMPH
(See How The Body Works, pp. 5–9.)

LYMPHATIC SYSTEM
(See How The Body Works, pp. 5–9.)

MALABSORPTION
Failure to absorb adequate nourishment even though the diet is satisfactory. Malabsorption may be temporary or permanent, and is a result of inflammatory bowel disease or disturbances of digestive enzymes.

MALAISE
A general term for feeling unwell. It may signify the onset of an infectious illness, or may be associated with an established illness. Symptoms include loss of appetite and energy, aching joints and muscles, weakness, difficulty in thinking clearly, and headache.

MALARIA
A tropical disease, marked by severe chills and fever, caused by a microscopic parasite called *Plasmodium* carried by mosquitoes and introduced into the human bloodstream through the mosquito's bite. The parasites invade the red blood cells and multiply, eventually causing the cells to burst. Symptoms include severe, regularly recurring bouts of fever and prostration. After repeated attacks of malaria, a person will develop anaemia and the liver and spleen will become enlarged. Quinine was once the only drug available for treatment but today new, more effective drugs have been developed to prevent and treat the disease. While the malaria mosquito is confined to certain regions of the world, it is important for travellers who intend visiting such places to take a course of preventative drugs.

MALIGNANT
The term used to describe a TUMOUR or growth that invades nearby organs or tissues and spreads to other parts of the body via the blood or lymph streams. The opposite of malignant is BENIGN.

MAMMARY GLANDS
The female breasts that produce milk in LACTATION. See also MASTECTOMY.

MANIA
A disorder marked by over-excited, over-confident behaviour, quick and excessive movement and a garrulous manner. Often it is associated with manic-depressive psychosis, a severe mental disorder in which the sufferer swings between moods of extreme excitement and profound depression. Manic-depressive psychosis needs specialist, long-term psychiatric care.

MARIJUANA
Also known as grass, tea, pot, it is the most widely used and abused of the hallucinogenic drugs. It is prepared from the leaves, stalks and flowers of the Indian hemp plant and usually smoked in cigarettes. The sticky resin, CANNABIS, is the most potent part of the plant. The drug usually creates a pleasurable feeling of well-being although mental and physical capabilities may be diminished. Marijuana is illegal.

MASOCHISM
An abnormal sexual state in which a person is sexually gratified by being physically or mentally abused. It is named after a 19th-century Austrian novelist, Leopold von Sacher-Masoch, whose life and work detailed the abnormality. In more general terms however, masochism is used to describe a self-destructive person who has little self-esteem, who unconsciously seeks punishment and humiliation through feelings of worthlessness, guilt and anxiety.

MASTECTOMY
Surgical removal of the breast. When tumours of the breast are found, it is usual for the doctor to perform a BIOPSY (removal of a piece of the tumour tissue) to find out whether the tumour is BENIGN (non-cancerous) or MALIGNANT (cancerous). If the tumour is malignant, and depending on the extent of the tumour and the opinion of the surgeon, either a

partial mastectomy may be performed where only that part of the breast containing the tumour is removed, or a total mastectomy is carried out to remove the entire breast. A radical mastectomy, which is performed less frequently these days, involves removing the breast, the underlying pectoral muscles and the lymph nodes in the nearby armpit. A successful outcome depends on the stage at which the cancerous growth is removed, whether or not it has spread to other parts of the body (known as METASTASIS) and the various combinations of hormone, drug and radiation therapy that may be given as necessary follow-up treatment to surgery. (See also Medical And Health Support Organisations.)

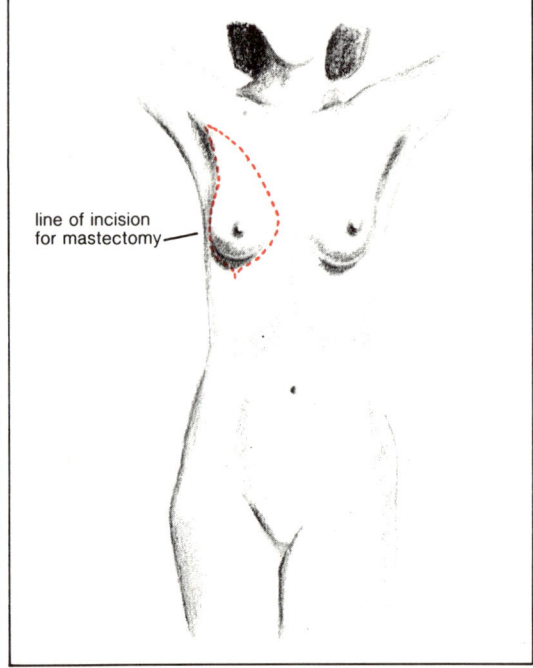

line of incision
for mastectomy —

In cases of cancerous tumour, the breast may be partially or wholly removed in a surgical operation known as mastectomy.

MASTITIS

Inflammation of the breast due to bacterial infection which causes the breast to become red and painful, with associated fever and malaise. Mastitis usually occurs in women who are lactating, the infection getting into the breast through a cracked nipple. It subsides rapidly with ANTIBIOTIC treatment.

MASTOIDITIS

Inflammation of the prominent bone just behind the ear, known as the mastoid process, due mostly to spread of infection from the middle ear. It causes headache, fever and local pain and swelling. It is usually successfully treated with antibiotics but if the complaint recurs, or the bone becomes chronically infected, it may be surgically removed in an operation called a mastoidectomy.

MASTURBATION

Stimulation of one's own genitals to achieve orgasm. It is a harmless, normal activity used by most people as a sexual outlet or to relieve emotional tension.

MEASLES

A common, highly infectious disease, usually occurring in childhood, caused by a virus. Although it can affect people of any age, most adults who had measles when they were children have lifelong immunity. Symptoms include high temperature, cough and runny nose in the first stage, then KOPLIK'S SPOTS appear inside the cheeks. A day or two later a pink rash appears on the face, neck and torso. The most common complications of measles are MIDDLE EAR INFECTION, BRONCHOPNEUMONIA and ENCEPHALITIS. A straightforward case of measles is treated with bedrest, a light diet, plenty of fluids and aspirin to reduce fever. Complications may require antibiotic treatment. VACCINATION against measles has been in use since 1968 and is usually given to a child in the second year of life. See IMMUNISATION.

MECONIUM

The dark green, thick bowel discharge of a baby in the first few days of life, consisting of bile and intestinal waste accumulated in the baby's intestine before birth.

MEGALOMANIA

In strict terms, a mental illness in which a person has delusions of grandeur or great power. In general terms, it is often used to describe a person who is inordinately ambitious with an intense drive to gain great public power.

MELANCHOLIA

Another name for DEPRESSION. Most cases respond to treatment with anti-depressant drugs.

MELANIN

The brown or black pigment that gives dark colouring to the skin, hair and iris of the eye.

MELANOMA

A dark brown-coloured tumour of the skin, due to overactivity of the melanin-producing cells. Any new brown or black swelling or mole that suddenly starts to grow should be promptly checked because melanomas can become MALIGNANT (cancerous) and may rapidly spread throughout the body.

MELENA
Unpleasant-smelling black stools due to blood in the FAECES indicating bleeding from PEPTIC ulceration, bowel tumours, or inflammation of the intestines. Melena may also be due to swallowed blood from a nosebleed but obviously it is a condition that should be checked by your doctor.

MENARCHE
The first MENSTRUATION, or monthly period, which occurs during puberty.

MENIÈRE'S DISEASE
A progressive disease of the inner ear caused by swelling and an increase of fluid in the internal part of the ear. Symptoms include bouts of dizziness, NAUSEA, vomiting, VERTIGO, ringing in the ears and deafness. The cause is unknown. While there is no definitive cure, a doctor may recommend appropriate drug treatment to alleviate the symptoms. However, many sufferers, who are mostly men over the age of 40, have only mild, occasional attacks which require little treatment.

MENINGITIS
Inflammation of the meninges (the membranes covering the brain and spinal cord) caused by either viral or bacterial infection. It is a serious illness which can affect all age groups but is mostly found in children. Symptoms include severe headache, fever, vomiting, sensitivity to light and stiffness and pain in the neck and back muscles. Examination of a sample of cerebrospinal fluid, taken by LUMBAR PUNCTURE, confirms the diagnosis and determines whether the cause is bacterial or viral because the symptoms of both are the same. If untreated, bacterial meningitis can lead to convulsions, coma and possible death. With prompt antibiotic treatment bacterial meningitis can be successfully cured. There is no specific drug treatment for viral meningitis, but recovery is often spontaneous.

MENOPAUSE
The time in a woman's life during which MENSTRUATION becomes irregular and finally ceases, also known as change of life or climacteric. It usually takes place between the ages of 40 and 55. During the menopause, the ovaries no longer release eggs and begin to curtail production of the female hormones. The change in the balance of the hormones causes the uterus to become smaller and the walls of the vagina thinner and drier, making sex difficult or painful. Characteristic bodily responses to oestrogen lack are hot flushes, headaches and palpitations, which may last from six months to three years. While some women find it physically and emotionally difficult, with modern treatment such as HORMONE REPLACEMENT THERAPY and considerate care from her family and doctor, the menopause need not be a time of great stress.

MENORRHAGIA
Excessive menstrual bleeding – more than 80 ml per MENSTRUATION. Causes include hormone imbalance, infections or tumours in the uterus, ovary or fallopian tube. Menorrhagia should be reported to your doctor so that the cause can be sought and corrected.

MENSTRUATION
Periodic bleeding in women which starts at the MENARCHE and finishes with the MENOPAUSE. The usual time between one period of menstruation and the next is about twenty-eight days. It is one stage in a constant cycle in which an egg, or OVUM, develops in the ovary and at a given time, about halfway through the cycle, is released into the FALLOPIAN TUBE (in a process called OVULATION) to travel down to the uterus. If the ovum is not fertilised, tissue and blood from the lining of the uterus (endometrium) is discharged from the vagina as the menstrual flow. See also AMENORRHOEA, MENORRHAGIA, DYSMENORRHOEA. (See How The Body Works, p. 26.)

MENTAL RETARDATION
A general term describing low intelligence as a result of either defective brain development, or infection or injury suffered during birth or early childhood. There are varying degrees of retardation. Most psychologists define intelligence as a person's ability to successfully adapt to the environment, and the capacity to learn and deal with abstract ideas. Even though low intelligence might be confirmed, there are many people in that category who have some encouraging, positive degree of ability to be productive and take care of themselves. Because mentally retarded people are slow learners, they need love, patience and understanding. Many specially equipped and staffed schools and workshops are now providing for these needs. (See Medical And Health Support Organisations.)

METABOLISM
(See How The Body Works, pp. 19–21.)

METACARPAL
One of the five long bones in the hand which join the fingers to the wrist.

METASTASIS
The spread of cancer cells from one part of the body, usually the site of a primary malignant growth, to other parts to form secondary or metastatic tumours.

METATARSAL
One of the five long bones in the foot which joins the toes to bones under the heel.

MIDDLE EAR INFECTION
Any infection of the part of the ear just inside the eardrum, usually as a complication of such disorders as infected ADENOIDS or TONSILS, COMMON COLD, INFLUENZA, MEASLES, SCARLET FEVER. Symptoms include severe earache, high temperature, vomiting, headache and drowsiness. OTITIS media, as it is called, responds promptly to appropriate antibiotic treatment.

MIGRAINE
An intense, throbbing headache, usually confined to one side of the head. Migraine is the result of spasm followed by dilation of blood vessels in the head, often triggered by stress, dietary factors or hormonal changes. Migraine may also occur at times of release of tension, such as weekends or holidays. Attacks may last for hours or days, and are often preceded by premonitory symptoms such as visual disturbances, weakness on one side of the body and hallucinations of smell. The onset of headache is usually accompanied by nausea and vomiting, running nose and flushing and sweating of the face, and sensitivity to noise, light and odours. Treatment during attacks includes rest, quiet and darkness, analgesics and specific anti-migraine medication.

Prevention of migraine may be helped by avoiding trigger factors, and the use of drugs to control hypersensitivity of blood vessels. All migraine sufferers are well advised to consult a neurologist or attend a headache clinic for personalised advice about how best to prevent or manage this disabling condition.

MISCARRIAGE
See spontaneous ABORTION.

MITRAL VALVE DISEASE
Disease of the heart's mitral valve which separates the left atrium from the left ventricle. Mitral valve disease usually occurs as a complication of RHEUMATIC FEVER with ENDOCARDITIS. If the inflamed valve becomes stretched it may fail to close properly, allowing blood to flow back into the atrium when the ventricle contracts. This is mitral incompetence. Mitral stenosis occurs when the valve opening is narrowed by scarring, reducing the amount of blood which can flow from atrium to ventricle. Each type of mitral valve disease causes a typical HEART MURMUR, and can lead to left-sided heart failure. In such cases, surgery is necessary to correct the valve defect or to replace the damaged valve with a plastic PROSTHESIS.

MOLE
See MELANOMA.

MONGOLISM
Another name for DOWN'S SYNDROME.

MONILIASIS
An infection caused by the fungus *Candida albicans*. This fungus is normally found in small quantities in the mouth, vagina, bowel, and on skin. When local conditions allow overgrowth of the fungus, monilial inflammation occurs. The common forms of moniliasis include thrush, which affects the mucous membranes of the mouth causing white patches on the inside of the cheeks; vaginal moniliasis, which is one of the commonest causes of irritating vaginal discharge in women (see VAGINITIS); and moniliasis of the skin, which produces an acute DERMATITIS in areas likely to remain moist, such as in the armpit, in the groin around the anus, and under babies' napkins. Moniliasis is successfully treated with specific anti-fungals by local application or by mouth.

MONONUCLEOSIS
Commonly known as glandular fever, mononucleosis is a contagious disease in which the blood contains an abnormally high number of large white blood cells. It is caused by a virus and spread is airborne. Glandular fever mostly affects people under the age of 35, especially those in colleges, hostels or communities where many people live closely together. Symptoms include sore throat, fever, headache, tiredness and swollen lymph glands in the neck, armpits and groin. Sometimes the spleen becomes enlarged and the liver affected, resulting in HEPATITIS and JAUNDICE. Most often infectious mononucleosis is a mild disorder, although symptoms may last or recur for weeks. There is no specific treatment. Rest and a good diet will speed up spontaneous recovery.

MORNING SICKNESS
The nausea, and in some cases, vomiting, that occurs early in pregnancy. Most women experience it on getting up in the morning, hence its name, although the nauseated feeling can occur any time during the day. It generally passes after two or three months.

MORPHINE
A NARCOTIC drug derived from opium and used in medicine as a powerful and effective pain reliever. Because of its addictive potential its use is strictly controlled.

MOTOR NEURONE DISEASE
Progressive deterioration of the nerve cells which

control the voluntary muscles, resulting in progressive paralysis. The cause is unknown.

MUCOUS MEMBRANE
(See How The Body Works, pp. 10–11, 16–17.)

MUCUS
The viscous fluid – made up of mucin (secreted by special cells in the mucous membrane), water, sloughed off cells, white blood cells and dissolved salts – that protects and lubricates the lining membranes of the respiratory and digestive systems. (See How The Body Works, pp. 10–11, 16–17.)

MULTIPLE SCLEROSIS (MS)
Also known as disseminated sclerosis, it is a CHRONIC disease of the nervous system in which the insulating sheaths around nerve fibres of the brain and spinal cord are affected. The disease, which is thought to be caused by a slow virus infection, begins in young adulthood and affects more women than men. Early symptoms include episodes of disturbed vision, pins and needles, muscular weakness, and clumsiness, which come and go – usually with long periods of normal health between attacks. The disease may progress over the years to loss of vision, loss of sensation and paralysis. There is no cure, but progress of MS can be slowed by the use of corticosteroid drugs, and physiotherapy helps when weakened muscles are recovering. (See Medical And Health Support Organisations.)

MUMPS
An epidemic viral infection which causes inflammation of the salivary glands. Symptoms are fever and painful swelling of the affected glands – usually those around the ear lobe and under the chin. Mumps is usually a mild illness with spontaneous recovery after a week or so. It is occasionally complicated by inflammation of the gonads (testes or ovaries) or LABYRINTHITIS. There is no specific treatment. Management consists of rest and bland diet; strongly flavoured or acid foods such as fruit juices aggravate the pain in the affected salivary glands. See IMMUNISATION.

MURMUR
See HEART MURMUR.

MUSCULAR DYSTROPHY
A group of inherited diseases characterised by progressive weakness and degeneration of skeletal muscle fibres without any evidence of nerve degeneration. There are several different types, each affecting muscles in a particular part of the body such as the calves, the face and shoulders, the shoulders only, and the pelvis. The disease often begins in childhood, causing a waddling gait, abnormalities of spinal curvature, frequent falling, and difficulty in standing up and in climbing stairs. There is no cure. Treatment involves massage, exercise and physiotherapy, plus counselling and advice for the family from support organisations. (See Medical And Health Support Organisations.)

MYASTHENIA GRAVIS
A chronic disorder of muscles, especially those of the head and neck, characterised by progressive tiredness and weakness of the muscles as the day goes on. For example, movements such as blinking, swallowing and coughing may be normal at the beginning of the day but rapidly deteriorate throughout the day. The cause is suspected to be an immunological disorder, associated with the THYMUS gland, which interferes with the chemical transmitters involved when stimulating impulses pass from nerves to muscles. Removal of the thymus gland often gives good results. If not, the use of drugs to improve nerve-to-muscle transmission is usually satisfactory, but this treatment must be kept up indefinitely. Sometimes spontaneous improvement occurs, but the condition usually relapses.

MYCETOMA
A chronic, slowly-spreading inflammation of the skin and underlying tissues caused by a variety of fungi. Mycetoma usually affects the feet, and occurs in tropical climates (where it is known as madura foot). The infection starts in or under the skin, from where it spreads to the deeper tissues and, in time, may destroy bone and muscle. The swelling which develops may discharge pus through multiple openings onto the skin. The condition is surprisingly painless unless secondary bacterial infection has occurred. Treatment is by the appropriate antibiotics or antifungals. When there has been widespread tissue destruction, amputation of the foot may be necessary.

MYELITIS (ACUTE TRANSVERSE MYELITIS)
Inflammation affecting the grey and white matter in one or several adjacent segments of the spinal cord. Myelitis may complicate ENCEPHALITIS, viral infections, SYPHILIS or MULTIPLE SCLEROSIS, but often no cause is found. Symptoms are sudden back pain followed by PARAPLEGIA or QUADRIPLEGIA, depending on the level of the affected part of the spinal cord. CORTICOSTEROID drugs may be given to decrease the inflammation. Recovery is sometimes complete, but more often there is some remaining loss of movement and sensation after the acute inflammation subsides.

MYELOMA
A rare MALIGNANT (cancerous) TUMOUR of the bone marrow, which is progressive and usually fatal.

MYOCARDIAL INFARCTION

Also known as HEART ATTACK, myocardial infarction is death or severe damage to an area of heart muscle due to blockage of one or more of the coronary arteries when the blood supply is cut off. The most common symptom is constricting pain in the chest which may spread into the left arm. Pain may also be felt between the shoulder-blades and in the right arm. Often it is associated with breathlessness, cold sweats, a panicky, frightened feeling and sometimes loss of consciousness. A doctor should be called immediately if heart attack is suspected. (See First Aid – HEART ATTACK.)

MYOCARDITIS

Another name for the heart disease called cardiomyopathy in which the heart muscle becomes inflamed. It occurs as a complication of such infections as DIPHTHERIA and RHEUMATIC FEVER in early life. Later it may be caused by a number of virus infections.

MYOPATHY

A general term referring to any disease in which muscle wastage occurs, either due to inherited factors as in MUSCULAR DYSTROPHY, in wasting disease such as CANCER, or associated with chronic illness such as DIABETES mellitus.

MYOPIA

Commonly known as short-sightedness, it is the ability to see things clearly only at close range. The opposite condition is hypermetropia, or long-sightedness.

MYXOEDEMA

A disease caused by the inability of the THYROID GLAND to secrete adequate amounts of the hormone thyroxine (HYPOTHYROIDISM). It affects more women than men and tends to appear in people around the age of 45. Symptoms include thickening of the skin (especially of the eyelids and cheeks, causing altered appearance), dry skin, thinning of the hair, slowing of speech, deepening of voice, listlessness and apathy, constipation, menstrual disturbance, muscular aches, and abnormal sensations (pins and needles). The onset of symptoms is usually insidious, making diagnosis difficult. Causes of myxoedema include autoimmune destruction of the thyroid gland, over-treatment of THYROTOXICOSIS, and pituitary disorders. It is rarely due to lack of iodine in the diet. Diagnosis is confirmed by blood tests. Treatment is by oral administration of thyroid hormone, usually for the rest of life.

NAEVUS

Any permanent, coloured skin blemish. The term is usually reserved for blemishes caused by abnormalities of blood vessels of the skin (see BIRTHMARK), but is sometimes used to describe certain moles.

NAPPY RASH

Red, inflamed patches of skin on the area covered by a baby's nappy. It is usually caused by the ammonia which forms in the baby's urine. At the first sign of nappy rash, apply a barrier cream to the affected areas and keep the skin as dry and clean as possible by changing the nappy frequently. Keep nappies bacteria free by soaking them in an antiseptic solution, then rinse them thoroughly. It also helps if the baby is left for an hour or two each day without a nappy so that the skin is exposed to the light and air. If nappy rash has not improved after 24 hours, see your doctor.

NARCOLEPSY

A chronic condition in which a person has a tendency to fall asleep at any time, usually for about 10 minutes or so, but can be easily roused. It is sometimes associated with sleep paralysis, where the person is awake but unable to move, and cataplexy, where the person feels weak, loses muscle tone and falls down. There is no known cause of narcolepsy and a person with the condition, which tends to recur, seems to suffer no ill effects. It can be treated with specific drugs but most doctors suggest that a person who has experienced narcolepsy shouldn't drive or operate potentially dangerous machinery.

NARCOSIS

A state of stupor or unconsciousness usually brought on by NARCOTIC drugs.

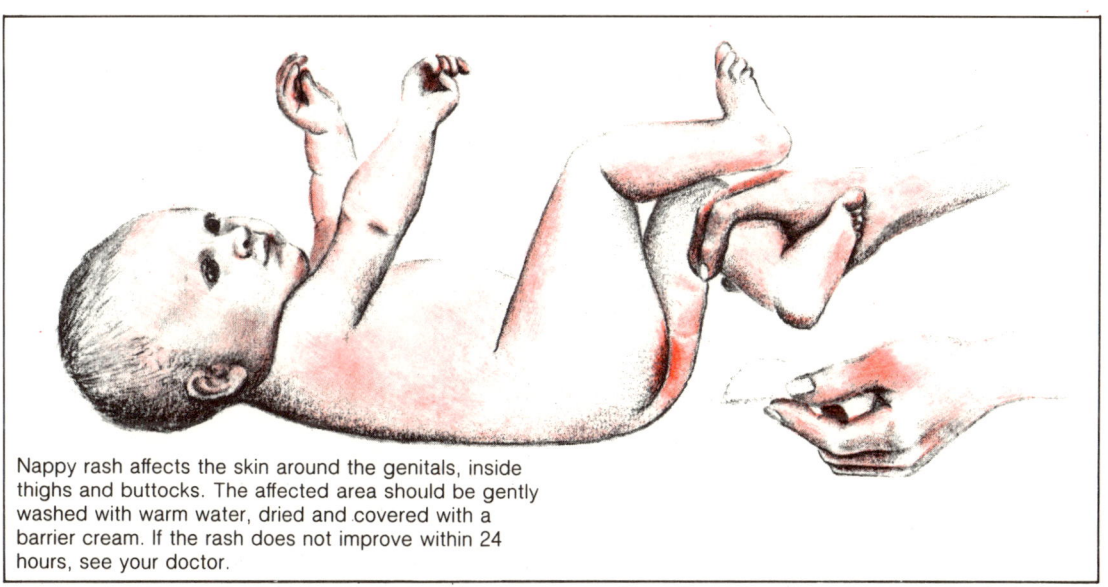

Nappy rash affects the skin around the genitals, inside thighs and buttocks. The affected area should be gently washed with warm water, dried and covered with a barrier cream. If the rash does not improve within 24 hours, see your doctor.

NARCOTIC

Any substance that produces stupor, dulling of the consciousness and relieves pain. Narcotics include opium and all its derivatives including MORPHINE and HEROIN. Pethidine and methadone, often used as analgesics, are synthetic narcotics. Because narcotic drugs induce addiction or dependence if used repeatedly, they are under strict legal and medical control. See also ADDICTION and DRUG ABUSE.

NASAL FEEDING

A method of feeding a person whose digestive system is working but who cannot swallow. A thin polythene naso-gastric tube is passed into the stomach through a nostril and the oesophagus (gullet). Liquid food is slowly passed into the stomach through the tube.

NATUROPATHY

Naturopathy, a system of alternative medicine based on the belief that people have within their bodies the resources not only to maintain good health but also to fight disease (orthodox medicine also believes this but calls it the immune system). Naturopathy advocates the use of certain 'natural food' diets, fasting, yoga, relaxation and breathing exercises, herbal therapy and remedies, and other diets and life-styles such as macrobiotic and vegetarianism.

NAUSEA

The medical term for the feeling of sickness that is usually relieved by VOMITING. Nausea may be caused by too much food, too much alcohol, foods that are too rich or too spicy, contaminated foods, tension and anxiety, MORNING SICKNESS, travel sickness and certain drugs such as some antibiotics. More seriously, nausea is a symptom of a large number of illnesses including GASTRITIS, FOOD POISONING, HEPATITIS, ENTERITIS, inflamed GALL-BLADDER and stomach CANCER. While the unpleasant effects associated with nausea may be relieved with certain drugs, the cause of the nausea should be determined and treated.

NEAR-SIGHTEDNESS

The common name for MYOPIA.

NECROSIS

The medical term describing the death of cells, tissue or part of an organ. It may occur after severe burns or injury or when the blood supply is cut off for a dangerous period as happens in INFARCTION and GANGRENE. Bacterial toxins may also cause necrosis, as in TUBERCULOSIS.

NEPHRECTOMY

The surgical operation to remove a KIDNEY, usually performed because of severe injury or disease such as HYDRONEPHROSIS or renal cancer. People with one healthy kidney remaining can lead a normal life.

NEPHRITIS (GLOMERULONEPHRITIS)

Nephritis (previously called Bright's disease) is an acute or chronic inflammation of the filtering units of the kidneys, caused by an abnormal reaction of the immune system. The reaction often occurs several weeks after a streptococcal infection (usually a sore throat). The immune system produces ANTIBODIES which overcome the bacterial infection but which later accumulate in the kidney, causing damage which results in leakage of blood into the urine and inadequate output of urine. In one type of nephritis, the damage is caused by autoimmune antibodies (see AUTOIMMUNE DISEASE). Acute nephritis is rare, but occurs most often in children. About one in 3000 school-age children develop nephritis. Symptoms include red-brown or smoky coloured urine of reduced amount, puffiness of the eyes and face, sometimes generalised OEDEMA, tiredness and backache. If your child develops these symptoms after a recent sore throat, see your doctor without delay. The diagnosis is made if there are typical abnormalities in the urine and blood together with raised blood pressure and oedema.

Treatment consists of bedrest, diet low in salt and protein, ANTIBIOTICS to get rid of any remaining infection and in some cases drugs such as DIURETICS to reduce oedema, drugs to reduce blood pressure if it is dangerously high and CORTICOSTEROIDS to reduce the inflammatory reaction. Usually recovery is complete within two or three weeks. In a few severe cases acute nephritis may become chronic, and may lead to renal failure and URAEMIA.

NERVOUS BREAKDOWN

A non-specific term describing an emotional disturbance that makes it impossible for a person to function normally. The condition may be the result of physical illness, bereavement, anxiety over some aspect of work or of an emotional relationship. Symptoms include loss of appetite, tiredness, depression, lack of self-esteem and lack of interest in life generally. In some cases, the doctor may recommend specific drugs such as anti-depressants and tranquillisers; in all cases, PSYCHOTHERAPY may help.

NERVOUS SYSTEM

(See How The Body Works, pp. 12–15.)

NETTLE RASH

Known medically as urticaria, this allergic skin complaint appears as itchy, raised red and white blotchy weals. It is a reaction to certain drug, food and contact allergens. It may be effectively treated with antihistamines and prevented in future by avoiding the allergen. See also HIVES, ALLERGY.

NEURALGIA

Pain, often intense, due to compression or inflammation of a nerve, often felt along the entire course of the nerve. The commonest form is trigeminal neuralgia in which there is intense jabbing pain in the jaws, cheeks and gums. SHINGLES is also associated with neuralgia.

NEURITIS

An inflammation of a nerve or nerves which may be caused by malnutrition, ALCOHOLISM, DIABETES, poisoning, ALLERGY or virus infection. Removing the cause is the first step in treatment. See also SCIATICA.

NEUROPATHY

A degenerative condition in which the peripheral nerves gradually lose their function. Symptoms may include tingling sensations, numbness and weakness often starting in the fingers and toes. Neuropathy may be caused by malnutrition, poisoning, ALCOHOLISM, poor blood supply, TRAUMA, compressed or stretched nerves, DIABETES or LEPROSY. Treatment involves getting to the source of the problem.

NICOTINE

A stimulant and poisonous alkaloid drug found in tobacco. See SMOKING.

NIGHT BLINDNESS

An inability to see adequately in the dark. It may be due to hereditary disorder of the retina, or may occur as the result of severe malnutrition with deficiency of vitamin A which is found in butter, egg yolks and green and yellow vegetables. There may be something to the old saying that eating carrots helps one see in the dark. See VITAMINS.

NIGHT SWEATS

Excessive sweating at night, to the extent that night-clothes and bedclothes are saturated. Night sweats are often a symptom of diseases which cause a nocturnal rise in temperature, such as TUBERCULOSIS and HODGKIN'S DISEASE.

NITS

The eggs of head and pubic LICE.

NOCTURIA

Frequent passing of urine during the night. In a healthy adult, the kidneys do not produce as much urine during sleep (it is much more concentrated) as they do during the day so that the bladder doesn't need emptying during the night. In some forms of kidney disease, the kidneys fail to properly concentrate the urine during sleep, with resulting nocturia. Other causes include increased irritability of the bladder as in CYSTITIS, and anything which reduces bladder capacity such as pregnancy, prostate enlargement, bladder tumours.

NON-SPECIFIC URETHRITIS (NSU)

Inflammation of the urethra from causes other than gonococcal infection. See URETHRITIS.

NOSEBLEED

See EPISTAXIS.

NYMPHOMANIA

Desire for excessive sexual activity in women, thought to be caused by emotional disorders such as feelings of anxiety and insecurity rather than by hormonal imbalance. Quite often, women with this disorder find less than average satisfaction in sexual relations. In men, the corresponding disorder is known as SATYRIASIS.

NYSTAGMUS

Involuntary movement of the eyes, usually in a constant side to side motion. It may be CONGENITAL or the result of a disorder of the inner ear or it may occur as a feature of such diseases as MULTIPLE SCLEROSIS and MENIERE'S DISEASE.

OBESITY

Obesity exists when bodyweight is 20 per cent greater than normal (taking into account the person's age, height, build and degree of physical activity). Over-eating is the cause. When a person eats more food than the body needs to supply energy to maintain activity, the result is excessive fat storage. Obesity is dangerous to health because it causes the heart and circulatory system to work harder. Excessively overweight people are more susceptible to HEART DISEASE, ATHEROSCLEROSIS, HYPERTENSION, DIABETES, OSTEOARTHRITIS and other serious illnesses. The most satisfactory treatment is an approved, nutritious diet and a sensible, individually tailored programme of exercise.

OBSESSION

An emotional disorder in which a person has a very strong belief, idea or compulsion that cannot be shaken or influenced by logical argument. Such a person may well recognise that a belief or compulsion has come to dominate his or her mind, but yet be unable to do anything about it.

OCCUPATIONAL DISEASE

A disease or disorder that is the result of the environment, either physical or emotional, in which a person works. Some people work in industries where there may be dangerous chemicals or dusts, some in jobs involving intense heat, or noise, or light, while others work in high pressure office jobs. All these work situations have the potential to cause an occupational disorder although industry and business are becoming increasingly conscious of the need to minimise the risks to the health and welfare of employees.

OCCUPATIONAL THERAPY

A form of treatment in which health is restored to physically or mentally ill people through selected constructive and creative activities. Handicapped or disabled people are helped through a form of occupational therapy called vocational rehabilitation.

OEDEMA

Accumulation of fluid in body cavities or tissues. It is not a disease itself but a symptom of disease, local disorders or general disturbance of fluid balance, such as in NEPHRITIS and HEART FAILURE. Local oedema occurs in inflammation, and in disturbances of venous or lymphatic drainage of the affected part. Generalised oedema (previously called DROPSY) may include ASCITES and PLEURAL EFFUSION. Usually oedema is corrected by treating the cause.

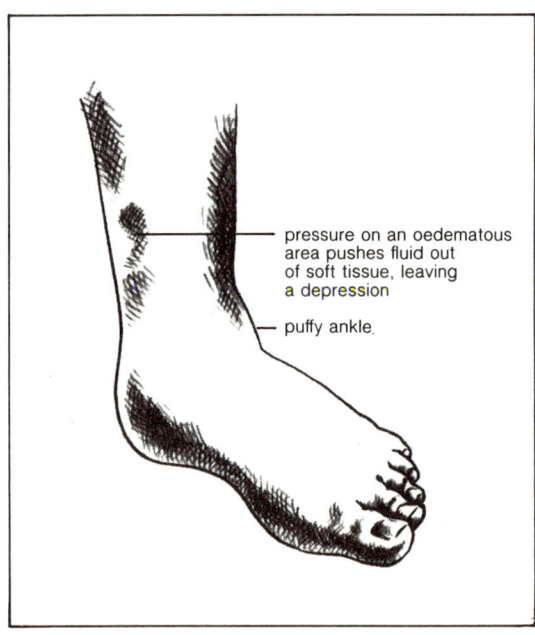

pressure on an oedematous area pushes fluid out of soft tissue, leaving a depression

puffy ankle

Oedema is an accumulation of fluid in the soft tissues, due to excess seepage from capillaries, or to interference with drainage. Ankle oedema is worse after standing or sitting for long periods.

OESOPHAGUS

Also known as the gullet, it is the muscular passageway from the throat which carries food to the stomach. (See How The Body Works, pp. 16–17.)

OESTROGEN

Female sex HORMONE produced by the OVARIES. Oestrogen controls the female primary and secondary sexual characteristics – the development of reproductive organs, breasts, pubic hair, and the distribution of subcutaneous fat. See MENOPAUSE, HORMONE REPLACEMENT THERAPY. (See also How The Body Works, p. 26.)

OOPHORECTOMY

The surgical removal of an ovary.

OOPHORITIS

Inflammation of both, or one, of the ovaries. It may be caused by TUBERCULOSIS, GONORRHOEA or other pelvic infections, or may occur as a complication of certain viral infections such as MUMPS.

OPHTHALMOSCOPE

An instrument used to examine the inside of the eye, particularly the RETINA. During a routine medical examination, the doctor will usually examine the eyes with an ophthalmoscope because the retina is the only place in the body where blood vessels and nerve tissue can be seen directly. Such an examination may indicate the early stages of such diseases as HYPERTENSION, DIABETES, ANAEMIA and LEUKAEMIA. It may also reveal CATARACTS and injuries to the eye, such as DETACHED RETINA. (See Medical Tests And Examinations – OPHTHALMOSCOPY.)

ORAL CONTRACEPTION

Also known as the contraceptive pill or simply the Pill, it is a method of birth control in which ovulation is prevented by regularly taking a combination of oestrogen and progestagen to inhibit egg maturation and release. See CONTRACEPTION.

ORCHITIS

Inflammation of the testes. Orchitis may be the result of spread of infection along the VAS DEFERENS from the URETHRA or PROSTATE. This is likely to happen if sexually transmitted diseases such as GONORRHOEA and NSU are not treated in their early stages. In such cases, it is often associated with epididymitis and the condition is known as epididymo-orchitis. Bacterial orchitis may also be the result of penetrating injuries of the testis or spread from infections of the scrotum. Orchitis may complicate general infections such as MUMPS and other viral illnesses, TUBERCULOSIS and SYPHILIS.

Mumps orchitis is the most common. About 1 in 4 boys with mumps will develop some degree of orchitis. If both testes are severely affected, sterility may result. Symptoms of orchitis are severe pain and swelling of the testis and redness and swelling of the scrotum, usually associated with fever, malaise and sometimes prostration. Treatment is with bedrest and painkillers, supportive bandaging for the affected testis, antibiotics for bacterial infection and sometimes CORTICOSTEROID drugs for severe viral orchitis. Most cases of orchitis respond to treatment within a few days. If abscess formation occurs, surgical drainage of pus may be necessary.

OSTEITIS DEFORMANS

See PAGET'S DISEASE.

OSTEOARTHRITIS

Degenerative inflammation of the joints resulting from wear-and-tear of the cartilage and bone ends of joints. The larger weight-bearing joints, such as the knee and hip, are most commonly affected. Osteoarthritis affects middle-aged and elderly people, and tends to be worse in OBESITY. Symptoms are stiffness of the joints and pain on movement. Treatment includes physiotherapy, anti-inflammatory and analgesic drugs, and, if necessary, a weight-loss plan.

OSTEOMA

A benign tumour of bone, often originating in the skull, lower jaw or the walls of the sinuses. Osteoma, may occur singly or in large numbers and are also found in the pelvic bones, the vertebrae and the long bones of the arms and legs. These tumours are removed if they cause pressure on surrounding structures or deformity.

OSTEOMALACIA

The adult equivalent of RICKETS.

OSTEOMYELITIS

Inflammation of the BONE and BONE MARROW caused by infection. Pus-forming BACTERIA usually reach the bone via the bloodstream when pyaemia complicates a primary infection such as a BOIL or ABSCESS, or through a deep, penetrating wound such as a compound FRACTURE. Children are more prone than adults to osteomyelitis, which usually has a sudden onset with FEVER and severe pain at the site of the inflammation. If treated promptly, osteomyelitis may be cured by antibiotics, though surgical drainage of pus may be necessary. If bone infection becomes chronic, it is extremely difficult to eradicate.

OSTEOPATHY

A system of treatment mainly by massage and

manipulation of bones and joints in an effort to find and correct any so-called structural abnormalities. Developed last century by an American named Andrew Taylor Still, the system is based on the theory that many pains, especially those in the back, are caused by faulty alignment of the bones.

OSTEOPOROSIS

Weakening of bones due to loss of both mineral content and structural framework. Throughout life bone is a very active tissue, undergoing constant breakdown and build-up to remodel the shape and strength of each bone as our bodies grow and our activities change. During adult life the reproductive hormones (oestrogen in women and testosterone in men) are essential in maintaining the balance between bone breakdown and build-up. Exercise and adequate calcium and protein in the diet are also essential for healthy bones. From middle age onwards, as hormone production decreases, bone rebuilding becomes less efficient so that there is an imbalance between bone loss and replacement. When breakdown exceeds build-up, the process of osteoporosis has begun. The imbalance develops more rapidly and severely in women than in men, because women lose their hormones suddenly at the menopause, whereas male hormones taper off gradually into old age. Osteoporosis weakens bones making them much more liable to break.

When bone loss from osteoporosis is slight, as it usually is in older men, there is not much increase in risk of fracture. When osteoporosis has advanced to the stage where bones break too easily, as happens in 1 out of 4 older women, fractures and their consequences cause much suffering, ill health and loss of life. The commonest sites of fracture due to osteoporosis are the hip, upper arm and wrist. Crush fractures of the vertebrae produce the dowagers' hump so common in elderly women. It is now clear that most osteoporosis can be prevented by exercise, adequate calcium in the diet, and HORMONE REPLACEMENT THERAPY (HRT) if appropriate for post-menopausal women.

OTITIS

Inflammation (usually infectious) of the ear. **Otitis externa** affects the *outer ear* and may be caused by ECZEMA, fungal or bacterial infections which result in the ear canal becoming red, painful and itchy, and often discharging. It is treated with drops containing antibiotics and anti-fungals. Corticosteroids may control inflammation due to eczema.

Otitis media occurs when infection enters the *middle ear* through the EUSTACHIAN TUBES, usually as a complication of upper respiratory infections, tonsillitis, enlarged adenoids or measles. Symptoms are severe earache, slight deafness, high temperature, and examination of the ear reveals a red,

bulging ear-drum. Otitis media can result in deafness due to ruptured ear-drum, or other serious complications such as MASTOIDITIS or MENINGITIS. It should be promptly treated with appropriate antibiotics, and with analgesics to relieve pain and reduce fever. See also MIDDLE EAR INFECTION.

OTOSCOPE

An instrument, used by doctors in most routine ear examinations, with a light and magnifying lens in a tube-like nozzle to allow inspection of the auditory canal and ear-drum.

OVARIAN CYST

A swelling in the ovary due to an encapsulated collection of fluid. Most ovarian cysts are benign (non-cancerous). They are usually caused by the retention of fluid within the ovarian follicles (see How The Body Works, p. 26), although some, filled with blood, are the result of ENDOMETRIOSIS. Most ovarian cysts are small (2–3 cm in diameter) and cause no health problems, and will subside without treatment. Even large cysts (7 cm or greater) may exist without causing symptoms, and may be discovered on routine examination. However, any cyst may cause symptoms by pressure on nearby structures, or by twisting, leaking, bleeding or rupturing. Symptoms are acute: severe lower abdominal pain, often with SHOCK. Treatment may be by aspiration of fluid through the laparoscope or by surgical removal of the cyst.

OVARY

(See How The Body Works, pp. 25–26.)

OVULATION

(See How The Body Works, pp. 25–26.)

OVUM

The medical name of the female egg that matures

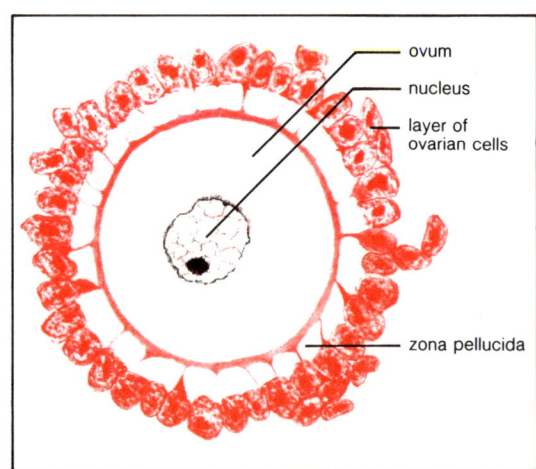

An unfertilised ovum.

inside the ovary. Once a month an ovum is released into the FALLOPIAN TUBE in the process called ovulation. (See also How The Body Works, pp. 25–26.)

OXYGEN
A colourless, odourless, tasteless, water-soluble gas that forms about 20 per cent of the air. Oxygen is essential to most forms of life. (See also How The Body Works, pp. 10–11.)

PACEMAKER

A group of special cells in the heart that initiate and set the rate of the heartbeat, causing it to increase during physical effort, fever or times of heightened emotion, and to slow down during rest periods. (See How The Body Works, pp. 8–9.) An artificial pacemaker is a very small electrical unit which is either implanted in the chest or attached to the chest to stimulate the heart to contract when the natural pacemaker fails to function properly.

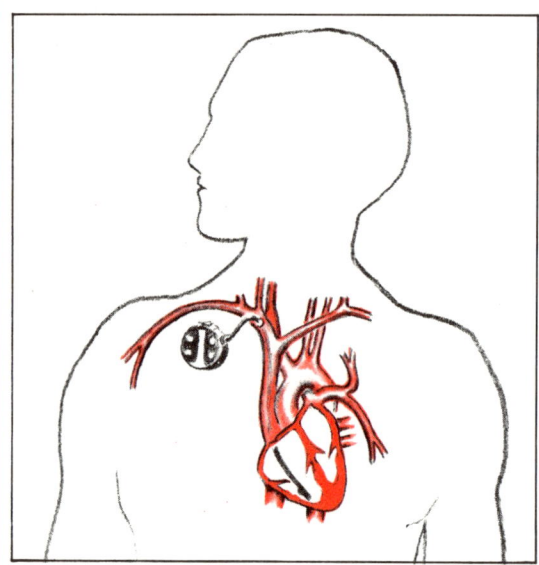

The wires from an external pacemaker are passed through the veins into the right ventricle. Here the pacemaker emits tiny electrical impulses which stimulate regular contractions of the heart muscle.

PAGET'S DISEASE

An insidious chronic disorder of bone remodelling which causes bones to become enlarged, soft, weak and deformed. Bones most commonly affected are the skull, spine, pelvis and legs. There is no known cause, but the disorder tends to run in families. Symptoms include constant dull pain in the bones, complaints of bone deformity (such as a larger hat size being needed), or symptoms due to pressure on nerves. Fractures are common. Paget's disease usually affects people over 50 and men more than women. By age 80, 10 per cent of people are affected. In recent years several new drug treatments have improved the outlook for Paget's sufferers.

PAIN

Pain is an unpleasant sensory and emotional experience usually associated with tissue damage or muscle spasm. The sensation of pain performs the important function of drawing attention to the fact that something is wrong, forcing the sufferer to take charge of the situation and to find out and do something about whatever is causing the damage. People differ in their sensitivity to pain. The same injury may be described as anything from mild discomfort to excruciating by different people or by the same person at different times. Sometimes pain may be felt in areas other than the damaged part of the body. This is known as REFERRED PAIN, an example being the pain felt in the arm in MYOCARDIAL INFARCTION. See also ABDOMINAL PAIN, BACKACHE, EARACHE.

PALLIATIVE

A drug or treatment that relieves symptoms of a disorder without curing it.

PALLOR

A term used to describe part or all of the body which lacks colour due to the blood draining away from the skin. Pallor of the face may indicate emotional states such as anger, fear, fatigue or shock. Pallor in the limbs usually means disturbance of blood supply. Generalised skin pallor occurs in most illnesses and is a particular symptom of ANAEMIA.

PALPITATIONS

Awareness of the heartbeat, usually because it is abnormally strong, rapid or irregular. Palpitations may be caused by strenuous exercise, fear or excitement, or may be a sign of HEART DISEASE or other circulatory disorder. See also TACHYCARDIA.

PALSY

Another term for PARALYSIS. See CEREBRAL PALSY, BELL'S PALSY.

PANCREAS

A gland which lies behind the stomach, producing the watery pancreatic juice which plays an important part in the digestion of proteins, fats and carbohydrates in food. The pancreas also produces the hormones INSULIN and glucagon which regulate metabolism of sugars. See DIABETES, HYPOGLYCAEMIA, HYPERGLYCAEMIA, PANCREATITIS. (See also How The Body Works, pp. 22–24.)

PANCREATITIS

Acute or chronic inflammation of the PANCREAS. Acute pancreatitis is characterised by high temperature, severe pain – in the middle or upper left abdomen – which runs through to the back, vomiting, rapid pulse and low blood pressure. Pancreatitis may occur when the pancreatic duct is blocked by a GALLSTONE (in which case there may be associated JAUNDICE), or there may be no discoverable cause. It may also lead to paralysis of the bowel, shock and collapse. Chronic pancreatitis may be associated with ALCOHOLISM, CYSTIC FIBROSIS or such virus infections as MUMPS and INFLUENZA, or may follow abdominal surgery. Symptoms are recurrent attacks of upper abdominal and back pain and vomiting, aggravated by food. Pancreatitis usually results in damage to the pancreas. If much pancreatic tissue is destroyed, it may lead to DIABETES. Treatment may include a low-fat diet, abstinence from alcohol, painkillers, special calcium and vitamin D supplements, and insulin therapy if diabetes is a complication.

PANDEMIC

An EPIDEMIC affecting many countries at the one time or affecting most people within a large area or country.

PAP SMEAR

See SMEAR TEST.

PAPILLOEDEMA

Swelling of the optic disc – the point where the retinal nerve fibres join to form the optic nerve – which can be inspected with an OPHTHALMOSCOPE. Papilloedema is a reliable sign of increased pressure within the skull. Causes of such pressure include brain haemorrhage, abscess or tumour, severe HYPERTENSION, MENINGITIS or kidney disease. Papilloedema, which usually affects both eyes, is relieved by treating the underlying cause.

PAPILLOMA

A usually benign (non-cancerous) TUMOUR which develops in skin or MUCOUS MEMBRANES. A WART is an example of a skin papilloma. Papillomas may also develop in the larynx, bladder and lungs.

PARAESTHESIA

Abnormal sensation, usually in the skin. Commonly known as 'pins and needles', paraesthesia is often described as a tingling, prickling feeling. Temporary paraesthesia may be caused by the build-up of pressure on a nerve, and often is felt when limbs have been held in a twisted or unusual position such as prolonged sitting with crossed or bent legs. If the feeling becomes frequent, consult your doctor because it may be an indication of nerve or blood vessel disorder.

PARALYSIS

Partial or complete loss of the power of movement in part or parts of the body. Paralysis is caused by damage to the nerve supply of muscles, often through injury or disorder of the brain or spinal cord. There are many different, individually named forms of paralysis. See STROKE, MULTIPLE SCLEROSIS and POLIOMYELITIS.

PARANOIA

A psychotic state in which a person suffers delusions of persecution believing, illogically and irrationally, that people are acting against him or her. It may accompany such disorders as DEPRESSION, DEMENTIA and SCHIZOPHRENIA. People suffering from severe paranoia require specialised psychiatric treatment.

PARAPLEGIA

PARALYSIS (and usually loss of sensation) affecting the legs and lower body and usually caused by injury to or disease of the spinal cord. (See Medical And Health Support Organisations.)

PARASITE

An organism that lives on or in a host animal or plant. While many parasites are microscopic, some that infect humans, such as worms, lice and fleas, are big enough to see with the naked eye. Some parasites are directly responsible for causing diseases in man such as malaria, amoebic dysentery, scabies.

PARATYPHOID

A highly infectious GASTROENTERITIS which is usually spread by food or water contaminated by the faeces of carriers. Symptoms include a pink rash on the chest, fever, vomiting, diarrhoea, headache and abdominal pain. Plenty of fluids and bedrest is the usual treatment. Antibiotics do not help the acute attack, but may be used to eliminate the disease from chronic carriers.

PARKINSON'S DISEASE

A CHRONIC, slowly progressive disease of the nervous system, also known as paralysis agitans or shaking palsy. Its manifestations are the result of degeneration of nerve ganglia at the base of the brain. There is no known cause of Parkinson's disease although it may follow ENCEPHALITIS or ATHEROMA. Parkinson's disease is rare before age 50, and affects more men than women. Early symptoms include fine tremors in the hands, arms and legs and involuntary nodding of the head. Later the facial muscles begin to tighten and the expression becomes fixed and mask-like. Gradually, as muscular tremors affect the whole body, limbs become stiff and walking increasingly difficult until it is reduced to a stooped shuffle of small, rapid steps.

There is no known cure for Parkinson's disease but some of the more distressing symptoms like stiffness and tremors may be relieved by specific drug treatment. Exercise and massage are also

People with Parkinson's disease have a characteristic stooped posture and fine tremor in the hands and arms.

helpful. In most cases, people suffering from this disease become depressed as their mobility and independence are curbed. Support agencies have been established to help both those people suffering from Parkinson's disease and their family members. (See Medical And Health Support Organisations.)

PARONYCHIA

Bacterial or fungal infection under the fold of skin at the side of a toenail or fingernail. The condition may be ACUTE or CHRONIC, and is common in those whose hands are frequently in water. Treatment is by appropriate local and/or antibiotic or antifungal medication. Pus which has accumulated under the skin fold may need to be drained.

PAROTITIS

Inflammation of the parotid glands (the salivary glands in the neck just near the ear lobe and the point of the jaw) most commonly as a result of MUMPS infection.

PARTURITION

Another term for birth. (See How The Body Works, pp. 28–30.)

PATHOLOGIST

A laboratory-based specialist in the branch of medicine dealing with those changes in the body causing or caused by disease. Such changes may be charted by the pathologist using the microscope, or by chemical and other forms of analysis of tiny samples of tissue, bodily fluids, secretions, and excretions.

PEDICULOSIS

The medical term for infestation by LICE.

PELLAGRA

A disease caused by deficiency of niacin (nicotinic acid), one of the vitamin B group, found in wholegrain cereals, yeast extracts, meat and fish. Symptoms include weakness, DERMATITIS, GASTRITIS and thought disorders. Pellagra is uncommon in Australia. It is corrected with vitamin supplements and an adequate diet. See VITAMINS.

PELVIC INFLAMMATORY DISEASE

See PID (PELVIC INFLAMMATORY DISEASE).

PEMPHIGUS

A rare, serious disease of skin and mucous membranes in which clusters of large, painful blisters develop. Pemphigus mainly affects people of middle age and beyond. The cause is unclear, although AUTOIMMUNE DISEASE is suspected. Treatment involves corticosteroid drugs, and expert nursing, usually in hospital.

PENIS
(See How The Body Works, pp. 26–27.)

PEPTIC ULCER
Ulceration of the intestinal lining which penetrates to involve the muscle layer, caused by the action of the acid and pepsin secreted by the stomach. Peptic ulcers are found in the stomach and duodenum and less commonly in hiatus HERNIA. Ulceration occurs when there is a disturbance of balance between production of gastric juice and factors protecting the intestinal lining such as mucus. Many influences can disturb this balance, including stress and certain drugs. The most common symptom is gnawing or burning upper abdominal pain, relieved by milk or antacids. Diagnosis is confirmed by BARIUM MEAL X-RAY or GASTROSCOPY. (See also Medical Tests And Examinations.) Many peptic ulcers heal by themselves when precipitating factors are corrected, and after a short period of treatment with antacids. Otherwise the outlook for ulcer sufferers has been vastly improved by the introduction of the histamine H_2 receptor blocking agents such as cimetidine, which reduce gastric secretion and promote healing of peptic ulcers. These medications have dramatically reduced the need for surgery, which is now performed only in emergency treatment of complications such as perforation and severe bleeding.

PERFORATION
A tear or hole in an organ or tissue caused by penetrating injury (as in perforated ear-drum) or a disorder (as in an ulcer perforating the stomach wall).

PERICARDITIS
Inflammation of the membranous sac, known as the pericardium, that lines the cavity containing the heart and forms the outer covering of the heart. It may be caused by infection or occur as a complication of CORONARY THROMBOSIS, MYOCARDITIS, RHEUMATIC FEVER. Symptoms of pericarditis include severe chest pain and shortness of breath. Pericarditis is treated according to the underlying cause.

PERINEUM
The region of the body between the ANUS and the SCROTUM or VULVA.

PERIODONTITIS
See PYORRHOEA.

PERISTALSIS
Slow, wave-like muscular contractions which force the contents of an organ or duct (for example, the gullet, intestines, the bile duct, the fallopian tubes) to move along in front of the wave of movement.

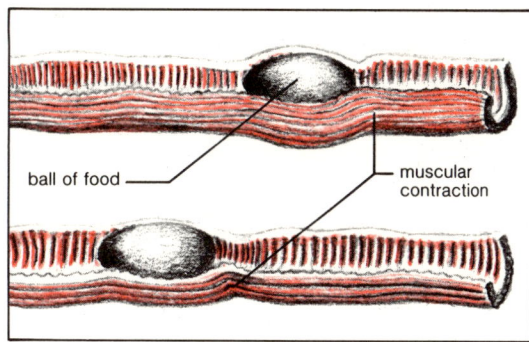

ball of food — muscular contraction

These cross-sectional diagrams of a hollow tubular organ show how the process of muscular contraction pushes the contents along the tube.

PERITONITIS
Inflammation of the membrane lining the abdominal cavity and surrounding the stomach, intestines and other abdominal organs. It may be the result of ruptured APPENDIX, ruptured ECTOPIC PREGNANCY or an ULCER that has perforated the stomach or intestines. Symptoms include severe abdominal pain, fever, prostration, nausea and vomiting. If peritonitis is suspected, call a doctor immediately. Untreated peritonitis can be fatal so prompt hospital treatment is necessary.

PERNICIOUS
Causing extreme, destructive or fatal harm. Pernicious ANAEMIA, for example, can have serious consequences if not properly treated.

PERTHES' DISEASE
Degeneration of the upper growing end (epiphysis) of the thigh bone (femur), which may occur in children, particularly boys, between the ages of 4 and 10. Perthes' disease is caused by disturbance of the blood supply to the epiphysis. The reason for this occurring is usually obscure. Symptoms include mild pain in the hip and sometimes in the knee, limping and restricted hip movement. A child promptly diagnosed as suffering from Perthes' disease can be successfully treated with bedrest and a caliper, or splint, fitted to the hip to take weight off the joint until healing is complete.

PERTUSSIS
Another name for WHOOPING COUGH.

PESSARY
Any device or solid medication introduced into the VAGINA. Rigid, ring-shaped pessaries which support the pelvic organs may be used to correct PROLAPSE of the uterus. Medicated pessaries include contraceptive spermicides and antibiotics or anti-fungals for the treatment of VAGINITIS.

PETIT MAL
A mild form of EPILEPSY.

PHARMACOLOGY
The study of the action of medicines, drugs and other substances on the body.

PHARYNGITIS
Inflammation the PHARYNX. Acute pharyngitis may be caused by infection (bacterial or viral), or by injury to the pharynx from sharp or too hot food. Symptoms include sore throat, fever, headache, swollen glands in the neck and a dry cough. Most pharyngitis clears up in a couple of days with rest, plenty of fluids and painkillers if necessary. Antibiotics are prescribed for bacterial complications. Chronic pharyngitis is usually the result of prolonged irritation by smoke, dust or other inhaled irritants causing the throat to become inflamed. Treatment involves removing the cause of irritation. See also TONSILLITIS.

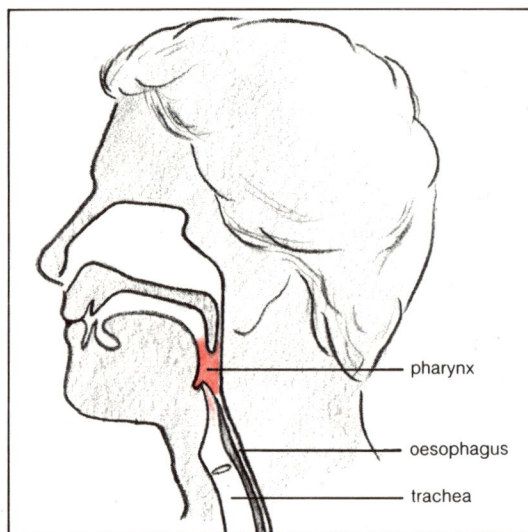

Sore throats due to pharyngitis commonly accompany upper respiratory tract infections.

PHARYNX
The tract that extends from the back of the throat to the top of the OESOPHAGUS, or gullet. Lined with MUCOUS MEMBRANE, it is the passageway for both food and air. (See How The Body Works, pp. 10–11, 16–17.)

PHENYLKETONURIA
An inherited abnormality in which there is a defect in the way the body uses certain proteins in food. Phenylketonuria (PKU) does not occur unless a defective gene has been inherited from both parents. If undetected, the accumulation of phenylalanine in the blood results in severe mental retardation. However, nowadays all new-born babies are screened for PKU, which may be successfully controlled with a special diet.

PHIMOSIS
Tightness of the foreskin so that it is difficult to draw it back over the glans penis without causing pain. It is corrected by CIRCUMCISION.

PHLEBITIS
Inflammation of a vein, occurring most commonly in the legs. The cause of phlebitis is sometimes unclear, though it is often associated with THROMBOSIS or injury to a vein. Phlebitis of arm veins is common in intravenous drug abusers. Symptoms include redness and pain around the vein, OEDEMA of the parts beyond and sometimes fever. Usual treatment is rest and supportive bandaging, as well as antibiotics and anticoagulants when appropriate.

PHLEGM
Excessive thick mucus produced in and coughed up from the respiratory tract, usually as a result of an inflammatory disorder of the bronchi or lungs.

PHOBIA
Abnormal, irrational fear of an object or situation, which may be so overwhelming that the sufferer may not be able to function normally. While fear helps us to avoid danger, phobias have no rational explanation or basis in reality. An example is obsessive dread of germs, leading to refusal to handle everyday objects like money, handrails or doorknobs. Other irrational fears involve open spaces (AGORAPHOBIA), crowded or confined spaces (CLAUSTROPHOBIA), high places (ACROPHOBIA). A person seriously disturbed by any unreasonable fear should discuss it with a doctor who may recommend PSYCHOTHERAPY.

PHOTOPHOBIA
An extreme sensitivity of the eyes to light, sometimes to the extent of causing pain. Photophobia is a common symptom of feverish illness and disorders such as MIGRAINE and CONJUNCTIVITIS.

PHTHISIS
Destruction of lung tissue resulting in cavities in the lung. Usually the result of chronic TUBERCULOSIS and rare these days, now that TB can be cured by antibiotics.

PHYSIOTHERAPY
A form of treatment of an injury or disability using massage, heat, controlled exercise, electricity, infrared radiation and other external means rather than drugs and surgery. Treatment may be given in a hospital, clinic, convalescence centre or at home by a

specially trained person called a physiotherapist. It is used with considerable success in the treatment of diseases or TRAUMAS that affect the muscles or joints and in the REHABILITATION of people who have suffered such disorders.

PICA
An abnormal craving for eating strange substances such as dirt, coal, paint, putty and plaster. Pica is occasionally found in small children and pregnant women. Pica is thought to indicate iron deficiency and may be treated accordingly.

PID (PELVIC INFLAMMATORY DISEASE)
Inflammation (usually infectious) of the pelvic reproductive organs: the uterus, tubes and ovaries in women and the prostate and seminal vesicles in men. The commonest cause of PID is thought to be sexually transmitted infection (GONORRHOEA and CHLAMYDIA), though it may also occur following childbirth or abortion, surgical procedures on the reproductive organs or lower urinary tract, or APPENDICITIS (especially ruptured). Like most STDs, PID has been diagnosed more often since the mid-1970s than previously. Symptoms of acute PID are severe lower abdominal pain, fever and often a foul discharge from the vagina or penis. There may be associated symptoms of CYSTITIS. The onset of chronic PID may be insidious, especially in women, who may experience few or no symptoms until the inflammatory process is well advanced. Whether acute or chronic, PID can lead to scarring and adhesions in the reproductive organs which may reduce fertility. Early diagnosis and vigorous treatment with appropriate antibiotics will reduce the risk of reproductive system damage.

PIGEON CHEST
An abnormally prominent breastbone (sternum), which may be present from birth or be due to calcium or vitamin B deficiency during childhood. Usually pigeon chest is harmless, but if the chest is so seriously deformed that heart and lung movement are restricted, surgical correction may be necessary.

PIGEON TOES
A condition in which the toes turn inwards, usually first noticed when a child begins to walk. It is the result of weakness in the leg muscles or in the arches of the feet. Specific exercises and built up shoes may help, but usually the condition corrects itself.

PIGMENT
An organic substance that colours material in the body. Some pigments have important biological functions. The red HAEMOGLOBIN in the blood carries oxygen from the lungs to the rest of the body: the retina of the eye contains visual purple and other pigments that are essential to sight, MELANIN in the skin offers protection against the sun's rays, bilirubin is one of the BILE pigments that gives urine its characteristic yellow colour.

PILES
Another name for HAEMORRHOIDS.

PILL, THE
See CONTRACEPTION.

PIMPLES
See ACNE.

PINS AND NEEDLES
A common name for PARAESTHESIA.

PITUITARY GLAND
(See How The Body Works, pp. 22–23.)

PITYRIASIS ROSEA
An inflammatory skin condition caused by an unidentified infectious agent (probably a virus). A week or so before the general outbreak, a single, or 'herald', patch appears. The eruption is patchy, scaly and sometimes itchy, occurring mainly on the trunk and upper arms. The disorder is self-limiting and clears up spontaneously within five or six weeks. A simple, soothing lotion such as calamine will relieve the itch.

PLACEBO
An inactive substance or treatment that has no biological effect. Placebos are used in studies which aim to test the effectiveness of new drugs or treatments. Any treatment accepted in the belief that it will relieve symptoms or cure disease is likely to bring about improvement of symptoms of some disorders. This is known as the placebo effect. When new drugs are being tested a 'placebo controlled' study is carried out as follows: a number of patients is randomly divided into two groups, with the first group being given the test drug and the second, or control, group being given a placebo which looks and tastes exactly the same. Neither the researchers nor the patients know who is taking drug or placebo until the study has been completed. In this way the researchers can properly determine the effectiveness of the drug against merely confidence that something is being done. Such is the power of placebo effect that in some complaints it produces as much relief as theoretically effective drugs.

PLACENTA
A disc-shaped spongy mass of tissue which develops in the uterus in about the third month of pregnancy. One side is closely attached to the uterus, normally

in the upper part; the other is connected to the UMBILICAL CORD through which the FOETUS obtains nourishment, oxygen and ANTIBODIES, and discharges carbon dioxide and waste products. The placenta remains undisturbed throughout the baby's development until the moment the baby takes its first breath, when the blood vessels in the cord close off. After delivery, the placenta is expelled as the afterbirth and the umbilical cord is cut.

PLACENTA PRAEVIA

An abnormal position of the placenta, when it is attached to the lower part of the uterine wall. In such a case, there is danger of the placenta obstructing the passage of the foetus and/or becoming prematurely detached before or during birth with resulting heavy bleeding. These days placenta praevia can be detected by ultrasound so that appropriate measures, such as caesarian delivery, can be taken to safeguard the well-being of mother and baby.

PLAGUE

Any epidemic disease, but usually used to describe an infectious disease caused by a bacterium called *Yersinia pestis* transmitted by fleas which have become infected from rats. The symptoms, which appear suddenly after an incubation period of two or four days, include high fever, swollen lymph glands, headache, vomiting, delirium and coma. A form of plague known as the 'Black Death' killed 25 million people in Europe in the 14th century. Although plague still breaks out in parts of Asia and Africa, epidemics are rare since a vaccine is available to protect people at high risk. Where plague does break out, it is treated with antibiotics and further curbed by eliminating the rats.

PLASMA

The liquid portion of blood. (See How The Body Works, p. 5.)

PLEURAL EFFUSION

An increased amount of fluid between the layers of the pleura. Pleural effusion may complicate infection or cancer of the lung, heart failure or kidney failure.

PLEURISY

Inflammation of the pleural membrane, which covers each lung and lines the chest cavity. Pleurisy may be due to viral or bacterial infection, or may be a complication of PNEUMONIA, LUNG CANCER or injury to the chest wall. There are two forms of pleurisy: dry, when the membranes become inflamed and chafe against one another which often happens as a complication of pneumonia; and wet, when an excess amount of fluid collects between the layers of the

pleura, forming a PLEURAL EFFUSION. The treatment of pleurisy is that of the underlying infection or condition.

PMS

See PREMENSTRUAL SYNDROME.

PMT (PREMENSTRUAL TENSION)

Another term for the psychological symptoms of the PREMENSTRUAL SYNDROME.

PNEUMOCONIOSIS

CHRONIC inflammatory lung disease caused by inhaling mineral dusts containing silicon, hard coal or asbestos particles. Pneumoconioses are occupational or environmental diseases. The inflammation caused by the particles where they come in contact with the lungs leads to destruction of respiratory tissue and its replacement by fibrous scar tissue. When this happens there is less lung available for exchange of oxygen with resulting shortness of breath, and it is harder for the right side of the heart to pump blood through the scarred lungs, which leads to right heart failure. See PULMONARY HEART DISEASE. There is no cure for the pneumoconioses. The aim of treatment is to prevent further damage and infection. Breathing exercises and carefully graded activity can make the most of the remaining undamaged lung tissue. See also EMPHYSEMA, BRONCHITIS, OCCUPATIONAL DISEASE.

PNEUMONECTOMY

Surgical removal of a lung, usually as a result of bronchial CARCINOMA or severe TRAUMA. The remaining lung can usually cope with everyday respiratory demands.

PNEUMONIA

Acute inflammation of the lungs in which the tiny air sacs become so filled with inflammatory EXUDATE that respiration cannot take place. It may be caused by bacteria, viruses, chemical damage from inhalation of certain gases, or from inhalation of vomit. Bacterial pneumonia, which may develop when resistance is lowered by colds, influenza or general poor health, may affect only one lung or one lobe of a lung, when it is called lobar pneumonia. When both lungs are affected it is called bilateral or double pneumonia. Symptoms of pneumonia, which often strikes without much warning, include very high fever, RIGOURS, headache, sharp chest pains, rapid shallow breathing, harsh dry cough followed by, perhaps, the bringing up of rust-coloured sputum containing blood and pus. Bacterial pneumonia can be successfully treated with antibiotics. Many cases of pneumonia, particularly in infants and the elderly, require admission to hospital so that appropriate nursing care is available day and night and so that oxygen can be administered if necessary. See also BRONCHOPNEUMONIA.

PNEUMOTHORAX

In health the pleural layer covering the lungs is in close contact with the pleural layer which lines the chest cavities, with only a thin film of fluid separating the two layers. Pneumothorax develops when air enters the pleural cavity. This may happen when the lung perforates due to an injury, or may occur as a result of perforating injuries of the chest wall. Rarely, pneumothorax can develop dramatically when an apparently healthy person takes a forceful, deep breath or bursts out laughing. The pressure of air in the pleural cavity causes the lung to collapse, preventing respiration on the affected side. Symptoms are sudden severe pain in the chest, shoulder tip pain and shortness of breath. Diagnosis is confirmed by chest X-ray. Pneumothorax is an emergency usually requiring hospital admission for oxygen administration and round the clock nursing care. Treatment is to correct the cause.

POLIOMYELITIS

Commonly called 'polio' and once known as infantile paralysis, poliomyelitis is an acute viral infection of the central nervous system. The disease is spread from the faeces of infected persons. The virus attacks the motor components of the brain and spinal cord. The effects range from mild weakness to total paralysis of muscles. Early symptoms include mild fever, sore throat and headache, vomiting, drowsiness and stiffness in the neck and back.

There is often complete recovery at this stage, leaving the patient with life-long immunity to further polio infection. If polio progresses, cramping muscle pains and spasms develop and the affected muscles may become weakened or paralysed. In young children paralysis of one limb is common, in older people more muscles are usually affected. There may be hoarseness and difficulty in swallowing. If the breathing or swallowing muscles become paralysed, the patient's life may be in danger. In some cases a respirator ('iron lung') may be necessary to help a patient breathe.

There is no specific treatment for poliomyelitis although with skilled hospital care, patients usually survive. Paralysis is permanent. The incidence of poliomyelitis in Australia has been greatly reduced by immunisation. However, in countries without immunisation programmes, 35 000 childhood deaths from polio were reported in one recent year. Irresponsible neglect of immunisation could lead to resurgence of the disease in this country. It is essential that infants are immunised to protect them against polio. Oral vaccine is given in three doses during the first year of life with a booster dose given around the age of 5. See IMMUNISATION. (See also Medical And Health Support Organisations.)

POLYP

A TUMOUR, in most cases benign (non-cancerous), that projects from the surface of a mucous membrane. Polyps occur most often in the nose, bladder, intestine or uterus. When necessary, polyps are removed by surgery.

POLYPOSIS COLI

A condition in which large numbers of POLYPS form on the lining of the large bowel. The cause is unclear, though it is believed that in some cases polyps form because of a malfunction of mucous cells in the bowel lining. Polyposis coli tends to run in families. Inflammatory diseases such as ulcerative COLITIS and CROHN'S DISEASE may also result in polyp formation. Symptoms include mild diarrhoea, plus discharge of blood and mucus from the anus when the bowels are opened. No treatment is necessary for polyposis unless complications such as anaemia develop. Rarely, there may be malignant change in a bowel polyp so the condition should be monitored regularly for early detection of cancer, for which the affected part of the bowel is removed surgically.

PORPHYRIA

A group of rare, inherited metabolic disorders of the breakdown of the blood pigment haemoglobin. The error of metabolism may occur in the liver or the bone marrow or both. The disorder becomes apparent in infancy or early childhood. Symptoms are caused by the accumulation of excessive porphyrins in the blood and urine, and by defective formation and excessive breakdown of red blood cells. Usual symptoms are abdominal pain, disturbances of the nervous system, sensitivity to sunlight, blistering of the skin. Characteristically, the urine turns dark brown if left standing for an hour or so. There is no specific treatment because the underlying metabolic fault cannot be corrected.

PORT WINE STAIN

A dark red, flat BIRTHMARK caused by a patch of abnormally dilated blood vessels in the skin. Port wine stains vary in size from very small to quite large. The stain will not spread, and only enlarges as the body grows. Nothing much can be done about a port wine stain. If it is very noticeable and causes embarrassment to a child, parents should offer loving support and encourage the child to accept it. Birthmarks on the face may be covered by an opaque cosmetic application specially prepared to blend with the individual's skin tone. Some of the new techniques of cosmetic surgery have been used successfully to disguise port wine stains. A specialist in dermatology will advise whether such treatments are suitable.

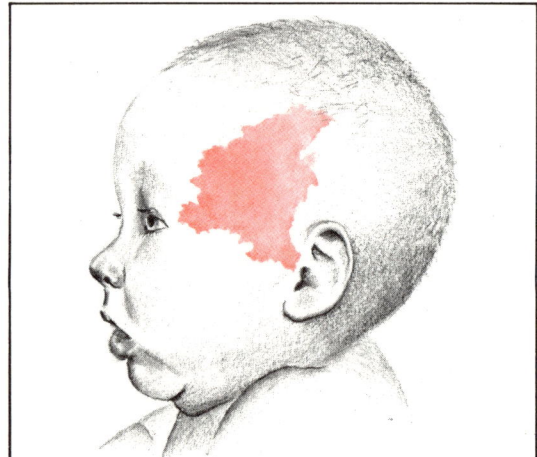

Port wine stains are present at birth and do not fade. However, they may be effectively concealed with special cosmetics.

POSTMATURITY

A pregnancy in which the baby has been in the uterus for more than the normal forty weeks. Since postmaturity may lead to neo-natal problems, it is common for doctors to induce labour if it has not commenced spontaneously by seven days after the expected date of confinement.

POST MORTEM

Also called an AUTOPSY, it is the examination of a dead body (corpse, cadaver) to determine the cause of death.

POSTPARTUM

Post-natal, or occurring after the delivery of a baby, and as a result of or connected with the pregnancy and delivery.

POT

One of several colloquial names for MARIJUANA. See also CANNABIS.

PREGNANCY

Pregnancy lasts about forty weeks from conception to labour. See EMBRYO, FERTILISATION, FOETUS, LABOUR, OVARY, OVULATION, OVUM, SPERM, UTERUS. (See also How The Body Works, pp. 28–30.)

PREGNANCY TESTING

(See Medical Tests and Examinations.)

PREMATURE BIRTH

Any birth occurring before full term (about forty weeks of gestation). When the date of conception is uncertain, prematurity is assumed if the baby weighs less than 2.5 kg.

PREMENSTRUAL SYNDROME (PMS)

A variety of physical and psychological symptoms which develop progressively during the one to two weeks before the onset of menstruation, and subside rapidly when the menstrual flow begins. PMS may be present from the MENARCHE or may come and go during the reproductive years. Most women notice symptoms at some time or other, although some women are never affected. A small proportion experience symptoms severe enough to seriously disrupt life and health. All sufferers agree that symptoms vary in nature and intensity from month to month, and tend to be worse at times of stress. Although it is known that PMS is associated with the rise and fall of reproductive hormones during the menstrual cycle, the biological factor responsible for the symptoms has not been precisely identified. Numerous studies have found no biochemical differences between sufferers and non-sufferers. Researchers believe that there is some metabolic or biochemical factor which makes part of the midbrain (the central controller of mood, daily rhythm, appetite and fluid balance) more sensitive to the fluctuation of hormone concentrations in the blood. Symptoms include moodiness, agitation, aggression, irritability, depression, tearfulness, headache, fatigue, slight weight gain, increased appetite, food cravings, painful breasts, constipation and increased or decreased libido. The emotional symptoms of PMS are often referred to as premenstrual tension (PMT).

A multitude of treatments have been recommended since this disorder was first described in 1931. So far, those treatments that have been studied in properly controlled trials have not produced significantly better results than PLACEBO. This confirms that because the precise cause is unknown, specific treatment has not yet been found. However, some women are vastly relieved by taking progestagens or other hormones during the last two weeks of the menstrual cycle, or by taking the contraceptive pill. Most sufferers are helped by a well-balanced diet rich in vitamins of the B group (see VITAMINS), a regular exercise programme, and avoiding stress during the ten days or so before menstruation. If PMS is disrupting your life, see your doctor about the prescription drugs that are worth trying.

PRIAPISM

Prolonged, usually painful erection of the penis unrelated to sexual arousal. Mild, painless priapism during sleep is normal but when it occurs at other times, a doctor should be consulted.

PREPUCE

Another name for the FORESKIN of the penis.

PRESBYOPIA

When the lens of the eye becomes less elastic during middle age, fine focusing distance becomes longer (long-sightedness). The onset of this natural process of ageing is very gradual. In the late 40s most people notice that in order to focus on the printed page, it must be held further and further from the eyes. Spectacles correct the focus for reading.

PRICKLY HEAT

An irritating rash which occurs in the folds of skin or on the neck, face, chest, back, thighs or in the armpits during hot, humid weather. Babies and overweight people are particularly susceptible. The rash is caused by excessive sweating which leads to swollen skin cells and blocked sweat ducts. It disappears when the weather cools but until that happens, the best treatment is frequent cool baths, without soap, and soothing applications of calamine lotion or non-irritating talcum powder.

PRIMAGRAVIDA

A woman who is expecting her first baby.

PROCTITIS

Inflammation of the lining of the RECTUM, which may be caused by infectious organisms, certain drugs, injury, or which may occur with ulcerative COLITIS, CROHN'S DISEASE, DIABETES, DYSENTERY or ALLERGY. Symptoms include discomfort felt in the rectum, diarrhoea (in which blood, mucus or pus may be present), pain while passing the loose motion and a repeated, and often unsuccessful, urge to empty the bowels (known as tenesmus). Treatment aims to correct the underlying cause, plus anti-spasmodic and anti-diarrhoeal drugs to relieve the symptoms, rest, and a light nourishing diet with plenty of fluids.

PROCTOSCOPE

An instrument used to examine the RECTUM.

PROGESTERONE

The female sex hormone which is secreted by the corpus luteum (the cells which fill the cavity in the ovary from which an ovum has been expelled during ovulation), and, in pregnancy, by the PLACENTA. Synthetic copies of progesterone are known as progestagens.

PROGNOSIS

The likely outcome of a disease or disorder based on knowledge and previous experience, the availability of treatment and the patient's general health, age, sex and circumstances.

PROLACTIN

A hormone secreted by the PITUITARY GLAND which stimulates milk production by the breast (mammary gland).

PROLAPSE

The forward or downward displacement of an organ from its usual place. The most common prolapses are of the rectum, bladder and uterus, which in severe cases may protrude from the body. Rectal prolapse may be associated with HAEMORRHOIDS and chronic constipation, or with polyps or other tumours of the large bowel. In post-menopausal women, when age and lack of oestrogen weaken the pelvic muscles and ligaments, prolapse of the uterus and bladder may be the delayed result of damage to the pelvic floor during childbirth. Your doctor will advise whether physiotherapy, surgery or other corrective treatment is necessary.

PROPHYLAXIS

Measures aimed towards prevention. Examples are immunisation against infections, use of ultraviolet sunscreens to prevent sunburn and skin cancer, and the use of condoms to prevent pregnancy and sexually transmitted diseases.

PROSTAGLANDINS

A family of hormone-like substances, produced in many body tissues and fluids which have a variety of regulating actions. These hormones have a powerful influence on the involuntary muscle in blood vessels and hollow organs, especially in the digestive, urinary and reproductive systems. The release of various prostaglandins in the full term, pregnant uterus helps to control the progress of labour. Synthetic prostaglandins may be used to induce abortion. Anti-prostaglandins may be used to relieve muscle spasm.

PROSTATE GLAND

A walnut-sized gland which lies beneath the bladder in males, and which produces a sugary fluid that is an essential part of SEMEN. In men over 50, the prostate gland may become enlarged, so that it presses on the neck of the bladder and narrows the urethra, making urination difficult. An enlarged prostate is usually the result of benign overgrowth within the gland. Symptoms include frequent night-time passing of urine, slow stream, small amounts of urine being passed, the feeling after urination that the bladder is not completely empty and prolonged, sometimes painful erections of the penis. Such symptoms should be investigated to be sure that there is no malignancy of the prostate. If benign enlargement of the prostate is causing significant obstruction to the flow of urine, removal (prostatectomy) is usually advised. These days this is a simple procedure, usually performed through the urethra using spinal anaesthesia. Only four or five days in hospital are needed for this type of prostatectomy.

PROSTATITIS

Inflammation of the PROSTATE GLAND, usually caused by bacterial infection which may be sexually transmitted or secondary to urinary infection. Symptoms include burning pain during urination, sudden frequent urination, cloudy, blood-stained or foul-smelling urine, low back pain and fever. In CHRONIC prostatitis, fever is usually absent. The usual treatment is by antibiotics, copious fluids and correction of any underlying cause.

PROSTHESIS

An artificial replacement for a part of the body. Prosthetic devices include dentures, artificial eyes, hands, arms, legs, breasts and even ears and noses.

PROSTRATION

Extreme physical or mental exhaustion.

PROTEIN

A complex chemical compound made up of substances called amino acids and forming an essential part of every living cell. When people eat foods rich in protein, such as meat, fish, eggs, milk, cheese and soy beans, ENZYMES in the digestive juices break down the proteins into their constituent amino acids. Protein is man's only source of nitrogen and is essential for the growth of new tissues and the repair of damaged tissues. While the body can manufacture some of the amino acids needed to form proteins, there are eight essential amino acids which must be supplied in protein foods. (See also How The Body Works, pp. 19–21.)

PRURITUS

The medical name for itching, leading to an urge to scratch the affected area. Pruritus may be caused by anything that irritates certain nerve endings in the skin, such as inflammation or chemical irritation (as in the pruritis associated with jaundice). Pruritis ani affects the anal area, perhaps as a result of HAEMORRHOIDS, WORMS or DERMATITIS; pruritis vulvae affects the female genitals, usually secondary to VAGINITIS; pruritus senilis is believed to be associated with the effects of ageing on the skin. Pruritus is relieved by treating the underlying cause of the complaint, and the application of antipruritic lotions or creams.

PSITTACOSIS

Also commonly known as parrot fever or parrot disease, psittacosis is a lung infection caused by a VIRUS-like organism which is transmitted to people by certain birds including lorikeets, cockatoos, budgerigars, finches, pigeons, ducks and chickens. Humans usually contract the disease by breathing in germs in the dust from feathers or dried droppings.

Symptoms range from those of a mild respiratory infection to those of PNEUMONIA and complicating ENCEPHALITIS. Nosebleeds are common. Untreated psittacosis may be fatal but treatment with antibiotics will prevent complications.

PSORIASIS

A chronic, recurring scaly eruption of the skin. The cause of psoriasis is unknown, but it is not infectious. It has a tendency to run in families, and usually begins between the ages of 5 and 25. The onset of an attack may be associated with arthritis, skin surgery, minor infections and anxiety. Psoriasis is characterised by itchy, red patches covered with silvery scales. It mostly appears on the scalp, trunk, forearms, elbows, knees and legs. Sufferers are usually otherwise healthy, but because of the disfigurement it causes, psoriasis may be socially disabling. There is no specific cure. However symptoms can be alleviated by ointments and lotions to reduce inflammation and relieve itch. Careful exposure to sunlight is also helpful.

PSYCHIATRY

The branch of medicine specialising in the diagnosis and treatment of emotional and mental disorders. A specialist in this field is called a psychiatrist.

PSYCHOANALYSIS

A method of studying and treating disorders of the mind, behaviour and personality developed by the Austrian psychiatrist Sigmund Freud in the early 1900s. It is one of a number of forms of PSYCHOTHERAPY. Psychoanalysis is based on the assumption that we are all born with instinctive drives that may come in conflict with the demands of family and society and be forced back into the UNCONSCIOUS mind. These repressed drives may find a disguised outlet through various kinds of irrational behaviour. A psychoanalyst (usually a doctor with psychiatric experience or a specialist in treating emotional disorders) endeavours to bring past emotions and experiences that have been repressed to the forefront of the patient's consciousness so that the person has an opportunity to understand and learn to deal effectively with his or her problems.

PSYCHOLOGY

The study of behaviour and the mental processes that govern behaviour. A specialist in this science is called a psychologist.

PSYCHOPATHY

A vague term that is used to denote abnormal, anti-social behaviour A psychopath is a person who believes himself to be under no obligation to obey the rules and conventions of society. Quite often such people, who are inclined to be irresponsible, impulsive and sometimes to commit harmful acts, are obsessive, withdrawn and without friends.

PSYCHOSIS

A group of serious emotional and mental disorders which cause disintegration of the personality, loss of contact with reality, delusions and hallucinations. Psychoses may have an organic cause such as SYPHILIS, prolonged ALCOHOLISM (known as Korsakoff's syndrome), TRAUMA or SENILITY, or they may have no known physical cause, being known then as 'functional'. Two such forms are schizo-phrenia and manic-depressive psychosis which may be the result of biochemical brain disorder. There is controversy about whether these disorders may be partly inherited. Treatment with modern drugs has greatly improved the outlook in psychiatric illness.

PSYCHOSOMATIC

Having both mental and physical elements, but with emotional factors predominating. Conditions such as mouth and stomach ulcers, eczema, asthma, ulcer-ative colitis, infertility, menstrual irregularities, heart trouble, hypertension and arthritis may be, wholly or in part, associated with or aggravated by emotional stress. Most health workers believe that all illness has important emotional components and consequences. The symptoms of psychosomatic ill-ness are as real as those of any other illness. The treatment of both the physical disorder and the emotions is emphasised in psychosomatic medicine.

PSYCHOTHERAPY

The treatment of psychological and behavioural problems largely through verbal means including counselling, suggestion, persuasion, psychoanalysis and behaviour therapy. Methods range from brief counselling, either singly or in groups, to intensive individual PSYCHOANALYSIS. The psychotherapist seeks to make the patient aware of the significance of his or her problems in the context of that person's personality. To a large extent, the success of the treatment depends on the strength and nature of the relationship between the therapist and the patient.

PTOMAINE

A group of substances produced by rotting vegetable or animal protein. Despite what most people believe, most ptomaines are not particularly troublesome to a healthy digestive system. It is noxious bacteria that sometimes accompany them that cause the problem. See also FOOD POISONING.

PTOSIS

Drooping of the upper eyelid caused by muscular

weakness which may be either congenital or a sign of a nervous disorder resulting in paralysis of the eyelid muscles. Treatment is that of the cause.

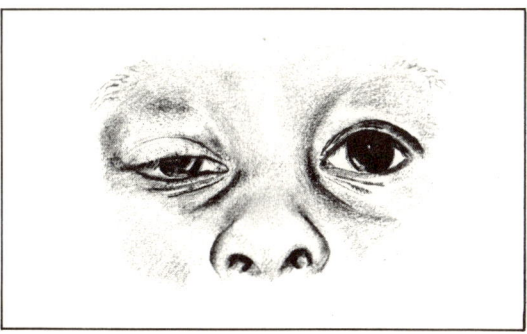

In ptosis the muscles controlling the upper lid are paralysed, making it impossible to fully open the eye. If and when the nerve supply to the muscle is restored to normal, the eye recovers.

PUBERTY

The progress from childhood to physical adulthood, during which the secondary sexual characteristics develop and reproductive functions mature. Adolescence usually refers to the progress from childhood to adult mentality, though the term is often used interchangeably with puberty. Bodily changes of sexual maturation are stimulated by an increase in the production of OESTROGEN and ANDROGEN by the reproductive glands (the OVARIES in women, the TESTES in men), in response to regulating hormones from the pituitary gland. The hormonal changes may cause skin problems like pimples and ACNE as well as emotional instability, moodiness, anxiety and over-excitement. Loving understanding and support from parents and family help an adolescent boy or girl to find a sexual and personal identity in the adult world.

PUERPERIUM

The period of about six weeks that follows childbirth, during which the reproductive organs return to normal.

PULMONARY

Relevant to or affecting the lungs. (See How The Body Works, p. 11.)

PULMONARY EMBOLISM

If one of the blood vessels to the lungs from the right side of the heart becomes blocked by EMBOLISM, the condition is known as pulmonary embolism. The blood clot develops somewhere else in the body, perhaps as a result of injury, or following surgery or childbirth, and is carried through the veins and heart into the lungs. Symptoms include a sudden cough, shortness of breath, chest pain, bluish lips, spitting of blood, shock and collapse. Pulmonary embolism is an emergency requiring immediate transfer to hospital.

PULMONARY HEART DISEASE
Enlargement of the heart secondary to obstruction of blood flow from the right side of the heart into the lungs as a result of PULMONARY EMBOLISM, EMPHYSEMA, PNEUMOCONIOSIS or any chronic inflammatory condition of the lungs. The right ventricle often fails to pump adequately against the obstruction, with resulting increase of venous blood pressure. Right heart failure often leads to OEDEMA, ASCITES, liver and kidney failure. Treatment is to correct the underlying cause, plus measures to improve the contractile power of the heart muscle.

PULSE
The alternating rise and fall in arterial blood pressure due to the pumping action of the heart. The three pulses most commonly taken are the radial pulse at the wrist, the carotid pulse in the neck and the femoral pulse in the groin. Generally the pulse rate is counted on the radial artery. The pulse rate can vary between different people but usually it is between 60–80 beats per minute in a healthy adult.

PUPIL
The opening in the centre of the coloured part of the eye (the iris) through which light passes to the retina.

PURPURA
A blood disorder in which blood leaks from subcutaneous blood vessels causing purple blotches under the skin. Purpura may be the result of a defect in the capillaries or defects of blood clotting usually due to insufficient platelets in the circulation. Contributing factors include vitamin deficiencies, certain drugs and some allergies. Treatment depends on the cause.

PUS
A thick yellow fluid found in abscesses and at the site of infections and inflammations. Produced by the body's defensive reaction against bacterial infection, pus is made up of dead white cells, blood serum, bacteria (both dead and alive) and damaged tissue.

PUSTULE
A blister that is filled with pus.

PYAEMIA
A form of SEPTICAEMIA, or blood poisoning, in which the blood is invaded by pus-forming bacteria which have spread from a site of infection elsewhere in the body. Pyaemia causes high fever, rigours and prostration and can be life-threatening unless promptly treated with antibiotics.

PYELITIS
An infection, usually bacterial, causing inflammation of the central part of the kidney where the ureter begins. Symptoms include pain in one or both sides of the lower back, fever, urinary difficulties and bloody or cloudy urine. Pyelitis should be promptly treated with antibiotics to prevent permanent kidney damage. See also PYELONEPHRITIS.

PYELONEPHRITIS
Although the term is sometimes used to describe any form of PYELITIS, strictly speaking pyelonephritis describes the serious condition in which the initial bacterial infection has spread from the central part of the kidney into surrounding parts of the organ. Pyelonephritis may be ACUTE, lasting a few days, or CHRONIC, persisting for many years. Chronic pyelitis is often a consequence of overuse of analgesic powders. If untreated, it can lead to kidney failure. Symptoms include pain in the lower back, fever, pain on urination and frequent urination. Treatment is with appropriate antibiotics.

PYLORIC STENOSIS
An obstruction of the pylorus, the strong muscular valve between the stomach and the duodenum. It may occur as a congenital condition in babies, or develop as a result of scarring from a long-standing gastric or duodenal ulcer in adults. Symptoms include colicky pain in the upper abdomen, severe projectile vomiting, weight loss, dehydration. Pyloric stenosis in both adults and babies usually requires surgical correction.

PYORRHOEA
Now called periodontitis, it is inflammation with pus formation in the gums around the roots of the teeth. Treatment is by drainage of pus, antibiotics to clear up infection, and appropriate oral hygiene.

PYREXIA
Raised body temperature, fever.

PYRIDOXINE
Vitamin B_6. See VITAMINS.

PYROSIS
The medical name for heartburn. See also INDIGESTION.

PYURIA
Pus in the urine, which may be seen as a cloudy fluid, indicating a bacterial infection somewhere in the urinary tract.

Q FEVER

An infectious disease of sheep, cows and goats, which may be transmitted to humans from an infected animal's excretions or by drinking its milk. Q fever is most commonly found among dairy farmers and abattoir workers. It cannot be passed from one human to another. Symptoms include fever, prostration and often chest pains, followed a few days later by pneumonia and a persistent cough. Q fever was first described in Queensland, but it occurs world-wide. It may be successfully treated with antibiotics. Prevention is by pasteurisation of milk, and by vaccination of those at occupational risk of infection.

QUADRIPLEGIA

Paralysis affecting all four limbs, the result of injury to or disease of the spinal cord in the neck. (See Medical And Health Support Organisations.)

QUARANTINE

The period of isolation of people or things which may be carrying infections that could be passed on to others. The purpose of quarantine, the length of which depends on the incubation period of the suspected diseases, is to protect other people, animals and plants from possible infection.

QUICKENING

The first signs of movement of a FOETUS that are felt by the mother, usually between the eighteenth and twentieth weeks of pregnancy.

QUINSY

An ABSCESS under the mucous membranes surrounding the tonsil. Quinsy is usually one sided, and is the result of spread of infection from acute bacterial TONSILLITIS. Symptoms include swelling and severe pain in the affected side of the throat, difficulty in swallowing and speaking, high temperature and spasm of the jaw muscles. Usual treatment is with antibiotics although in severe cases the abscess may need to be opened under local anaesthetic to drain the pus.

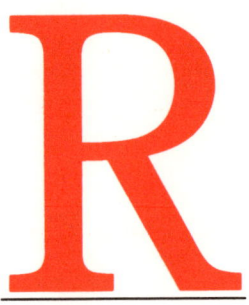

RABIES

Also known as hydrophobia, rabies is an acute viral disease that is endemic in dogs, cats, foxes, bats and even cattle. It is transmitted to humans when saliva from an infected animal enters the body through an open wound, usually a bite. Symptoms appear when the virus has reached the brain, and include fever, muscle spasms, extreme irritability, convulsions, paralysis and, if untreated, death within two or three days. Rabies is arrested by passive immunisation immediately following a bite from an infected animal. The disease does not occur in Australia and New Zealand due to strict animal QUARANTINE.

RADIATION SICKNESS

An illness caused by over-exposure to the high-energy radiation given off by RADIOACTIVE substances. Symptoms, which may follow accidental exposure or the use of radiotherapy in the treatment of cancer, include vomiting, diarrhoea and weakness, sore mouth and throat, fever and hair loss. Though severe accidental exposure may be fatal, recovery is usually spontaneous within one week after exposure is ceased.

RADIOACTIVE

Giving off rays or particles that are able to penetrate most substances and so affect living cells. The most powerful and potentially harmful (if not handled carefully), are X-RAYS and gamma-rays. Radium and uranium are naturally radioactive elements.

RADIOLOGY

The branch of medicine in which X-RAYS and radioactive substances are used to diagnose and treat certain diseases. A specialist in the field is called a radiologist.

RADIOTHERAPY

The treatment of diseases, such as certain types of TUMOURS and CANCER, using X-RAYS and other radioactive substances. While radiation can damage any living tissue, it is more destructive to cells that are rapidly multiplying (as do cancer cells) than to normal, slower growing cells. Used in conjunction with anti-cancer drugs, radiation can be effective in killing off malignant cells. However in some cases such treatment has unpleasant side-effects of mild RADIATION SICKNESS.

RASH

A temporary skin eruption due to inflammation of the skin, which may be caused by infection, allergy, chemical irritation, physical injury (such as sunburn, chafing), disorders of blood or blood vessels and nervous disorders. Rashes may be local (confined to a specific area) or general (occurring anywhere on the skin). In generalised rashes the cause is usually distributed by the bloodstream. Most rashes involve redness, with or without swelling, in spots or patches of varying shape and size. As well there may be itching, blistering, weeping, crusting, scabbing or peeling of the affected areas. Many rashes (for example those seen in infectious diseases such as CHICKEN-POX, MEASLES, SCARLET FEVER) are characteristic of the cause, so that diagnosis can be made on the appearance and distribution of the rash. If any rash persists, especially if accompanied by other symptoms such as fever and headache, consult your doctor. The treatment of rashes is that of the underlying cause, plus measures to relieve itching.

RAYNAUD'S DISEASE

A condition in which the blood supply to the hands and feet is temporarily restricted resulting in the affected parts becoming numb, white and then blue, followed by flushing when the circulation returns to normal. Raynaud's disease is the result of hypersensitive reaction to cold causing spasm of arteries in the extremities. When the affected part is warmed, symptoms subside in 15–30 minutes. If the spasm is not reversed, there may be permanent damage to the part and, in extreme cases, GANGRENE. Treatment includes keeping the extremities warm, avoiding other factors (such as smoking, holding vibrating tools, certain drugs) which may aggravate arterial spasm, the use of vasodilators, and expert advice on care of the feet from a podiatrist.

RECTOCELE
PROLAPSE of part of the rectum into the vagina or through the vaginal opening. Rectocele may be found after the pelvic floor has been damaged during childbirth and may be aggravated by further weakening of this area after the menopause. Often there are no symptoms. However, large rectoceles may cause difficulty in emptying the bowel or may be uncomfortable because of their size. In such cases treatment is by surgical repair.

RECTUM
That lower part of the large bowel which terminates at the ANUS. (See How The Body Works, p. 18.)

REFERRED PAIN
A pain that originates in one part of the body, but which is felt in another part supplied by nerves from the same region of the spinal cord.

REFLEX
A specific and involuntary response to a stimulus. The most well-known is the knee jerk where the stimulus of a tap on the tendon below the knee sends an impulse along a sensory nerve to the spinal cord. Here it triggers a return impulse for action resulting in the leg being kicked forward without either message having reached the brain. Another example is the contraction and dilation of the pupil of the eye according to the available light.

REGRESSION
The stage in which a disorder is subsiding or getting better. The term is also used in psychiatry to describe a return to childlike behaviour, perhaps indicating a desire to escape problems and emotional stress.

REGURGITATION
The flow of fluid or matter in the opposite direction to normal. Examples are the bringing up of partly-digested food in vomiting and the backwards flow of blood through a poorly functioning heart valve.

REHABILITATION
The process in which people who have been deprived of the routine of their normal life through illness or injury are reintroduced to their regular routine and environment. They may be given PHYSIOTHERAPY, instruction from an occupational therapist, counselling and access to support groups in order to learn to cope with a disability.

REITER'S DISEASE
A disease which affects men, characterised by DIARRHOEA, URETHRITIS, CONJUNCTIVITIS and ARTHRITIS. Although the causes are not exactly known, Reiter's disease is thought to be sexually transmitted and is usually associated with infections of the bowel or urethra or occurs as a complication of DYSENTERY. Symptoms include painful joints, backache, discharge from the urethra, painful red eyes and small mouth ulcers. It is treated with anti-inflammatory drugs and, if specific infection is identified, appropriate antibiotics.

RELAPSE
A return or worsening of symptoms after apparent partial or total recovery.

REMISSION
A period in which the symptoms of a disease lessen or abate although the condition has not been cured. Remission may be spontaneous or may follow treatment, and may last for days or weeks to many years.

RENAL CALCULUS
A stone in the kidney. See KIDNEY STONE.

RENAL FAILURE
Failure of the kidneys to perform their main functions of filtering waste products from the blood, controlling salt and water balance, and controlling blood pressure and red blood cell formation, ridding the body of fluid wastes. Kidney failure leads to URAEMIA in which the waste products, many of them poisonous, accumulate in the body. There are many possible causes of both ACUTE renal failure and CHRONIC renal failure. Acute renal failure may occur when the kidney is deprived of blood (as in HAEMORRHAGE or HEART ATTACK) or it may be the result of acute NEPHRITIS, which damages the kidneys' filtering units. The most obvious early symptom is the very small amount of urine passed in a day. Others include loss of appetite, nausea, vomiting, and, as uraemia develops, drowsiness, confusion, convulsions and coma. Treatment is according to the cause.

Chronic renal failure may be caused by chronic nephritis or PYELONEPHRITIS, KIDNEY STONES and CYSTS or over-use of certain ANALGESICS. Symptoms, which appear gradually, include frequent urination, fatigue and lethargy. If specific treatment proves to be unsuccessful, chronic renal failure may progress to the stage in which the kidneys can no longer sustain life. The only treatment then is with DIALYSIS (which is also used in some cases of acute renal failure) or kidney transplant. With modern technology and drug treatment, renal failure is not inevitably fatal as it once was. See also KIDNEY MACHINE.

REPETITIVE STRAIN INJURY (RSI)

A form of TENDINITIS or TENOSYNOVITIS resulting from repeated strain, injury or excessive unaccustomed exercise of particular muscles or muscle groups.

REPRESSION

A term used in PSYCHOANALYSIS to describe the mechanism by which those desires and impulses that prompt feelings of guilt or anxiety are forced out of a person's conscious mind and into the UNCONSCIOUS mind. They may emerge from the unconscious mind in a disguised form.

RESECTION

Surgical removal of the diseased part of an organ. For example a diseased section of intestine may be removed and the remaining cut ends joined or connected to a STOMA in the abdominal wall.

RESPIRATORY SYSTEM

(See How The Body Works, pp. 10–11.)

RESUSCITATION

Emergency measures to revive a person whose heart or breathing has stopped as a result of drowning, choking, electric shock, drug overdose or heart attack. (See also First Aid.)

RETENTION (URINARY)

The inability to pass urine from the bladder. Retention is common among older men who have an enlarged PROSTATE GLAND. Other causes include CYSTITIS, obstruction of the urethra by a stone, paralysis of the bladder muscle due to brain or spinal injury. Urinary retention requires urgent treatment. Immediate treatment is to drain the urine through a catheter. Prevention of further retention is by treating the underlying cause.

RETINA

The light-sensitive layer which lines the back of the eyeball. The retina contains millions of tiny cells, known as rods and cones, that detect and register light and send nerve impulses to the brain, giving rise to the sensation of sight. When fluid from within the eye leaks through a hole in the retina, it separates the retina from its underlying tissue in a condition known as DETACHED RETINA.

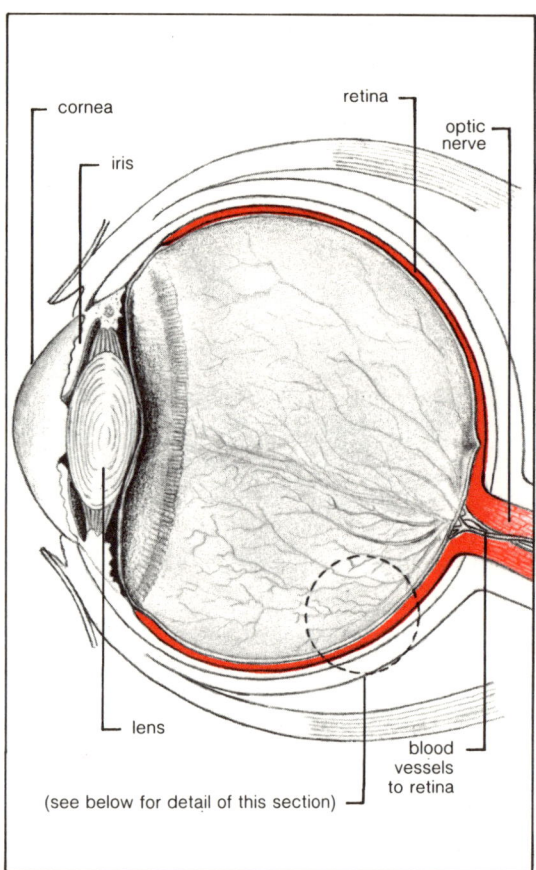

(see below for detail of this section)

Cross-sectional diagram of the middle of the eye. The rods and cones (see detail) of the retina pick up light rays and transmit them via the optic nerve to the brain.

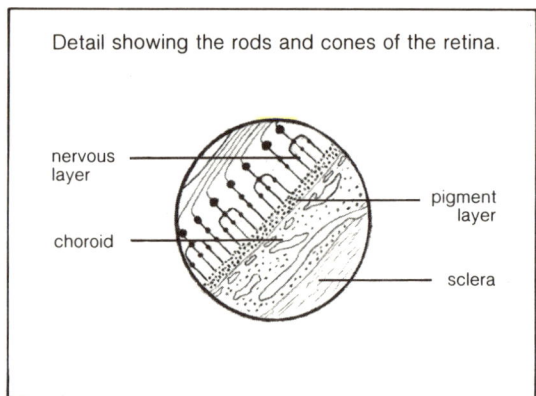

Detail showing the rods and cones of the retina.

RHESUS (Rh) FACTOR

A factor found on the surface of red blood cells which was first identified in the rhesus monkey, hence its name. Most people, (over 80 per cent) have this factor in their blood so are said to be Rh-positive.

People who do not have the factor are Rh-negative. The presence or absence of the Rh factor is inherited, and is important in blood transfusion. The rhesus factor is particularly important in pregnancy. If an Rh-negative mother has an Rh-positive baby, some of the baby's red blood cells may pass into the mother's circulation causing the production of Rh antibodies. In subsequent pregnancies, these antibodies can enter the blood of the foetus and, if it is Rh-positive, destroy its red cells. The presence or absence of the Rh factor is checked before blood transfusion and during pregnancy. Treatment with ANTI-D ANTIBODY is now given to Rh-negative mothers at the time of delivery of any Rh-positive baby to prevent the formation of antibodies which might affect a subsequent pregnancy. Nowadays very few babies die of Rh incompatibility.

RHEUMATIC FEVER

A disease, most commonly found in children, which causes inflammation of the connective tissue and the inner lining and valves of the heart. It may occur a week or two after a throat infection, such as TONSILLITIS, PHARYNGITIS or SCARLET FEVER, caused by streptococcal bacteria. Symptoms include fever, swollen and painful joints, nosebleed, a rash on the trunk and limbs and involuntary writhing movements of face, arms and body (ST VITUS'S DANCE). Treatment is bedrest and antibiotics. Although in most cases there is complete recovery, rheumatic fever can damage the heart valves resulting in MITRAL VALVE DISEASE. Since rheumatic fever tends to recur, antibiotics are usually prescribed long-term to prevent streptococcal infections, which might lead to another attack.

RHEUMATISM

A general term for pain and soreness, with or without stiffness, in the muscles and joints. It may be caused by a large number of diseases including ARTHRITIS, RHEUMATOID ARTHRITIS, RHEUMATIC FEVER, BURSITIS, OSTEOARTHRITIS, FIBROSITIS and GOUT.

RHEUMATOID ARTHRITIS

A progressive, slowly destructive disease of unknown origin that leads to CHRONIC inflammation of initially the small joints of the hands and feet and later, the larger joints of the wrists, knees, shoulders, ankles and elbows. Rheumatoid arthritis usually begins between the ages of 25 and 55, and affects twice as many women as men. As well as the swelling, pain and stiffness in the joints, there may be loss of appetite, fever and general malaise. Eventually the affected joints, especially in the hands, develop the characteristic knobby and twisted deformities. Rheumatoid arthritis, which can be diagnosed through blood tests and X-rays, is

treated with steroids, other anti-inflammatory drugs and PHYSIOTHERAPY. (See also Medical And Health Support Organisations – ARTHRITIS.)

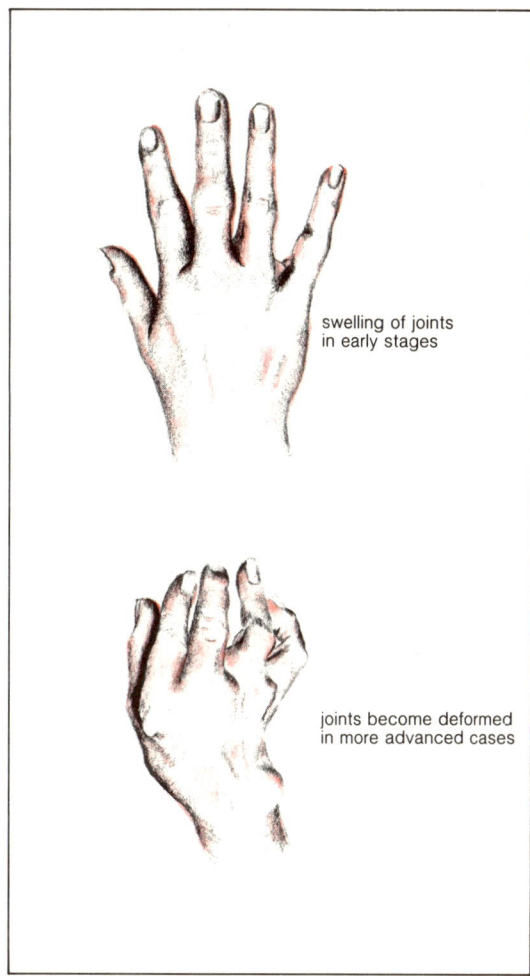

swelling of joints in early stages

joints become deformed in more advanced cases

Rheumatoid arthritis is an autoimmune disease which causes chronic and progressive inflammation of the joints. Severe deformity may now be prevented by treatment in the early stages.

RHINITIS

Inflammation of the mucous membranes of the nose causing running nose, CATARRH, sneezing, cough and headache. It may be caused by virus infections such as the COMMON COLD or by allergic reactions such as HAY FEVER.

RHINOPHYMA

Reddening and thickening of the skin and underlying tissues of the nose, leading to gross enlargement and disfigurement. Rhinophyma occurs as a complication of ROSACEA.

RHYTHM METHOD

A method of CONTRACEPTION which relies on calculating precisely the time in a woman's menstrual cycle when the egg is released by the ovary (ovulation). The period from seven days before to 48 hours after ovulation is known as the 'unsafe' or fertile time. During the unsafe time, a couple must avoid intercourse to avoid pregnancy.

RICKETS

A children's disease caused by vitamin D deficiency, the result being that not enough calcium salts are deposited in the developing bones. Children with rickets, seen rarely here these days, have a characteristic prominent forehead, swollen and deformed wrists, knees and ankles, bow legs and knock knees and pain in the affected bones. It is treated initially with supplements of vitamin D, followed by a diet adequate in vitamin D and plenty of carefully controlled time in the sun. See VITAMINS.

RIGORS

The severe, shivering and chattering of the teeth, which often accompanies the development of a high FEVER.

RINGING IN THE EARS

See TINNITUS.

RINGWORM

The common name for a contagious skin infection caused by fungi. This name is misleading since there is no worm present, but the appearance of ringworm – an itchy circular eruption with a red, spreading edge – is partly suggested by the name. Treatment is by application of anti-fungal creams or lotions. Scalp ringworm, difficult to treat in the past, is now easily cured by the new oral antifungals such as griseofulvin and ketoconazole.

RODENT ULCER

Another name for the SKIN CANCER known as basal cell carcinoma (BCC). It is a slow-growing malignant tumour that occurs mostly on the face and neck. A rodent ulcer starts as a raised, firm, light pink swelling with a pearly surface. As the lesion grows, the centre becomes ulcerated and the edge raised, red and curling. If untreated it can lead to mutilating destruction of adjacent tissue and bone. Early diagnosis and treatment by a dermatologist is nearly always effective in curing rodent ulcer.

RORSCHACH TEST

A psychological test, devised by Swiss psychiatrist Hermann Rorschach early this century, popularly known as the inkblot test. A series of inkblots of varying shapes and colours are shown to a patient who must describe what each one suggests. The answers give an indication as to the person's emotional, intellectual and social state.

ROSACEA

A chronic disease of the skin of the nose, forehead and cheeks. It begins with flushing, followed by permanent blotchy redness due to dilatation or breaking of capillaries. Later, acne-like pimples develop. Rosacea mostly affects women of middle age and beyond. Younger men may be affected, often more severely. The condition may progress to RHINOPHYMA. The cause of rosacea is unknown, but it is thought to be associated with hypersensitivity and lack of harmony in the control of blood flow to the face – a localised version of the menopausal hot flushes. Rosacea is aggravated by eating or drinking foods which cause flushing of the face (strong tea, coffee, spicy food) or over-indulgence in alcohol. It is also aggravated by exposure to cold winds, sunburn, or by constant exposure to heat, such as when cooking. Anxious people seem to be more susceptible. There is no specific treatment for rosacea. Removal of any aggravating factors, hormone replacement to eliminate hot flushes, careful use of sunscreens, application of astringents to reduce blood vessel dilatation and sedatives for the relief of anxiety may help to slow progress. If pustules develop on the red skin or the eyes become inflamed, antibiotics may be prescribed.

ROUNDWORMS

A common intestinal parasite, often found in children and particularly common in tropical regions. They are one of the largest parasites, looking rather like earthworms and varying from several centimetres up to 30 centimetres in length. The condition, known as ascariasis, is caused by swallowing the eggs in contaminated food or water or by ingesting soil which contains the microscopic eggs. Infested children suffer malnutrition and have stunted growth. Often the worms are found in an infected child's stools. Drugs such as piperazine provide rapid and effective treatment.

RSI

See REPETITIVE STRAIN INJURY.

RUBELLA

Commonly called German measles, this is an infectious virus illness, usually of childhood, characterised by a pink rash on the face, neck and body. The symptoms of rubella are mild, indeed many people do not realise that they have been infected. After an incubation period of two to three weeks, there may be fever and tenderness in the lymph nodes, with the rash appearing the following day. The rash disappears after two or three days and spontaneous recovery usually follows. Rubella is not usually serious unless contracted by a woman during the first three months of pregnancy, when it may cause serious defects in the foetus involving the ears, eyes and heart. A pregnant woman, who has not had rubella or who has not been immunised against the disease, should be kept away from anyone with rubella during the early months of her pregnancy. An effective vaccine against rubella became available in 1969, and today most adolescent girls are immunised routinely at age 13. See IMMUNISATION.

RUPTURE
A break or tear occurring either through injury, as when the spleen may be ruptured in a sporting or road accident, or through a disorder such as APPENDICITIS, when the infected appendix may rupture, due to inflammatory destruction of its wall. Abdominal HERNIA is sometimes called rupture, because it occurs through a break in the abdominal wall.

SADISM
Pleasure, especially sexual pleasure, derived from making others suffer pain. It is named after the 18th-century French aristocrat, the Marquis de Sade, who described it in his writings.

SAFE PERIOD
Another name for the RHYTHM METHOD of contraception. See also CONTRACEPTION, OVULATION.

ST VITUS'S DANCE
A disorder characterised by irregular, jerky, involuntary twitching of parts of the body. It was originally given this name because, in the 14th century, people suffering from the disease used to pray to St Vitus. It is now known as Sydenham's chorea. Other symptoms include weakness and lack of muscular coordination, confusion, and emotional ups and downs. It is thought to be due to a complication of streptoccocal infection and, as in RHEUMATIC FEVER, to which it is related, HEART DISEASE may be a further complication. Rheumatic fever and St Vitus's dance are becoming increasingly rare as they can both be prevented by early antibiotic treatment of streptococcal TONSILLITIS.

SALIVA
A mixture of mucus and fluid produced by the salivary glands found in the cheeks, under the tongue and in the lower jaw. Normally every person produces, each day, about two litres of saliva which is secreted in a reflex action in response to the thought, sight or smell of food. Saliva contains an enzyme called ptyalin which helps dissolve starches in the first step of digestion. Mouth or throat infections usually result in the saliva becoming contaminated, so if a person with such an infection coughs or sneezes, the infection may be spread to others through a shower of tiny drops of saliva. MUMPS is one infection which may involve the salivary glands.

Non-cancerous tumours and stony masses known as calculi may also form in the salivary glands, causing the ducts to become blocked and the glands to become swollen. Both may be successfully removed in a relatively simple, minor operation.

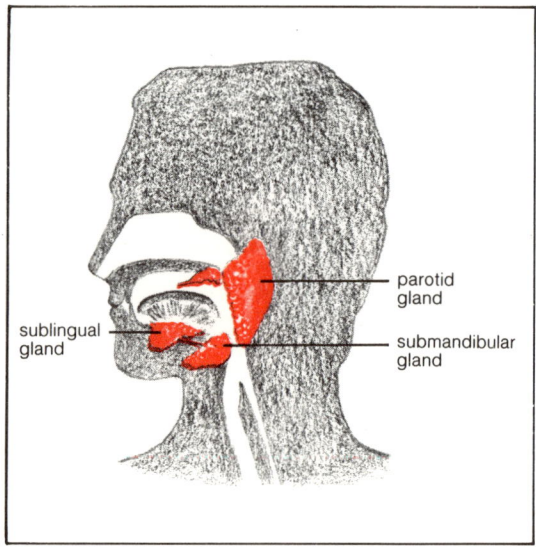

Saliva produced by three pairs of salivary glands keeps the mouth moist and lubricates food for chewing and swallowing. The glands can be activated by thought, sight, smell and taste.

SALMONELLA
A group of BACTERIA that live in the intestines and cause a variety of different diseases including TYPHOID, PARATYPHOID, SEPTICAEMIA, GASTROENTERITIS, FOOD POISONING. See also SALMONELLOSIS.

SALMONELLOSIS
A type of FOOD POISONING caused by BACTERIA of the SALMONELLA group. It is contracted through contaminated food.

SALPINGECTOMY

Surgical removal of one or both FALLOPIAN TUBES. The commonest reasons for this operation are severe infection and ECTOPIC PREGNANCY. If both tubes are cut or removed, fertilisation of egg cells cannot take place and permanent sterility results.

SALPINGITIS

Inflammation, usually due to infection, of the FALLOPIAN TUBE. The infection often also involves the ovaries and uterus, when it is known as PID (PELVIC INFLAMMATORY DISEASE). Symptoms include pain in the lower abdomen, vaginal discharge, painful intercourse, heavy and, in some cases, irregular periods and high fever. It may be caused by TUBERCULOSIS, infection following abortion or delivery, sexually transmitted infection such as GONORRHOEA or CHLAMYDIA, or may complicate acute APPENDICITIS. In many cases no obvious cause is found. Salpingitis may be acute and last only a few days if treated early, or chronic and last for months. If both tubes are affected in chronic salpingitis, infertility may be the result. Effective treatment is by ANTIBIOTICS. When large quantities of pus have accumulated in the tube, surgical drainage or SALPINGECTOMY may be necessary.

SARCOIDOSIS

A chronic disease in which small granular lumps form in the tissues, most often in the lungs, lymph glands, skin and eyes. Sarcoidosis in the lungs often resembles TUBERCULOSIS. There may be no symptoms although in severe cases there is usually fever, weight loss, joint pains, weakness. There is no known cause of sarcoidosis which, although it occurs around the world, is more prevalent in African races. There is no specific treatment. Cortisone is often prescribed to arrest progress of the disease. About two thirds of cases of sarcoidosis recover spontaneously.

SARCOMA

A MALIGNANT tumour of the connective tissues, such as muscle and bone. Definitive names indicate the tissue involved, as in liposarcoma (fat), osteo-sarcoma (bone). It is a less common type of cancer than carcinoma which originates in the covering and lining membranes of the body and in glands such as the breast, prostate and thyroid.

SATYRIASIS

An abnormal psychological condition in which a man has an excessive desire for sexual intercourse. In women, the similar condition is known as NYMPHOMANIA.

SCABIES

A skin infection caused by infestation by the mite *Sarcoptes scabiei* which lays its eggs in the outer layer of the skin. The mites' secretions cause intense itching (the common name for scabies being 'the itch'). Small red spots or lines are seen on the skin's surface where the mites have burrowed in to lay their eggs. When scratched, the spots often become infected. Scabies is contracted through close body contact with an infected person or through infested bedding or clothing. It is treated by the application of benzyl benzoate solution or gamma benzene hexachloride. Even though only one person may be affected, all members of the household should be treated. Mites and eggs in clothing and bedding can be killed by laundering and drying in the open air.

SCARLET FEVER

An acute infectious disease, now quite rare, caused by the same type of streptococcal bacteria that causes TONSILLITIS and PHARYNGITIS. Symptoms include, initially, nausea, vomiting and headache and then fever, sore throat, a rash of tiny spots which spreads over the body, a coated tongue which becomes bright red and – once the rash fades – perhaps peeling skin. Typically a disease of childhood (although it can affect adults), scarlet fever often used to result in complications such as RHEUMATIC FEVER, ear infections and NEPHRITIS. Through the use of antibiotics, scarlet fever is less serious these days than it once was.

SCHIZOPHRENIA

A chronic mental disorder, or PSYCHOSIS, characterised by disintegration of the personality. The condition is marked by irrational thinking and behaviour, emotional disturbances and an inability to relate to people. There are four main forms of schizophrenia which vary somewhat, although there may be no definite dividing line between them. People suffering from simple schizophrenia show a gradual mental deterioration and are usually apathetic and introverted. Paranoid schizophrenics are suspicious, believe they are being persecuted and may suffer from delusions and hallucinations. Hebephrenic schizophrenics generally behave in a bizarre manner, laughing and crying at inappropriate moments and using meaningless speech. CATATONIC schizophrenia is marked by fluctuations in behaviour, from extreme apathy to hyperactivity, often accompanied by strange and repetitive postures and gestures.

The cause of schizophrenia is not known but it is thought to be related to a genetic metabolic disorder. About one person is 1000 is affected, usually first between the ages of 18 and 30. Although some people suffering from schizophrenia require hospital treatment, modern drug treatment is helping many sufferers to lead more normal lives. (See also Medical And Health Support Organisations – MENTAL HEALTH & DISABILITY.)

SCIATICA

Pain felt along the course of the sciatic nerve, which runs down the leg from the sacral spine. It is usually the result of abnormal pressure on the nerve, caused by a slipped disc or by strain or injury of the lower back. The usual treatment is by correcting the cause, plus bedrest and analgesics to relieve the pain.

SCIATIC NERVE

The sciatic nerves, the largest in the body, run down each leg from the sacral spine. The sciatic nerve may become inflamed, as in NEURITIS, or it may be subject to pressure causing SCIATICA.

SCLEROSIS

Hardening of tissues due to infiltration with dense fibrous tissue, which may displace or destroy the functional tissue of the part, such as nerve, muscle or gland cells.

SCOLIOSIS

Abnormal, sideways curvature of the spine which may be congenital, or caused by poor posture, serious bone disease in the hip or spine or muscular imbalance due to paralysis of muscles in part of the trunk or legs. It is a common consequence of POLIOMYELITIS. While most cases improve by correcting the cause, severe cases may need physiotherapy, plaster casts or corrective surgery.

SCROFULA

A now rare childhood disease which is a type of TUBERCULOSIS affecting the lymph nodes, particularly in the neck. In many cases the germs come from infected milk, entering the system through the tonsils. The lymph nodes swell and later abscesses form, break through the skin and cause large weeping sores. If untreated the sores leave nasty scars. It is treated by anti-tuberculosis drugs, and prevented by pasteurisation of milk.

SCROTUM

The soft pouch hanging from below the base of the penis containing the TESTES. In ORCHITIS, the scrotum may become inflamed and red and swollen, or it may be affected by varicose veins, as in VARICOCELE. (See How The Body Works, pp. 26–27.)

SCURVY

A disease, now rare in the western world, caused by a severe lack of vitamin C, which is essential in maintaining healthy connective tissue in the skin, muscles and lining of the blood vessels. Indications of scurvy include bruising of the skin unrelated to injury, inflamed gums and eventually anaemia. People most at risk are alcoholics, the dispossessed and bottle-fed babies. Established scurvy is treated with large dose vitamin C tablets, but it can be easily prevented with a healthy diet including plenty of fresh fruit and vegetables. See VITAMINS.

SEBACEOUS CYST

A painless lump, usually found in the hairy skin of the scalp, face, neck, back and groin, arising in the sebaceous glands due to blockage of their ducts. Sebaceous cysts contain a dense yellowish-white accumulation of sebum which may become infected and painful. Such cysts do not go away on their own but can be easily and permanently removed surgically. See CYST.

SEBACEOUS GLAND

Glands found alongside the roots of all body hairs, and which produce a protective oily substance called SEBUM.

SEBORRHOEA

Abnormally oily skin due to excessive production of SEBUM from the SEBACEOUS GLANDS. It is not known precisely what causes the over-production of sebum but it is believed to be due to an excess of male hormones (ANDROGENS) or hypersensitivity of the sebaceous glands to androgens. Seborrhoea is often associated with ACNE, ECZEMA and DANDRUFF. Oily cosmetics should be avoided because they tend to aggravate the condition. The skin should be washed regularly with a gentle, mild soap. If seborrhoea is severe, consult a dermatologist.

SEBUM

The protective, oily substance produced by the SEBACEOUS GLANDS in the skin. See SEBORRHOEA.

SEDATIVE

Any drug that depresses the central nervous system. Sedatives are often used to give relief from agitation, anxiety, irritability, over-excitement and emotional stress. In a moderate dose, sedatives induce calmness and in larger doses, induce sleep.

SEIZURE

See CONVULSION.

SEMEN

(See How The Body Works, pp. 26–27.)

SENILITY

The deterioration of mental and physical capabilities that sometimes occurs in the natural process of ageing.

SEPSIS

Bacterial infection of the blood or tissues.

SEPTICAEMIA

A condition in which pathogenic (disease-causing) bacteria circulate and multiply in the blood causing high fever, rigours, weakness, sweating, low blood pressure and sometimes delirium. The organisms may settle in tissues or organs to cause localised infections. See BLOOD POISONING.

SERUM SICKNESS
The common name for an allergic reaction to an injection of animal serum which may occur seven to twelve days after the injection. It is characterised by mild fever, HIVES or pains in the joints and swollen lymph glands. Injections of human serum rarely cause serum sickness.

SEX ACT
Another name for coitus, copulation or SEXUAL INTERCOURSE.

SEX HORMONE
Any of the hormones which control and regulate sexual development and reproduction. Sex hormones (ANDROGENS in men, OESTROGENS and PROGESTERONES in women) are secreted under the influence of master hormones produced by the PITUITARY GLAND. See also How The Body Works, pp. 25–27.)

SEXUAL INTERCOURSE
The act of sexual union, coitus or copulation. We all have powerful instincts and reflexes, mostly outside conscious control, which lead to sexual attraction, sexual desire (LIBIDO) and sexual arousal. The main biological purpose of sexual intercourse is insemination of the female through ejaculation of semen into the vagina. The mating instincts and the shared past and anticipated pleasures of sexual arousal and sexual intercourse are important factors in maintaining the bonds of a relationship. (See also How The Body Works, p. 27.)

SEXUALLY TRANSMITTED DISEASES (STD)
Also known as venereal diseases, these are infectious diseases transmitted through contact with genital organs or secretions. Contrary to some popular myths, the organisms that cause these diseases survive only a few minutes outside the body so the chances of contracting such a disease from a toilet seat or a towel are very slight. Common sexually transmitted diseases include GONORRHOEA, SYPHILIS, genital HERPES, TRICHOMONIASIS, THRUSH, non-specific URETHRITIS, CHLAMYDIA and genital WARTS. See also AIDS (and Medical And Health Support Organisations).

SHINGLES
The common name for herpes zoster. This disease is the result of viral inflammation of the root of a sensory nerve. Shingles is caused by the same virus that causes chicken-pox in children. It is thought that after chicken-pox, the virus remains dormant in some or all nerve roots, only becoming active to cause shingles in states of severely reduced immunity. Shingles is marked by clusters of small blisters and severe pain along the course of the nerve. The redness and scabs remaining after the blisters break usually last two to three weeks. In some cases the pain along the course of the nerve may last for some months after the blisters have disappeared. There is no specific treatment for shingles, but rest and analgesics will help to relieve symptoms. The new anti-viral drugs will shorten the course of an attack.

SHOCK
A general term used to describe a set of symptoms associated with failure of the circulatory system. Shock may result from many severe disturbances including TRAUMA, HAEMORRHAGE, SEPTICAEMIA, MYOCARDIAL INFARCTION, severe DIARRHOEA, severe burns, overwhelming allergic reactions such as may occur following bee and wasp stings. Indications of shock include weakness, pallor, cold and sweaty skin, weak and fast pulse, low blood pressure, rapid, shallow and irregular breathing, thirst and sometimes unconsciousness. Anyone with a severe injury or burn may suffer delayed shock so should be closely watched for some hours after the injury. People showing signs of shock should be kept still and warm while waiting for medical attention. (See also First Aid.)

SHORT-SIGHTEDNESS
See MYOPIA.

SHOULDER
The ball-and-socket joint where the arm joins the shoulder bone. These bones are held together by

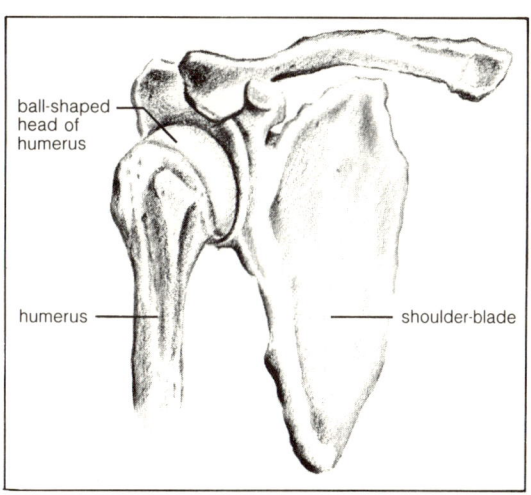

ball-shaped head of humerus

humerus

shoulder-blade

The ball-shaped head of the humerus can rotate in almost any direction in the socket formed by the shoulder-blade.

muscles, tendons and ligaments. The shoulder joint has a greater range of movement than any other joint in the body. (See also How The Body Works, pp. 2–3.)

SIAMESE TWINS

Identical twins born joined together, usually at the head, chest or hip. So-named because the first such twins (described medically as conjoined) to receive widespread publicity were born in Siam, now Thailand, last century. Such babies can usually be separated surgically unless they share a common heart, liver or other vital organ.

SICKLE-CELL ANAEMIA

A congenital disorder of the red blood cells in which the HAEMOGLOBIN is abnormal, causing the cells to be abnormally shaped. The sickle cells are fragile and break up easily, leading to haemolytic ANAEMIA. Also, the abnormal cells cannot pass properly through capillaries, with resulting THROMBOSIS and INFARCTION. Sickle-cell anaemia is found only in black-skinned people. If the gene is inherited from both parents, the condition is severe and usually fatal in childhood. If inherited from only one parent the carrier is usually normal or only mildly affected.

SILICOSIS

An occupational lung disease caused by breathing in rock dust, such as that from quartz or silica, over a period of time. Miners, sandblasters and quarry workers are most frequently affected. The dust particles cause an inflammatory reaction in the lungs, with subsequent destruction of tissue and scarring. Symptoms include shortness of breath, repetitive dry cough and later BRONCHITIS and EMPHYSEMA. Silicosis can't be cured but may be largely prevented by special ventilation of work sites, breathing masks and regular health checks. See PNEUMOCONIOSIS, OCCUPATIONAL DISEASE.

SINUS

A hollow space or cavity, generally in bone, and usually used to describe the paranasal sinus, the four sets of air-filled cavities in the bones of the skull. Such cavities may become infected in SINUSITIS. The term 'sinus' is also used to describe a passage or channel between a site of infection and the surface of the skin or a mucous membrane.

SINUSITIS

Inflammation of the mucous membranes of one or more of the paranasal sinuses, the air-filled bony cavities of the skull which are connected with the nasal cavity. It may be ACUTE or CHRONIC. Acute sinusitis may be associated with the COMMON COLD or other upper respiratory tract infections, or may be secondary to allergic RHINITIS or infected teeth in the upper jaw. Symptoms include pain in the front of the head or cheeks, green or yellow discharge from the nose, blocked nose on the affected side, raised temperature, heavy, watering eyes, sore teeth and tenderness over the affected sinus.

Home remedies include analgesics to relieve the pain, inhalations of menthol in steam and decongestant medicines, nasal sprays or drops. Antibiotics may be prescribed to clear up the infection. Chronic sinusitis is characterised by a persistently blocked nose, discharge from one or both nostrils, reduced sensitivity to taste and smell and recurrent or persistent pain in the front or the head and face. Usual treatment is a complete course of antibiotics although in some cases surgical drainage of pus from the infected sinus may be necessary. People suffering from either acute or chronic sinusitis should avoid tobacco smoke and other inhaled irritants.

SKELETON

(See How The Body Works, pp. 2–3.)

SKIN

(See How The Body Works, p. 4.)

SKIN CANCER

There are three types of skin cancer: RODENT ULCER (basal cell carcinoma), malignant MELANOMA and squamous cell carcinoma. Like other skin cancers, squamous cell carcinoma usually occurs in sun-damaged skin, so is mostly found on the hands, head, face, ears, lips and neck. It is more common after middle age. It often develops in thickened, scaly or corn-like patches known as hyperkeratoses. Malignant change is indicated by the hard patches of skin enlarging to eventually develop into an ulcer, which may bleed. There is usually little or no pain. Effective, permanent treatment is by surgical removal of the growth.

SKIN GRAFT

A method used to repair a badly damaged area of skin, as in burns, injury or surgery, whereby healthy sections of a patient's skin are taken from the thigh, back or abdomen and placed over the damaged areas of the body. Skin grafting is the oldest and most successful type of tissue transplant since there is no problem of rejection with a self-graft and new skin grows readily over the area from which the graft has been taken.

SKULL

The bones that frame the head and enclose the brain and the organs of sight, smell, taste and hearing. (See How The Body Works, pp. 2–3.)

SLEEPING PILL

See BARBITURATE, SEDATIVE.

SLEEPING SICKNESS

A disease caused by an organism spread by the tsetse fly and found only in tropical Africa. Symptoms include fever, swollen glands, headache and eventually inflammation of the brain, resulting in lack of vitality, tremors, convulsions, prolonged bouts of sleeping, then coma and death. Early treatment by CHEMOTHERAPY, before any brain damage has occurred, is effective in stopping progress of the disease.

SLEEPLESSNESS

See INSOMNIA.

SLEEP-WALKING

The common name for somnambulism. This is a condition in which a person, usually a child, moves about and carries out various actions while asleep, usually during the first third of the night. Sleep-walking is no cause for concern although sensible precautions, such as a gate at the top of a staircase, should be taken to protect a child from injury. Most children stop sleep-walking as they grow older.

SLIPPED DISC

This condition occurs when the soft centre of one of the rubbery, shock-absorbing intervertebral discs bulges out through a weakened section of its cartilage casing and presses on a spinal nerve, causing severe pain. Injuries and strains are progressively more likely to result in slipped disc after the age of 25, when the discs have begun the gradual process of degeneration which continues throughout adult life. A sudden sharp movement, a strain or an ill-considered attempt to lift a heavy object may cause the cartilage to split, allowing the enclosed disc to protrude. The discs in the lower back are most likely to be affected. Symptoms include severe pain which may spread down one or both legs, and which may become worse on bending, getting up from a sitting position, coughing, or movements involving the back. Sometimes the pain is associated with PARAESTHESIA and weakness of leg muscles. Immediate treatment is by analgesics and complete rest of two to six weeks on a firm bed. Physiotherapy is important in restoring strength and flexibility to the spinal muscles and joints. Anyone who has already suffered a slipped disc, or who may be vulnerable to the condition occurring, should minimise the risk by avoiding twisting the body and lifting at the same time. When lifting an object, keep the back straight and bend at the knees. See also BACKACHE.

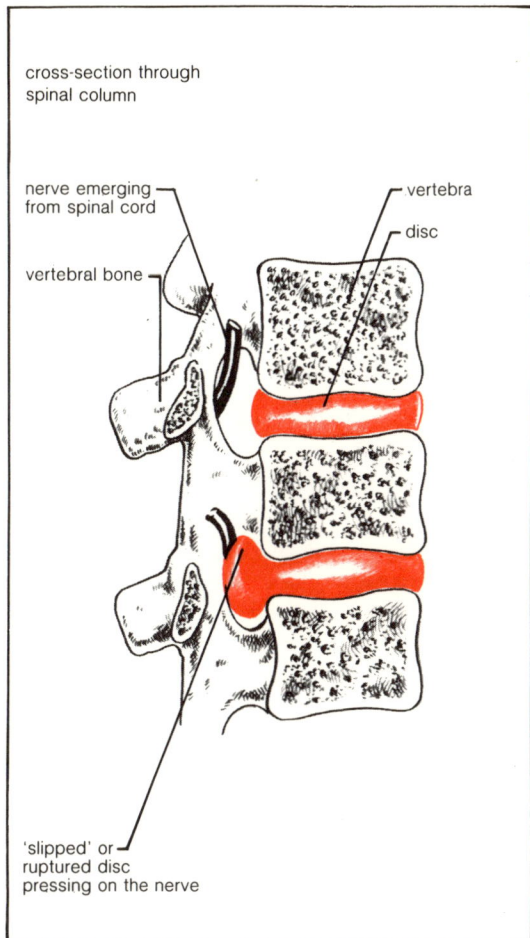

cross-section through spinal column

nerve emerging from spinal cord

vertebra

disc

vertebral bone

'slipped' or ruptured disc pressing on the nerve

The soft centre of an intervertebral disc may be forced through its cartilage capsule by injurious movements of the spine.

SMALLPOX

A highly contagious infectious disease caused by a virus spread by contact with an infected person. The onset of smallpox is heralded by fever, headache, sore throat, cough and nausea. Three or four days later the characteristic spots appear on the face and hands, then over most of the body. The spots resemble the chicken-pox rash in appearance, but differ in that on healing, after about three weeks, they leave the skin pitted and scarred. Once a killer disease, smallpox is now kept under control by vaccination programmes and strict public health safeguards. It was officially declared eradicated by the World Health Organisation in 1979. Vaccination is no longer regarded as necessary, especially in western countries, although the World Health Organisation has a stock of vaccine to guard against any possible outbreaks of the disease.

SMEAR TEST (PAPANICOLAOU OR PAP SMEAR)

Microscopic examination of a scraping of cells from any part of the body. Dr Papanicolaou invented the stain used in this test to differentiate various features of cells. The term is usually used to refer to the examination of cells from the cervix of the uterus in order to check for pre-cancerous changes. Cancer of the cervix (the neck of the uterus) is one of the most common cancers in women, but if pre-cancerous changes are detected early, it can be prevented. Doctors recommend that every woman should have a cervical smear test every two or three years. Smear tests are also used to detect cancer cells in secretions from the digestive and respiratory systems. (See also Medical Tests And Examinations.)

SMEGMA

A mixture of dead skin cells and SEBUM which tends to collect in the skin folds around the CLITORIS and under the foreskin of the PENIS. A daily bath or shower, with particular attention to these areas, prevents the accumulation of smegma.

SMOKING

Smoking is one of the most dangerous, and potentially lethal, habits of modern society. Tobacco smoke has been found to contain some 300 chemical compounds including nicotine, which acts as a stimulant to the nervous system, sixteen substances capable of causing cancer in animals, carbon monoxide, cyanide and other dangerous irritant substances. In Australia more than 16 000 people die each year as a direct result of smoking-related diseases. In America more than 300 000 people die each year for the same reason. A man who smokes and who dies as a result of this habit loses an average of fifteen years of life. In Australia 90 per cent of all deaths from LUNG CANCER and chronic BRONCHITIS are thought to be caused by smoking. The risk is directly proportional to the number of cigarettes smoked. Smokers are twice as liable as non-smokers to develop certain types of HEART DISEASE. In Australia, 25 per cent of all deaths from heart disease are estimated to be caused by smoking. According to the Royal College of Physicians in England, smoking is now just as great a cause of death as were the once-devastating epidemics of typhoid, cholera and tuberculosis.

The risk of developing such diseases as lung cancer, bronchitis and heart disease decreases progressively after a person gives up smoking. After ten years of not smoking, a person runs no greater risk of contracting such diseases than does a person who has never smoked. Unfortunately there is no easy way to give up smoking. Hypnotherapy, psychotherapy, group therapy and anti-smoking aids may all be helpful, but the bottom line is determination with motivation and willpower. Many health and education agencies run helpful motivational and support campaigns to assist people to stop smoking.

SNEEZING

An involuntary reflex action, triggered by irritation in the nasal passages, which forcibly expels air from the nose and throat. The irritation may be caused by dust or pollen or it may be the result of inflammation as in the COMMON COLD or other causes of RHINITIS.

SOMNAMBULISM

See SLEEP-WALKING.

SORE THROAT

Although smoking or too much talking may result in a sore throat, the condition is usually a warning sign that germs are invading the throat. Sore throat is associated with, among others, the COMMON COLD, TONSILLITIS, QUINSY, PHARYNGITIS, LARYNGITIS, MUMPS and VINCENT'S ANGINA. If a sore throat persists for more than two or three days, see your doctor.

SPASM

Sudden powerful, involuntary contraction of muscle. Muscle spasms may be caused by circulatory or metabolic disturbances, infection, injury or obstruction of hollow organs. See TIC, CRAMP, CONVULSION.

SPASTIC

A term used to describe conditions, usually the result of central nervous system damage, in which muscles are in a persistent state of spasm or uncoordinated, involuntary movements. The term usually refers to the spastic paralysis of CEREBRAL PALSY, caused by defective development or by brain damage occurring before, during or shortly after birth. Spastic hemiplegia is another type of spastic paralysis affecting one side of the body, the most common cause being STROKE. (See Medical And Health Support Organisations – CEREBRAL PALSY.)

SPECTACLES

Eye glasses with specially made lenses to correct defects of vision, most often those associated with short-sightedness (myopia), long-sightedness and astigmatism. Short-sightedness and long-sightedness may be the result of a mis-shapen eyeball or be due to an inability of the lens of the eye to change shape for focusing. Astigmatism is the result of an inability to focus vertically and horizontally at the same time and is generally caused by defects in the shape of the cornea. See also MYOPIA, ASTIGMATISM, EYE DISORDERS.

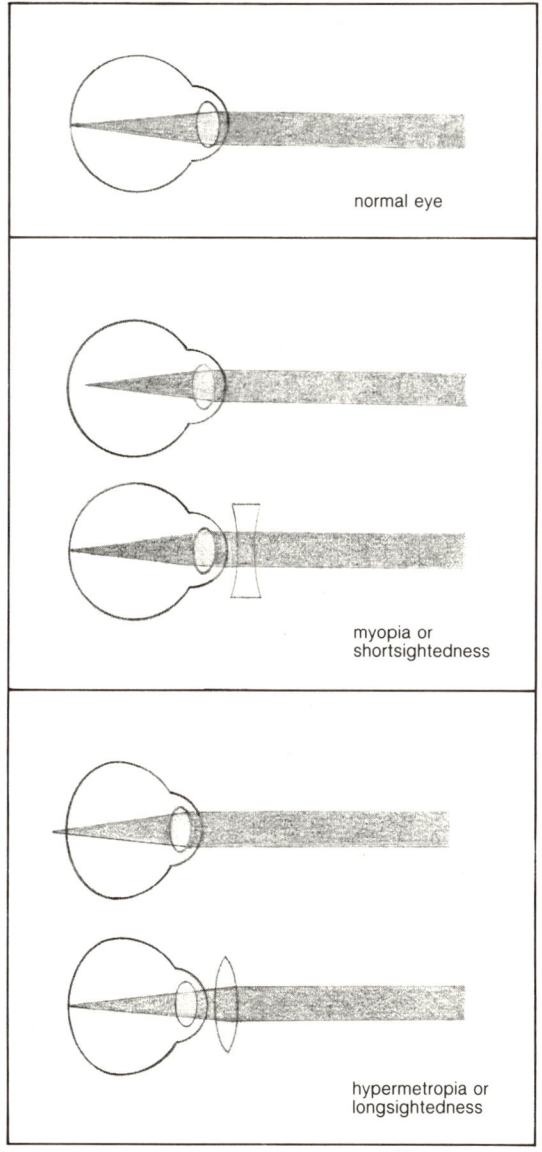

normal eye

myopia or
shortsightedness

hypermetropia or
longsightedness

The use of appropriate lenses in spectacles can correct
shortsightedness and longsightedness by focusing light
on the retina.

SPECULUM
A medical instrument to separate the walls of an
opening or passageway of the body so that a doctor
may more easily make an internal inspection.

SPEED
See AMPHETAMINES.

SPERM
(See How The Body Works, pp. 26–27.)

SPERMICIDE
Any substance which kills sperm. Commercially
available contraceptive spermicides contain
detergent-like chemicals which damage the sperm
cell membrane. See CONTRACEPTION.

SPHINCTER
A circular band of muscle around an orifice.
Sphincters may be opened under voluntary or
involuntary control to allow the passage of solids or
fluids through the orifice. For example, the sphincter
of the BLADDER is normally closed but opens, under
conscious control, to allow urine to flow out. The
pyloric sphincter, separating the stomach and
duodenum, relaxes automatically to allow the
passage of food from the stomach to the
intestines.

SPHYGMOMANOMETER
An instrument used for measuring BLOOD PRESSURE.
A rubber cuff connected to the instrument is placed
around the upper arm and inflated to compress the
arm until the flow of blood is stopped. As the cuff is
deflated the systolic and diastolic blood pressures
can be measured. See SYSTOLE, DIASTOLE.

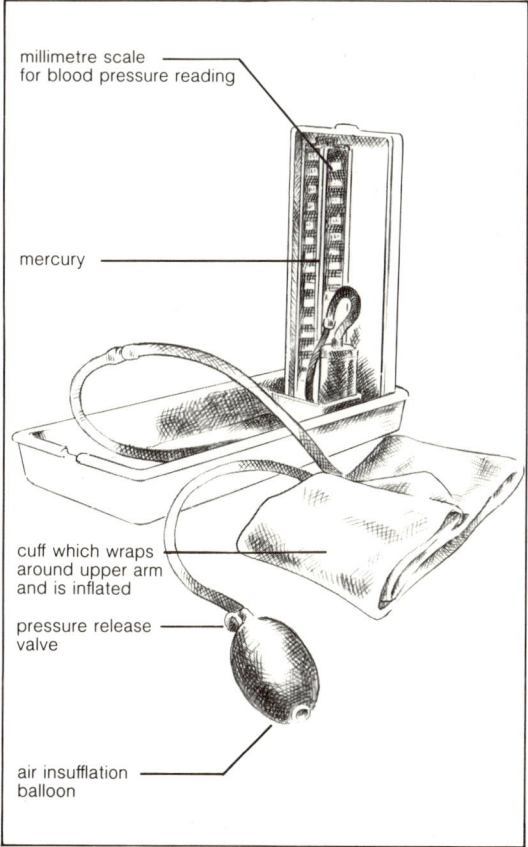

millimetre scale
for blood pressure reading

mercury

cuff which wraps
around upper arm
and is inflated

pressure release
valve

air insufflation
balloon

SPINA BIFIDA

A CONGENITAL deformity in which the bones of the spine, usually in its lower part, fail to join properly so that nervous tissue in the area is exposed and unprotected, and thus defective. The nerves in this part of the body control the muscles of the legs, the bladder and bowel, so that a child born with this deformity will usually have some degree of paralysis of the legs, and incontinence. The condition may be very mild, cause no problems and show up only on X-ray. Severe cases are characterised by a sac protruding from the middle of the back containing membranes and nerve fibres, PARALYSIS of the legs, INCONTINENCE,, hydrocephalus (excess fluid in the cavities of the brain) and mental retardation. Between the two is a range of disability ranging from minimal to severe. The exact causes of spina bifida are not known. There is no cure: nothing can be done to reverse the defective changes in the spinal cord and nerves. If a sac protrudes from the back, it will be repaired by surgery shortly after birth. Otherwise treatment is mainly aimed at preventing infections of the bladder and meningitis, with physiotherapy to prevent further deformities in the paralysed legs. There are special schools and centres which offer support to such children and their families. (See Medical And Health Support Organisations.)

SPINAL CORD

A thick, soft cord of white and grey matter which comprises the nervous tissue extending from the brain to the first lumbar vertebrae. Enclosed within the spinal canal, it makes up, with the brain, the central nervous system. (See How The Body Works, pp. 12–15.)

SPINAL CURVATURE

An abnormal curving, to the back or front or to either side, of the spine. It may be caused by congenital abnormality or disease of the bones of the spine or lower limbs, or disorders of the muscles and ligaments which support these bones. See BACKACHE, KYPHOSIS, SCOLIOSIS, SPONDYLITIS.

SPINAL PUNCTURE

See LUMBAR PUNCTURE.

SPINAL TAP

Another name for LUMBAR PUNCTURE.

SPINE

The bony, movable column of twenty-four vertebrae plus the sacrum and coccyx which support the trunk of the body. (See How The Body Works, pp. 2–3.)

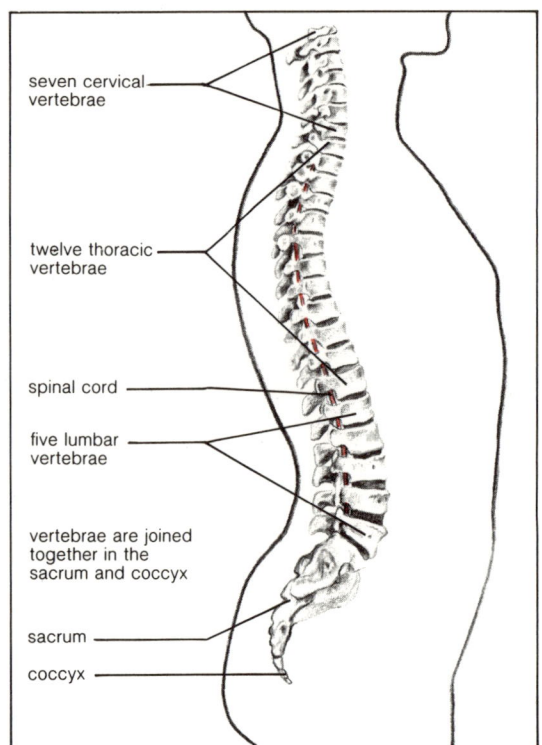

seven cervical vertebrae

twelve thoracic vertebrae

spinal cord

five lumbar vertebrae

vertebrae are joined together in the sacrum and coccyx

sacrum

coccyx

The intervertebral joints allow bending and rotation of the spine. The slightest movement, even breathing, involves the spine, which is why the pain of acute spinal injuries is so distressing.

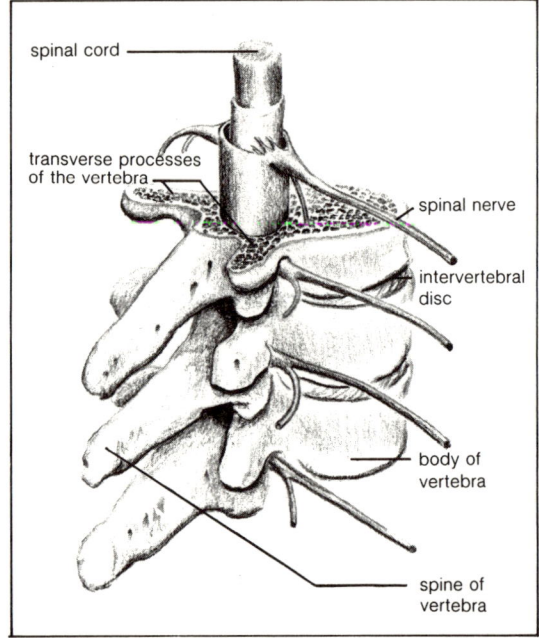

spinal cord

transverse processes of the vertebra

spinal nerve

intervertebral disc

body of vertebra

spine of vertebra

Detail of vertebrae and spinal cord.

SPLEEN

A lymphoid and blood-forming organ in the upper left-hand part of the abdomen. Weighing about 227 grams, it is made up of a pulpy, blood-filled mass of lymphoid tissue and red blood cells in a fibrous framework. The spleen is a centre for the formation of red and white blood cells in the foetus. In adults, it helps fight infection and removes old, worn out or damaged red blood cells and other particles from the blood. The spleen may become enlarged in a number of diseases such as MALARIA, TYPHOID, MONONUCLEOSIS, CIRRHOSIS of the liver, RHEUMATOID ARTHRITIS, LEUKAEMIA and HODGKIN'S DISEASE. A ruptured or diseased spleen may be removed surgically in an operation known as splenectomy.

SPONDYLITIS

Inflammation of the bones in the spine. Spondylitis may be the result of injury, infection or disorders such as OSTEOARTHRITIS, TUBERCULOSIS. It may lead to stiffness of the intervertebral joints such as SPONDYLOSIS, or deformity such as KYPHOSIS. See ANKYLOSIS.

SPONDYLOSIS

Arthritis of the joints between the vertebrae, often associated with degeneration of the discs. Spondylosis most commonly affects the neck. Symptoms are stiffness and pain (often radiating down the arms), which may be aggravated by spasm of the muscles surrounding the spine. Diagnosis is confirmed by X-ray. In most cases, treatment involves physiotherapy to relax and strenthen muscles, perhaps a short period in a neck support collar, and anti-inflammatory and analgesic medication. See SPONDYLITIS.

SPRAIN

A sudden, wrenching injury causing stretching or tearing of a ligament. Sprains result in swelling, tenderness, pain and restricted movement in the affected part. Rest and a firm bandage around the injured joint help the healing process which may take up to fourteen days in severe sprains.

SPRUE

A CHRONIC disease of the small intestine in which food and essential nutrients are inadequately absorbed. The condition is common in the tropics as a result of repeated or chronic bowel infections. Symptoms include flatulence after meals, diarrhoea and abdominal pain, poor appetite and weight loss. Treatment is with a diet high in kilojoules and proteins and low in gluten, as well as vitamin supplements and, in some cases, antibiotics to eliminate any remaining infection.

SQUINT

A common name for STRABISMUS.

STAMMER

A speech impediment, also known as a stutter, in which there is an interruption to the normal flow of speech as well as repetition of the first syllables of words. It is most often caused by a lack of confidence, anxiety and other underlying emotional problems. Quite often it is more noticeable as the sufferer feels increasingly stressed or flustered. Rarely is a stammer a sign of neurological disease. It is treated by speech therapy.

STAPHYLOCOCCUS

A member of a common group of BACTERIA that cause boils and other ABSCESSES as well as a type of FOOD POISONING.

STEATORRHOEA

Large and pale foul-smelling stools that may be difficult to flush away. Steatorrhoea may be a symptom of SPRUE and COELIAC DISEASE, and may be the result of any disorder which disrupts the proper digestion of food in the small intestine.

STENOSIS

The tightening or narrowing of any hollow organ or structure, such as an artery, heart valve, duct or passageway of the body. See PYLORIC STENOSIS, MITRAL VALVE DISEASE..

STERILISATION

A term that has several meanings when used in medicine. Usually it refers to a procedure in which medical instruments and dressings are made germ-free by treatment with dry heat, boiling water, radiation or steam.

It may also refer to surgical techniques used to induce permanent infertility. In men the procedure is VASECTOMY; in women the FALLOPIAN TUBES are removed, cut, tied, clamped or closed by diathermy in an operation known as tubal sterilisation.

STERILITY

The inability of a man or woman to have children either through natural INFERTILITY or as a result of an operation such as VASECTOMY or HYSTERECTOMY.

STEROID

A general term for any of a large group of drugs or naturally produced substances that have a similar chemical structure. The SEX HORMONES (androgens and oestrogens) and the hormones secreted by the cortex of the ADRENAL GLANDS (CORTICOSTEROIDS) are naturally occurring steroids. Synthetic corticosteroid drugs such as cortisone, together with the natural corticosteroids, have profound effects on the body's chemistry. Their main function is to reduce inflammation although some steroids suppress the immune responses of the body and so are used following transplant surgery. Another important use of corticosteroids is to reduce symptoms and prevent chronic tissue damage in acute or chronic non-infectious inflammatory diseases.

STETHOSCOPE

An instrument used to listen to the sounds of the heart, lungs, large blood vessels and other internal organs in order to detect any signs of disease or abnormality.

STILL'S DISEASE

A type of ARTHRITIS which affects children and which is similar to RHEUMATOID ARTHRITIS.

STINGS

(See First Aid – BITES AND STINGS.)

STITCH

A sharp pain below the ribs, usually on the left-hand side, which occurs when running or soon after a meal. It is caused by muscle spasm and disappears on resting.

STITCHES

See SUTURE.

STOKES-ADAMS ATTACKS

Named after two Irish doctors, these attacks of loss of consciousness, sometimes with convulsions, occur in people with complete heart block. If the slowly beating heart misses a couple of beats or suddenly beats even slower, the sudden reduction of blood supply to the brain is the cause of the blackout.

STOMA

A small opening, usually made surgically in the abdominal wall as in an ILEOSTOMY or COLOSTOMY.

STOMACH

A muscular bag at the lower end of the OESOPHAGUS which is the reservoir for food and the organ of digestion. (See How The Body Works, pp. 16–18.)

STOMACH-ACHE

See ABDOMINAL PAIN, INDIGESTION.

STOMACH CANCER

A malignant disease, more common in men over the age of 40 than in women. Symptoms include DYSPEPSIA initially, followed by loss of appetite, weight loss, pain in the upper abdomen, abdominal distension, vomiting, and bleeding causing vomiting of blood and leading to ANAEMIA. Diagnosis is

confirmed by BARIUM MEAL and GASTROSCOPY (see Medical Tests And Examinations). Stomach cancer is usually treated by surgical removal of the tumour and surrounding parts of the stomach, but in most cases, the outlook is not good.

STOMATITIS

Inflammation of the lips and the inside of the mouth. The causes are many, including nutritional deficiencies, irritating substances such as tobacco, certain drugs or bad oral hygiene. Thrush (MONILIASIS), trench mouth or VINCENT'S ANGINA, GINGIVITIS and oral HERPES simplex are all forms of stomatitis. The condition is often also associated with debilitating diseases such as pernicious ANAEMIA, LEUKAEMIA, prolonged feverish illnesses and PURPURA.

STONE

See CALCULUS. See also GALLSTONES, KIDNEY STONE.

STOOL

The individual sections of the solid wastes of the body (FAECES). The appearance of the stools may indicate the presence of a particular condition, and laboratory examination is often used to detect blood, mucus, germs and parasites which indicate specific diseases.

STRABISMUS

Another name for squint, a condition in which one or

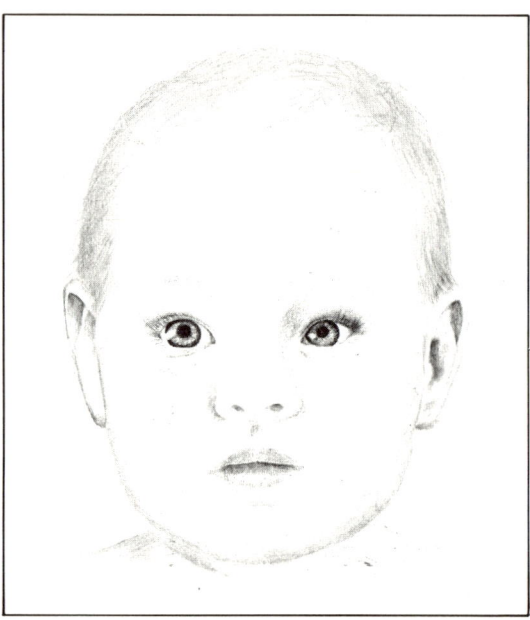

Strabismus (squint) is not usually noticed in the first weeks of life. Most childhood squints are easily corrected.

both eyes cannot be focused on the same spot at the same time; in other words, the two eyes do not look in the same direction at once. A squint may be convergent (where one or both eyes are turned towards the nose) or divergent (where one or both eyes are turned out towards the ears). Squint is generally present at birth although it may be difficult to detect in a tiny baby. Corrective spectacles, eye exercises and sometimes surgery in severe cases are all used in the treatment of squint.

STREP THROAT
A common term describing a throat infection caused by a type of streptococcal bacteria. It is always accompanied by fever and requires prompt treatment with antibiotics.

STREPTOCOCCUS
A member of a large group of spherical bacteria, many of which cause infections such as TONSILLITIS, SCARLET FEVER, STREP THROAT, RHEUMATIC FEVER and some forms of NEPHRITIS and ENDOCARDITIS. Many streptococci are harmless.

STRETCH MARKS
These form when the body grows from within faster than the skin can stretch to accommodate it. The deeper layers of the skin can stand only so much stretching. If rapid growth continues, many small breaks occur in the fibrous and elastic tissue of these layers. The breaks are comparable to a surgical incision beneath the surface layers of the skin and heal by the formation of scar tissue. At first the stretch marks are wide, purple-red lines. After six to twelve months they fade to a fine silvery lines, but no amount of massage or any application will make them disappear. Stretch marks are most likely during rapid growth of breasts, buttocks and thighs during puberty, and over the lower abdomen and breasts during pregnancy. They tend to be worse where there is the added strain of gravitational pull on the skin, so they can be reduced by wearing a firm bra and an abdominal support during pregnancy.

STRICTURE
The localised narrowing or contraction of the walls of a hollow organ or duct. The term most often refers to the URETHRA, where stricture results in difficulty or inability to pass urine.

STROKE
Also known as APOPLEXY and cerebrovascular accident, stroke refers to the brain damage that results from a blocked artery or a ruptured artery in the brain. Strokes, which are uncommon before the age of 50, may be associated with HYPERTENSION (high blood pressure), ARTERIOSCLEROSIS and

VALVULAR DISEASE OF THE HEART. Symptoms include paralysis or weakness of face, arm and leg on one side of the body, difficulty in swallowing and speaking, confusion and drowsiness, sometimes loss of consciousness or COMA, involuntary urination and defaecation. Immediate treatment in the case of a suspected stroke, and while waiting for the doctor, involves keeping the person quiet and warm and, if the person is conscious, giving reassurance. A person with stroke is usually taken to hospital for tests to determine the exact cause. In the case of blood clot, anticoagulants may be prescribed. In some cases of haemorrhage, an operation may be necessary to stop bleeding. The long-term prospects for a person who has had a stroke depend on the extent of the brain damage and the person's level of physical and mental fitness beforehand. Once the immediate problems are under control, PHYSIO-THERAPY and OCCUPATIONAL THERAPY are started.

STUTTER
Another name for STAMMER.

STYE
A common condition caused by infection in the root of an eyelash or in a sebaceous gland in the eyelid. A painful red swelling appears, which may progress to form a pus-filled cyst. The lower lid is more often affected. Usually a stye can be treated successfully at home by applying moist, very warm compresses to it, so making the cyst come to a head and discharge spontaneously. A stye should never be fiddled with as it may spread the infection. If a stye has not subsided within several days, consult your doctor.

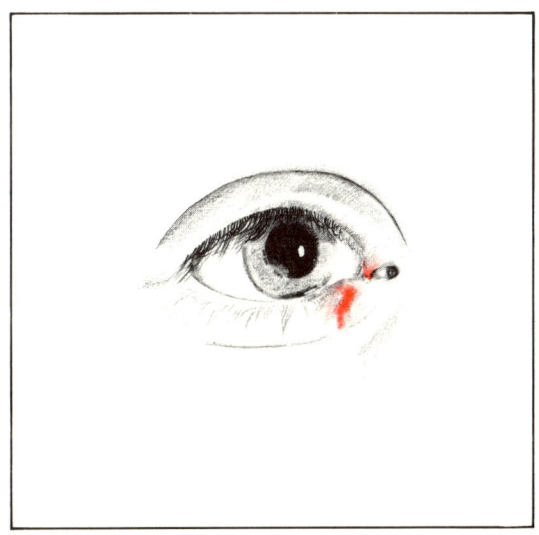

Stye is the common name for an infection in one of the glands of the eyelid.

SUBARACHNOID HAEMORRHAGE

Sudden bleeding on the surface of the brain, usually from the site of congenital weakness or ANEURYSM of a cerebral vessel. There is usually no apparent reason for rupture of the vessel, although the weakness has probably been present since birth. Symptoms, which depend on the extent and duration of bleeding, include sudden severe headache, nausea and vomiting, stiff neck, drowsiness, sometimes unconsciousness and paralysis. The diagnosis is confirmed by head X-ray, lumbar puncture and perhaps brain scan. Treatment is by admission to hospital for intensive care and expert nursing with life support systems until bleeding stops, after which recovery proceeds over some weeks. If possible, surgical closure of the affected vessel is usually attempted to prevent future haemorrhage.

SUDDEN INFANT DEATH SYNDROME

See COT DEATH.

SUNSTROKE

Serious upset of the body's cooling system due to excessive heat or exposure to the sun combined with a loss of fluid and salt. Symptoms include headache and dizziness, high fever, hot dry skin, lack of perspiration, vomiting, convulsions and even coma. Sunstroke is a serious condition needing urgent medical attention. Ice bags and cold baths are used to bring the temperature down and an intravenous drip of fluids containing salt and sedatives are given if necessary.

SUPPOSITORY

A drug, antiseptic or other medication given in the form of a soft pellet or cone which is inserted into the RECTUM or VAGINA.

SUPPURATION

The formation of PUS. A wound that discharges pus is described as suppurating.

SUTURE

The technique used to close surgical incisions and wounds, cuts and gashes by drawing the edges of the wound together using silk or nylon thread, catgut, wire and metal clamps. Suturing encourages rapid, more effective healing resulting in less disfiguring scars. The materials used in suturing, such as thread and clamps, are also called sutures. The sutures used in deep tissue or internal organs are absorbed by the body so do not have to be removed while the surface sutures are usually taken out after seven to fourteen days.

SWAB

A small stick with a piece of cotton wool or gauze wrapped around it used for cleaning out small body cavities or taking samples of discharge and secretions for laboratory analysis; or a small wad of gauze used to mop up blood during an operation.

SWEAT

Also known as perspiration, this fluid is secreted by the sweat glands in response to sympathetic nervous system stimulation as a reaction to heat, fear, pain, exertion, nausea and certain drugs. Sweating plays an important part in the body's temperature control system. Sweat is odourless until it comes in contact with bacteria.

SYDENHAM'S CHOREA

See ST VITUS'S DANCE.

SYMPATHETIC NERVOUS SYSTEM

(See How The Body Works, pp. 12–15.)

SYMPTOM

A noticeable change, often discomfort and pain, in a body organ or function indicating a disorder or disease. When a change indicating a problem is noticed on examination but not complained of by the patient, it is properly called a sign. The term symptom also applies to changes in behaviour indicating emotional stress or mental illness.

SYNCOPE

Another name for FAINTING.

SYNDROME

A collection of symptoms, signs and test findings which, occurring at the same time, are characteristic of a particular disease or disorder.

SYPHILIS

A venereal disease caused by the spiral-shaped bacterium called *Treponema pallidum*. Syphilis is usually acquired through sexual transmission, although it may be passed from an infected pregnant woman to her baby. There are three clear stages. In the first or primary stage a CHANCRE – hard, painless ulcer – develops, usually on the genitals, but sometimes on the fingers or lips, a few days after infection. The lymph glands draining the area – usually in the groin – become enlarged and tender. The chancre, which is highly infectious, heals spontaneously in two to four weeks. The secondary stage appears between six weeks and six months after exposure: a general rash appears together with sore throat, headache, swollen lymph nodes and elongated ulcers (snail track ulcers) in the mouth and on the tongue. The disease is highly infectious during this second stage which lasts for several weeks. The third, or tertiary stage, may become apparent within months or it may take years. Masses of rubbery tumours called gummas may form in a number of organs including the skin, brain and liver and testes. Tertiary syphilis also attacks and damages the heart, the blood vessels and the brain, resulting in disturbances of the circulation and neurological disorders, blindness, degeneration of the spinal cord, paresis (paralysis) and GPI (general paralysis of the insane).

Diagnosis of syphilis and treatment with appropriate antibiotics in the primary, secondary and latent (between the secondary and tertiary) stages results in complete cure. The potential problem of congenital syphilis can be detected during pregnancy by testing the mother's blood. If an infected mother is adequately treated with penicillin, the baby will not be affected.

SYSTOLE
The rhythmic contraction of the heart muscles during which blood is pumped out of the VENTRICLES and through the circulatory system. See DIASTOLE. (See also How The Body Works, pp. 5–9.)

TACHYCARDIA

Rapid heart rate. An increase in the rate of the heartbeat is a normal response to the increased demands on the circulation during physical exertion, fever, and in certain emotions such as fear. Tachycardia may also be a sign of disorders such as THYROID disease, HEART DISEASE, ANAEMIA or ANXIETY. In paroxysmal tachycardia, the heart suddenly starts to beat up to three times faster than its normal rate and then returns to normal just as suddenly. The cause of this is usually obscure, though it is thought to be due to disturbance of control of the PACEMAKER of the heart. Certain drugs, such as amphetamines, caffeine, alcohol and nicotine, may cause tachycardia. Severe tachycardia is often associated with PALPITATIONS, and if the heartbeat is so rapid that insufficient blood is ejected from the heart at each stroke, HEART FAILURE may result. The treatment of tachycardia is to correct the cause. Until this is achieved, the heart rate may be slowed with specific drugs.

TACHYPNOEA

An increase in the normal rate of breathing beyond the usual rate of 12–16 breaths per minute in adults. Tachypnoea is the normal response to increased demand for oxygen during exertion. It may also be a sign of such disorders as lung disease (especially the pneumonias), heart disease, anaemia, thyrotoxicosis, anxiety and hysteria.

TALIPES

See CLUBFOOT.

TAPEWORM

A long, flat parasitic intestinal worm. The most common tapeworms found in man occur as the result of eating undercooked beef, pork or fish from infected animals. Of the three, only the beef tapeworm is found to any extent in Australia. Generally people with a tapeworm suffer no symptoms although some may have abdominal discomfort or pain, diarrhoea or suffer from ANAEMIA or weight loss. The life cycle of tapeworms involves an animal swallowing the worm eggs which then hatch to form dormant cysts in that animal's muscles. When a person eats the flesh of an infected animal, the cysts develop into mature egg-producing worms in the human intestine. Segments of a mature tapeworm may be seen in an infected person's faeces, and the eggs can be detected by the microscope. There are a number of effective prescription drugs which will kill tapeworms.

TARTAR

A substance that collects around the teeth, especially along the gum line, consisting of plaque which has become calcified by mineral salts in the saliva. Tartar build-up should be regularly removed by the dentist for good dental hygiene.

TB

The abbreviation for TUBERCULOSIS.

TEETH

We have two sets of teeth: primary, or first teeth, in early childhood which are gradually replaced by permanent teeth from about the age of 6 onwards. Around the age of 12 most of the primary teeth have fallen out to make way for the permanent teeth. There are twenty primary teeth, ten in both the upper and lower jaws. Each jaw has two central incisors, two lateral incisors, two canines, two first molars and two second molars. The primary teeth begin to form months before a baby is born with the first teeth usually appearing when the baby is about six months old and the last ones, the second molars, usually appearing at the age of about two-and-a-half. There are thirty-two permanent teeth, sixteen in both the upper and lower jaws. Each jaw has two central incisors, two lateral incisors, two canines, four bicuspids, two first molars, two second molars

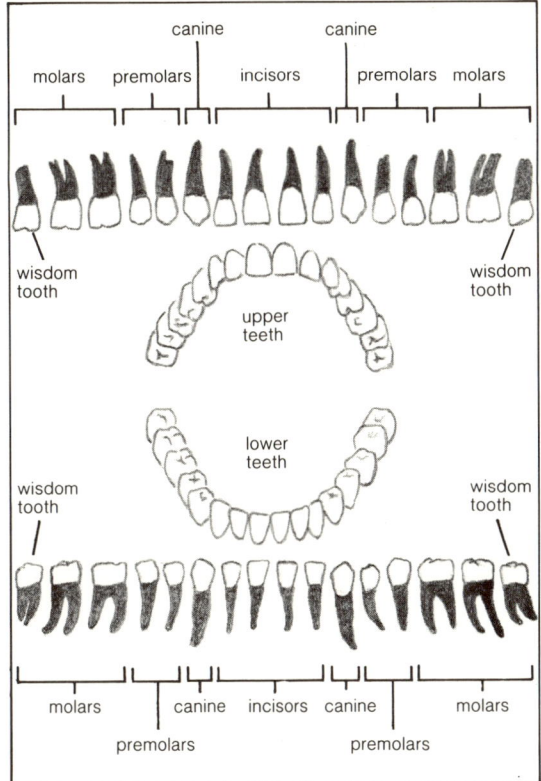

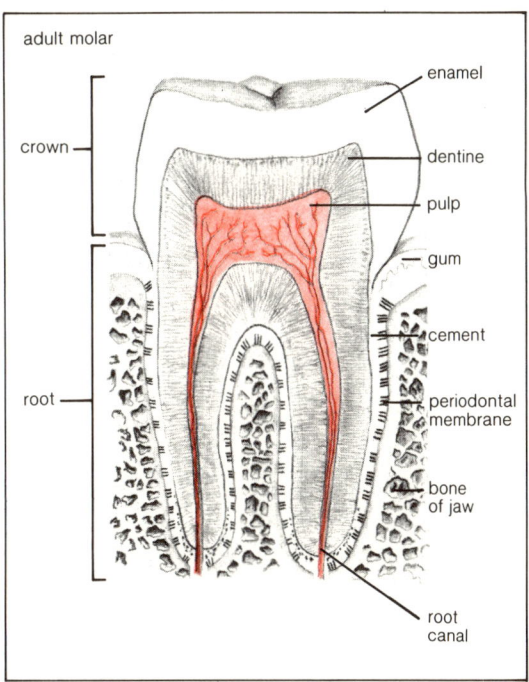

The 32 permanent teeth have usually appeared by age twenty-four. The third molar (wisdom tooth) is most likely to cause problems as it erupts.

and two wisdom teeth. The replacement of primary teeth with permanent teeth is usually a painless process. It is important that children have regular dental checks because the primary teeth play an important role in guiding the permanent teeth.

TEMPERATURE
A measure of the heat of the body. The normal range of body temperature is 36.7°–37.2°C (98°–99°F). A raised temperature usually indicates the presence of infection, while a lowered temperature may be the result of shock, large blood loss and MYXOEDEMA. See also FEVER, HYPOTHERMIA.

TENDINITIS
Inflammation of a TENDON, usually as a result of excessive – and often unaccustomed – use. The tendon becomes painful and tender, often with a stiff, creaking feeling when the affected part is moved. Treatment is with rest, analgesic or anti-inflammatory drugs, and physiotherapy. Severe cases may require injection into the tendon of local anaesthetic or corticosteroid. Tendinitis is often associated with TENOSYNOVITIS.

TENDON
The strong fibrous cord connecting muscles to bones. Tendons may be thick and short (as in those

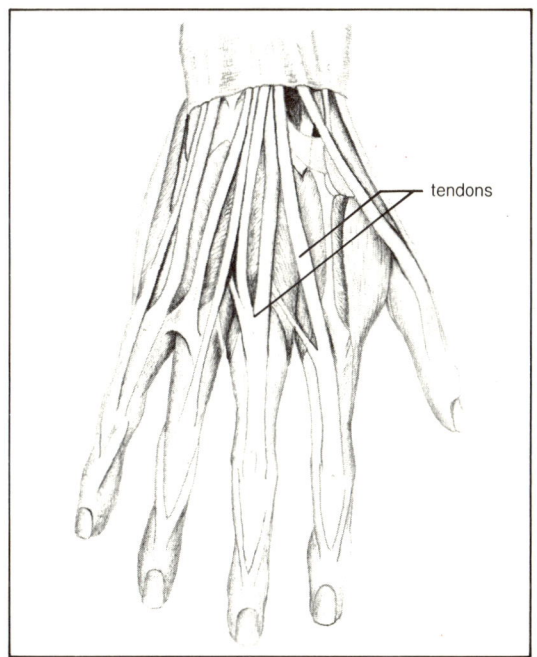

The long delicate tendons of the hand connect the muscles of the forearm to the fingers and control fine finger movements.

attaching the biceps arm muscles to the shoulder) or long and slender (as in those running from the forearm across the back of the hand to the fingers). Some tendons are surrounded by sheaths containing a lubricating fluid to reduce friction during movement. Inflammation of a tendon causes TENDINITIS, inflammation of the tendon sheath causes TENOSYNOVITIS.

TENNIS ELBOW
Inflammation of the tendons connecting the muscles of the forearm with the elbow. This condition is caused by over-use and jarring of the forearm muscles following unaccustomed activity such as a vigorous game of tennis, hence the name. Pain in the elbow may be severe, and often extends down the forearm. The pain is aggravated by twisting movements of the forearm. The best treatment is rest, analgesic and anti-inflammatory drugs, and PHYSIOTHERAPY. Hydrocortisone and a local anaesthetic may be injected into the most tender part to reduce inflammation and pain. In some severe cases, the elbow may need to be immobilised in a plaster cast for up to six weeks.

TENOSYNOVITIS
Inflammation of the sheath surrounding a tendon, most often found in the wrist, ankle or shoulder, which may be caused by over-use of the affected tendon or by RHEUMATOID ARTHRITIS. The usual symptoms are pain and tenderness in the tendon and a creaking sensation when the affected part is moved. Treatment is the same as for TENDINITIS and TENNIS ELBOW.

TESTES
The male gonads, or sex glands, which are situated in the scrotum. Production of sperm cells and SEX HORMONES begins at puberty, stimulated by hormones produced by the PITUITARY GLAND. Disorders of the testes include inflammation, known as ORCHITIS, possibly as a complication of MUMPS. They may also become infected by GONORRHOEA. Very occasionally, a testis, the VAS DEFERENS and its arteries may become twisted in a condition known as torsion of the testis. This causes severe pain and sometimes SHOCK, and quite often requires an emergency operation to avoid the blood supply to the gland being cut off. Usually the testes descend from the abdomen into the scrotum before birth, but sometimes when a new-born baby boy is examined it is found that one or both are undescended. In half of such cases, the testis will descend normally before the baby is four weeks old. Sometimes the condition may be corrected with hormone injections but if not, it is necessary for undescended testes to be brought down into the scrotum by surgery. If the testes are left in the abdomen, sperm cannot be produced,

resulting in INFERTILITY. As well, testes remaining in the abdomen are at higher risk of developing malignant tumours later in life.

TESTOSTERONE
The male SEX HORMONE produced by the TESTES. Testosterone is responsible for male secondary sex characteristics which develop in adolescent boys. (See How The Body Works, pp. 26–27.)

TEST TUBE BABY
See IN-VITRO FERTILISATION.

TETANUS
A serious disease caused by infection with bacteria called *Clostridium tetani*, which exist as spores in soil and animal faeces. The bacteria can only develop in tissue without oxygen, for example damaged flesh such as occurs in deep penetrating wounds, burns, animal bites or crush injuries beneath lacerations. Symptoms of tetanus, which are caused by the powerful toxin produced by the bacteria, begin with spasms of the voluntary muscles, usually beginning with clamping together of the jaws, hence the common name for the disease: lockjaw. Other symptoms include difficulty in swallowing, raised temperature, headache, sweating, stiffness of other muscles, convulsions and severe spasms in which the whole body becomes arched backwards.

The usual incubation period is six to fifteen days, shorter periods indicating more severe infection. Tetanus requires hospital treatment, where an injection will be given to neutralise the poison produced by the tetanus bacteria, plus appropriate drugs to control muscle spasm. In severe cases, where breathing is threatened, a breathing tube may be inserted into an opening – called a TRACHEOTOMY – made in the windpipe. This technique has dramatically reduced the number of tetanus deaths due to respiratory failure. Widespread immunisation of children and adults has helped reduce the number of cases of tetanus. For children anti-tetanus is included in the three routine triple antigen injections given in the first twelve months with boosters on starting and leaving school. Adults who have not been immunised should have a full course of three injections. See IMMUNISATION.

TETANY
A disorder in which abnormally low levels of calcium in the blood cause excessive irritability of the nerves, resulting in muscle spasms which may affect the hands, feet and face, and sometimes also cause CONVULSIONS. Tetany may develop for several reasons: hyperventilation (overbreathing) which temporarily lowers the amount of active calcium in the bloodstream, vitamin D deficiency, inadequacy of the parathyroid gland and excessive, prolonged

diarrhoea (which may drain the body of calcium). Treatment is by correction of the cause. Tetany should not be confused with TETANUS, which has some similiar symptoms.

THALASSAEMIA (MEDITERRANEAN ANAEMIA)

An inherited blood disease found mostly in Mediterranean countries and parts of Africa and Asia. In thalassaemia the red blood cells contain an abnormal form of HAEMOGLOBIN which gives the cells an abnormal shape and causes them to be broken down in a shorter time than the usual 120 days, leading to ANAEMIA. There are two main forms of the disease: **thalassaemia major** occurs when the gene responsible for the disease is inherited from both parents. Symptoms include jaundice, weakness, fever and the other indications of anaemia. Thalassaemia major may often be fatal, especially in children, and the only treatment is regular blood transfusion. **Thalassaemia minor** occurs when the condition is inherited from only one parent. People with this form of the disease can usually lead normal lives with few, if any, symptoms of anaemia.

THIAMINE

Another name for vitamin B_1, found in yeast and liver. See VITAMINS.

THREADWORM

Also known as pinworm, this common condition is caused by a small, parasitic worm, about 6–10 mm long, which infests the large intestine, and which can be seen around the anus and in faeces as tiny white, cotton-like strands. Symptoms include intense itching around the anus at night (when the female worms have made their way there to lay up to 10 000 eggs), abdominal pain and nausea. People with threadworms tend to scratch the itchy area and so pick up the eggs on their hands and under their fingernails. In this way the eggs may be passed back to the person's mouth or transferred to other people. The eggs may also be picked up from bed linen. Effective drugs are available to kill the worms. Even though only one person may have detectable threadworms, all members of a household should be treated at the same time.

THROMBOSIS

The formation of a blood clot (thrombus) inside a blood vessel. If the clot becomes detached from the wall of the blood vessel and is carried to another part of the body, it is known as an embolus. A thrombus may eventually block the blood vessel, with serious consequences. Thrombosis of a main artery in the arm or leg may lead to GANGRENE, especially if the person is elderly with poor circulation. Thrombosis in an artery supplying the brain results in STROKE.

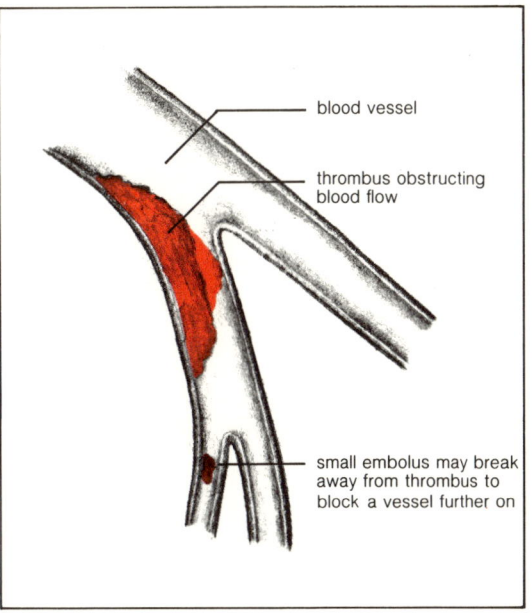

blood vessel

thrombus obstructing blood flow

small embolus may break away from thrombus to block a vessel further on

A thrombus usually starts on one side of a blood vessel wall. Further build-up of the blood clot may lead to blockage of the vessel.

Thrombosis in the coronary arteries (CORONARY THROMBOSIS) may cause ANGINA or heart attack (MYOCARDIAL INFARCTION). Thrombosis of the veins is most common in the vessels of the leg (DEEP VENOUS THROMBOSIS) and the pelvis, but may also occur in the portal vein which carries blood from the intestines to the liver. The wall of the vein around a thrombosis may become inflamed in the painful condition of thrombophlebitis. Thrombosis is treated by anticoagulant medication and sometimes by surgical removal of the thrombus in an operation known as thrombectomy. See also EMBOLISM.

THROMBUS

The medical term for a BLOOD CLOT in a blood vessel or the heart cavity. See THROMBOSIS.

THRUSH

The common name for MONILIASIS, inflammation caused by the fungus *Candida albicans* of the lining membranes of the mouth and vagina.

THUMB-SUCKING

A widespread habit among children. It usually starts in babyhood with most children outgrowing the habit by the age of 4. It should not concern parents since thumb-sucking rarely disturbs the normal growth of the teeth, unless the child continues the habit beyond the sixth year when the second set of teeth begin to appear.

THYMUS

A lymphoid organ in the neck which is essential to the development and maturation of immune function. The thymus is large and active during childhood but gradually shrinks after puberty.

THYROID GLAND

An ENDOCRINE GLAND in the neck in front of the trachea. It produces the hormones thyroxine and triiododthyronine which regulate the body's metabolism and influence growth rate and development. The hormone-releasing role of the thyroid gland is itself regulated by a hormone secreted by the PITUITARY GLAND. If the thyroid gland produces too little thyroxine before birth and during childhood, the result may be CRETINISM; too little thyroxine in later life may lead to MYXOEDEMA. Too much thyroxine may lead to THYROTOXICOSIS. Enlargement of the thyroid gland is known as GOITRE. (See How The Body Works, pp. 22–23.)

THYROTOXICOSIS

A condition in which there is an over-production of the thyroid hormone thyroxine, causing a speeding up of all chemical reactions in the body. This affects mental as well as physical processes. For unknown reasons, the condition affects about five times more women than men. EXOPHTHALMOS and Graves' disease are forms of thyrotoxicosis. Symptoms include bulging eyes, enlarged thyroid gland, agitation, hyperactivity, tremors, heat intolerance, sweating, weight loss in spite of increased appetite, rapid pulse, palpitations, diarrhoea and menstrual disorders. Diagnosis is confirmed by blood tests and thyroid scans. There are several successful forms of treatment including antithyroid drugs which control the secretion of the thyroid hormone, surgical removal of part or all of the gland and radioactive iodine solution by mouth, which inactivates much of the overactive thyroid tissue.

TIC

Intermittent spasm of a particular muscle or group of muscles, resulting in characteristic twitches. Tic douloureux is an extremely painful condition due to neuralgia of a nerve supplying one side of the face. See TRIGEMINAL NEURALGIA.

TINEA

A contagious fungal infection of the skin, often additionally described according to its site (for example, tinea pedis on the feet, tinea corporis on the body, tinea capitis on the scalp). RINGWORM is a form of tinea. All tinea may effectively be treated with anti-fungal applications.

TINNITUS

Buzzing or ringing in the ears when there is no external source of noise. It may be the result of a build-up of ear wax, high blood pressure, congestion or inflammation of the middle or inner ear, MENIERE'S DISEASE or the progressive loss of hearing that accompanies ageing. It can be a very distressing symptom. Treatment is that of the cause, and in some cases (Menière's disease for example), the ringing noises can be controlled by drugs. Organisations such as Better Hearing Australia can help with information on the latest research developments. (See Medical And Health Support Organisations – DEAFNESS; HEARING DISABILITIES.)

TONSILLECTOMY

Surgical removal of the tonsils. Since tonsils are part of the body's defence system against infection, their removal is controversial. In many cases swollen or infected tonsils may be controlled with antibiotics until the swelling subsides towards the end of childhood. When tonsils are affected by severe, chronic or recurrent disorders such as QUINSY, recurrent OTITIS media (middle ear infection) and repeated TONSILLITIS, most surgeons recommend removal.

TONSILLITIS

Inflammation of the TONSILS, most often found in children but also occurring in adults. Tonsillitis may be caused by numerous viruses and bacteria, and is often a symptom or complication of a number of infectious diseases such as MEASLES, GERMAN MEASLES, INFLUENZA, DIPHTHERIA and GLANDULAR FEVER.

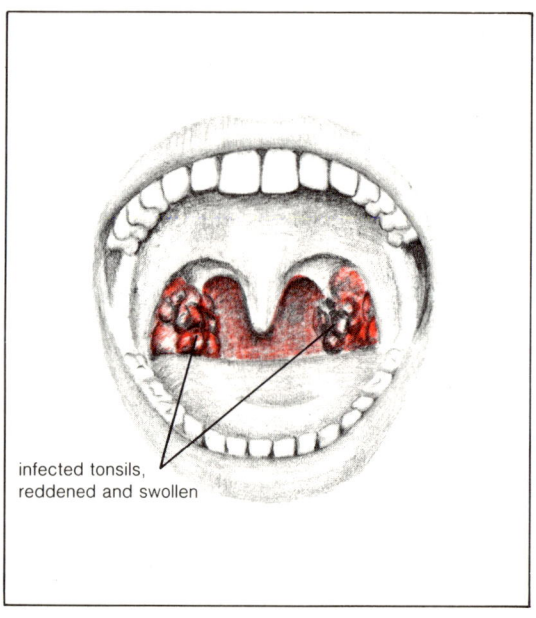

infected tonsils, reddened and swollen

In bacterial infection, pus may be seen on the surface of the tonsils.

Symptoms include sore throat, difficulty in swallowing, high temperature, dry cough, flecks of pus on the red, inflamed tonsils and back of the throat, swollen neck glands and white coated tongue. Any persistent sore throat, especially if associated with fever, should be checked by your doctor. If the source of the infection is bacterial, the usual treatment is with antibiotics.

TONSILS

A pair of flat oval nodules of lymphatic tissue which lie on either side of the entrance to the throat. The tonsils play an important role in protecting the body against the entrance of infection via the nose and mouth. The tonsils may become infected and enlarged, especially in childhood. See TONSILLITIS.

TOOTH DECAY

See CARIES.

TORTICOLLIS

The medical term for wryneck. This condition may be the result of muscles on one side of the neck being overstretched or injured during birth. Contraction of scar tissue in the damaged muscle later in infancy causes the head to tilt to one side while the face is turned to the other. Torticollis may also be due to severe burn or may be result of repeated intense head movements as occurs in some occupations. PHYSIOTHERAPY or surgery may help alleviate the condition.

TOXAEMIA

Also known as blood poisoning, it describes the presence of any poisonous substance in the circulating blood. It may be associated with DIPHTHERIA, FOOD POISONING, URAEMIA. Toxaemia in pregnancy is known as ECLAMPSIA.

TOXIC SHOCK SYNDROME

A relatively new and extremely rare condition, often associated with the use of tampons during menstruation, but also occurring after delivery and in people with large wounds covered by dressings. It is thought to be caused by toxins released from a staphylococcal infection in the vagina, uterus or under the wound dressing. Symptoms include sudden high temperature, vomiting and diarrhoea, dehydration, pallor, collapse, rapid pulse and other signs of shock. If such symptoms occur, remove any tampons or wound dressings and call a doctor immediately. Toxic shock is an emergency needing admission to hospital so that fluids and antibiotics may be given intravenously.

TOXIN

Any poisonous substance. However, the term usually refers to poisons produced by living things, either by bacteria inside or outside the body, or by waste products which accumulate through liver or kidney failure. An example of disease caused by a bacterial toxin produced outside the body is BOTULISM. The body's defence system produces antitoxins to neutralise the effects of some bacterial toxins.

TOXOCARIASIS

Infection by a roundworm that is primarily a parasite of cats and dogs but which can be passed to humans through contact with soil contaminated by faeces from an infected animal. If eggs have been in soil long enough to incubate, and are then swallowed by humans, they hatch into larvae and circulate through the body in the bloodstream. Small children who play in unclean sandpits are particularly at risk. Symptoms are often mild or non-existent, although clues to the disorder include unexplained fever, rash, vomiting, muscular aches and sometimes convulsions. A serious complication of toxocariasis can occur when the parasite gets into the eye, causing inflammation which may progress to blindness. Appropriate drugs will kill the worms but prevention is better than cure. Family pets should be regularly wormed; children's sandpits and play areas should be fenced to keep out cats and dogs.

TOXOPLASMOSIS

A serious infection of animals, most often sheep, cattle, cats and dogs, by the protozoan organism *Toxoplasma gondii*. The infection may be picked up by people through eating under-cooked meat from infected animals or by coming into contact with the animals' faeces or fouled soil. The disease affects the central nervous system, the lymph nodes, the spleen and eyes. Often there are no symptoms and the disease remains undetected and harmless. In more severe infections there may be symptoms similar to those of MONONUCLEOSIS (glandular fever). When a pregnant woman is infected with toxoplasmosis, there is a high risk of the infection being transferred to the foetus, with serious consequences. The pregnancy may miscarry, or the new-born may be affected by fever, jaundice, convulsions and eye and brain disorders. Most toxoplasmosis infections, including those during pregnancy, respond well to treatment with antibiotics.

TRACHEA

The windpipe, the tube made up of muscle, cartilage and membrane that is the main air passage stretching from the larynx to the chest where it divides into the right and left bronchi. (See How The Body Works, pp. 10–11.)

TRACHEITIS

Inflammation of the trachea, usually as a result of

bacterial, viral or fungal infections, or allergic reactions. The inflammation often also involves the throat and bronchi.

TRACHEOSTOMY

Another name for TRACHEOTOMY. The term tracheostomy is used when the lining of the trachea is joined to the skin to create a permanent air passage when there is irreversible blockage of the upper airways, such as permanent paralysis of the vocal chords.

TRACHEOTOMY

An operation to make an opening into the trachea through the skin and tissue of the neck just below the Adam's apple. A small tube, or air pipe, is inserted through the incision to allow air to reach the lungs without passing through the mouth and upper airways. Tracheotomy may be performed, often as an emergency measure, when there is obstruction of the upper airways such as can occur when the larynx is paralysed in diphtheria. Tracheotomy may also provide an airway for artificial respiration after head or chest injury, drug overdose or stroke. When normal breathing has been restored, the tube is removed and the wound closed.

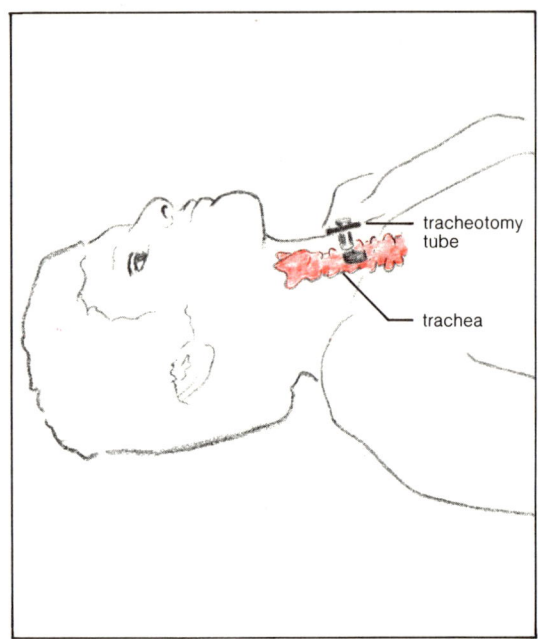

tracheotomy tube

trachea

A tracheotomy tube is inserted to allow air flow into the lungs when there is an obstruction in the larynx or upper trachea.

TRACHOMA

A contagious and serious eye disease that is ENDEMIC through Mediterranean countries, the Middle and Far East and parts of central Australia. It is the result of infection by the organism *Chlamydia trachomatis*, and is spread by contaminated hands, towels and such like. The infection causes severe CONJUNCTIVITIS and BLEPHARITIS, with copious discharge of pus from the eyes. If not treated, trachoma may progress to deformity of the eyelids due to scarring, and inflammation and opacities in the cornea leading to blindness. Early treatment with antibiotics, however, usually results in complete recovery. Simple hygiene (hand washing, keeping towels clean and not sharing them) is the best way to prevent the spread of trachoma.

TRANQUILLISERS

A number of different drugs which calm mental and emotional agitation without causing drowsiness or inhibiting the body's response to stimuli. While tranquillisers have greatly helped to relieve the symptoms of some emotional disorders and psychoses, they are not a cure. They may be either habit-forming or create dependency, and most tranquillisers have various side-effects. Tranquillisers must be taken under the supervision of a doctor.

TRANSFUSION

The intravenous infusion of blood from a donor to a recipient who has lost blood by HAEMORRHAGE, or who is severely ANAEMIC. Donors of blood must be in good health because diseases such as hepatitis, malaria, syphilis and AIDS (acquired immune deficiency syndrome) can be transmitted to others through blood transfusion. See also BLOOD GROUP.

TRANSIENT ISCHAEMIC ATTACK (TIA)

A mild transient form of STROKE, the result of temporary blockage of one of the blood vessels in the brain by spasm, or a small THROMBUS or patch of ATHEROMA. The attack subsides when the spasm abates or the thrombus or atheroma disperses. TIAs occur as a complication of HYPERTENSION, ATHEROMA and other disorders of the circulation, and are most common among elderly people. Symptoms include sudden weakness on one side of the face or in one leg or arm, a tingling sensation in the affected part, impaired vision and speech, and sometimes loss of consciousness.

There is no permanent damage, although a fifth of people who suffer from transient ischaemic attacks eventually suffer a full stroke. The rate of recurrence of this disorder varies. Some people suffer several attacks a day, others only rarely. Treatment is that of the underlying cause, often with the addition of long term use of drugs such as aspirin which reduce the risk of thrombosis. People who have suffered TIAs should not drive cars or operate potentially dangerous machinery.

TRANSPLANT

The surgical replacement of a diseased or damaged organ by transplanting a healthy one, taken from a donor, in its place. The most common transplanted organ is the cornea (see KERATOPLASTY), one of the few living tissues which can be transplanted with no risk of rejection because the cornea, having no blood vessels, is not affected by the immune defences which act through the bloodstream. There is also no risk of rejection in the grafting of blood vessels, heart valves and bone because the non-cellular fibres of the grafted tissues are rapidly invaded by living cells from the recipient's body. Kidney transplants are now carried out quite frequently, heart and liver transplants to a much lesser extent, although there have been a number of successful such transplants.

There are two major problems involved in transplants. Firstly there are not enough donor organs available for all the transplants that are needed. Secondly the body's own defence mechanisms, which reject any foreign tissue. Rejection can be prevented or reduced by a number of drugs called IMMUNOSUPPRESSANTS, which interfere with the body's normal immune mechanisms. However when immune mechanisms are reduced the body is also open to infection, so a careful balance must be drawn. Anyone who is given a transplant must accept the considerable risks of lifelong suppression of immunity.

TRANSSEXUAL

A person who believes that, despite belonging genetically to one sex, he or she should belong to the opposite sex. A transsexual usually dresses and behaves as, and adopts the life-style of, the desired sex. After intense psychological counselling and gender identity therapy, a transsexual may undergo hormone therapy and surgery to his or her external genital organs to enhance resemblance to the desired sex.

TRANSVESTITE

A person who derives sexual pleasure and emotional satisfaction from dressing in clothes of the opposite sex.

TRAUMA

There are two types of trauma, physical and emotional. A physical trauma is a wound or injury caused by an outside force; an emotional or psychological trauma is the result of an experience which leaves a profoundly painful or damaging impression on the mind of the sufferer.

TREMOR

Involuntary trembling or quivering of the muscles.

TRENCH MOUTH

An infection of the gums and possibly the membranes lining the mouth and throat and usually occurring in people with poor health and poor dental hygiene. See VINCENT'S ANGINA.

TRICHOMONIASIS

Infection by the protozoan parasite *Trichomonas vaginalis* (trich or TV for short), which causes VAGINITIS in women and URETHRITIS in men. The infection is spread by sexual contact, and is highly contagious. Trich produces an intense inflammation, a profuse, greenish-yellow, foul-smelling discharge and maddening irritation. Incubation period from contact to the appearance of symptoms ranges from a few days to three weeks. Ninety per cent of cases can be cured by a single dose of tinidazolde or a week's treatment with metronidazole tablets. All sexual contacts should be treated at the same time.

TRIGEMINAL NEURALGIA

The trigeminal nerves supply sensation to the face, teeth, mouth and nasal cavity, and control some movements of the jaw. In trigeminal neuralgia, intense pain is usually felt in one side of the mouth, lower jaw, gums, cheek or temple. Attacks may be triggered simply by touching the face, by a particular facial movement, by exposure to cold, by chewing, or may be the result of disturbance of the bite or other dental problems. The pain may last for seconds or minutes, and while it lasts it can be agonising. Attacks may occur every few minutes over several days or weeks, gradually becoming less intense and frequent. Some cases are accompanied by spasm of the facial muscles, when the condition is known as TIC douloureux. Trigeminal neuralgia is rare before age 50. The exact cause is not known. Treatment involves regular use of specific drugs which will prevent or reduce attacks in most cases. Sometimes the nerve may have to be destroyed by injection or operation. In some cases, the condition spontaneously disappears.

TRISOMY 21

See DOWN'S SYNDROME.

TUBERCULOSIS

Infection by the tubercle bacillus, *Mycobacterium tuberculosis*. Tuberculosis is now rare in Australia, but is still found in under-developed countries. It can affect all parts of the body but most frequently affects the lungs. More rarely tuberculosis is found in kidneys, bones, bowel, fallopian tubes and lymph glands, and as a cause of MENINGITIS. Infection is usually contracted through breathing in the germs in infected droplets of sputum or by swallowing contaminated food, especially milk. Many people are exposed to the tubercle bacillus but few develop tuberculosis. Healthy people usually overcome and develop immunity to the bacillus at first contact. The infection has a better chance of becoming established when the body's defences are weakened by other disease, poor nutrition, insanitary living conditions, or immunosuppression by drugs or disease such as AIDS.

Symptoms of active pulmonary (lung) tuberculosis include persistent cough producing yellowish and blood-stained sputum, weight loss, chest pain, breathlessness, night sweats, general ill health. In its early stages, there may be no symptoms and it may be detected only with the aid of X-rays. Miliary tuberculosis occurs when large numbers of bacilli spread through the bloodstream to many parts of the body. Specific drug treatment effectively destroys the tubercle bacilli. Due to efficient X-ray screening, pasteurisation of milk, drug treatment and vaccination, tuberculosis has ceased to be the killer disease it once was.

TUMOUR

An abnormal growth of tissue that forms a lump or swelling. It may be BENIGN or MALIGNANT.

TURNER'S SYNDROME

A congenital, chromosomal disorder in which growth and sexual development are disturbed. A person suffering from Turner's syndrome appears to be female but lacks one of the usual female sex chromosomes, being XO instead of the normal XX. The ovaries are absent, or non-functional remnants only. Without ovarian oestrogen, there is little or no development of secondary female sex characteristics.

TWINS

Twins occur about once in every eighty births and tend to run in families. Fraternal, or non-identical, twins develop from two different egg cells which happen to be fertilised at the same time. They may be of the same or opposite sex and are only as like one another as any other siblings in the family.

Identical twins develop from a single fertilised egg. At a very early stage, the fertilised egg divides to create two individuals with the same genetic make-up. Identical twins are always the same sex with the same blood group and the same eye colour. Identical twins who are not completely separated are known as conjoined or SIAMESE TWINS.

TYPHOID

An infectious disease of the intestines caused by the bacteria *Salmonellae typhi* and *S. paratyphi*. Typhoid is spread from sewage contaminated by the faeces of infected persons or seemingly healthy people, who harbour the germs in their gall-bladder and gut, and act as carriers. Flies carry the disease from the sewage to food. About 3 per cent of people become carriers after they have recovered from the disease. The incubation period is about ten to fourteen days. Symptoms include prolonged fever, headache, confusion, abdominal pain and red spots which appear on the chest and abdomen during the second week. There may be constipation or diarrhoea. If typhoid is not treated in time, serious complications may occur such as intestinal haemorrhage and PERITONITIS. The disease may be effectively treated with antibiotics and good nursing care. People planning to travel where typhoid is widespread should be immunised against the disease.

TYPHUS

A group of infectious diseases caused by various rickettsia micro-organisms and spread by ticks, lice, fleas and mites. EPIDEMIC typhus is found in temperate climates and was at one time responsible for thousands of deaths. ENDEMIC typhus is caused by a different kind of rickettsia and is more common in hot climates. Typhus has an incubation period of one to two weeks, followed by severe headache, fever, nervous and mental disturbances, RIGOURS, pain in the limbs and a rash which appears first in the armpits. It is prevented with good sanitation, the use of insecticides, control of rats and vaccination for people at high risk. Typhus is effectively treated with antibiotics.

U

ULCER

An inflamed open sore, or breech, of the skin surface or the membrane lining a body cavity. There are many different kinds of ulcers. The most common, from which almost everyone suffers, from time to time, are mouth ulcers. Called aphthous ulcers, they may form as a result of stress and general poor health, or following an injury or scratch. Aphthous ulcers usually heal without any form of treatment, though proprietary pain-relieving applications may relieve symptoms. Persistent mouth ulcers may indicate serious disease and so should be checked by your doctor. Skin ulcers may develop as a result of poor circulation in the lower limbs and be associated with such conditions as VARICOSE VEINS, DIABETES and ARTERIOSCLEROSIS. Other common ulcers include BEDSORES, RODENT ULCERS, PEPTIC ULCERS, GASTRIC ULCERS and DUODENAL ULCERS.

ULCERATIVE COLITIS

A disorder in which ulcers and inflammation occur in the colon (large intestine). See COLITIS.

ULTRASOUND

A diagnostic, investigative technique in which high frequency sound waves are used to examine the deep tissues of the body. It operates on the same principle as radar. Ultrasound scans, which have no damaging effect on the tissues, are used in situations where X-RAYS would be harmful, such as the examination of the FOETUS. (See Medical Tests And Examinations.)

ULTRAVIOLET LIGHT

Light of extremely short wavelength that is present in sunlight and which causes sunburn after careless, prolonged exposure. It produces vitamin D in the skin and is sometimes used to aid the treatment of ACNE and PSORIASIS.

UMBILICAL CORD

The cord-like structure connecting the FOETUS to the PLACENTA. The foetus receives nourishment and discharges waste through the two arteries and a vein which are contained in the umbilical cord. After birth, the cord is cut and tied off near its attachment to the baby while the rest is expelled with the PLACENTA or afterbirth. The navel, or umbilicus, marks the place where the cord was attached to the body. (See also How The Body Works, p. 30.)

ulcer at lower end of oesophagus

stomach

gastric ulcer

duodenal ulcer

Common sites of peptic ulcers are the lower end of the oesophagus, the stomach, and the duodenum.

UNCONSCIOUS

Referring to either the state of being insensible, or to the unconscious mind which, according to psychoanalytic theory, stores those repressed feelings that the conscious mind cannot usually summon up at will. It has great influence on a person's emotions and behaviour and is also known as the subconscious mind. The contents of the unconscious mind may have an influence on our dreams, our unconscious actions and speech as in so-called slips of the tongue. Repressed feelings, especially those of hate, guilt and anxiety, may contribute to neurotic emotional disorders. See UNCONSCIOUSNESS.

UNCONSCIOUSNESS

A state in which a person is insensible and cannot be roused. Unconsciousness may be caused by a blow to the head, fainting, electric shock, loss of blood, poisoning, drowning, sunstroke, stroke, heart attack, diabetes, drug or alcohol overdose. It is important to discover the exact cause so that the correct treatment can be given. See CONCUSSION, HAEMORRHAGE, COMA, FAINTING. (See also First Aid.)

UPPER RESPIRATORY INFECTION

An acute infection affecting the nose, throat and larynx, often also affecting the upper air passages to the lungs (larynx and trachea). Infection may be either bacterial or viral. Viral upper respiratory infections such as the COMMON COLD are by far the most common. There are over 100 separately identifiable viruses, and many more still untyped, which produce typical symptoms including sore throat, headache, stuffy feeling in the head, runny nose, cough, lack of appetite and general lethargy. Bedrest for three or four days is the usual treatment although your doctor may prescribe antibiotics if a secondary bacterial infection develops causing OTITIS media, SINUSITIS, BRONCHITIS or PNEUMONIA. See also LARYNGITIS, PHARYNGITIS, SORE THROAT.

UPSET STOMACH

See INDIGESTION, ABDOMINAL PAIN.

URAEMIA

When the kidneys are unable to perform their function of filtering toxic substances from the blood, a type of poisoning develops due to the accumulation of waste products in the blood. Although uraemia is usually the result of RENAL FAILURE due to disease of the kidneys, it can be a complication of any disorder (such as kidney stones, pregnancy complications, vitamin D overdose, injury to the kidney), which interferes with the way the kidneys normally function. Symptoms include headache, nausea, vomiting, drowsiness, shortness of breath and, if untreated, convulsions, coma and death. Usual management is to discover and treat the underlying cause and to purify the blood by DIALYSIS.

URETER

The tubes which carry urine from each of the kidneys to the bladder. An obstruction such as a KIDNEY STONE in the ureter may cause severe colicky abdominal pain and blood in the urine. (See How The Body Works, p. 18.)

URETHRA

The final part of the URINARY TRACT through which urine leaves the bladder and is discharged from the body. The female urethra is short, about 5 cm, while the male urethra is longer, about 20 cm, and also serves as a passageway for the ejaculation of SEMEN.

URETHRITIS

Inflammation of the URETHRA, the tube through which urine is emptied from the bladder. The most common causes of urethritis in men are sexually transmitted diseases such as GONORRHOEA and non-specific urethritis (NSU). Symptoms include discharge, usually containing pus, from the penis and a burning sensation on passing urine. Treatment is with antibiotics. Urethritis in women may be ACUTE or CHRONIC as an accompaniment of CYSTITIS. Infectious organisms usually enter the lower urinary tract from the vagina or bowel, entry often being precipitated by sexual intercourse. Sexually transmitted urethritis (caused by CHLAMYDIA and gonorrhoea) may also occur in women. Symptoms include burning pain on passing urine, frequent urination, painful intercourse and in some cases, blood-stained urine. Treatment is with antibiotics. Sometimes in women the symptoms of urethritis are not caused by infection but by inflammation of the urethra secondary to trauma during sexual intercourse. This is most likely to happen when there is penetration without sufficient lubrication.

URINARY TRACT

The system of organs through which urine, produced by the kidneys, is expelled from the body. It consists of the KIDNEYS, URETERS, BLADDER and URETHRA. Blood filters through the kidneys which extract excess water and waste products to form urine. The urine passes down the ureters to be stored in the bladder, from where it is discharged from the body through the urethra. The urinary tract is subject to two main disorders: those of obstruction, as in KIDNEY STONES, TUMOURS, congenital abnormalities, enlarged PROSTATE GLAND, and inflammations and infections such as NEPHRITIS, PYELONEPHRITIS, PYELITIS, CYSTITIS and URETHRITIS.

URINE

The yellowish liquid wastes of the body comprised mostly of water, together with waste products from the blood such as uric acid, urea, ammonia and creatine. Urine is produced in the kidneys, carried by the ureters to the bladder where it is stored, then finally discharged out of the body through the urethra. The urine may contain other substances such as blood, bile, pus and sugar and identifiable bacteria, hormones and certain drugs. Consequently it is frequently analysed in an effort to diagnose or detect certain conditions and illnesses.

URTICARIA

Another name for HIVES or NETTLE RASH.

UTERUS

In women, the hollow, muscular organ in the pelvis, also known as the womb. The uterus is subject to several fairly common disorders and diseases including painful and excessive MENSTRUATION, (DYSMENORRHOEA, MENORRHAGIA), FIBROIDS, PROLAPSE and CANCER of the endometrium. Symptoms of this cancer, which is more common after the MENOPAUSE, include intermittent period-like pains and unexpected bleeding or brown discharge from the vagina. Women should routinely have a pelvic examination and smear test every two years. If detected early enough, cancer of the endometrium is relatively easily and successfully treated. (See also How The Body Works, pp. 25–26.)

VACCINATION

A technique of making a person resistant to an infectious disease by introducing into the body a VACCINE which stimulates the production of ANTIBODIES to counteract infectious agents or disease toxins. Vaccination may be by injection, as in DIPHTHERIA and TETANUS, by oral administration, as in POLIOMYELITIS, or it may be introduced through a scratch on the skin as in SMALLPOX. IMMUNISATION is the desired result.

VACCINE

A specific preparation, made up of dead, weakened or altered living VIRUSES or BACTERIA or containing modified toxins (poisonous material made by germs), which is introduced into a person's body to provide immunity against a particular disease. The proteins of the vaccine, known as ANTIGENS, stimulate certain white blood cells and other elements of the immune system to produce ANTIBODIES. Later when the person is exposed to the micro-organism, the appropriate antibodies go into action to prevent the development of disease. Different vaccines are given at different times during childhood. See also IMMUNISATION.

VACCINIA

Also called cowpox, vaccinia is a viral disease of cows' udders, which is transmitted to humans by direct contact, or through VACCINATION for SMALLPOX. The smallpox vaccine is based on the modified cowpox virus which gave its name to the technique of vaccination.

VAGINA

The hollow organ leading from the CERVIX to the VULVA (the female external genitals). (See How The Body Works, pp. 25–26.)

VAGINISMUS

Painful, spasmodic contraction of the muscles around the entrance to the VAGINA, which prevents sexual penetration or gynaecological examination. Most cases of vaginismus have a psychological basis, arising from fear of or aversion to sexual intercourse, or fear of pregnancy. Women suffering from vaginismus need the help of a therapist experienced in disorders of sexual function.

VAGINITIS

Inflammation of the VAGINA, which may be caused by infection, chemical or mechanical injury, allergy, or weakening of the tissues due to ATROPHY after the menopause. The most common vaginal infections are those due to THRUSH, certain bacteria and TRICHOMONIASIS. Symptoms include itching, burning, and soreness of the lower vagina and vulva, pain on intercourse and increased discharge which may be white, yellow or green, frothy or lumpy, and may have an offensive smell. Treatment is for the underlying cause.

VALVE

A flap-like section of membrane lining a blood vessel, duct or other hollow organ which serves to maintain a one-way flow through the lumen. The most important valves in the body are those in the heart, the veins and the lymphatic system.

VALVULAR DISEASE OF THE HEART

Diseases that lead to defects in the VALVES of the heart include RHEUMATIC FEVER, SYPHILIS, bacterial ENDOCARDITIS and some congenital abnormalities. There are two forms of valvular disease: stenosis, or narrowing of the valve, and incompetence, where the valve allows backflow. Either condition can lead to severe disorder or failure of the circulation. When the function of a heart valve is seriously defective, it may need to be replaced or repaired by surgery.

VARICELLA

The medical term for CHICKEN-POX.

VARICOCELE

The presence of VARICOSE VEINS around the spermatic cord in the scrotum, usually of unknown cause and more common on the left side than the right. Generally varicocele causes no problems, and the patient is unaware of its existence until it is discovered on routine examination. In most cases, no treatment is required. If swelling due to the varicocele causes discomfort, or if sperm production is reduced because the blood in the dilated veins raises the temperature of the testis, varicocele may be removed surgically.

VARICOSE VEINS

Abnormal dilatation of veins, usually found in the legs but also occurring in the rectum where they are known as HAEMORRHOIDS, and in the scrotum, where they are called VARICOCELE. Varicose veins result when there is partial obstruction to the flow of blood, and/or the VALVES in the veins become weakened and incompetent, allowing backflow. The increased pressure in the vein leads to stretching and weakening of its wall, which becomes distended. Common causes of obstruction to venous blood flow from the legs are constipation, pregnancy, pelvic tumours. Varicose veins are more common in women than in men, in people who spend a lot of time standing, and in overweight and older people. They often first develop during pregnancy, or if already present, they may become much worse. As well as the unsightly knotted, swollen appearance of the veins, other symptoms include aches and pains in the legs, swollen ankles after standing and tiredness in the legs, especially when walking.

Treatment may include special injections to shrink and close the veins or, in severe cases, surgical removal of the affected veins. There are some simple methods of relieving symptoms and minimising progression in less severe cases. People with varicose veins should take the weight off their feet as much as possible, elevate their legs when they can, wear support stockings, walk instead of driving, eat a healthy, balanced, high-fibre diet to maintain a sensible weight and prevent constipation.

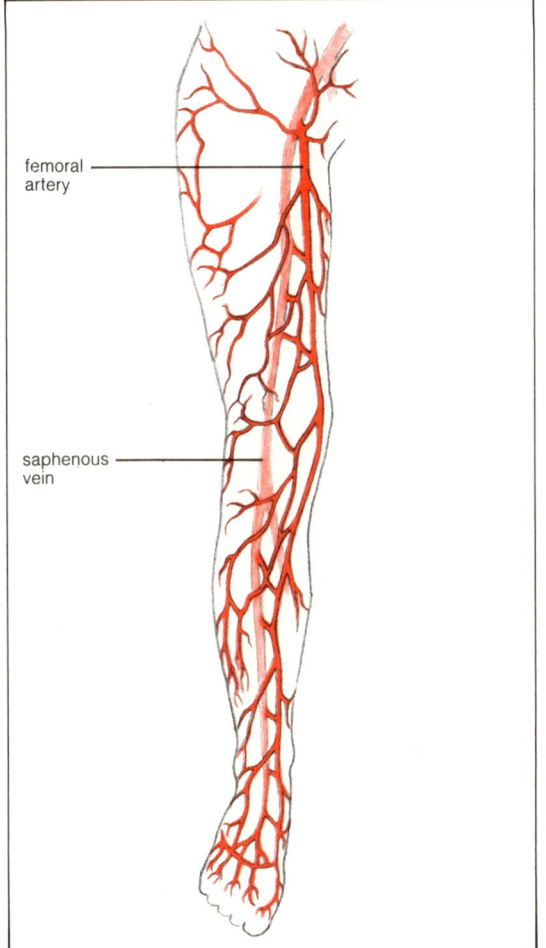

femoral artery

saphenous vein

Backflow of blood in veins is prevented by the valves. Damage to the valves leads to increased pressure within the veins and stretching of their walls. The long saphenous vein beneath the skin in the back of the leg is the most commonly affected by this disorder.

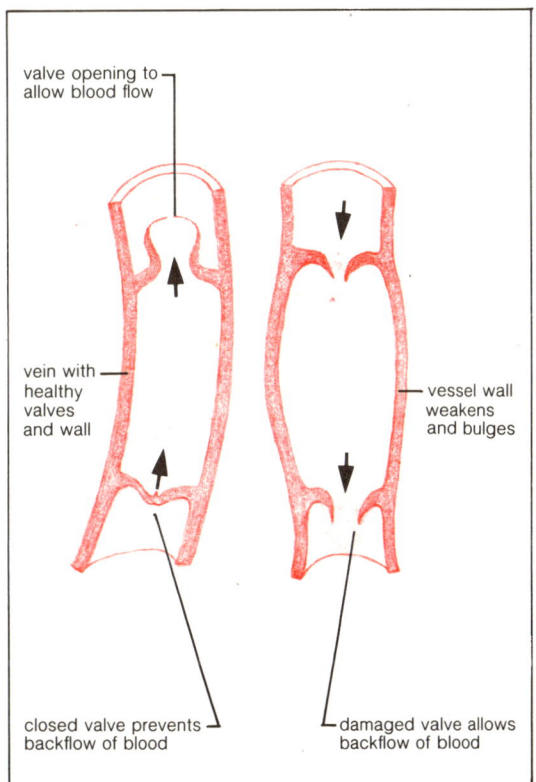

valve opening to allow blood flow

vein with healthy valves and wall

vessel wall weakens and bulges

closed valve prevents backflow of blood

damaged valve allows backflow of blood

VAS DEFERENS

One of a pair of tubes which carries sperm cells from the TESTES through the scrotum into the pelvis and on to the PROSTATE. (See How The Body Works, pp. 26–27.)

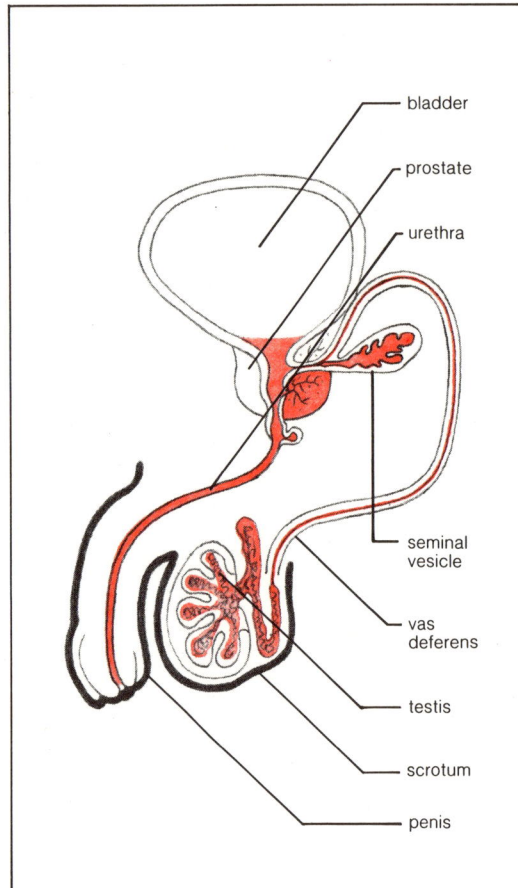

- bladder
- prostate
- urethra
- seminal vesicle
- vas deferens
- testis
- scrotum
- penis

The vas deferens joins the urethra in the prostate. In vasectomy the vas deferens is blocked by cutting and tying its scrotal part, to prevent sperm from entering the semen.

VASECTOMY

The procedure of dividing, removing or otherwise blocking the VAS DEFERENS in the scrotum in order to make a man infertile by preventing sperm from entering the semen. Vasectomy is a simple operation that is usually performed under local anaesthetic with return to work possible the following day. It has no effect on virility, orgasm or ejaculation. There are many reports of vasectomy being successfully reversed, but because this cannot be guaranteed, vasectomy should not be considered until the man has fathered as many children as he will ever want.

VASOCONSTRICTION

The constriction of blood vessels which may be caused by certain drugs (called vasoconstrictors) used to relieve local congestion (as in HAY FEVER) and to reduce minor bleeding when surgery is performed under local anaesthesia. Vasoconstriction in certain parts of the body may also result from stimulation of the sympathetic nervous system (see How The Body Works, pp. 12–15).

VASODILATION

The dilation, or widening, of blood vessels which may be caused by certain drugs (called vasodilators) used, for example, in the treatment of HYPERTENSION, ANGINA, CLAUDICATION and RAYNAUD'S DISEASE, or by the stimulation of the parasympathetic nervous system (see How The Body Works, pp. 5–9).

VD

Short for venereal disease. See SEXUALLY TRANSMITTED DISEASES.

VEIN

A vessel that returns blood to the heart from all parts of the body. (See How The Body Works, pp. 5–9.)

VENA CAVA

The largest VEIN in the body. It has two main branches: the superior vena cava returns blood from the head, neck, arms and shoulders to the upper right chamber of the heart, and the inferior vena cava carries blood from the abdomen and legs. (See How The Body Works, pp. 5–9.)

VENEREAL DISEASE

See SEXUALLY TRANSMITTED DISEASES.

VENTRICLES

The two large, muscular chambers of the heart. The right ventricle receives blood from the right ATRIUM and pumps it to the lungs through the pulmonary artery; the more muscular left ventricle receives blood from the left atrium and pumps it through the aorta and around the body. (See How The Body Works, pp. 5–9.)

VENTRICULAR FIBRILLATION

A disturbance of the normal heart rhythm in which the VENTRICLES beat very fast, irregularly and inefficiently. This disturbance may result from any serious disorder of the heart muscle (myocardium) such as MYOCARDIAL INFARCTION, ischaemic heart disease (see ISCHAEMIA), MYOCARDITIS or HEART FAILURE. The onset of fibrillation may be marked by breathlessness, pallor, collapse, shock or loss of consciousness. The pulse usually cannot be detected. Ventricular fibrillation may lead to sudden death. If fibrillation is suspected, start cardiopulmonary resuscitation immediately (see First Aid – RESUSCITATION), and continue until an ambulance arrives. Once in hospital the patient's heartbeat is restored by a defibrillating machine. Having survived such an emergency, the outlook is, in many cases, good.

VERNIX CASEOSA
The creamy layer, made up of sebaceous secretions, that covers new-born babies.

VERRUCA
The medical term for a WART.

VERTEBRA
A bone of the SPINE.

VERTIGO
Extreme dizziness or, more exactly, the sensation of being whirled about in space or that one's surroundings are spinning around. It may be accompanied by NAUSEA and VOMITING. Vertigo is a symptom of disturbance of the organs of balance in the inner ear, and may be the temporary result of certain rides at amusement parks. As a symptom of disease, it may be caused by OTITIS media, otitis interna, LABYRINTHITIS, MENIÈRE'S DISEASE, HYPERTENSION, ARTERIOSCLEROSIS. Persistent vertigo can be extremely disabling. Usual treatment is with specific anti-vertigo drugs.

VESICLE
A small blister that is filled with clear fluid and occurring in such diseases as CHICKEN-POX and HERPES.

VINCENT'S ANGINA
Commonly known as trench mouth, this is an infection of the gums and sometimes the membranes lining the lips, cheeks and throat. It is usually associated with poor dental hygiene or a generally run-down physical state. It is thought that particular germs that are always present in small numbers in healthy mouths are responsible for the infection. Symptoms include bleeding gums, sores and ulcers, fever, swollen lymph glands and bad breath. Treatment is with antibiotics and oral and dental hygiene.

VIRILISM, VIRILISATION
The presence or development in a woman of male characteristics such as hair on the chest and face, increased muscle mass, deep voice. Menstruation may also cease. Virilism occurs as a result of hormonal disorder due to ovarian failure, tumours of the ovary or adrenal gland and treatment with certain

drugs. The condition is corrected by treatment of the cause.

VIRUS
Any of a large variety of minute organisms, some of which may cause many different infections, from the common cold to smallpox. Viruses are so small that they can be seen only with the aid of an electron microscope. They consist of complex molecules of protein and nucleic acid and while they show no life-like activity, they have the ability to replicate inside a living cell. Viruses, and therefore virus diseases, are not affected by ANTIBIOTICS and in general, the control of such diseases depends on the development of vaccines. Recently some anti-viral drugs have been developed which, although they cannot eradicate viral infection, can reduce or prevent viral replication in host cells.

VISCERA
Another term for the major organs of the thorax and abdomen, including the lungs, heart, stomach, liver and intestines.

VISION
Eyesight. See EYE DISORDERS.

VITAMINS
An adequate supply of vitamins in the diet is essential for good health. A diet which includes a variety of animal and plant foods, including fresh fruits and vegetables, contains more than enough vitamins, and supplements are quite unnecessary. The following list of the main vitamins describes their known functions, the foods they are found in, and the features of deficiency and excess.

A (retinol)
Vitamin A is necessary for growth and for the maintenance of healthy skin and lining membranes of the body. It is essential for vision in low light because of the part it plays in the chemical reactions that take place in the eye's retina when it is stimulated by light. Vitamin A occurs naturally in fish liver oil, milk, butter, eggs, spinach and carrots. Symptoms of deficiency include hard and corny skin, dry and ulcerated eyes, inflamed gums, low resistance to infection and poor night vision. It is used to treat night blindness and, in some cases, acne. Excessive amounts of Vitamin A can lead to loss of hair, loss of appetite, weight loss, menstrual irregularities, fatigue, irritability, disorders of the nervous system, bone and joint pain, and enlarged liver and spleen.

B_1 (thiamine)
Essential for growth, sugar breakdown and release of energy, and assists in the functioning of the brain, nerves and muscles. It is found in pork, liver, wholemeal cereals and green vegetables. Deficiency

is indicated by loss of appetite, tiredness, irritability, confusion and heart disturbances. This deficiency disease is called beri beri, and is easily reversed by giving vitamin B_1 by mouth. There are no reports of overdose from vitamin B_1 taken by mouth. Excessive doses by injection may cause hypersensitivity (allergy-like reactions).

B_2 (riboflavine)
Required for growth, maintaining body tissues and assisting in the breakdown of food to provide energy. Riboflavine is found in eggs, yeast, liver, kidney and green vegetables. Riboflavine deficiency may result in cracking at the corners of the mouth, inflammation of the tongue and lips, and certain skin and eye disorders. It is used to correct such conditions. It has no toxic effects.

B_3 (niacin, nicotinamide, nicotinic acid)
Niacin assists in proper sugar utilisation and intestinal function. It is abundant in yeast, wheat germ, liver, kidney and fish. Severe deficiency results in PELLAGRA, digestive upsets, diarrhoea and anxiety. Excess can cause flushing, itching, liver damage, skin disorders, GOUT, mouth and skin ulcers and blood sugar disturbances.

B_5 (pantothenic acid)
This vitamin is essential to some of the body's metabolic processes. It is found in many foods, particularly liver, yeast and eggs. Deficiency, although rare, may play a part in some skin disorders. Generally, it has no toxic effects.

B_6 (pyridoxine)
Plays an important part in the body's efficient use of amino acids and fatty acids. It is found in most foods, particularly meat, fish, wheat germ and yeast. Symptoms of deficiency, which is very rare, include irritation of the skin and dry lips, nervous disorders, anaemia and convulsions in babies. Pyridoxine has been used to relieve nausea, vomiting, RADIATION SICKNESS, some side-effects of the oral contraceptive and the PREMENSTRUAL SYNDROME. Excessive amounts may cause headache, abnormal sensory nerve function and depression.

B_{12} (cobalamin)
Essential for blood formation and a healthy nervous system. This vitamin is abundant in liver and kidney but is absent in vegetables. Deficiency results in some nervous disorders and pernicious ANAEMIA. People who suffer inadequate absorption of the vitamin are treated by injections at about four-weekly intervals. Excessive use may lead to a rare allergy.

C (ascorbic acid)
Important in tissue and blood formation, it plays an essential part in the development of cartilage, bone and teeth and in the healing of wounds. It is found naturally in many fruits and vegetables, especially grapefruit, oranges and lemons. Deficiency results in scurvy, characterised by coarse skin, swollen and bleeding gums, teeth loss, muscular pain and weakness, and bleeding disorders. It is used to supplement inadequate diet, given to bottle-fed babies and used to promote healing following surgical operations. Larger doses are also said to prevent and reduce cold symptoms, although such effects are still being studied. Although usually well tolerated, excessive amounts of this vitamin may cause diarrhoea, dyspepsia, dental erosion, kidney stones and disturbances of iron storage.

D (calciferol)
Plays an important part in bone formation and the utilisation of calcium by the body. Vitamin D is sometimes called the sunshine vitamin because it is produced in skin which is exposed to sunlight. It is also found in oily fish and fish oils, butter and eggs. Deficiency may lead to RICKETS in children. It is used to correct deficiency effects on bone. Prescribed amounts of vitamin D must be taken strictly as the doctor recommends. Overdose is much more common than deficiency, and may result in loss of appetite, nausea, weakness, deposits of calcium in the tissues, kidney stones, kidney failure and high blood pressure.

E (tocopherol)
Not a great deal is known about the role this vitamin plays. It is believed to be important in red blood cell function, and possibly plays a part in muscle development and fat processing. It is present in most foods and particularly wheat germ and dark green, leafy vegetables. There is an increased need for it in diets that are high in polyunsaturated fats. Its use has been tried to prevent or reduce scarring, to promote healing, and in cases of habitual ABORTION, MUSCULAR DYSTROPHY and cardiac disease. Overdose is rare although some recorded symptoms include dyspepsia, diarrhoea, muscle weakness, inflammation of the mouth, bleeding tendency and blurred vision.

Folic acid (PGA or pteroylglutamic acid)
Essential to a number of different chemical reactions that take place in the nucleus of every cell in the body. It assists in red blood cell formation and in the normal formation of new cells. It is plentifully found in liver, yeast, mushrooms and green, leafy vegetables. Deficiency may be due to malabsorption or ALCOHOLISM and may result in ANAEMIA. It is used to either treat or prevent anaemia, particularly in pregnancy. Folic acid is generally well tolerated.

H (biotin)
Biotin is one of the least understood vitamins, but it is thought to be necessary for a healthy skin and in body utilisation of fats, carbohydrates and many

other body processes. Vitamin H is found abundantly in liver and yeast. Symptoms of deficiency are similar to many of those characterised by lack of the B group vitamins. Overdosage has not been recorded.

K (phytomenadione)
Necessary for the production of prothrombin, an essential factor in the blood-clotting process. It is found in green, leafy vegetables and is also formed by bacteria present in the intestine. Deficiency is characterised by internal and external bleeding. It may be given to prevent haemorrhage in new babies born to women who have a known deficiency or it may also be used to counteract an overdose of some ANTICOAGULANTS. Severe reactions, such as flushing, sweating, vascular collapse and jaundice in the new-born, have been reported following intravenous administration of the vitamin.

VITILIGO
A common skin disorder resulting from patchy loss of the pigment MELANIN. Well-defined, round or irregular shaped patches, which may enlarge, can appear anywhere on the body. The patches are especially susceptible to sunburn, and may be accentuated if the surrounding skin becomes tanned. The cause is unknown. Until recently, the only measures available for vitiligo were the use of cover cosmetics and sunscreens. Since the introduction of the psoralen drugs, some cases can be corrected by the use of oral tablets followed by careful exposure to sunlight. A dermatologist will advise whether this treatment is suitable.

VOCATIONAL REHABILITATION
See OCCUPATIONAL THERAPY.

VOICE-BOX
See LARYNX.

VOLVULUS
The twisting of the intestines into a loop, causing obstruction and usually cutting off the blood supply to the loop. It may occur in the small or large intestine, with middle-aged and elderly people being most susceptible. Volvulus causes sudden, severe abdominal pain, vomiting, distension of the abdomen and often shock or collapse. Immediate surgery is necessary to correct the condition.

VOMITING
Expulsion of the stomach contents through the mouth as a result of reversed direction of muscular contractions which force up and out the food and any other matter in the stomach, usually following the sensation of NAUSEA. Vomiting is a very common symptom, which may occur in most bowel disturbances and in many other illnesses. Infections, fever, headache such as MIGRAINE, travel sickness and MORNING SICKNESS are some of the other disorders frequently associated with vomiting.

VULVA
The external female genitals, surrounding the entrance to the VAGINA, comprised on each side of two folds of skin called the labia majora and the labia minora. The inner folds of the labia minora meet in front of the CLITORIS with the urethral opening just behind. See VULVITIS.

VULVITIS
Inflammation of the VULVA, called vulvitis, is quite common. Causes include irritation by tight underclothes, poor hygiene, local allergic reaction and infections such as THRUSH. Symptoms include intense itching, burning, swelling and weeping of the vulval skin. It is treated by correcting the cause. See VAGINITIS.

WARTS

Warts are pale, raised, rough-surfaced lesions which can appear on the skin anywhere on the body. They are due to infection by a virus which causes local overgrowth in the surface layers of the skin. Different types of wart appear on different parts of the body. It is believed that each type is caused by one of the many different strains of the wart virus. The most common warts, usually found in children and young people, occur on the hands and fingers, elbows, knees and face. Plantar warts, which occur on the sole of the foot, are deeply embedded and may be painful. Warts around the anus and genitals have a cauliflower-like appearance and are often multiple. They are usually acquired from a sexual partner. Genital warts can be transferred to the cervix of the uterus, where they may be associated with abnormal SMEAR TESTS. Most warts will eventually disappear of their own accord but those that are painful, unsightly, or growing in a troublesome place may be removed by painting with special solutions to destroy them, or by freezing or cautery.

WASSERMANN TEST

One of the first tests used to detect SYPHILIS. The Wassermann reaction was not completely specific, and sometimes came up positive when there was no syphilis infection. It has now been replaced by more specific tests known as STS (Serological Tests for Syphilis).

WASTING

A decrease in muscle size and tone accompanied by weight loss. It is a feature of any type of muscular paralysis, MUSCULAR DYSTROPHY, and of any chronic debilitating disease. Wasting may also be the result of prolonged inactivity such as occurs in bedridden people. PHYSIOTHERAPY helps minimise its development and effects.

WATERBRASH

The belching of acidic fluids from the stomach. It is one of the symptoms of DYSPEPSIA.

WAX

The medical name for wax in the ear is cerumen. It is a normal secretion which traps dust and other matter to prevent any particles from reaching the eardrum. Ear wax normally drains slowly out of the ear but sometimes a hardened plug accumulates (in the canal) causing discomfort or reducing hearing. It should be properly removed by a doctor, never with a match or hairpin.

WEAL

A temporary raised red area on the skin, such as occurs following a sharp blow or in allergic reactions such as HIVES and NETTLE RASH.

WEIGHT

A person's weight can be a clue to state of health. Bodyweight depends on a person's height, build and age. OBESITY, or being overweight, is usually caused by over-eating although it may indicate a metabolic disorder. Sudden weight loss may be evidence of a disease or disorder such as chronic DIARRHOEA, THYROTOXICOSIS, ANOREXIA NERVOSA, FEVER, TUBERCULOSIS and untreated DIABETES. Anyone who suffers sudden unexplained weight loss should see a doctor. Anyone planning to go on a weight reduction diet should also seek the advice of a doctor.

WEN

Another name for a SEBACEOUS CYST.

WHIPLASH

A sudden strain or tearing of ligaments or muscles in the neck, often the result of violent jerking back of the head, rather like the action of a whip being cracked, hence its name. The commonest victims of whiplash are occupants of motor vehicles that abruptly come to a jerking halt when a collision occurs. Whiplash injury may also involve damage to the bones of the neck, to the discs between the bones, to the nerves within the spinal column and the nerves running from between the cervical vertebrae down the arms. Symptoms include headache, a painful and stiff neck, pins and needles in the arms and hands and feelings of weakness in the arms and shoulders. The neck of a person who has suffered whiplash injury may have to be supported by a special collar for several weeks. PHYSIOTHERAPY and anti-inflammatory drugs also help.

WHITE BLOOD CELL
(See How The Body Works, p. 5.)

WHITEHEAD
A tiny white lump which forms when sebum becomes trapped in a sebaceous gland of the skin. See ACNE.

WHITES
A common name for the white or yellowish discharge from the vagina, known as LEUCORRHOEA.

WHITLOW
A bacterial infection of the soft pad at the tip of a finger. The finger tip becomes swollen, red and very painful as pus accumulates under the skin. Antibiotics may help stop the whitlow progressing, but once an ABSCESS forms, it will need to be lanced and drained.

WHOOPING COUGH
An acute, very contagious disease of childhood – known medically as pertussis – affecting the bronchi and the upper respiratory passages. Infection is spread by droplets breathed out into the air by an infected child. The incubation period is seven to fourteen days. In the early stages, symptoms are similar to those of a heavy cold with fever and a persistent cough. As the child's condition worsens so does the cough which develops into a characteristic barking, rather than whooping, sound. Vomiting may follow a coughing spasm with the result that the patient may also suffer loss of fluid, nutrition and sleep. The disease may last from three weeks to three months or more, and may be complicated by BRONCHOPNEUMONIA and OTITIS media. Whooping cough and its complications may be effectively treated with antibiotics. Whooping cough is uncommon where all children are immunised, but in communities with no immunisation programmes or where immunisation is neglected, dangerous epidemics may occur. See IMMUNISATION.

WIND
Air or gas accumulated in the stomach or intestines leading to belching, rumblings, passing wind and a bloated feeling. The most common cause of wind is swallowing air. We all swallow some air, but excess air is likely to be swallowed by nervy, anxious people and when drinks are gulped or food is bolted. Wind is also a symptom of INDIGESTION. Some foods, such as beans, onions, cabbage and Brussels sprouts, are likely to cause wind because they are usually not fully broken down by the digestive juices and the residue collects in the bowel where it ferments, producing gas. People who suffer from wind should avoid such foods, and should sit down to a meal in a relaxed state, and eat and drink slowly.

WORMS
A term used to describe a parasitic infestation of man. See THREADWORM, TAPEWORM, TOXACARIASIS.

WOMB
Another name for the UTERUS.

XANTHOMA

Small yellow plaques on the skin caused by lipid (fatty) deposits in its deeper layers. They are most commonly found on the eyelids, around joints and over some tendons. Xanthomas are usually quite benign and cause no problems, but if unsightly they may easily be removed in a minor surgical procedure.

X CHROMOSOME

The female sex chromosome. Every normal person has two sex chromosomes in each cell, females having two X chromosomes (XX) and males having XY. There are certain congenital defects associated with abnormal numbers or combinations of sex chromosomes such as TURNER'S SYNDROME and KLINEFELTER'S SYNDROME.

X-RAYS

A form of radiated energy similar to light but with finer and extremely short wavelengths. The properties of X-rays that are important medically are their ability to penetrate soft tissue, and their ability to register on photographic plates but be stopped by calcium or lead. Thus X-ray pictures show bones clearly. Using special techniques with X-rays, doctors can examine any part of the body. Large doses of X-rays will destroy certain tissues so they are now used to bombard and damage cancer cells in a treatment called RADIOTHERAPY. (See Medical Tests And Examinations.)

YAWS

A tropical disease, usually occurring in children, caused by a spiral-shaped bacteria of the spirochaete family. In the first stage, there is a raspberry-like eruption, called the mother yaw, which usually develops on the leg. The mother lesion heals, but weeks to months later similar multiple yaws appear in skin and sometimes deeper tissues and bones. It is effectively treated with penicillin.

Y CHROMOSOME

The sex chromosome associated with maleness. Every normal person has two chromosomes in each cell and at least one of them is an X CHROMOSOME. If the other is a Y chromosome, the person is male (XY)

while the combination XX results in a female.

YELLOW FEVER

An acute virus disease carried to humans by mosquitoes. It is ENDEMIC in tropical Africa and the northern parts of South America. Outbreak may affect thousands of people, although now that an effective vaccine is available, epidemics are rare. There is an incubation period of three to six days followed by headache and fever and in more severe cases, conjunctivitis, haemorrhage, jaundice and kidney failure. There is no specific treatment but people who recover from one attack have immunity for life. People planning to travel to tropical Africa and America should be immunised against yellow fever.

Z

ZOONOSIS
Disease or infection that primarily affects animals, but which can be transmitted to humans. See Q FEVER.

3

MEDICAL TESTS AND EXAMINATIONS

MEDICAL TESTS AND EXAMINATIONS — INDEX

The words in SMALL CAPITAL LETTERS within the separate entries in this chapter generally refer to the Basic Tests on pages 180–182. Occasionally, however, they refer to tests in other sections of this chapter, and may be found by consulting the following alphabetical contents list. The Basic Tests are in BOLD type in the contents list; the twelve section headings are in upper and lower case letters.

One of the most important advances in health care during the 20th century (and especially since 1950) has been the development of technology to aid in the accurate diagnosis of disease and to monitor various body functions. New specialties (such as various branches of pathology, diagnostic radiology and nuclear medicine) have evolved which are devoted to medical testing.

The judicious use and interpretation of tests helps your doctor to gain a knowledge and understanding of the nature, cause and progress of your illness. This means that the correct treatment can be started early and its effectiveness monitored. Even when results are negative, testing has fulfilled the valuable functions of reassuring you and your doctor that nothing is wrong, and preventing unnecessary treatment.

Most samples of body fluids and tissues can be collected in your doctor's consulting room and sent to a laboratory for testing. X-rays, ultrasounds and CAT scans must be done at special centres. A few tests require an overnight stay in hospital.

There are some negative aspects to diagnostic testing. Some tests are uncomfortable or painful, a few are risky and most are expensive. Also, health authorities are worried that doctors are ordering too many tests for too many patients. Unnecessary testing may subject you to needless pain, worry, risk and expense. Doctors are not the only culprits in the overuse of medical testing. Patients may ask for extensive investigations in the belief that the more tests they get, the better the treatment. Requests for multiple testing when there are no symptoms or signs of disease often indicate a health neurosis. A pile of negative test results does nothing to allay fears, and may even aggravate anxiety.

No test is fool-proof. A test is only as good as the quality and reliability of the equipment used, the competence of those who perform and interpret it, and the reliability of measures used to record and communicate data about tests. Tests should always be considered in the light of the clinical findings (history and examination), and should be repeated if unexpected abnormalities are found.

The majority of illnesses can still be diagnosed by taking a thorough history and by careful physical examination. Many doctors use tests as a sort of 'second opinion', to confirm that their treatment – or non-treatment – is based on a sound diagnosis. In some disorders the appropriate use of tests is crucial to proper diagnosis and treatment.

Most doctors will explain why they are recommending a test. If not, here are some important questions to ask. Is the test necessary? What is it testing for? How is it done? Who will perform it? Where will it be done and how long will it take? What are the benefits, risks, side-effects? Is it painful? How conclusive are the results? How accurate? When will results be available? Who will explain the results to you? What is the cost? (Not all tests are refundable on health insurance.)

Be sure to tell your doctor, or whoever performs the test, if you suffer from any allergies (an allergy to iodine, for example, will disqualify you from some diagnostic procedures). Also tell your doctor if you have any fears or uncertainties about a recommended test. Apprehension can have an adverse effect on some body functions, and may cause misleading results.

In this section the main categories of medical tests are described, followed by information about how these and other special tests may be used to diagnose disorders of the systems and organs of the body.

BASIC TESTS

BIOPSY

The removal of a small piece of tissue for laboratory examination. The technique used to obtain the tissue depends on its site. Samples from tissues on or near the body surface are easily obtained, using local anaesthetic and a simple incision. Tissues and organs deeper in the body may be sampled by needle biopsy. Local anaesthetic is injected into the skin. A hollow needle is inserted into the organ or tissue (sometimes using X-RAY or ULTRASOUND to guide the procedure) and rotated while slight suction is applied. This draws fragments of the tissue into the bore of the needle. Fragments of the lining membranes of the hollow organs may be taken during ENDOSCOPY.

Biopsy specimens are treated in one of two ways. In most cases, the tissue is placed in preservative immediately. In the laboratory, it is embedded in wax and finely sliced. The slices of tissue are mounted on a glass slide, stained to demonstrate various characteristics, and examined under a microscope. This process takes about two days. If information about the tissue is needed more quickly (for example, during an operation a surgeon may need to know whether a tumour is benign or malignant) the tissue may be snap-frozen, sliced and examined under the microscope immediately. This is the frozen section technique, which provides results within minutes.

BLOOD TESTS

As well as giving information on the condition of the blood itself, blood tests are also important in diagnosing disorders of other organs and systems of the body. Collection of a blood sample is usually performed by your doctor, and – apart from the slight discomfort of the needle puncturing the skin – is quick and painless. The sample is usually taken from the veins in the bend of the elbow or on the back of the hand. In babies, the scalp veins may be used. Arterial blood is collected only when blood gases need to be measured (see BLOOD GAS ANALYSIS). For most tests, blood can be collected at any time of the day. However, some tests of metabolism require blood to be sampled after a 12-hour fast or at certain times after a measured amount of food is taken.

The majority of blood analyses are carried out on serum. Blood is sent to the laboratory in a plain glass or plastic tube which allows the blood to clot. If the blood cells or plasma are to be examined, some of the sample is placed into a special tube containing a chemical which prevents the blood from clotting. This is a whole blood sample. The cells and clot may be separated from the plasma or serum by spinning the tube in a centrifuge.

The blood may be analysed by several different laboratories. Haematology deals with the blood cells, blood groups and clotting functions. Biochemistry measures the concentration of the many chemicals contained in the serum. Highly specialised laboratories measure hormones and antibodies in serum. Sometimes blood may be sent to microbiology laboratories to test for the presence of bacteria or viruses.

Most of the common blood tests are now performed by machines called autoanalysers, and results are available within 24 hours of the sample reaching the laboratory. Unusual or highly specialised tests are performed in batches once or twice per week, so that results may take longer to obtain.

CAT SCAN

CAT stands for computer axial tomography, a recently developed X-ray technique which has greatly advanced the early diagnosis of certain cancers. A very fine X-ray beam is used to take a series of pictures at fractionally different depths of tissue. The pictures are analysed by a computer to produce images composed of dots, with the density of dots corresponding to the density of the tissue through which the X-ray beam has passed. Comparison of tissue density at different depths allows differentiation between normal tissue, blood clots, abscesses and tumours. (Conventional X-ray cannot do this.)

CAT scanning is quick and safe, does not invade the body, and does not need the injection of radiopaque dyes. The procedure is particularly useful for examination of the brain, and is sometimes the only way that malignant tumours of soft tissues such as the lungs, liver and pancreas can be diagnosed early.

CONTRAST X-RAYS

A special modification of X-ray technique is the contrast X-ray which is used to study the outline of the interior of hollow organs. Solutions of special radiopaque dyes (which do not transmit X-rays) are introduced into the organs under investigation, and a series of pictures taken as the dye moves through the organs. Contrast X-rays demonstrate irregularities in the walls of hollow organs, and any partial or total obstruction of their lumens. See PLAIN X-RAYS.

ENDOSCOPY

The technique of looking inside the body, using special instruments (generally called endoscopes) which illuminate and magnify the area under examination. Endoscopes rely on special flexible fibreoptic cables, which can transmit light around bends in the cable without loss of light intensity or quality. Endoscopes specially designed to examine particular parts of the body are named accordingly. For example, the interior of the stomach is examined by a gastroscope. A bronchoscope is used for the bronchi and lungs, and an arthroscope examines the inside of joints.

Endoscopes are usually introduced into the body through anatomical openings, such as the mouth, anus or urethra, but for some examinations a small incision must be made through the skin. Some endoscopic examinations are performed in the doctor's consulting rooms, with no preparation or only mild sedation. Others must be performed in a hospital under operating theatre conditions, some needing general anaesthetic. Many endoscopes are equipped with built-in devices for taking biopsy specimens and for removing small benign tumours such as polyps.

Endoscopy is a great advance in the diagnosis of disorders of the lining membranes of the body.

INFRA-RED THERMOGRAPHY (IRT)

This is a method of measuring the amount of heat radiated by various parts of the body. The part to be tested is photographed, using special heat-sensitive film. Different colours on the developed film indicate different temperatures. The technique locates tissues such as tumours and areas of inflammation which have greater blood flow than their surroundings and are therefore warmer. Areas of inadequate blood supply can also be located.

Thermography is quick, simple, non-invasive and relatively cheap.

ISOTOPE SCAN (NUCLEAR SCAN)

A technique for monitoring the activity of organs or tissues by measuring the amount of radioactive isotopes taken up. Isotopes are unstable radioactive forms of chemical elements which show up on photographic film or may be detected by scanners. The isotope used for a particular test must be of a chemical (or attached to a chemical by the technique of 'tagging') which is specifically used, absorbed or concentrated by the tissue being investigated. For example, a radioactive form of iodine (which is stored by the thyroid) is used for isotope scans of the thyroid. Radioactive iodine may be used to tag fibrinogen – the blood protein which is the main constituent of blood clots – to locate blood vessel obstruction by thrombosis or embolism.

Isotope scans are very safe. The dose of radiation is less than that received in a single X-ray, and the isotopes are rapidly broken down and excreted from the body. A scan can be performed as an outpatient procedure.

MICROBIOLOGY

This branch of pathology deals with the identification and testing of infectious organisms. Specimens of blood, urine, faeces, sputum, discharges, pus, cerebrospinal fluid, fluid aspirated from joints, cysts and other body cavities, biopsies or tissue scrapings are sent to the microbiology laboratory. The usual procedure is to immediately examine fresh and stained smears under the microscope. If many organisms are present, as for example in pus, it may be possible to identify the cause of the infection at once. Some of the specimen is then added to one or more culture mediums (often a broth or a jelly) specially prepared to nurture particular organisms. The cultures are then incubated for various periods before being examined to see whether organisms have grown. If so, the organism is then identified by microscopic examination or by immunological means. If certain bacteria are cultured they are tested against a range of antibiotics to see whether they are sensitive or resistant to antibiotic action.

The use of these techniques of culture and sensitivity testing has made the diagnosis of many infectious diseases very accurate, and has saved much futile and unnecessary antibiotic treatment. Culture and sensitivity testing for bacteria takes 48 hours. Fungi may be identified immediately in a fresh specimen, but may take several weeks to culture. Some viruses can be quickly identified by immunological tests, but may take weeks to culture.

NUCLEAR MAGNETIC RESONANCE SCAN (NMR)

A recently developed technique that allows doctors to see through human tissue. Many doctors believe it is even more effective than the CAT scan at providing clear images of deep tissues. The process by which the NMR works is highly technical, involving computer analysis of the electro-magnetic signals emitted by different tissues. The end result is, like the CAT scan, a cross-sectional image of the tissues under examination which allows precise assessment of any variation from the normal. Since it involves none of the risks of X-rays, the NMR is completely safe. Cost is the major drawback to NMR scanning. The NMR machine costs twice as much as a CAT scanner and it must be housed in a special, magnetically-isolated room.

PLAIN X-RAYS

X-rays are used to examine tissues inside the body. The rays are directed through the area to be examined from one side and recorded on a photographic plate on the other side. Dense tissues such as bone transmit fewer X-rays and thus project a paler image on the photographic film than the soft tissues. X-ray pictures taken without any special preparation are called plain X-rays. These are of great value in the diagnosis of disorders of the bones and joints. Chest X-rays are useful to demonstrate the size and shape of the heart and any changes in density of the lungs. See CONTRAST X-RAYS.

ULTRASOUND

Ultrasound is a method of examining tissues deep inside the body by means of high-frequency sound waves. Ultrasound waves bounce off tissues at different rates according to the density of the tissue. The waves are generated by a small device which is held or moved over the area to be examined. This device also records the echoes of the reflected waves, which are transmitted to a computer where they are analysed and transformed to an image on the computer screen. Interpretation of the image on the screen, or photographs or printouts taken from it, allows tissues of different density to be distinguished.

Because the sound waves have no effect on the tissues being examined, the scan can be continued over a period of time to observe the movements of structures within the body, such as the beating of the heart or the progress of a biopsy needle towards its target. Continuous observation under ultrasound is called real time ultrasound. Ultrasound scans are quick and safe, and the results are available immediately. The procedures can be done in an out-patient clinic or radiology centre. Because of its safety, ultrasound is of great value in examining the pregnant uterus.

X-RAY

See PLAIN X-RAYS and CONTRAST X-RAYS.

BONES, JOINTS AND MUSCLES

(See also How The Body Works, pp. 2–4.)

ARTHROGRAPHY

A CONTRAST X-RAY procedure performed to determine the extent of joint derangement from injury or disease. After injecting local anaesthetic, a needle is inserted into a joint, fluid is withdrawn and then a special radiopaque dye is injected. The patient is instructed to move the joint while X-rays are taken. There may be slight discomfort when the needle is inserted and the dye injected. The procedure takes from 30 to 60 minutes.

BLOOD TESTS FOR ARTHRITIS

BLOOD TESTS for antinuclear factor and ESR aid in the diagnosis of rheumatoid arthritis. The level of uric acid in the serum is raised in gout.

BONE BIOPSY

A sample of bone is taken – usually from the breastbone or the pelvis – to examine the bone under the microscope, and for analysis of its structural framework and mineral content. Local anaesthetic is injected into the skin and through to the bone surface. A special bone biopsy instrument, which punches out a fragment from the surface of the bone, is introduced through a tiny incision in the skin.

Usually the patient is admitted to hospital overnight for this relatively quick procedure. There may be some pain as the sample is punched from the bone, but this settles quickly. See BONE MARROW BIOPSY and BIOPSY.

JOINT ASPIRATION

When swelling and pain occur due to accumulation of excess fluid between the membranes lining a joint, a sample of the fluid may be withdrawn for testing. A small area of skin over the joint is cleaned with antiseptic, and anaesthetised with a special 'freezing' spray. A needle is inserted into the joint cavity and a sample of the fluid is aspirated into a syringe and sent to a laboratory for analysis. This may reveal infection or other cause of the joint disorder. The procedure takes 5–10 minutes. Momentary pain may be felt during insertion of the needle. There is a rare risk of infection or bleeding into the joint.

JOINT BIOPSY

When the cause of severe joint inflammation is in doubt, a small piece of the synovial membrane which lines the joint, together with some synovial fluid, may be removed for laboratory examination. The procedure is the same as for JOINT ASPIRATION (above), except that local anaesthetic is injected and it may take a few minutes longer. See also BIOPSY.

MUSCLE BIOPSY

Used as an aid in the diagnosis of muscle-wasting diseases such as muscular dystrophy. Under local anaesthetic, a small incision is made in the skin to give access to an affected muscle. Examination of the biopsied tissue under a microscope may reveal the cause of the disorder. It is a relatively quick, straightforward procedure. The incision is closed with a stitch or two. See BIOPSY.

X-RAY

PLAIN X-RAY is the most valuable means of diagnosing disorders of bones and joints. Fractures are clearly demonstrated as are disorders of bone such as osteoporosis, rickets, and bone tumours. Disorders of joints and cartilage due to injury, arthritis and gout are also well demonstrated by X-ray pictures.

THE CIRCULATORY SYSTEM

(See also How The Body Works, pp. 5–9.)

ANGIOGRAM, ARTERIOGRAM, VENOGRAM

A radiopaque dye is used to obtain a CONTRAST X-RAY

picture of blood vessels (arteries or veins). Arterial angiography may be used to detect obstruction due to thrombosis or embolism, or distortions of the vessel wall due to arteriosclerosis, atheroma or aneurysm. Venography is usually performed to detect deep venous thrombosis in the legs. The dye is injected into the vessel to be examined (see CARDIAC ANGIOGRAPHY). The procedure is relatively quick and is painless.

CARDIAC CATHETERISATION/CARDIAC ANGIOGRAPHY

A specialised CONTRAST X-RAY technique used to determine how much the blood supply to the heart has been affected by such conditions as coronary artery disease. It is often performed when by-pass surgery is considered. This test is carried out in hospital. Preparation includes a physical examination and ECG, and a 6-hour fast before the procedure. The patient lies on an X-ray table and electrodes are taped to the wrists and ankles. A catheter, or thin tube, is inserted into an artery in the groin or arm, usually under local anaesthetic and mild sedation (although sometimes full anaesthetic is used). The catheter is gently pushed through the artery towards the heart. Its progress is monitored on an X-ray screen. When the catheter reaches the heart, a radiopaque dye is injected. X-rays are taken as the dye passes through the coronary arteries (coronary angiography).

The patient may feel faint or nauseated as the catheter is moved through the artery, and will usually feel hot as the dye is injected. With this test there is a small risk of complications, which should be discussed with your doctor. The procedure is lengthy, usually taking an hour or more.

CARDIAC ENZYMES

A BLOOD TEST carried out when a minor heart attack is suspected. In the days following myocardial infarction, three enzymes are released into the blood in a set order as a result of breakdown of the damaged heart muscle. The appearance of the enzymes confirms infarction, and their concentration in the blood reflects the extent of damage to the cardiac muscle.

CARDIOVASCULAR NUCLEAR (ISOTOPE) TEST

This helps in the diagnosis of many heart disorders and diseases not usually detected in conventional tests. A solution containing radioactive material is injected into a vein in the arm. A special scanning camera takes pictures as the blood passes through the heart, revealing its structure and pumping efficiency. During part of the test, the patient is asked to move and change positions, and to exercise. An ECG may be taken simultaneously. The test is painless and harmless, and takes between 30 and 60 minutes. See also ISOTOPE SCAN (NUCLEAR SCAN).

ECG (ELECTROCARDIOGRAM)

This tests the degree to which the heart is healthy by measuring its electrical activity. Electrodes are fastened (with adhesive tape) to the wrists, ankles and chest wall, and the monitoring device is turned on. One of the several electrodes attached to the chest is moved in succession to five or six different places on the chest. The electrical impulses which control the contraction of various parts of the heart muscle are recorded on a moving strip of paper. The ECG gives valuable information about the condition of the cardiac pacemaker, the heart's conducting system and the cardiac muscle. It is particularly useful in the accurate diagnosis of the nature of cardiac arrhythmias and the extent of myocardial infarction. The test, which is painless and harmless, takes about 5 minutes.

ECHOCARDIOGRAPHY

Real time ultrasound echocardiography allows observation and recording of the movements of the cardiac muscle and valves during the heartbeat. The ultrasound pictures (which are studied in conjunction with an ECG taken simultaneously) also provide information about the size, shape and flexibility of the atria, ventricles, heart valves and aorta. The procedure, which is painless and harmless, takes between 15 and 60 minutes. See also ULTRASOUND.

LIPIDS

The measurement and interpretation of the levels of various lipids (fats) in the serum (performed as a routine by the autoanaliser, see BLOOD TESTS), is often used to predict the risk of cardiovascular disease. Sometimes apparently healthy people have abnormally high fat levels which may predispose them to heart attack, atherosclerosis or stroke. The finding of abnormal lipid levels or ratios may encourage changes in diet and life-style which are believed to reduce cardiovascular risk.

OPHTHALMOSCOPY, RETINOSCOPY

Examination of the retinal blood vessels can provide valuable information about the condition of blood vessels elsewhere in the body. See RETINOSCOPY.

STRESS TEST (EXERCISE ECG)

This test may be carried out on people with suspected coronary artery disease, heart muscle disorder or cardiac arrhythmia. The procedure is the same as for an ECG except that the person is asked to walk on a treadmill, ride an exercise bike or climb up and down a small set of steps. The ECG is recorded before, during and after the exercise to see how well the heart responds to an increase in the demand for blood. It is painless and takes between 15 and 30 minutes. In some cases the patient may experience some chest pain, weakness, dizziness or irregular heartbeat. The ECG readings are constantly monitored during the test, which is stopped at the first sign of cardiac distress.

THE RESPIRATORY SYSTEM

(See also How The Body Works, pp. 10–11.)

BLOOD GAS ANALYSIS

A test in which the concentration of oxygen and carbon dioxide in the blood is measured. It gives valuable information about the efficiency of the lungs in such conditions as severe asthma, emphysema and pneumoconiosis. Arterial blood (which contains the oxygen absorbed from the air in the lungs) is taken from the arm, wrist or groin using a needle and syringe. No tourniquet is used but a local anaesthetic may be given because the procedure is more painful than that when blood is collected from a vein. It takes around 5 minutes. See BLOOD TESTS.

BREATHING AND LUNG CAPACITY TESTS

A series of tests carried out to measure the efficiency of breathing. The most commonly used test is the peak flow estimation, which involves the patient blowing hard and quickly into a device (a peak flow meter) which records on a dial the rate at which the air is expelled. Several readings may be taken at intervals to get a good average. If the meter shows that breathing efficiency is reduced (which often happens in conditions such as asthma, emphysema and chronic bronchitis) special hospital laboratory tests may be necessary. Such a test is the vitalograph which, when attached by a face mask to the patient, measures the amount of air taken in and exhaled during each breath, both during rest and exercise. The information provided by these tests helps doctors to establish the progress of a particular lung disorder and to decide on the most appropriate form of treatment.

BRONCHOGRAPHY

A technique of CONTRAST X-RAY in which a catheter is inserted into the trachea through the nose or mouth (sometimes through a needle into the windpipe) and then pushed carefully through the bronchi, its progress being monitored on the X-ray machine. A radiopaque dye is introduced and X-rays are then taken to demonstrate parts of the bronchial tree. The patient is admitted to hospital, fasts overnight and is sedated before the procedure. In some cases,

an anaesthetic is given. Time involved varies between 30 and 90 minutes.

BRONCHOSCOPY

Endoscopic examination (see ENDOSCOPY) of the interior of the bronchi using a special instrument called a bronchoscope. This procedure is used in the investigation of respiratory diseases such as chronic pneumonia or lung tumours. Sputum and biopsy samples may be collected during bronchoscopy. The patient is admitted to hospital and fasted for at least 6 hours before the procedure. A sedative is given and the throat and airways anaesthetised. The test is unpleasant and sometimes rather frightening. It takes about 30 minutes.

NUCLEAR ISOTOPE TESTS

Another CONTRAST X-RAY investigation which may aid in the diagnosis of chest and lung conditions by studying the blood flow through the lungs. Radioactive material is injected into the arm, then scanners photograph the flow of blood through the lungs. In such a way, pulmonary embolism, for example, may be diagnosed. Radioactive xenon gas may also be inhaled to further determine the efficiency of the lungs. The procedure, which is painless and harmless, takes about 30 minutes. See ISOTOPE SCAN (NUCLEAR SCAN).

PULMONARY ANGIOGRAPHY

A CONTRAST X-RAY technique used to demonstrate the blood vessels of the lungs. It is useful in the diagnosis and location of pulmonary embolism. The technique is similar to that used for CARDIAC ANGIOGRAPHY, except that the catheter is inserted into the pulmonary artery. A full anaesthetic may be used. As in a cardiac angiography, the patient may feel faint or sick as the catheter is moved through the artery and feel hot as the dye is injected. The test takes from 30 to 60 minutes.

SKIN TESTS

Used to test whether a person may be immune to such diseases as tuberculosis or diphtheria. In the Mantoux test, which establishes whether there is immunity to tuberculosis, a solution containing dead tubercle bacilli is injected into the skin, usually on the forearm. If immunity exists, a red, raised swelling about 1–2 cm across, forms at the site of the injection. The reaction is due to the activity of antibodies to the tubercle bacillus at the site of the injection. A similar test for immunity to tuberculosis is the Heaf multiple-puncture tuberculin test, which is based on the action of antibodies to the toxin (tuberculin) of the tubercle bacillus. In the Schick test, which determines immunity to diphtheria, a small amount of a weak solution of the toxins produced by the diphtheria bacteria is injected into the skin on the forearm. If antibodies are present, the toxin will be neutralised and no reaction occurs. People without sufficient immunity (and thus needing immunisation) develop, within three or four days, a red inflamed area at the site of the injection.

SPUTUM TESTS

Microscopic examination of secretions from the lungs are used to diagnose respiratory disorders. Usually a sample is simply obtained by collecting the sputum coughed up by the patient. If there is difficulty in producing sputum during a medical consultation, the patient may be given a specimen jar for overnight collection. Sometimes, the back of the throat may be tickled to stimulate coughing or a tube inserted in the windpipe to collect a sample. If infection is suspected the sputum will be sent to a MICROBIOLOGY laboratory to see whether microorganisms are present. Sputum may also be examined for the presence of cancer cells.

X-RAY/TOMOGRAPHY (CAT SCAN)

Chest X-rays are the most common means used to examine the condition of the lungs. Areas of inflammation and the presence of fluid in the lungs and pleural cavities are clearly demonstrated by chest X-ray. These changes and the presence of other abnormal shadows in the lung fields may aid in the diagnosis of such conditions as pneumonia, bronchitis and lung cancer. Tomography (CAT SCAN) is a valuable aid in the diagnosis of early cancers too small to be detected on ordinary X-ray. See also PLAIN X-RAYS.

THE NERVOUS SYSTEM

(See also How The Body Works, pp. 12–15.)

AUDIOGRAM

A test to determine how well a person can hear. The patient puts on a pair of headphones through which sounds of varying pitch and volume are sent to each ear, one at a time. The results (which are recorded on a graph) give the doctor a good indication about the type and cause of deafness. Audiograms are performed in special sound- and vibration-free rooms, and take 30-60 minutes.

CEREBRAL ANGIOGRAPHY

This CONTRAST X-RAY test is most often used to examine the arteries of the brain in cases of stroke, or to reveal the presence of clots, bleeding and other disorders of the circulation of the neck and head. This is a hospital procedure. The patient lies on an X-ray table and a general anaesthetic is given. A catheter is inserted either into the carotid artery or the femoral artery in the groin. In the latter case, a fine flexible tube must be carefully pushed all the way to the neck. A radiopaque dye is injected through the catheter and X-rays are taken as the dye flows through the blood vessels in the head. The test takes an hour or more to perform.

COLOUR VISION TESTS

Specially designed coloured plates, depicting several objects made up of slightly differently coloured dots, are used to detect colour blindness.

COMPUTERISED AXIAL TOMOGRAPH

The CAT SCAN is used to detect blood clots, abscesses, tumours and other structural changes in the brain. The patient places his or her head in a rubber helmet-like device attached to a special camera. The procedure is painless, safe and quick, taking between 15 and 60 minutes.

ELECTROENCEPHALOGRAM (EEG)

A technique used to measure the electrical activity within the brain in order to diagnose over- or under-activity, tumours, seizures and abscesses. The patient lies flat, and up to eight electrodes are placed around the head. As the patient rests, or even sleeps, the electrodes convert the brain's electrical impulses into signals which are recorded on a moving strip of paper. The procedure is painless and takes between 30 and 60 minutes.

ELECTROMYOGRAPHY AND NERVE CONDUCTION TEST

A test carried out to measure the electrical activity of the muscles to determine whether paralysis is due to a disorder of nerve or of muscle. An electrode is passed through the skin into the muscle. Any flow of electricity within the muscle is picked up by the electrode and recorded on a moving strip of paper or projected on to a computer screen. A nerve conduction test is performed in a similar way except that the electrode is taped to the skin over the nerve. There is momentary pain or discomfort as the electrode needle is inserted while the electric current may cause a strange sensation which can last up to 24 hours. The tests take between 30 and 60 minutes.

MYELOGRAPHY

A CONTRAST X-RAY technique used to detect abnormalities of the contour of the spinal canal, such as tumours, fractures, or other deforming disorders of the vertebrae or intervertebral discs, or conditions which result in swelling or shrinkage of the spinal cord. Myelography is performed in hospital. A sedative is usually given before the test: in some cases general anaesthetic is used. Radiopaque dye is injected into the space surrounding the spinal cord via a SPINAL TAP. The patient lies on a table which can be tipped so that the radiopaque dye can be distributed along the length of the spinal cord. X-rays are then taken. As in the spinal tap, this procedure involves some discomfort, with the possibility of headache afterwards. It takes between 30 and 90 minutes.

NUCLEAR BRAIN SCAN (ISOTOPE SCAN)
This scan is used in stroke to locate obstruction to brain blood vessels by thrombosis or embolism. Radioactive isotope-tagged fibrinogen is injected into the patient's arm. It then circulates to the brain and is concentrated in thrombi, which then show up clearly on photographic film. The technique may also demonstrate certain tumours. The patient must keep his or her head still while the special camera takes pictures. This painless procedure takes between 45 and 60 minutes. See ISOTOPE SCAN (NUCLEAR SCAN).

NUCLEAR MAGNETIC RESONANCE SCAN (NMR)
If available, the NUCLEAR MAGNETIC RESONANCE SCAN may be used for the same diagnostic purposes as the CAT SCAN.

OCULAR TENSION
The measurement of the pressure within the eye. A sensitive pressure gauge called an ocular tonometer is used. Ocular tension is a routine part of any eye examination, for the purpose of early detection of pressure rises which may herald the development of glaucoma. Early treatment may prevent loss of vision from glaucoma.

OPHTHALMOSCOPY
Examination of the eye using an ophthalmoscope – a small device, held by hand, which shines a beam of light into the eye. By rotating a series of lenses attached to the ophthalmoscope, the focus of the light beam may be extended so that all the structures of the eye, from the cornea to the retina, are clearly focused, illuminated and magnified for inspection. Ophthalmoscopy provides important information about conditions of the front of the eye, such as strabismus (squint), glaucoma and cataracts. The retina (also called the fundus of the eye) can also be inspected, as well as the retinal blood vessels and the beginning of the optic nerve. When special examination of the retina is required, the retinoscope is used (see RETINOSCOPY). The ophthalmoscope is also used to determine how efficiently the cornea and lens of the eye refract light. Depending on the results, the doctor may prescribe glasses or contact lenses to correct defects in vision.

RETINOSCOPY
Examination of the retina using a device called a retinoscope (which is similar to an ophthalmoscope, but is more sensitive and provides higher magnification). The fundus of the eye is the only place in the body where blood vessels and nerves can be directly inspected. The retinal blood vessels reflect many vascular disorders, including the changes of atherosclerosis, arteriosclerosis and diabetes. Before retinoscopy or OPHTHALMOSCOPY the patient may be given eye-drops containing atropine which dilates the pupil so that the doctor can see a wider expanse of the inner eye clearly. If atropine eye-drops are used, the patient may have disturbed vision for an hour or two after the examination.

SPINAL TAP (LUMBAR PUNCTURE)
A technique of obtaining a sample of the cerebrospinal fluid (CSF). Laboratory examination of the CSF gives important diagnostic information about disorders such as stroke, subarachnoid haemorrhage, multiple sclerosis, meningitis and encephalitis. This test is performed in hospital. The patient lies on his or her side, legs bent at the knees and drawn up to the abdomen, chin resting on chest so that the spine is stretched and the spaces between the vertebrae are opened up. Local anaesthetic is injected into the skin and deeper tissues before the fine needle is inserted into the space between the third and fourth, or fourth and fifth lumbar vertebrae into the subarachnoid space, where the cerebrospinal fluid circulates. After the pressure of the cerebrospinal fluid is measured, a sample of the fluid is withdrawn. The patient is then required to lie flat for several hours. There is some discomfort during and after a lumbar puncture, and some people experience a severe headache for up to 24 hours afterwards. The procedure takes about 15 minutes.

ULTRASOUND
The ULTRASOUND may be used to detect clots, tumours and collections of fluid in the brain. It is painless and quick, taking between 15 and 30 minutes.

VISUAL ACUITY
A series of tests to determine the extent and nature of defects in vision. The patient is asked to read a chart on which the letters become smaller and smaller. A person with normal vision should be able to read letters 6 cm high at a distance of 6 metres. After the doctor or optometrist has recorded the visual acuity, the patient is asked to read the chart again through varous combinations of lenses. The most effective combination is then made into glasses or contact lenses.

THE DIGESTIVE SYSTEM

(See also How The Body Works, pp. 16–18.)

AMYLASE

This is a BLOOD TEST for the enzyme amylase, which is produced by the pancreas to assist in the digestion of carbohydrates. Injuries or conditions which disrupt the pancreas, such as pancreatitis, may cause an increase in the release of amylase into the bloodstream.

BARIUM SULPHATE X-RAY STUDIES

The radiopaque dye, barium sulphate, is used to obtain CONTRAST X-RAYS of the interior of the digestive tract as an aid in the diagnosis of such disorders as ulcers, tumours, hernias, colitis and diverticulitis. If the upper digestive tract (oesophagus, stomach and duodenum) is being examined, the patient fasts for 6 hours, and then swallows a porridge-like, chalky drink of barium sulphate solution. The progress of the barium down the oesophagus is observed and photographed, and the patient is asked to move around a little as the doctor presses on the stomach while further X-rays of the stomach and duodenum are taken.

If the lower digestive tract is being examined, the patient is given a laxative on the previous evening and then fasts until the test is done. Barium solution is passed into the rectum through an enema tube. The doctor may also pump some air into the rectum to make the walls of the intestine more clearly defined in X-rays. The procedures, which take between 15 and 60 minutes, involve more discomfort than pain. Constipation may follow a barium meal. Cramps and a strong urge to defaecate follow a barium enema.

CHOLECYSTOGRAM/CHOLANGIOGRAM

A CONTRAST X-RAY procedure used to demonstrate the interior of the gall-bladder and bile ducts in order to detect gallstones, to check for any malfunction of these organs or to check for tumour or other obstruction in the bile ducts. The night before the examination the patient is given tablets containing a radiopaque dye which is absorbed into the blood from the intestine and excreted by the liver into the bile. By the following morning, the dye has concentrated in the gall-bladder. An X-ray is taken, and then a fatty meal is given to stimulate the gall-bladder to deliver bile into the common bile duct and thence into the duodenum. Any obstruction to the flow of bile from the gall-bladder can be accurately located. If the flow of bile from the liver to the gall-bladder is to be examined (or if the patient cannot swallow or keep down tablets) the dye is given by injection into

the arm 20–30 minutes before the test. These tests take between 1 and 4 hours.

COLONOSCOPY

Endoscopic examination of the large intestine using a sigmoidoscope or colonoscope (see ENDOSCOPY). The shorter sigmoidoscope is used for the lower third of the colon, and the proctoscope for the rectum and the anus. This examination allows early and accurate diagnosis of such conditions as ulcerative colitis, malignant tumours or polyps. The patient is given a laxative (sometimes an enema) and then fasts or takes only clear fluids until the test is performed. Occasionally sedation is given beforehand. The procedure, which can take up to an hour, causes some discomfort.

DIGESTIVE TRACT BIOPSY

Tests in which samples of tissue are taken from the lining of the digestive tract to diagnose such conditions as peptic ulcer, cancer and colitis. They are performed during ENDOSCOPY of the digestive tract. A fine wire, with two tiny pincer-like cutters at the end, is inserted through the fibreoptic tube of the endoscope to obtain the BIOPSY specimen. When it reaches the designated area, the doctor moves a lever activating the cutters which snip off a small piece of tissue. Small polyps in the digestive tract may be removed in this way, avoiding the need for further surgery. These tests take 15–90 minutes.

GASTROSCOPY

Endoscopic examination of the oesophagus, stomach and upper digestive tract using a flexible gastroscope (see ENDOSCOPY). This procedure may be used in the diagnosis of conditions such as peptic ulcer, inflammation and tumours of the upper digestive tract. It is usually performed in hospital. The patient fasts overnight, and is given a sedative before the test, and local anaesthetic is applied to the mouth and throat to minimise discomfort as the fibreoptic tube is passed through the mouth and into the stomach. General anaesthetic may be used. Samples of gastric secretions and BIOPSY specimens may be obtained through the gastroscope. The examination takes 15–60 minutes. This technique has largely replaced oesophagoscopy, in which a rigid tube that works rather like a periscope, is passed into the stomach.

LIVER BIOPSY

A sample of liver tissue is taken to assist in the diagnosis of infection, cirrhosis, tumours and other liver disorders. It is usually performed in hospital, often with an overnight stay. Local anaesthetic is injected into the skin between the lower ribs on the right side for insertion of the BIOPSY needle into the liver to obtain the biopsy specimen. There may be a dull pain when the liver is punctured. The procedure takes only about 5 minutes.

NUCLEAR ISOTOPE LIVER SCAN

A test used to study the efficiency and functioning ability of the liver, and to detect disturbances of the anatomical structure of the liver and the presence of cysts. In tests of function, radioactive material which is metabolised in the liver is injected into the arm. Pictures are taken of the liver and gall-bladder every 15 minutes or so for 2 hours. In structural tests, a different radioactive material is used in the same way, but the scanner takes pictures over a 12-hour period in order to detect cysts, tumours, scar tissues. The test is painless and safe, and takes between 2 and 12 hours.

A similar procedure may be carried out to examine the pancreas. See ISOTOPE SCAN (NUCLEAR SCAN).

PROCTOSCOPY

Endoscopic examination of the rectum and anal canal. See COLONOSCOPY and ENDOSCOPY.

SIGMOIDOSCOPY

Endoscopic examination of the lower third of the colon. See COLONOSCOPY and ENDOSCOPY.

ULTRASOUND

ULTRASOUND examination may be used to detect tumours, stones, cysts, and signs of inflammation in the pancreas, liver and gall-bladder. The procedure takes between 15 and 30 minutes and is safe and quite painless.

METABOLISM

(See also How The Body Works, pp. 19–21.)

BLOOD SUGAR TESTS

Measurement of the blood level of glucose may be performed if diabetes is suspected. Random blood sugar measures the level of glucose in a blood specimen collected at any time. If this is abnormally raised, a fasting blood sugar will be measured on blood collected after a 12-hour fast. If the fasting blood sugar is raised, a glucose tolerance test will be recommended. A fasting blood sample is collected, and then the patient is given a drink containing a measured amount of glucose. Samples of blood are collected by finger prick at half-hourly intervals for the next 3 hours. The glucose level of all samples is measured and the results plotted on a graph. The shape of the resulting blood sugar curve reflects the insulin response to glucose absorbed from the digestive tract and indicates whether or not the patient is diabetic.

LIVER FUNCTION TESTS

Measurement of the concentration of certain constituents of the blood is a reliable guide to the metabolic function of the liver. The levels of plasma proteins, certain enzymes and bilirubin (a pigment derived from the breakdown of red blood cells and metabolised in the liver to form bile pigment) are disturbed in conditions such as hepatitis and cirrhosis, which result in liver malfunction. BLOOD TESTS can also determine whether jaundice is due to obstruction of the bile ducts or liver cell damage. These tests can be performed by an autoanalyser on a routinely collected blood sample.

THE ENDOCRINE SYSTEM

(See also How The Body Works, pp. 22–24.)

CORTISOL BLOOD TEST

A test to determine the blood level of the steroid hormone, cortisol, produced by the adrenal glands. An increased level of cortisol is thought to be associated with such conditions as diabetes, hypertension, obesity and Cushing's syndrome. A decrease in the level of cortisol is associated with Addison's disease.

HORMONE LEVEL TESTS

A variety of different laboratory tests are used in the investigation of many endocrine disorders and diseases to determine the level of certain hormones in urine and blood. Because the normal release of some hormones varies over each 24-hour period, samples may need to be collected at particular times of the day, depending on the hormone and function being assessed. Because hormone measurements involve complex methods of analysis which are performed only in specialist laboratories, results may not be available for up to two weeks after the sample reaches the laboratory.

RADIOACTIVE IODINE UPTAKE (RAIU) AND SCANNING

This test is carried out to determine whether the thyroid gland is producing normal amounts of the hormone thyroxine, and to detect tumours and cysts. The patient is given radioactive iodine, either in tablet form, by injection or by inhalation, and the rate at which it is absorbed by the thyroid is recorded by passing a scanner over the gland. The amount of iodine absorbed indicates how much hormone the thyroid is producing. Measurements are taken at 2-, 4-, 6- and/or 24-hour intervals after administration of the radioactive iodine. Every measurement takes between 15 and 30 minutes. The test is painless and harmless.

THYROID ECHOGRAPHY

ULTRASOUND examination may be used to accurately detect and locate tumours and cysts of the thyroid gland. The procedure is painless and harmless and takes about 30 minutes.

THE URINARY SYSTEM

(See also How The Body Works, p. 18.)

BLOOD UREA TEST

A BLOOD TEST to determine the serum level of urea, a chemical produced by the liver as a by-product of protein metabolism, and normally excreted by the kidneys. A high level of urea in the blood indicates that the kidneys are not functioning properly.

CATHETERISED URINE COLLECTION

A sample of urine may be collected directly from the bladder. A hollow, flexible tube is passed through the urethra into the bladder and some urine allowed to flow into a sterile jar for MICROBIOLOGY tests. The catheter may cause a little discomfort with some burning or stinging but the procedure takes only a few minutes.

CYSTOGRAM

A CONTRAST X-RAY test to detect abnormalities of the internal contours of the bladder and urethra. The dye is introduced through a thin tube which is inserted through the urethra into the bladder. The patient may also be asked to urinate while further X-rays are taken, to demonstrate whether there is any obstruction to the flow of the urine such as may occur in prostatic hypertrophy and urethral stricture. The procedure takes about an hour and causes some discomfort and embarrassment.

CYSTOSCOPY

Endoscopic examination of the bladder to establish the presence of growths, stones or other disorders of the bladder lining (see ENDOSCOPY). The instrument used, called a cystoscope, is inserted through the urethra and passed carefully into the bladder. Local or general anaesthetic may be used. Stones and small benign tumours found during cystoscopy may often be removed through the cystoscope. There may be burning or stinging in the urethra after cystoscopy. The procedure takes 20–60 minutes.

PROTEINURIA TEST

A test to determine the amount of protein in the urine to help in the diagnosis of kidney disease or infection. Initially the doctor will test a urine sample in the surgery using a simple dipstick which is sensitised to react to the presence of protein. If an abnormally high quantity of protein is indicated by the changing colour of the dipstick, a urine sample will be sent to a laboratory for further, more exact measurement of protein loss in urine.

PYELOGRAM

A CONTRAST X-RAY technique to detect cysts, stones, congenital abnormalities and other deforming disorders of the kidneys and ureters. A radiopaque dye is injected (usually into the arm) which then travels through the blood to the kidneys and outlines their shape and size as they filter the dye from the blood. X-rays are taken at significant stages of this process. The rate at which the dye travels to the ureters and bladder may be recorded as a measure of the kidneys' efficiency. In preparation for the procedure, which usually takes about half an hour, the patient is asked to fast overnight.

RENAL BIOPSY

A BIOPSY sample of kidney tissue is taken in order to determine the exact nature of kidney disorders and renal failure. It is a hospital procedure. Local anaesthetic is given and, guided by X-rays or ULTRASOUND, a special biopsy needle is passed through the lower back and into the kidney.

URINALYSIS

The most common urine test is done on a mid-stream sample. After washing the genitals, a small amount of urine is passed into the toilet, then 5–10 ml are passed into a sterile collection jar and then the urine remaining in the bladder is emptied into the toilet. The sample is sent to a laboratory where it is tested for the presence of sugar, protein, blood, pus, crystals, bile and any other abnormal constituents. Microscopy, culture and sensitivity are also performed to detect any organisms that may be causing urinary tract infections such as cystitis, pyelitis or pyelonephritis. See MICROBIOLOGY.

THE BLOOD AND LYMPH SYSTEMS

(See also How The Body Works, pp. 5–9.)

BONE MARROW BIOPSY

A sample of the bone marrow, usually taken from the breastbone or the pelvic bone, may be examined under the microscope to give valuable diagnostic information in disorders of blood cell formation such as leukaemia and certain anaemias. The procedure involves some discomfort, in spite of the local anaesthetic, so a mild sedative is usually given beforehand. Marrow biopsy takes 15–60 minutes. See BIOPSY.

CLOTTING (COAGULATION) TESTS

Tests to establish how long it takes for blood to clot, and to measure the levels of the many factors involved in the clotting process. Clotting tests are carried out to monitor the effects of anticoagulant treatment which is used in cases where the formation of blood clots must be prevented. They may also be used to test liver function, to investigate the causes of excessive bruising or bleeding (as may happen in haemophilia and thrombocytopoenia) and as a screening device before surgical procedures which may result in bleeding.

ESR (ERYTHROCYTE SEDIMENTATION RATE)

Often carried out in conjunction with a FULL BLOOD COUNT, the ESR determines the rate at which red blood cells settle out from plasma. It gives an indication of the presence of infection, inflammation and malignancy.

FULL BLOOD COUNT

The most common of all BLOOD TESTS, in which the numbers of red cells, white cells and platelets in a cubic mm of whole blood are counted. These days the count is performed by an autoanalyser, which also measures the amount of haemoglobin per 100 ml of blood, the proportion of cells to plasma, the average size of the red cells and the average amount of haemoglobin in each red cell. The proportion of each of the five types of white cell and the form (shape) of the red cells is reported after examining a stained film of blood under the microscope.

LYMPH NODE BIOPSY

A procedure in which a whole lymph node is removed for examination to assist in the diagnosis of various diseases such as Hodgkin's disease, or to check on the spread of malignant cells or certain infections from elsewhere in the body. The skin over the node to be removed is anaesthetised (in children, general anaesthetic is used) after which an incision is made and the node dissected out from its surroundings. The incision is closed with one or more stitches. There is very little pain associated with the procedure, which takes 15 to 30 minutes, although the area may be sore for several days. See BIOPSY.

LYMPHANGIOGRAM

A CONTRAST X-RAY technique is used to help in the diagnosis of disorders of the lymph system such as Hodgkin's disease. The radiopaque dye is injected into one of the lymph vessels, usually on the foot.

The dye spreads through the nodes, glands and channels of the lymph system and is recorded on X-rays. This painless procedure takes between 90 minutes and 2 hours.

SCHILLING TEST

A test carried out to find out how efficiently the body absorbs vitamin B_{12}, usually to detect anaemia and some neurological disorders. The patient is given two doses of vitamin B_{12}, one by injection, the second in tablet form.

All the person's urine is collected over a 24-hour period and, after a series of analysis, measurements and calculations, any deficiency in vitamin B_{12} absorption can be gauged. If a deficiency is noted, another similiar test is carried out to establish whether the person is suffering from pernicious anaemia.

SERUM IRON AND IRON BINDING CAPACITY

Tests to measure the amount of iron carried in the plasma and the capacity of the blood to carry iron are important in the accurate diagnosis of the cause of anaemia.

REPRODUCTION AND PREGNANCY

(See also How The Body Works, pp. 25–30.)

AMNIOCENTESIS

Removal of a sample of the amniotic fluid during pregnancy for the purpose of testing the foetal cells it contains, to see whether genetic or other foetal disorders exist. The fluid is obtained by inserting (under local anaesthetic and with ULTRASOUND monitoring) a hollow needle through the abdominal wall and the wall of the uterus into the amniotic sac. Amniocentesis cannot be performed until the fifteenth week of pregnancy or later. It is carried out if a woman has a high risk of having an abnormal baby (for example, women over 39, those who have previously given birth to an abnormal baby and women who have a family history of inherited birth defects). There is a little discomfort (a brief pinching pain when the needle is inserted) involved in this procedure which takes about 10–15 minutes. A more recently developed technique of ante-natal diagnosis, chorionic villus sampling, (CVS) allows removal of a fragment of the outer wall of the amniotic sac by passing a slender instrument through the mother's cervical canal. This can be performed before the twelfth week of pregnancy – a more satisfactory time for the diagnosis of foetal abnormalities. Both amniocentesis and CVS involve slight discomfort, take 10–15 minutes to perform, and carry a slight risk of causing miscarriage.

BREAST BIOPSY

A needle BIOPSY is taken from a lump in the breast to determine whether the lump is malignant. The procedure, which takes 5–10 minutes is performed with local anaesthetic and causes only a little discomfort.

COLPOSCOPY

A test carried out after a Pap smear has shown abnormalities. The colposcope is like a microscope – it illuminates and magnifies the view of the surface membranes of the cervix and vaginal walls. A speculum is inserted into the vagina to bring the cervix into view. The colposcope is moved into position about 15 cm outside the entrance to the vagina and the focus moved so that the cervix and vagina can be inspected at ×10–15 magnification. By painting the cervix with solutions of water and vinegar and water and iodine, the abnormal area(s) can be clearly defined, and a small BIOPSY taken from any suspicious spot. Colposcopy is a painless procedure that takes around 15–20 minutes.

HORMONE TESTS

The measure of the levels in blood and urine of hormones produced by the pituitary, the ovaries, the testes and the adrenal gland, are important for the diagnosis of many disorders of the male and female reproductive systems. Blood for reproductive hormone testing may need to be collected at particular times of the day, and in women, at particular times of the menstrual cycle. Hormone measurements are performed in special laboratories so that the results take up to two weeks to return.

HYSTEROSALPINGOGRAM

A CONTRAST X-RAY examination of the interior of the uterus and fallopian tubes, usually performed to see whether or not the tubes are blocked. A thin tube is inserted through the vagina and into the cervical canal. Radiopaque dye is injected through the tube into the uterus. If the tubes are not blocked, the dye passes freely through them and spills out into the peritoneal cavity. X-ray pictures are taken as the dye flows into the tubes so that the location and extent of any blockage can be studied. The procedure takes 10–20 minutes and often causes some uterine cramps, and occasionally pain felt at the shoulder tip.

HYSTEROSCOPY

Endoscopic examination (see ENDOSCOPY) of the interior of the uterus, using a hysteroscope. Hysteroscopy may be used to aid in the diagnosis of disorders of uterine cavity and the endometrium, and to obtain BIOPSY samples. The procedure is usually performed with general anaesthesia, and takes 15–30 minutes.

INFRA-RED THERMOGRAPHY (IRT)

INFRA-RED THERMOGRAPHY is used to confirm a diagnosis of breast cancer and to locate the tumour. Cancerous areas give off more heat than surrounding tissue. The test is painless and takes about 15 minutes.

LAPAROSCOPY

Endoscopic examination (see ENDOSCOPY) of the internal reproductive organs to detect tumours and cysts, and to diagnose ectopic pregnancy and reasons for pain, menstrual irregularities and other gynaecological symptoms. It is a hospital procedure carried out under general anaesthetic. The doctor makes a small incision in the abdomen just below the navel through which the laparoscope is inserted into the abdominal cavity. The laparoscope often has surgical and BIOPSY tools built into it so that the doctor may take tissue samples for further analysis, perform a tubal ligation (sterilisation) or loosen any adhesions. Laparoscopy takes about 30 to 45 minutes.

MAMMOGRAPHY

X-ray examination of the breast for the purpose of detecting cysts, benign tumours and cancer. The woman sits or lies down while low dosage X-rays are taken. If a lesion is found, further X-rays are taken to pinpoint the area for biopsy. Mammography takes between 15 and 20 minutes.

PREGNANCY TESTS

The technology for detecting early pregnancy has advanced rapidly in the past decade or two. There is now a blood test which will reliably diagnose normal pregnancy before a period is missed. The means of detecting a fertilised egg before implantation in the uterus is on the horizon. Both urine and blood tests pinpoint the presence of a hormone produced by the placenta. Measurable quantities of this hormone (human chorionic gonadotrophin – hCG for short) can be found in the mother's blood about four days after implantation – that's three days before the period is due. The presence of hCG can be found in the mother's urine about eight days (sometimes sooner) after the missed period by the 2-hour tube tests, and twelve to fourteen days after the missed period by the 2-minute slide test. The 2-hour test is available in kits that can be used at home, and is very reliable.

SEMEN ANALYSIS

In the investigation of all subfertile couples, a

specimen of semen will be sent to the laboratory for examination of the number, motility and normality of form of the spermatozoa.

SMEAR TEST (PAP SMEAR)

The purpose of the Pap smear is the early detection of conditions of the cervix which might later become cancerous. Removal of suspicious tissue prevents the development of cervical cancer, which is still one of the common cancers of the female reproductive system. A Pap smear should be performed soon after the first sexual intercourse, and then at intervals of six months to three years, depending on a woman's age and the results of previous smears. The test is simple to perform. A doctor or nurse inserts a speculum into the vagina so that the cervix can be seen. A plastic or wooden spatula is used to wipe some cells from the region where the cervical canal meets the membrane covering the vaginal surface of the cervix. The cells are transferred to a glass slide which is then sprayed with or immersed in preservative solution. The slide is later sent for microscopic examination. The test takes about 2 minutes to perform, and apart from the intrusive feeling of the speculum, is painless. If abnormal cells are found, COLPOSCOPY is recommended. Certain infections and inflammatory conditions of the cervix and vagina may also show up on a Pap smear.

ULTRASOUND

ULTRASOUND is very useful for confirming the diagnosis of ovarian and other pelvic cysts, pelvic abscesses, and other disorders of the female reproductive organs. A full bladder is necessary for this safe, painless procedure, which takes between 15 and 45 minutes.

ULTRASOUND is also widely used for examination of the pregnant uterus. It is used to demonstrate the size, position and growth rate of the foetus, to check for multiple pregnancy and to check for any abnormalities in the foetus or placenta. The beating of the foetal heart can be seen on real time ultrasound from the sixth week of pregnancy.

THE IMMUNE SYSTEM

(See also How The Body Works, pp. 31–32.)

ANTIBODY TESTS

BLOOD TESTS can determine the presence in serum of specific antibodies produced in response to infectious organisms or other antigens. The finding of antibodies indicates previous exposure to the antigen, but not necessarily continuing infection. A newsworthy example of antibody testing is the test for antibodies to the AIDS virus.

ANTIGEN TESTS

The presence in serum of the antigen of a particular organism indicates that the active organism still exists in the body (in contrast to the presence of antibodies which indicate past – and in some instances continuing – infection). An example is the Australia antigen test (so called because the test was developed in Australia) which detects the antigen on the surface of the hepatitis B virus. The presence of Australia antigen, after the symptoms of the first infection have subsided, indicates chronic infection and the carrier state. When an antigen test for the AIDS virus is developed, it will be possible to tell which carriers of the AIDS antibody are infectious and may develop AIDS.

AUTOANTIBODY TESTS

Antibodies to particular types of the body's own tissues are produced by the immune system in autoimmune disease. For example, antithyroid antibodies are found in autoimmune thyroiditis, and anti-nuclear antibodies are present in rhematoid arthritis. The Coombes test identifies the auto-antibodies responsible for autoimmune haemolytic anaemia.

IMMUNOGLOBULINS (GAMMA GLOBULINS)

The measurement over time of the amounts of the various antigen-specific immunoglobulins in serum can give an indication of the progress of infectious disease. For example, the presence of specific immunoglobulin G (IgG) indicates past reaction to an antigen. The additional presence of specific immunoglobulin M (IgM) indicates continuing infection or reinfection.

T CELL COUNTS

Counts of the numbers and proportions of the several types of T lymphocytes (T3, T4, T8, T11) in blood are used to estimate the efficiency of the immune system. The progress of these counts over time reflects the progress of immune deficiency states such as AIDS.

4

FIRST AID
FOR
EMERGENCIES

FIRST AID FOR EMERGENCIES — INDEX

First aid is the immediate care given to victims of sudden illness or injury. Often it involves knowing how to treat the 101 minor accidents and medical situations that occur in everyday life. But sometimes it involves a sudden life-threatening event. The aim of this first aid section is to help you deal effectively with both.

When faced with an emergency, whether minor or major, you need to:
• be able to recognise symptoms and signs of physical malfunction or distress
• be able to recognise the *pattern* of certain symptoms and signs, using the pattern as a clue to the cause of distress
• know how to treat the sufferer
• know in what *order* to carry out the treatment.

Most of us find we are surprisingly vague about the correct procedures for treating minor medical events, even though many of these mainly require common sense. We find we do not know whether the doctor should be called immediately when a guest develops asthma in the middle of the night (see ASTHMA) or whether we should apply ice packs, massage or bandages for a strained muscle and in what order (see SPRAINS, STRAINS and DISLOCATIONS). Knowing the correct steps can markedly lessen the pain, discomfort and duration of an everyday medical occurrence.

In a major medical emergency, adherence to a clearly defined order of procedure can mean the difference between life and death. In this situation you *must* know that restoration of breathing and circulation takes precedence over treating any other medical condition. And you must be able to take the following steps.

1 Immediately decrease the danger of the situation (to yourself as well as to the casualty); this may involve knowing how to move the injured person (see MOVING AN INJURED PERSON).

2 Recognise unconsciousness and know how to position the unconscious person to minimise the dangers of that condition (see UNCONSCIOUSNESS).

3 Clear the casualty's airway and establish whether breathing and circulation are functioning (see RESUSCITATION).

4 Administer expired air resuscitation and cardiopulmonary resuscitation (see RESUSCITATION).

5 Control severe bleeding (see BLEEDING).

The first aid section of this book has been written with the help and advice of The St John Ambulance Association. These instructions are intended as a guide only and are in no way meant to be a replacement for a certified first aid course. You should practise the most important first aid techniques with a qualified first aider, but reading the following pages — now, rather than when a crisis, large or small, occurs — will help you to diagnose and treat those medical conditions we all encounter in our daily lives. For details of first aid courses available contact The St John Ambulance Association in your nearest city or town.

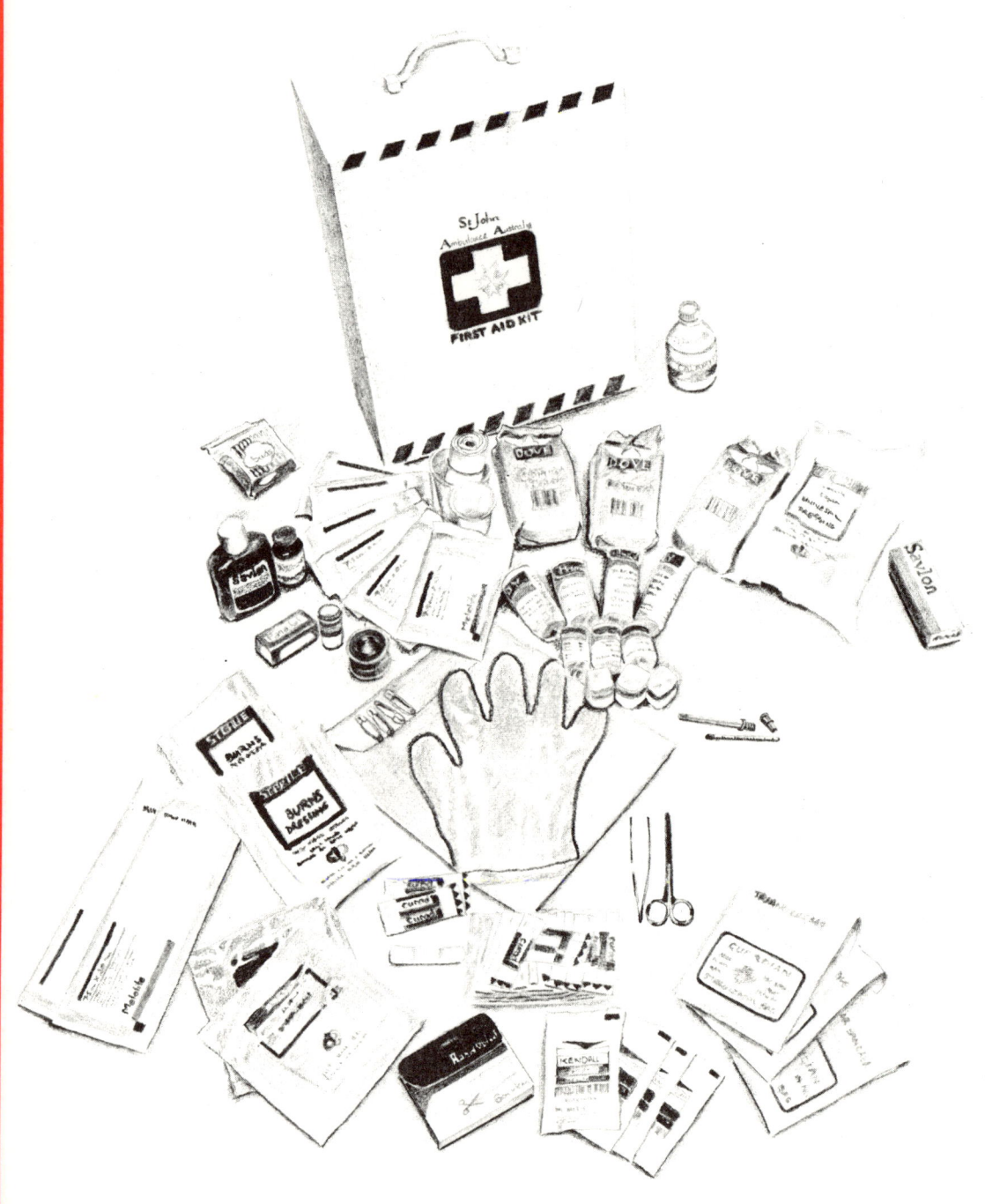

Every home should keep a first aid kit ready for emergencies. It should contain all the materials and equipment necessary for treating everyday accidents and illnesses. Keep separate kits in your car and boat and for hiking or camping. You can buy a ready-made kit from most chemists or make your own, using, for example, a plastic box. You should:

• keep it in a handy place, but *out of children's reach*
• make sure you replace items as they are used
• label the kit clearly 'First Aid'
• tape a card to it, giving details of blood group, allergies and special problems for each member of the household
• *not* keep any medicine for any length of time. You should safely dispose of a prescribed medicine once the course is completed.

A basic kit should contain the following items.

Cotton wool (*remember* that cotton wool must always be dampened before use, otherwise fibres will adhere to the wound)
Adhesive tape to secure dressings and bandages
Analgesic tablets such as paracetamol and children's soluble aspirin
Assorted **adhesive strip plasters** for minor cuts, grazes and scratches
Adhesive dressing that may be cut into various lengths
Antiseptic for cleaning wounds
Calamine lotion for sunburn, itchy bites and rashes
Cotton buds for swabbing and cleaning
Measuring glass or spoon for medicines
Roller bandages of various sizes and widths
Triangular bandages for head bandages, slings, splints, padding and to act as broad bandages for wounds and fractures

Pressure bandages for venomous bites and for holding dressings in place
Safety pins
Sharp scissors with rounded ends
Sterile non-adhesive absorbent dressings
Sterile gauze swabs for cleaning or dressing wounds
Thermometer
Splinter forceps
Sterile non-adhesive eye pads
Sterile non-adhesive dressings for burns
Sterile plastic gloves
Antiseptic cream
Beaker to hold, for example, antiseptic

The St John Ambulance Association supply a wide range of first aid kits for the home, the car, the workplace and for leisure activities such as boating and camping.

ASPHYXIA

Asphyxia occurs when the blood is deprived of oxygen, and carbon dioxide builds up. Unless the warning signs are recognised, the causes removed and resuscitation applied, if necessary, the casualty will die. Asphyxia can be caused by suffocation (see DROWNING and SUFFOCATION); strangulation and hanging; foreign bodies lodged in the airway (see CHOKING); lack of oxygen in the air because of a gas leak, fire or toxic fumes (see POISONING — inhaled poisons); some chest infections and conditions, such as asthma (see ASTHMA).

The symptoms and signs common to most cases of asphyxia are:
• laboured, noisy breathing
• swollen neck and head veins
• sweating
• blueness of face, fingernails and toenails
• pulse is fast, then is weak, then stops
• restlessness and confusion
• breathing turns into shuddering spasms, then ceases
• casualty becomes unconscious and cannot be aroused.

1 Treat the cause of the asphyxia (see SUFFOCATION, CHOKING, DROWNING, POISONING — inhaled poisons, ASTHMA).

2 Clear the casualty's airway and begin resuscitation (see RESUSCITATION): expired air resuscitation if there is no breathing; cardiopulmonary resuscitation if there is no pulse.

3 If pulse and breathing return but the casualty remains unconscious, follow the procedures outlined in UNCONSCIOUSNESS.

4 Seek immediate medical aid.

ASTHMA

Asthma sufferers experience difficulty in breathing. During an attack the muscles of the air passages in the lungs go into spasm and these tubes swell and become blocked with mucus. Many attacks occur at night when the sufferer is lying down. Occasionally asthma may be fatal, so it should be treated immediately. Symptoms and signs include:
- loud, laboured, wheezy breathing and heaving chest
- difficulty in talking and moving
- sufferer is distressed and alarmed
- pallor and sweating
- mental confusion, if oxygen is depleted in severe attack.

1 Sit sufferer upright with her arms resting on a table, chair or pillow. Open the windows, but do not let her become cold.

2 If the asthmatic is carrying any medication, it should be given immediately.

3 Unless the attack is very transitory, medical help should always be sought.

4 Calm the sufferer, and assure her that medical aid will soon arrive. A warm drink may be relaxing.

BANDAGES, DRESSINGS AND PADS

Bandages are used to keep dressings and splints in place (see SPLINTS); to prevent and reduce swelling; to maintain the pressure needed to control bleeding; to support an injured limb or joint (see SLINGS) or to immobilise it. Bandages are available commercially in a variety of sizes, shapes and materials (usually calico, crepe or gauze), but can be improvised from items, such as sheets, pillowcases, stockings and belts.

The two most used types are the **triangular bandage** (see below), which may be folded in various ways to become a dressing, pad, pressure bandage or sling, and the traditional **roller bandage** (see below), available in many different widths and lengths. **Crepe bandages** are particularly suitable as compression bandages for immobilising parts of the body affected by bites and stings (see BITES AND STINGS — pressure immobilisation). **Elasticated bandages** can be used to support injured joints, such as sprained ankles or wrists (see SPRAINS, STRAINS AND DISLOCATIONS). Seamless **tubular gauze bandages** are easier to apply than other bandages because they do not need to be tied.

All bandages should be either secured with a safety pin or adhesive tape or tied (see below). They should be applied firmly enough to control bleeding and to prevent dressings or splints from slipping, but should not be too tight. Loosen the bandage if toes, fingers or the areas around the wound become numb or bluish-white.

DRESSINGS
Before bandaging a wound, place a dressing over it. Dressings are a protective cover applied to a wound to control bleeding, prevent infection, ease swelling, absorb blood and discharges and prevent further damage. Commercial sterile dressings, gauze dressings and adhesive plasters with dressings attached are available, but many non-stick materials, such as folded triangular bandages, disposable baby napkins, towels or handkerchiefs can be used as emergency dressings. *Do not* place materials, such as cotton wool, that are likely to shed fibres, in direct contact with a wound.

Attach the dressing to the wound with a bandage or piece of clean material. Take care to prevent germs or dirt from entering the wound. Before touching the wound and dressing wash your hands carefully. *Do not* touch the wound or dressing more than necessary or expose them to the air. Try not to cough, sneeze or breathe on them.

PADS
Pads of gauze or clean material are sometimes used on top of dressings to increase the pressure and absorption. They are particularly useful for wounds involving protruding bones or foreign bodies. Firm pads may be improvised from a folded triangular bandage, an unwrapped roller bandage or firmly folded clothing.

A triangular or narrow bandage can also be made into a **ring pad** to hold the bandage away from a wound with a foreign object buried in it or to increase pressure to stop bleeding. Wind one end of a narrow bandage once or twice around your fingers to make a loop. Bring the other end of the bandage through the loop and continue passing it over and through until all the bandage is used and a firm ring made.

ROLLER BANDAGES

These have the advantage of shaping to the body and being easy to apply. Ideally, the size of the bandage should be related to the size of the injured limb: finger bandages should be small, body bandages wide.

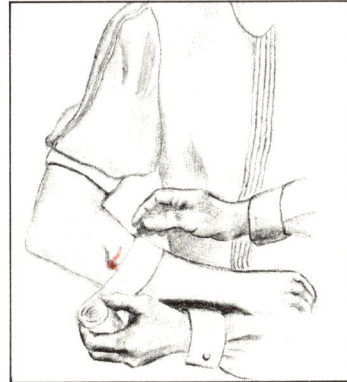

1 Stand or sit opposite the casualty, supporting the injured part while bandaging. Hold the roll in one hand and apply the outer surface of the bandage to the hurt area, unrolling a few centimetres at a time. Start just below the injury, bandaging outwards from the casualty's body and maintaining an even pressure. Finish just above the injury, overlapping each turn slightly for maximum support.

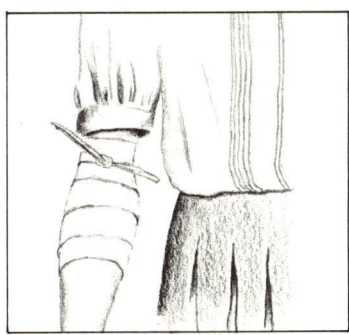

2 If tying, cut the end into two strips and make a reef knot. If using a safety pin or adhesive tape, fold the end of the bandage in and apply. Check that the bandage is not so tight that it impedes circulation.

TRIANGULAR BANDAGES

These can be made from squares of firm material, 50–100 cm wide, cut diagonally. They are very adaptable and can be used as slings (see SLINGS) or to protect shoulder, elbow, hand, chest, back, foot or the scalp (see HEAD, FACE AND JAW INJURIES). They can be folded to make either broad or narrow bandages or used as pads.

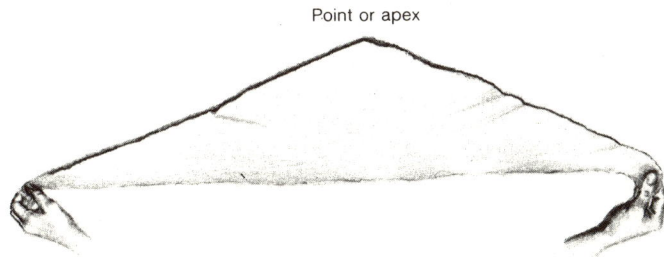

Point or apex

1 Lay the triangle on a flat surface.

2 Fold the top point of the triangle (known as the point or apex) over to meet the middle of the base edge.

3 Fold over again in the same direction. For a narrow bandage, fold material one more time. Use as a roller bandage. If the wound is large, several overlapping triangular bandages may be needed. Secure with a reef knot and tuck the ends in firmly.

BITES AND STINGS

Bites from non-poisonous animals, such as dogs and people, are not serious, but *must* be treated to prevent infection. Unless the sufferer has had a tetanus injection recently, one must be given. Bites from venomous creatures, such as snakes, spiders, insects and marine life, need immediate emergency action.

Some people may develop allergic reactions to bites and stings. Allergic reactions may involve:
- local pain
- local swelling and itchiness
- puffy eyelids
- wheezy breathing.

But they may also have a life-threatening effect on breathing and the heart. Medical help must be sought immediately, if an allergic person is bitten or stung. The most common threats are stings from bees and wasps.

PRESSURE IMMOBILISATION
Pressure immobilisation prevents venom reaching the bloodstream. It was introduced as a technique for treating snake bite, but is recommended for most other bites and stings, *except* poisoning by red-back spider and venomous fish.

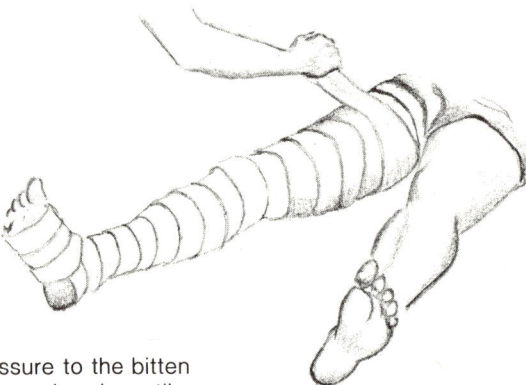

1 Apply pressure to the bitten area with your hands, until you can use a firm bandage, preferably crepe, or improvise with pantyhose or strips of torn clothing or material. Starting at the bitten area, bandage limb down to fingers or toes. Return and cover limb up to armpit or groin.

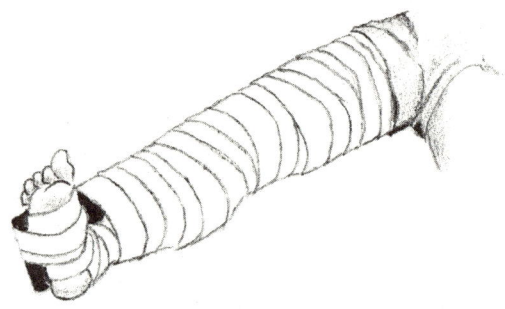

2 Splint or immobilise limb (see SPLINTS). If the bite is on the upper arm, immobilise the limb in an arm sling (see SLINGS).

3 Rest the patient, keeping splint and bandages in place.

4 Bring medical aid or transport to the casualty, rather than moving him.

SNAKES

Some snakes are not venomous; others, such as the brown snake, tiger and taipan, are particularly poisonous. Serious poisoning is rare because the snake usually does not inject enough venom, but medical aid must always be sought immediately.

Although there will be signs of puncture marks on the skin, other signs and symptoms may not be immediate. They can take from 15 minutes to 2 hours to appear. Symptoms and signs may include:

- nausea
- vomiting
- headache
- double vision
- giddiness
- drowsiness
- tightening in the chest
- diarrhoea
- sweating
- breathing difficulty.

1 Reassure the casualty rather than identify the snake because venom detection kits are now available.

2 Rest the victim in a comfortable position. *Do not* move him or raise the bitten limb — this will only spread the venom.

3 *Do not* wash the venom off the skin, as it may help identification later. *Do not* cut or cauterise the bite or try to suck the venom out.

4 Apply pressure immobilisation (see above).

5 Regularly check breathing and pulse (see PULSE). Give expired air resuscitation if breathing stops or cardiopulmonary resuscitation if pulse stops (see RESUSCITATION).

6 Seek medical attention urgently.

SPIDERS

There are only two dangerous spiders in Australia: the funnel-web, found in Sydney, and the red-back, found in all Australian States.

The **funnel-web**'s bite is intensely painful and the casualty is likely to be most distressed and frightened. Antivenom is available. Symptoms and signs include:

- tingling round the mouth
- muscular spasm or weakness
- excessive sweating
- profuse salivation
- nausea
- abdominal pain
- numbness
- coughing up of secretions entering lungs
- weeping eyes
- coldness and shivering
- breathing difficulty.

Funnel-web spider

1 Treat as for snake bite (see above).

2 Seek medical aid urgently.

The **red-back**'s bite can be intensely painful, but is not always so. An antivenom is available. Symptoms and signs include:

- tingling round the mouth
- generalised pain
- nausea
- vomiting
- profuse sweating
- weakness and faintness
- swelling round the bite
- rapid pulse.

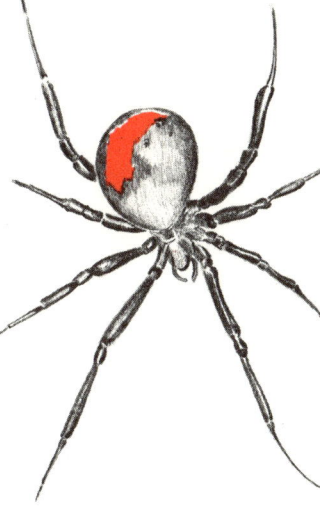

Red-back spider

1 Apply an ice cube wrapped in damp material to the bite to relieve the pain. Reapply as needed, but *do not* freeze or damage the skin.

2 *Do not* apply pressure immobilisation.

3 Seek medical aid urgently.

4 Watch for signs of shock and treat (see SHOCK).

BITES AND STINGS

BEES AND WASPS

1 Remove the bee sting by scraping it sideways with a fingernail or the side of a knife. *Do not* pull or squeeze the poison sac attached to the sting.

2 Wipe the affected area clean and apply ice (see treatment for red-back spider bite, p. 201).

3 If the casualty suffers a strong allergic reaction (see above), apply pressure immobilisation (see above).

4 Seek medical attention urgently, if reaction is severe.

5 Regularly check breathing and pulse (see PULSE) in serious cases. Give expired air or cardiopulmonary resuscitation as required (see RESUSCITATION).

SCORPIONS AND CENTIPEDES

The bites from these are very painful, but not normally dangerous. Symptoms and signs include:
• immediate, intense burning pain
• throbbing and numbness of afflicted area.

1 Apply ice to the bitten area (see above).

2 Seek medical attention.

TICKS

Most bites occur in the spring and summer when ticks are most active. Only the **bush tick** is potentially dangerous. Its habitat is the eastern Australian coastal strip. It usually shelters in foliage and drops on its victim when its surroundings are disturbed. The venom can cause irritation and a skin nodule. Occasionally, if bush tick bite is untreated, paralysis can occur. Symptoms and signs include:
• pin-prick sensations and irritation of the affected area
• double vision
• unsteadiness
• weakness of the face and eyelids, which can progress to the upper limbs and breathing muscles.

1 Apply a drop of kerosine or olive oil to the tick. This may make it drop off.

2 *Do not* try to pull it off, cut it out or squeeze it. Slide the two open blades of splinter forceps around the sides of the tick and lever it outwards. Make sure that the mouth is not left in the skin.

3 Search carefully in hair and body crevices for other ticks.

4 Wash bitten area with soap and water. Dry gently.

5 Seek medical attention promptly, if any of the symptoms listed occur.

BLUE-RINGED OCTOPUS AND CONE SHELL

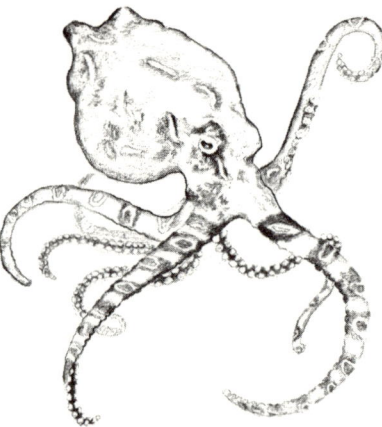

Blue-ringed octopus

These are often found in rock pools along the Australian coastline. The bite of the blue-ringed octopus may be painless, although that of the cone shell may be very painful. Their venoms are extremely potent and act rapidly. Symptoms and signs include:
• numbness of lips and tongue within minutes
• muscular weakness
• respiratory failure.

1 Reassure the casualty.

2 Send for medical aid urgently, but *do not* leave the casualty unattended.

3 Apply pressure immobilisation (see above).

4 Apply expired air resuscitation (see RESUSCITATION) as soon as breathing weakens. Eventually the sufferer will depend completely on expired air resuscitation, so be careful to continue it until the task is taken over by a medical helper.

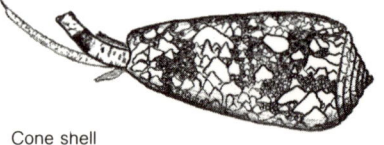

Cone shell

STONEFISH AND BULLROUT

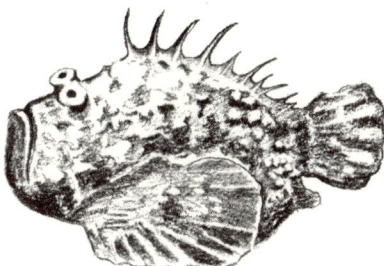

Stonefish

These fish are found along Australia's tropical coastline. Symptoms and signs of their stings include:
- intense pain, which spreads along the limb
- blue or grey discolouration
- swelling
- sweating
- signs of shock (see SHOCK).

1 Relieve pain by soaking affected area in hot water.

2 Remove any foreign body.

3 Seek medical attention urgently.

4 Reassure the sufferer.

5 *Do not* apply pressure immobilisation as this increases pain and can cause tissue destruction.

Bullrout

JELLYFISH

Jellyfish

The most dangerous species is the **box jellyfish** found in tropical waters. Extensive stinging can result in respiratory and circulatory failure within minutes. Tissue death occurs along the line of the stings after 24–48 hours. An antivenom is available. Symptoms and signs include:
- immediate intense pain
- characteristic 'frosted ladder' pattern
- irrationality
- breathing is difficult and often stops.

1 *Do not* attempt to remove the tentacles with your hands or rub the affected area.

2 Flood the stings with vinegar, which immediately makes the tentacles harmless, and apply a firm compression bandage to the area.

3 If no vinegar is available, apply a firm compression bandage *above* the sting. Gently remove any tentacles with splinter forceps (*not* fingers), then apply a firm compression bandage to the area.

4 Watch breathing and pulse (see PULSE) and apply expired air or cardiopulmonary resuscitation, if necessary (see RESUSCITATION).

5 Seek medical aid urgently.

STING-RAY

Sting-ray

The sting is attached to the long, lash-like tail and can cause death. Symptoms and signs include:
- immediate searing pain
- breathing difficulty, if the chest has been stung.

1 Carefully remove the barb, if left.

2 Bathe area with hot (but *not* scalding) water.

3 Apply pressure immobilisation (see above), if general symptoms occur.

BLEEDING

Any bleeding can look alarming, but most healthy people can afford to lose about 20 per cent of their blood without any serious effects. Bleeding from a small wound usually stops naturally after about a minute. Most cases are not fatal provided the wound is treated straight away.

However, **severe or continued bleeding** can lead to shock (see SHOCK) or death in a very short time. Therefore, severe bleeding *must* be treated before any other injuries.

Internal bleeding is always serious and must receive immediate hospital treatment. Symptoms and signs of severe bleeding include:
- pale, clammy skin, particularly on the face and lips
- shallow breathing
- weak, rapid pulse
- casualty complains of nausea, pain, thirst, faintness and shortness of breath
- casualty may cough up bright red or dark blood, if lungs or intestines are bleeding.

1 *Do not* move casualty until bleeding has been controlled, unless it is essential to avoid further danger (see MOVING AN INJURED PERSON).

2 Lay casualty down, unless he is suffering from a chest wound (see CHEST INJURIES).

3 Look for escaping blood and check over the body carefully. Tenderness or muscle rigidity may indicate internal bleeding.

4 If the bleeding is external, check for any embedded foreign body. *Do not* remove a foreign body (unless it is surface dirt). Instead, apply a ring pad (see BANDAGES, DRESSING AND PADS) and seek medical aid.

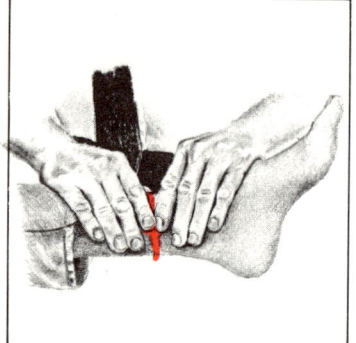

5 If there is no embedded foreign body, apply direct pressure to the bleeding area. Quickly press down with your hands or with a pad of clean, absorbent material. Any suitable firm, bulky object will do but, if possible, cover the wound with a sterile or clean dressing. Try to squeeze the edges of the wound together. Keep pressure on the wound until the bleeding stops.

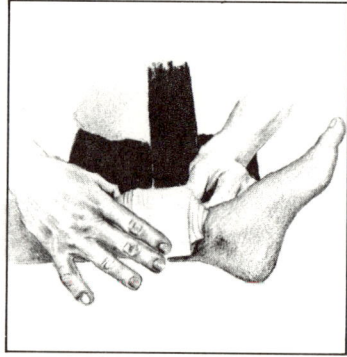

6 If blood leaks through the pad, leave the dressing in place but replace the pad. *Do not* disturb the dressing or pad after the bleeding stops.

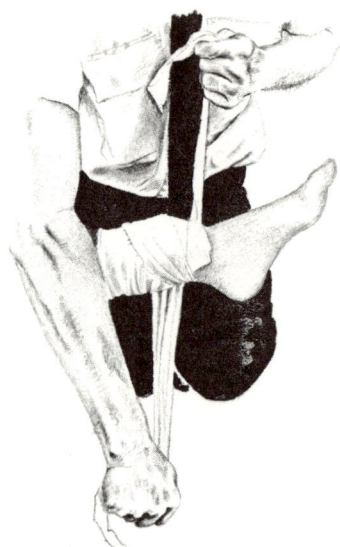

7 Tie pad in place with a bandage, belt, tie or scarf. Immobilise the part with another bandage, sling (see SLINGS), pillowcase or piece of clothing or material. Raise the wounded area if it is an arm, leg or head, unless you suspect a fracture (see FRACTURES).

8 Seek medical aid urgently, but *do not* leave the casualty unattended. If internal bleeding is suspected, arrange for the casualty to be taken to hospital immediately.

9 Reassure the casualty, ensure that he remains resting and loosen any tight clothing.

10 *Do not* give anything to eat or drink.

11 Watch for signs of shock (see SHOCK). Regularly check breathing and pulse (see PULSE).

SEVERE BLEEDING FROM THE PALM

at the base of the thumb for tying. Bring the length of bandage across the back of the hand, down over the bent fingers to the thumb side and around over the short end of the bandage to secure it.

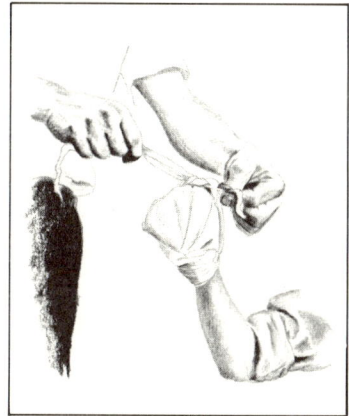

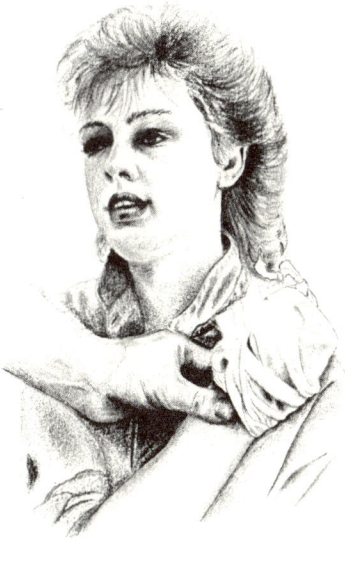

1 Apply pressure to whole palm of hand by getting the casualty to hold a pressure pad in place. Folded or rolled bandages or material make good pressure pads. A small object, such as a matchbox or stone, or a few fingers of the uninjured hand may be wrapped in clean cloth and used. Elevate the hand and begin bandaging, leaving a short end of bandage

2 Continue bandaging the fist by bringing the length across the back of the hand and down over the fingers. Tie the two ends at the top of the fist.

3 Place the forearm across the chest, with the injured hand resting against the shoulder, and support with an elevation sling (see SLINGS).

BRUISES

Falls or blows against hard objects can cause internal bleeding under the unbroken skin, resulting in discolouration and swelling. Bruises turn from red to dark blue to greenish-yellow in the ten to fourteen days following the injury.

1 Check for fractures or sprains of ligaments or tendons, which often accompany bruising (see FRACTURES and SPRAINS, STRAINS AND DISLOCATIONS).

2 Rest the casualty in a comfortable position, getting him to support the injury to prevent further bleeding under the skin.

3 Apply ice packs to help reduce the swelling (see SPRAINS, STRAINS AND DISLOCATIONS).

4 Wind a compression bandage around the injured part.

5 Support an injured arm with a sling (see SLINGS). Prop up a leg or bruised body with pillows.

BURNS AND SCALDS

Burns are caused by the dry heat of flames, radiation (see SUNBURN), hot metals, lightning and electricity (see ELECTRIC SHOCK) and chemicals (see below). Scalds are caused by the moist heat of steam or boiling water: they are the most common cause of heat injury in the home.

First aid is the same for both and involves removing the casualty from the source of heat and cooling the affected area to reduce the pain, further damage and the risk of infection.

Deep burns are the least painful because they usually destroy the nerve ends. Layers of skin and tissue may be totally destroyed and look black and charred. **Superficial burns** are red and blistered on the outer layers of the skin. They are more painful and can result in serious fluid loss. **Extensive burns**, which cause fluid loss over a period of time, can lead to progressive shock (see SHOCK).

WHEN CLOTHES ARE ON FIRE

1 Remove the casualty from danger, but take care not to become burnt yourself. (If the burns are caused by electric shock, follow the safety procedures for rescuing a casualty outlined in ELECTRIC SHOCK.) Hold a rug or piece of clothing in front of you as you approach the casualty whose clothes are on fire.

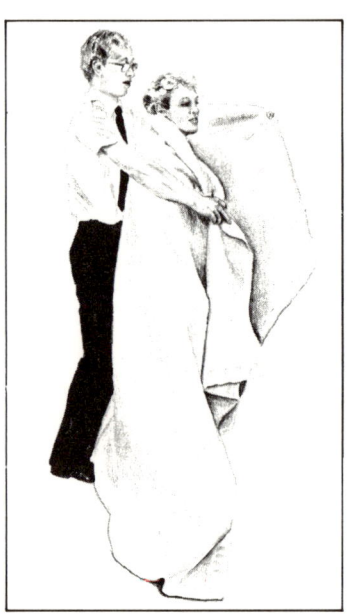

2 Envelop the casualty in the rug or piece of clothing.

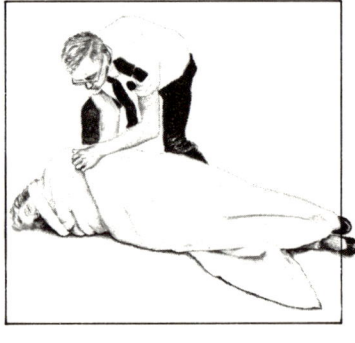

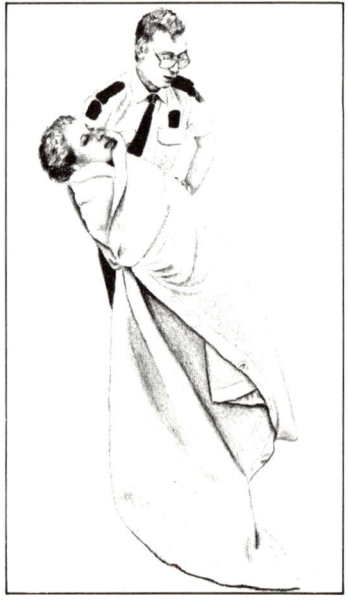

3 Wrap it tightly around the casualty to smother the flames as you begin to lower her to the ground.

4 Lay her on the ground. (Water from a hose or bucket can also be used to put out the flames, but *do not* throw water in a manner likely to create scalding steam.) Try to keep the casualty still to prevent flames from spreading.

5 Remove hot clothing that comes off easily, but *do not* remove any fragments sticking to the skin.

GENERAL TREATMENT

1 Cool the burnt area with cold water. The burn should be placed under running cold water for at least 10 minutes.

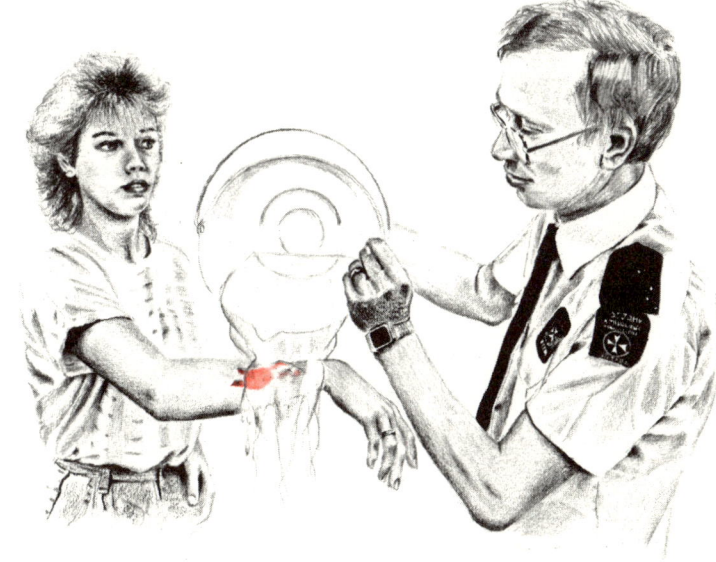

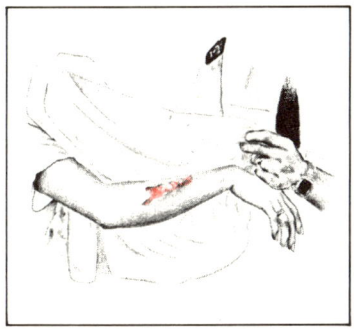

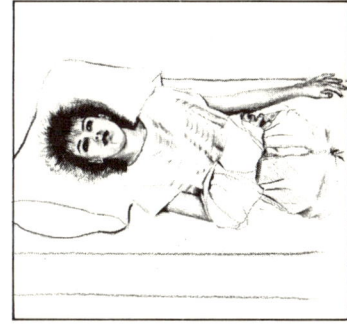

2 *Do not* prick or break any blisters. *Do not* apply any lotions, ointments or oily dressings. Instead, where possible, cover the burnt area with a sterile or clean non-adhesive dressing. Then apply a triangular bandage, soft towel or bedroom linen.

3 Bandage the burnt area lightly. If the face if burnt, cut holes in the dressings for the eyes, mouth and nose.

4 Rest the casualty comfortably. Support an injured arm across the body or prop on a pillow. If the casualty's face is burnt, place her in a sitting position to reduce swelling, fluid loss and shock. Raise injured legs and feet on cushions.

5 *Do not* give alcohol. Give frequent sips of water or milk to replace fluids.

6 Seek urgent medical aid.

7 Watch for signs of shock (see SHOCK) and monitor breathing and pulse (see PULSE). Give expired air or cardiopulmonary resuscitation, if necessary (see RESUSCITATION).

BURNS AND SCALDS

CHEMICAL AND CORROSIVE BURNS

1 Wash substance off immediately with a large amount of flowing water from a tap or hose.

2 Remove contaminated clothing, protecting your hands with rubber gloves or a piece of material.

3 Continue washing the burn for at least 20 minutes until all traces of chemical have disappeared.

4 Cover the burnt area with a clean dressing.

5 Seek medical aid immediately. If possible, supply medical helpers with information about the chemical involved.

CHEST INJURIES

Most chest injuries are caused by car accidents. They are also likely to occur as a result of stab wounds, gunshot and crushing. Watch any victim of an accident who has breathing difficulties. Chest injuries can range from simple bruising (see BRUISES) with a little pain in the chest, to serious threats to the vital organs that control breathing and circulation. Collapsed lungs and fractured ribs are among the most common chest injuries. If any injury or fracture is suspected, take the casualty to hospital immediately. Symptoms and signs include:
- pain in the chest and on touching the injured area
- difficult, short, gasping breathing
- casualty may cough up bright red, frothy blood.

CLOSED WOUNDS
If a rib has been fractured and enters a lung without penetrating the chest wall, the wound is known as a closed wound.

1 Place the casualty in a half-sitting position, leaning downwards on his injured side.

2 Pad the injured side with plenty of clean padding. Place the upper arm beside the injured side and bandage across it and around the body just firmly enough to hold the pad in place.

3 Place the casualty's arm on the injured side across his chest, so that his hand rests on the opposite shoulder. Immobilise the arm against the chest wall, using an elevation sling (see SLINGS).

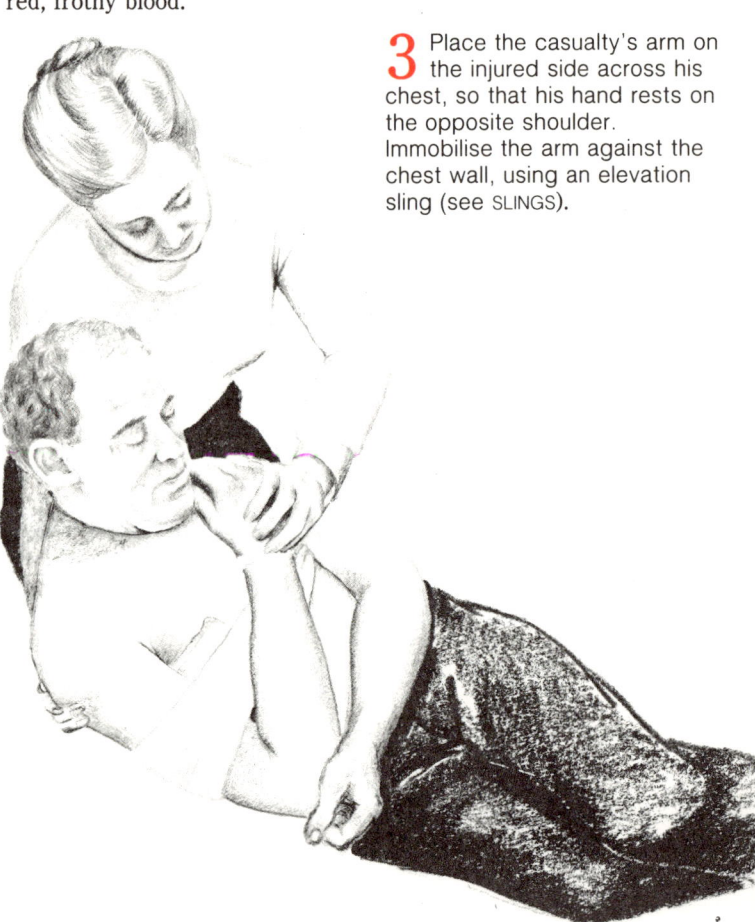

SUCKING WOUNDS

Sucking wounds are caused by a fractured rib or sharp object protruding through the chest wall. Air is drawn into the chest cavity, making a sucking noise, and may cause a lung to collapse. Symptoms and signs include:
- restricted breathing
- blood bubbling from the wound
- blue lips
- pain
- increasing shortness of breath
- casualty lapses into unconsciousness.

1 Place the casualty in a half-sitting position, leaning downwards on his injured side.

2 Remove or cut away any clothing around the injury.

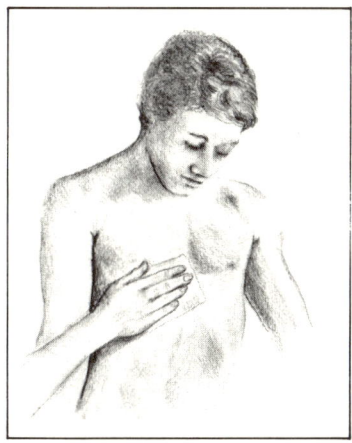

3 Immediately place your hand over the wound to stop the bleeding, then use a dressing or bandage. *Do not* press down if you suspect fractured ribs.

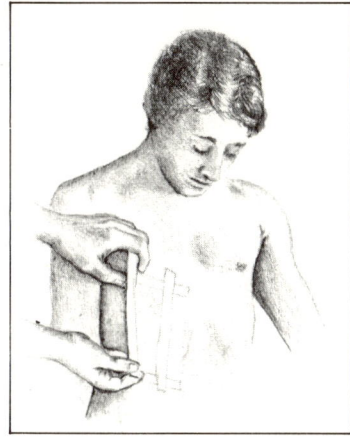

4 The main aim is to seal the wound to prevent air entering the chest cavity. Cover the wound firmly with an airtight dressing of plastic, aluminium foil or cloth. Secure with adhesive tape on all four sides.

5 Place the arm on the injured side across the victim's chest, and support it in an elevation sling (see SLINGS).

6 Seek immediate medical help.

7 Watch breathing and be prepared to give expired air resuscitation (see RESUSCITATION)

CHOKING

Choking is usually caused by a foreign body becoming stuck in the airway, obstructing respiration. It is crucial to remove the object immediately. Choking can be caused by inhaling lumps of food or splinters of bone or teeth. In the case of children, it can occur when they run with a toy or other object in their mouth and stumble. Peanuts or toys with small detachable parts should never be given to young children — they are a common cause of choking. In addition to those listed in ASPHYXIA, symptoms and signs include:
- a fit of coughing
- agitated attempt to breathe, which often has the effect of more firmly fixing the obstruction.

1 Check the airway and remove any visible obstruction (see RESUSCITATION — clearing the airway). If the obstruction is not visible and the casualty is still conscious, get him to cough.

2 If this fails, the casualty should bend over a chair to bring the head lower than the body and help expel the foreign object. Or he should lie on his side while you administer two or three sharp slaps between the shoulder-blades, using the heel of your hand. In the case of an **infant or child**, hold him by the legs upside down or place him across your knees, head-down, and smack the shoulders smartly with the heel of your hand.

3 If choking continues, try to blow air past the obstruction by gently using the expired air resuscitation technique (see RESUSCITATION).

4 Seek medical help urgently, if obstruction is not dislodged.

CONCUSSION

A blow to the head or a heavy fall can shake and disturb the brain, causing concussion. Symptoms and signs include:
- breathing becomes shallow
- pallor
- nausea
- vomiting
- dizziness
- nervousness
- temporary unconsciousness
- shock (see SHOCK)
- loss of memory.

1 Lay the casualty down.

2 Keep warm and comfort.

3 *Do not* give any drinks.

4 Apply a cold compress to the part of head that was knocked.

5 If unconsciousness occurs, place the casualty in the coma position (see UNCONSCIOUSNESS).

6 Seek medical attention.

7 Watch for signs of serious injury to the brain: deepening unconsciousness, constant vomiting, double vision or persistent severe headache.

CONVULSIONS

Convulsions are the result of a disturbance of brain function. Some people suffer regular convulsions. Others experience a convulsion as the result of a particular medical event, such as head injury or poisoning. Small children, aged 1–4 years, often experience seizures, termed febrile convulsions, associated with a raised body temperature resulting from infection. Convulsions can be frightening to observe, so those connected with the sufferer will need to be reassured.

EPILEPTIC SEIZURES
Signs include:
- sufferer cries out, falls to the ground (often injuring himself) and lies rigid for some seconds with back arched and jaws clamped shut
- face and neck become congested and blue because breath is held
- jerking muscular movements and returning colour as breathing begins again
- frothing at the mouth
- tongue-biting, sometimes
- possible bowel and bladder loss of control
- confusion, after sufferer has regained consciousness, and loss of memory of the event
- exhaustion afterwards.

1 Protect the sufferer from injury, but *do not* restrain.

2 Remove false teeth, if possible, but *do not* pry open the mouth or force objects into it.

3 Place in coma position (see UNCONSCIOUSNESS), if this is possible, and monitor breathing and pulse (see PULSE) while the casualty is unconscious or asleep.

4 Seek medical aid. If the casualty is a known epileptic, he should be asked, when he recovers, whether he wants to consult a doctor and his wishes followed.

FEBRILE CONVULSIONS
Signs may include:
- body rigidity
- twitching
- arched head and back
- rolling eyes
- congested face and neck and bluish face and lips.

1 Ensure the airway is clear, turning the child on his side, if necessary (see RESUSCITATION).

2 Remove all clothing.

3 Bathe in or sponge with tepid water.

4 Fan the child.

5 When the child's temperature has been reduced (see TEMPERATURE), cover him lightly.

6 Seek medical aid.

DROWNING

Drowning is a form of suffocation: water or another liquid enters the airway, blocking the air supply, often causing spasm of the larynx and resulting in asphyxia. If the near-drowning person is promptly rescued and the oxygen supply to the brain restored by immediate resuscitation, his life may still be saved. However, many unnecessary drownings occur each year when people attempt a rescue beyond their swimming capabilities. *Do not* attempt a rescue if you are a poor swimmer or untrained in lifesaving techniques.

CRAMP

Cramp is a sudden, painful, involuntary contraction of a muscle or a group of muscles. The cause of the common sort of cramp is unknown, although it is often associated with old age, varicose veins, arthritis and pregnancy. It may be the result of poor blood supply, lack of salt or over-exertion. It often occurs during exercise, such as swimming, in the cold or during exertion in hot conditions which produce a lot of sweating. Severe diarrhoea and vomiting may also cause cramp.

When cramp occurs, gently stretch the stiffened muscle until straight. Sometimes, in calf or foot cramp, for instance, the sufferer can treat himself by straightening his leg and standing firmly.

If cramp occurs when the casualty is in water, get him out and cover with a blanket.

In hot weather or conditions producing much sweating, give plenty of water to drink, adding glucose and a small amount of salt — ½ teaspoon to about a litre of water.

CUTS AND SCRATCHES

Minor cuts and scratches may not require medical attention unless infection has set in or penetrating foreign bodies are embedded in the wound. The main treatment is to control the bleeding and prevent the spread of infection. The amount of bleeding and length and depth of the wound usually indicate whether it is serious (see WOUNDS).

1 Control bleeding by pressing gently on the wound with a clean cloth or dressing, provided there are no foreign bodies in the wound. Bodies, such as gravel, on the surface of the wound may be lightly brushed off after bleeding has stopped, but embedded objects must be attended to by a medical helper.

2 Clean the skin around the wound by wiping away from the cut without touching it, using clean swabs, lukewarm water and a little disinfectant or soap.

3 Gently dry around the cut with a clean cloth and apply an adhesive dressing or bandage.

4 Any large or gaping lacerations require medical attention and possibly stitches. If a cut is dirty or infected a tetanus injection may be necessary.

In addition to displaying the symptoms and signs described in ASPHYXIA, the near-drowning person will:
• make erratic movements in the water
• gradually sink down
• swallow water and air, which causes vomiting
• cough
• sometimes develop laryngeal spasm, which blocks the airway.

1 If the casualty is within reach of land, you may be able to hold out to her a strong stick, blanket or piece of clothing. Or you may be able to throw her an object, such as a beach ball, that will keep her afloat. Hold on to a firmly anchored object while you pull her ashore.

DROWNING

2 If you are rescuing a victim in the water who is unconscious and not breathing, begin mouth-to-nose expired air resuscitation there, if possible (see RESUSCITATION). Support her as much as the depth of water allows. Either stand at the side of her head and support her body with one hand, tilting her head with the other, or kneel on the bottom with one knee raised to support the middle of her back. Only strong swimmers and experienced lifesavers should make an attempt to resuscitate a non-breathing victim in deep water, as they will need to tread water.

3 Near-drowning casualties often vomit because of the large amounts of water swallowed. Begin clearing the airway as soon as you are in the shallows or on land, by sweeping any vomit or loose matter, such as seaweed, out of her mouth with your hands. Once on firm ground, turn her on her side to continue the process (see RESUSCITATION — clearing the airway) and to check breathing. *Do not* attempt to drain water from the lungs.

4 Resume or begin expired air resuscitation. Cardio-pulmonary resuscitation may be necessary, if there is no pulse (see RESUSCITATION). If the victim is still suffering from spasm of the larynx, gently blow past the spasm, but *do not* blow so vigorously that you distend the stomach. If she vomits during resuscitation, turn her on her side again promptly.

5 Continue resuscitation until breathing and pulse begin or medical aid arrives. Once the victim is breathing, place her in the coma position (see UNCONSCIOUSNESS). Cover her with blankets or towels, and treat any injuries.

6 Continue to observe her closely, and monitor breathing and pulse until medical aid arrives. Although at first victims of immersion may appear to have been successfully resuscitated, their condition frequently deteriorates. All casualties who have lost consciousness or required resuscitation must be sent to hospital.

DRUG OVERDOSE

Drug overdose requires immediate medical attention. Be prepared to give expired air or cardiopulmonary resuscitation until medical help arrives or the casualty is taken to hospital. Symptoms and signs vary according to the amount and type of drug taken, but may include:
- a feeling of faintness
- slurred speech
- convulsions
- rapid, weak pulse and shallow or gasping breathing, if narcotics, such as morphine or heroin, are involved
- loss of consciousness, breathing and pulse, leading to death.

1 It is vital to establish which drug has been taken and whether it has been swallowed, inhaled or injected. Look for injection marks in the veins of the arms and legs. Also look for containers, ampoules or syringes. Send any you find to the hospital with the casualty, along with any samples of his vomit, packed in a clear container or plastic bag.

2 *Do not* induce vomiting unless instructed to do so by a doctor or your local Poisons Information Centre (see Medical And Health Support Organisations).

3 If the casualty is unconscious place him in the coma position (see UNCONSCIOUSNESS). Monitor his breathing and pulse (see PULSE). Give expired air or cardiopulmonary resuscitation as required (see RESUSCITATION).

4 Seek immediate medical aid, even if the casualty appears to have recovered, and be ready to take him to hospital.

EAR INJURIES

Ear injuries are often caused by cuts, foreign bodies or infection which may be effectively treated. However, they are sometimes serious and can affect the vital hearing function and balance of the body. If they are associated with severe head injuries, urgent medical attention is required. Symptoms and signs include:
- bleeding or fluid from the ear, which can indicate a fractured base of the skull or a ruptured ear-drum
- deafness
- pain in the ear.

BLEEDING OR FLUID SECRETION

1 *Do not* plug the ear canal or give any ear drops.

2 Place the casualty in the coma position (see UNCONSCIOUSNESS), with the affected ear facing downwards and resting on a clean pad.

3 Seek medical aid urgently.

FOREIGN BODY

1 Check to see how firmly it is lodged, but *do not* probe.

2 Seek medical aid.

TRAPPED INSECT

1 Reassure the sufferer.

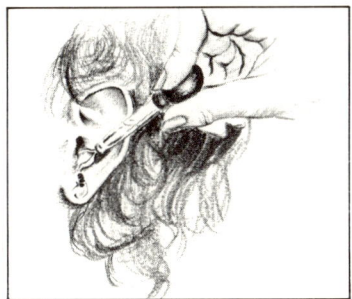

2 Using an eye dropper, place a little lukewarm water or oil in the ear canal.

3 If the insect does not float out, seek medical aid.

ELECTRIC SHOCK

The effects of electric shock can vary from a mild sensation of tingling to death. The seriousness of the effect depends on the strength of the electric charge, the length of time the victim is exposed to it and how well he is insulated. Death by electrocution is most likely to occur if the victim is in contact with water.

The main danger of electric shock is immediate heart failure. High voltage injuries also cause muscle spasms and severe burns.

1 Never approach a victim if there is a risk of shock to yourself. If he is still in contact with the source of electricity, make sure the power is cut off before the casualty is touched. If the accident involves a **low voltage current** — as used in house, shop and office lighting and heating — turn off the power at the nearest switch or the mains and pull out the plug. If this is not possible, *do not* touch the casualty directly. Stand on insulated material, such as rubber, if possible, and push the victim away from the source of electricity with a piece of dry wood. **High voltage currents** from, for example, power lines or industrial equipment can travel through the ground for some distance, so *do not* touch the casualty until an expert turns off the power.

2 As soon as the victim is freed from the current, burning clothes must be smothered with a blanket or similar material (see BURNS AND SCALDS).

3 Check breathing and pulse (see PULSE). Start expired air or cardiopulmonary resuscitation, if necessary (see RESUSCITATION).

4 If the casualty is breathing but unconscious, place him in the coma position (see UNCONSCIOUSNESS).

5 Treat any burns by cooling them with water and bandaging (see BURNS AND SCALDS).

6 Treat for shock (see SHOCK).

7 Seek immediate medical help.

EXPOSURE, HYPOTHERMIA AND FROSTBITE

OVER-EXPOSURE

Exposure to wind and rain or immersion in water without adequate body protection can cause physical and mental fatigue, even in young, fit and healthy people. When heat loss from the body is greater than heat gain, severe problems may occur. If not treated, the condition can be fatal.

Babies, young children and the elderly are particularly susceptible. The degree of over-exposure depends on clothing, temperature, wind speed, moisture, fatigue, hunger, anxiety and length of exposure. Symptoms and signs include:

• extreme fatigue
• drowsiness, with the danger that the sufferer may not be aware of the significance of this
• cramps
• shivering
• uncoordinated movements
• slurred speech
• confusion
• blurred vision
• increasingly slow mental and physical response.

1 If the casualty is unconscious, place in the coma position (see UNCONSCIOUSNESS).

2 Remove to a warm, dry place, if possible, or protect from the weather.

3 Put the casualty in warm, dry clothes, blankets or a warmed sleeping bag. Windproof material like aluminium foil or plastic, if available, provides extra protection.

4 If conscious, give warm drinks, but *not* alcohol.

5 If possible, place the casualty in a warm bath heated to about 37° Celsius and slowly raise the temperature to about 45° Celsius — *but never* place someone suffering from hypothermia (see below) in a warm bath. If a bath is not possible, a companion stripped to his underwear can share the casualty's sleeping bag to help warm his torso. It is essential that the warming process be slow. *Do not* try to speed up the process in front of a fire or heater.

6 Seek medical aid and remain with the casualty until it arrives.

HYPOTHERMIA

This is a dangerous development of over-exposure. After several hours of exposure, loss of the body's surface heat is followed by cooling of the deep tissues and organs. It often occurs after prolonged immersion in cold water. Immobilisation combined with exposure to cold, particularly in the case of the elderly, babies and the injured or ill, can also result in hypothermia. Drugs and alcohol decrease the response of the temperature-regulating mechanism of the brain. Symptoms and signs include:

- cold to the touch
- slow pulse
- slow and shallow breathing
- babies become quiet and refuse food
- unconsciousness, especially in the elderly.

1 If unconscious, place in the coma position (see UNCONSCIOUSNESS). If conscious, keep the casualty lying down.

2 Remove to a warm, dry place, if possible.

3 Place between blankets so that body temperature can rise gradually. A companion stripped to his underwear can share a sleeping bag to warm the casualty. *Do not* massage extremities or try to warm by a fire or heater.

4 If conscious, give warm, sweet drinks, but *no* alcohol.

5 Seek medical aid urgently.

6 Remain with the casualty until help arrives.

FROSTBITE

In severe cases, exposure can lead to frostbite. This is the local freezing of body tissue, particularly in exposed parts, such as the nose, ears, face, fingers and toes. As a part cools, the blood vessels become constricted, cutting off circulation to the area. Symptoms and signs include:

- the part is painless until warmed
- numbness and tingling of area
- white, waxy skin
- firm to touch
- possible blistering.

1 Warm the affected area slowly with your hands until circulation returns. *Do not* rub or massage the frostbitten area.

2 *Do not* apply snow, cold water or direct heat.

3 *Do not* give alcohol.

4 Keep the casualty dry and warm.

5 Cover any blisters with a dry, clean dressing. Put padding between fingers and toes and secure with a triangular bandage (see BANDAGES, DRESSINGS AND PADS). Cover the whole foot or affected area with a blanket.

6 Seek medical aid urgently.

EYE INJURIES

All eye injuries are potentially serious and require medical attention. A casualty should never rub or touch an injured eye, eyelid or eyebrow. A damaged eye should never be opened or examined, as further damage could be done. If a casualty is wearing contact lenses, *do not* remove. This is a skilled task best left to the casualty or medical helper.

BLACK EYE

Bleeding and bruising will lead to blue, green and yellow discolouration of the skin round the eye.

1 Check that there is no damage other than bruising.

2 Ice packs applied intermittently for 2–3 hours will help reduce the swelling. *Do not* apply ice directly to the eye: wrap it in a damp material first. Leave pack on for a maximum of 20 minutes, then remove it for a minimum of 20 minutes.

CHEMICAL INJURIES

Burns to the eye can be caused by chemicals, heat and the flash from arc welding, if the eye is unprotected. Symptoms and signs include:

- severe watering of the eye
- spasm of the eyelids
- reddening of the eyeball
- possible swelling of the eyelids
- a feeling of grit in the eye, in the case of flash burns.

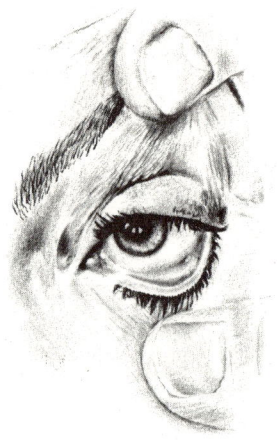

1 Chemical and heat burns — but *not* flash burns — must be washed. It is imperative to act immediately in the case of corrosive burns to prevent further damage. To irrigate the eye: tilt the casualty's head to the affected side, with the eye down; hold eyelids apart between thumb and forefinger; flood the eye with gently flowing lukewarm water for at least 20 minutes. Make sure that the flow of water is away from the other eye. When thoroughly washed clean of the chemical, dry gently with a clean cloth.

2 Cover eyes affected by arc flash, and washed chemical and heat burns, with a clean dressing.

3 Seek medical help.

FOREIGN BODIES

Loose lashes, insects, specks of grit and pieces of metal or glass lodged in the eye can cause extreme irritation and sometimes pain. Symptoms and signs include:
- reddening of eye
- weeping
- eye partly or completely closed
- sensitivity to light
- twitching or spasm of the eyelids.

Treatment for **surface foreign objects** is as follows.

1 *Do not* try to remove an object from any part of the eye other than the white.

2 Tilt the casualty's head to the affected side, with the eye down. Hold the eyelids apart between thumb and finger (see above).

3 Flood with gently flowing, lukewarm water. Try to make the casualty blink under the water.

4 If bathing does not work, gently push back the lashes of the eyelid and try to dislodge the object with a moist pad of clean material. Ask the casualty to look up, if it is under the lower lid, or down, if it is under the upper.

EMBEDDED FOREIGN BODIES AND PENETRATING WOUNDS

1 *Do not* try to remove an object embedded in the eye — this must be done by a doctor.

2 Lay the casualty down and reassure.

3 Cover both eyes with pads and gauze or clean material held in place by a light bandage. Make sure that pad is not pressing on the injured eye.

4 Seek medical attention immediately.

FAINTING

A temporary drop in the blood supply to the brain can cause people to faint. It may happen in a hot, stuffy atmosphere or be the result of emotional shock or over-exertion. It usually occurs when a person has been standing still in a crowded situation for a long time or suddenly stands up after sitting or crouching. Sometimes there can be a more serious cause, such as illness or injury. In this case, medical attention should be sought. However, fainting is not usually serious and consciousness usually returns when the casualty is placed in a position where his head is in line with his body. Symptoms and signs may include:
- pale and clammy skin
- beads of sweat on face, neck and hands
- casualty yawns frequently, showing he is short of air
- casualty feels dizzy, hot and cold, and weak
- slow and weak pulse
- blurred vision.

1 If the casualty is breathing normally and has a regular pulse (see PULSE), lay him down, with his legs raised higher than his head. He should remain lying down for a few minutes after recovering before attempting to rise.

2 Loosen any tight clothing. Make sure that the casualty is not crowded and has plenty of fresh air.

3 Check for any illness or for an injury that might have occurred when he fell.

4 If the casualty does not recover spontaneously within a few minutes, turn him on his side in the lateral position (see UNCONSCIOUSNESS) and seek medical aid.

FISH HOOK

Although as a rule penetrating foreign bodies should not be touched, an embedded fish hook may be removed.

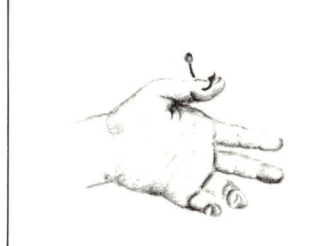

1 *Do not* try to pull the hook out the way it went in, as the barb will damage the tissue. Push the embedded barb out through the skin.

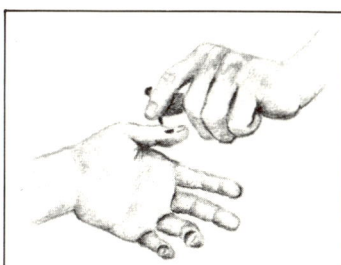

2 Either cut off the shank of the hook and then pull the hook out by the barb or cut off the barb and pull the hook out by the shank.

3 Control bleeding by applying a clean pad to the wound.

4 Bandage firmly.

5 Seek medical aid.

FOOD POISONING

Food poisoning is usually caused by bacteria that have grown in food kept at warm temperatures — particularly chicken, ham, fish and milk products. The main problem is the dehydration resulting from persistent vomiting and diarrhoea, especially with very young children and elderly people. Symptoms and signs include:
- cramping stomach pains
- vomiting
- diarrhoea.

1 Rest as much as possible.

2 Give sips of sweetened fluid, such as boiled water, with a small amount of added glucose or sugar.

3 Gradually increase intake of fluids as symptoms lessen; eventually, as sufferer improves, small amounts of solid food may be given.

4 Seek medical attention, if the vomiting and diarrhoea persist.

TROPICAL FISH POISONING
One form of food poisoning in Australia is caused by eating tropical fish containing ciguatoxin. Symptoms and signs include:
- sweating
- tingling of the hands and around the mouth
- diarrhoea
- pain in the joints, muscles and abdomen.

1 Give plenty of fluids to drink, but *do not* give anything containing alcohol.

2 Seek urgent medical attention.

FRACTURES

A fracture is a broken bone. The break is usually complete but, in the young, the bone can be bent without breaking completely. This is called a **greenstick fracture**. There are two other main kinds of fracture: closed fractures and compound or open fractures.

In **closed fractures** the skin around the fracture is unbroken, although blood lost into the tissues can cause heavy bruising. Closed fractures can be complicated, that is, the bone damages tissue. For example, rib fractures may injure the lung. Or they can be simple, that is, they cause no damage to surrounding body tissue.

Compound or **open fractures** have a bone protruding through the skin or an open wound over the fracture site. There is a risk of serious blood loss and of germs entering the wound, causing infection.

All doubtful cases should be treated as fractures and medical attention given as soon as possible. Symptoms and signs include:
- the snap of a breaking bone
- pain near the site of the injury, which is made worse by movement of that part
- tenderness when gentle pressure is applied to affected part
- swelling from blood loss around the fracture
- deformity of limb, inability to move it, or unnatural movement of the injured part
- crepitus — the dry, grating noise of broken ends of fractured bone rubbing together.

1 Treat a suspected fracture gently and move as little as possible. Warn the casualty not to move the injured limb. If there are suspected back or neck fractures, *do not* move the casualty, unless he is in immediate danger, to avoid damaging the spinal cord.

2 Carefully remove clothing from any open wound over the break. Cover the wound with a clean or sterile dressing. Control bleeding (see BLEEDING).

3 Support a fractured limb in a position giving as much comfort as possible.

4 Immobilise the fracture as soon as possible and before moving the casualty. Use bandages, slings and splints (see SLINGS and SPLINTS). The body of the injured person can also be used as a splint (see SPLINTS). If the fractured limb is too badly deformed, it may not be possible to splint it in the usual straight position.

5 Seek medical attention.

6 Check the tightness of bandages every few minutes because swelling may occur.

HEAD, FACE AND JAW INJURIES

No head injury should ever be disregarded. All head injuries from sporting or motor accidents, blows or falls must always be carefully watched, in case of complications. Injuries that may prove to be fatal do not always immediately show. Unconsciousness or concussion may not occur until several hours later (see UNCONSCIOUSNESS and CONCUSSION).

Head injuries can range from minor cuts (see CUTS AND SCRATCHES) and bruises (see BRUISES) to damage of the skull, brain, neck (see SPINAL INJURIES), tissues of the scalp and face, bones of the face and jaw, teeth (see TEETH INJURIES), tongue and the sensory organs of eyes (see EYE INJURIES), ears (see EAR INJURIES) and nose.

If the skull is fractured, there is the risk that internal bleeding may place increasing pressure on the part of the brain that controls vital body functions, such as consciousness, breathing, pulse rate and blood pressure. Medical attention must be sought after even slight unconsciousness.

Although the casualty with head injuries may appear to be quite well at first, the following symptoms and signs may develop:
- headache
- nausea
- blurred vision
- loss of memory, particularly of the accident
- weakness down one side
- restlessness
- abnormal responses and incoherent speech
- noisy breathing
- twitching of the limbs or convulsions
- wounds to the scalp or face
- congestion of the face
- bruising around the eyes
- dilated pupils
- vomiting
- clear fluid escaping from the nose and ear.

1 *In all cases*, place the casualty in the coma position, as if unconscious (see UNCONSCIOUSNESS). Support the head and neck and handle gently, in case of neck or back injuries (see SPINAL INJURIES).

2 Clear the airway (see RESUSCITATION — clearing the airway). If there is serious facial injury you may need to keep the airway open with your fingers.

3 Monitor breathing and pulse (see PULSE) and be prepared to give expired air or cardiopulmonary resuscitation, if necessary (see RESUSCITATION).

4 Control any external bleeding (see BLEEDING), but *do not* exert pressure on a suspected skull fracture. To bandage scalp injuries apply a bulky, clean dressing and secure in place with a bandage. If using an open triangular bandage, stand behind the casualty and place the long side across the forehead with the point hanging down the back of the neck. Bring the other two ends back over the point. Cross them and bring around to the front of the head. Tie in a reef knot on the forehead. Gently steady the head and pull the point down, then turn it up over the bandage at the back and pin it. Lightly cover any eye injuries with a clean pad (see EYE INJURIES).

JAW FRACTURE OR DISLOCATION

Only one side of the jaw is usually affected. Symptoms and signs include:
- tender, swollen and painful jaw
- deformity and misalignment of jaw and teeth
- drooling of saliva
- if dislocated, tenderness over the joint and pain in front of the ear.

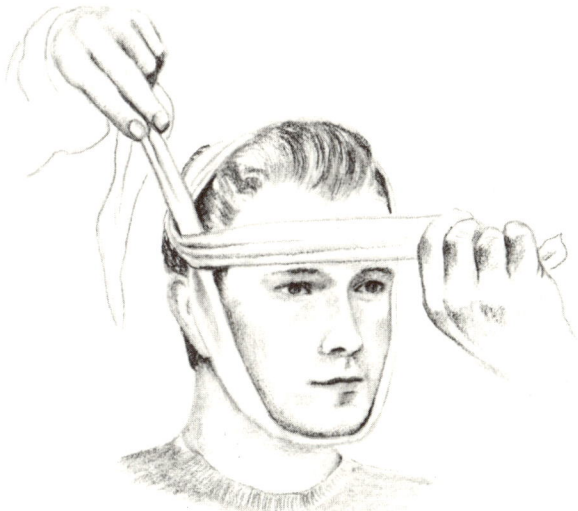

1 Make sure the mouth is clear of any blood or debris and remove any dentures.

2 If the casualty is suffering from shock (see SHOCK), is unconscious or has swelling or nausea, lay him down in the coma position (see UNCONSCIOUSNESS), supporting his jaw with your hand. Check that the jaw is pulled forward to keep the airway open.

3 Provided the casualty is conscious and not in shock, help him to support his jaw with his hand or apply a jaw bandage. *Do not* try to close his mouth. To tie a jaw bandage, sit the casualty down and ask him to lean forward. Support the lower jaw with the palm of your hand. Carefully move the lower jaw up to meet the upper jaw. Centre a narrow bandage under the chin and bring the two ends up the sides of the face. Carry the end on the injured side across the head to meet and cross the other end at eye level on the uninjured side. Carry the short end round the forehead, above the eyebrows, to the injured side. Bring the long end around the back of the head to meet it. Tie.

HEART ATTACK AND HEART FAILURE

HEART ATTACK

A heart attack (coronary occlusion) occurs when the flow of blood in the heart's own arteries is blocked by the narrowing or hardening of the arteries or by blood clots that occur as a result of hardening. The symptoms and signs include:

• pain or discomfort in the centre of the chest, lasting more than 10 minutes, which can become severe and radiate to the arms, neck and jaw
• pale, clammy skin
• vomiting
• irregular pulse
• anxiety
• shortness of breath
• nausea
• possibly an irregular pulse
• shock (see SHOCK)
• sometimes an immediate collapse, leading to the heart stopping (cardiac arrest).

1 Check the casualty's breathing and pulse (see PULSE). If necessary, give expired air or cardiopulmonary resuscitation (see RESUSCITATION).

2 Place the casualty in the most comfortable position and loosen his clothing at the neck, chest and waist. Ensure that he has plenty of fresh air. If the casualty is breathing, but unconscious, place him in the coma position (see UNCONSCIOUSNESS).

3 Comfort the casualty and keep him quiet.

4 Seek medical attention urgently. If possible send him by ambulance to the nearest hospital with a coronary care unit.

HEART FAILURE

Sometimes following a heart attack, or with advanced age, the heart becomes less able to pump blood around the body so that the blood banks up, causing congestion of the lungs and other organs. Symptoms and signs include:

• noisy, gurgling breathing
• rapid, weak pulse
• severe shortness of breath
• bluish lips and extremities
• congested neck veins and swollen neck, legs and ankles
• sometimes frothy, blood-stained sputum.

1 If conscious, sit the casualty up. If unconscious, place in the coma position (see UNCONSCIOUSNESS).

2 Loosen clothing round neck, chest and waist. Ensure plenty of fresh air.

3 Seek urgent medical aid.

4 Reassure the sufferer.

HEAT EXHAUSTION AND HEAT STROKE

HEAT EXHAUSTION

Heat exhaustion occurs in hot climates when people become dehydrated or lose excessive amounts of body salts through perspiration. It often results from hard physical exercise. The young and the elderly are more susceptible because their heat-regulating mechanism is more likely to break down under stress. Symptoms and signs include:
- exhaustion and faintness
- headache
- nausea
- muscle and stomach cramps
- muscular weakness and lack of coordination
- pale and clammy skin
- rapid pulse
- sweating
- irritability and confusion.

1 Rest the casualty in a cool, airy place.

2 Check temperature and pulse (see TEMPERATURE and PULSE).

3 Undress the sufferer and sponge down with tepid water.

4 Give frequent small drinks of lemonade or water with glucose and ½ teaspoon of salt per litre added.

5 If the sufferer does not recover promptly or has vomiting which continues, seek medical aid.

HEAT STROKE

Heat stroke is a complete breakdown of the body's heat-regulating mechanism. It is more serious than, and often follows, heat exhaustion. It is less common, but must be treated immediately as it is frequently fatal. Infants left in closed cars on hot days, athletes running long distances in hot weather, old people and unfit workers not used to heat are likely victims. Symptoms and signs include:
- body temperature of 40° Celsius or more (see TEMPERATURE)
- hot, flushed, dry skin
- rapid onset of nausea
- restlessness
- headache
- rapid breathing
- confusion
- loss of consciousness
- strong and rapid pulse
- dilated pupils.

1 Move the casualty to a cool place.

2 If he is unconscious, place in the coma position (see UNCONSCIOUSNESS).

3 Undress him. Douse him with cold water or carefully rub cold ice over his body. Apply cold packs or ice to the neck, groin and armpits. Cover him with a wet sheet and fan him to increase air circulation.

4 Seek medical aid. (The casualty will probably need to be hospitalised to control body levels of salt and fluid.)

5 Check body temperature every 5 minutes. When the casualty is cool to the touch and temperature is lowered to 38° Celsius, stop the cooling procedures.

6 When casualty is fully conscious give fluids, such as water or lemonade, to which glucose and ½ teaspoon salt per litre have been added.

HICCUPS

Hiccups are involuntary spasms of the diaphragm that can occur from eating too much or too quickly or from nervousness. Occasionally they are caused by disorders of the digestive system or lungs. If an attack is persistent, the casualty should see a doctor.

1 Instruct the casualty to hold his breath or breathe into a *paper* bag several times.

2 Give him water to sip slowly or ice to suck.

MOVING AN INJURED PERSON

You should only move an injured person if he is in immediate danger from oncoming traffic, fire, leaking gas, falling debris, extreme weather or difficult terrain; or to place him in the coma position (see UNCONSCIOUSNESS) or on his back for expired air or cardiopulmonary resuscitation, if either of these is needed (see RESUSCITATION).

DRAGGING
If you are on your own, you will have to drag the badly injured or unconscious person to safety. (Even if several people are handy, lifting can be dangerous unless done so that the neck, back and any injured limbs are supported properly.)

1 Crouch down behind the head of the prostrate casualty. Place her arms by her side and take hold of her clothing by the shoulders, provided it is strong and will stay in place. You may also drag a casualty by the wrists, but this puts more strain on her extended arms and may cause further damage to any arm injuries. If the casualty is in a confined space, you may only be able to grasp her by her heels.

2 Move backwards, sliding her gently. Keep her body as horizontal with the ground as possible to avoid wrenching and bending her neck and back. *Do not* let her head bump.

HUMAN CRUTCH
Use yourself as a crutch to move a person who can walk with assistance.

1 Place yourself beside her, on her injured side (unless she has an arm, shoulder or hand injury).

2 Bring your near arm across her back and grip the clothes at the hip on the uninjured side.

3 Bring her arm on the injured side around your neck and support her with your shoulder. Unless you need a free hand to control bleeding, hold her hand to maintain this position.

4 Step off together. As you and the casualty walk, both move your inside and outside foot in unison, starting on the inside foot.

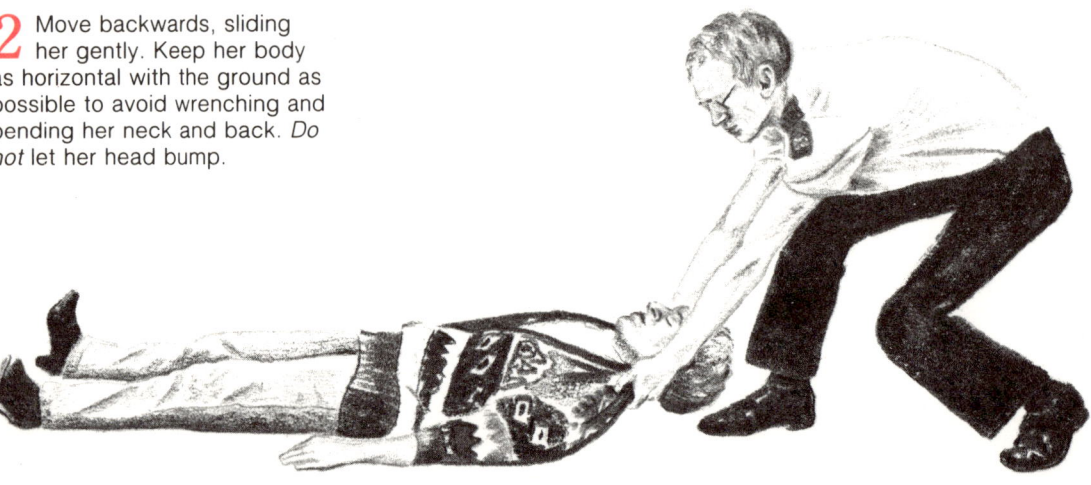

NOSEBLEEDS

Bleeding from the nose is very common and is usually caused by a nasal blood vessel bursting just inside the nose. It can result from a knock, high blood pressure or the nose being blown too hard, or it can start spontaneously.

If the casualty is unconscious and the blood escaping from the nose is combined with clear fluid, suspect serious head injuries and seek medical aid immediately (see HEAD, FACE AND JAW INJURIES).

1 Sit the casualty down, with his head slightly forward.

2 Loosen any tight clothing round the neck, chest and waist.

3 Instruct him to pinch his nostrils together with his thumb and fingers for approximately 10 minutes and to breathe through his mouth. He should *not* blow his nose.

4 Keep the casualty cool and apply cold, wet towels to the neck and forehead.

5 If the bleeding does not stop within 30 minutes, tell the victim to keep pinching his nose, and seek medical aid.

POISONING

Poisons exist in food (see FOOD POISONING), household substances and industrial products. (And see also BITES AND STINGS.) They may be swallowed, inhaled or injected.

It is vital to find out as much as possible about the type and amount of poison taken. Search for any empty bottles or pill containers to send to the hospital with the casualty.

Seek medical help without delay. Generally the poisons that act most quickly are those injected, but treat all cases as urgent. Telephone your nearest Poisons Information Centre (see Medical And Health Support Organisations) or your local doctor immediately. Symptoms and signs vary according to the type of poison taken, but may include:
- odours of poison on the breath
- bite or injection marks
- abdominal pain
- vomiting
- nausea
- drowsiness
- burning pains
- ringing in the ears
- blurred vision
- burns around the mouth and tongue
- change of skin colour and breathing difficulties (see ASPHYXIA)
- loss of consciousness.

ALL CASES OF POISONING

1 If the casualty is unconscious, place in the coma position (see UNCONSCIOUSNESS) and check that his airway is clear.

2 Monitor breathing and pulse (see PULSE) constantly. If he is not breathing, give expired air resuscitation; if the pulse becomes shallow or ceases, begin cardiopulmonary resuscitation (see RESUSCITATION).

3 Seek urgent medical aid.

UNKNOWN OR CORROSIVE SUBSTANCES

Corrosives are acids or alkalis, such as battery acid, oven cleaners and strong disinfectants, that burn tissues.

1 *Do not* induce vomiting.

2 Give the casualty plenty of sips of milk or water to dilute the poison, and seek medical aid.

PETROLEUM-BASED PRODUCTS

1 *Do not* induce vomiting.

2 Wipe the substance away from the mouth and face.

3 Give nothing by mouth. Seek medical aid.

MEDICINAL OR GENERAL SUBSTANCES

1 If casualty is conscious, induce vomiting: stimulate the back of his throat with fingers *or* give syrup of ipecacuanha according to instructions on the bottle. *Do not* give salt or soapy water to drink.

2 Keep a sample of the vomit in a clean jar to send to the hospital.

INHALED POISONS

1 Remove the casualty from fumes or turn fumes off at the source, in cases such as gas. Take care not to be the next victim. Hold a deep breath when entering a fume-filled room or wear a wet handkerchief over your nose and mouth. Call the fire brigade if the atmosphere is too badly contaminated.

2 Carry the casualty into the fresh air or open the windows.

3 Loosen any tight clothing.

POISONING

POISONS ABSORBED THROUGH THE SKIN

1 Remove the casualty's clothes. Get him to shower or wash thoroughly.

2 Watch the casualty carefully for any signs or symptoms of poisoning.

3 Make sure that the contaminated clothing is washed separately from other clothes.

PULSE

Taking the pulse is crucial in an emergency as it measures the heartbeat. The pulse rate varies a lot and can be governed by fitness. The normal pulse is regular and strong. In adults the average resting rate is 60–80 beats per mimnute, but this can accelerate to 180 during exercise or excitement. Babies and children have a much faster heartbeat. A child's resting pulse rate is up to 100 beats per minute, and a baby's up to 140 beats.

The pulse changes considerably with illness or injury. It may be:
● weak and rapid, possibly indicating bleeding (see BLEEDING) and/or shock (see SHOCK)
● slow and bounding, possibly indicating brain injury (see HEAD, FACE AND JAW INJURIES)
● irregular, possibly indicating a heart condition (see HEART ATTACK AND HEART FAILURE).

The pulse may be checked at two points of the body: the neck (the carotid pulse); and the wrist (the radial pulse). When applying first aid to a seriously injured or ill person monitor the pulse every few minutes. If the pulse stops, administer cardiopulmonary resuscitation (see RESUSCITATION). The carotid pulse rather than the radial can be easier to check in a life-threatening emergency: it can be taken while first aid is being given near the casualty's head.

CAROTID PULSE

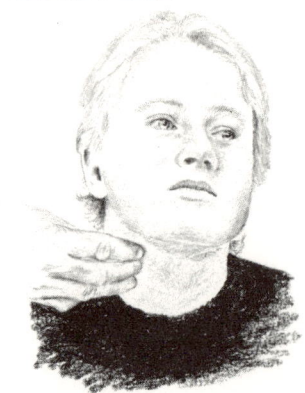

1 Place the tips of the three middle fingers of one of your hands over the casualty's Adam's apple. Move them gently to one side of her neck until they slip into the hollow there. You should now be able to feel the pulse. *Do not* press on the other side of the neck while feeling for the pulse or counting the beats.

2 Count the beats for 1 full minute.

RADIAL PULSE

1 Gently press the tips of three fingers over the underside of the wrist, about 25 mm below the base of the thumb and 10 mm in from the side.

2 Count the beats for 1 full minute. If the casualty is seriously ill or injured, the radial pulse may be difficult to feel.

RESUSCITATION

It is essential when someone seems unconscious, as the result of serious injury or illness, to establish whether breathing or circulation has stopped. If one or both functions have ceased, it is vital to begin resuscitation immediately. Death or major brain damage may result after 3 minutes, if the brain does not receive oxygen. Therefore, maintenance of the airway and resuscitation *always* take precedence over treating any of the casualty's other medical problems.

ASSESSING THE CASUALTY

1 Remove the casualty — and yourself — from danger, if necessary (see MOVING AN INJURED PERSON).

2 Gently shake the casualty and speak to him loudly. If he fails to respond, he is unconscious. (If the casualty does respond, proceed to administer first aid for his injury or illness — see alphabetical listings, p. 194.)

3 Check that the airway of the unconscious casualty is not blocked, preventing breathing (see below). The airway is the passage, from the nose and mouth to the lungs, by which air enters the body.

4 Check that breathing has in fact stopped. Look for the rise and fall of the lower chest and abdomen. Then listen and feel for breathing by placing your ear close to the casualty's nose and mouth. (If the casualty is breathing, place him in the coma position and proceed as discussed in UNCONSCIOUSNESS).

5 Start expired air resuscitation to restore breathing: give 5 full breaths quickly within 10 seconds (see description of procedure below).

6 Check carotid pulse (see PULSE). If the pulse is present, continue with expired air resuscitation. If absent, begin cardiopulmonary resuscitation (see below).

CLEARING THE AIRWAY

1 Place the casualty on her side in the lateral position (see UNCONSCIOUSNESS).

2 Tilt the head backwards, face turned slightly downwards, to allow fluid to drain out of the mouth and to make the tongue fall forwards.

3 Open mouth and check gently for foreign bodies.

4 Clear out any foreign bodies with your fingers.

5 Remove dentures, *if* they are loose or broken.

EXPIRED AIR RESUSCITATION

Mouth-to-mouth resuscitation is the easiest and most successful method of expired air resuscitation. Mouth-to-nose resuscitation is used mainly when: the jaw is clenched or injured; the mouth is obstructed; a corrosive or poisonous substance is still on the lips; or the casualty has to be revived in deep water.

RESUSCITATION

Mouth-to-mouth resuscitation

1 Where possible, place the casualty on her back and kneel beside her head. Tilt her head back, using the neck thrust or jaw thrust method.

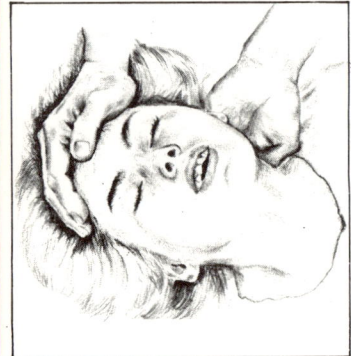

Neck thrust method: place one of your hands on her forehead and the other under the back of her neck; press her head firmly but gently backwards, while lifting the neck upwards.

Jaw thrust method: again use one hand on the forehead to tilt the head backwards, but support her jaw with your other hand, keeping your fingers from pressing on her throat, and lift the jaw upwards and forwards. Make sure in all cases that the casualty's mouth is *slightly* open — if the mouth is wide open the airway will be obstructed.

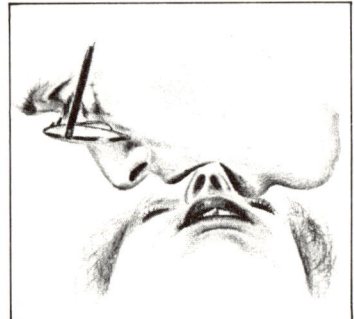

2 Take a deep breath and place your wide-open mouth over the casualty's, making an airtight seal. Your cheek must be against her nostrils to seal off the nose, also. (Alternatively, you can pinch her nostrils between your fingers and thumb to prevent air escaping.) Keeping her head tilted, breathe into her mouth until her chest rises, giving 5 full breaths within 10 seconds.

3 Remove your mouth, place your ear close to her mouth and listen and feel for exhaling air.

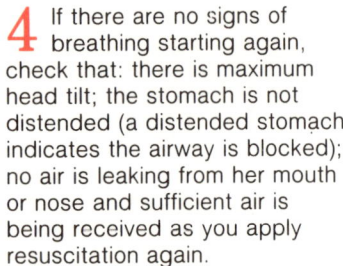

4 If there are no signs of breathing starting again, check that: there is maximum head tilt; the stomach is not distended (a distended stomach indicates the airway is blocked); no air is leaking from her mouth or nose and sufficient air is being received as you apply resuscitation again.

5 Give 5 full breaths within 10 seconds, then continue at the normal breathing rate of 12–14 breaths per minute until the casualty starts breathing for herself.

6 Check the pulse after 1 minute of resuscitation and continue to monitor at least every 2 minutes. If there is no pulse, begin cardiopulmonary resuscitation (see below).

7 When breathing begins independently, place the casualty in the coma position (see UNCONSCIOUSNESS).

Mouth-to-nose resuscitation

1 Clear airway and place casualty on his back with his head maintained in the tilted position described for mouth-to-mouth resuscitation.

2 Close the casualty's mouth and place the thumb of your hand that is supporting his jaw against his bottom lip to keep his lips together.

3 Taking a deep breath, place your wide-open mouth over his nose. Take care it completely covers the bridge of his nose, but does not press on the soft part. Blow into his nose until his lower chest rises.

4 Lift your mouth from his nose and peel down his lower lip to allow him to exhale.

5 Proceed as for mouth-to-mouth resuscitation, steps 4–8. The mouth-to-mouth method should be substituted, if air continues to leak.

Babies and small children

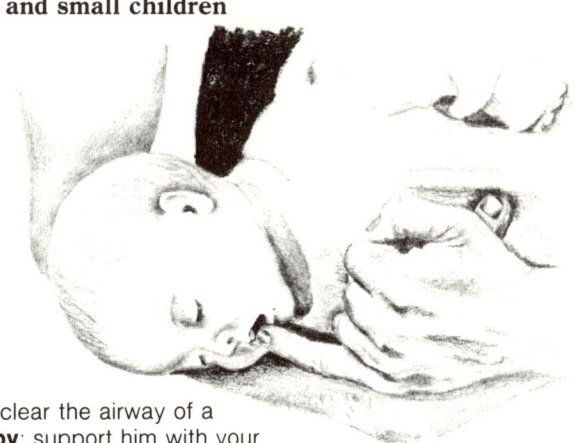

1 To clear the airway of a **baby**: support him with your arm, placing him on his side with his head lower than his feet. Clear away any matter from his mouth with the little finger of your free hand. Clear the airway of a **child** as for adults. If this fails, the child may be placed head-down and given several firm hits between the shoulder-blades.

2 Place the baby or small child on his back with his head positioned horizontally, not tilted, and his jaw supported by your hand.

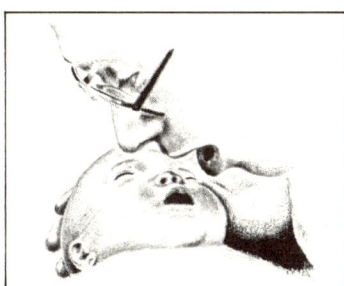

3 Apply expired air resuscitation, but more gently and quickly than for adults — over-blowing will distend the stomach. Babies and children under 2 years are given **mouth-and-nose resuscitation**: place your wide-open mouth over the infant's nose and slightly opened mouth. Puff gently from your cheeks, providing just enough air pressure to make the baby's chest rise.

4 Lift your head to listen and feel for exhaling air from the infant's mouth and nostrils and to look for the fall of the chest. Check whether the stomach is distended: if so, check the mouth and nostrils for any obstruction.

5 Repeat the shallow breaths into his mouth and nose at the rate of 20 times a minute.

6 Check his pulse every 2 minutes.

7 When he starts breathing for himself, nurse him on his side.

CARDIOPULMONARY RESUSCITATION

If the heart has stopped beating, the casualty will be unconscious, breathing will have stopped and there will be no pulse (see procedure for assessing the casualty, above). Cardiopulmonary (heart–lung) resuscitation *must* be given without delay. It is a combination of expired air resuscitation (see above), and external cardiac compression, which allows oxygen to reach the vital organs, preventing death and brain damage. By compressing the casualty's heart between breastbone and spine, it is possible to artificially pump blood to the brain and other organs.

Cardiopulmonary resuscitation is a tiring technique that is best performed by two people working together. It should be learnt from a qualified instructor. The operator needs to give at least 4 completed cycles per minute. Each 15–second cycle is made up of 15 compressions followed by 2 breaths, so the operator gives 1 compression every three-quarters of a second. A pair of operators need only give 1 compression every second because, working together, two people can complete 12–15 cycles per minute.

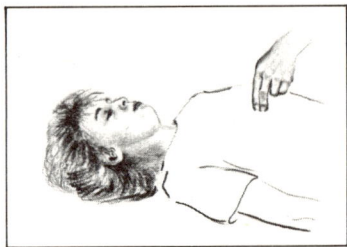

1 Place the casualty on her back and kneel beside her. Quickly find the lower end of her breastbone: move the fingers of both your hands in from the lowest rib on either side to meet at the midline. Place the index and middle fingers of your hand that is farther from her head directly above the lower end of the breastbone.

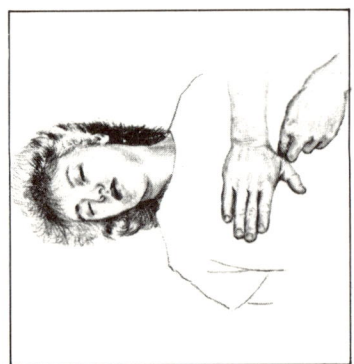

2 Place the heel of your near hand on her chest immediately above these two fingers. Slightly raise all the fingers of this hand.

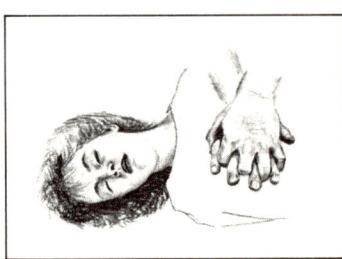

3 Remove the index and middle fingers of your far hand and place that hand over the near one, interlocking the fingers of both.

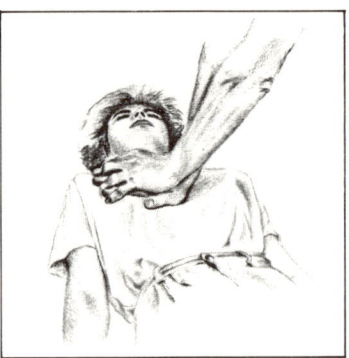

4 Keeping your arms straight and using only the heel of your hand, begin compressions. Depress the breastbone about 5 cm. Relax to allow the chest to expand properly, but do not remove your hands. Continue doing this rhythmically. If there is only yourself available, give 15 compressions in 10–12 seconds, followed by 2 breaths within 3–5 seconds. If you have a helper, one of you should apply the compressions while the other gives the expired air resuscitation. Give 5 compressions and 1 breath within 5 seconds. The person applying compression needs to count the 5 compressions of each cycle aloud, so that the other person can give a breath as the fifth compression starts to avoid a break between cycles.

5 After 1 minute check the pulse. If it is still not present, continue cardiopulmonary resuscitation. At all times ensure that the airway is clear (see above).

6 If the pulse is restored, but the casualty still does not breathe independently, stop cardiopulmonary resuscitation and apply expired air resuscitation (see above).

7 Once both pulse and breathing have begun, place the casualty in the coma position (see UNCONSCIOUSNESS). Check her continually until medical help arrives.

Children 1–8 years

1 Find the middle of the breastbone: place the index finger of your hand which is nearer the child's head at the notch at the top of the breastbone; place the index finger of your farther hand at the bottom of the breastbone where the ribs join; keeping both index fingers in position and using both thumbs, divide the breastbone in half.

2 Leave your farther index finger and thumb in place and put the heel of the nearer hand between them.

3 Remove the index finger and thumb and place the farther hand over the nearer hand, interlocking the fingers of both.

4 Depress the chest about 2–3 cm at the rate of 80–100 times per minute. After every 15 compressions give 2 breaths, covering the child's nose and mouth with your mouth and using less force and less volume of air than you would for an adult. If you have a helper, give 5 compressions to 1 breath, as for an adult.

Babies

1 Find the middle of the breastbone as for children.

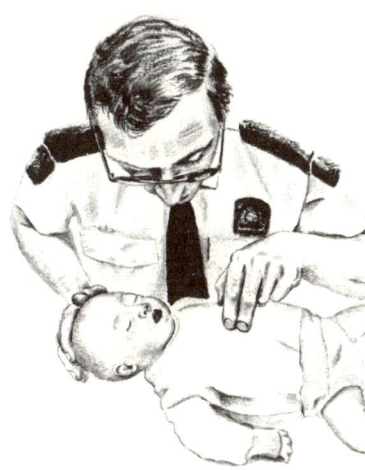

2 Apply compression with the tips of your index and middle fingers. Depress the chest 1.5 cm. Proceed as for children.

The first few minutes at the scene of an accident are vital. People may survive the initial impact, only to die because their airway is obstructed by their tongue or foreign matter. They may also bleed to death. Therefore, prompt action taken by the first person to arrive may prevent loss of life or brain damage.

1 Make the situation as safe as possible. Ensure that your car and any others that arrive are parked at a safe distance. Turn on hazard warning lights and headlights. Keep clear, if the crashed vehicle is on fire or there are fallen electricity wires across it. *Do not* smoke. Immobilise the crashed vehicle by turning off the ignition, pulling on the handbrake and chocking the wheels, if it is on a slope.

2 Check to see if anyone is injured. *Do not* move a casualty unless he is in immediate danger or it is necessary to clear his airway or give expired air or cardiopulmonary resuscitation. Follow the instructions given in MOVING AN INJURED PERSON, if you do need to move someone. Splint any fractures before the casualty is moved, if possible. Remove any **trapped casualty**, if this can be done easily and gently — rarely the case. *Remember* that expired air resuscitation may still be applied even if the casualty is trapped. If possible, remove the object crushing a **crush casualty** and send for emergency medical services immediately.

3 Attend to the unconscious casualty first. Place the victim in the coma position and clear his airway (see UNCONSCIOUSNESS and RESUSCITATION — clearing the airway). If the casualty is trapped, tilt the head backwards, supporting the jaw, so that the airway remains open. Check breathing and pulse and, if needed, apply expired air or cardiopulmonary resuscitation (see RESUSCITATION). Continue to monitor airway, breathing and pulse.

4 Check the unconscious casualty for bleeding and try to control (see BLEEDING). Then attend to all wounds (see WOUNDS and also specific injuries listed alphabetically, p. 194) and immobilise any fractures (see FRACTURES).

5 Reassure any conscious casualties and help them into comfortable positions. Make sure they can breathe freely and loosen any tight clothing. Control bleeding, attend to any wounds and immobilise fractures as for the unconscious person. Monitor breathing and circulation.

6 Check the area of the accident in case someone has been thrown clear of the vehicle or is wandering around in a state of shock (see SHOCK).

7 *Do not* give casualties anything to eat or drink.

8 Cover casualties with a light blanket or piece of clothing.

9 Stay with the casualties if possible, and send a bystander to call the ambulance, police or other emergency services, making sure that they receive precise information about exact location; nature of the accident; number of injuries; severity of injuries; whether anyone is trapped; and any special services, such as the fire brigade or electricity authorities, which are needed.

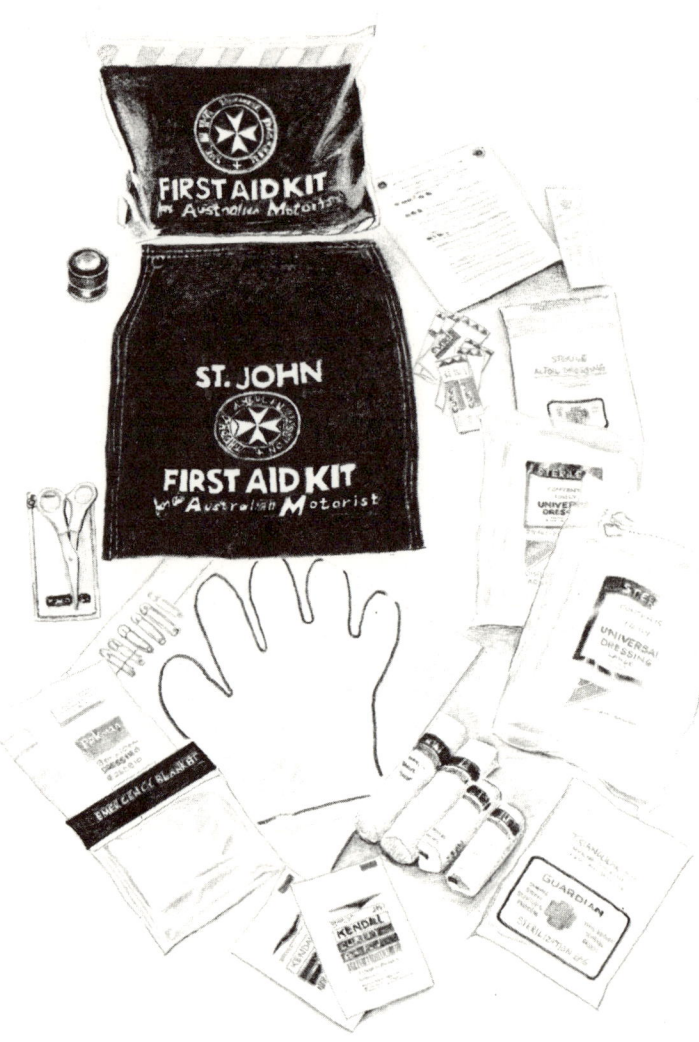

SEVERED LIMBS

Quick action in preserving a severed limb, finger or toe may mean that it can be successfully replaced, given recent advances in micro-surgery. However, save the casualty first. *Never* try to restore the amputated limb yourself, as it will cause the casualty a lot of pain and may damage the tissues.

1 Lay the casualty down, propping the injured part on a pillow or your knee.

2 Control the flow of bleeding by pressing a large pad of gauze or clean material on the raw area.

3 Fix the pad in place with a roller bandage or adhesive tape.

4 Seek medical aid urgently.

5 Keep the casualty calm and still.

6 If you can find the severed part, wrap it in sterile or clean material and place it in a plastic bag. Inflate and seal the bag and send it with the casualty to hospital.

SHOCK

The term shock is often confusing. We sometimes use the word to describe a person's extreme psychological reaction to fright, grief or joy. This is *not* the medical condition known as shock.

Shock is the condition in which there is insufficient circulation of blood to the brain and body, possibly resulting in death. It is caused by: severe bleeding; heart attack; fluid loss from major burns, diarrhoea and vomiting; spinal injury; some kinds of poisoning; or overwhelming infection. Watch for shock whenever there is severe injury or illness.

It is a *progressive* condition. The casualty at first may look only slightly pale, feel a little cold and have a rapid pulse, but after a while may lapse into unconsciousness, develop an extremely weak pulse and perhaps die. Symptoms and signs include:

- faintness or dizziness
- restlessness
- pale face and lips
- cold, clammy skin
- shallow or gasping breath
- weak and rapid pulse
- nausea
- thirst
- bluish extremities
- ultimately, drowsiness, confusion and unconsciousness.

1 Remember that shock results from major illness or injury, so try to *diagnose and treat the cause* (see, for example, BLEEDING, HEART ATTACK AND HEART FAILURE, BURNS AND SCALDS, SPINAL INJURIES, POISONING).

2 Lay the casualty down, with his head low and his legs (unless there is a fracture) resting on a pillow to maintain the blood supply to the brain. The unconscious casualty is placed in the coma position (see UNCONSCIOUSNESS) to ensure the airway is kept clear.

3 Reassure the casualty.

4 Loosen any tight clothing and make him comfortable.

5 Maintain body temperature at all times, but *do not* over-heat the casualty.

6 *Do not* give anything to eat or drink. You may moisten the casualty's lips or he may suck on an ice cube.

7 Carefully monitor the casualty's breathing and pulse, remembering that the condition is progressive. Apply expired air or cardiopulmonary resuscitation, if needed (see RESUSCITATION).

8 Seek medical aid urgently.

SLINGS

Slings are used to rest, support or immobilise an injured hand, arm, shoulder or chest after it has been treated. They can be bought ready-made or adapted from a triangular or a narrow bandage. They can also be improvised from a large square of folded material, from a towel or pillowcase or from a belt, tie or scarf. If none of these is available, turn up and pin the bottom of the casualty's shirt or jacket or pin his sleeve to the front of his clothes. As a last resort, tuck his wrist inside his buttoned shirt or jacket.

ARM SLING

Made from a triangular bandage (see BANDAGES, DRESSINGS AND PADS), an arm sling supports an injured forearm in a position roughly parallel to the ground. It is particularly useful for supporting an arm with a heavy splint.

1 The casualty supports her injured arm, with the wrist and hand raised higher than the elbow. Place an open triangular bandage between her chest and forearm, its point stretching well beyond the elbow and its top point hanging over her shoulder on the uninjured side.

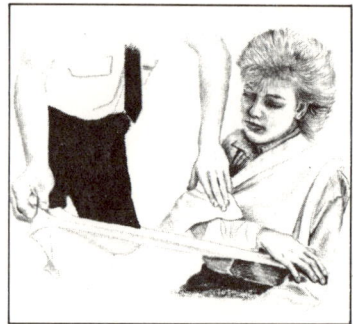

2 Bring the point round the elbow and tuck between the arm and the sling.

3 Bring the base point of the triangular bandage up over the hand and forearm on the injured side and the top point around the back of the neck.

4 Tie the two ends in a reef knot in the hollow just above the collar bone on the injured side. Keep the casualty's fingernails free and check their circulation: if they are turning white or blue, loosen the bandage or alter the position of the hand.

ELEVATION SLING

The elevation or St John sling supports the elbow and keeps the hand resting comfortably on the shoulder of the uninjured side. It provides support for shoulder injuries, without causing pressure on the shoulder or upper chest.

1 Place the casualty's upper arm by her side, with the elbow flexed and the forearm raised across her chest, the fingers pointing to the shoulder of the uninjured side. (BLEEDING shows an injured hand in position for the sling.)

2 Cover the forearm and hand with an open triangular bandage, its point towards the bent elbow and its uppermost edge parallel to the forearm resting across the chest. The top point of the triangle goes over the shoulder, the base point hangs down, parallel to the body.

3 Hold the casualty's hand and the bandage over her shoulder by tucking your thumb under her wrist, bringing the bandage with it. Using your other hand, tuck the point firmly under the upper arm. Then sweep the same hand, palm facing towards you, under the part of the bandage hanging down. Bring it up under the upper arm, tucking in the folds in your hand.

COLLAR AND CUFF SLING

This is used if the casualty does not have an injured wrist or forearm. Made from a narrow bandage or a belt, tie or scarf, it supports the wrist towards the neck, while allowing gravity to pull an upper arm fracture into alignment.

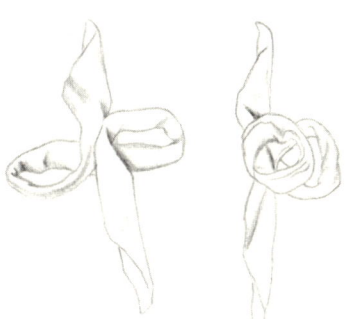

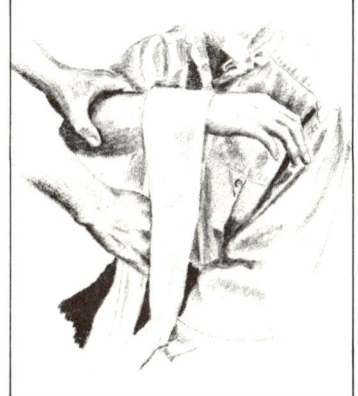

1 Hold the injured arm parallel to the chest. Drape the bandage over the forearm, with its two lengths hanging down on either side.

3 Alternatively, you can make a clove hitch with the bandage first, then slip it over the wrist. To tie a clove hitch, make two loops in a narrow bandage, one towards the body and one away, leaving one end longer than the other. Bring the loops together with your hands.

4 Bring the end of the bandage across the back to meet the other end at the shoulder on the uninjured side. Adjust the height of the sling, then tie the ends in a reef knot in the hollow above the collar bone. Check circulation.

2 Make a clove hitch on the forearm as follows. Leave the outside length dangling. Bring the inside length back towards the elbow. Then bring it forward over the wrist and loop it around. Tuck the end between the cross-over folds of the bandage on the wrist.

4 Place the casualty's forearm across her chest with her hand resting against the shoulder of her uninjured side. Tie the ends of the bandage in the hollow just above the collar bone on either side.

SPINAL INJURIES

Spinal injuries may be the result of direct force, such as a blow to the back, or indirect force, such as a blow to the head that injures the neck. They are often caused by car accidents, surfing, diving and skiing accidents, heavy falls from heights or blows from falling objects.

Spinal injuries should always be regarded as serious, but injuries to the 33-bone (vertebra) spinal column are less serious than those to the spinal cord that it protects. Damage to the cord can result in paralysis below the injury. Always suspect neck injury following a head injury. If neck injury is high, paralysis may prevent breathing and circulation and be life-threatening.

It is crucial to handle the casualty carefully. Twisting or bending an injured spinal column can dangerously affect the extent of the permanent damage.

Injury to the spine *must always* be suspected in unconscious casualties (see UNCONSCIOUSNESS).
Symptoms and signs include:
• pain, tenderness and a tingling sensation over or below the injury site
• loss of movement or feeling
• sometimes deformity of the neck or spine
• loss of bladder and bowel control
• breathing difficulties
• signs of shock (see SHOCK).

1 *Do not* move casualties with suspected neck or back injuries unless they are in immediate danger from, for example, oncoming traffic (see MOVING AN INJURED PERSON). Leave lifting and carrying to ambulance attendants with the right equipment. If a diving accident has occurred, use a surfboard or flat piece of wood to support the casualty before moving him from the water, and leave him on it until examined by a medical helper.

2 If the casualty is unconscious, place in the coma position (see UNCONSCIOUSNESS), carefully supporting the head and neck during the movement.

3 If a neck injury is suspected, carefully support the head and neck in your hand until a cervical collar can be improvised from a folded towel, newspaper or bulky dressing held in place around the neck with, for example, a tie or scarf.

4 Reassure the conscious casualty, loosen any tight clothing and cover with a blanket.

5 Seek medical attention urgently.

6 Monitor breathing and pulse (see PULSE) and be prepared to administer expired air or cardiopulmonary resuscitation, if necessary (see RESUSCITATION).

SPLINTERS

Small pieces of wood or glass, prickles or other foreign bodies embedded in the skin can cause infection, if they are not removed. If the splinter is not protruding from the skin, *do not* try to remove it yourself, but seek medical aid.

1 Sterilise a pair of splinter forceps (see FIRST AID KIT) by quickly burning the ends over a flame or with a match. Alternatively, boil in a saucepan of water for 5 minutes.

2 Clean the area around the splinter, washing away from the wound.

3 Grasp the protruding end of the splinter with the splinter forceps. If the splinter does not come out, seek medical aid.

4 When it has been removed, wash around the wound with antiseptic and dry gently with a clean cloth.

5 Cover with an adhesive dressing.

6 If the area swells or becomes painful, seek medical advice.

SPLINTS

Splints are used to support or immobilise limbs. Padded wooden splints can be bought ready-made, but splints can also be improvised from any rigid article, such as a piece of wood, cardboard or firmly folded newspaper or magazine. A tightly rolled blanket can be used as a splint for an arm or leg. An injured leg can be immobilised by tying it with bandages against the other leg at the feet and knees. The trunk of the body can be used to splint a fractured upper arm.

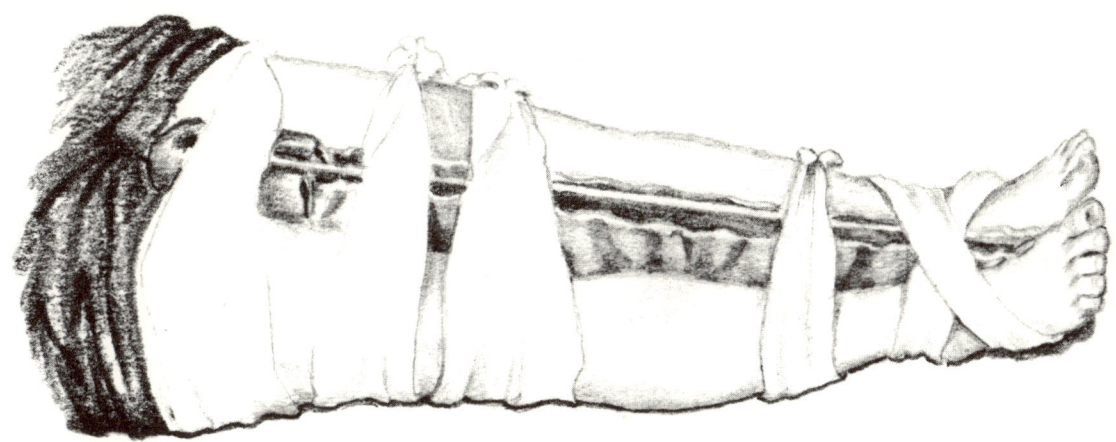

1 *Do not* remove clothing to apply a splint and move the injured limb as little as possible.

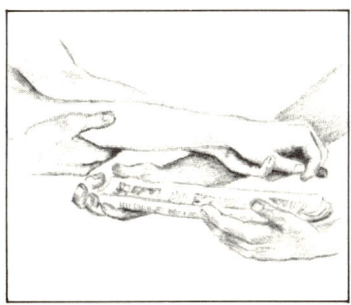

2 Make sure that the splint is rigid and long enough to immobilise the joints above and below the fracture.

3 Pad it well with gauze or clean material, unwrapped roller bandages, folded triangular bandages or firmly folded clothing (see BANDAGES, DRESSINGS AND PADS). Place padding between the splint and natural hollows. Make sure that bony points, such as ankles, are covered (see illustration of leg splint).

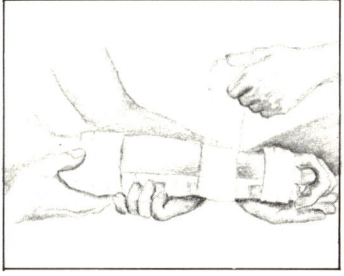

4 Tie the splint to the limb firmly at the top and bottom and at regular intervals in between, but not over the site of the wound.

5 Check the bandages every 15 minutes to ensure that they are firm enough to immobilise the limb, without affecting the circulation or causing pain.

SPRAINS, STRAINS AND DISLOCATIONS

Sprains occur when ligaments connected to joints are wrenched or torn. Strains happen to muscles or tendons when they are over-stretched. Dislocation occurs when the bones of a joint are forced out of contact with each other. Almost any joint can be dislocated. Sprains and dislocations are often associated with fractures and have the same symptoms.

SPRAINS

The ligaments of the ankle and knee joints are the ones most frequently affected. Sprains often result from sporting activities. Symptoms and signs include:
- pain and tenderness round the joint
- swelling
- inability to move the joint
- rapid bruising
- deformation of the joint.

1 Remove or loosen clothing around the injury. If there is *any* suspicion that a fracture may also be involved, proceed as described in FRACTURES.

2 If there is not, apply an ice pack to the affected area to reduce pain, swelling and tissue damage. *Do not* apply ice directly to bare skin: wrap it in a damp material first. Leave the pack on for a maximum of 20 minutes, then remove it for a minimum of 20 minutes.

3 Bandage firmly over the ice pack.

4 Elevate the part.

STRAINS

Muscles usually become strained as the result of unaccustomed physical activity or a fall. Symptoms and signs include:
- sudden, sharp pain in the muscle
- local tenderness
- inability to move the muscle.

1 Make the casualty comfortable. Handle the injured muscle gently and support it carefully.

2 Apply an ice pack to the affected area, as for sprains (see above), to control any tissue bleeding.

3 Bandage firmly.

4 Encourage gentle exercise, if possible, to reduce painful spasm and any shortening of the muscle, but *do not* massage.

DISLOCATIONS

Symptoms and signs are as for sprains (see above).

1 Rest the joint in the most comfortable position. *Never* try to push a dislocated bone back into place, but treat as if it were broken (see FRACTURES).

2 Using soft padding, splint the joint (see SPLINTS) in the position in which it was found.

SUFFOCATION

Suffocation results when oxygen is prevented from entering the airway. It is often caused by the casualty's nose and mouth being blocked by a plastic bag or pillow. Liquids, smoke and toxic gases are other causes of suffocation. For symptoms and signs see ASPHYXIA.

1 Remove any object blocking the mouth and nose — a plastic bag should be torn open. If the victim has been suffocated by liquids, smoke or fumes, follow procedures outlined in DROWNING and POISONING — inhaled poisons.

2 If the casualty has stopped breathing or has no pulse (see PULSE) apply expired air or cardiopulmonary resuscitation (see RESUSCITATION).

3 If the casualty continues to be unconscious after normal breathing has resumed, turn him on his side in the coma position (see UNCONSCIOUSNESS).

4 Seek medical aid and monitor airway, breathing and pulse carefully until it arrives.

SUNBURN

Sunburn is caused by exposure to strong sunlight, particularly in the middle of the day. People with fair complexions and young children are more susceptible, even on cloudy days and in the shade. The skin becomes reddened, prickles and is hot to the touch. In severe cases it may be swollen and blistered. After a few days it becomes dry and usually peels. Long-term effects can be permanent freckling, blotching and premature ageing of the skin.

1 Relieve the burning with cool baths or showers or apply cool compresses to the head and affected areas. *Do not* chill the sufferer by using ice packs. If the sufferer is perspiring heavily, a fan may help the cooling process.

SWALLOWED OBJECTS

A swallowed object which lodges in the airway and impedes breathing must be treated immediately (see CHOKING for symptoms and signs and treatment).

Most smooth swallowed objects no bigger than a cent will pass through the system without any problems. However, sharp objects, such as pins, needles, bones, matchsticks, nails and glass splinters, may lodge in the tonsils, throat or oesophagus. They may have to be removed surgically. Symptoms and signs indicating the need for treatment include:
- gagging
- pain in throat or chest
- abdominal pain
- vomiting
- difficulty in swallowing.

1 *Do not* give fluids or food.

2 Seek medical aid.

2 *Do not* allow him to go back into the sun without covering the burnt parts with light, loose clothing, such as a T-shirt.

3 Mild cases can be soothed by applying calamine lotion, commercial ointments or a paste of baking soda and tap water.

4 If the sunburn is severe, especially in young children, seek medical attention.

5 If necessary, give paracetamol for pain, according to the dosage prescribed on the packet.

6 Take care not to cause extra discomfort and to delay healing by breaking any blisters.

TEETH INJURIES

If a permanent tooth is knocked out of the mouth, it can be saved by quick action (although baby teeth should not be replaced). Even if teeth are replaced several hours after an accident, they can often last for years.

1 Cleanse the tooth either by having the casualty suck it or by washing it at room or refrigerator temperature in either saliva or milk. Washing it under a tap is a last resort.

2 Replace it in the mouth in its original position. Hold it there for 2 minutes.

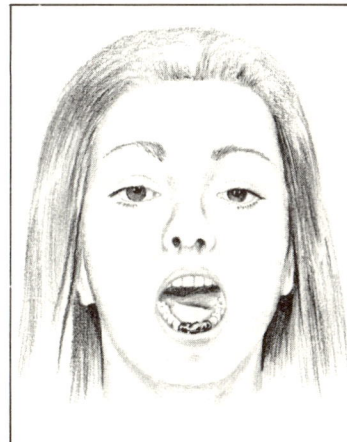

3 Splint the tooth by wrapping aluminium foil or similar material around it and a tooth on either side. Once the splint is moulded to the three teeth, get the casualty to bite firmly on it. (Similarly, a loosened tooth may be kept in place with an aluminium foil splint.) If the tooth cannot be replaced, keep the tooth moist in the casualty's mouth or in saliva or milk at room temperature and seek dental aid urgently.

4 If the replaced tooth is dirty, advise the casualty to have an anti-tetanus injection.

5 Seek dental aid as soon as possible.

TEMPERATURE

The average body temperature is 37° Celsius, but temperature may vary during the course of the day, even in healthy people. It may be lower in the early morning and higher in hot weather or after hot meals or physical exertion. However, a raised or lowered temperature may be an indicator of illness or malfunction. Low temperatures can occur after shock (see SHOCK), severe bleeding (see BLEEDING) or exposure (see EXPOSURE, HYPOTHERMIA AND FROSTBITE). High temperatures often indicate severe infection.

If the victim's skin is hot and moist, it may be a sign of fever, but it is impossible to accurately estimate temperature by look or touch. A thermometer reading is always necessary.

Before using a thermometer, wash and dry it and shake the mercury column down until it is below 37° Celsius. Check by rotating the thermometer slowly between your fingers until you can see the top of the mercury column against the scale on the side.

Temperatures can be taken under the arm, in the groin, in the rectum and in the mouth. The mouth is usually used for adults and children over 5 years old. Rectal temperature taking is particularly suitable for babies and toddlers. Taking the temperature under the arm is also preferable to taking a mouth reading where small children are concerned because they may bite the thermometer.

TEMPERATURE | UNCONSCIOUSNESS

MOUTH TEMPERATURE TAKING

1 Place the bulb of the thermometer under the tongue, to one side of the mouth. Ask the casualty to close her lips, but not her teeth, and to keep the thermometer in place.

2 Read the thermometer after 3 minutes.

RECTAL TEMPERATURE TAKING

1 Lubricate the bulb of the *rectal thermometer* with petroleum jelly.

2 Spread the buttocks with the thumb and forefinger of one hand so that the anal opening is visible.

3 Insert the thermometer gently. There should be no discomfort.

4 Support the buttocks and thermometer for 2–3 minutes before withdrawing the thermometer to read the temperature.

Unconsciousness occurs when the brain completely or partly fails to respond to its normal messages. There are three levels of unconsciousness:
• the casualty can be easily aroused, although he slips back into a sleepy state
• the casualty is drowsy and can only be aroused with difficulty
• the casualty cannot be aroused at all.
The casualty may remain at one level of consciousness or may get worse over time.
The unconscious person is unable to:
• communicate
• perceive danger and protect himself
• clear his airway by coughing or swallowing — this inability is always serious because relaxation of the muscles during unconsciousness allows the tongue to fall backwards blocking the airway, if the casualty is lying on his back.

Because unconsciousness therefore indicates malfunction of the brain and enhances the likelihood of breathing difficulties, it is crucial to act quickly and to seek medical aid, even if unconsciousness is only temporary.

1 Check whether the casualty is conscious by speaking loudly to him and shaking his shoulders. If he does not respond, he is unconscious.

2 Shift him only if he is in immediate danger (see MOVING AN INJURED PERSON).

3 Seek immediate medical aid, but *do not* leave the victim alone.

4 Check that his airway is clear (see RESUSCITATION — clearing the airway) and that he is breathing and has a pulse (see PULSE). Apply expired air or cardiopulmonary resuscitation, if necessary (see RESUSCITATION).

5 If the casualty is breathing and has a pulse, place him immediately in the coma position or the lateral position (see below) and maintain the position to ensure that the airway is kept clear. The coma position is more comfortable if the casualty has to lie for any length of time.

6 *Do not* give anything to eat or drink.

7 Loosen tight clothing.

8 Attend to any injuries.

9 Monitor airway, breathing and pulse continually until medical aid arrives.

COMA POSITION

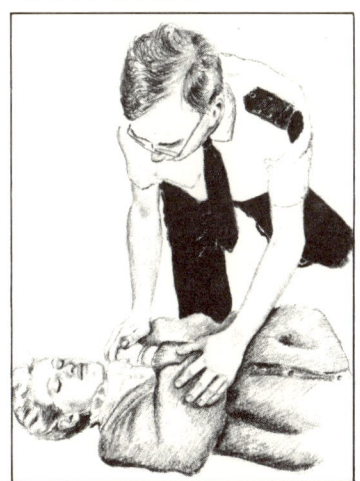

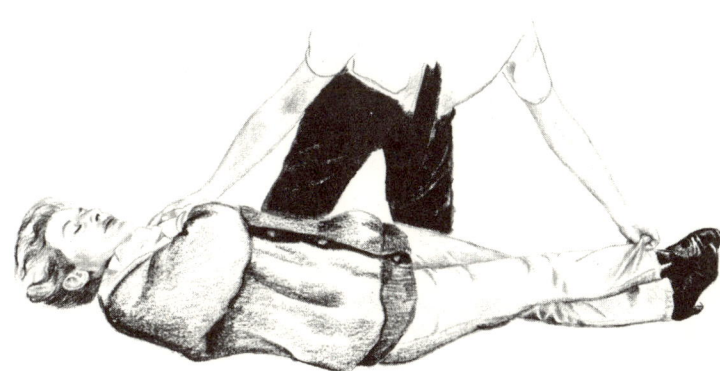

1 Place the casualty on her back. Kneel beside her. Place her nearer arm, palm up, under her buttocks. Place the farther arm across her chest.

2 Cross the farther leg over the nearer one.

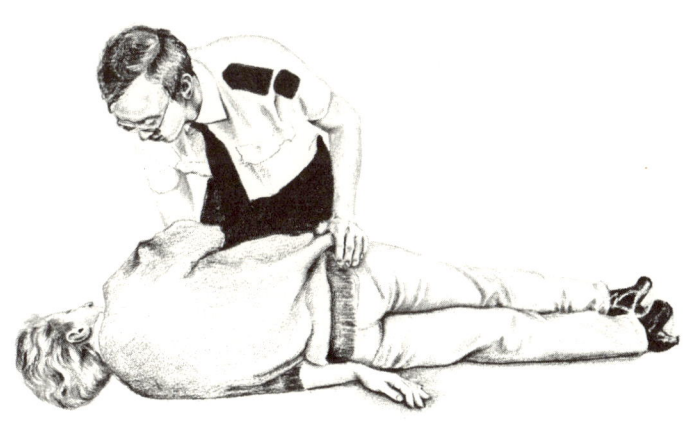

3 Supporting the casualty's head and neck with your hand that is nearer her head, place your other hand on her farther hip and turn her over until she is resting against your knees.

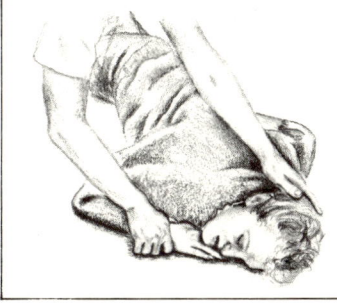

4 Place the nearer upper leg at right angles to the casualty's body.

5 Remove the casualty's farther arm from under her body and flex the elbow. Move her head back and place the hand of the nearer arm under the chin.

UNCONSCIOUSNESS

LATERAL POSITION

1 Place the casualty on his back. Kneel beside him. Bring his farther arm out at right angles to his body.

2 Bring the nearer arm, bent at the elbow, across the chest.

3 Bend the knee of the nearer leg to bring its upper part at right angles to the body, keeping the farther leg straight.

4 Holding the casualty's nearer shoulder and hip, roll him on to the side farther from you. His back is straight and his bent leg rests on the ground, not on the straight leg.

5 Place the nearer arm across the farther one at the latter's elbow.

6 Place the head in a backwards tilt, with the face slightly downwards. Support the jaw.

WOUNDS

A break in the tissues of the body is called a wound.

OPEN WOUNDS

If bleeding is on the outside of the body, it is known as an open wound. There are five types of open wound:
- abrasions caused by direct contact with a rough surface, for example gravel
- incised wounds or cuts caused by a sharp object — because of the tendency for these to be deep they often bleed profusely and become infected
- lacerations torn by a jagged object, such as metal, barbed wire, animal claws or machinery — these are often dirty and therefore prone to infection, and the area may be bruised
- bites
- penetrating wounds caused by sharp objects, such as bullets, nails or needles — these have a small entry so may look minor, but they are in fact dangerous because of the internal injury inflicted and the possibility of deep-seated infection.

See BITES AND STINGS, BRUISES, CHEST INJURIES, CUTS AND SCRATCHES, EAR INJURIES, EYE INJURIES, FISH HOOK, HEAD, FACE AND JAW INJURIES and SEVERED LIMBS for different open wounds and their specific treatments. The following treatment applies for open wounds in general.

1 Control bleeding (see BLEEDING).

2 Cut away or remove clothing covering the wound.

3 Clean the wound to prevent infection, if it is possible to do so without causing the bleeding to start again. *Do not* attempt to remove any foreign body except surface dirt or gravel.

4 Apply a sterile or clean dressing with washed hands, trying not to breathe, cough or sneeze on it. Pad *round* an implanted foreign object or apply a ring pad (see BANDAGES, DRESSINGS AND PADS).

5 Seek medical aid for all serious open wounds.

CLOSED WOUNDS

Here the bleeding is internal: it does not occur through the skin. The types of closed wound are:
- contusions (bruises)
- sprains, strains and closed fractures. Some fractures result in very severe bleeding.

See BRUISES, FRACTURES and SPRAINS, STRAINS AND DISLOCATIONS for the symptoms, signs and treatment for these two types of closed wound.

MEDICAL AND HEALTH SUPPORT ORGANISATIONS

5

INTRODUCTION

Knowing who to contact or where to turn for advice, information, or simply moral support, can make all the difference to many of life's crises. A wide range of useful support groups and medical and community services has been collated in this section. They have been organised under topics such as ASTHMA, CHILD ABUSE, DIABETES, and arranged alphabetically for easy reference, State-by-State for Australia and under four main regions for New Zealand.

These groups range from long-established organisations such as The St John Ambulance Association to small self-help groups, sometimes virtually run by one or two dedicated individuals.

For the sufferers of some diseases and disabilities, moral support over a long period can be just as important to their well-being as medical treatment. Simply knowing that others

have experienced the same problems and gone through similar emotional reactions can greatly help people who have had, for example, a colostomy or mastectomy, or who are suffering from diseases such as multiple sclerosis, cancer, Parkinson's disease or epilepsy. Support groups can also offer practical help and information gained from the experience of others.

Some afflictions place just as much or more stress on the families of sufferers than the sufferers themselves. Special support groups for the families of alcoholics, drug addicts and the mentally disabled are included.

A comparatively new concept in community support organisations are the many telephone information and counselling services which now exist world-wide. This directory includes such vital services as poisons information, as well as

counselling services for child abuse, rape and sexual assault and information on AIDS. Many of these telephone services operate on a 24-hourly basis.

A third major group of organisations included could be broadly classified as community services such as family planning clinics, marriage guidance bureaus and general counselling on sex education and human relationships. Drug dependency counselling groups, emergency dental services, sexually transmitted disease clinics, and organisations offering advice on pregnancy, abortion and contraception are among the other community health services listed.

The telephone numbers and addresses of all the following organisations were checked at the time of publication, but no responsibility can be taken by the publishers for subsequent changes.

AUSTRALIA

AUSTRALIAN CAPITAL TERRITORY

ABORTION
See PREGNANCY, ABORTION, CONTRACEPTION

AGEING
ACT Council on the Ageing
Hughes Community Centre,
Wisdom St, Hughes, 2605
Tel: (062) 82 3777, 81 2985

AIDS
(Acquired Immune Deficiency Syndrome)

AIDS Reference Centre
Woden Valley Hospital,
Yamba Dr., Garran, 2605
Tel: (062) 84 2184, 84 2231

See also SEXUALLY
TRANSMITTED DISEASES

ALCOHOL & DRUG DEPENDENCE
Al-Anon Family Groups
Health Promotion Centre,
Childers St, Canberra City,
2600
Tel: (062) 48 8651

Al-A-Teen
Health Promotion Centre,
Childers St, Canberra City,
2600
Tel: (062) 48 8651

Alcohol & Drug Dependence
Foundation ACT Inc.
Health Promotion Centre,
Childers St, Canberra City,
2600
Tel: (062) 47 4747

Alcoholics Anonymous
Health Promotion Centre,
Childers St, Canberra City,
2600
Tel: (062) 49 1340

Narcotics Anonymous
PO Box 2091, Canberra City,
2601

We Help Ourselves Fellowship
19 Keira St, Narrabundah, 2604
Tel: (062) 95 6865

ARTHRITIS
Arthritis Foundation of Australia
ACT
Health Centre, Phillip, 2606
Tel: (062) 81 6814

ASTHMA
ACT Asthma Association
c/- SHOUT Office, Hughes
Community Centre, Wisdom St,
Hughes, 2605
Tel: (062) 81 2983
(9.30 am–2 pm)

BLINDNESS
Blind Society of the ACT Inc.
Griffin Centre, Bunda St,
Canberra City, 2600
Tel: (062) 47 4580

Royal Blind Society of NSW
6 Kennedy St, Kingston, 2604
Tel: (062) 95 3333

Guide Dog Association of the
ACT
Griffin Centre, Bunda St,
Canberra City, 2600
Tel: (062) 49 8445

BLOOD BANK
Blood Bank
c/- Woden Valley Hospital,
Yamba Dr., Garran, 2605
Tel: (062) 84 2915

CANCER
Cancer Society ACT
Health Promotion Centre,
Childers St, Canberra City,
2600
Tel: (062) 48 0477

Breast Cancer Support Group
c/- Cancer Society (see above)

CEREBRAL PALSY
Cerebral Palsy Association
c/- Spastic Centre of ACT &
Southern District
31 Fitzmourice St, Kaleen,
2617
Tel: (062) 41 5652

CHILDBIRTH & BREASTFEEDING
Australian Multiple Birth
Association
PO Box 15, Scullin, 2614
Tel: (062) 31 9816

Nursing Mothers Association of
Aust.
Tel: (062) 58 8928

Still Births, Miscarriages &
Neo-Natal Death Association

7 McQueen Place, Charnwood,
2615
Tel: (062) 58 6531

COELIAC DISEASE
Coeliac Society of the ACT
34 Tanumberine St, Hawker,
2614
Tel: (062) 54 8457

CONTRACEPTION
See FAMILY PLANNING

COT DEATH
See SUDDEN INFANT DEATH
SYNDROME

CYSTIC FIBROSIS
Cystic Fibrosis Association of
ACT
c/- SHOUT Office, Hughes
Community Centre, Wisdom St,
Hughes, 2605
Tel: (062) 81 2983
(9.30 am–2 pm)

DEAFNESS
Australian Deafness Council
c/- SHOUT Office, Hughes
Community Centre, Wisdom St,
Hughes, 2605
Tel: (062) 81 2983
(9.30 am–2 pm)

DISABLED
Disabled Adults Residential
Establishment
c/- SHOUT Office, Hughes
Community Centre, Wisdom St,
Hughes, 2605
Tel: (062) 81 2983
(9.30 am–2 pm)

DRUG DEPENDENCE
See ALCOHOL & DRUG DEPENDENCE

DYSLEXIA & LEARNING DIFFICULTIES
SPELD (ACT Inc.)
c/- SHOUT Office, Hughes
Community Centre, Wisdom St,
Hughes, 2605
Tel: (062) 81 2983
(9.30 am–2 pm)

FAMILY PLANNING
Family Planning Association
Health Promotion Centre,
Childers St, Canberra City, 2605
Tel: (062) 47 3077

See also SEX EDUCATION, COUNSELLING & HUMAN RELATIONSHIPS

FIRST AID

Red Cross Society, ACT
Hobart Place, Canberra City, 2605
Tel: (062) 47 8675, 47 8514, 47 9524, 47 7026

St John Ambulance Association
Cnr Canberra Ave & Dominion Crt, Forrest, 2603
Tel: (062) 82 2399

GOVERNMENT HEALTH DEPARTMENTS

ACT Health Authority
ACT Health Authority Building, Cnr Moore & Alinga Sts, Canberra City, 2605
Tel: (062) 45 4111

HEARING DISABILITIES
See DEAFNESS

HEART DISEASE

National Heart Foundation (ACT)
51 Northbourne Ave, Canberra City, 2605
Tel: (062) 47 7100

HOMOSEXUALITY

ACT Gay Contact
PO Box 214, Woden, 2606
Tel: (062) 47 2726

Gayline
Kingsley St, Acton, 2601
Tel: (062) 47 2726

INTELLECTUAL DISABILITY
See MENTAL HEALTH & DISABILITY

KIDNEY DISEASE

ACT Renal Group
c/- SHOUT Office, Hughes Community Centre, Wisdom St, Hughes, 2605
Tel: (062) 81 2983
(9.30 am–2 pm)

LEUKAEMIA
See CANCER

MENTAL HEALTH & DISABILITY

Intellectual Handicap Service
Health Centre, Phillip, 2606
Tel: (062) 83 5211

National Association on Intellectual Disability
Block E, Acton House, Edinburgh Ave, Canberra City, 2601
Tel: (062) 47 6022

Schizophrenia Fellowship of ACT
Hughes Commonwealth Centre, Hughes, 2605
Tel: (062) 81 6781

MULTIPLE SCLEROSIS

Multiple Sclerosis Society of the ACT
PO Box 38, Hughes, 2605
Tel: (062) 81 2921

MUSCULAR DYSTROPHY

Muscular Dystrophy Association of Canberra
11 Broadby Close, Spence, 2615
Tel: (062) 58 3891

PARAPLEGIA & QUADRIPLEGIA

Paraplegic & Handicapped Association
Tel: (062) 47 8668

POISONS INFORMATION

Poisons Information Service
Royal Canberra Hospital, Acton, 2601
Tel: (062) 43 2154 (24 hours)

PREGNANCY, ABORTION, CONTRACEPTION

Pregnancy Support Service
Garema Place, Canberra City, 2600
Tel: (062) 47 5050

See also FAMILY PLANNING, SEX EDUCATION, COUNSELLING & HUMAN RELATIONSHIPS

QUADRIPLEGIA
See PARAPLEGIA & QUADRIPLEGIA

RAPE/SEXUAL ASSAULT

Rape Crisis Line
Tel: (062) 47 2525

RHEUMATISM
See ARTHRITIS

SCHIZOPHRENIA
See MENTAL HEALTH & DISABILITY

SEX EDUCATION, COUNSELLING & HUMAN RELATIONSHIPS

Canberra Marriage Counselling Service
Savings House, Petrie Place, Canberra City, 2600
Tel: (062) 48 0530

See also HOMOSEXUALITY, RAPE/SEXUAL ASSAULT

SEXUALLY TRANSMITTED DISEASES

Venereal Disease Telephone Information
Tel: (062) 45 4316

See also AIDS, SEX EDUCATION, COUNSELLING & HUMAN RELATIONSHIPS

SPASTIC
See CEREBRAL PALSY

SUDDEN INFANT DEATH SYNDROME

Sudden Infant Death Association (ACT)
c/- SHOUT Office, Hughes Community Centre, Widsom St, Hughes, 2605
Tel: (062) 81 2983
(9.30 am–2 pm)

VACCINATIONS
(Immunisation and vaccinations for overseas travel) See GOVERNMENT HEALTH DEPARTMENTS

WOMEN'S HEALTH
See CHILDBIRTH & BREASTFEEDING, FAMILY PLANNING, RAPE/SEXUAL ASSAULT

ABORTION

See PREGNANCY, ABORTION, CONTRACEPTION

AGEING

NSW Council on the Ageing
34 Argyle Place, Sydney, 2000
Tel: (02) 27 4857

AIDS

(Acquired Immune Deficiency Syndrome)

Albion Street Centre,
150 Albion St, Surry Hills, 2010
Tel: (02) 332 4000

See also SEXUALLY TRANSMITTED DISEASES

ALCOHOL & DRUG DEPENDENCE

Alcoholism Advisory Telephone Service
591 South Dowling St, Moore Park, 2010
Tel: (02) 33 4532

Alcoholics Anonymous
127 Edwin St, Croydon, 2132
Tel: (02) 799 1199

Al-Anon Family Groups
262 Pitt St, Sydney, 2000
Tel: (02) 264 9255

Alcohol & Drug Information Service
St Vincent's Hospital, Victoria St, Darlinghurst, 2010
Tel: (02) 331 2111 (24 hours)

Bourke Street Drug Advisory Centre
(Sydney Health Service)
703 Bourke St, Surry Hills, 2010
Tel: (02) 698 7688

Drug & Alcohol Coordination Unit
(Northern Metropolitan Area)
8a McIntosh St, Chatswood, 2067
Tel: (02) 411 4099

ALZHEIMER'S DISEASE

Alzheimer's Disease & Related Disorders
PO Box 139,
Ryde, 2002
Tel: (02) 80 3325

ANOREXIA NERVOSA & BULIMIA

Bulimia & Anorexia Nervosa Society (BANS)
PO Box 1398, Crow's Nest, 2065
Tel: (02) 705 5802 (Wed. & Fri.), 438 2871 (Mon.)

ARTHRITIS

Arthritis Foundation of Australia (NSW)
32 York St, Sydney, 2000
Tel: (02) 290 3499

Arthritis Foundation of Australia
411 Wingello House, Angel Place, Sydney, 2000
Tel: (02) 221 2456

ASTHMA

Asthma Foundation of NSW
3rd Floor, 1–12 Angel Place, Sydney, 2000
Tel: (02) 235 1293

AUTISM

Autistic Association of NSW
545 Pacific Hwy, Artarmon, 2064
Tel: (02) 412 4766
Counsellors & Librarian
41 Cook St, Forestville, 2087
Tel: (02) 452 4041

BATTERED BABY SYNDROME

See CHILD ABUSE

BLINDNESS

Braille Library
4 Mitchell St, Enfield, 2136
Tel: (02) 747 6622

Guide Dog Association of NSW,
5 Northcliff St, Milsons Point, 2061
Tel: (02) 922 4211

Royal Blind Society of NSW
4 Mitchell St, Enfield, 2136
Tel: (02) 744 6622

Royal NSW Institute for Deaf & Blind Children
361 North Rocks Rd, North Rocks, 2151
Tel: (02) 871 1233

Sydney Eye Hospital
Sydney Hospital, Sir John Young

Crescent, Woolloomooloo, 2011
Tel: (02) 230 0111

BLOOD BANK

Red Cross Blood Transfusion Service
153 Clarence St, Sydney, 2000
Tel: (02) 290 2555

BULIMIA

See ANOREXIA NERVOSA & BULIMIA

CANCER

Australian Cancer Society
3rd Floor, Angus & Coote Building,
500 George St, Sydney, 2000
Tel: (02) 267 1944

Camp Quality
Camping Programme for Children with Cancer
5 Taylor St, West Pennant Hills, 2120
Tel: (02) 872 5454

Cancer Information & Support Society
1/65 Bay Rd, Waverton, 2060
Tel: (02) 922 2334

Cancer Patients' Assistance Society of NSW
17 Ocean Ave, Double Bay, 2028
Tel: (02) 32 2430

CanTeen
The Australian Teenage Cancer Patients' Society,
PO Box 1000, St Pauls, 2031
Tel: (02) 399 4604

Children's Leukaemia & Cancer Foundation
Prince of Wales Children's Hospital, High St, Randwick, 2031
Tel: (02) 399 2766

Skin & Cancer Foundation of NSW
c/- St Vincent's Medical Centre, 376 Victoria St, Darlinghurst, 2010
Tel: (02) 357 4480

CEREBRAL PALSY

The Spastic Centre of NSW
Medical Treatment & Education Centre, 6 Queen St, Mosman, 2088
Tel: (02) 969 1666

CHILD ABUSE

Camperdown Children's Hospital
Pyrmont Bridge Rd,
Camperdown, 2050
Tel: (02) 519 0466 (24 hours)

Child Abuse Prevention Services
Randwick Community Centre,
33 Bundock St, Randwick, 2031
Tel: (02) 344 5111, 344 7646

CHILDBIRTH & BREASTFEEDING

Australian Multiple Birth
Association
1 Chedley Place, Marayong, 2148
Tel: (02) 621 2424

Childbirth Education Association
of Aust. (NSW) Ltd
127 Forest Rd, Hurstville, 2220
Tel: (02) 57 4927

Nursing Mothers' Association of
Aust.
2 Queens Rd, Asquith, 2078
Tel: (02) 477 5934

CHILDREN

Association for the Welfare of
Children in Hospital
158 Hawkesbury Rd,
Westmead, 2145
Tel: (02) 633 1988, 46 4811
(after hours advisory service)

COELIAC DISEASE

The Coeliac Society
10 Diana Ave, West Pymble,
2073
Tel: (02) 498 2593

COLOSTOMY

Colostomy Rehabilitation
Association of NSW
630 George St, Sydney, 2000
Tel: (02) 264 2741

CONTRACEPTION

See PREGNANCY, ABORTION,
CONTRACEPTION

COT DEATH

See SUDDEN INFANT DEATH
SYNDROME

CYSTIC FIBROSIS

Cystic Fibrosis Association of
NSW
40 Milton St, Ashfield, 2131
Tel: (02) 799 9100

DEAFNESS

See HEARING DISABILITIES

DENTAL CARE

(emergency)

Dental Hospital of Sydney
14 Chalmers St, Sydney, 2000
Tel: (02) 211 4322

Dental Emergency Information
Service
Australian Dental Association
NSW,
332 Pitt St, Sydney, 2000
Tel: (02) 267 5919

DIABETES

Diabetes Australia NSW
250 Pitt St, Sydney, 2000
Tel: (02) 264 6909

Diabetes Education &
Assessment Programme,
74 Herbert St, St Leonards,
2065
Tel: (02) 438 4584

Juvenile Diabetes Foundation
Australia
370 Victoria Ave, Chatswood,
2067
Tel: (02) 411 4087

DISABLED

Community Services for the
Developmentally Disabled
Cnr Belgrave & Railway Pde,
Kogarah, 2217
Tel: (02) 587 2444

Disabled Persons' International
Resource Centre
7 Franklin St, Glebe, 2037
Tel: (02) 552 1411

Handicapped Children's Centre
NSW
PO Box 29, Sutherland, 2232
Tel: (02) 521 2966

See also MENTAL HEALTH &
DISABILITY, MULTIPLE SCLEROSIS,
MUSCULAR DYSTROPHY, PARAPLEGIA
& QUADRIPLEGIA

DOWN'S SYNDROME

Down's Syndrome Association
31 O'Connell St, Parramatta, 2150
Tel: (02) 683 4333

DRUG DEPENDENCE

See ALCHOHOL & DRUG
DEPENDENCE

DYSLEXIA & LEARNING DIFFICULTIES

SPELD (NSW)
16 Coronation Ave, Mosman,
2088
Tel: (02) 969 7433

EPILEPSY

Epilepsy Association of NSW
468 Pennant Hills Rd, Pennant
Hills, 2120
Tel: (02) 875 1855

FAMILY PLANNING

Natural Family Planning Services
Polding House, 276 Pitt St,
Sydney, 2000
Tel: (02) 264 7211

St Vincent's Private Hospital
Victoria St, Darlinghurst, 2010
Tel: (02) 339 1111

St Margaret's Hospital
435 Bourke St, Darlinghurst, 2010
Tel: (02) 339 0466

Family Planning Association of
NSW
161 Broadway, Broadway, 2007
Tel: (02) 211 0244

See also SEX EDUCATION,
COUNSELLING & HUMAN
RELATIONSHIPS, VASECTOMY

FIRST AID

Australian Red Cross Society
159 Clarence St, Sydney, 2000
Tel: (02) 290 2622

St John Ambulance Australia
6 Hunt St, Surry Hills, 2010
Tel: (02) 212 1088

GOVERNMENT HEALTH DEPARTMENTS

Commonwealth Health Dept
Commonwealth Govt Centre,
Chifley Square, Sydney, 2000
Tel: (02) 239 3000

Health Dept of NSW
McKell Building, Rawson Place,
Sydney, 2000
Tel: (02) 217 6666

HAEMOPHILIA

Haemophilia Society of NSW
39 La Boheme Avenue,
Caringbah, 2229
Tel: (02) 524 3540

HEARING DISABILITIES

Adult Deaf Society of NSW
123 Cambridge St, Stanmore,
2048
Tel: (02) 560 6433

Better Hearing Aust. (Sydney)
Limited
288 Unwins Bridge Road,
Sydenham, 2044
Tel: (02) 516 3322

Deaf Education Federation for
Juniors
235 Enmore Rd, Marrickville,
2204
Tel: (02) 550 1066

Hearing Clinics (See NSW
Government Health Dept,
Sydney *White Pages* phone
directory)

National Acoustic Laboratory.
Stockland House,
175 Castlereagh St, Sydney, 2000
Tel: (02) 267 8055

Royal NSW Institute for Deaf &
Blind Children
361 North Rocks Road, North
Rocks, 2151
Tel: (02) 871 1233

HEART DISEASE

Heart Foundation
Cardiac Rehabilitation,
Counselling
Tel: (02) 212 4965

National Heart Foundation of
Aust. (NSW Division)
343 Riley St, Surry Hills, 2010
Tel: (02) 211 5188

HOME NURSING

Home Care Service of NSW
31 Macquarie St, Parramatta,
2150
Tel: (02) 689 2666

Sydney Home Nursing Service
36 Boyce St, Glebe, 2047
Tel: (02) 660 1166

HOMOSEXUALITY

Gay Counselling Service
51 Holt St, Surry Hills, 2010
Tel: (02) 211 1177

Homosexual Acceptance Centre
57 Holt St, Surry Hills, 2010
Tel: (02) 212 5247

HUNTINGTON'S CHOREA

Huntington's Disease
Association
74 Hunter Avenue, St Ives,
2075
Tel: (02) 449 9796

HYPERACTIVITY

Hyperactivity Association
(NSW)
Voluntary Support Service,
29 Bertram St, Chatswood, 2067
Tel: (02) 411 2186

ILEOSTOMY

Ileostomy Association of NSW
Outpatients Department,
Lewisham Hospital,
Lewisham, 2049
Tel: (02) 568 2800

INTELLECTUAL DISABILITY

See MENTAL HEALTH & DISABILITY

KIDNEY DISEASE

The Australian Kidney
Foundation
(basically research organisation)
1 York St, Sydney, 2000
Tel: (02) 27 1436

Sydney Dialysis Centre
'Duntrim', 37 Darling Point Rd,
Darling Point, 2027
Tel: (02) 32 5978

LEUKAEMIA

See CANCER

MASTECTOMY

Mastectomy Rehabilitation
Service
c/- State Cancer Council,
500 George St, Sydney, 2000
Tel: (02) 264 8888

See also CANCER, WOMEN'S HEALTH

MENTAL HEALTH & DISABILITY

Association of Relatives &
Friends of the Mentally Ill
165 Blues Point Rd, McMahons
Point, 2060
Tel: (02) 698 8216

NSW Association for Mental
Health
62 Victoria Rd, Gladesville, 2111
Tel: (02) 816 1611

NSW Council for Intellectual
Disability
4 Doig Avenue, Denistone East,
2112
Tel: (02) 807 1411

Schizophrenia Fellowship of NSW
c/- 8 Dunmore Ave, Carlingford,
2118

MULTIPLE SCLEROSIS

Multiple Sclerosis Society of
NSW
5 Bryson St, Chatswood, 2067
Tel: (02) 412 1577

MUSCULAR DYSTROPHY

Muscular Dystrophy Association
PO Box 10, Strawberry Hills,
2012
Tel: (02) 698 9555
(enquiries, c/- NSW Society for
Crippled Children)

PARAPLEGIA & QUADRIPLEGIA

Paraplegic & Quadriplegic
Association of NSW
33 Burlington Rd, Homebush,
2140
Tel: (02) 764 4166

PARKINSON'S DISEASE

Parkinson's Syndrome Society
Uniting Church, Palmer St,
Parramatta, 2150
Tel: (02) 630 1192

POISONS INFORMATION

Poisons Information Centre
(antidotes)
Royal Alexandra Hospital,
Pyrmont Bridge, Camperdown,
2050
Tel: (02) 519 0466

POLIOMYELITIS

NSW Society for Crippled
Children
Cnr Chalmers & Bedford Sts,
Sydney, 2000
Tel: (02) 698 9555

PREGNANCY, ABORTION, CONTRACEPTION

Bessie Smythe Foundation
Family Planning
80 Wentworth Rd, Homebush,
2140
Tel: (02) 764 4885

Every Woman's Health Centre
164 Flood St, Leichhardt, 2040
Tel: (02) 569 9522

Pregnancy Counselling &
Support Strathfield
56 Mosley St, Strathfield, 2135
Tel: (02) 745 2904

Pre-Term Foundation
50 Cooper St, Surry Hills, 2010
Tel: (02) 699 9211

Population Services
International (A/Asia) Ltd
25 Challis Ave, Potts Point,
2011
Tel: (02) 357 1066

See also FAMILY PLANNING, SEX
EDUCATION, COUNSELLING & HUMAN
RELATIONSHIPS, WOMEN'S HEALTH

QUADRIPLEGIA
See PARAPLEGIA & QUADRIPLEGIA

RAPE/SEXUAL ASSAULT
Rape Crisis Centre
Tel: (02) 819 6565 (24 hours)

Rape/Sexual Assault Clinics can
be found at the following
hospitals:

King George V Memorial
Hospital
Missenden Rd, Camperdown,
2050
Tel: (02) 516 6111

Royal North Shore Hospital
Pacific Hwy, St Leonards, 2065
Tel: (02) 438 7111

St George Hospital
Belgrave St, Kogarah, 2217
Tel: (02) 588 1111

Prince of Wales Children's
Hospital
High St, Randwick, 2031
Tel: (02) 399 0111

RHEUMATISM
See ARTHRITIS

SCHIZOPHRENIA
See MENTAL HEALTH & DISABILITY

SEX EDUCATION, COUNSELLING & HUMAN RELATIONSHIPS
Family Planning Association of
NSW
161 Broadway, Broadway, 2007
Tel: (02) 211 0244

Sex Education & Family Life
Family Life Movement of
Australia,
16 Jersey Road, Strathfield, 2135
Tel: (02) 745 1288

Sex Information Help Line
Tel: (02) 389 0469

Marriage Guidance Council of
NSW
226 Liverpool Rd, Enfield, 2136
Tel: (02) 745 4411

See also HOMOSEXUALITY,
RAPE/SEXUAL ASSAULT

SEXUALLY TRANSMITTED DISEASES
Sexually Transmitted Diseases
Clinic
Nightingale Centre, Sydney
Hospital, Macquarie St,
Sydney, 2000
Tel: (02) 27 4851

See also AIDS, SEX EDUCATION,
COUNSELLING & HUMAN RELATIONSHIPS

SPASTIC
See CEREBRAL PALSY

SPINA BIFIDA
Spina Bifida Association of NSW
Shop 2–3, 14–20 Station Street,
Harris Park, 2150
Tel: (02) 633 1311

SUDDEN INFANT DEATH SYNDROME
Sudden Infant Death Association
(SIDA)

c/- 36 Toolang Rd, St Ives, 2075
Tel: (02) 44 6128, 982 3915

TUBERCULOSIS
Anti-Tuberculosis Association of
NSW
169 Albion St, Surry Hills, 2010
Tel: (02) 331 4113

VACCINATIONS
(Immunisation and vaccination
for overseas travel) See
GOVERNMENT HEALTH
DEPARTMENTS – Commonwealth

VASECTOMY
Vasectomy Medical & Research
Centre
11a Howard St, Randwick, 2031
Tel: (02) 399 3900

Family Planning Association
Vasectomy Clinic, 92 City Rd,
Chippendale, 2008
Tel: (02) 698 9499

WOMEN'S HEALTH
Royal Hospital for Women
188 Oxford St, Paddington,
2021
Tel: (02) 339 4111

Clinic – St Andrew's House,
Sydney Square, Sydney, 2000
Tel: (02) 264 7388, 267 5274

King George V Breast Clinic
Missenden Rd, Camperdown,
2050
Tel: (02) 516 6111

Rachel Forster Hospital Breast
Clinic
150 Pitt St, Redfern, 2016
Tel: (02) 699 3222

Women's Health Centres
See Health Dept of NSW for
centres in your district

See also CHILDBIRTH &
BREASTFEEDING, FAMILY PLANNING,
MASTECTOMY, RAPE/SEXUAL
ASSAULT

ABORTION
See PREGNANCY, ABORTION, CONTRACEPTION

AIDS
(Acquired Immune Deficiency Syndrome)

NT AIDS Clinical Advisory Group
Royal Darwin Hospital,
Rocklands Drive, Tiwi, 5792
Tel: (089) 20 7211

See also SEXUALLY TRANSMITTED DISEASES

ALCOHOL & DRUG DEPENDENCE

Alcoholics Anonymous
2 Water St, Northcliffe, 5790
Tel: (089) 85 4479

Banyan House
2 Fay Court, Rapid Creek, 5792
Tel: (089) 85 2479

Darwin & Districts Alcohol & Drug Dependence Foundation Inc.
155 Stuart Hwy, Parap, 5790
Tel: (089) 81 8030

NT Drug & Alcohol Bureau
79 Smith St, Darwin, 5790
Tel: (089) 80 2911

BLINDESS

NT Association for the Blind & Visually Impaired
53 Ross Smith Ave, Parap, 5790
Tel: (089) 81 7579

Guide Dogs for the Blind Association
(as above)

BLOOD BANK

Red Cross Society
19 Lambell Terrace,
Larrakeyah, 5790
Tel: (089) 41 1555

CANCER

NT Anti-Cancer Foundation
15 Peel St, Darwin, 5790
Tel: (089) 81 3556

CHILDBIRTH & BREASTFEEDING

Childbirth Education Association
Trower Rd, Casuarina, 5792
Tel: (089) 27 2575

Nursing Mothers' Association
6 Woolwonga Court, Anula,
5793
Tel: (089) 27 9461

CONTRACEPTION
See FAMILY PLANNING

DEAFNESS

Deafness Association of the NT
Rapid Creek, Darwin, 5790
Tel: (089) 85 1762

DENTAL CARE
(emergency)

Dental Clinic
48 Mitchell St, Darwin 5790
Tel: (089) 81 9688

DISABLED

The Disabled Persons Bureau
Cnr Trower Rd & Banderlin
Drive, Casuarina, 5792
Tel: (089) 20 3213

Handicapped Persons Association
Albatross St, Winnellie, 5789
Tel: (089) 84 3206

DOWN'S SYNDROME

Down's Syndrome Association
10 Witherden St, Nakara, 5792
Tel: (089) 27 9408

DRUG DEPENDENCE
See ALCOHOL & DRUG DEPENDENCE

FAMILY PLANNING

Family Planning Association, NT
133 Mitchell St, Larrakeyah,
5790
Tel: (089) 81 5335

Natural Family Planning Association
Tel: (089) 85 1540

See also PREGNANCY, ABORTION, CONTRACEPTION

FIRST AID

Red Cross Society
19 Lambell Terrace,
Larrakeyah, 5790
Tel: (089) 81 4499

St John Ambulance Association
PO Box 40221, Casuarina, 5792
Tel: (089) 27 9111
(headquarters);
27 9000 (ambulance)

GOVERNMENT HEALTH DEPARTMENTS

Commonwealth Dept of Health
MLC Building, 81 Smith St,
Darwin, 5790
Tel: (089) 80 2911

Health Dept of NT
Darwin Central Office,
The Mall, Darwin, 5790
Tel: (089) 80 2911, 80 2753

HEARING DISABILITIES
See DEAFNESS

HEART DISEASE

National Heart Foundation
Cavanagh St, Fannie Bay, 5790
Tel: (089) 81 1966

KIDNEY DISEASE

Renal Dialysis Unit
Nightcliffe Community Health
Centre, Darwin, 5790
Tel: (089) 85 3876

LEUKAEMIA
See CANCER

MULTIPLE SCLEROSIS

Multiple Sclerosis Society of SA & NT
Tel: (089) 27 1744

POISONS INFORMATION

Poisons Information Centre
(antidotes)
Rocklands Drive, Tiwi, 5792
Tel: (089) 27 4777

PREGNANCY, ABORTION, CONTRACEPTION

Pregnancy Help
90 Smith St, Darwin, 5790
Tel: (089) 81 8526

See also FAMILY PLANNING, WOMEN'S HEALTH

RAPE/SEXUAL ASSAULT

Rape Crisis Centre
Garden Hill Crescent, Darwin,
5790
Tel: (089) 81 4454

Royal Darwin Hospital
Tel: (089) 20 7211

SEXUALLY TRANSMITTED DISEASES

Venereal Disease Information Service

Peel St, Darwin, 5790
Tel: (089) 81 5460;
20 7211 (AH)
See also AIDS

VACCINATIONS
(Immunisation and vaccination
for overseas travel) See

GOVERNMENT HEALTH
DEPARTMENTS – Commonwealth

VASECTOMY
See FAMILY PLANNING

WOMEN'S HEALTH
Women's Information Centre

Tel: (089) 27 7166

See also CHILDBIRTH &
BREASTFEEDING,
FAMILY PLANNING,
RAPE/SEXUAL ASSAULT

ABORTION
See PREGNANCY, ABORTION, CONTRACEPTION

AGEING
Qld Council on the Ageing
Empire House, 1 Walsh St,
Brisbane, 4000
Tel: (07) 832 2262

AIDS
(Acquired Immune Deficiency Syndrome)
See SEXUALLY TRANSMITTED DISEASES

ALCOHOL & DRUG DEPENDENCE
Alcoholics Anonymous
453 Ann St, Brisbane, 4000
Tel: (07) 221 7920

Al-Anon Family Groups
308 Edward St, Brisbane, 4000
Tel: (07) 229 2501 (24 hours)

Alcohol & Drug Dependence
Services
Information & Counselling
Tel: (07) 229 6566 (24 hours)

Alcohol & Drug Foundation
119 Leichhardt St, Spring Hill,
4004
Tel: (07) 832 3798

ALZHEIMER'S DISEASE
ADARDA Qld Inc.
GPO Box 2188, Brisbane, 4001
Tel: (07) 846 2676

ARTHRITIS
Arthritis Foundation
Coronation Drive,
Auchenflower, 4066
Tel: (07) 371 9755

ASTHMA
Asthma Foundation of Qld
PO Box 227, Broadway, 4006
Tel: (07) 356 9699

AUTISM
Autistic Children's Association
of Qld
437 Hellawell Rd, Sunnybank
Hills 4109
Tel: (07) 273 2222

BATTERED BABY SYNDROME
See CHILD ABUSE

BLINDNESS
Guide Dogs for the Blind
Association of Qld
139 Wharf St, Brisbane, 4000
Tel: (07) 831 2500

Lady Nell Seeing Eye Dogs
10 Cronin St, Annerley, 4103
Tel: (07) 391 5271

Qld Society of Blind Citizens
247 Vulture St, Sth Brisbane,
4101
Tel: (07) 844 4111

BLOOD BANK
Red Cross Society
Blood Transfusion Service,
409 Adelaide St, Brisbane, 4000
Tel: (07) 832 2541

CANCER
Cancer Society & Children's
Leukaemia
24 Rennie St, Indooroopilly,
4068
Tel: (07) 870 2731

Qld Cancer Fund
50 Water St, Spring Hill, 4004
Tel: (07) 839 7077

CEREBRAL PALSY
Qld Spastic Welfare League
Spastic Centre, 55 Oxlade
Drive, New Farm, 4005
Tel: (07) 358 3011

CHILD ABUSE
Department of Family & Youth
Services,
PO Box 339, North Quay, 4002
Tel: (07) 227 7111

CHILDBIRTH & BREASTFEEDING
Nursing Mothers' Association
Ross St, Northgate, 4013
Tel: (07) 266 3119

CHILDREN
Royal Children's Hospital
Herston Rd, Herston, 4006
Tel: (07) 253 8111

COLOSTOMY
See ILEOSTOMY

CONTRACEPTION
See FAMILY PLANNING

COT DEATH
See SUDDEN INFANT DEATH SYNDROME

CYSTIC FIBROSIS
Cystic Fibrosis Association of
Qld Ltd
32 School St, Kelvin Grove, 4059
Tel: (07) 352 6322

DEAFNESS
See HEARING DISABILITIES

DENTAL CARE
(emergency)
Dentists' Emergency Service
131 Elizabeth St, Brisbane, 4000
Tel: (07) 221 8957 (24 hours)

DIABETES
Diabetic Association of Qld
Cnr Albert & Elizabeth Sts,
Brisbane, 4000
Tel: (07) 229 1986

DISABLED
Disabled Persons' Service
'Mawarra', 50 Albert St,
Brisbane, 4000
Tel: (07) 224 5411,
(008) 17 7120 (toll free)

See also MENTAL HEALTH &
DISABILITY, MULTIPLE SCLEROSIS,
PARAPLEGIA & QUADRIPLEGIA

DOWN'S SYNDROME
Down's Syndrome Association
101 Highgate St, Cooper Plains,
4108
Tel: (07) 275 1947

DRUG DEPENDENCE
See ALCOHOL & DRUG DEPENDENCE

DYSLEXIA & LEARNING DIFFICULTIES
SPELD (Qld)
27 McDougall St, Milton, 4064
Tel: (07) 369 6100

EPILEPSY
Epilepsy Association of Qld
Penney's Building, 210 Queen
St, Brisbane, 4000
Tel: (07) 229 3606

FAMILY PLANNING
Family Planning Association of
Qld

100 Alfred St, Fortitude Valley,
4006
Tel: (07) 52 5151

Natural Family Planning Clinic
(Catholic)
Morgan St, Fortitude Valley,
4006
Tel: (07) 52 8585

See also SEX EDUCATION,
COUNSELLING & HUMAN
RELATIONSHIPS

FIRST AID

Red Cross Society
393–409 Adelaide St, Brisbane,
4000
Tel: (07) 832 2551

St John Ambulance Association
& Council
St John House, 225 St Paul's
Terrace, Fortitude Valley, 4006
Tel: (07) 52 2092;
52 3450 (ambulance)

GOVERNMENT HEALTH DEPARTMENTS

Commonwealth Dept of Health
232 Adelaide St, Brisbane, 4000
Tel: (07) 225 0122

Qld Government Health Dept
State Health Building, Charlotte
St, Brisbane, 4000
Tel: (07) 227 7111

HEARING DISABILITIES

Better Hearing Aust. (Brisbane
Branch), 51 Edmondstone St,
South Brisbane, 4101
Tel: (07) 844 5065

Qld Deaf Society
34 Davidson St, Newmarket,
4051
Tel: (07) 356 8255

HEART DISEASE

National Heart Foundation of
Australia
557 Gregory Tce, Fortitude
Valley, 4006
Tel: (07) 854 1696

HOME NURSING

St Luke's Nursing Service
District Nursing Association,
Cnr Hale St & Milton Rd,
Brisbane, 4000
Tel: (07) 369 7700

HOMOSEXUALITY

Homosexual Counselling &
Welfare Service
Brunswick St, Fortitude Valley,
4006
Tel: (07) 852 1414

Homosexual Information &
Advice Service – Gayline
379 George St, Brisbane, 4000
Tel: (07) 221 9373

HUNTINGTON'S CHOREA

Huntington's Disease
Association (Qld)
12 Lucy St, Moorooka, 4105
Tel: (07) 848 2802

HYPERACTIVITY

Hyperactivity Association (Qld)
480 Ipswich Rd, Annerley, 4103
Tel: (07) 848 2321

ILEOSTOMY

Ileostomy Association
62 Newmarket Rd, Windsor,
4030
Tel: (07) 357 7570

INTELLECTUAL DISABILITY

See MENTAL HEALTH & DISABILITY

KIDNEY DISEASE

The Australian Kidney
Foundation
416 Queen St, Brisbane, 4000
Tel: (07) 831 0530

LEUKAEMIA

See CANCER

MASTECTOMY

Mastectomy Rehabilitation
Service
Arthur Cooper Hospital
18 Whyenbah St, Hamilton, 4007
Tel: (07) 268 4322

See also CANCER

MENTAL HEALTH & DISABILITY

GROW (Qld) Community Mental
Health
43 Crown St, Holland Park,
4121
Tel: (07) 394 4344

Schizophrenia Fellowship of
South Queensland

Box 1567, GPO Queen St,
Brisbane, 4001

MULTIPLE SCLEROSIS

Multiple Sclerosis Society of Qld
286 Gladstone Rd, Dutton Park,
4102
Tel: (07) 844 6801

PARAPLEGIA & QUADRIPLEGIA

Paraplegic Welfare Association
of Qld
Horan St, West End, 4101
Tel: (07) 844 7311

POISONS INFORMATION

Poisons Information Centre
(Antidotes)
Royal Children's Hospital,
Herston Rd, Herston, 4006
Tel: (07) 253 8233 (24 hours)

PREGNANCY, ABORTION, CONTRACEPTION

See FAMILY PLANNING, SEX
EDUCATION, COUNSELLING & HUMAN
RELATIONS, WOMEN'S HEALTH

QUADRIPLEGIA

See PARAPLEGIA & QUADRIPLEGIA

RAPE/SEXUAL ASSAULT

Rape Crisis Centre
Tel: (07) 844 4008 (24 hours)

RHEUMATISM

See ARTHRITIS

SCHIZOPHRENIA

See MENTAL HEALTH & DISABILITY

SEX EDUCATION, COUNSELLING & HUMAN RELATIONSHIPS

Marriage Guidance Council
159 St Paul's Terrace,
Brisbane, 4000
Tel: (07) 831 2005 (regional &
suburban offices)

See also HOMOSEXUALITY,
RAPE/SEXUAL ASSAULT

SEXUALLY TRANSMITTED DISEASES

Venereal Disease Clinics
484 Adelaide St, Brisbane,
4000
Tel: (07) 227 7091 (male);
227 7095 (female)

See also AIDS

SPASTIC

See CEREBRAL PLASY

SPINA BIFIDA

Spina Bifida Association of Qld
387 Old Cleveland Rd,
Coorparoo, 4151
Tel: (07) 394 3822

SUDDEN INFANT DEATH SYNDROME

Queensland Sudden Infant Death
Research Foundation
GPO Box 1987, Brisbane, 4001
Tel: (07) 224 7390

VACCINATIONS

(Immunisation and vaccination
for overseas travel) See
GOVERNMENT HEALTH
DEPARTMENTS – Commonwealth

VASECTOMY

See FAMILY PLANNING

WOMEN'S HEALTH

Women's Information Service
Department of the Prime
Minister, 280 Adelaide St,
Brisbane, 4000
Tel: (07) 229 1580

Women's Health Centre
86 Stephens Rd,
Highgate Hill,
4101
Tel: (07) 844 1944

Royal Women's (Maternity)
Hospital
Bowen Bridge Road, Herston,
4029
Tel: (07) 253 8111

See also CHILDBIRTH &
BREASTFEEDING, FAMILY PLANNING,
MASTECTOMY, RAPE/SEXUAL
ASSAULT

ABORTION
See PREGNANCY, ABORTION, CONTRACEPTION

AGEING
SA Council for the Ageing
23 Coglin St, Adelaide, 5000
Tel: (08) 212 2057

AIDS
(Acquired Immune Deficiency Syndrome)

Sexually Transmitted Disease Services
275 North Terrace, Adelaide, 5000
Tel: (08) 218 3668

See also SEXUALLY TRANSMITTED DISEASES

ALCOHOL & DRUG DEPENDENCE
Alchoholics Anonymous
AA House, 11 Rundle St, Kent Town, 5067
Tel: (08) 42 2977

Al-Anon/Alateen Family Groups
First Floor, 31 Gilbert Place, Adelaide, 5000
Tel: (08) 51 2959

Alcohol & Drug Foundation (SA)
33 Pirie St, Adelaide, 5000
Tel: (08) 231 0822

Drug & Alcohol Service Council (DASC)
3/161 Greenhill Rd, Parkside, 5063
(outpatient clinics throughout the state)
Tel: (08) 274 3333

Narcotics Anonymous
PO Box 479, Norwood, 5067
Tel: (08) 223 7228

ALZHEIMER'S DISEASE
ADARDS SA Inc.
PO Box 202, Eastwood, 5063
Tel: (08) 274 1684

ANOREXIA NERVOSA & BULIMIA
Anorexia Bulimia/Nervosa Aid (ABNA)
c/- Mental Health Resource Centre, 35 Fullarton Rd, Kent Town, 5068
Tel: (08) 42 6772

ARTHRITIS
Arthritis Foundation of Aust. (SA Inc.)
99 Anzac Highway, Ashford, 5035
Tel: (08) 297 2488

ASTHMA
The Asthma Foundation of SA
33 Pirie St, Adelaide, 5000
Tel: (08) 51 4272

AUTISM
Autistic Children's Association of SA Inc.
3 Fisher St, Myrtle Bank, 5064
Tel: (08) 79 6976

BATTERED BABY SYNDROME
See CHILD ABUSE

BLINDNESS
Blind Welfare Association of SA
84 Archer St, North Adelaide, 5006
Tel: (08) 267 3333

Guide Dogs for the Blind Association of SA & NT
250 Flinders St, Adelaide, 5000
Tel: (08) 223 1413

Royal Society for the Blind of SA
Blacks Rd, Gilles Plains, 5086
(includes Braille & Talking Book Library)
Tel: (08) 261 4611

BLOOD BANK
Red Cross Blood Bank
301 Pirie St, Adelaide, 5000
Tel: (08) 223 1333

BULIMIA
See ANOREXIA NERVOSA & BULIMIA

CANCER
Anti-Cancer Foundation
24 Brougham Place, North Adelaide, 5006
Tel: (08) 267 5222

Cancer Care & Resource Centre
Cnr Sussex Tce & Monmouth Rd, Westbourne Park, 5041
Tel: (08) 272 2014

Cancer Support Fellowship
43 Franklin St, Adelaide, 5000
Tel: (08) 212 2599

CEREBRAL PALSY
Cerebral Palsy Self-Help Group of SA
c/- 1-3 Old Treasury Lane, Adelaide, 5000
Tel: (08) 232 0407

CHILD ABUSE
Adelaide Children's Hospital
King William Rd, North Adelaide, 5006
Tel: (08) 267 7000

CHILDBIRTH & BREASTFEEDING
Childbirth Education Association, Adelaide (Inc.)
1140a South Rd, Clovelly Park, 5042
Tel: (08) 276 9810

Nursing Mothers' Association of Australia (SA)
c/- 11 Oliver St, Crafers, 5152
Tel: (08) 339 6783, 332 4094

CHILDREN
Adelaide Children's Hospital
King William Rd, North Adelaide, 5006
Tel: (08) 267 7000

COELIAC DISEASE
Coeliac Society of SA
176 Port Rd, Hindmarsh, 5007
Tel: (08) 46 3114

COLOSTOMY
Colostomy Association of SA
Adelaide Hospital, North Terrace, Adelaide, 5000
Tel: (08) 223 3338, 278 1327

CONTRACEPTION
See PREGNANCY, ABORTION, CONTRACEPTION

COT DEATH
See SUDDEN INFANT DEATH SYNDROME

CYSTIC FIBROSIS
Cystic Fibrosis Association of SA (Inc.)
GPO Box 1914, Adelaide, 5000
Tel: (08) 332 3635

DEAFNESS
See HEARING DISABILITIES

DENTAL CARE

Adelaide Dental Hospital
Frome Rd, Adelaide, 5000
Tel: (08) 223 9211

Emergency Dental Care
Tel: (08) 79 7878

DIABETES

The Diabetic Association of SA
Eleanor Harrald Building,
Frome Rd, Adelaide, 5000
Tel: (08) 223 7848

Diabetic Education Centre
Ashford Community Hospital,
18 Alexander Avenue, Ashford,
5035
Tel: (08) 297 1777

DISABLED

Disability Information &
Resource Centre
195 Gilles St, Adelaide, 5000
Tel: (08) 223 7522

Disabled People's International
SA Branch:
Rose Terrace, Thebarton, 5031
Tel: (08) 227 0088
National Office: 208 Wattle St,
Unley, 5061
Tel: (08) 271 8483

The Independent Living Centre
180 Daws Rd, Daws Park, 5041
Tel: (08) 276 3455

See also MENTAL HEALTH &
DISABILITY, MULTIPLE SCLEROSIS,
MUSCULAR DYSTROPHY, PARAPLEGIA
& QUADRIPLEGIA

DOWN'S SYNDROME

Down's Children
PO Box 65, Burnside, 5066
Tel: (08) 275 5326

DRUG DEPENDENCE

See ALCOHOL & DRUG DEPENDENCE

DYSLEXIA & LEARNING DIFFICULTIES

SPELD (SA)
298 Portrush Rd, Kensington,
5068
Tel: (08) 31 1655

EPILEPSY

Epilepsy Association of SA
471 Regency Rd, Prospect, 5082
Tel: (08) 269 3511

FAMILY PLANNING

Catholic Family Planning Centre
33 Wakefield St, Adelaide, 5000
Tel: (08) 223 6313

Family Planning Association of
SA Inc.
17 Phillips St, Kensington, 5068
Tel: (08) 31 5177

Queen Victoria Hospital
Family Planning Clinic
160 Fullarton Rd, Rose Park,
5067
Tel: (08) 332 4888

See also SEX EDUCATION,
COUNSELLING & HUMAN
RELATIONSHIPS

FIRST AID

Australian Red Cross Society
211 Childers St, North
Adelaide, 5006
Tel: (08) 267 4277

St John Council for SA Inc.
216 Greenhill Rd, Eastwood,
5063
Tel: (08) 274 0281

GOVERNMENT HEALTH DEPARTMENTS

Commonwealth Govt Health
Dept
33 King William St, Adelaide,
5000
Tel: (08) 216 3911

Health Commission of SA
52 Pirie St, Adelaide, 5000
Tel: (08) 218 3211

Health Hotline
Tel: (08) 1 1644

Patient Information & Advisory
Service
Tel: (08) 218 3555,
(008) 218 8115 (toll free)

HAEMOPHILIA

Haemophilia Society of SA Inc.
PO Box 146, Rundle Mall,
Adelaide, 5000
Tel: (08) 228 5038,
298 1472 (AH)

HEARING DISABILITIES

Hearing Advisory Centre
Better Hearing Australia,
139 Franklin St, Adelaide, 5000
Tel: (08) 51 2996

National Acoustic Laboratories
Adelaide Hearing Centre,
33 King William St, Adelaide,
5000
Tel: (08) 216 3911

Royal South Australian Deaf
Society
262 South Terrace, Adelaide,
5000
Tel: (08) 223 3335

HEART DISEASE

Heartbeat Inc.
Tel: (08) 49 1883

National Heart Foundation
(SA Inc.)
155–159 Hutt St, Adelaide,
5000
Tel: (08) 223 3144

HOME NURSING

Royal District Nursing Society
of SA
139 Kensington Rd, Norwood,
5067
Tel: (08) 332 6444

HOMOSEXUALITY

Gay Counselling Service Inc.
Tel: (08) 268 4675, 268 5577

HUNTINGTON'S CHOREA

South Australian Huntington's
Disease Association
14 Shepard St, Hove, 5048
Tel: (08) 296 6781, 337 4339

HYPERACTIVITY

Hyperactivity Association of SA
Inc.
18 King William Rd, North
Adelaide, 5006
Tel: (08) 267 5551

ILEOSTOMY

Ileostomy Association of SA Inc.
Memorial Hospital, Pennington
Terrace, North Adelaide, 5006
Tel: (08) 267 3200

INTELLECTUAL DISABILITY

See MENTAL HEALTH & DISABILITY

KIDNEY DISEASE

Kidney Foundation SA Branch,
124 Waymouth St, Adelaide, 5000
Tel: (08) 210 1212

LEUKAEMIA
See CANCER

MASTECTOMY

Mastectomy Rehabilitation
c/- Anti-Cancer Foundation,
24 Brougham Place, North
Adelaide, 5006
Tel: (08) 267 5222

See also CANCER, WOMEN'S HEALTH

MENTAL HEALTH & DISABILITY

Australian Association for the
Mentally Retarded
1 Finniss St, North Adelaide,
5006
Tel: (08) 239 0179

Association of Relatives &
Friends of the Mentally Ill
35 Fullarton Rd, Kent Town,
5067
Tel: (08) 42 6772

Schizophrenia Fellowship of
South Australia,
223a Hutt St, Adelaide, 5000
Tel: (08) 224 0414

MULTIPLE SCLEROSIS

Multiple Sclerosis Society of SA
& NT
274 North East Rd, Klemzig,
5087
Tel: (08) 266 2311

MUSCULAR DYSTROPHY

Muscular Dystrophy Association
of SA
251 Morphett St, Adelaide,
5000
Tel: (08) 212 6694

PARAPLEGIA & QUADRIPLEGIA

Paraplegic & Quadriplegic
Association of SA Inc.
211 Portrush Rd, Maylands,
5069
Tel: (08) 364 0555

Wheelchair Sports Association
of SA Inc.
PO Box 144, Greenacres, 5086
Tel: (08) 349 6366

PARKINSON'S DISEASE

Parkinson's Syndrome Society
of SA

150 Young St, Parkside, 5063
Tel: (08) 274 1944

POISONS INFORMATION

Poisons Information Centre
Adelaide Children's Hospital,
King William Rd, North
Adelaide, 5006
Tel: (08) 267 7000

POLIOMYELITIS

Poliomyelitis Welfare
Association Inc.
42 Nelson St, Stepney, 5069
Tel: (08) 363 0355

PREGNANCY, ABORTION, CONTRACEPTION

Pregnancy Support
597 South Rd, Everard Park,
5035
Tel: (08) 297 4422

See also FAMILY PLANNING, SEX
EDUCATION, COUNSELLING & HUMAN
RELATIONSHIPS, WOMEN'S HEALTH

QUADRIPLEGIA
See PARAPLEGIA & QUADRIPLEGIA

RAPE/SEXUAL ASSAULT

Rape Crisis Centre
PO Box 903, Norwood, 5067
Tel: (08) 363 0233

Sexual Assault Referral Centre
Queen Elizabeth Hospital,
Woodville Rd, Woodville South,
5011
Tel: (08) 45 0222

RHEUMATISM
See ARTHRITIS

SEX EDUCATION, COUNSELLING & HUMAN RELATIONSHIPS

Centre of Personal Encounter
Inc. (COPE)
116 Hutt St, Adelaide, 5000
Tel: (08) 223 3433

Marriage Counselling Service
Adelaide Central Mission,
Pitt St, Adelaide, 5000
Tel: (08) 212 2599

Marriage Guidance Council of
SA
55 Hutt St, Adelaide, 5000
Tel: (08) 223 4566

See also HOMOSEXUALITY,
RAPE/SEXUAL ASSAULT

SEXUALLY TRANSMITTED DISEASES

Sexually Transmitted Disease
Services
275 North Terrace, Adelaide, 5000
Tel: (08) 224 5246

See also AIDS, SEX EDUCATION,
COUNSELLING &
HUMAN RELATIONSHIPS

SPASTIC
See CEREBRAL PALSY

SPINA BIFIDA

Spina Bifida Association of SA Inc.
GPO Box 349, Adelaide SA, 5000
Tel: (08) 337 4066

SUDDEN INFANT DEATH SYNDROME

Sudden Infant Death Syndrome
Association of SA
301 Payneham Rd, Royston
Park, 5070
Tel: (08) 363 1963

TUBERCULOSIS

Tuberculosis Services
Government Health Dept,
275 North Terrace, Adelaide,
5000
Tel: (08) 223 0230

VACCINATIONS
(Immunisation and vaccinations
for overseas travel) See
GOVERNMENT HEALTH
DEPARTMENTS – Commonwealth

VASECTOMY
See FAMILY PLANNING

WOMEN'S HEALTH

Adelaide Women's Community
Health Centre Inc.
64 Pennington Terrace, North
Adelaide, 5006
Tel: (08) 267 5366

Queen Victoria Hospital
160 Fullarton Rd, Rose Park,
5067
Tel: (08) 332 4888

See also CHILDBIRTH &
BREASTFEEDING, FAMILY PLANNING,
MASTECTOMY, RAPE/SEXUAL
ASSAULT

ABORTION
See PREGNANCY, ABORTION, CONTRACEPTION

AGEING
Tasmanian Council on the Ageing
Cnr St John's Avenue & New Town Rd, New Town, Hobart, 7008
Tel: (002) 28 1897

AIDS
(Acquired Immune Deficiency Syndrome)

AIDS – Information & Counselling
Tel: (008) 005 188 (toll free)

See also SEXUALLY TRANSMITTED DISEASES

ALCOHOL & DRUG DEPENDENCE
Alcoholics Anonymous
Tel: (002) 34 8711

Al-Anon Family Groups
Tel: (002) 23 4244

Alcoholics & Drug Dependency Services
John Edis Hospital, Creek Rd, New Town, 7008
Tel: (002) 28 8220

Alcohol & Drug Foundation
John Edis Hospital, Creek Rd, New Town, 7008
Tel: (002) 28 8256

ALZHEIMER'S DISEASE
ADARDS Tasmania
GPO Box 1606, Hobart, 7001
Tel: (002) 28 1897

ARTHRITIS
See RHEUMATISM

ASTHMA
Asthma Foundation of Tas.
82 Hampden Rd, Battery Point, 7000
Tel: (002) 23 7725

BLINDNESS
Royal Guide Dogs for the Blind
Cnr Argyle & Lewis Sts, North Hobart, 7002
Tel: (002) 34 4666

Royal Tasmanian Society for the Blind & Deaf
Argyle St, North Hobart, 7002
Tel: (002) 34 3076

Vision Hotline
Tel: (008) 13 5811 (toll free)

BLOOD BANK
Red Cross Society
Blood Transfusion Service,
53 Collins St, Hobart, 7000
Tel: (002) 34 6143

CANCER
Tasmanian Cancer Committee
43 Collins St, Hobart, 7000
Tel: (002) 34 2866

CEREBRAL PALSY
Tasmanian Spastics Association
47 Sandy Bay Rd, Sandy Bay, 7005
Tel: (002) 31 0466

CHILDBIRTH & BREASTFEEDING
Childbirth Education Association
212 Roslyn Ave, Blackman's Bay, 7152
Tel: (002) 29 5211

Nursing Mothers' Association of Australia
Tel: (002) 48 6738 (counselling); 29 5461 (enquiries)

COLOSTOMY
See ILEOSTOMY

CONTRACEPTION
See FAMILY PLANNING

COT DEATH
See SUDDEN INFANT DEATH SYNDROME

DEAFNESS
See BLINDNESS – Tasmanian Society for the Blind & Deaf

DIABETES
Australian Diabetes Foundation
65 Davey St, Hobart, 7000
Tel: (002) 34 5223

DISABLED
Action Group for Children with Disabilities
Community House,

Hampden Rd, Battery Point, 7000
Tel: (002) 23 7841

Australian Council for Rehabilitation of the Disabled
Community House,
Hampden Rd, Battery Point, 7000
Tel: (002) 23 6086

Tasmanian Association of Disabled Persons
20 Creek Rd, Lenah Valley, 7008
Tel: (002) 28 3164

See also MENTAL HEALTH & DISABILITY, MULTIPLE SCLEROSIS

DRUG DEPENDENCE
See ALCOHOL & DRUG DEPENDENCE

DYSLEXIA & LEARNING DIFFICULTIES
SPELD (Tas.)
370 Argyle St, Hobart, 7000
Tel: (002) 34 8489

EPILEPSY
Epilepsy Association of Tas.
86 Hampden Rd, Battery Point, 7000
Tel: (002) 34 6967

FAMILY PLANNING
Family Planning Association of Tas.
73 Federal St, North Hobart, 7002
Tel: (002) 34 7200

Family Planning (Natural)
CentaCare, 23 Stoke St, New Town, 7008
Tel: (002) 23 1000

See also SEX EDUCATION, COUNSELLING & HUMAN RELATIONSHIPS

FIRST AID
Red Cross Society
53 Collins St, Hobart, 7000
Tel: (002) 34 3477

St John Ambulance
Campbell St, Hobart, 7000
Tel: (002) 34 8299;
34 3131 (ambulance)

GOVERNMENT HEALTH DEPARTMENTS

Commonwealth Govt Health Dept
Kirksway House, 2 Kirksway Place, Battery Point, 7000
Tel: (002) 20 5011

Government of Tasmania Health Dept
34 Davey St, Hobart, 7000
Tel: (002) 30 8022

HEART DISEASE

National Heart Foundation of Aust. (Tas.)
86 Hampden Rd, Battery Point, 7000
Tel: (002) 34 5330, 34 5199

HOME NURSING

District Nursing Service
1 St John's Ave, New Town, 7008
Tel: (002) 28 1320, 28 7377

ILEOSTOMY

Ileostomy/Colostomy Association Tasmania
PO Box 415, Sandy Bay, 7005
Tel: (002) 23 2974

INTELLECTUAL DISABILITY

See MENTAL HEALTH & DISABILITY

KIDNEY DISEASE

Australian Kidney Foundation
65 Murray St, Hobart, 7000
Tel: (002) 34 4325

LEUKAEMIA

See CANCER

MENTAL HEALTH & DISABILITY

Retarded Citizens' Welfare Association
11–13 Morrison St, Hobart, 7000
Tel: (002) 23 6644

GROW (mental health support group)
82 Hampden Rd, Battery Point, 7000
Tel: (002) 23 6284

MULTIPLE SCLEROSIS

Multiple Sclerosis Society of Tas.
90 Letitia St, North Hobart, 7002
Tel: (002) 34 5305

PARKINSON'S DISEASE

Parkinson's Disease Association of Tas.
82 Hampden Rd, Battery Point, 7000
Tel: (002) 44 5192

POISONS INFORMATION

Poisons Information Centre (antidotes)
Tel: (002) 38 8485

PREGNANCY, ABORTION, CONTRACEPTION

Pregnancy Support Service
82 Hampden Rd, Battery Point, 7000
Tel: (002) 34 5787

See also FAMILY PLANNING, SEX EDUCATION, COUNSELLING & HUMAN RELATIONSHIPS

RAPE/SEXUAL ASSAULT

Rape Crisis Information Centre
Tel: (002) 34 7200

RHEUMATISM

Rheumatism & Arthritis Foundation of Tas.
84 Hampden Rd, Battery Point, 7000
Tel: (002) 34 6489

SEX EDUCATION, COUNSELLING & HUMAN RELATIONSHIPS

Marriage Guidance & Family Counselling

23 Stoke St, New Town, 7008
Tel: (002) 23 1000

See also RAPE/SEXUAL ASSAULT

SEXUALLY TRANSMITTED DISEASES

Venereal Disease Information Service
Tel: (002) 38 8799

See also AIDS, SEX EDUCATION, COUNSELLING & HUMAN RELATIONSHIPS

SPASTIC

See CEREBRAL PALSY

SPINA BIFIDA

Spina Bifida Association of Tas.
82 Hampden Rd, Battery Point, 7000
Tel: (002) 23 4537

SUDDEN INFANT DEATH SYNDROME

SID Society
Contact 'Lifeline'
Tel: (002) 34 5600 (24 hours)

VACCINATIONS

(Immunisation and vaccination for overseas travel) See GOVERNMENT HEALTH DEPARTMENTS – Commonwealth

VASECTOMY

See FAMILY PLANNING

WOMEN'S HEALTH

Women's Information Service
Dept of the Prime Minister, 169 Liverpool St, Hobart, 7000
Tel: (002) 34 2166

See also CHILDBIRTH & BREASTFEEDING, FAMILY PLANNING, RAPE/SEXUAL ASSAULT

ABORTION

See PREGNANCY, ABORTION, CONTRACEPTION

AGEING

Do Care
(volunteers visiting older people)
148 Lonsdale St, Melbourne, 3000
Tel: (03) 662 2044

Victorian Council on the Ageing
449 Swanston St, Melbourne, 3000
Tel: (03) 663 6199

AIDS
(Acquired Immune Deficiency Syndrome)

AIDS Clinic
Communicable Diseases Centre, 364 Little Lonsdale St, Melbourne, 3000
Tel: (03) 602 4900

AIDS Hotline
(counselling, advice, information)
Tel: (03) 347 3000

AIDS Support Group
The Peter Knight Centre, 117 Johnston St, Collingwood, 3066
Tel: (03) 417 1759

See also SEXUALLY TRANSMITTED DISEASES

ALCOHOL & DRUG DEPENDENCE

Alcohol & Drug Dependence Recovery Centre
36 Pine Crescent, Boronia, 3155
Tel: (03) 762 4733, 762 4200 (counselling)

Alcoholics Anonymous
658 Bridge Rd, Richmond, 3121
Tel: (03) 429 1833

Al-Anon Family Groups & Al Teen
238 Flinders Lane, Melbourne, 3000
Tel: (03) 63 3368

Alcohol & Drug Foundation
153 Park St, South Melbourne, 3205
Tel: (03) 690 6000

Alcohol & Drug Direct Line
(counselling, information)
Tel: (03) 614 1999

Narcotics Anonymous
459 Punt Rd, South Yarra, 3141
Tel: (03) 266 2878

Odyssey House
(Community Involvement Centre)
173 Greville St, Prahran, 3181
Tel: (03) 51 5394

ALZHEIMER'S DISEASE

Alzheimer's Disease & Related Disorders
Society of Vic. (ADARDS)
84 Eastern Rd, South Melbourne, 3205
Tel: (03) 696 1789

ANOREXIA NERVOSA & BULIMIA

Anorexia and Bulimia Nervosa Fellowship of Vic.
1 Cookson St, Camberwell, 3124
Tel: (03) 813 1352

ARTHRITIS

Arthritis Foundation of Vic.
Yarra Boulevard, Kew, 3101
Tel: (03) 862 2555

Parents of Arthritic Children
10 Carramar Ave, Glen Waverley, 3150
Tel: (03) 560 9035

ASTHMA

Asthma Foundation
2 Highfield Grove, Kew, 3101
Tel: (03) 861 5666

AUTISM

Autistic Children & Adults' Association
80 Maling Rd, Canterbury, 3126
Tel: (03) 836 3514

Autistic Citizens Residential & Resources Society of Victoria
143 Victoria Ave, Albert Park, 3206
Tel: (03) 699 3815

BATTERED BABY SYNDROME

See CHILD ABUSE

BLINDNESS

Association for the Blind
7 Mair St, Brighton Beach, 3186
Tel: (03) 598 8555

Braille & Talking Book Library
31 Commercial Rd, South Yarra, 3141
Tel: (03) 267 6022

Deaf/Blind Care Association
600 Nicholson St, North Fitzroy, 3068
Tel: (03) 482 1155

Royal Victorian Eye & Ear Hospital
32 Gisborne St, East Melbourne, 3002
Tel: (03) 665 9666

Royal Guide Dogs for the Blind
Chandler Hwy, Kew, 3101
Tel: (03) 860 4444

Royal Victorian Institute for the Blind
557 St Kilda Rd, Melbourne, 3004
Tel: (03) 529 3544

Vision Information Hotline
Tel: (03) 598 8555;
(008) 13 5811 (toll free)

BLOOD BANK

Red Cross Blood Bank
Cnr Kavanagh & Balston Sts, South Melbourne, 3205
Tel: (03) 616 0111

BULIMIA
See ANOREXIA NERVOSA & BULIMIA

CANCER

Anti-Cancer Council of Vic.
(can supply names of support groups)
1 Rathdowne St, Carlton South, 3053
Tel: (03) 662 3300

Breast Cancer Support Service
1 Rathdowne St, Carlton, 3053
Tel: (03) 662 3300, ext. 253

Ian Gawler
The Living Centre
360 Mont Albert Rd, Mont Albert, 3127
Tel: (03) 890 2209

Peter MacCallum Hospital

481 Lt Lonsdale St, Melbourne, 3000
Tel: (03) 602 1333

CEREBRAL PALSY

Spastic Society of Vic.
135 Inkerman St, St Kilda, 3182
Tel: (03) 537 2611

Yooralla Society of Vic.
52 Thistlethwaite St, South Melbourne, 3205
Tel: (03) 699 2066

CHILD ABUSE

Community Services Vic.
Regional Child Protection Unit, 333 Clarendon St, South Melbourne, 3205
Tel: (03) 690 1266, 690 4544

Parents Anonymous
Tel: (03) 654 4654

Royal Children's Hospital
Flemington Rd, Parkville, 3052
Tel: (03) 345 5522 (24 hours)

CHILDBIRTH & BREASTFEEDING

Australian Multiple Birth Association
71 Valley Rd, Park Orchards, 3114
Tel: (03) 876 4188

Childbirth Education Association of Aust. (Vic.)
PO Box 133, Malvern, 3146
Tel: (03) 359 4868

Childbirth & Parenting Association of Vic.
PO Box 219, Mooroolbark, 3138
Tel: (03) 725 4832

Nursing Mothers' Association of Aust.
5 Glendale St, Nunawading, 3131
Tel: (03) 878 3304

CHILDREN

Royal Children's Hospital
Flemington Rd, Parkville, 3052
Tel: (03) 354 5522

COELIAC DISEASE

Coeliac Society of Vic.
104 Grimwade Crescent, Frankston, 3199
Tel: (03) 783 8899

COLOSTOMY

Colostomy Association of Vic.
98 Elizabeth St, Melbourne, 3000
Tel: (03) 63 1210

CONTRACEPTION

See PREGNANCY, ABORTION, CONTRACEPTION

COT DEATH

See SUDDEN INFANT DEATH SYNDROME

CYSTIC FIBROSIS

The Cystic Fibrosis Association of Vic.
125 Central Rd, Blackburn, 3130
Tel: (03) 878 0091

DEAFNESS

See HEARING DISABILITIES

DENTAL CARE

(emergency)

Royal Dental Hospital
Cnr Elizabeth St & Flemington Rd, Melbourne, 3000
Tel: (03) 341 0222

DIABETES

Diabetes Foundation (Vic.)
100 Collins St, Melbourne, 3000
Tel: (03) 654 8777

DISABLED

Council of Disabled Persons (Vic.)
24 Macauley Place, Bayswater, 3153
Tel: (03) 729 3188

Community Services
Office of Intellectual Disability Services (including information bureau), 555 Collins St, Melbourne, 3000
Tel: (03) 616 7777

Disability Resources Centre
791 High St, Thornbury, 3071
Tel: (03) 480 2877

See also MENTAL HEALTH & DISABILITY, MULTIPLE SCLEROSIS, MUSCULAR DYSTROPHY, PARAPLEGIA & QUADRIPLEGIA

DISABLED (CHILDREN)

Noah's Ark Toy Library for Children with Special Needs
28 The Avenue, Windsor, 3181
Tel: (03) 529 1466

Parent Support for Parents of Children Who are Disabled
c/- 2/105 Severn St, Box Hill, 3128
Tel: (03) 898 6559

DOWN'S SYNDROME

Down's Syndrome Association of Vic.
55 Victoria Parade, Collingwood, 3066
Tel: (03) 419 1653

DRUG DEPENDENCE

See ALCOHOL & DRUG DEPENDENCE

DYSLEXIA & LEARNING DIFFICULTIES

SPELD (Vic.)
494 Brunswick St, Fitzroy, 3065
Tel: (03) 489 4344

EPILEPSY

The National Epilepsy Association of Aust.
184 Main St, Lilydale, 3140
Tel: (03) 735 0211

FAMILY PLANNING

Action Centre: Family Planning Adolescent Counselling
268 Flinders Lane, Melbourne, 3000
Tel: (03) 654 4766

Action Pregnancy Problem Centre
228 Clarendon St, East Melbourne. 3002
Tel: (03) 419 7622

Family Planning Association of Vic.
270 Church St, Richmond, 3121
Tel: (03) 429 1177

Natural Family Planning Centre
27 Alexandra Pde, North Fitzroy, 3068
Tel: (03) 481 1722

See also SEX EDUCATION, COUNSELLING & HUMAN RELATIONSHIPS

FIRST AID

Australian Red Cross Society
(Vic.)
171 City Rd, South Melbourne,
3205
Tel: (03) 616 9911

St John Ambulance Association
285 La Trobe St, Melbourne,
3000
Tel: (03) 67 5576

GOVERNMENT HEALTH DEPARTMENTS

Commonwealth Govt Health
Dept
Commonwealth Govt Centre,
Cnr Spring & La Trobe Sts,
Melbourne, 3000
Tel: (03) 662 2999

Victorian Health Commission
555 Collins St, Melbourne, 3000
Tel: (03) 616 7777

HAEMOPHILIA

Haemophilia Society of Vic.
76 Lynch St, Hawthorn 3122
Tel: (03) 819 1366

HEALTH ADVISORY SERVICE

CALL (Complaints Advisory
Link Line)
Tel: (03) 663 3773,
(008) 013 338 (toll free)

HEARING DISABILITIES

Better Hearing Australia (Vic.)
5 High St, Prahran, 3181
Tel: (03) 51 1577

Deafness Foundation (Vic.)
340 Highett Rd, Highett, 3190
Tel: (03) 555 8816

Eye & Ear Hospital
32 Gisborne St, East
Melbourne, 3002
Tel: (03) 665 9666

The Victorian Deaf Society
104 Wellington Parade South,
East Melbourne, 3002
Tel: (03) 63 1164

HEART DISEASE

National Heart Foundation
464 William St, West
Melbourne, 3003
Tel: (03) 329 8511

HOME NURSING

Royal District Nursing Service
452 St Kilda Rd, Melbourne,
3004
Tel: (03) 266 8791

HOMOSEXUALITY

Gayline Support Service
PO Box 1801, GPO Melbourne,
3001
Tel: (03) 329 5555

Gay & Married Men's
Association (GAMMA)
PO Box 41, Richmond, 3121
Tel: (03) 899 0509

HUNTINGTON'S CHOREA

Huntington Disease Association
333 Waverley Rd, Mt Waverley,
3149
Tel: (03) 277 6144

HYPERACTIVITY

ACTIVE
Hyperkinetic Children's
Association
PO Box 17, East Doncaster,
3108
Tel: (03) 842 6428

ILEOSTOMY

Ileostomy Association (Vic.)
3rd Floor, 290 Collins St,
Melbourne, 3000
Tel: (03) 63 9040

INTELLECTUAL DISABILITY

See MENTAL HEALTH & DISABILITY

KIDNEY DISEASE

Dialysis & Transplant
Association of Vic.
80 Plenty Rd, Preston, 3072
Tel: (03) 480 3088

Kidney Foundation of Aust.
459 Collins St, Melbourne,
3000
Tel: (03) 614 3921

LEUKAEMIA

See CANCER

MASTECTOMY

ENCORE (support group)
YWCA, 489 Elizabeth St,
Melbourne, 3000
Tel: (03) 329 5188

Mastectomy Association of Vic.
c/- 13/1 Duncraig Ave,
Armadale, 3143
Tel: (03) 509 3619

See also CANCER, WOMEN'S HEALTH

MENTAL HEALTH & DISABILITY

Association of Relatives &
Friends of the Emotionally &
Mentally Ill (ARAFEMI) Vic.
Inc.
615 Camberwell Rd,
Camberwell, 3124
Tel: (03) 29 3733, 29 1777

Helping Hand Association for
Mentally Retarded Children
65 Sutherland Rd, Armadale,
3143

Schizophrenia Fellowship of
Victoria
17 Cromwell Rd, South Yarra,
3141
Tel: (03) 241 8150, 240 9795

Victorian Mental Awareness
Council
Victorian Health Commission,
555 Collins St, Melbourne, 3000
Tel: (03) 616 7777

MULTIPLE SCLEROSIS

Multiple Sclerosis Society of
Vic.
Dorset Rd, Boronia, 3155
Tel: (03) 762 8922

MUSCULAR DYSTROPHY

Muscular Dystrophy Association
208 Union Rd, Ascot Vale,
3032
Tel: (03) 370 0889

PARAPLEGIA & QUADRIPLEGIA

Australian Quadriplegic
Association Ltd
70 Station St, Fairfield, 3078
Tel: (93) 489 0777

Paraplegic & Quadriplegic
Association of Vic.
229 Burwood Rd, Hawthorn,
3122
Tel: (03) 819 4055

PARKINSON'S DISEASE

Parkinson's Disease Association
of Vic.

583 Ferntree Gully Rd, Glen
Waverley, 3150
Tel: (03) 562 0411

POISONS INFORMATION

Poisons Information Centre
Tel: (03) 345 5678 (24 hours)

Royal Children's Hospital
Flemington Rd, Parkville, 3052
Poisons Information (antidotes)
Tel: (03) 345 5555

POLIOMYELITIS

Yooralla Society
52 Thistlethwaite St, South
Melbourne, 3205
Tel: (03) 698 5222

PREGNANCY, ABORTION, CONTRACEPTION

Fertility Control Clinic
118 Wellington Pde, East
Melbourne, 3002
Tel: (03) 419 2922,
419 3449 (AH)

See also FAMILY PLANNING, SEX
EDUCATION, COUNSELLING & HUMAN
RELATIONSHIPS, WOMEN'S HEALTH

PSORIASIS

Skin & Psoriasis Foundation
37 Swanston St, Melbourne,
3000
Tel: (03) 63 3755

QUADRIPLEGIA

See PARAPLEGIA & QUADRIPLEGIA

RAPE/SEXUAL ASSAULT

Rape Crisis Intervention
Queen Victoria Medical Centre,
172 Lonsdale St, Melbourne,
3000
Tel: (03) 665 5111 (24 hours)

RHEUMATISM

See ARTHRITIS

SCHIZOPHRENIA

See MENTAL HEALTH & DISABILITY

SELF-HELP GROUPS

COSHG (Collective of Self-Help
Groups) Represents over 700
organisations
65 Gertrude St, Fitzroy, 3065
Tel: (03) 417 6266

SEX EDUCATION, COUNSELLING & HUMAN RELATIONSHIPS

Citizens Welfare Service of
Victoria
Counselling
197 Drummond St, Carlton,
3053
Tel: (03) 663 6733

Marriage Guidance Council of
Vic.
46 Princess St, Kew, 3101
Tel: (03) 861 8512

See also HOMOSEXUALITY,
RAPE/SEXUAL ASSAULT

SEXUALLY TRANSMITTED DISEASES

Communicable Diseases Centre
VD Clinic, 364 Little Lonsdale
St, Melbourne, 3000
Tel: (03) 602 4900

See also AIDS, SEX EDUCATION,
COUNSELLING & HUMAN
RELATIONSHIPS

SPASTIC

See CEREBRAL PALSY

SPINA BIFIDA

Spina Bifida Association

52 Thistlethwaite St, South
Melbourne, 3205
Tel: (03) 698 5222

SUDDEN INFANT DEATH SYNDROME

Sudden Infant Death Research
Foundation
2a Barkly Ave, Armadale, 3143
Tel: (03) 509 7722

TUBERCULOSIS

Victorian Government Health
Dept
Tuberculosis Services,
555 Collins St, Melbourne, 3000
Tel: (03) 616 7777

VACCINATIONS

(Immunisation and vaccinations
for overseas travel) See
GOVERNMENT HEALTH
DEPARTMENTS – Commonwealth

VASECTOMY

See FAMILY PLANNING

WOMEN'S HEALTH

Breast Cancer Support Service
Anti-Cancer Council
1 Rathdowne St, Carlton,
3053
Tel: (03) 662 3300, ext. 253

Queen Victoria Medical Centre
172 Lonsdale St, Melbourne,
3000
Tel: (03) 665 5111

Royal Women's Hospital
132 Grattan St, Carlton, 3053
Tel: (03) 344 2000

See also CHILDBIRTH &
BREASTFEEDING, FAMILY PLANNING,
MASTECTOMY, RAPE/SEXUAL
ASSAULT

ABORTION
See PREGNANCY, ABORTION, CONTRACEPTION

AGEING
WA Council on the Ageing
11 Freedman Rd, Mt Lawley,
6050
Tel: (09) 272 2133

AIDS
(Acquired Immune Deficiency
Syndrome)

AIDS Information Line
Tel: (09) 11 642

See also SEXUALLY TRANSMITTED
DISEASES

ALCOHOL & DRUG DEPENDENCE
Alcoholics Anonymous
2nd Floor, 251 Hay St East,
Perth, 6000
Tel: (09) 325 3566

Al-Anon Family Groups
2nd Floor, 251 Hay St East,
Perth, 6000
Tel: (09) 325 7528

Adult Children of Alcoholics
c/- Holyoake Institute,
65 Newcastle St, Perth, 6000
Tel: (09) 328 9733

Alcohol & Drug Information
Service
79 Collins St, West Perth, 6005
Tel: (09) 481 1088

Nar-Anon Family Group
c/- Cyrenian House,
419 Newcastle St, West Perth,
6005
Tel: (09) 328 9200

Narcotics Anonymous
PO Box 668, Subiaco, 6008
Tel: (09) 328 1619

ALZHEIMER'S DISEASE
Alzheimer's Disease & Related
Disorders (ADARDA)
PO Box 266, Subiaco, 6008
Tel: (09) 382 3652

ARTHRITIS
WA Arthritis & Rheumatism
Foundation
42 Jersey St, Jolimont, 6014
Tel: (09) 387 7066

ASTHMA
Asthma Foundation of WA
Suite 2, Heytesbury House,
61 Heytesbury Rd, Subiaco,
6008
Tel: (09) 382 1666

AUTISM
Association for Autistic Children
in WA
Unit 114, 396 Scarborough
Beach Rd, Osborne Park,
6017
Tel: (09) 444 6933

BATTERED BABY SYNDROME
See CHILD ABUSE

BLINDNESS
The Blind Association
61 Kitchener Ave, Victoria
Park, 6100
Tel: (09) 362 8202

Royal Guide Dogs for the Blind
Association
c/- 245 Burwood Rd, Hawthorn,
Melbourne, Vic.
Tel: (008) 33 8183 (toll free)

BLOOD BANK
Blood Transfusion Service
Australian Red Cross
357 Murray St, Perth,
6000
Tel: (09) 321 0321

CANCER
Breast Cancer Support Services
Information Centre, 1st Floor,
32 St Georges Terrace, Perth,
6000
Tel: (09) 325 9620, 321 6224

Cancer Foundation
705 Murray St, West Perth,
6005
Tel: (09) 321 6224

Cancer Support Association
80 Railway St, Cottesloe, 6011
Tel: (09) 384 3674

CEREBRAL PALSY
Spastic Welfare Association of
WA Inc.
106 Bradford St, Coolbinia,
6050
Tel: (09) 443 0211

CHILD ABUSE
Princess Margaret Hospital for
Children,
Roberts Rd, Subiaco, 6008
Tel: (09) 382 8222

CHILDBIRTH & BREASTFEEDING
Nursing Mothers' Association of
Australia
41 Lichfield St, Victoria Park,
6100
Tel: (09) 361 5716

CHILDREN
Association for the Welfare of
Children in Hospital
c/- Merrilinga, 1186 Hay St,
West Perth, 6005
Tel: (09) 321 4821

COELIAC DISEASE
Coeliac Society of WA
PO Box 219, Mt Lawley, 6050

COLOSTOMY
Colostomy & Ileostomy
Association
15 Guildford Rd, Mt Lawley,
6050
Tel: (09) 272 1833

CONTRACEPTION
See PREGNANCY, ABORTION, CONTRACEPTION

COT DEATH
See SUDDEN INFANT DEATH SYNDROME

CYSTIC FIBROSIS
Cystic Fibrosis Association of
WA
14 Cook St, West Perth, 6005
Tel: (09) 321 9422

DEAFNESS
See HEARING DISABILITIES

DENTAL CARE
(emergency)
Perth Dental Hospital
196 Goderich St, Perth, 6000
Tel: (09) 325 3452

DIABETES
Diabetic Association of WA
48 Wickham St, East Perth,
6000
Tel: (09) 325 7699

DISABLED

People with Disabilities WA Inc.
Disability Resource Centre,
80 Railway St, Cottesloe, 6011
Tel: (09) 384 3222

See also MENTAL HEALTH &
DISABILITY, MULTIPLE SCLEROSIS,
MUSCULAR DYSTROPHY, PARAPLEGIA
& QUADRIPLEGIA

DOWN'S SYNDROME

Down's Syndrome Association of
WA
110 Bessell Ave, Como, 6152
Tel: (09) 443 3628

DRUG DEPENDENCE
See ALCOHOL & DRUG DEPENDENCE

DYSLEXIA & LEARNING DIFFICULTIES

SPELD (WA)
PO Box 26, Scarborough, 6019
Tel: (09) 446 9400

EPILEPSY

Epilepsy Association Inc. (WA)
14 Bagot Rd, Subiaco, 6008
Tel: (09) 381 1187

FAMILY PLANNING

Family Planning Association of
WA
104 Collins St, West Perth,
6005
Tel: (09) 321 6607

See also SEX EDUCATION,
COUNSELLING & HUMAN
RELATIONSHIPS

FIRST AID

Australian Red Cross Society
357 Murray St, Perth, 6000
Tel: (09) 321 0321

St John Ambulance Brigade
298 Wellington St, Perth, 6000
Tel: (09) 277 8899;
000 (ambulance emergency)

GOVERNMENT HEALTH DEPARTMENTS

Commonwealth Dept of Health
2 St Georges Terrace, Perth,
6000
Tel: (09) 323 5711

Health Dept of WA
Curtin House, 60 Beaufort St,
Perth, 6000
Tel: (09) 328 0241

HAEMOPHILIA

Haemophilia Society of WA
37 Essex St, Wembley
Tel: (09) 446 6331 (afternoons)

HEARING DISABILITIES

Better Hearing Australia (WA)
Inc.
29 West Parade, East Perth,
6000
Tel: (09) 328 7938

Deaf Society of WA Inc.
16 Brentham St, Leederville,
6007
Ph (09) 443 2677

HEART DISEASE

Heart Foundation of Australia
(WA)
43 Stirling Hwy, Nedlands, 6009
Tel: (09) 386 8926

HOMOSEXUALITY

Gay Counselling Service
GPO Box G406, Perth, 6000
Tel: (09) 328 9044

HUNTINGTON'S CHOREA

Australian Huntington's Disease
Association
Marjorie Guthrie Centre,
81 Manning Rd, Bentley, 6012
Tel: (09) 350 5444

HYPERACTIVITY

Hyperactive Help
77 Fernhurst Crescent, Balga,
6061
Tel: (09) 446 1718

ILEOSTOMY
See COLOSTOMY

INTELLECTUAL DISABILITY
See MENTAL HEALTH & DISABILITY

KIDNEY DISEASE

Dialysis & Renal Transplant
Association of WA
209 Fremantle Rd, Gosnells,
6110
Tel: (09) 398 7949

Kidney Foundation of Australia
240 St Georges Tce, Perth, 6000
Tel: (09) 322 1354

LEUKAEMIA
See CANCER

MASTECTOMY

Support Groups for Mastectomy
14 Dalry Rd, Darlington, 6070

See also CANCER, WOMEN'S HEALTH

MENTAL HEALTH & DISABILITY

Association of Relatives &
Friends of the Mentally Ill
2 Nicholson Rd, Subiaco, 6008
Tel: (09) 381 4747

Health Dept of WA
Division for Intellectually
Handicapped,
53 Ord St, West Perth, 6005
Tel: (09) 322 2499

GROW
(Mental Health Self-help Group)
142 Beaufort St, Perth, 6000
Tel: (09) 328 3344

MULTIPLE SCLEROSIS

Multiple Sclerosis Society
288 Nicholson Rd, Subiaco,
6008
Tel: (09) 381 1308

MUSCULAR DYSTROPHY

Muscular Dystrophy Research
Association of WA Inc.
Queen Elizabeth II Medical
Centre, Verdun St, Nedlands,
6009
Tel: (09) 382 2700

PARAPLEGIA & QUADRIPLEGIA

Paraplegic & Quadriplegic
Association of WA Inc.
10 Selby St, Shenton Park,
6008
Tel: (09) 381 0111

PARKINSON'S DISEASE

Parkinson's Association of WA
Inc.
Unit 5, 154 Hampden Rd,
Nedlands, 6009
Tel: (09) 386 6485

POISONS INFORMATION

Poisons Information Centre
Roberts Rd, Subiaco, 6008
Tel: (09) 381 1177

POLIOMYELITIS

Poliomyelitis Immunisation Unit
16 Rheola St, West Perth
Tel: (09) 321 6161, 321 7191

PREGNANCY, ABORTION, CONTRACEPTION

Pregnancy Help
459 Hay St, Perth, 6000
Tel: (09) 325 5592

See also FAMILY PLANNING, SEX
EDUCATION, COUNSELLING & HUMAN
RELATIONSHIPS, WOMEN'S HEALTH

QUADRIPLEGIA

See PARAPLEGIA & QUADRIPLEGIA

RAPE/SEXUAL ASSAULT

Queen Elizabeth II Medical
Centre
Sir Charles Gardner Hospital,
Nedlands, 6009
Tel: (09) 389 3333

Rape Support Group
PO Box 138 Aberdeen St,
Perth, 6000

Rape Crisis Line
Tel: (09) 382 3323

Children: Princess Margaret
Hospital
Roberts Rd, Subiaco, 6008
Tel: (09) 382 8222

RHEUMATISM

See ARTHRITIS

SELF-HELP GROUPS

WA Institute of Self Help
(WISH) Represents over 320
organisations
80 Railway St, Cottesloe, 6011
Tel: (09) 383 3188

SEX EDUCATION, COUNSELLING & HUMAN RELATIONSHIPS

Marriage Guidance Council of
WA
32 Richardson St, West Perth,
6005
Tel: (09) 322 4755

See also HOMOSEXUALITY,
RAPE/SEXUAL ASSAULT

SEXUALLY TRANSMITTED DISEASES

VD Clinic
74 Murray St, Perth, 6000
Tel: (09) 220 1122

See also AIDS, SEX EDUCATION,
COUNSELLING & HUMAN
RELATIONSHIPS

SPASTIC

See CEREBRAL PALSY

SPINA BIFIDA

Spina Bifida Association of WA
364 Cambridge St, Wembley,
6014
Tel: (09) 387 3431

SUDDEN INFANT DEATH SYNDROME

Sudden Infant Death Syndrome
Foundation
PO Box 119 Inglewood,
6052
Tel: (09) 451 4607

TUBERCULOSIS

Chest & Tuberculosis Services
Health Dept of WA, Perth Chest
Clinic,
17 Murray St, Perth,
6000
Tel: (09) 325 3922

VACCINATIONS

(Immunisation and vaccination
for overseas travel) See
GOVERNMENT HEALTH
DEPARTMENTS – Commonwealth

VASECTOMY

See FAMILY PLANNING

WOMEN'S HEALTH

Women's Health Care
Association
Women's Health Care House,
92 Thomas St, West Perth,
6005
Tel: (09) 321 2383

See also CHILDBIRTH &
BREASTFEEDING, FAMILY PLANNING,
MASTECTOMY, RAPE/SEXUAL
ASSAULT

NEW ZEALAND

AGEING

AgeConcern
Auckland Old People's Welfare
Council (Inc.)
305 Queen St, Auckland 1
Tel: (09) 774 844

AIDS

(Acquired Immune Deficiency
Syndrome)

NZ Aids Foundation
Burnett Clinic, Wallace Block,
Auckland Hospital, Auckland
Tel: (09) 33 124

Hotline
Tel: (09) 395 560 (toll free,
24 hours)

See also SEXUALLY TRANSMITTED
DISEASES

ALCOHOL & DRUG DEPENDENCE

Al-Anon Family Group
Information Service
96 Hobson St, Auckland
Tel: (09) 794 871

Alcoholics Anonymous
2nd floor, Town Hall, Queen St,
Auckland
Tel: (09) 734 294 (24 hours)

Community Alcohol Services (CAS)
77 Carrington Rd, Pt Chevalier,
Auckland 2
Tel: (09) 860 808, 862 932

Drug Dependency Clinic
393 Great North Rd,
Auckland 2
Tel: (09) 765 272

Eden Clinic
13 Gilgit Rd, Epsom,
Auckland 3
Tel: (09) 687 023

National Society on Alcohol &
Drug Dependence (NSAD)
Medical Centre, 4/115 Church
St, Otahuhu
Tel: (09) 276 7192, 276 7193

Odyssey House Trust
46 St Georges Bay Rd, Parnell,
Auckland 1
Tel: (09) 396 714

Presbyterian Support Services
Private Bag, GPO, Auckland 1
Tel: (09) 775 654

Alcohol Centre:
408 Mt Eden Rd, Mt Eden,
Auckland 3
Tel: (09) 686 111

Salvation Army Bridge
Programme
15 Ewington Ave, Mt Eden,
Auckland 3
Tel: (09) 608 389

Segar House
Carrington Hospital
Tel: (09) 893 720, 893 730

ALLERGY

Allergy Awareness Association
Inc.
PO Box 12–701, Auckland
Tel: (09) 267 6030

ALZHEIMER'S DISEASE

Alzheimer's Disease & Related
Disorders Society (Auck.) Inc.
(ADARDS)
PO Box 5587, Wellesley St,
Auckland 1
Tel: (09) 601 213

ANOREXIA NERVOSA & BULIMIA

Eating Disorder Support Group
Trust Inc.
(Anorexia & Bulimia Family
Support Group)
PO Box 21–489, Henderson,
Auckland 8
Tel: (09) 678 493

ARTHRITIS

Arthritis Foundation of NZ
14 Erson Ave, Royal Oak,
Auckland 3
Tel: (09) 655 372, 654 949

ASTHMA

Auckland Asthma Society Inc.
PO Box 27–124, Mt Roskill,
Auckland 4
Tel: (09) 675 195

AUTISM

Autistic Association of NZ (Auck.)
33 Sylvia Rd, St Heliers,
Auckland 5
Tel: (09) 558 733

BLINDNESS

Royal NZ Foundation for the
Blind

545 Parnell Rd, Parnell,
Auckland 1
Tel: (09) 774 389

NZ Association of the Blind &
Partially Blind
6 Titoki St, Parnell, Auckland 1
Tel: (09) 779 215

BLOOD BANK

Auckland Regional Blood Centre
Park Ave, Grafton, Auckland 1
Tel: (09) 31 949

Waikato Blood Donor Centre
83 Pembroke St, Hamilton
Tel: (071) 393 679

BULIMIA

See ANOREXIA NERVOSA & BULIMIA

CANCER

Cancer Society of New Zealand
(Auckland Division)
41 Gillies Ave, Epsom, Auckland 3
Tel: (09) 540 023

Breast Cancer Support Society
67 Hillside Rd, Papatoetoe
Tel: (09) 278 5751

Cancer Call
Tel: (09) 779 224

Child Cancer Foundation
PO Box 152, Auckland 1
Tel: (09) 544 051

CEREBRAL PALSY

Cerebral Palsy Society
14 Erson Ave, Royal Oak,
Auckland 3
Tel: (09) 658 069

CHILDBIRTH & BREASTFEEDING

Auckland Homebirth Association
PO Box 7093, Wellesley St,
Auckland 1
Tel: (09) 787 614

Auckland Infertility Society Inc.
PO Box 68–428, Auckland 1
Tel: (09) 451 244 (day),
817 4678 (evening)

La Leche League
26 Beihlers Rd, Weymouth,
Manurewa
Tel: (09) 860 752

Royal NZ Plunket Society Inc.
96 Symonds St, Auckland 1
Tel: (09) 774 365

CHILDREN

Auckland Parents Centre
PO Box 74–110, Market Rd,
Epsom, Auckland
Tel: (09) 659 181

**Auckland Toy Library for
Children With Special Needs**
14 Erson Ave, Royal Oak,
Auckland 3
Tel: (09) 656 177

Contact (Auckland)
(support group to help children
and families with communication
and/or coordination handicaps)
PO Box 9277, Newmarket,
Auckland 1
Tel: (09) 797 624

**National Children's Health
Research Foundation (NCHRF)**
PO Box 6450, Wellesley St,
Auckland 1
Tel: (09) 735 026

**Parent Help & Child Abuse
Prevention Society**
PO Box 37–577, Parnell,
Auckland 1
Tel: (09) 601 052 (office),
32 122 (24 hours)

**Princess Mary Children's
Hospital**
Park Rd, Grafton, Auckland 1
Tel: (09) 797 440

COELIAC DISEASE
See CHRISTCHURCH REGION

COLOSTOMY
See OSTOMY

COT DEATH
See SUDDEN INFANT DEATH
SYNDROME

CYSTIC FIBROSIS

**Cystic Fibrosis Association of
NZ (Auckland Branch)**
PO Box 6460, Wellesley St,
Auckland 1
Tel: (09) 298 4594

DEAFNESS

Auckland Deaf Society Inc.
164 Balmoral Rd, Auckland 3
Tel: (09) 606 980

Deafness Research Foundation
PO Box 6726, Auckland 1
Tel: (09) 733 674

NZ Association of the Deaf (Inc.)
Suite 315, 3rd floor, T & G
Building,
Cnr Wellesley & Elliott Sts,
Auckland 1
Tel: (09) 799 331, 395 993

**NZ Federation for Deaf
Children Inc.**
51A View Rd, Henderson,
Auckland 8

**National Foundation for the
Deaf Inc.**
Suite 315, 3rd floor, T & G
Building,
Cnr Wellesley & Elliott St,
Auckland 1
Tel: (09) 399 830, 393 109

The Hearing Association Inc.
8 St Vincent Ave, Remuera,
Auckland 5
Tel: (09) 549 847

DENTAL CARE
(emergency)

Auckland Hospital
Park Rd, Grafton, Auckland 1
Tel: (09) 797 440, ext. 670

St John Ambulance
Tel: (09) 599 099 (dentist
after-hours, weekends etc.)

DIABETES

Auckland Diabetic Society
97A Grafton Rd, Auckland 1
Tel: (09) 798 383

DIETICIANS

NZ Dietetic Association
c/- Dietary Department,
Middlemore Hospital,
Private Bag, Otahuhu,
Auckland 6
Tel: (09) 276 1999, ext. 8090

DISABLED (ADULT)

Disabled Citizens' Society Inc.
PO Box 56–083, Dominion Rd,
Auckland 3
421 Dominion Rd, Auckland 3
Tel: (09) 688 153

Independent Living Centre
14 Erson Ave, Royal Oak,
Auckland 3
Tel: (09) 658 069

**Laura Fergusson Trust for
Disabled Persons**
224 Great South Rd, Auckland

Tel: (09) 548 882

NZ Neurological Foundation
National office: HB Building,
Cnr France St & Karangahape
Rd, Auckland 1
Tel: (09) 798 470
Auckland Division: PO Box
6314, Auckland 1
Tel: (09) 760 368

**NZ Society for the Intellectually
Handicapped Inc.**
35 Graham St, Auckland 1
Tel: (09) 770 394

Rehabilitation League NZ (Inc.)
PO Box 8533, Symonds St,
Auckland 1
Tel: (09) 686 103

DISABLED (CHILDREN)

NZ Crippled Children's Society
Dadley Foundation Building,
1–9 Mount St, Auckland 1
Tel: (09) 735 026

DRUG DEPENDENCE
See ALCOHOL & DRUG DEPENDENCE

DYSLEXIA & LEARNING DIFFICULTIES

SPELD
14 Erson Ave, Royal Oak,
Auckland 3
Tel: (09) 658 069

EPILEPSY

NZ Epilepsy Association (Auck.)
PO Box 5714, Wellesley St,
Auckland 1
Tel: (09) 687 639

EUTHANASIA

**Voluntary Euthanasia Society
(Auck.) Inc.**
14 Quay St, Auckland 1
PO Box 77–029, Mt Albert,
Auckland 3
Tel: (09) 734 351

FAMILY PLANNING

Family Planning Association
214 Karangahape Rd, Auckland
Tel: (09) 775 049

**NZ Association of Natural
Family Planning Inc.**
c/- Mater Hospital, 98 Mountain
Rd, Epsom, Auckland 3
Tel: (09) 605 451

FIRST AID

Red Cross Society (NZ) Inc.
85 Wakefield St, Auckland 1
Tel: (09) 774 175

St John Ambulance Association
(Auck.)
Private Bag, Panmure,
Auckland 6
Tel: (09) 591 015

GOVERNMENT HEALTH DEPARTMENTS

Department of Education
Gillies Ave, Newmarket,
Auckland 1
Tel: (09) 541 989

Department of Health
Bledisloe State Building,
Wellesley St West, Auckland 1
Tel: (09) 792 900

Department of Social Welfare
State Insurance Building,
Wakefield St, Auckland 1
Tel: (09) 799 011

HAEMOPHILIA

NZ Haemophilia Society Inc.
PO Box 122, Auckland 1
Tel: (09) 884 912 (day),
884 981 (evening)

Haemophilia Clinic
Auckland Hospital
Tel: (09) 797 440, ext. 705

HEARING DISABILITIES
See DEAFNESS

HEART DISEASE

Heart Mothers of NZ
PO Box 9067, Newmarket,
Auckland 1
Tel: (09) 788 266 (support
group)

National Heart Foundation of
NZ
17 Great South Rd, Greenlane,
Auckland 5
Tel: (09) 546 005

HOME NURSING

District Nursing Service
Auckland Hospital Board
See telephone book

HOMOSEXUALITY

Gayline
Tel: (09) 33 584

Lesbian Support Group
PO Box 47–090, Ponsonby,
Auckland 1
Tel: (09) 888 325

HUNTINGTON'S CHOREA

Huntington's Disease Inc.
(Auckland Association)
PO Box 5001,
Auckland
Tel: (09) 689 679

HYPERACTIVITY

Auckland Hyperactivity
Association
PO Box 36–099, Northcote,
Auckland 6

HYPNOTHERAPY

Psychotherapy and
Hypnotherapy Institute of NZ
(Inc.)
PO Box 2054, Auckland
Tel: (09) 485 505

ILEOSTOMY
See OSTOMY

INTELLECTUAL DISABILITY
See MENTAL HEALTH & DISABILITY

KIDNEY DISEASE

National Kidney Foundation
(Auckland Branch)
PO Box 6976, Wellesley St,
Auckland 1

LEUKAEMIA
See CANCER

MENTAL HEALTH AND DISABILITY

Mental Health Foundation of NZ
Inc.
272 Parnell Rd, Parnell,
Auckland 1
Tel: (09) 31 516, 31 517

Parents Association of the
Mentally Handicapped Inc.
PO Box 19–267, Avondale,
Auckland 7
Tel: (09) 867 400

MULTIPLE SCLEROSIS

Multiple Sclerosis Society of
Auckland Inc.
Box 24–042, Royal Oak,
Auckland 3
Tel: (09) 658 069

MUSCULAR DYSTROPHY

Muscular Dystrophy Association
of NZ Inc.
PO Box 56–123, Auckland 3
Tel: (09) 688 931

OSTOMY

Auckland Ostomy Society
51 Wairiki Rd, Auckland 3
Tel: (09) 607 738

PARKINSON'S DISEASE

Parkinsonism Society of NZ Inc.
67 Canberra Ave, Lynfield,
Auckland 4
Tel: (09) 676 919

POISONS INFORMATION

National Poisons & Hazardous
Chemicals Information Centre
Dunedin
Tel: (024) 740 999

PSORIASIS

Auckland Psoriasis Society
PO Box 3062, Auckland
Tel: (09) 278 6326

RAPE/SEXUAL ASSAULT

Help Foundation
PO Box 68–165, Newton, Auckland 1
Tel: (09) 399 185

Rape Crisis
63 Ponsonby Rd, Auckland 1
Tel: (09) 764 404

RHEUMATISM

NZ Rheumatism Association
Department of Rheumatology,
Auckland Hospital, Grafton Rd,
Auckland 1
Tel: (09) 797 440, ext. 751

SEX EDUCATION, COUNSELLING & HUMAN RELATIONSHIPS

Marriage Guidance Council
3rd floor, Hampton Court,
Cnr Wellesley & Federal Sts,
Auckland 1
Tel: (09) 790 025

3A Gibbons Rd, Takapuna,
Auckland 9
Tel: (09) 498 349

Suite 5, 89 Great South Rd,
Papatoetoe
Tel: (09) 278 9396

270

See also FAMILY PLANNING, HOMOSEXUALITY

SEXUALLY TRANSMITTED DISEASES

Sexually Transmitted Disease
Information Service
PO Box 5442, Auckland 1
Tel: (09) 33 123

STD Clinic
Auckland Hospital,
Park Rd, Grafton, Auckland 1
Tel: (09) 797 440, ext. 9402 or
470

STD Clinic
Manukau City Health Centre,
Opposite Manukau City
Shopping Centre
Tel: (09) 277 9660, ext. 79

See also AIDS, SEX EDUCATION, COUNSELLING & HUMAN RELATIONSHIPS

SPASTIC

See CEREBRAL PALSY

SPINA BIFIDA

NZ Spina Bifida Trust
PO Box 68–454, Newton,
Auckland 1
Tel: (09) 278 1428

SUDDEN INFANT DEATH SYNDROME

National Child Health Research
Foundation, Cot Death Division
5 Clonbern Rd, Remuera,
Auckland 5
Tel: (09) 548 597

TUBERCULOSIS

Auckland Tuberculosis & Chest
Diseases Association Inc.
c/- Greenlane Hospital,
Greenlane Rd, Epsom,
Auckland 3
Tel: (09) 600 051 (afternoon)

WOMEN'S HEALTH

Auckland Women's Health
Centre
63 Ponsonby Rd, Auckland 1
Tel: (09) 764 506, 765 173
(information, advice)

National Women's Hospital
Claude Rd, Epsom, Auckland 3
Tel: (09) 689 919

Supportline
(support and help for victims of
domestic violence plus refuge)
PO Box 16–192, Sandringham,
Auckland 3
Tel: (09) 396 167

Women's Refuge Auckland
PO Box 78–016, Grey Lynn,
Auckland 2
Tel: (09) 787 635

For smaller centres contact the above or see WELLINGTON REGION.

CHRISTCHURCH REGION

AGEING

Canterbury Aged People's
Welfare Council
PO Box 2355, Christchurch
Tel: (03) 849 299

AIDS

(Acquired Immune Deficiency
Syndrome)

NZ Aids Foundation
PO Box 21–285, Edgeware,
Christchurch
Tel: (03) 65 865 (local hotline)
Clinic: Christchurch Hospital,
Riccarton Ave, Christchurch
Tel: (03) 792 900

See also SEXUALLY TRANSMITTED
DISEASES

ALCOHOL & DRUG
DEPENDENCE

Al-Anon Family Group
Information Service
PO Box 1314, Christchurch

Alcohol & Drug Dependence
Centre
258 Armagh St, Christchurch
Tel: (03) 50 983, 50 139

Alcoholics Anonymous
Room 1, 1st floor, 1 New
Regent St, Christchurch
Tel: (03) 790 860

National Society of Alcohol &
Drug Dependence (NSAD)
Contact through Hokitika
Probation Office

Odyssey House Trust
100 Greers Rd, Fendalton,
Christchurch 5
Tel: (03) 587 791

Presbyterian Support
Services
236 Hereford St, Christchurch
Tel: (03) 65 472

Salvation Army Bridge
Programme
35 Collins St, Addington,
Christchurch 2
Tel: (03) 382 743

ALLERGY

Allergy Awareness Association
Support Group
203 Hoon Hay Rd, Hoon Hay,
Christchurch 2

ALZHEIMER'S DISEASE

Alzheimer's Disease & Related
Disorders (ADARDS)
Canterbury Inc.
PO Box 2355, Christchurch
Tel: (03) 385 059, ext. 801

ANOREXIA NERVOSA

Eating Disorder Clinic
Princess Margaret Hospital
Cashmere Rd, Cashmere,
Christchurch 2
Tel: (03) 39 169

Anorexia and Bulimia Aid Group
Hagley High School, Chilton
House, 486 Hagley Ave,
Christchurch 1
Tel: (03) 67 725

ARTHRITIS

Arthritis Foundation of NZ
(Canterbury Division)
PO Box 1065, Christchurch
Tel: (03) 67 852

Canterbury Arthritis Society
Inc.
PO Box 1801, Christchurch
Tel: (03) 68 383

ASTHMA

Canterbury Asthma Society Inc.
PO Box 13–091, Armagh,
Christchurch
Tel: (03) 487 896

AUTISM

Canterbury Autistic
Association
PO Box 7305, Sydenham,
Christchurch
Tel: (03) 370 550

BLINDNESS

Royal NZ Foundation for the
Blind
86 Bristol St, Christchurch
Tel: (03) 559 005

Association of the Blind &
Partially Blind
79 Teesdale St, Burnside,
Christchurch 5
Tel: (03) 582 255

BLOOD BANK

Blood Transfusion Service
36 Cashel St, Christchurch
Tel: (03) 790 010

Blood Bank
Christchurch Hospital
Riccarton Avenue, Christchurch
Tel: (03) 792 900

BULIMIA

See ANOREXIA NERVOSA & BULIMIA

CANCER

Cancer Society of NZ
(Canterbury/Westland Division)
221 Gloucester St, Christchurch
Tel: (03) 795 835

CEREBRAL PALSY

Adult Cerebral Palsy Society
Inc.
3/8 Peer St, Christchurch 4
Tel: (03) 485 740

CHILDBIRTH &
BREASTFEEDING

Royal NZ Plunket Society Inc.
211 Oxford Tce, Christchurch
Tel: (03) 60 765

Christchurch Home Birth
Association
PO Box 2806, Christchurch

Christchurch Infertility Society
PO Box 29–188, Christchurch

La Leche League
6B Kaputone Place, Belfast,
Christchurch 5
Tel: (03) 23 8506

CHILDREN

Christchurch Parents Centre
PO Box 28–056, Christchurch
Tel: (03) 35 185

Contact (Canterbury) Inc.
(for children with
communication and/or
coordination disabilities)
PO Box 1537, Christchurch
Tel: (03) 328 304

National Children's Health
Research Foundation
See AUCKLAND REGION

NZ Childcare Association
32 Tomrich St, Christchurch

NZ Toy Library Federation
See WELLINGTON REGION

COELIAC DISEASE

Coeliac Society of NZ Inc.
15 Stenness Ave, Somerfield,

Christchurch 2
Tel: (03) 34 793

COLOSTOMY
See OSTOMY

DEAFNESS

NZ Association of the Deaf
(Inc.)
195 Gloucester St,
Christchurch
Tel: (03) 795 074

Canterbury Parents of Deaf
Children Inc.
PO Box 19–687, Christchurch

The Hearing Association Inc.
11 Beveridge St, Christchurch
Tel: (03) 63 303

DENTAL CARE
(emergency)
St John Ambulance Association
Dental/Medical Emergencies
Tel: (03) 69 133

DIABETES

Christchurch Diabetic Society
PO Box 2527, Christchurch

Diabetes Centre
Arts Centre, Hereford St,
Christchurch
Tel: (03) 63 742

DIETICIANS

NZ Dietetic Association
c/- Dietary Department,
Christchurch Hospital,
Riccarton Ave, Christchurch
Tel: (03) 792 900

DISABLED (ADULTS)

Laura Fergusson Trust for
Disabled Persons
279 Ilam Rd, Christchurch
Tel: (03) 516 047

NZ Neurological Foundation Inc.
(Canterbury/Westland Division)
PO Box 984, Christchurch
Tel: (03) 555 464

NZ Society for the Intellectually
Handicapped Inc.
7 Liverpool St, Christchurch
Tel: (03) 793 980

Rehabilitation League NZ
(Inc.)
PO Box 643, Christchurch
Tel: (03) 488 989

DISABLED CHILDREN

NZ Crippled Children's
Association
27 Kilmarnock St, Riccarton
Tel: (03) 488 974

DRUG DEPENDENCE
See ALCOHOL & DRUG DEPENDENCE

**DYSLEXIA & LEARNING
DIFFICULTIES**

SPELD (Canterbury)
23 Glenburn Place,
Christchurch 4
Tel: (03) 34 039

SPELD NZ Centre
(research/testing)
15 Rastrick St, Christchurch
Tel: (03) 841 486

EPILEPSY

NZ Epilepsy Association Inc.
PO Box 2468, Christchurch
Tel: (03) 798 175

EUTHANASIA
See WELLINGTON REGION

FAMILY PLANNING

Family Planning Association
Arts Centre, 301 Montreal St,
Christchurch
Tel: (03) 790 514

NZ Association of Natural
Family Planning
21 Caledonian Rd, St Albans,
Christchurch 1
Tel: (03) 68 281

FIRST AID

St John Ambulance Association
Tel: (03) 64 776

St John Ambulance Brigade
55–61 Peterborough St,
Christchurch
Tel: (03) 64 776

North Canterbury Red Cross
Centre
33 Cashel St, Christchurch
Tel: (03) 798 158

**GOVERNMENT HEALTH
DEPARTMENTS**

Department of Education
25 Cranmer Square,
Christchurch 1
Tel: (03) 798 800

Department of Health
Reserve Bank Building, 158
Hereford St, Christchurch 1
Tel: (03) 799 480

Department of Social Welfare
Housing Corporation Building,
Cathedral Square,
Christchurch 1
Tel: (03) 795 100

HEART DISEASE

National Heart Foundation of
NZ
Health Education Officer &
Medical Director
c/- Nurses Hostel, Princess
Margaret Hospital, Cashmere
Rd, Christchurch 2
Tel: (03) 39 169, ext. 6965

Regional committee: PO Box
696, Christchurch
Tel: (03) 797 010

HOME NURSING

Christchurch Nursing &
Karitane Bureau
10 Northcroft St, Hoon Hay,
Christchurch 2
Tel: (03) 382 184

Coordinator for Geriatric and
Domiciliary Services
21 Mansfield Ave, St Albans,
Christchurch 1
Tel: (03) 559 169

Nurse Maude District Nursing
Association
15 Mansfield Ave, St Albans,
Christchurch 1
Tel: (03) 556 089; 556 139

HOMOSEXUALITY

Gay Health Group
PO Box 21–285, Edgeware,
Christchurch
(Information, advice, research &
support)

Gay Information Centre
Room B12, Arts Centre,
Hereford St, Christchurch
Tel: (03) 65 577
Gay Information Line
Tel: (03) 65 577

Gayline
PO Box 2470, Christchurch
Tel: (03) 794 796 (Mon.
8–9pm, Wed. 11.30am–2pm,
Sat. 7–10pm)

Lesbianline/Lesbian Support Group
PO Box 21–069, Christchurch
Tel: (03) 794 796 (Thurs.
7.30–10.30pm)

HUNTINGTONS CHOREA

Huntingtons Disease Inc.
PO Box 25–088, Christchurch

HYPNOTHERAPY
See AUCKLAND REGION

ILEOSTOMY
See OSTOMY

INTELLECTUAL DISABILITY
See MENTAL HEALTH & DISABILITY

KIDNEY DISEASE

National Kidney Foundation
119 Roydvale Ave, Christchurch

LEUKAEMIA
See CANCER

MENTAL HEALTH & DISABILITY

Community Mental Health Centre
301 Montreal St, Christchurch
Tel: (03) 792 934

MULTIPLE SCLEROSIS

Multiple Sclerosis Society of NZ
Inc.
PO Box 4091, Christchurch

MUSCULAR DYSTROPHY

Muscular Dystrophy Association
of NZ

PO Box 20–164, Bishopdale,
Christchurch 5

OSTOMY

Canterbury Ostomy Society
PO Box 2568, Christchurch

PARKINSON'S DISEASE

Parkinsonism Society of NZ Inc.
189A Mountain View Rd,
Timaru
Tel: (056) 60 870

POISONS INFORMATION

National Poisons & Hazardous
Chemicals Information Centre
Dunedin
Tel: (024) 740 999

RAPE/SEXUAL ASSAULT

Rape Crisis and Incest Survivors
PO Box 13–476, Christchurch
Tel: (03) 796 202, 797 047
(includes Women's Refuge,
Women Against Pornography)

RHEUMATISM

NZ Rheumatism Association
Christchurch Clinical School of
Medicine,
PO Box 4345, Christchurch
Tel: (03) 792 900

SEX EDUCATION, COUNSELLING & HUMAN RELATIONSHIPS

Family Planning Association
See FAMILY PLANNING

Marriage Guidance Council
PO Box 13–003, Christchurch
Tel: (03) 68 804

See also HOMOSEXUALITY

SEXUALLY TRANSMITTED DISEASES

STD Information
Tel: (03) 792 999

STD Clinics
St Andrews Outpatients Clinic,
Christchurch Hospital,
16 Tuam St, Christchurch
Tel: (03) 792 900, ext. 490

See also AIDS

SPASTIC
See CEREBRAL PALSY

SUDDEN INFANT DEATH SYNDROME
See AUCKLAND REGION

TUBERCULOSIS

Canterbury Tuberculosis &
Respiratory Diseases
Association
76 Hereford St, Christchurch

WOMEN'S HEALTH

Christchurch Women's Hospital
885 Colombo St, Christchurch
Tel: (03) 790 890

The Health Alternative for
Women (THAW)
PO Box 884, Christchurch
Tel: (03) 796 970

AGEING

AgeConcern (Otago)
The Octagon, Dunedin,
PO Box 5355, Dunedin

AIDS

(Acquired Immune Deficiency
Syndrome)

STD Clinic, Dunedin Hospital
Tel: (024) 740 999

NZ Aids Foundation Hotline
Tel: (09) 395 560 (toll free, 24
hours)

STD Answerphone
(024) 777 083

See also SEXUALLY TRANSMITTED
DISEASES

ALCOHOL & DRUG DEPENDENCE

Presbyterian Support Services
415 Moray Place, Dunedin
Tel: (024) 777 115

Community Health Services
Dunedin Hospital, Great King
St, Dunedin
Tel: (024) 740 999

ALLERGY

Allergy Awareness Association
Inc.
Support Group
2 Heath St, Andersons Bay,
Dunedin
Tel: (024) 44 549

ARTHRITIS

Arthritis Foundation of NZ Inc.
PO Box 2015, Dunedin
Tel: (024) 777 599

ASTHMA

Otago Asthma Society
PO Box 5494, Dunedin

AUTISM

Autistic Association Otago
Branch
245 Pine Hill Rd, Dunedin
Tel: (024) 737 209

BLINDNESS

Association of the Blind &
Partially Blind
57 Sommerville St, Andersons
Bay, Dunedin
Tel: (024) 43 102

Royal NZ Foundation for the
Blind
Cnr Hillside Rd & Law St,
Dunedin
Tel: (024) 51 154

BLOOD BANK

Otago Blood Donor Centre
Dunedin Hospital
Cumberland St, Dunedin
Tel: (024) 740 999, ext. 8320

Smaller centres: refer to local
hospital for details.

CANCER

Cancer Society of NZ (Otago
Division)
c/- Deloitte Haskins & Sells,
NZ Mutual Funds Building,
11 Bond St, Dunedin
Tel: (024) 777 042

CHILDBIRTH & BREASTFEEDING

Dunedin Home Birth Association
PO Box 6124, Dunedin

Dunedin Infertility Support
Group
60 Queen St, Dunedin
Tel: (024) 740 940

La Leche League
13 Station St, Alexandra
Tel: (024) 88 969

Royal NZ Plunket Society Inc.
472 George St, Dunedin
Tel: (024) 770 110

CHILDREN

Dunedin Parents Centre
PO Box 6037, Dunedin
Tel: (024) 34 281

National Children's Health
Research Foundation (NCHRF)
See AUCKLAND REGION

NZ Childcare Association
46A Kenmure Rd, Belleknowes,
Dunedin

NZ Toy Library Federation
See WELLINGTON REGION for
national office and information.

COLOSTOMY

See OSTOMY

COT DEATH

See SUDDEN INFANT DEATH
SYNDROME

DEAFNESS

NZ Association of the Deaf
(Inc.)
660 George St, Dunedin
Tel: (024) 771 033

Otago Association for Deaf
Children
24 Granville Terrace, Dunedin

The Hearing Association Inc.
7 Malcolm St, Dunedin North
Tel: (024) 779 710

DENTAL CARE

(emergency)

St John Ambulance Association
17 York Place, Dunedin
Tel: (024) 777 111

DIABETES

Dunedin Diabetic Society
PO Box 5154, Moray Place,
Dunedin

NZ Diabetes Association Inc.
National office: PO Box 54,
Oamaru
Tel: (0297) 48 100

DIETICIANS

NZ Dietetic Association
c/- Dietary Department,
Dunedin Hospital
201 Great King St, Dunedin
Tel: (024) 740 999

DISABLED ADULTS

NZ Neurological Foundation Inc.
PO Box 914, Dunedin
Tel: (024) 777 371

NZ Society for the Intellectually
Handicapped Inc.
Forbury Corner, St Clair,
Dunedin
Tel: (024) 877 018

Rehabilitation League NZ (Inc.)
PO Box 249, Dunedin
Tel: (024) 770 877

DISABLED CHILDREN

NZ Crippled Children's Society
514 Great King St, Dunedin
Tel: (024) 774 117

EPILEPSY

NZ Epilepsy Association (Inc.)
(Otago Branch)
PO Box 1142, Dunedin
Tel: (024) 771 751

FAMILY PLANNING

Family Planning Association
NML Building, The Octagon,
Dunedin
Tel: (024) 775 850

NZ Association of Natural
Family Planning Inc.
Dunedin Hospital Hostel
300 Castle St, Dunedin
Tel: (024) 894 381, 740 940

FIRST AID

Otago Regional Red Cross
Centre
31 York Place, Dunedin
Tel: (024) 771 527

St John Ambulance Association
17 York Place, Dunedin
Tel: (024) 777 111

GOVERNMENT HEALTH DEPARTMENTS

Department of Education
Administration: John Wickliffe
House, Princes St, Dunedin
Tel: (024) 740 152

Advisory Services: Capital
Building, Princes St, Dunedin
Tel: (024) 772 381

Psychological Services: Public
Trust Building, 442 Moray
Place, Dunedin
Tel: (024) 778 610

Department of Health
State Insurance Building,
Cnr Princes & Rattray Sts,
Dunedin
Tel: (024) 770 213

Department of Social Welfare
Government Life Insurance
Building,
Cnr Rattray & Princes Sts,
Dunedin
Tel: (024) 748 499

HEART DISEASE

National Heart Foundation of
NZ
PO Box 1243, Dunedin
Tel: (024) 778 634

HOME NURSING

Community Health Services
Dunedin Hospital
201 Great King St, Dunedin
Tel: (024) 740 999

HOMOSEXUALITY

Gayline
PO Box 1382, Dunedin
Tel: (024) 772 077 (Fri.
7pm–12am)

Lesbianline
Tel: (024) 778 765 (Mon.
7–10pm)

HUNTINGTON'S CHOREA

c/- Sister Breda Shannon, Social
Worker,
Dunedin Hospital
201 Great King St, Dunedin
Tel: (024) 740 999

ILEOSTOMY

See OSTOMY

KINDEY DISEASE

Southland Branch
National Kidney Foundation
Southland Hospital, Invercargill

LEUKAEMIA

See CANCER

MENTAL HEALTH & DISABILITY

Community Health Services
Dunedin Hospital
201 Great King St, Dunedin
Tel: (024) 740 999

MULTIPLE SCLEROSIS

Multiple Sclerosis Society
PO Box 2220, Dunedin

OSTOMY

Otago Ostomy Society
Harrier Rd, St Leonards,
Dunedin

PARKINSON'S DISEASE

Parkinsonism Society of NZ Inc.
93 Glenpark Ave, Maryhill,
Dunedin

POISONS INFORMATION

National Poisons & Hazardous
Chemicals Information Centre
Tel: (024) 740 999

RAPE/SEXUAL ASSAULT

Rape Crisis
Corso Building, Moray Place,
Dunedin
Tel: (024) 741 592

RHEUMATISM

NZ Rheumatism Association
PO Box 913, Dunedin

SEX EDUCATION, COUNSELLING & HUMAN RELATIONSHIPS

Marriage Guidance Council
603 George St, Dunedin
Tel: (024) 776 766

See also FAMILY PLANNING,
HOMOSEXUALITY

SEXUALLY TRANSMITTED DISEASES

STD Clinic
Dunedin Hospital
Tel: (024) 740 999

STD Answerphone (024) 777 083

See also AIDS

SUDDEN INFANT DEATH SYNDROME

See AUCKLAND REGION

TUBERCULOSIS

Southland Tuberculosis & Chest
Diseases Association
PO Box 169, Invercargill

WOMEN'S HEALTH

Women's Resource Centre
Tel: (024) 739 767

Dunedin Women's Refuge
PO Box 5239, Dunedin
Tel: (024) 771 229

For refuges in smaller centres
contact the above, or the
National Collective of
Independent Women's Refuges,
see WELLINGTON REGION.

AGEING

AgeConcern (Wellington)
Anvil House, Wakefield St,
Wellington
Tel: (04) 720 130

AIDS

(Acquired Immune Deficiency
Syndrome)

NZ Aids Foundation
Awhina Aids Clinic, 35 Mein St,
Newtown
Tel: (04) 893 169

See also SEXUALLY TRANSMITTED
DISEASES

ALCOHOL & DRUG
DEPENDENCE

Alcoholics Anonymous
25 Arthur St, Wellington
Tel: (04) 846 499

National Society of Alcohol &
Drug Dependence (NSAD)
Head office: PO Box 54–146,
Plimmerton
Tel: (04) 338 056
Regional office: 1st floor, 259
Wakefield St, Wellington
Tel: (04) 851 517

Presbyterian Support Services
144b Abel Smith St, Wellington
Tel: (04) 850 309

Salvation Army Bridge
Programme
1 Tasman St, Wellington
Tel: (04) 850 395

ALZHEIMER'S DISEASE

Alzheimer's Disease & Related
Disorders Society (ADARDS)
PO Box 16–049, Wellington

ANOREXIA NERVOSA &
BULIMIA

Eating Disorder Unit
Wellington Hospital
Tel: (04) 855 999

Anorexia and Bulimia Support
Group
PO Box 10–016, Wellington
North

ARTHRITIS

Arthritis Foundation of NZ
PO Box 10–020, Wellington
Tel: (04) 721 427, 726 709

(National office)
174 Hutt Rd, Petone
(Wellington Division)
Tel: (04) 691 125

ASTHMA

Asthma Society Inc.
PO Box 11–159, Wellington
Tel: (04) 837 006

AUTISM

Autistic Association of New
Zealand
119 Tirohanga Rd, Lower Hutt
Tel: (04) 698 346

BLINDNESS

Association of the Blind &
Partially Blind
35 Ava St, Petone
Tel: (04) 683 243

Royal NZ Foundation for the
Blind
67 Hankey St, Wellington
Tel: (04) 865 755

BLOOD BANK

Wellington Blood Donor Service
Tasman St, Wellington
Tel: (04) 896 531

BULIMIA

See ANOREXIA NERVOSA & BULIMIA

CANCER

Cancer Society of NZ
52/62 Riddiford St, Newtown
Tel: (04) 898 332

CHILDBIRTH &
BREASTFEEDING

Royal NZ Plunket Society Inc.
3 Moncrieff St, Wellington
Tel: (04) 844 973

La Leche League
c/- Alison Craig, 5 Cranwell St,
Wellington 4
Tel: (04) 785 213

Wellington Homebirth Association
PO Box 19–011, Wellington
Tel: (04) 837 637

Wellington Infertility Society
PO Box 20–011, Wellington

CHILDREN

National Children's Research
Foundation
See AUCKLAND REGION

NZ Childcare Association
(National Office)
PO Box 3402, Wellington
Tel: (04) 846 947

NZ Childcare Association
(Branch)
42 Ngaio Rd, Kelburn,
Wellington 5

The Federation of Parents'
Centres Inc.
PO Box 11–310, Wellington
Tel: (04) 766 950

NZ Toy Library Federation
PO Box 216, Waikanae
Tel: Dannevirke (0653) 4633

Parentline
PO Box 2014, Palmerston
North
Tel: (063) 62 679

Wellington Parents' Centre
PO Box 688, Wellington
Tel: (04) 764 081

COELIAC DISEASE
See CHRISTCHURCH REGION

COLOSTOMY
See OSTOMY

DEAFNESS

NZ Association of the Deaf
(Inc.)
106 Courtenay Place,
Wellington
Tel: (04) 849 682

The Hearing Association Inc.
8 Scarborough Terrace,
Wellington
Tel: (04) 847 017

Wellington Association for Deaf
Children
21 Roseneath Terrace,
Wellington
Tel: (04) 848 924

DENTAL CARE
(emergency)

Dental Association
Tel: (04) 727 072

DIABETES

Wellington Diabetic Society
PO Box 3304, Wellington

DIETICIANS

NZ Dietetic Association
c/- Dietary Department,

Wellington Hospital,
Riddiford St, Wellington
Tel: (04) 855 999

DISABLED (ADULTS)

Laura Fergusson Trust for
Disabled Persons
18 Hammerton St, Naenae,
Lower Hutt
Tel: (04) 676 024

NZ Neurological Foundation Inc.
PO Box 3168, Wellington
Tel: (04) 797 213

NZ Society for the Intellectually
Handicapped
National office: 153 Featherston
St, Wellington
Tel: (04) 722 247
Regional office: 62 Ghuznee St,
Wellington
Tel: (04) 857 868

Rehabilitation League NZ (Inc.)
PO Box 6296, Te Aro,
Wellington
Tel: (04) 851 349

DISABLED CHILDREN

NZ Crippled Children's Society
National office: 86–90 Vivian St,
Wellington 1
Regional office: 14–16
Frankmoore Ave, Johnsonville,
Wellington 4, PO Box 13–220,
Johnsonville
Tel: (04) 789 291

DRUG DEPENDENCE
See ALCOHOL & DRUG DEPENDENCE

DYSLEXIA & LEARNING DIFFICULTIES

SPELD
PO Box 27–112,
Wellington
Tel: (04) 757 914

EPILEPSY

NZ Epilepsy Association Inc.
PO Box 55–107, Waitangirua,
Porirua
Tel: (04) 359 228

EUTHANASIA

The Voluntary Euthanasia
Society
95 Melrose Rd, Island Bay,
Wellington 2
Tel: (04) 837 752

FAMILY PLANNING

Family Planning Association
Todd Building, 110-116
Courtenay Place, Wellington
Tel: (04) 849 743

NZ Association of Natural
Family Planning Inc.
PO Box 13–056, Johnsonville,
Wellington 4
Tel: (04) 733 295

FIRST AID

NZ Red Cross Society Inc.
14 Hill St, Wellington
Tel: (04) 723 750

Wellington Regional Red Cross
Centre
7–9 Donald McLean St,
Wellington South
Tel: (04) 899 103, 899 104

St John Ambulance Association
St John House, 99 The Terrace,
Wellington
Tel: (04) 731 315

Wellington Free Ambulance
6–9 Cable St, Wellington 1
Tel: (04) 722 999

GOVERNMENT HEALTH DEPARTMENTS

Department of Education
Head office: Government
Buildings, Lambton Quay,
Wellington
Tel: (04) 735 499

Regional office: Rossmore
House, Molesworth St,
Thorndon, Wellington 1
Tel: (04) 735 299

Department of Health
Head office: T. G. McCarthy
Trust Building, 140–150
Lambton Quay, Wellington
Tel: (04) 727 627

Wellington District Health Office
Education House, 178–182
Willis St, Wellington
Tel: (04) 858 769

Department of Social Welfare
Head office: Charles Fergusson
Building, West Block, Bowen St,
Wellington
Tel: (04) 727 666
District office: 141 Manners St,
Wellington

HAEMOPHILIA

Haemophilia Support Group
49 Somme Rd, Upper Hutt
Tel: (04) 283 347

HEART DISEASE

National Heart Foundation of
NZ
7 Taranaki St, Wellington
Tel: (04) 849 698

HOME NURSING

Wellington Hospital Board
Community Health
Services
Tel: (04) 897 069

See also FIRST AID

HOMOSEXUALITY

Gay Switchboard
Tel: (04) 728 609 (Tues., Wed.,
Fri., Sat., Sun. 7–10pm)

Gay Task Force
PO Box 9561,
Wellington

Lesbianline
Tel: (04) 898 082 (Tues. &
Thurs. 7–10pm)

HUNTINGTONS CHOREA

Huntingtons Disease Inc.
6 Kahu St, Paraparaumu
Tel: (058) 70 164

HYPERACTIVITY

Wellington Hyperactivity &
Allergy Association
93 Waipapa Rd, Haitaitai,
Wellington 3

HYPNOTHERAPY
See AUCKLAND REGION

ILEOSTOMY
See OSTOMY

KIDNEY DISEASE

The National Kidney Foundation
of NZ
National office: PO Box 10–431,
The Terrace, Wellington
Tel: (04) 724 951

National Kidney Foundation
Wellington branch
49 York St, Lower Hutt

LEUKAEMIA
See CANCER

MULTIPLE SCLEROSIS

National Multiple Sclerosis
Society of NZ Inc.
Room 501, Bonaventure House,
Panama St, Wellington
Tel: (04) 722 347

MUSCULAR DYSTROPHY

Muscular Dystrophy Association
of NZ
65 Calcutta St, Khandallah,
Wellington 4

OSTOMY

Wellington Ostomy Society
6 Lincoln St, Tawa,
Wellington

PARKINSON'S DISEASE

Parkinsonism Society of NZ
PO Box 10–138,
Wellington
Tel: (04) 849 364

POISONS INFORMATION

National Poisons & Hazardous
Chemicals Information Centre

Dunedin
Tel: (024) 740 999

RAPE/SEXUAL ASSAULT

Rape Crisis
PO Box 12–253, Wellington
Tel: (04) 730 116, 842 299

RHEUMATISM

NZ Rheumatism Association
Wellington Region Rheumatic
Diseases Unit,
Hutt Hospital, High St, Lower Hutt
Tel: (04) 666 999

SEX EDUCATION, COUNSELLING & HUMAN RELATIONSHIPS

Marriage Guidance Council
8 Roxburgh St, Wellington
Tel: (04) 851 729

See also FAMILY PLANNING,
HOMOSEXUALITY

SEXUALLY TRANSMITTED DISEASES

Sexually Transmitted Diseases

Clinic
Hospital Rd, Wellington
Tel: (04) 855 996 (men),
855 997 (women)

See also AIDS

SUDDEN INFANT DEATH SYNDROME

See AUCKLAND REGION

WOMEN'S HEALTH

Wellington Women's Resource
Centre
PO Box 11–669, Wellington

National Collective of
Independent Women's Refuges
Inc.
Reid House, Cnr Cuba & Vivian
Sts, Wellington 1
PO Box 6386, Te Aro
Tel: (04) 856 768

Wellington Women's Refuge
PO Box 16–079, Wellington
Tel: (04) 736 280

For refuges in smaller centres
contact the above.

GENERAL INDEX

Page numbers in **bold** type refer to main entries, while page numbers in *italics* refer to illustrations.

A